DATE DUE

PLANNING AND MANAGEMENT
FOR A CHANGING ENVIRONMENT

PLANNING AND MANAGEMENT FOR A CHANGING ENVIRONMENT

A Handbook on Redesigning Postsecondary Institutions

Marvin W. Peterson
David D. Dill
Lisa A. Mets
and Associates

Foreword by Burton R. Clark

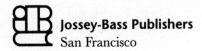
Jossey-Bass Publishers
San Francisco

Substantial discounts on bulk quantities of Jossey-Bass books are available to corporations, professional associations, and other organizations. For details and discount information, contact the special sales department at Jossey-Bass Inc., Publishers (415) 433–1740; Fax (800) 605–2665.

For sales outside the United States, please contact your local Simon & Schuster International Office.

Jossey-Bass Web address: http://www.josseybass.com

Manufactured in the United States of America on Lyons Falls Turin Book. This paper is acid-free and 100 percent totally chlorine-free.

Library of Congress Cataloging-in-Publication Data

Peterson, Marvin W.
    Planning and management for a changing environment : a handbook on
redesigning postsecondary institutions / Marvin W. Peterson, David D.
Dill, Lisa A. Mets, and associates : foreword by Burton R. Clark.—
1st ed.
        p. cm.—(The Jossey-Bass higher and adult education series)
    Includes bibliographical references and index.
    ISBN 0-7879-0849-5 (alk. paper)
        1. Universities and colleges—United States—Administration—
Handbooks, manuals, etc.   2. Postsecondary education—United
States—Planning—Handbooks, manuals, etc.   3. Educational change—
United States—Handbooks, manuals, etc.   I. Dill, David D., date.
II. Mets, Lisa A.   III. Title.   IV. Series.
LB2341.P438   1997
378.1′01—dc21   96-50208
                                                                  CIP

FIRST EDITION
HC Printing 10 9 8 7 6 5 4 3 2 1

CONTENTS

PART FOUR: RENEWING INSTITUTIONS AND PLANNING FOR ACADEMIC CHALLENGES   403

FOREWORD

Throughout the world beginning in the mid-1980s, universities initiated numerous experiments in how best to transform their character. From Australia and Hong Kong to Finland and the Czech Republic, with the United States included, universities have been and are today actively searching for new combinations of capabilities that will enable them to survive and prosper.

Clark Kerr took sharp note in the early 1990s of how much the international arena of higher education has heated up, stressing that "for the first time, a really international world of learning, highly competitive, is emerging" (1993, p. 33). Kerr emphasized that if higher education institutions want to get into this emerging international orbit, they have to do so on merit. Politics will not do the job. Rather, nations "have to give a good deal of autonomy to institutions for them to be dynamic and to move fast in international competition" (p. 33). Institutions have to develop entrepreneurial leadership that makes active use of their autonomy.

Without doubt, the tools of institutional self-development now move to center stage in higher education. How do we, in our own institutions, energize the many departments, research centers, and interdisciplinary programs—the operational sites of research, teaching, and learning—to the point where they continuously explore new options and selectively carry forward and enhance those things they have traditionally done well? Can the institution's basic units develop effective organizational capacities to relate changing internal strengths to rapidly altering constraints and opportunities in their immediate environments, as, for example, in the case of the medical school, the chemistry department, and even the many departments of the humanities and social sciences?

If operational departments located in the university's academic heartland can be largely strengthened by means of stimulated self-development, how is broader institutional development to be handled? One university after another finds that a strengthened, steering core is needed, one central body or several interlocked central groups of administrators and academic staff who can legitimately and effectively assert the interests of the university as a whole (Clark, 1996a). As departments learn how to flexibly plan their way, and intermediate faculties and schools do so in their individual realms, responsible central bodies find medium- and long-term orientations increasingly necessary. Central groups become more planning-oriented: they review the capabilities of the university as a whole, size up changing environmental opportunities, and make best bets—selective investments of resources—for getting from here to there, to a desirable and sustainable institutional character for the early decades of the twenty-first century.

There will be no surcease in the churning turmoil increasingly experienced by universities in the conditions of their existence. Student access steadily becomes more complicated: not only more students but also different kinds of students appear at the door. The connections of universities to labor markets on the output end become extremely segmented: not only are larger numbers of graduates at multiple degree levels to be turned out but they are to be graduates trained as experts in a vast array of occupational specialties. The patronage of universities diversifies: in public universities, nigh-total budgetary support by a single patron, national or state government, is replaced by a half-dozen or more changing income streams; in private universities, income from tuition and fees, endowment, and alumni largess constitute major sources of support alongside funds variously obtained from governments, foundations, and international organizations.

Arguably the most important and irresistible pressure calling for university adaptation, if the one least remarked, is the veritable explosion of knowledge that rolls on in a self-propelling fashion in one field of knowledge after another. As old fields diversify and fragment their knowledge base and new ones rapidly arise, the highly selective choice of which segments to pursue and which ones to downplay— or totally ignore—becomes more pressing in even the wealthiest universities. The need for tougher decision making steadily grows in the domains of history and literature, anthropology and political science, as well as in physics and engineering. Substantive focusing becomes a planning priority all along the line, from department to university to university sector to a whole national system of higher education (Clark, 1996b).

To picture the rising tide of complexity in only slightly different terms, modern universities are pressed to transform themselves so that they can (1) simultaneously perform elite and mass functions in a welter of differently constituted structures and programs, (2) directly relate to private industry, nonprofit organizations, professional associations, and various segments of the general population, as well as to local, regional, national, and transnational governments, and (3) broadly commit themselves to relevant knowledge and useful learning as well as to knowledge for its own sake and learning that has no immediate utility. "Missions" multiply and conflict; "purposes" fill a portfolio of desires. Many forms of planning arise in different parts of universities and higher education systems to cope with such increasing complexity.

In efforts to regulate universities, patrons may step forward in one period and back in another (Neave and van Vught, 1991). Governmental patrons in particular are fickle partners: they have different and highly changeable sets of interests from those of higher education institutions. But sooner or later, generally after much backing and filling, major patrons encourage the search for the *self-regulating, responsive university*, even the *entrepreneurial university*. Then the planning of pathways of development is not left to the global outlook of state officials and system administrators, nor even to those who sit astride the university as a whole. Entrepreneurial responsiveness is increasingly lodged both in the decentralized structure of the academic heartland and in an expanding developmental periphery of outreach offices and programs particularly oriented to development of environmental linkages. Not only does the university as a whole struggle to stay on its feet, but so, too, do a growing number of constituent units. Wise subunits plan their way, always on the lookout for new, viable directions in research, teaching, and learning.

A central tension in the entrepreneurial university is the need to reconcile new managerial values with traditional academic values. Academics are quite properly suspicious of the jargon and outlook of a hard managerialism imported from industry without regard for the vast, fundamental differences between university and nonuniversity forms of organization. The bottom-heaviness of universities has to be understood not as a defect but as a natural feature of organizations in which disciplinary and professional lines of affiliation and authority crisscross the institutional lines that predominate in most public and private organizations (Clark, 1983). Members of the physics department are first of all physicists; their value to the university lies in their capability to do research and teach and provide service in their particular realm, including exploration of linkages with neighboring fields old and new. As subject territories become more complicated and esoteric, their supporting "tribes" within universities have a stronger rather than weaker need for autonomous self-development (Becher, 1989). If capabilities are to be propagated in the basic units, ongoing devolution becomes a virtual necessity. Hence, decentralization from state to university and from university to basic unit is much on the international agenda as we turn toward the twenty-first century.

Planning strategies must be based on this fundamental recognition. Managerially driven schemes ought to encourage new and old basic units to find their own best pathways into the future. No matter how much universities attempt to run a tight ship administratively, they work from a platform of operational diversity. Beyond the multiversity lies the emerging academic conglomerate or federal university, in which parts proceed in different directions and use different methods. Medical schools, more than ever, are pushed to be tubs on their own bottoms, even splitting off as privatized components of public universities. In many countries, business schools now become essentially two organizations: a first-degree segment supported by the state and a set of advanced-degree programs (M.B.A. and executive-training endeavors) that pay their own way from tuition and fees. One major part of a university—for example, some engineering departments—may largely live off industrial research contracts, a form of support in which student head counts play no part, while another major segment, the humanities, depends on governmental and institutional support computed mainly on the number of students enrolled, sometimes supplemented by such output measures as the number of degrees awarded.

With the clash between new managerial-and-planning approaches and traditional academic-professional outlooks at the center of organizational tension, the ultimate Gordian knot in the entrepreneurial university is how to plan for unplanned change. Answers seem to lie in the counterbalancing construction of self-directing units and overarching administrative frameworks that assert broad institutional interests. Valuable unplanned change lies largely in the realm of the university understructure. The centrifugal force of initiatives taken at this level plows pathways from the present to unknown futures. Subfaculties, internal colleges, departments, research centers, and interdisciplinary programs all make their bets in a rolling wager, seeking the benefits of good choices and suffering the consequences of bad judgments. Planned change lies largely in the realm of larger administrative frameworks that, in the name of broad institutional interests, will decide, for example, to back certain new departments and programs while closing others. Central groups particularly need to seek symbolic expression of unified character, persistently maintaining that an oddly shaped conglomerate of disparate operations, stretching from the classics department to the medical school, is actually a united organization that knows what it is doing.

Facing the twenty-first century, Americans need to be mindful of the extent to which university planning should take into account what is occurring elsewhere in the world. Clearly, American universities have been leading the way during the last half of the twentieth century. Observers from other nations have come to our shores, and will continue to do so, to learn how we do certain things, from operating an open-door system of mass higher education to constructing world-class research universities. But Americans should not assume that there are no useful lessons they can learn from current efforts in reform and institution building in higher education elsewhere. Other national systems are working hard to catch up with and stay abreast of the forefront of "the international orbit of learning," to recall Clark Kerr's phrase. In many regions of the world—a good example is Europe—considerable analysis and transfer of ideas is taking place across national lines. In shirking from such learning, American higher education experts need to recall the painful experience of American industry in the myopic days of the recent past, before trips to Osaka and major restructuring became commonplace. This historic error need not be repeated in higher education, especially among those committed to better planning. Currently, Europe alone is a sufficient treasure trove of university experimentation. The volume of papers before us, which so richly extends our working knowledge of contemporary university restructuring in American higher education, has its value extended when American findings are placed alongside insights gained in the study of university transformation in other societies.

What we find as we search for change agents and processes of change in the higher education systems of the world is enormous tension between planning frameworks and the virtual "anarchy of production"—a necessary disorder—that generally exists at the level of the individual academic preoccupied with doing a good job in the give-and-take, and now rapidly changing, milieu of research and teaching. Everywhere in postsecondary education systems, a spontaneous road to order follows from the interacting competencies of thousands of faculty specialists, as well as from the spontaneous mobility of students who are able to choose institutions and fields of study. This road is difficult for all of us to understand, and one that is especially difficult for responsible government officials to recognize and approve. As higher education becomes more complicated, the order provided by state-imposed organizational frameworks and regulations can carry us only part of the way. Large grids of assignment and demarcation among institutions and disciplines, as in state master plans, can be redrawn from time to time, usually after much political struggle. At the same time, the broad river of established, connected practices rolls on, influenced in shape and flow by marketlike interactions and profession-led changes that may be only barely touched by planning frameworks. Greater sophistication about essentially unplanned lines of development can hardly come about too soon, since public concerns about postsecondary education everywhere stimulate the urge to micromanage from outside and microevaluate from on high. As we attempt to work out planning strategies, we need a better grasp of how state officials and academic staff make use of market-type interactions and how, in turn, various markets shape formal frameworks and professional behavior. Many interacting forms of coordination serve as lines of continuity and as engines of change.

What will universities be like in the year 2025? No one knows. Since there is no market for the unknown, and neither officials nor academics can design it, flexible openness remains essential. Higher education institutions need to ratchet their way across time, from one newly secured handhold to another, as they actively test and manipulate their environments, assess and alter internal capabilities, and accept risk portfolios as the price of long-term effectiveness. We shall soon see whether the 1990s have ushered in a golden age of experimentation and desirable change.

References

Becher, T. *Academic Tribes and Territories: Intellectual Enquiry and the Cultures of Disciplines.* Stony Stratford, Milton Keynes, England: Society for Research into Higher Education & Open University Press, 1989.

Clark, B. R. *The Higher Education System: Academic Organization in Cross-National Perspective.* Berkeley and Los Angeles: University of California Press, 1983.

Clark, B. R. "Case Studies of Innovative Universities: A Progress Report." *Tertiary Education and Management,* 1996a, *2*(1), 52–61.

Clark, B. R. "Substantive Growth and Innovative Organization: New Categories for Higher Education Research." *Higher Education,* 1996b, *31*(1), 1–14.

Kerr, C. "Universal Issues in the Development of Higher Education." In J. B. Balderston and F. Balderston (eds.), *Higher Education in Indonesia: Evaluation and Reform.* Berkeley: Center for Studies in Higher Education, University of California, 1993.

Neave, G., and van Vught, F. (eds.). *Prometheus Bound: The Changing Relationship Between Government and Higher Education in Western Europe.* New York: Pergamon Press, 1991.

February 1997   Burton R. Clark
                                                    Allan M. Cartter Professor Emeritus
                                                    of Higher Education and Sociology
                                                    University of California, Los Angeles

PREFACE

As we approach the twenty-first century, institutions of higher education are facing challenges they have never faced before. Clark Kerr (1987) observed that there has been a revolutionary rather than an evolutionary change in the environment of colleges and universities, and that these challenges represent a "new age" for higher education. In the decade since Kerr's observation, the external changes have only accelerated.

In this new context, higher education institutions need to critically examine their programs and processes, adapting where possible and reorganizing and restructuring where necessary. Most critical to the long-term effectiveness of higher education is thoughtful attention to the design of institutional processes for planning, management, and governance. The ability of colleges and universities to adapt successfully to the revolutionary challenges they face depends a great deal on an institution's collective ability to learn, successfully implement appropriate change, and continuously improve the core technologies of the organization.

The challenges facing institutions require a new paradigm for how we think about postsecondary education. Our institutions are beginning to exist in a fundamentally changed context, from a loose system of postsecondary institutions to one that might better be described as a postsecondary knowledge industry. That industry is marked by intensified competition among postsecondary institutions and from business both in the United States and globally, increasing governmental regulation, a more diverse clientele, and rapidly changing technology. Institutions need to respond to demands for more emphasis on nontraditional students, extended modes of delivery, more extensive relationships with government and business, more concern for learners and learning needs, and more interdisciplinary and cross-disciplinary scholarship.

These challenges call for a revolutionary redesign in many of our institutions, which requires a *redefinition* of a postsecondary knowledge industry and our institution's role in it, *redirection* of our institutional missions and external relationships, *reorganization* of educational programs and delivery systems, and *renewal* of the academic workplace. These extensive challenges require of our institutions a renewed commitment to planning and to a new mode of planning—contextual planning—that is broader in scope and capable of introducing extensive change in our institutions. Institutional planning and resource allocation processes are assuming crucial importance in the new environment. How to effectively design, implement, and carry out planning is increasingly a critical test of institutional leadership.

The emergence of the new age of higher education is not unrelated to global economic, political, and technological changes that are affecting all our lives. Access to higher education is now seen as critical to the "life chances" of a majority of the population, not only in the United States but in most developed countries of the world. True worldwide communication, a result of both technological advances in communication and cultural changes in language, have created a genuinely international market, not only for conventional products but also for "knowledge professionals," research, and educational services. As a consequence, higher education is under rapid expansion everywhere, and in this process governments are encouraging major reforms of their higher education systems, aggressively seeking effectiveness *and* efficiency, access *and* innovation. The result is unprecedented change in the environment of higher education, the nature and degree of which is revolutionary. It does not affect every institution in the same way, but it is likely to affect every institution.

The significance of the new competitive environment becomes even more evident when we examine the explicit challenges this new environment poses to higher educational institutions. We must accommodate or respond to demands for increased diversity; for wisely utilizing information, telecommunications, and computer technology; for increasing the quality of education and management; for contributing to economic productivity; for relearning in all areas of society; for a more global approach; and for new research agendas. Finally, these changes have to be performed in an environment of increasing competition and resource scarcity.

The intent of this book is to examine the challenges of the changing environment, the new approaches to planning that are necessary to respond to these challenges, and some planning strategies and management approaches to address the emerging issues of the new millennium. This book is addressed to presidents and other executive officers who want to understand how to redefine, redirect, reorganize, and renew their institutions; to planners, institutional researchers, and administrators who want to introduce new approaches and techniques to reform their institutions; and to higher education scholars interested in organizational behavior—in governance, planning, management, and institutional research for the decades ahead.

The collection has been designed as an authoritative handbook. The authors for each chapter are noted experts on their topic, and the chapters are written for the nonspecialist, providing a comprehensive overview of each topic with suggestions for further reading. The organization of the volume is from the general to the specific. Part One, "Redefining the External Context for Postsecondary Education," addresses some of the broad contextual changes and challenges facing postsecondary education and some of the external organizations, agencies, and dynamics that influence planning at the institutional level. Part Two, "Redirecting Institutions Through Contextual Planning," introduces a broader, more proactive approach to planning for this new environment and suggests how the primary elements of planning can be used to redirect our institutions. Part Three, "Reorganizing Management Support for Planning," examines how our various management and analytic functions can help reshape our institutions. Part Four, "Renewing Institutions and Planning for Academic Challenges," focuses again on approaches to some emerging planning issues that all institutions will face in the decade ahead.

As we move into the next century, colleges and universities throughout the world are grappling with the changing environmental forces systematically described in this volume. At every institution there is and will be vigorous debates about how planning and management should best be conducted in this new context. As suggested throughout this book, these debates matter in a way that has not been true in the past. Our goal has been to contribute to these critical discussions on the future forms of higher education by providing this thoughtful collection of essays codifying what has been learned from research and experience on planning in colleges and universities.

Acknowledgments

We are most grateful to four important groups of individuals who played very different but equally significant roles in turning into reality our proposal for a new book with a fresh look at planning. First, we are most indebted to the thirty-four authors who contributed chapters to this volume. Their eagerness to join in this venture and their enthusiasm throughout the process sustained an energetic momentum that kept the project on task. Their patience and grace under pressure were more than we deserved. Second, we extend our sincerest appreciation to the three anonymous reviewers for their extremely thoughtful, thorough, and helpful suggestions for improvement of the manuscript. Third, a project of this magnitude would not have been possible without the continuing support of the editors at Jossey-Bass. Gale Erlandson provided unwavering encouragement with the words, "If anyone can pull this off, they can!" Rachel Livsey always cheerfully provided the needed editorial assistance in helping us steer this rather large vessel into port. Fourth, we are certain the chapter authors will join us in acknowledging the support of clerical staff, graduate students, and other support staff who typed manuscripts, searched literatures, and provided support in other invaluable ways. We are especially indebted to Margaret Plawchan at the Center for the Study of Higher and Postsecondary Education at the University of Michigan for her backup support to our efforts. Finally, we are indebted to Burton R. Clark for his thoughtful and provocative foreword. The strengths of this volume can all be attributed to their efforts; any weaknesses are ours.

Reference

Kerr, C. "A Critical Age in the University World: Accumulated Heritage Versus Modern Imperatives." *European Journal of Education*, 1987, *22*(2), 183–193.

February 1997

Marvin W. Peterson
Ann Arbor, Michigan
David D. Dill
Chapel Hill, North Carolina
Lisa A. Mets
Ann Arbor, Michigan

THE AUTHORS

Paul T. Brinkman is director of planning and policy studies and adjunct professor of higher education at the University of Utah. During the 1980s, he was a senior associate at the National Center for Higher Education Management Systems. He holds a Ph.D. in higher education administration from the University of Arizona and has written books and articles on the economics of higher education and comparative data issues.

Ellen Earle Chaffee is the president of Mayville State University and of Valley City State University, two autonomous North Dakota institutions. She was national president of the Association for the Study of Higher Education and of the Association for Institutional Research. Her four books and two dozen articles focus on quality, strategy, and leadership. She received a B.A. degree in English from the University of Kentucky, an M.S. degree in counseling from North Dakota State University, and M.A. and Ph.D. degrees in administration and policy analysis from Stanford University.

Burton R. Clark is Allan M. Cartter Professor Emeritus of Higher Education and Sociology at UCLA. He took his Ph.D. in sociology at UCLA in 1954. During a long and distinguished career he has taught at five leading American research universities (Stanford, Harvard, Berkeley, Yale, and UCLA) in departments of sociology and graduate schools of education and has received national awards for distinguished scholarship from the American Educational Research Association, the American College Testing Program, the Association for the Study of Higher Education (ASHE), and Division J, Postsecondary Education, American Educational Research Association.

David William Cohen is professor of anthropology and history and director of the International Institute at the University of Michigan. He has done research—and published five books—on the historical anthropology of the lakes plateau region of eastern and central Africa.

Eric L. Dey is assistant professor of higher education at the University of Michigan's Center for the Study of Higher and Postsecondary Education. He received his Ph.D. degree in higher education at UCLA. His research centers on the influence that institutions have on students and faculty and the interconnections between social trends and higher education.

David D. Dill, associate editor, is professor of public policy analysis and education at the University of North Carolina at Chapel Hill. He received his B.A. degree from Oberlin College, his M.A. degree from the University of Chicago, and his Ph.D. degree in higher education from the University of Michigan. He has served as president of the Society for College and University Planning and as editor of *Planning for Higher Education.* He has written numerous books and articles on academic organization, management, and planning and is currently doing research on public policy in higher education.

Elaine El-Khawas is professor of education at UCLA and a former vice president for policy analysis and research at the American Council on Education. She received her B.A. degree from George Washington University and her M.A. and Ph.D. degrees from the University of Chicago, all in sociology. She has published several articles and chapters on accrediting agencies and other quality assurance organizations, particularly in comparative perspective.

Rhonda Martin Epper is a research associate with the State Higher Education Executive Officers (SHEEO). Her work at SHEEO has focused on technology policy, state coordination and governance, and finance issues. Epper holds a Ph.D. degree in higher education from the University of Denver, an M.B.A. degree from the University of Denver, and a B.B.A. degree in finance from the University of Texas at Austin.

Peter T. Ewell is senior associate at the National Center for Higher Education Management Systems (NCHEMS) in Boulder, Colorado. He received his Ph.D. degree in political science from Yale and completed his undergraduate study at Haverford College. He frequently consults, writes, and speaks on assessment and accountability policy for higher education for national and international audiences.

Ira Fink is president of Ira Fink and Associates, Inc., University Planning Consultants, in Berkeley, California. He specializes in university land and facilities planning, development, and management. Fink, a licensed architect, is a fellow of the American Institute of Architects. He holds master's and Ph.D. degrees in city and regional planning from the University of California, Berkeley. Fink is the author of more than forty books and articles on university planning and development.

Dorothy E. Finnegan received her Ph.D. degree in higher education from Pennsylvania State University. She is an assistant professor in the higher education program at the College of William and Mary. She currently serves as secretary for Division J of the American Educational Research Association. Her primary research interests are faculty careers and roles and higher education history, law, and finance.

Fred J. Galloway is project director for the Direct Student Loan Evaluation at Macro International. Before joining Macro, Galloway was director of federal policy analysis at the American Council on Education, where he represented the interests of the higher education community before the Executive and Legislative branches of the federal government. He has also been a faculty member in the Economics Department at San Diego State University and in the School of Business at the University of San Diego. Galloway received his B.A. and M.A. degrees from the University of California, San Diego, and his doctoral degree from Harvard University.

Harvey A. Goldstein is professor of city and regional planning at the University of North Carolina at Chapel Hill. He received a B.S. degree in engineering from Columbia University and M.A. and Ph.D. degrees from the University of Pennsylvania. His principal areas of teaching and research are economic development policy, regional labor markets, and economic impact assessment methods.

William H. Graves earned a Ph.D. degree in mathematics from Indiana University. Shortly thereafter, he joined the faculty at the University of North Carolina at Chapel Hill, where he is professor of mathematics and professor of information and library science. He is serving as interim chief information officer in a new position that consolidates the University's central information technology services. He has given over three hundred invited presentations on the role of information technology in higher education and has written and edited extensively on the subject.

Patricia J. Gumport is the executive director and principal investigator of the National Center for Postsecondary Improvement (NCPI), which is sponsored by the U.S. Department of Education's Office of Educational Research and Improvement (OERI). She concurrently serves as director of the Stanford Institute for Higher Education Research (SIHER) and associate professor in the School of Education at Stanford University. She holds a Ph.D. degree in education and a master's degree in sociology, both from Stanford. She has received the Early Career Scholar Award and the Dissertation of the Year Award, both from the Association for the Study of Higher Education (ASHE), and the Outstanding Teaching Award from Stanford University.

Raymond M. Haas is University Professor in the McIntire School of Commerce at the University of Virginia. He was formerly vice president for administration at both the University of Virginia and West Virginia University. His doctorate degree in business administration is from Indiana University.

Terry W. Hartle is vice president for governmental relations at the American Council on Education (ACE). Before joining ACE, he was the education staff director of the U.S. Senate Committee on Labor and Human Resources chaired by Senator Edward M. Kennedy. Hartle also has been a resident fellow and director of social policy studies at the American Enterprise Institute for Public Policy Research and a research scientist for the Educational Testing Service. Hartle received a B.A. degree from Hiram College, a master's degree from the Maxwell School at Syracuse University, and a doctoral degree from George Washington University.

Robert G. Henshaw is a program manager for institutional partnering initiatives at the Institute for Academic Technology in Research Triangle Park, North Carolina. He also manages a faculty support program for instructional use of the Internet at the University of North Carolina at Chapel Hill. He holds a B.A. degree in economics and an M.S. degree in information science from the University of North Carolina at Chapel Hill.

Richard B. Heydinger is a partner with the Public Strategies Group, a consulting firm in St. Paul, Minnesota, that specializes in the redesign of education and government services. He holds a Ph.D. degree from the University of Michigan and has written a number of monographs and articles.

Sylvia Hurtado is assistant professor of higher education at the University of Michigan's Center for the Study of Higher and Postsecondary Education. She holds a Ph.D. degree in higher education from UCLA. She received her B.A. degree from Princeton University and her M.Ed. degree from Harvard University. Her teaching and research interests focus on equity issues in higher education and the impact of campus racial climates on students and student development.

Sarah Williams Jacobson is an assistant professor in the College of Business at North Dakota State University in Fargo. She received a B.A. degree in biology from Grinnell College, an M.B.A. degree from the University of Connecticut, and a Ph.D. degree in organizational studies from the University of Massachusetts, Amherst. Her research and publications have focused on issues in international research on organizations and management, women in management, and work/private life concerns.

Dennis P. Jones is president of the National Center for Higher Education Management Systems (NCHEMS). He received his undergraduate and graduate degrees in engineering management from Rensselaer Polytechnic Institute. His work at NCHEMS has focused on supporting strategic decision making, planning, budgeting, and resource allocation and state policy regarding higher education.

George Keller is a Baltimore-based higher education consultant, editor, and author. He received his A.B. and M.Ph. degrees from Columbia University. He has authored more than one hundred articles, reviews, and book chapters, and the best-selling book *Academic Strategy: The Management Revolution in American Higher Education.* He currently edits the quarterly *Planning for Higher Education.* He has received several national awards for his education writing and editing and the K. C. Parsons Award from the Society for College and University Planning for "distinguished achievements in the field of higher education."

R. Sam Larson is a doctoral candidate in educational administration at Michigan State University. She has worked in the Office of Planning and Budgets and the Graduate School at Michigan State and is a consultant to the W. K. Kellogg Foundation.

Bruce A. Loessin received his B.A. degree from the University of Southern California and his M.A. degree in political science from the University of Wisconsin.

He has extensive experience in teaching, research, and administration as well as in fundraising, capital support, public relations, advertising, news and publications, graphic design, broadcasting, special events, continuing education, international studies, and federal relations. Mr. Loessin joined Case Western Reserve University in 1991 as vice president for development and alumni affairs.

Michael I. Luger is the Carl H. Pegg Professor of City and Regional Planning and chairman of the curriculum in public policy analysis at the University of North Carolina at Chapel Hill. He received an M.C.P. and Ph.D. (economics) degrees from the University of California, Berkeley, and M.P.A. and A.B. (architecture and planning) degrees from Princeton University. His research focuses in the areas of economic development, urban economics, infrastructure finance, and public policy.

Theodore J. Marchese is vice president of the American Association for Higher Education (AAHE) and editor of *Change* magazine and the *AAHE Bulletin*. He holds a B.A. degree in English from Rutgers University, a J.D. degree from Georgetown University, and a Ph.D. degree from the University of Michigan's Center for the Study of Higher Education.

Lisa A. Mets, associate editor, is associate director of the Center for Research on Learning and Teaching and is a candidate in the Ph.D. program in the Center for the Study of Higher and Postsecondary Education (CSHPE) at the University of Michigan. She received her B.A. degree in French from the University of Michigan and her M.A. degree in theoretical linguistics from Indiana University. Mets is coeditor of the sourcebook *Key Resources on Higher Education Governance, Management, and Leadership,* and two sourcebooks in the series *New Directions for Institutional Research.*

James R. Mingle is executive director of the State Higher Education Executive Officers (SHEEO). He completed his Ph.D. degree at the Center for the Study of Higher Education at the University of Michigan and his bachelor's and master's degrees in history from the University of Akron in Ohio. Mingle's scholarly work has focused on numerous public policy issues facing the states and the nation.

Anthony W. Morgan is vice president for budget and planning and professor of higher education at the University of Utah. He received a B.S. degree in political science from the University of Utah, an M.A. in political science from UCLA, and a Ph.D. in higher education from the University of California, Berkeley. He is currently a principal investigator of a major assistance project for higher education planning in Hungary.

James L. Morrison is professor of educational leadership at the University of North Carolina at Chapel Hill. His publications focus on futures research and planning. He founded and serves as editor of *On the Horizon: The Environmental Scanning Publication for Educational Leaders.*

Anna Neumann is associate professor of education at Michigan State University. She holds a Ph.D. degree in higher education from the University of Michigan and has published numerous articles and books on academic leadership, institutional cultures, and research methods and inquiry.

John L. Oberlin is interim executive director for Academic Technology and Networking Services at the University of North Carolina at Chapel Hill. He holds a B.A. degree in quantitative economics and decision sciences from the University of California, San Diego, and an M.B.A. degree from University of North Carolina at Chapel Hill.

Anne S. Parker currently serves as interim executive director for policy and planning for the University of North Carolina at Chapel Hill's information technology services division. She is completing a Ph.D. degree in information science at University of North Carolina at Chapel Hill.

Marvin W. Peterson, editor, is professor of higher education at the University of Michigan, a research program director in the National Center for Postsecondary Improvement, and former director of the Center for the Study of Higher and Postsecondary Education at the University of Michigan. He has served as president of the Association for the Study of Higher Education, the Association for Institutional Research, and the Society for College and University Planning, and as editor of the *New Directions for Institutional Research* monograph series.

Brian Pusser is a doctoral candidate in the School of Education at Stanford University and a research associate in the National Center for Postsecondary Improvement at Stanford.

Frans van Vught is professor of public policy at the University of Twente in the Netherlands. He is also director of the Center for Higher Education Policy Studies (CHEPS), Europe's leading higher education research center. During the years

1997–2001, he will serve as rector of the University of Twente. Van Vught has studied in the Netherlands and in the United States.

Ian Wilson is a principal of Wolf Enterprises in San Rafael, California, specializing in scenarios-based strategic management. For nearly fifty years, he has been engaged in corporate planning, beginning with his development for GE of its pioneering environmental analysis effort. He is a graduate of Oxford University.

PART ONE

REDEFINING THE EXTERNAL CONTEXT FOR POSTSECONDARY EDUCATION

Planning has many definitions for institutions and systems of higher education as it does for other societal organizations. But all these definitions share three critical concerns about the external world on which planning must focus: the nature of an institution's relevant environment, how that environment is changing, and the relationship of the institution to that changing environment. The major challenge, as institutions contemplate this external world, is to comprehend how the environment is changing and whether those changes will require the institution to adopt fresh perspectives or paradigms to understand how the environment is being redefined and what new planning issues they must address.

The chapters in Part One address this changing external environment for postsecondary institutions. Following an introductory overview in Chapter One, subsequent chapters focus on a particular environmental segment. Each addresses three common questions: (1) how is this segment of the environment changing? (2) what are the implications for institutional planning? and (3) what are some likely future issues emanating from changes in this segment of the environment for which planners need to be prepared?

Chapter One focuses on the changing nature of postsecondary education as a competitive system—a perspective that we accept as given in the United States and about which we make implicit assumptions that need to be seriously reconsidered. External societal challenges are seen as forces that are redefining the nature of postsecondary education as an emerging "postsecondary knowledge industry." This suggests a new and broader set of planning questions that institutions need to address and a new conceptual approach to planning: contextual planning (discussed in Part Two).

Chapters Two, Three, and Four examine the federal and state roles in shaping postsecondary education and the changing nature of our postsecondary buffer organizations, which mediate between institutions, the government, and the larger environment. The focus is on how governmental and nongovernmental activities are being shaped by the forces that are shaping this emergent postsecondary knowledge system or industry, and how these entities and their responses may affect planners as they design their institutional responses.

Chapters Five and Six offer insights into and implications for various institutional segments and the nature of colleges and universities as organizations as they attempt to plan for this environment. Chapter Five examines the possible impacts on traditional institutional contexts of community colleges, four-year colleges, and comprehensive institutions and how increasing competition within and among these sectors and with new external organizations is likely to influence the nature of planning. Chapter Six suggests some broad models and guidelines for thinking about substantially reconfiguring institutions for a more fluid postsecondary knowledge industry.

Part Two has a more institutionally oriented perspective on planning. Chapters in this part focus on new approaches to planning and how planning activities can be more responsive to some of the external changes discussed in Part One. The chapters in Part Three examine how planning relates to critical internal governance, management, and leadership processes. Part Four addresses some of the critical new planning challenges, which were identified as redefining our postsecondary system and our institutions in Chapter One, and suggests planning approaches or strategies for responding to them.

CHAPTER ONE

UNDERSTANDING THE COMPETITIVE ENVIRONMENT OF THE POSTSECONDARY KNOWLEDGE INDUSTRY

Marvin W. Peterson and David D. Dill

"Drift." "Reluctant accommodation." And "belated recognition that while no one was looking, change had in fact taken place." Using these words, Frederick Rudolph concluded his scholarly, insightful, and entertaining history of American higher education prior to 1950 (Rudolph, 1962). But the history of change in higher or postsecondary education in the past four decades has been decidedly more guided. Federal, state, and institutional initiatives have all directed attempts to expand, guide, and even control our systems and our institutions. Planning at the state and institutional levels has received particular attention as attempts to devise plans and develop planning structures, processes, and approaches have become commonplace.

While our definitions of, perspectives on, and approaches to planning have been varied, the primary focus of planning has been to examine environmental change and to develop institutional strategies for *responding* or *adapting*. Our traditional approaches to long-range and strategic planning assume that we compete in a system or industry consisting of other higher and postsecondary institutions. From this perspective, institutional planning involves understanding these broader environmental changes and how to compete more effectively with other postsecondary institutions.

As we approach the twenty-first century, this chapter argues that the nature of our postsecondary system itself is changing, that major forces in the larger societal environment are reshaping the nature of postsecondary education, changing it to a "postsecondary knowledge system" or industry that cuts across many of our traditional notions of system boundaries. These forces portend the growth of a postsecondary knowledge industry that delivers knowledge, information, and the capacity to teach and learn in a vast and flexible knowledge network. It also involves the active participation of many different types of institutions in the development and even educational use of this network. Postsecondary institutions are challenged not only to understand the nature of this new industry but to reconsider their institutional role and mission, their academic and administrative structure, and their academic processes.

This shift from a system of postsecondary institutions to one of a postsecondary knowledge system or industry suggests the need for a new paradigm in our thinking about the external and internal context of our institutions. Externally, it suggests competing and/or collaborating with non-postsecondary institutions and firms. Internally, it suggests potentially radical changes in the academic structure, the educational process, the conduct of research, and even the meaning of academic work in our institutions—the core of our institutional culture. A new approach to planning, *contextual planning*, is suggested (and elaborated in Chapter Seven). Chapter One provides a perspective on our changing postsecondary system. We examine the challenges reshaping postsecondary education, the nature of the emerging postsecondary knowledge network or industry, its internal and external institutional implications for planning, and a new set of planning questions that suggest the need for a new approach to planning: contextual planning.

An Expanded Planning Perspective: Society, Industry, and Institution

The literature on higher and postsecondary governance, management, and planning has long recognized our institutions as complex organizations functioning as open systems and subjected to many external societal forces and conditions. Planning is often seen as the attempt to deal with issues of the fit between institution and environment. Similarly, as a country we have prided ourself on our diverse and decentralized higher and postsecondary system; we have often viewed it as a comprehensive, loosely defined national system made up of subsets or segments of differing institutional types with somewhat more formally organized state-level governance or coordinating systems. However, we seldom focus on the nature of our higher or postsecondary education system as an industry—and the implications for institutional planning. Yet industry, as a concept that clusters similar organizations in society and differentiates them from those in other industries, is an appropriate focus—especially when the structure of the industry within which one exists is changing rapidly. Such is the case, this chapter argues, in post-secondary education today. The concept of an *industry* provides a useful tool for examining the changing nature of competition among colleges, universities, and other organizations.

The industry concept is implicitly understood and seldom discussed, yet of critical importance to postsecondary education. An industry is often defined as a set of competing organizations that utilize similar resources or attract similar clients, and that produce similar products and services. There are two critical features to the notion of an industry. First, it helps us define our competitive market or segment of it. Second, it is often the focus of attempts at governmental control or regulation. Clearly, we can recognize our higher or postsecondary education system as a major industry in our society.

Changing Perspectives

In understanding our current and future contexts, it is important to note that our system or industry has not been stable. This is suggested in Figure 1.1.

Traditional Higher Education. Prior to 1950, the higher education system or industry was viewed primarily as the public and private degree-granting, four-year, comprehensive, and university institutions in the country. Two-year institutions were still few in number and not considered core competitors. Planning was not a major institutional function or activity.

Mass Higher Education. The release of the Truman Commission Report in 1948, which recommended higher education for everyone who graduated from high school (a population whose numbers were increasing rapidly), spawned the rapid expansion of community colleges from the 1950s through the mid-1970s, as well as increasing enrollments in most other types of institutions. The industry was expanded by including a broader array of students (clients) who were absorbed in the growth of existing institutions, in the rapid expansion of two-year institutions, and in the addition of many new public four-year and university institutions. Institutional planning became a focal concern as plans were developed for new institutions, and forecasting growth and resource needs gave rise to long-range planning efforts.

Postsecondary Education. The higher education amendments of 1972 redefined the system or industry in two important ways. First, they transferred federal student aid from institutions to students who could demonstrate financial need. Second, they broadened the definition of which institutions were eligible to receive

FIGURE 1.1. REDEFINING OUR INDUSTRY.

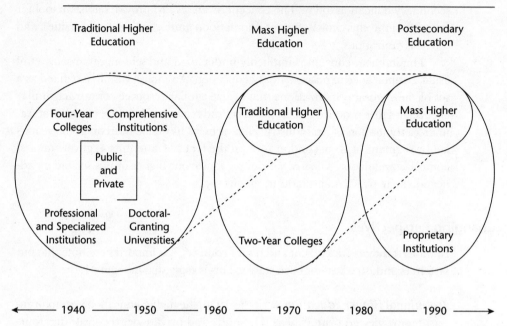

students with federal aid by including nondegree-granting postsecondary institutions and proprietary institutions. The shift in government student aid policy from institutions to students and the expanded definition of which institutions could compete for students or clients who received federal funds redefined the competitive relationship and nature of the industry. The increasingly competitive market-oriented environment of the 1970s and the constrained resources of the 1980s reinforced institutional interest in planning and led to the expanded interest in strategic planning that continues into the 1990s.

These changes in the nature of our system and the structure of our industry, from traditional to mass higher education and then to postsecondary education, suggest the role of governmental action in redefining the "related organizations" in the industry and in increasing the array of "similar clients." The transitions to mass and then to postsecondary education both had the effect of expanding the industry. But it was still an industry of institutions delivering education beyond high school.

A Model of the Forces Reshaping Institutional Planning

In order to better comprehend the factors in our changing environment that will influence institutional and state-level planning in higher and postsecondary education, it is important to understand the shift from an industry composed of postsecondary educational institutions to a postsecondary knowledge system or industry. To do so it is helpful to examine both the forces that reshape an industry and the changing societal conditions that affect the industry itself. (See Figure 1.2.) For example, the nature of competition in the postsecondary education industry will be affected by new customer or client needs for new educational services, by possible new entrants to the industry such as telecommunications companies seeking to offer degrees over the World Wide Web, and even by improvements within the industry itself. But the structure of the industry is being reshaped by larger forces: government regulation or deregulation, and the trend toward globalization of services and products.

While the planning challenges to individual institutions are clear, it is also important to examine their impact on the industry and less-direct implications for institution planning. To clarify the nature of these impacts, it is useful to examine the specific forces that govern competition in an industry. Porter (1980) has outlined a useful model for analyzing the structure of an industry (Figure 1.3). This schema, slightly revised to reflect education as a service industry, helps to reveal the forces that redefine the composition of an industry and reshape the competition within it. Those basic forces are (1) the threat of entry into the industry by new organizations, (2) the bargaining power of suppliers (for example, student clientele), (3) the bargaining power of customers (for example, employers, funding sources), and (4) the threat of substitute services. We have added a fifth force to Porter's model to reflect the potentially rapid changes occurring in how teaching, research, and service are being transformed by technology: (5) technical innovation in the core processes of the industry. Each of these forces in turn affects (6) the overall degree of rivalry or competition among institutions in the industry, which changes the external environment in which institutions must plan.

The model of institutional planning that emerges thus needs to reflect how changing societal conditions impact our industry as well as our postsecondary institutions directly. The institutional impacts of the societal changes affect both the internal nature of our institutions and the character of their external relationships. Thus, the planning perspectives institutions must have as we approach the twenty-first century are shaped both by the changing industry as well as the changing societal conditions.

This model guides the remaining discussion in this chapter. The next section examines changing societal conditions or challenges that are reshaping our industry and impacting our institutions. Then the nature of an emerging postsecondary knowledge industry and its institutional implications are discussed. The chapter concludes with a new set of institutional planning questions and suggests the need for a broader contextual approach to planning.

FIGURE 1.2. INFLUENCES ON INSTITUTIONAL PLANNING.

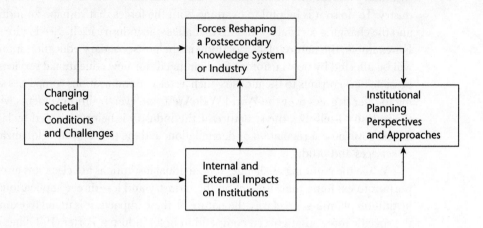

FIGURE 1.3. FORCES SHAPING COMPETITION IN AN INDUSTRY.

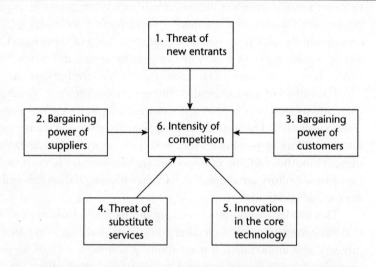

Source: Adapted from Porter, 1980.

Societal Conditions and Challenges

It is beyond the scope of this chapter to deal with the infinite array of trends, issues, and possibilities that forecasters, scanners, and futurists have identified that can affect postsecondary institutions. However, many of them coalesce around a series of discrete challenges to postsecondary educational institutions. We present here six challenges that have emerged in the 1990s and that promise to continue into the new century. They are quite different in nature from the demands and challenges that reshaped our industry in its transition from traditional to higher education and then to postsecondary education. These challenges require us to revise our thinking extensively about postsecondary education, the basic nature or structure of our institutions, and the nature and meaning of academic work.

More importantly, these challenges impact postsecondary education at a time when our institutions face a common, critical condition that amounts to a seventh, overarching challenge: *constrained resources.* For example, the costs of higher education are exceeding the willingness of taxpayers, governments, parents, employers, or students to pay; there are other societal priorities for funds; and many campuses are already financially strained. Resource-constraint issues are already so well documented that they are not discussed separately as a challenge in this chapter but rather are assumed. The following is a brief description of the six other challenges, their influence on the forces reshaping our industry, and their internal and external impacts on and implications for our institutions.

Changing Patterns of Diversity

The challenge of dealing with cultural diversity and its concomitant educational and economic deprivation is widely recognized as a social reality, a public policy issue, and an institutional reality. We have had some success in the past three decades in improving access to postsecondary education for various disadvantaged groups, but our record of successful retention and graduation is still inadequate in many fields and at the graduate level (Carter and Wilson, 1993; Mintz, 1993; Musil, 1995).

There are several lessons from our experience to date. First, the operant definition of cultural diversity is constantly changing. The initial concern for African American minorities in the 1960s has expanded to include numerous other racially underrepresented groups, and even to various subdivisions within them. Issues of gender, sexual preference, and economic or educational disadvantage have further expanded and/or fragmented the definition and focus of diversity as an issue. Second, our public policy and institutional responses have shifted: from separate-but-equal to nondiscrimination, to affirmative action, to preferences, and now to attempts to dismantle affirmative action. Third, members of most minority groups have become well organized and are gaining effective political voice both on campuses and in government.

While these lessons seem clear, so are the trends. The numbers of almost all of minority groups are increasing and will continue for the foreseeable future. Their differential rate of educational attainment or improvement is leading to conflict among disadvantaged groups. The debates about affirmative action are likely to be heated and continual. But the impacts both on our industry and in our institutions are revealing.

At the *industry level* (Table 1.1), potential customers for postsecondary learning opportunities—both the number of individuals and the categories defined as educationally disadvantaged—continue to grow. As a client group influencing public policy, the increasing presence of minority political caucus groups at the institutional, state, and national levels makes them a more powerful force. Although there have been few new institutions of postsecondary education founded as minority institutions in recent decades (except those for American Indians), the number of institutions becoming de facto minority institutions is increasing rapidly: approximately one in five postsecondary institutions has an enrollment in which ethnic minority students exceed 50 percent. Several new minority-oriented professional associations have been founded to serve these institutions and groups and to represent their interests. Within postsecondary institutions, the increase of minority-oriented academic and support programs has often been seen as adding substitute services. Although not directly affecting the core technology of postsecondary education, the advent of minority programs, new faculty staffing patterns, new student interaction patterns, and new academic perspectives and research agendas have influenced the processes of teaching and research in significant ways. Clearly, pressure to enhance diversity has created intensive competition for scarce resources, among students seeking limited financial support and admission slots, and among institutions to attract increased numbers of more diverse students, faculty, and staff.

The *impacts on institutions* largely reflect the changes impacting the industry (Table 1.2). Externally, governmental and political issues reflect the growing number and influence of minority political groups that demand attention. Competition both from minority and nonminority institutions for minority students, faculty, and funds is now a reality. The lessons within our institutions are even more telling. Dealing with issues of racism, discrimination, and pluralism requires addressing not only student conduct and classroom behavior but also issues of course, program, and discipline content, of research agendas, and of faculty behavior and staffing.

TABLE 1.1. CHALLENGES AND FORCES RESHAPING THE POSTSECONDARY INDUSTRY.

Changing Societal Conditions or Challenges	Forces Reshaping an Industry					
	Bargaining Power of Customers	Bargaining Power of Suppliers	Threat of New Organization Entrants	Threat of Substitute Services	Innovation in Core Technology	Intensity of Competition
Patterns of diversity	More defined groups; increasing numbers	Stronger and more numerous political groups	Minority institutions and associations	New programs and services	New academic and research perspectives	Among students and among institutions
Telematics Revolution	More access and numbers; individualized needs	Telematics firms control key educational resources	Telecommunications, computing, and information firms	Training firms and merger of entertainment and telecommunications	New interactive, individualized T/L/R potential	New cross-industry competition
Quality Reform	Increased focus on learner needs	Increased attention to client demands	—	Minor new training options	New mode of management; limited use by academics	Improvements in efficiency and effectiveness
Economic Productivity	Increased career oriented pressure	Government and industry needs	New role or interorganizational patterns	Many new groups and government agencies	May redirect teaching and research	New regional, state, or national
Postsecondary Relearning	New groups of postsecondary learners	Employer-based funding sources	Many new forms emerging	Corporate and governmental education programs	Emphasis on personalized content and delivery	Ill-defined market; potential of many sources
Globalization of Scholarship	Not clearly defined; highly specialized	Potentially, nations and institutions	Currently informal or limited arrangements	Emergent use of technology	Traditional or new technology	Yet to be determined

TABLE 1.2. EXTERNAL AND INTERNAL INSTITUTIONAL IMPACT OF CHANGING CONDITIONS.

Changing Conditions and Challenges	Institutional Impacts	
	Internal	*External*
Changing Patterns of Diversity	Pluralism, curricular content, research perspectives, faculty role	Rise of minority political power groups, institutions, and associations
Telematics Revolution: Telecommunications, Computing, and Information Resource Firms	Teaching/research, delivery modes, new faculty and student roles	Cross-industry links: educational, information, telecommunications and entertainment firms
Academic and Institutional Quality	Academic outcomes, value added and assessment; culture of academic quality improvement	Business-government collaboration; tide of TQM/CQI
Improving Societal Economic Productivity	Resource partner, or leadership role; new managerial and academic priorities	Business government, and higher education collaboration
Postsecondary Relearning markets	Client-driven modular content, external delivery, faculty role	Growing adult and professional postsecondary market; academic collaboration and new competitors
Globalization of Scholarship and Education	Interdisciplinary and transnational colleagues, problems, and research paradigms	Multidisciplinary cross-industry and and transnational research groups; Multinational institutions

Regardless of its definition, diversity is clearly a condition and challenge that will not abate soon. Indeed, the new debates about affirmative action force us to take a hard look at dealing with and responding to issues of educational disadvantage versus social, cultural, or economic disadvantage, and whether it is to be addressed as a group problem, an individual issue, or both. Diversity is an issue that is reshaping our industry and affecting its institutions. In addressing it, we need to be aware of how it is changing the nature of this postsecondary industry, the external political realities of our institutions, and the internal influences on curriculum, teaching, research, and tension over our "political ambivalence" (Smelser, 1993) about the concept itself.

The Telematics Revolution: Reinventing or Supplementing the Core Technology

Probably the most pervasive challenge to our industry and institutions is the rapid expansion and influx of interactive telecommunications networks, which link students and faculty to extensive data resources via workstations and computers capable of integrating information, sound, and video images. Whether it will lead to a sweeping reinvention of how students and faculty teach, learn, and conduct scholarship or whether it is merely a technical substitute is the source of heated debate on most campuses. There are several unique features about the current revolution: (1) its rapid development and rate of change, (2) the extent to which applications are being adopted in all areas of modern life beyond the campus, (3) its spread to national—even global—availability in a short time span, (4) its potential for use with few constraints of time and location, and (5) the increased affordability of ever more powerful technology. These features make it imperative that institutions adopt it as a tool of postsecondary education. But the capacity for use of telematics as a technology for learning (not just a teaching or communication technology) is perhaps the most critical challenge facing postsecondary institutions. The irony and difficulty is that this technology, which was spawned in universities, has taken on a life of its own. With so many societal as well as educational applications and implications, it has created its own industry as new computer hardware and software, telecommunications, and information-handling products and techniques are developed. The impacts on our postsecondary industry and our institutions will be extensive, and perhaps central, in the next decade (Green and Gilbert, 1995; Twigg, 1994; see also Chapter Twenty-Two, which provides a focused treatment of this challenge).

At the *industry level* (Table 1.1), this revolution has a vast potential for increasing the options for accessing electronic learning opportunities, for reaching a significant array of new customers (students or scholars), and for extending an institution's teaching potential. On the other hand, it has in many instances reversed the client relationship of postsecondary institutions with the telematics firms. Rather than those firms being the client seeking an institution's research results or trained students, they have become both the creator and supplier of information-handling tools, which makes the postsecondary institution the client—effectively reversing roles and making postsecondary institutions increasingly dependent on their former clients. An even bigger threat is the potential for new non-postsecondary institutions to enter the postsecondary educational arena. A small number of institutions offering postsecondary education via interactive telecommunications have emerged, and others are beginning to experiment with this mode. Large companies are adopting these technologies for their own internal postsecondary training programs. Of greater possible significance is the merger of entertainment and telecommunication firms, further enhancing the potential of the packaging and delivery of postsecondary knowledge. (Will they make education entertaining, or entertainment more educational?)

Clearly, what makes this change so revolutionary is that it constitutes an alteration of the core technology of teaching, learning, and research. Colleges and universities cannot afford *not* to utilize it. But the critical issue for faculty is whether that will be as a substitute service for some portions of their teaching and scholarly activities, or an adoption of it as a more central mode.

One of the things that make this technological revolution so critical is the extent to which it interacts with all the other societal challenges. It enhances the capacity to reach both new and current student-customers differently. It also influences the way academics work and students learn. This technology is just beginning to reshape the way postsecondary institutions compete with each other for students and compete or cooperate with firms in other industries (telematics, entertainment, training) to deliver their educational products. New patterns of competition and cooperation in delivering educational services with firms that were not part of our postsecondary industry are emerging as they and we become part of a postsecondary knowledge industry.

At the *institutional level* (Table 1.2), the implications are also extensive. Externally, universities will either find themselves collaborating with public and private educational corporations, telecommunications companies, and information-based firms and even entertainment enterprises in designing educational and knowledge-delivery systems, or competing with them. Already, researchers have the capacity to collaborate with scholars around the globe; they will increasingly do so.

Within the institution, students have access to extensive content material, educational resources, and other students and faculty without constraints of time or location. Such an educational network suggests a very different teaching-learning process. In addition to their traditional role, faculty may serve as learning facilitators, network guides, or learning-resource designers. The nature of the faculty role, the student-faculty relationship, and the course or classroom may change as the campus becomes part of a teaching-learning network.

While the investment in hardware and software for wide-scale use will strain the budgets of all institutions, its influence on faculty and the processes of teaching and research constitutes a major internal challenge to redefine the nature of academic work within the academy. The major external challenge is to develop new interinstitutional ties with various telematics firms.

Academic and Institutional Quality: A Focus on Learning and Improvement

Thus far in the 1990s, the demand for educational quality has already become pervasive (Ewell, 1991). The meaning of academic quality, however, has changed in recent decades. In the 1960s and 1970s, academic quality was associated with the level and nature of institutional resources. In the 1980s, a new meaning evolved: assessment, with a focus on assessing results (outcomes, goal achievement, value-added). In the mid-1990s, academic quality has become associated with public accountability and a focus on student learning, faculty productivity and performance, program effectiveness, and even institutional evaluation. The debate about the definition of, criteria for, and means of improving educational quality shows no signs of diminishing and will be a continuing challenge both in government policy circles and in academic and institutional discussions (Dill, 1995a).

A more recent focus on quality is the concern for Total Quality Management (TQM) or Continuous Quality Improvement (CQI) (Dill, 1992). While those ideas emerged in the private sector and have had the support of political leaders, the primary emphasis and application in postsecondary education to date has been in administrative activities and functions. Unlike the more educationally focused notions of quality, this approach suggests a comprehensive emphasis on developing an institutional culture that stresses policies and practices promoting (1) an environment of continuous improvement, (2) customer- or client-centeredness, (3) a rational approach to decision making using intensive measurement and benchmarking, (4) a focus on process design, (5) collaboration and teamwork, and (6) individual empowerment. Such a comprehensive approach promises to clash with strong traditions of academic individualism when applied to academic areas. But if this perspective can be successfully adapted to academic settings, it may also lead to rethinking our teaching, learning, and research processes and how we utilize the new technology for educational purposes. The fact that the Baldrige Award was recently extended in 1995 to postsecondary education suggests that TQM/CQI will have a continued emphasis in academic as well as administrative areas. (Chapter Twenty-Five addresses the concerns of planning for quality in greater detail.)

To date, the quality challenge has not had an extensive impact on our *post-secondary industry*, but it may increase as competition within the industry increases (Table 1.1). The quality challenge does force an institution to refocus on defining and differentiating its stakeholders (customers with needs and clients making demands) and designing its services (academic or administrative) with them in mind rather than with disciplinary, professional, or faculty concerns being primary. This particular challenge has not yet prompted new organizations to enter postsecondary education except in the narrow area of TQM/CQI training programs. Quality or continuous-improvement approaches initially seemed to represent a new mode of management rather than a revision of core academic technology or provision of a substitute service. However, as competition requires postsecondary institutions to attend more to cost and productivity, quality approaches may become associated with reengineering (a focus on process), downsizing, and/or prioritizing of services. As such, they are more a response to resource constraint designed to enhance institutional competitiveness than a force changing the competitiveness in the industry.

At the *institutional level* (Table 1.2), the major external dynamics suggest that as the public image of postsecondary education continues to decline, the emphasis both on educational quality and TQM/CQI will likely increase. Internally, the varying approaches to assessment, reinforced by accreditation and political pressures, are increasingly used for collegial accountability, redesign, or improvement (Romer, 1995). The advent of the Baldrige Award for education will no doubt also reinforce the use of TQM and CQI in administrative arenas. Whether concerns for educational quality and assessment can effectively merge with total-quality and continuous-improvement approaches will be a major management and planning challenge for the future.

Improving Economic Productivity: New Emphasis or New Function?

The contribution of postsecondary education to economic development has been the primary drive for the rapid and continuous expansion of postsecondary education (Leslie and Brinkman, 1988). Colleges and universities produced well-trained students, provided appropriate professional programs, and conducted pure and applied research that contributed to society's well-being and improvements in the standard of living. But the decline of U.S. economic fortunes, and particularly the loss of dominance in key manufacturing industries in the global marketplace, has led to a new emphasis on enhancing economic productivity both at the national and state levels.

In the development of federal government priorities and state-level plans for economic development, it has been implicitly assumed that higher education, government, and the private business community are all key players. Postsecondary institutions have historically played, and been satisfied with playing, a "knowledge development" function, serving as primary providers of academic and professional training and of pure and applied research. In recent decades, serving as consultants and as sites for campus research parks, they have participated more directly in the "technology transfer" function. A more recent and aggressive form of this function is reflected in the growth of campus-affiliated incubator parks for new-product and new-company development. Most recently, postsecondary institutions have participated in developing "state or regional economic development strategies" (Dill, 1995b). In all of these roles, their participation can vary from resource institution to partner, or to manager of the function (Peterson, 1995). Increasingly, institutions are pressured to take on all three roles and to become a leader of the effort. The difficulty is that becoming a manager of technology transfer or economic development may involve an institution in an activity for which it is not well suited and one in which it may not be able to succeed (Feller, 1990). Yet political and economic pressures to show greater institutional accountability for and contribution to this area is likely to increase as long as our economy falters or fails to meet political expectations or promises. (See Chapter Twenty-Two for an extended examination of this challenge.)

At the *industry level* (see Table 1.1), this challenge has little direct effect on our primary customers (students), but it is probably reflected in their career-oriented priorities and concerns about useful programs. However, it does subject the industry to increasing demands from its primary clients (government and industry), especially in the public sector. The expansion of concern for economic productivity also introduces new entrants into postsecondary education—public and private technology development organizations—that may be better positioned than postsecondary institutions themselves are to compete for public applied research and development funds, and better staffed to carry out such activities. It may also require institutions to subsidize risky economic development activities with other funds traditionally used for academic functions (Feller, 1990). In effect, a new mode of organization is created (the economic development agency or the technology transfer partnership) to provide a new service. In order to compete in this emerging service activity, institutions may be pressed to redirect effort away from some of the traditional postsecondary emphasis on teaching and research to supply the knowledge and trained students for economic development to active organizers of economic development activity. In most instances, this pressure for economic development involves postsecondary education directly in a new realm of competition: interregional, interstate, or even international, an arena in which it was previously only indirectly engaged.

At the *institutional level* (see Table 1.2), the press for economic development involves the institution in potentially different types of partnerships that cut across industry boundaries in order to engage in complex public-private corporate arrangements and to develop a new or previously peripheral function. These may be collaborative arrangements, or they may subject the institutions to new governmental controls and regulations. Internally, extensive involvement in economic development activity may require new managerial roles and approaches to engage in more entrepreneurial (for example, technology transfer) or political development activity. It may also realign faculty effort or require hiring of faculty more skilled in these less scholarly or academic realms (Fairweather, 1996).

Postsecondary Relearning: New Markets, Modes, and Models of Continuing Education

In recent decades, expanded educational services have been directed toward increasing traditional student enrollments and increasing service to underrepresented groups: minorities, women, older students. Modifications in schedules (evenings, weekends) or locale (off campus) were used to deliver traditional courses or programs to the part-time, nontraditional student. Continuing education was often an ancillary function, or primarily related to professional and occupational programs. Yet in today's increasingly competitive and technologically turbulent world, products, companies, and careers can change rapidly. The need for technological retooling and postsecondary reeducation is increasing in a wide variety of professions (Reich, 1991).

The demand for postsecondary relearning by older individuals is an exploding market. It comprises three identifiable groups. One is the post-high school but pre-baccalaureate group who need further education to reenter the job market or remain viably employed. One study (Grubb, forthcoming) suggests there are 20–30 million individuals between twenty-five and fifty years of age in this category. A second is the postbaccalaureate group who have college degrees but may need further education (but less than a full graduate degree) to remain viably employed or to change fields. While not as large as the previous group, it is rapidly growing as the proportion of degree holders continues to grow. Finally, there are the graduate and professional degree holders who need more than traditional continuing education to advance or change fields. In addition to their size and growth, these three market segments have much in common. Their educational interests and/or those of their employers often focus on professional competencies, individual educational needs, learning modules, off-campus delivery, and willingness to use distance-education modes of transmission (including technology) rather than on traditional courses, degrees, or programs.

At the *industry level* (see Table 1.1), these numbers suggest three substantial groups of potential customers for postsecondary reeducation. While some may pay for their own education, there is a sizable set of employer organizations that may be potential clients for such educational services for their employees. This market is currently served by internal corporate educational units, specialized training and development firms, and numerous postsecondary institutions, although often in traditional courses, programs, and delivery modes (Eurich, 1985). It is a market with significant potential for new industry entrants and in which some substitute services in the form of non-postsecondary institutions are expanding. But this market is still somewhat amorphous, with patterns of competition that are not well defined, especially by traditional postsecondary institutions.

At the *institutional level* (see Table 1.2), this is a substantial market. If traditional postsecondary institutions fail to respond, they risk losing a growing, sophisticated market for postsecondary, professional, and even postgraduate reeducation (beyond traditional continuing education in this field). But responding to this market requires working closely, even collaboratively, with the client and customer (or their employees). Within the institution, organizing, delivering, and financing customer-based education is often a complex new endeavor. It requires a responsive mode of curriculum design, new or individualized content modules, willingness to provide nontraditional delivery modes, and a substantial change of faculty roles.

Globalization: Breaking Bonds and Boundaries

The challenge of international and global perspectives as we approach the twenty-first century needs little exposition; nor is it a new phenomenon. Models of international student and faculty exchange programs, attempts to emphasize and improve foreign language instruction, and introducing global perspectives into our curriculum are widespread if not completely effective. But two emergent phenomena suggest that the need for greater global emphasis could take on new boundary-spanning forms in the near future.

While knowledge and scholars have always resisted regional and national boundaries, a new form of international network may be emerging. One author (Cohen, 1994) has coined the term "international civil societies" to describe a form of network consisting of university scholars, governmental policy researchers, and private-sector experts organized around major significant social problems or issues (for example, global warming, AIDS, human rights, etc.). These civil societies are interdisciplinary, cross-national, and cross-industry groups. Their work may combine research, learning, action or policy, and formulation. They often rely on technology and have access to a wide array of information and expertise, but they often have little managerial structure. In effect, they reflect how the knowledge and technology explosion can rewrite scholarly boundaries without institutional structure.

Another form of globalization that may emerge is more similar to the multinational corporation. While loosely structured, institutional exchange programs and research alliances crossing national boundaries are common, the prospects for a multinational university are worth contemplating. Some universities now have their own campuses in other countries. Many institutions have partnerships with multinational technology firms. Some countries such as those of the European Union have supported cross-national postsecondary alliances. A move to more formalized international consortia, degree-granting federations among institutions in different countries, and even the possibility of a multinational university, while a daunting challenge, are likely in the decade ahead. (See Chapter Twenty-Seven, which provides further insights on planning for this challenge.)

At the *industry level* (see Table 1.1), new forms of global organization would markedly intensify competition in postsecondary education (Dill and Sporn, 1995). Clearly, scholars, researchers, and many students who now participate in the less formal arrangements are a specialized customer group who could be attracted. Some countries as clients might support limited forms of cross-national organizations, and institutions with an extensive international mission or presence could emerge. A truly multinational focus would be an intriguing new entrant to our postsecondary industry, providing an alternate form of global and international opportunity for study and scholarship, and an interesting addition to the competitive mix.

At the *institutional level* (see Table 1.2), the prospect of organizing a multinational institution or participating in a multinational partnership requires development of new mechanisms for collaboration with or competition in different cultures and in dealing with multiple government bureaucracies. The problems of internal management require guiding a more entrepreneurial, multicultural network form of organization—a skill to be advanced by those who develop such enterprises.

The Emerging Postsecondary Knowledge Industry: A New Perspective

As we face the twenty-first century, the changing societal conditions discussed earlier are all likely to continue. Each promises to have a major impact on both our postsecondary institutions and our industry (Tables 1.1 and 1.2).

In the previous transitions from higher education to mass education to a postsecondary industry, only one or two societal conditions created the need for transition, and the necessary industry change was usually expansion of clientele (students) or institutions. However, the six societal conditions discussed above affect all of the forces that reshape an industry. The resulting alteration in our notion of a postsecondary industry promises to be extensive and to call for a new paradigm: the postsecondary knowledge industry. While the exact nature of this new industry is only nascent, a review of how the forces reshaping an industry are affected by societal conditions provides some glimpses into our industry's possible evolution (Table 1.3).

Core Technology

Perhaps the most influential force is the potential for innovation in our core technology: the development, transmission, and dissemination of knowledge in society and in turn in our postsecondary industry. Postsecondary institutions have long believed they were the preeminent knowledge industry for postsecondary teaching, learning, and research. However, the telematics revolution has introduced a powerful new interactive information-handling technology that offers potentially revolutionary changes in moving from traditional modes of teaching, learning, and research to varied, responsive, flexible, interactive, and individualized modes. More critically, the telematics revolution makes it easier to respond to most of the other societal conditions affecting the industry (diversity, quality, economic productivity, postsecondary relearning, and globalization); and the revolution enhances all the other forces acting upon the industry (new organizational entrants, the power of customers and suppliers, the threat of substitute services, and the intensity of competition).

New Organizational Entrants

While the extent of use and effectiveness of information technology is key to our core processes of postsecondary education, the threat of new organizational entrants is perhaps the most tangible way of visualizing the reconfigured industry. Figure 1.1 reflects the institutional changes as our industry moved from traditional to mass education and then to postsecondary concepts. However, all of these transitions have primarily added students (customers) and new types of postsecondary educational institutions. Postsecondary now includes a broad array of public, private, and proprietary educational organizations providing varied educational offerings. But all are primarily educational organizations. Focusing on the organizations that are critical to a postsecondary knowledge industry perspective suggests the addition of many types of organizations previously thought to be part of other industries: telecommunications companies; computer software and

TABLE 1.3. A NEW PARADIGM FOR THE POSTSECONDARY KNOWLEDGE INDUSTRY.

Industry Forces	Postsecondary Industry	Postsecondary Knowledge Network
Innovation in core technology	Traditional teaching, learning, research modes	Interactive information technology network for T, L, & R
Threat of new organizational entrants	Traditional colleges, universities, and proprietary institutions	Telecommunications, computing hardware and software, information resource, corporate and government education and training, and entertainment firms
Bargaining power of customers (students)	Traditional and nontraditional degree students	Growing minority and postsecondary relearning markets for individual learning needs
Bargaining power of suppliers (clients)	Primarily as employers, funding sources, and purchasers of services	Providers of information resources, educational technology, and communications networks; as pressure groups, partners, or competitors
Threat of Substitute services	Limited	More extensive
Intensity of competition	Among existing postsecondary institutions or segments	Cross-industry more competitive

hardware firms; information resource organizations; corporate and governmental organizations engaged in education, training, and professional development; and, perhaps, even "entertainment" firms. Figure 1.4 portrays this new extended industry that includes all the organizations in the postsecondary knowledge network. As our previous discussion has suggested, these new organizations are often no longer either just suppliers to, or customers of, postsecondary institutions. They are now effectively part of our postsecondary knowledge development, dissemination, and education system and need to be viewed as potential collaborators or competitors.

The Power of Customers

The analysis of societal conditions also suggests a change in perspective on our potential customers for postsecondary education (students). The shift is from a focus on traditional and nontraditional students seeking regular courses and degree offerings via traditional delivery modes to a broader view of the entire market for postsecondary education, which includes those potential student customers who are interested in non-degree-oriented learning and often in nontraditional modes of delivery. The key shift in the postsecondary knowledge industry perspective is to focus on students as learners with individualized educational needs rather than as potential students for courses and programs designed and delivered by postsecondary institutions.

The Power of Suppliers and the Threat of Substitute Services

The inclusion of potential new organizational entrants in the new postsecondary knowledge industry both enlarges and suggests their increased power as suppliers. They are no longer just the customers who are employers of graduates and purchasers of our knowledge products and services or sources of funding. They are often key suppliers, providers of valuable information resources, new educational technology and advances, and access to critical communication networks. Another major shift is to recognize that in the new postsecondary knowledge environment suppliers may be not merely resource providers for and purchasers of services from postsecondary institutions but also sources of substitute (educational) services. Further, they are now potential pressure groups, educational partners, or competitors—not merely suppliers. It is clear that in a postsecondary knowledge environment other knowledge-based firms do have greater power, both as suppliers of resources or as sources of substitute services, because of the ease of access to knowledge and its utilization.

FIGURE 1.4. THE EMERGING POSTSECONDARY KNOWLEDGE INDUSTRY.

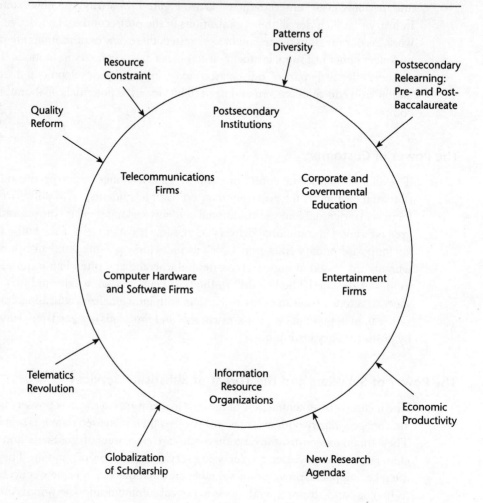

Competition

Finally, it is also apparent that in the postsecondary knowledge industry competition is likely to intensify. Clearly, competition among existing postsecondary institutions is intensified by the challenges to increase diversity, to improve quality, to constrain costs, and to enter the expanding postsecondary relearning markets. What is likely to be qualitatively different is competition in the knowledge industry that cuts across old industry boundaries. For instance, competing in the knowledge industry with organizations from the telecommunications, computing, or the corporate education and training world is far more entrepreneurial and fast-paced than in the traditional postsecondary world. Also, competition to engage in economic development or new global arrangements may entail both creative risks and new governmental controls or regulatory environments.

Thus, it is apparent that a postsecondary knowledge industry is substantially different from one composed only of postsecondary educational institutions. Participating in this new environment or industry requires a continued attempt to understand its evolving character and the role that traditional postsecondary institutions will play in it.

Institutional Challenges: A Contextual Planning Perspective

Discussion of changing societal conditions has implicitly identified many of the internal and external impacts on postsecondary institutions and the forces that are shaping the emerging postsecondary knowledge industry (Tables 1.1 and 1.2).

A brief review highlights the challenges for institutional leaders and planners as they provide new perspectives to their institutions in the decade ahead. First, there is the need to plan for a period of substantial external change and uncertainty in which the nature not only of our postsecondary system but of our postsecondary knowledge industry is changing. The foremost challenge is to understand the critical societal conditions and forces that are reshaping our postsecondary knowledge industry. Second, one needs to understand how interactive, technology-based information and knowledge systems will reshape our industry and our institutions. Third, there is an even more diverse array of potential educational customers needing postsecondary educational services: the growing minority and educationally disadvantaged populations, new cadres of postsecondary learners, etc. Fourth, there is an increasingly diverse and powerful set of constituent groups and organizations demanding various educational services: a more proactive business community, more varied and changing governmental interest, and a complex labyrinth of telematics and information-resource firms. Fifth, many of these external business and governmental organizations are now also potential competitors for or collaborators with existing postsecondary institutions for both the new postsecondary markets and as an alternative or substitute for our more traditional undergraduate, graduate, and professional education and research functions. Sixth, the growing diversity of customers or student clientele includes postsecondary learners interested in or willing to use interactive technology as modes of educational transmission delivered to noncampus settings and packaged in nontraditional content or competency modules rather than traditional programs or degrees. Seventh, on the educational side, there is a shift in emphasis from teaching—from faculty and instructional development—to learning, learners, learning needs, and learning development. Eighth, the nature and bounds of research are likely to be more transdisciplinary and collaborative but less limited to geographic, institutional, or even national spheres. Finally, most of these challenges call for rethinking the basic educational delivery and research processes and functions. They focus more on change in the teaching-learning process, the research process, and faculty-to-student and faculty-to-faculty relationships. They suggest extensive changes in faculty roles and behaviors—in essence, changing the academic culture of the workplace.

This set of planning challenges suggests extensive change in how we view our institutions both externally and internally. Externally it requires a planning perspective focused on the broader notion of a postsecondary knowledge industry or network rather than an industry or system of higher or postsecondary institutions. This suggests an external environment of increasing diversity and complexity, recognizing that many other types of organizations are engaged in the development, dissemination, and utilization of knowledge that is postsecondary in character. Internally, the planning perspective must recognize the potential need for extensive change in the academic structure and function and even in the nature of academic work. In essence, the societal challenges to postsecondary institutions and this new paradigm of a postsecondary knowledge industry may require extensive institutional change. This suggests a need for planning which will address the following questions:

Redefinition: What is the nature of a postsecondary knowledge industry, and what is our institution's role in it?

Redirection: How should our institution's mission change to reflect these new realities, and what new external relationships should we develop?

Reorganization: How should we redesign our academic processes and structures and reorganize our management functions?

Renewal: How do we renew or re-create our academic workplace and institutional culture? Our preparation of future faculty?

In an environment of extensive and often unpredictable change that mandates rethinking the nature of our system or industry and considering the need for major institutional adaptation, current approaches to planning may be inadequate. Long-range and strategic planning typically begins with the assumption that one functions within an existing system of institutions or an industry, and that evolutionary change will allow an institution to adapt to environmental constraints and opportunities. However, in a situation in which the industry context is being reshaped and the institution may need to change drastically, a more proactive mode of planning that seeks to participate in shaping the industry and offers the possibility of more radical redesign of the institution may be called for. Contextual planning, discussed in Chapter Seven, offers an approach to addressing these broader questions of redefinition, redirection, reorganization, and renewal.

Further Reading

Those interested in exploring the changing nature of society and its implications for postsecondary education in the information age will find Peter Drucker's "The Age of Social Transformation" (1994) and *Managing for the Future* (1992) provocative and insightful. For a perspective on the changing nature of institutions as organizations, *Organizing for the Future,* by Jay Galbraith and others (1993), is an interesting generic treatment for those interested in planning postsecondary institutions. Two thought-provoking books that provide new ways of thinking about organizations in a postindustrial information age are Sally Hegelson's *The Web of Inclusion* (1995) and Margaret Wheatley's *Leadership and the New Science* (1992). Two edited volumes that focus more explicitly on our current and changing world of postsecondary education are David Dill and Barbara Sporn's *Emerging Patterns of Social Demand and University Reform: Through a Glass Darkly* (1995) and *Higher Education in American Society* (1994, third edition, but a fourth is planned), edited by Philip Altbach, Robert Berdahl, and Patricia Gumport. These volumes feature well-prepared chapter contributions that focus on the external conditions influencing postsecondary institutions (Dill and Sporn, 1995) and on a comprehensive examination of our current postsecondary system or industry and how it is changing (Altbach, Berdahl, and Gumport, 1994). Readers are also encouraged to identify a broadly focused publication or other information source that scans and examines external forces or internal changes in postsecondary education. *On*

The Horizon, edited by James Morrison and published by Jossey-Bass, is such a useful resource focusing on education. Readers with more focused interests in the challenges to postsecondary education discussed in this chapter will want to identify a resource related to their particular interest.

References

Altbach, P. G., Berdahl, R. O., and Gumport, P. J. *Higher Education in American Society.* (3rd ed.) Amherst, N.Y.: Prometheus, 1994.

Carter, D. J., and Wilson, R. *Minorities in Higher Education: American Council on Education Eleventh Annual Status Report.* Washington, D.C.: American Council on Education, 1993.

Cohen, D. W. "The Constitution of International Expertise." *Journal of the International Institute.* Ann Arbor, Mich.: University of Michigan International Institute, 1994.

Dill, D. D. "Quality by Design: Towards a Framework for Academic Quality Management." In J. Smart (ed.), *Higher Education: Handbook of Theory and Research,* Vol. VIII. New York: Agathon Press, 1992.

Dill, D. D. "Through Deming's Eyes: A Cross-National Analysis of Quality Assurance Policies in Higher Education." *Quality in Higher Education,* 1995a, *1*(2), 95–110.

Dill, D. D. "University-Industry Entrepreneurship: The Organization and Management of American University Technology Transfer Units." *Higher Education,* 1995b, *29*(4), 369–384.

Dill, D. D., and Sporn, B. "The Implications of a Postindustrial Environment for the University: An Introduction." In D. D. Dill and B. Sporn (eds.), *Emerging Patterns of Social Demand and University Reform: Through a Glass Darkly.* New York: Pergamon Press, 1995.

Drucker, P. *Managing for the Future: The 1990s and Beyond.* New York: Dutton, 1992.

Drucker, P. "The Age of Social Transformation." *Atlantic Monthly,* November 1994, pp. 53–80.

Eurich, N. P. *Corporate Classrooms, the Learning Business.* Princeton: Princeton University Press, 1985.

Ewell, P. T. "Assessment and Public Accountability: Back to the Future." *Change,* 1991, *23*(6), 12–17.

Fairweather, J. *Faculty Work and Public Trust: Restoring the Value of Teaching and Public Service in Academic Life.* Needham Heights, Mass.: Allyn & Bacon, 1996.

Feller, I. "Universities as Engines of R&D-Based Economic Growth: They Think They Can." *Research Policy,* 1990, *19*(4), 335–348.

Galbraith, J. R., Lawler, E. E., III, and Associates. *Organizing for the Future.* San Francisco: Jossey-Bass, 1993.

Green, K. C., and Gilbert, S. W. "Great Expectations: Content, Communications, Productivity, and the Role of Information Technology in Higher Education." *Change,* 1995, *27*(2), 8–18.

Grubb, W. N. *Working in the Middle: Strengthening the Sub-Baccalaureate Labor Force.* San Francisco: Jossey-Bass, forthcoming.

Hegelson, S. *The Web of Inclusion: A New Architecture for Building Great Organizations.* New York: Doubleday, 1995.

Leslie, L., and Brinkman, P. T. *The Economic Value of Higher Education.* New York: American Council on Education and Macmillan, 1988.

Mintz, S. D. (ed.). *Sources: Diversity Initiative in Higher Education.* Washington, D.C.: American Council on Education, 1993.

Morrison, J. L. (ed.). *On the Horizon: The Environmental Scanning Publication for Leaders in Education.* San Francisco: Jossey-Bass, 1996.

Musil, C. M. *Diversity in Higher Education: A Work in Progress.* Washington, D.C.: Association of American Colleges and Universities, 1995.

Peterson, M. W. "Images of University Structure, Governance, and Leadership: Adaptive Strategies for the New Environment." In D. Dill and B. Sporn (eds.), *Emerging Patterns of Social Demand and University Reform: Through a Glass Darkly.* New York: Pergamon Press, 1995.

Porter, M. E. *Competitive Strategy.* New York: Free Press, 1980.

Reich, R. *The Work of Nations: Preparing Ourselves for 21st Century Capitalism.* New York: Knopf, 1991.

Romer, R. *Making Quality Count in Undergraduate Education.* Denver: Education Commission of the States, 1995.

Rudolph, F. *The American College and University: A History.* New York: Random House, 1962.

Smelser, N. "The Politics of Ambivalence." *Daedalus,* 1993, *122*(4), 37–54.

Twigg, C. A. "The Need for a National Learning Infrastructure." *EDUCOM Review,* 1994, *29*(5), 16–20.

Wheatley, M. J. *Leadership and the New Science: Learning About Organization from an Orderly Universe.* San Francisco: Berrett-Koehler, 1992.

CHAPTER TWO

FEDERAL GUIDANCE FOR A CHANGING NATIONAL AGENDA

Terry W. Hartle and Fred J. Galloway

These are extraordinary times for America's colleges and universities. There is widespread belief that these durable institutions are entering a period that will fundamentally transform what they do and how they do it.

There is no shortage of evidence that the times are changing colleges and universities. The demand for the kinds of services offered on a college campus—the creation and transmission of knowledge—are way up, but the revenues to finance these services are stable or declining. Rapid shifts in the demographics of American society are altering the nature of the student body. The workload and employment protection given to faculty are under constant scrutiny. The pressure for more accountability has never been greater. Technology has made it increasingly possible for new competitors to offer the kinds of services that historically have been provided by colleges.

The simple fact is that many colleges and universities have lost much of their ability to determine their own future. It used to be that offering a good, solid education at a reasonable price would ensure the well-being of an institution. That remains the central task, but colleges and universities now get enormous sums of money—and considerable regulation—from federal and state governments. As long as colleges depend on public-sector support, decisions by government policy makers will have a significant impact on the shape and structure of American colleges and universities.

The Changing Political Landscape

The American political landscape is in the midst of a fundamental transformation, and there is no telling where it will end. At the heart of this change is a belief that the federal government has become too big and too intrusive, and that "politics" no longer benefits average Americans.

While most Americans still believe that the structure of the nation's political institutions is fine, they are not so sanguine about the people who control the levers of political power. In the 1990s, a "throw the bums out" mentality has become an increasingly powerful undercurrent of public opinion. In November 1994, the voters did just that, turning control of Congress over to the Republican party. The start of the 104th Congress in January 1995 marked the first time in forty-two years that the Republican party controlled both houses of Congress.

The changing attitudes toward government are the product of many factors. First, the end of the Cold War removed the central rudder that had steered American public policy for two generations. When the Soviet Union crumbled, the role and priorities of the federal government—and other governments around the world—came under searching examination. In many countries, voters concluded that the political structures and actors that had served them through "the long, twilight struggle" against communism were no longer what they wanted.

At the same time, the American public began to conclude that their government was not working. In two especially important areas, education and crime, the public was confronted with unmistakable evidence that government was unable to provide what the public wanted: good schools and safe streets.

Public approval of government also fell as economic insecurity became a way of life for millions of middle-class Americans. Earnings inequality increased in the 1980s as the rich got richer and the poor got poorer (Levy and Murnane, 1992). Rapid technological change and globalization ended lifetime employment. Blue-collar jobs disappeared and labor unions were unable to protect the middle-class existence of their members. Once again, government seemed unable to reverse the trend or to provide meaningful help to those who had lost their jobs.

Finally, the communications revolution made the transmission of news and information almost instantaneous. The proliferation of communications media has provided a host of new ways to share discontent and unhappiness. The Internet, the World Wide Web, computer bulletin boards, radio talk shows, and cable channels are a cornerstone of the New Populism. Many of these developments—such as conservative talk radio shows—fly below the radar of political elites until they are within striking distance in very clear and unambiguous ways. That's exactly what happened in the election of 1994.

The "Contract with America" and the New Populism

Many members of the new Republican majority in the House of Representatives based their 1994 election campaigns on a document called the "Contract with America." This document actually was a list of ten politically popular ideas—including a constitutional amendment to balance the federal budget, term limits for members of Congress, legal reform, and welfare reform—that the Republicans promised to bring to a vote in the first one hundred days of the new Congress.

The Republicans kept their promise and brought all of the items to a vote on the floor of the House. However, few provisions of the "contract" were written into law. Only two of the items were enacted, and two others (the balanced budget amendment and term limits) were defeated. The rest were approved by the House but died in the Senate.

The contract itself has begun to fade into insignificance. However, as a metaphor for changing attitudes about government, the contract is fundamental to understanding the direction in which public policy is likely to move. Americans want a different government than the one they have had. The Contract with America suggests a government that will be much less interventionist and regulatory (if you are a conservative) or nurturing and supportive (if you are a liberal) than ever before. Either way, it'll be different.

The political environment we are living in is neither conservative nor liberal. It is populist, in that it is focused on helping the proverbial man in the street, and on a belief that large institutions—any large institution—may ignore or trammel the common folk.

Populism is likely to remain a central feature of American politics, no matter which party controls Congress and the executive branch. Populism is anti-elite and antiprivilege. It can be good and it also can be bad. And populist does not always mean progressive. The wave of populism that swept the nation from the 1890s through the 1920s featured such positive developments as the establishment of regulatory agencies to reign in big business, women's suffrage, and the direct election of senators. It also featured the birth of Jim Crow laws and very restrictive immigration policies, as well as the nation's first witch-hunt for communist infiltrators. This populist current is very likely to shape future debates about the size and role of the federal government in all areas of social policy, including higher education.

The Expansion of Federal Aid to Higher Education

University planners must keep several things in mind about federal support for higher education. First, it involves both sponsored research and student aid. Second, support for both has grown substantially over the last thirty years, and the health of higher education is intrinsically related to federal efforts in these areas.

Student Aid

A significant federal role in student aid can be traced to the Higher Education Act (HEA) of 1965. Earlier support for college students (the Serviceman's Bill of Rights [1944] and the National Defense Education Act [1958], or NDEA) had used access to higher education as a means to an end. In the case of the GI Bill, the goal had been to facilitate veterans' readjustment into the civilian labor force. The NDEA was an effort to increase capabilities in math and science in order to enhance our national security.

The Higher Education Act of 1965 had a different objective: to open the doors of higher education to the academically talented but financially needy. It did this through grant and work-study programs for low-income students and a loan program aimed at middle-class families. These programs have undergone numerous major changes since their creation, but they still constitute a visible and important part of federal student aid policy. Indeed, loans are by far the largest form of federal student aid—hardly what was intended when the program was created three decades ago.

As shown in Table 2.1, the student loan program has been expanded to include both subsidized and unsubsidized loans for students, as well as an unsubsidized loan program for parents (called the Parental Loans for Undergraduate Students, or PLUS, program). In 1994–95, over $24 billion was borrowed through these programs ($15.2 billion in subsidized loans, $7.8 billion in unsubsidized loans, and $1.8 billion in PLUS) (College Board, 1995). More importantly, over the last few years borrowing in these programs has exploded; of the $183 billion borrowed in the nearly thirty-year history of the student loan program, 22 percent has been borrowed in the last two years alone.

In the last decade, students also have become increasingly reliant on the array of campus-based programs that originally were begun in the late 1950s and 1960s. Both the work-study and Perkins loan programs have seen increases in the number of recipients, despite the fact that in real terms average awards have fallen over the last ten years. The same is true for the Supplemental Educational Opportunity Grant (SEOG) program; while the number of recipients increased from

TABLE 2.1. ANNUAL LOAN VOLUME IN THE STUDENT LOAN PROGRAM.

Year	Total Federal Student Loans		Subsidized Stafford Student Loans		Unsubsidized/SLS Student Loans		Parental Loans (PLUS)	
	Loans	Dollars	Loans	Dollars	Loans	Dollars	Loans	Dollars
1980–81	2,905	$6,202	2,904	$6,200	0	$0	1	$2
1981–82	3,162	$7,219	3,135	$7,150	6	$15	21	$54
1982–83	3,020	$6,696	2,942	$6,497	31	$80	47	$119
1983–84	3,269	$7,576	3,147	$7,260	57	$148	65	$168
1984–85	3,722	$8,609	3,546	$8,144	84	$222	92	$243
1985–86	3,729	$8,839	3,536	$8,328	102	$269	91	$242
1986–87	7,510	$9,102	3,499	$8,330	191	$520	91	$252
1987–88	4,371	$11,385	3,595	$9,119	629	$1,830	147	$436
1988–89	4,595	$11,985	3,626	$9,319	757	$2,015	212	$651
1989–90	4,546	$12,151	3,619	$9,508	670	$1,835	257	$808
1990–91	4,588	$12,669	3,689	$10,002	601	$1,710	298	$957
1991–92	4,935	$13,993	3,889	$10,805	690	$2,022	356	$1,165
1992–93	5,191	$14,914	3,883	$10,937	920	$2,698	388	$1,279
1993–94	6,505	$21,182	4,527	$14,123	1,636	$5,510	342	$1,550
1994–95	6,998	$24,673	4,551	$15,193	2,096	$7,819	351	$1,830

Note: Loans in Thousands, Dollars in Millions

Source: College Board, 1995.

686,000 in 1985–86 to almost one million in 1994–95, the real value of the average award declined by more than 30 percent over the same period (College Board, 1995).

In 1972, the HEA was amended to create what is now called the Pell Grant program (originally named Basic Educational Opportunity Grants). Designed to provide a foundation grant for low-income students, Pell Grants represent the basic building block of federal student aid. Although the real value of these grants has eroded over time, the federal government spent more than $5.6 billion in 1994–95 to make Pell Grants available to over 3.7 million financially needy students (College Board, 1995).

Pell Grants have helped millions of students enroll in higher education. Unfortunately, as both inflation and college costs have increased, the purchasing power of Pell Grants has fallen. For example, in 1975, the average Pell Grant covered 48 percent of college costs; in 1985, it covered just 32 percent; and in 1995, the average Pell Grant covered only 20 percent of college costs. To fill the gap between Pell Grants and the cost of college, millions of students began to borrow money.

The rapidly growing imbalance between grants and loans, illustrated in Table 2.2, has been a major financial aid concern of the 1990s. In 1977–78, roughly $1.7 billion was borrowed under the loan program and $1.5 billion was awarded in Pell Grants (College Board, 1995). Thus, a little over one dollar was borrowed for every dollar of grants. The difference widened during the 1980s, so that by 1989–90, two and a half dollars were borrowed for every dollar of Pell Grants.

Today, thanks to the recent surge in borrowing, the ratio between grants and loans has changed dramatically. Preliminary estimates for 1994–95 show that $5.6 billion was awarded in Pell Grants, while over $24 billion was loaned out, making the loan-to-grant ratio 4.4 to 1 (College Board, 1995). Not since 1973–74, the first year of the Pell Grant program, when just $48 million was awarded, has the ratio been this skewed.

Although the last thirty years have seen an increase in the federal commitment to financial aid, the recent shift in emphasis from grants to loans has undermined the social compact that assumed that the adult generation would pay for the next generation's college education. Furthermore, the growing dependence on loans may well undermine the federal commitment to ensure access to higher education for low- and middle-income students. Given the reluctance of some ethnic groups to borrow large sums of money, any movement away from grants toward loans may well reduce access to college for the groups that need it the most.

TABLE 2.2. THE PELL GRANT/STUDENT LOAN IMBALANCE.

Year	Total Federal Student Loans		Total Pell Grants		Ratio: Amount Borrowed to Pell Grant Dollars
	Loans	Dollars	Grants	Dollars	
1977–78	1,014	$1,737	2,011	$1,524	1.1 : 1
1978–79	1,277	$2,360	1,893	$1,541	1.5 : 1
1979–80	1,940	$3,926	2,538	$2,357	1.7 : 1
1980–81	2,905	$6,202	2,708	$2,387	2.6 : 1
1981–82	3,162	$7,219	2,709	$2,300	3.1 : 1
1982–83	3,020	$6,696	2,523	$2,421	2.8 : 1
1983–84	3,269	$7,576	2,759	$2,797	2.7 : 1
1984–85	3,722	$8,609	2,747	$3,053	2.8 : 1
1985–86	3,729	$8,839	2,813	$3,597	2.5 : 1
1986–87	7,510	$9,102	2,660	$3,460	2.6 : 1
1987–88	4,371	$11,385	2,882	$3,754	3.0 : 1
1988–89	4,595	$11,985	3,198	$4,476	2.7 : 1
1989–90	4,546	$12,151	3,322	$4,778	2.5 : 1
1990–91	4,588	$12,669	3,405	$4,935	2.6 : 1
1991–92	4,935	$13,993	3,786	$5,793	2.4 : 1
1992–93	5,191	$14,914	4,002	$6,176	2.4 : 1
1993–94	6,505	$21,182	3,756	$5,651	3.7 : 1
1994–95	6,998	$24,673	3,718	$5,632	4.4 : 1

Note: Loans and Grants in Thousands, Dollars in Millions

Source: College Board, 1995.

Research and Development

As with student aid, federal support for research and development also has increased over the last thirty years. In FY 1996, for example, federal R&D expenditures will total $72.1 billion, compared with $31.8 billion in 1980 and $15.8 billion in 1970 (American Association for the Advancement of Science, 1995). Although federal R&D spending declined as a percentage of the overall budget over this period (from 8.1 percent in 1970 to 4.5 percent in 1996), federal R&D expenditures increased from 12.7 percent to 13.2 percent of the discretionary portion of the budget.

Of the total federal investment in research and development in 1996, over 57 percent ($41.6 billion) was devoted to development activities, while 40 percent ($29 billion) went to research (American Association for the Advancement of Science, 1995). Less than 3 percent was spent on R&D facilities. Of the $29.1 million in federal funds going just to research, support is split almost equally between basic and applied research, with 19.9 percent ($14.5 billion) allocated for basic research and 20.1 percent ($14.6 billion) for applied research. In terms of trends, this can be contrasted with 1980, when over 60 percent of R&D expenditures were devoted to development and only 35 percent to research. Even more important, however, is the increasing federal commitment to basic research, which accounted for less than 15 percent of the R&D budget in 1980.

Not all of the federal R&D dollars go to colleges and universities. As shown in Table 2.3, in 1995 roughly $16.5 billion went to higher education, up from $13.3 billion in 1990 and $6 billion in 1980 (U.S. Department of Education, 1995a). Most of the money going to universities is for research. In 1995, for example, 79 percent of the R&D dollars flowing to higher education were for research and only 16 percent were for development. As has been the case for the last ten years, most of the federal research money going to colleges was spent on basic research (67 percent in 1985, 68 percent in 1994) rather than applied (33 percent in 1985, 32 percent in 1995) (U.S. Department of Education, 1995b).

A substantial amount of federal research dollars flow through the National Science Foundation (NSF) and the National Institutes of Health (NIH), which operate as the primary funding agencies for basic research. Together, they support research in all major scientific and engineering fields through grants, contracts, and other forms of assistance. The NSF accounts for about 25 percent of all federal support for basic research going to academic institutions; in 1994 it awarded approximately twenty thousand grants and contracts to researchers at

TABLE 2.3. FEDERAL BUDGET AUTHORITY FOR RESEARCH AND DEVELOPMENT AND FEDERAL RESEARCH AND DEVELOPMENT FUNDING TO COLLEGES AND UNIVERSITIES, FY 1980–1996.

Fiscal Year	Federal Budget Authority	Federal Funding for Colleges and Universities
1980	$33,000	$6,029
1981	$37,300	$6,714
1982	$37,600	$7,054
1983	$38,800	$7,617
1984	$44,000	$8,331
1985	$51,800	$9,483
1986	$54,600	$9,573
1987	$58,600	$11,194
1988	$61,000	$12,083
1989	$64,300	$12,864
1990	$66,400	$13,260
1991	$68,700	$14,650
1992	$71,900	$14,948
1993	$72,900	$15,804
1994	$71,100	$16,411
1995 (est.)	$73,100	$16,470
1996 (budget)	$72,600	n/a

Source: American Association for the Advancement of Science, 1995, U.S. Department of Education, 1995a.

two thousand universities, colleges, academic institutions, and small businesses nationwide (American Association for the Advancement of Science, 1995). The amount of funds awarded by the National Institutes of Health (NIH) has increased steadily over the last fifteen years. NIH is now the largest single federal provider of research funds to academic institutions.

The Changing Public Policy Environment for Higher Education

Rapidly changing political dynamics make it impossible to predict how public policy will change in the years ahead. However, several public policy themes seem likely to reshape politics and higher education in the near future. All colleges will be affected by these changes. But the impact will vary considerably from campus to campus, depending on any number of local variables, including geographic locale and the mission and financial health of the college. College and university officials need to reflect on the implications for their institutions and begin to plan accordingly.

The Drive to Balance the Federal Budget Will Continue

The new Republican majority on Capitol Hill and the Clinton administration both have committed themselves to balancing the federal budget. Their timetables and priorities differ, but the fact is that achieving this goal has been adopted as a central policy objective by both Republicans and Democrats.

Regardless of the timetable or the specific priorities, balancing the federal budget will require deep cuts in federal spending. The Republican balanced budget plan vetoed by President Clinton in December 1995, for example, assumed that entitlement spending would be reduced by $626 billion over the next seven years and domestic discretionary spending would decline by 30 percent after inflation. It is possible that the current Congress, or a future one, will decide that it does not wish to balance the budget or does not wish to do so on this timetable. Still, prudent campus planning requires an assumption that the effort to balance the federal budget will continue and that this will reduce the federal funds available for both student aid and research.

The impact of reduced federal spending on individual institutions also will vary depending on the amount and type of federal funds the institution receives. Research universities must be concerned about the adequacy of federal support for research. The University of Washington, for example, receives almost 30 percent of its funding from federal sources, and most of that funding is for research. This situation is not unusual, and any major research university is likely to be deeply affected by federal cutbacks in research support. Higher education institutions of all kinds must be concerned about student aid funding. At many small liberal arts colleges, federal student aid is critical to the financial health of the institution.

The effort to balance the budget will set the context for everything else the federal government does in the next decade. The simplest description of the public policy process in Washington is that "budget drives policy." This has long been the case, and it will be even truer in the years ahead.

Making progress toward reducing the federal budget deficit will be a negative-sum game; less money will be available for everything the federal government does. It is possible that those programs of primary concern to higher education—student aid and research—will be of continuing interest to members of Congress because they are visible investments that produce long-term dividends. However, in an era in which substantial budget cutting will be required, even important and valuable programs will face the budget ax.

Everything the Federal Government Does Will Be Subjected to Greater Scrutiny

As the federal government moves toward a balanced budget, everything it supports will be the subject of careful analysis to determine whether it can and should continue to engage in the activity. Given the overarching financial pressures, we are likely to see extensive "reengineering" of the sort that many private-sector corporations have been through in the last decade. As this happens, some long-standing federal functions may be eliminated, and long-established details of federal policy may be altered forever.

Evidence abounds that the federal government—especially the Republican majority on Capitol Hill—is rethinking the role and place of virtually all federal activities. Much of the Republican effort to balance the budget has focused on programs that are not working or that, in Republican eyes, should be managed by state and local officials. For example, federal support for elementary and secondary education has been targeted for reductions. Federal budget cuts, such as a reduction in funding for elementary and secondary education, may impose additional financial burdens on state governments; this in turn may increase competition for scarce resources at the state level. For example, many Republicans have proposed to turn Medicaid—which provides funds for health care for the poor—into a block grant to the states. In the past decade, annual expenditures for this entitlement, driven by rapid increases in health care costs, have increased by over 260 percent (U.S. Bureau of the Census, 1994).

The implication for colleges and universities is that rapid changes in federal policy making could alter significantly the environment in which colleges and universities operate, even if the legislation is not usually thought of as involving higher education policy. For example, major changes in Medicare reimbursement may sharply reduce the amount of money paid to teaching hospitals to train the next generation of medical professionals, a step that would have a huge impact on hospitals affiliated with university medical schools. The revisions to the Telecommunications Act also may affect colleges by either limiting their access to affordable telecommunications, which would complicate the development of distance-learning technologies, or by eliminating the current process through which excess funds are transferred from regulated telecommunications companies to educational and public interest organizations. Either way, the challenge for colleges and universities will be to monitor a wide variety of federal policy developments more carefully than ever and to take action to address matters of particular importance.

One question likely to be asked by policy makers in these debates is how the costs and benefits of public policy are allocated. Who pays and who benefits are the most basic questions in public policy making, and they are being asked with increasing frequency as federal (and state) officials seek to ensure that whenever possible the beneficiaries of public policies pay for them. In the debates over the federal student loan program, for example, advocates of cutting federal support regularly pointed out that those who received a higher education would, on average, earn substantially more money over their lifetimes than those who did not, and that this justified reductions in federal aid. The historic counterarguments that colleges have used—that higher education is an investment in the next generation of citizens, that student aid helps open doors to college, and that individuals who get a higher education earn more money and pay substantially more in taxes than those who do not get a college education—often are brushed aside.

Much of the rationale for public sector support for higher education rests on the notion that investing in the production and transmission of knowledge will have important long-term societal benefits. To the extent that policy making is reduced to a simple cost-benefit equation or becomes a matter of exacting user fees, it greatly complicates the efforts to make the case that investing in higher education will pay handsome, though unknowable, dividends in the future.

State Governments' Shifting Budget Priorities Make Increased Support for Higher Education Uncertain

In addition to the increasingly constrained federal budgetary climate, the shifting budget priorities of state governments make increased support for higher education highly uncertain. State spending on higher education fell from 14 percent of state budgets in 1990 to 12.5 percent in 1994 (Gold and Ritchie, 1995). Meanwhile, spending on corrections and Medicaid rose from 14 percent to 19 percent of state budgets. During the same period, thirty-six states increased spending on corrections and forty-four increased spending on Medicaid, but just seven expanded support for higher education.

A historical review of state appropriations for higher education suggests that it has not always been this way: annual percentage gains averaged almost 20 percent in the 1950s and 1960s, then fell to about 15 percent in the 1970s, and into the single digits in the 1980s. However, between 1992 and 1993, state support for higher education actually declined slightly, before rebounding to a 7.5 percent increase between 1993 and 1995 (State Higher Education Executive Officers, 1995).

This trend is unfortunate, but it has a logic to it. States face huge and growing bills for Medicaid, Medicare, elementary and secondary education, and corrections. Armed with evidence that college pays off financially for those who get it, many states have decided to reduce operating support for higher education in favor of increasing tuitions. In some states, the reductions in operating support and the increase in tuitions have been striking. For example, in Massachusetts, appropriations for higher education declined by 21 percent between academic years 1989–90 and 1992–93, prompting a 34 percent increase in tuition and fees in the following two years. In California, where state appropriations declined by 12 percent over the same period, tuition increases averaged 33 percent between 1992–93 and 1994–95 (U.S. Department of Education, 1995a).

Colleges also have responded to declining state support by eliminating some academic programs, increasing class size, using more part-time faculty members, reducing the number of classes taught, and reducing expenditures for libraries and other instructional materials. *Campus Trends,* a 1995 survey of changes taking place in the academic and administrative practices of American colleges and universities, found that larger classes were "possible" or "very likely" at 75 percent of the institutions surveyed, and fewer course sections were either "possible" or "very likely" at 70 percent (American Council on Education, 1995).

Changing Demographic Pressures Will Further Complicate Access to Higher Education

As federal and state financial support stagnates, increasing the financial pressure on colleges and universities, demographic pressures will further complicate access to higher education. After dropping significantly over the last two decades, the number of high school graduates—and thus the number of individuals seeking to enroll in college—is now increasing. Between 1995 and 2005, the annual number of high school graduates is projected to jump by 22 percent (U.S. Department of Education, 1995b). In some states, the increases will be much steeper. For example, the number of public high school graduates annually is expected to grow over this period by almost 28 percent in the Western region, led by Nevada (64 percent), Washington and Colorado (32 percent), Arizona (31 percent), and California (30 percent). In this last state, an estimated 3.1 million public high school students are expected to graduate within the next ten years.

More students graduating from high school will inevitably mean more students applying to college. Patrick Callan, director of the California Higher Education Policy Center, recently estimated that the number of students who want to attend college in California alone will increase by almost five hundred thousand over the next decade. To gain some perspective, that's one hundred thousand more students than are currently enrolled in all nine campuses of the University of California and all twenty-two campuses of the California State University system combined.

Coping with such a surge of new students is almost unimaginable after twenty years of relatively modest enrollment increases. Where will the students enroll? How will colleges meet the educational needs of a much more ethnically and racially diverse student body? These are only two of the most obvious questions that policy makers and campus leaders must begin to address. But there is scant evidence that educators and policy makers have begun to tackle them. Economist David Breneman has called the situation "the collapse of thought about the future, as if the dimensions of the problem have simply overwhelmed policy makers." The coming enrollment surge, he said, is "the proverbial elephant in the corner of the room, ignored by all" (Breneman, 1995).

Implications for College and University Planners

For nearly half a century, the most basic goal of the federal government's role in higher education has been to open the doors of higher education to all qualified students. Increased access to higher education has enjoyed bipartisan support that reflects a shared consensus that the nation's long-term national security, economic growth, and social progress depend on an educated citizenry. Widespread public enthusiasm for opening the doors to higher education made it easy for policy makers to support more access to higher education.

These efforts have resulted in substantial expenditures on student aid. Over the last thirty years, colleges and universities have become increasingly dependent on federal aid to help students meet the costs of enrollment. As the amount of money involved has grown, so have the stakes to the colleges. A deep cut in federal student aid or changes in terms that make the aid less generous to students will have very real consequences for college enrollments.

The future of federal support for research on our nation's campuses presents a different set of challenges. Although a relatively small number of colleges and universities receive such support, those deeply committed to research risk losing their ability to attract the world's best students and professors, and to continue performing cutting-edge research. And the constrained federal budgetary climate makes it much harder for colleges and universities who seek to expand their research capabilities.

The future of federal aid to higher education will be decided a long way from most college campuses, and it will be decided for the most part by individuals who are not well connected with the institutions. The challenge for college and university planners is to learn enough about the nature of student aid and research support that they can follow events in state capitals and Washington and be in a position to intervene effectively when the occasion arises.

Further Reading

Readers interested in a more in-depth discussion of the financing of higher education might want to examine McPherson and Schapiro (1991) for an excellent review of the effects of twenty years' worth of student aid policies; Gladieux and Hauptman (1995) for a look at access, quality, and the federal role in higher education; and Breneman (1994) for a look at the future of liberal arts colleges. For those readers interested in research funding issues at colleges and universities, the annual American Association for the Advancement of Science reports (1995) provide a wealth of information.

References

American Association for the Advancement of Science. *AAAS Report XX: Research and Development FY 1996.* Washington, D.C.: American Association for the Advancement of Science, 1995.

American Council on Education. *Campus Trends 1995.* Washington, D.C.: American Council on Education, 1995.

Breneman, D. W. *Liberal Arts Colleges: Thriving, Surviving, or Endangered?* Washington, D.C.: Brookings Institution, 1994.

Breneman, D. W. *A State of Emergency? Higher Education in California.* Sacramento: California Higher Education Policy Center, 1995.

College Board. *Trends in Student Aid: 1985 to 1995.* New York: College Board, 1995.

Gladieux, L., and Hauptman, A. M. *The College Aid Quandary: Access, Quality, and the Federal Role.* Washington, D.C.: Brookings Institution and College Board, 1995.

Gold, S. D., and Ritchie, S. "How State Spending Patterns Have Changed." *State Fiscal Brief No. 31.* Washington, D.C.: Center for the Study of the States, Nelson Rockefeller Institute of Government, 1995.

Levy, F., and Murnane, R. "U.S. Earnings Levels and Earnings Inequality: A Review of Recent Trends and Proposed Explanations." *Journal of Economic Literature,* 1992, *30*(3), 1333–1381.

McPherson, M., and Schapiro, M. *Keeping College Affordable: Government and Educational Opportunity.* Washington, D.C.: Brookings Institution, 1991.

State Higher Education Executive Officers. *State Higher Education Appropriations 1994–95.* Denver, Colo.: State Higher Education Officers, 1995.

University of Washington. Unpublished data, 1995.

U.S. Bureau of the Census. *Statistical Abstract of the United States: 1994.* (114th ed.) Washington, D.C.: GPO, 1994.

U.S. Department of Education. Office of Educational Research and Improvement, National Center for Education Statistics. *Digest of Education Statistics 1995.* Washington, D.C.: GPO, 1995a.

U.S. Department of Education. Office of Educational Research and Improvement, National Center for Education Statistics. *Projections of Education Statistics to 2005.* Washington, D.C.: GPO, 1995b.

CHAPTER THREE

STATE COORDINATION AND PLANNING IN AN AGE OF ENTREPRENEURSHIP

James R. Mingle and Rhonda Martin Epper

A variety of social, economic, and political factors are reshaping the landscape of statewide coordination and governance. Still relying on concepts forged in the 1950s and 1960s, state boards are entering a new period marked by a focus on student consumers and their learning productivity, increasing competition brought about by developments in information technology, and changing public attitudes about government bureaucracies. New structures, less formal and more ad hoc, are emerging in this environment to replace those of an earlier age. In the paper that follows, we discuss the historical origins, structures, and functions of state coordination; the current social, economic, and political context; the emerging values that are affecting state boards; and the long-term implications for both states and institutions.

Statewide Coordination: Origins, Structures, and Functions

Statewide coordination of higher education contains a rich history of characters, cultures, and, above all, conflict. Conflict inevitably arises from differing views about the purposes of statewide coordination. Glenny and Hurst (1971b) defined *statewide coordination* from three perspectives. From the view of the state, coordination means more effective use of appropriations; from the view of state colleges, coordination means a fairer share of appropriations; and from the view of state universities, it means restricting the state colleges from any encroachment on their university research and graduate programs. With expectations so diverse and rising pressures from all sides in the 1990s, a new order of change can be expected. A brief examination of the origins and functions of statewide coordination offers guideposts for the changes ahead.

Until the 1940s, state government remained comfortably distant from higher education institutions. But as higher education began to grow in size and public importance, so grew the interest of government. States became increasingly interested in "coordinating" the complex resource requirements of their higher education institutions. Thus, the trend since the 1940s has changed "toward greater state intervention" (Glenny and Schmidtlein, 1983, p. 133).

In his landmark study of statewide coordination in 1959, Lyman Glenny cited two forces that gave rise to coordination of higher education: the increasing complexity of higher education and the increasing size of state government. Prior to the 1950s, institutions attempted to increase their appropriation through intensive lobbying of local legislators. Even when legislators tried to rationally determine the needs of complex institutions, reports too voluminous and technical to interpret were required. This situation left legislators "bewildered as to the real needs of any institution and of higher education in general" (Glenny, 1959, p. 13). As a partial solution, some states began to centralize control of higher education institutions.

In addition to the increasing complexity of higher education, state government also began to grow in cost, size, and complexity. New programs for highways, police, corrections, welfare, mental health, public health, and industry regulation created more competitors for funds in the legislature. These two forces generally underlay more immediate motives that actually brought the central coordination systems into existence: "economy, efficiency, and the reduction of competition among institutions for state funds" (p. 263). Glenny was concerned that the impetus for coordination came from shortsighted views on the part of both legislatures and institutions. "The more positive purpose of promoting a better, more vigorous system of higher education has usually been overlooked" (p. 23). Glenny accurately forecast greater state needs for centralized planning and coordination.

By 1950, seventeen state boards for higher education had been established. Most early boards were consolidated governing boards for senior public institutions; the exceptions were the New York Board of Regents (1784), the Florida Board of Education (1885), the Kentucky Council on Public Higher Education (1934), and the Oklahoma Board of Regents (1941) (Millard, 1981). Boards created between 1960 and 1975, many of the "coordinating" type, were given greater responsibilities than what Glenny had witnessed prior to 1960. Among their functions were keeping expenditure rates in balance and perspective, providing for budgetary equity among institutions, ensuring diversity among institutions within the state, avoiding unnecessary duplication of programs, and balancing institutional operations with political and social realities (Millard, 1981).

Although much of the rise in state coordination can be attributed to external forces, the academy itself had much to gain from these new arrangements. As Mingle (1995) explained: "We may have been pressed to centralization by governors and legislators seeking a 'single voice' instead of the cacophony of competing interests, but many within the academy saw the advantages as well. Regional institutions joined the umbrella of the system, not only to protect themselves from external intervention, but to gain the economic, political, and educational advantages of the system. Salaries improved, working conditions improved, new programs were obtained, federal support was leveraged, and access was extended to the unwashed masses of students rejected by the small, elite, autonomous campus of our colonial past" (p. 3).

Coordinated "systems," whether their governance structures were primarily consolidated governing boards or coordinating boards, evolved as a solution to a pressing need from *both* states and institutions for rational planning, coordinating, and equitably distributing the extraordinary outpouring of public financial support for higher education following the end of World War II.

In tracing the evolution of state coordination, Robert O. Berdahl (1971) found four distinct developmental periods:

1. Complete autonomy of institutions lasting from colonial days to the late nineteenth century
2. Creation of single statewide governing boards beginning in the late nineteenth century, reaching a peak in the first two decades of this century . . .
3. Creation of voluntary arrangements gaining impetus in the 1940s and 1950s
4. Creation of statewide coordinating boards beginning in the 1950s . . . (Pliner, cited in Berdahl, 1971, p. 26)

One might conclude that we entered a fifth period beginning in the 1980s: a period of broadened responsibilities for statewide coordination that includes an interest in academic quality and measurable outcomes for higher education. For higher education, the decade of the 1980s has been described as a period of "resurgence of the states" (Callan, 1993). McGuinness (1994) noted fundamental shifts in state boards as governors and legislators became interested in the quality of higher education. Four policy mechanisms were introduced in the 1980s and used by coordinating agencies to meet demands from various constituencies: (1) setting a policy agenda and serving as agents for change; (2) incentive, competitive, or targeted funding; (3) state requirements for assessment of student learning; and (4) new performance-oriented accountability reports (McGuinness, 1994). Moreover, state boards have had to increase their expertise and legitimacy in areas formerly reserved to faculty, such as curriculum and assessment, and in professional areas (for example, health-related fields) and applied research (Mingle, 1987). The key issue in the 1990s is whether agencies originally created to control expansion have come to take on more functions than their structures and staff are adequately equipped to handle.

Agency Structures and Functions

In his 1971 study, Berdahl created the classification system most commonly used in the literature on statewide coordination. He identified three basic types of statewide boards: the voluntary association, the coordinating board, and the consolidated governing board. Also in the early 1970s, the Education Commission of the States began surveying its members on the basic legal structures and responsibilities of state coordinating and governing agencies. Now known as the *State Postsecondary Education Structures Handbook*, this resource classifies state boards into the following categories: consolidated governing boards, coordinating boards (both regulatory and advisory), and planning agencies.

Consolidated Governing Boards. Some states structure their higher education systems by assigning coordinating responsibility to boards that also govern institutions. These are known as consolidated governing boards. In general, consolidated governing boards:

- Head a single corporate entity encompassing all institutions within the system
- Have authority both to develop and implement policy
- Appoint and evaluate system and institutional chief executives
- Set faculty personnel policies and usually approve tenure
- Have authority to allocate and reallocate resources among institutions within their jurisdiction
- Establish policies and, in some cases, set tuition and fees (adapted from McGuinness, 1994, p. 6)

The strengths of this type of structure are in its full range of authority to govern individual campuses in the system. Its weaknesses are that the board remains vulnerable to political influences, and its members are often concerned with immediate management concerns rather than systemwide planning. In addition, its decision-making structures are often elaborate and cumbersome, brought about ironically from a commitment to collegial decision making and not hierarchy (Mingle, 1995). Millett (1984) found public disillusionment and dissatisfaction in several states with this model of coordination. This phenomenon was described as "the paradox of power and loyalty" by Graham (1989): "Precisely because consolidated governing boards are empowered (as coordinating boards generally are not), they turn for political support toward their natural constituency, which is the institutions themselves—not toward the governor and legislature, whose role it is to fund them" (p. 95).

Millett recounted governors and legislators complaining of the central boards becoming spokespersons, and even "cheerleaders" for the institutions, and not making the tough decisions for which they were created (pp. 108–109).

Coordinating Boards. Some states assign responsibility for statewide coordination to a board other than one of the institutional governing boards. Regulatory coordinating boards have authority to approve academic programs, where advisory coordinating boards have authority only to review and make recommendations regarding academic programs to the institutional governing boards. In general, coordinating boards:

- Do not govern institutions
- Usually do not have corporate status independent of state government
- Focus more on state and system priorities than on advocating particular institutional interests
- Appoint and evaluate only the agency executive officer and staff
- May review and make recommendations on budgets
- May review and/or approve proposals for new academic programs
- May have authority to require institutions to review existing programs (adapted from McGuinness, 1994, pp. 6–7)

Strengths of a coordinating board include the comprehensive scope of its authority and its close identification with the interests of the state. Its drawbacks are lack of authority to implement a master plan and lack of political constituency (Millett, 1984). Furthermore, when pushed by hostile legislators, these boards can fall into a regulatory mode and forget their advocacy responsibilities (Mingle, 1995).

Planning Agencies. Planning agencies perform coordinating functions consisting primarily of voluntary planning and convening institutions and sectors around policy issues of mutual concern. In structure and activity they are similar to many coordinating boards, especially those without regulatory responsibilities. Their strengths include an emphasis on long-range planning, policy analysis, and consumer advocacy (Mingle, 1987). Glenny (1959) held these boards in low regard, stating that they are "dominated by the oldest and largest institutions, tend to preserve the status quo in numbers and types of institutions, and are insufficiently accountable to a lay board or the legislature for statewide educational planning and programming" (pp. 264–265). In his national study in the 1980s, however, Millett unexpectedly found "vitality and influence" among state advisory boards (planning agencies). Several of the advisory board states he investigated were found to be "especially vigorous and to exercise considerable impact upon the legislative deliberations of their respective states" (pp. 248–249).

Currently twenty-three states and the District of Columbia have consolidated governing boards. Twenty-six states are coordinating board states, and five states and the District of Columbia have planning agencies (McGuinness, Epper, and Arredondo, 1994). The dividing lines among these three types are not distinct, however, and can cause some confusion. Functions of these boards vary by state and type of board, but together they can include long- and short-range planning, program review, budget review, administration of student aid and other programs, and information collection and management. These five functions were proposed as the minimum powers necessary in the 1970s for successful coordination of a system of higher education (Glenny, Berdahl, Palola, and Paltridge, 1971a). For the 1990s, these functions have expanded to include setting a policy agenda, providing policy studies and analyses, defining missions, creating accountability or performance indicator systems, and most recently, serving as change agents. Gordon Davies, director of the State Council of Higher Education for Virginia, described this role as "keeping people creatively restless" (Lively, 1993b). This new order of change for statewide coordination will be explored further in the next section.

The Changing Political and Economic Context for Coordination and Planning

During the 1990s, higher education has been faced with a significantly different economic and political context for policy making. Looming behind most issues, especially financial ones, has been the growing federal deficit and changing public attitudes about the value of government-sponsored programs. The recession of the early 1990s brought the first absolute drops in state support for higher education, possibly since the Great Depression (Hines, 1993). With the return of economic growth in 1994, state support for higher education once again turned upward, but the long-term decline of higher education as a funding priority for state governments remained. Halstead (1994) documents this decline as beginning in the early 1980s and continuing to the present day. Much of the declining priority is attributed to the effects of both public concerns about crime and the rise of health care costs fueled by an aging population (Gold, 1990).

States were not only pressed by increasing social welfare costs but were also greatly constrained in their taxing policy. Snell (1993) was among the first to note the structural problems with state tax systems that, because of their heavy reliance on sales taxes that exempted services, no longer captured growth even when it did occur. Revenue problems also were exacerbated in such states as Oregon, California, and Michigan, which shifted much of the cost of school finance from the local level to the state level.

Additional problems with state government finance can be anticipated with efforts to lower the federal deficit. In 1996, many governors were apparently willing to take less federal support in return for more flexibility for the nearly six hundred categorical federal programs which they administer. The cumulative effect of this strategy could be substantial. With higher education as the biggest discretionary item in state budgets (and often the last item decided in the process), it will be tempting for states to make up for these losses from higher education, especially during recessionary periods.

The past decade has also seen a significant change in public attitudes about college costs. In the 1990s, legislators allowed institutions to compensate for cutbacks in state support with sharp tuition hikes. The College Board (1995) reported that the cost of attendance (tuition, fees, and room and board costs) in public universities had risen 23 percent over inflation from 1985–86 to 1994–95. This was compared with per capita disposable income increases of about 12 percent and a *decrease* in median family income of about 1 percent from 1985 to 1993. The College Board report also noted the extraordinary increase in student borrowing to finance these increased costs.

The debate over tuition strategies centered around the efficacy of the high-tuition/high-aid strategy versus the more traditional low-tuition approach taken by most states. Wallace (1993) argued vigorously for the high-tuition/high-aid approach in Illinois, and movements led by the private sector in Minnesota and Washington pushed for increasing public-sector tuition (with compensations in student aid programs) closer to two-thirds of costs. Among the most powerful arguments among this group was the similar socioeconomic characteristics of students in "elite" publics and privates. On the other hand, analysts in states like Vermont, which has the highest tuition in the nation, cautioned that such a strategy results in underfunding of low-income groups. Mingle (1992) suggested a "tiered" approach for the public sector, with the share of costs rising in research universities while remaining low in regional state universities and community colleges.

Meanwhile, more out of necessity than philosophy, many state boards allowed institutions to increase tuition and fees incrementally over the decade.

Rising college costs have clearly affected public attitudes about higher education. Interestingly, public polls do not show the same concern about quality in higher education that is expressed regarding K–12 schools, but there is great anxiety about the price. "The people in our states are proud of their colleges and universities," the Southern Regional Education Board (SREB) notes in its 1994 report, *Changing States*, "and believe their quality is generally high. But that support is also shallow. There is too little understanding of higher education's strengths and problems. For the most part, people worry about only one higher education issue: the prospect that rising tuition costs will make it impossible for them or their children to go to college." Similarly, in a review of thirty public-opinion polls that touched on higher education, the American Council on Education found that "higher education enjoys a huge reservoir of public goodwill," which is accompanied by growing worry about costs. According to the study's findings, "'Sticker shock' is a real phenomenon in the public mind, and people believe that costs are escalating beyond the reach of the middle class" (Harvey and Immerwahr, 1995, p. iii).

The 1980s and 1990s also saw the emergence of economic development as a primary concern of policy makers at the state level. This was apparent in the changing language used in state reports on higher education, which emphasized the role that state systems play in making their state competitive in a global market (Thompson, 1994). Typical of this approach was the one taken by the Ohio Board of Regents (1988), calling basic and applied research the "cornerstones of economic growth" and promoting its "eminent scholars program."

This concern with global economic competitiveness continues to dominate the national scene and state agendas. "To compete and win in the global economy," to borrow President Clinton's phrase, remains the single national goal that unites Democrats and Republicans. The impact on higher education can be seen in the tremendous interest in and demand for vocational and professional education that leads quickly to graduation and employment. But the 1990s have seen a distinct shift away from the research role in economic development to an emphasis on "workforce preparation" (Rodriguez, 1992). Recent data seem to reinforce this trend. A national study of employers found a lack of confidence in the ability of schools and colleges to prepare young people for the workplace (National Center on the Educational Quality of the Workforce, 1995). In this new mode, states are focusing on the skills of individual students to be economically productive rather than on technology transfer and research issues.

In the spirit of "reinventing government" (Osborne and Gaebler, 1992) that has swept the nation, policy makers and higher education officials alike have suggested ways to privatize or deregulate state systems of higher education. In 1993, the governor of Florida stunned the higher education community when he asked the state university system to plan for "privatization." The ten-campus system was asked to study how it might operate if its budget stayed the same but half of its employees were removed from the state payroll (Lively, 1993a). In Oregon, the 1995 legislature considered a bill to convert the state system of higher education (OSSHE) into a public corporation. Repeated budget cuts prompted OSSHE officials to propose such a change in hopes of eliminating duplicative layers of oversight and providing greater flexibility to deliver its services more efficiently. Only portions of this deregulation bill, however, were finally adopted. Similar proposals were debated in Virginia, Washington, and Maryland. While the more radical of these privatization initiatives may involve political gambit more than substance, they are indicative of a public mood, skeptical of government services, that is likely to have long-term effects on both state boards and institutions.

Intergovernmental Issues

Historically, state and federal policies toward higher education have operated on relatively separate tracks. Since the 1960s, the federal government has assumed two primary roles: providing need-based student aid and support for research, especially basic research. The state role has been to add modestly to these student aid programs and to provide the infrastructure for an expanding public higher education system. Direct relationships between state and federal government have been limited to the management of student loan programs through the state guarantee agencies, data collection issues, and state administration of a small number of federal categorical grant programs.

The territory shifted significantly in 1992, however, when Congress authorized a new and more complex method of reviewing institutional eligibility to participate in Title IV student aid programs. A new body, the State Postsecondary Review Entity, or SPRE, was created to carry out federal oversight activities. Hearings sponsored by Senator Nunn (D-Ga.) in 1990 (U.S. Congress, 1990) had highlighted a variety of abuses in student aid programs. These findings, combined with public reports of high levels of student loan default, high dropout rates among student athletes, and abuses in federally sponsored research programs, all contributed to an atmosphere of "reform" during the debate over reauthorization of the Higher Education Act. In place of a loosely controlled and relatively ineffective system that divided responsibilities among the federal government, the states, and the accrediting bodies, Congress created a system that required the three partners (what had become known as the "triad") to duplicate a variety of reviews (Hauptman and Mingle, 1994). The increased role of the states to review eligibility was the most controversial. States were asked to establish standards across a wide range of issues including financial and administrative capacity, consumer information, student performance, and institutional quality. Reviews that would ultimately determine an institution's ability to participate in Title IV were to be conducted by the states for those institutions referred by the secretary of education on the basis of congressionally established review criteria such as high levels of student loan default.

In the minds of many institutional leaders, especially from private colleges and universities, this new state role was an inappropriate and intrusive intervention into the oversight of a federal program (Manegold, 1994). They also reacted negatively to the prescriptive approach to accreditation standards and processes. Many states also were reluctant to take on this added responsibility, given the likely legal and political costs in such a controversial program. Others saw it as integral to their primary licensing and consumer-protection functions in higher education.

Whether this new partnership between the federal government and the states for institutional accountability was sustainable was called into serious question by the congressional elections of 1994. Suddenly the atmosphere changed, and both the administration and the Congress began looking for regulatory relief for institutions. At the urging of the higher education community, Congress eliminated funding for the program and the U.S. Department of Education began rethinking its approach to Title IV oversight without a significant state role. Reauthorization of the Higher Education Act in 1998 will likely bring a final end to the SPRE saga. Of more lasting value, however, will be the work done at the state level in developing a standard-setting process and quantifying outcome measures. These issues, no doubt, will resurface in the future in other policy venues at both the state and federal levels.

Structures and Values for the Years Ahead

Whether out of necessity or choice, we can expect substantial change to the structures and underlying values of statewide planning and coordination in the years ahead. Planning and regulatory structures will be aimed not so much at establishing limits but creating opportunity, especially in an increasingly competitive system of delivering higher education that includes a host of new "alternative" providers. The distinctions between public and private higher education institutions will continue to blur, and this will be reflected in public policy. Planning and coordination will also continue to be affected by an increasingly conservative state legislative agenda with little stake in past statewide structures. At best, higher education will benefit from "benign neglect" as state policy makers continue to focus their attention on the schools and other social systems such as health care and criminal justice. More likely, higher education policy will become more partisan and politicized as the commitment to coordinating structures weakens. The increasing demands for retraining will shift the focus of public policy away from youth and toward adults, and away from general baccalaureate education to technical and professional curricula. (Countering this trend may be the growing number of aging baby boomers who could demand a more sophisticated liberal arts curriculum to occupy them in their spare time, and the small but consistent market for the experience of liberal education in a small college.) Technology will be a force for "deinstitutionalization" of public policy as the location of delivery shifts from the campus to the home and workplace and many new providers compete with traditional institutions for the continuing education market.

Evidence of this new context can be seen emerging in a number of state policies affecting coordination and planning: a focus on the student, not the institution; the decline of the "role and mission" approach to planning; increased use of competitive and incentive funding; decentralization, deregulation, and privatization initiatives; an emphasis on "private benefits"; greater student mobility and choice; and new forms of coordination. We now explore each of these policy trends in greater depth.

A Focus on the Student, Not the Institution

Information provided by state (and federal) agencies to improve consumer choices is increasingly seen as a substitute for regulatory approaches. The federal "student right to know" legislation, which requires institutions to report the graduation rates of various cohorts of students and statistics on the incidence of crime on campus, was aimed at better informing the choices of students and parents. (Outside of occasional press reports, this data has yet to have much public impact, however.) At the state level, coordinating and governing boards have developed student record databases that track students through the system. Most states now have such systems (Russell, 1995) and use them for a variety of purposes, including legislative accountability and feedback on student performance to high schools.

Information on student performance is most relevant in vocational and professional programs. The one-stop, all-purpose career centers for career information and job counseling proposed by the U.S. Department of Labor may be the forerunner of this trend. The concept was first outlined by Marshall and Tucker (1992) in their book *Thinking for a Living: Education and the Wealth of Nations.* "Report cards" on the performance of higher education are another. These report cards dovetail with the assessment movement, which began its course in the mid-1980s at the state level. Prominent examples of general purpose "reporting" of performance information to consumers are Tennessee's "Challenge 2000," South Carolina's Act 255/Institutional Effectiveness Report, Colorado's "Scorecard," and the Virginia Plan for Higher Education (Ewell, 1994).

In 1993, Bruce Johnstone, then chancellor of the State University of New York, coined the phrase "learning productivity" to express the growing need to move students through the system more quickly and with a higher level of achievement. This was in distinct contrast to the emphasis in many states on faculty productivity (Russell, 1992). Several states also explored ways to shorten time-to-degree, with the result that some acted to limit the total number of credit hours associated with a baccalaureate degree. For example, beginning in the fall of 1994, undergraduate students in North Carolina were assessed a 25 percent tuition surcharge when taking more than 140 credits to complete a four-year baccalaureate degree. Montana implemented a related policy in 1993; students who have attempted 170 or more credits in the Montana University System and have not obtained a baccalaureate degree are charged nonresident tuition for subsequent courses attempted (Blanco, 1994). Similar limits, either through institutional or state policy, have been imposed in Florida, Georgia, Oregon, Virginia, and Wisconsin (State Higher Education Executive Officers, 1996).

The Decline of the "Role and Mission" Approach to Planning

At the heart of many statewide plans has been the role-and-mission statement, which delineated a territorial approach to program development. Geographic or programmatic service areas guided the assignment of new academic programs, especially high-cost graduate and professional programs. Already we are seeing an erosion of this practice due to pressing demands from adults for access. For example, state-level policy decisions in Virginia and Utah have made it possible to deliver selected baccalaureate programs to community college campuses. This trend will only be accelerated by technology, which shows little respect for the political boundaries negotiated within the system. In fact, technology may ultimately make moot public policy distinctions on role and mission at both the state and national levels. In 1995, Maine struggled with this issue as it debated the future of its distance-education delivery structure. In the past, autonomous campuses in the Maine system had not dealt with students wanting to use resources from multiple campuses. To address this problem, the Education Network of Maine proposed to coordinate all distance delivery by becoming an eighth degree-granting institution in the state. This model may never be fully tested in Maine because it has been plagued with controversy and faculty resistance (Epper, 1996). But it will have a lasting impact on policy decisions. "No longer do we allow new programs based only on geographic need," stated a Maine system representative. "If a geographic area has enough demand to justify a program, it doesn't mean they will get it. We may bring it in from somewhere else" (Tolsma, 1995). It is not entirely clear what state boards will substitute for this role-and-mission approach; most likely institutional capacity and entrepreneurship will be the guiding decision points.

Other states, such as Georgia and Utah, which have put considerable emphasis on interactive video delivery systems, are exploring consortial approaches to program development and struggling with a wide variety of new policy issues in this electronic age. When programs are delivered at a distance, who should earn the state subsidy and the tuition: the sending site or receiving one? (And what if both send and receive?) Transfer of credit, an issue receiving attention by the proposed Western Governors University, is also likely to be a major problem as students collect credits from a wider range of providers.

State boards are beginning to use the "request for proposal" approach for program development, especially programs that are electronically delivered. This encourages both intrastate and interstate cooperation. Rather than waiting for new programs to emerge from individual departments and then saying yea or nay (based on predetermined mission statements and program review criteria), we can expect centralized offices to solicit proposals for new programs and to encourage collaboration across institutions and sectors. For example, in 1993 and 1994 the Oregon State System of Higher Education awarded over half a million dollars in grant monies to faculty and campus-based projects that emphasized interinstitutional collaboration. The program's goal, in part, was to increase course sharing among campuses and to evaluate new "mergers" between disciplines such as computer science and mathematics. In 1995, both the Utah System of Higher Education and the Georgia Board of Regents received special appropriations for curriculum development of distance learning, which encourages cross-institution and cross-sector collaboration.

Increased Use of Competitive and Incentive Funding

A general public skepticism about the priorities of higher education has led many state legislators to increased use of categorical, competitive, or incentive funding (Folger and Jones, 1993). Typically, such funding has been directed at strongly held state priorities such as the improvement of undergraduate education, preparation of teachers and programs that link K–12 and higher education, application of research to specific state problems such as environmental quality, provision of health care to rural areas or inner cities, and the enhancement of economic development. More recently, technology and distance learning have been the target of categorical grants. A few states, such as Tennessee and Ohio, have provided additional appropriations for improved student or institutional performance. In 1993, the Colorado legislature added a new dimension to the concept of incentive funding by passing a law requiring policy makers and higher education leaders to agree each year on five priority areas to receive new funding. Institutions still receive their base allocations, but additional funds are distributed (some by formula, some by competitive grants) only within the five priority areas. The five areas identified in 1996 were (1) providing students with a high-quality, accelerated undergraduate education, (2) linking K–12 and higher education, (3) workforce preparation and training, (4) using technology to lower costs and improve quality, and (5) improving operational productivity and effectiveness (Colorado General Assembly, 1996). The Texas Higher Education Coordinating Board proposed a performance-funding plan in 1991 but failed to gain legislative support in the face of institutional opposition (Bateman and Elliott, 1994). On the other hand, legislators have endorsed performance funding in several other states. Arizona, Arkansas, Connecticut, Florida, Kentucky, Minnesota, Missouri, Nebraska, and Tennessee all have adopted performance funding in some fashion (Layzell and Caruthers, 1995).

Decentralization, Deregulation, Privatization

Beginning with the publication of *Reinventing Government* (Osborne and Gaebler, 1992) and the Total Quality Management movement, states and systems have shown an increasing interest in more entrepreneurial, decentralized systems of higher education. This trend is not expected to diminish in the foreseeable future as institutions and systems seek greater fiscal and management autonomy through "privatization" of public higher education (Association of Governing Boards, 1996). Examples of such deregulation initiatives abound. The North Dakota University System adopted a systemwide TQM effort (Isaak, 1993), and other states such as New Jersey were caught up in the Republican political agenda to downsize state government, resulting in a much smaller and less regulatory coordinating board. The State Council of Higher Education in Virginia initiated a statewide effort to free institutions from control by state agencies of purchasing, cash management, and personnel matters. In 1995, the Oregon State System of Higher Education sought "public corporation" status from the legislature, which came in response to a statewide downsizing caused by property tax relief. This proposed status, while not fully adopted, implied a far more autonomous higher education system and, not coincidentally, less state support. Armajani, Heydinger, and Hutchinson (1994) went even further by recommending a disaggregated enterprise system of public corporations to carry out various functions of the universities and relate to other functions as customers. The trends in governance, however, have been quite mixed around the country (MacTaggart, 1996). Such states as Maryland, Alaska, and Minnesota have merged institutions into consolidated governing boards; some analysts argue for the continuation of this trend. The adage that "each state is unique" may best describe the current governance environment.

An Emphasis on "Private Benefits"

Ironically, the evidence most often used for the benefits of postsecondary education, namely the increased earning power of graduates, appears to be undermining societal commitment to the financing of higher education. Rationing proposals (recently suggested by Breneman, 1995, to cope with state financing cutbacks in California) and increasing tuition may further limit societal commitment. While many states continue to place emphasis on access issues, others appear to be moving away from commitments made in previous years. Admissions standards are rising in the public flagship universities, and remedial work is being limited to the two-year sector. Unspoken, but clearly evident, is a belief by many state legislators that, given high attrition rates, too many students may be attending traditional four-year institutions. Enrollment management is now a goal of several systems struggling with burgeoning demand and constrained resources. At the same time, costs and an interest in job skills are increasing enrollment in two-year institutions independently of state policy.

Student Mobility and Choice

Technology is predicted to significantly increase the number and diversity of providers of postsecondary credentials, a condition which is already prompting states to reconsider their regulatory environment to allow more out-of-state providers (Western Cooperative for Educational Telecommunications, 1995). The problem of transferability of credits led the Minnesota Higher Education Coordinating Board to recommend a statewide "credit bank" to certify skills gained both inside and outside of higher education. If the debate in K–12 spills over to higher education, expect a growing interest in "student voucher" systems at the state level as a replacement for institutional funding. This would open up at least limited state subsidies to a wider range of for-profit and corporate providers of higher education as well as out-of-state public institutions delivering courses electronically.

Removing geographic barriers to access was one goal of a group of western governors who, in 1996, advanced a plan to create a regional "virtual" university. Besides delivering courses electronically to local "franchise" receive sites, the new entity is expected to provide a means for learners to obtain formal assessment and recognition of skills and knowledge obtained outside traditional higher education institutions (Western Governors University Design Team, 1996). Within the framework of the Western Governors University, the flow of educational commerce across state lines will only increase.

Meanwhile, many institutions, with explicit or tacit state approval, continue to set their out-of-state tuition rates higher and higher as a means of generating additional revenue. This strategy is in distinct contrast to the European community, where student mobility across national borders is increasing, not declining. But ever higher in-state tuition for the well-off will make out-of-state tuition moot, except for those depending on financial aid. This provincial approach of many states could be countered by an activist federal government, although there seems to be little sentiment for such an approach in the 1996 political environment.

New Forms of Coordination

Emerging forms of voluntary coordination and coalition building may not be so much new as a return to old forms with new wrinkles. Voluntary associations, which Glenny once held in such disdain and Millett later commended, may yet become a powerful force in state-level policy making. The statewide telecommunications councils now being formed to coordinate the development of technology policy in the states are the precursors. These councils cross sectors that often involve other branches of state government and the K–12 system. Some may evolve into new delivery systems. Examples of such associations (both voluntary and with statutory authority) exist in Minnesota, Utah, and Florida and are being developed in several other states as well. The rising political and consumer interest in "workforce preparation" programs will also challenge the current forms of coordination which have, for the most part, focused their energies on traditional higher education institutions. Federal efforts to "devolve" job training responsibilities through block grants to the states will add to this pressure to expand coordination to the training sector.

Implications for States and Institutions

In the environment described above, the need for state coordination is likely to change significantly but not disappear. In fact, one might argue that a public or quasi-public body which is concerned primarily with the "public purposes" of higher education will be an even greater necessity in this age of entrepreneurship. Growing populations of minorities and immigrants will demand and need the benefits of a postsecondary education. State boards, as in the past, will need to be their own advocates in a sometimes biased and unresponsive system. An employment crisis in the United States similar to what Europe is currently experiencing among young people will put more, not less, pressure on higher education to provide access to high-quality programs leading to concrete outcomes such as employment and economic success. Equally powerful forces from employees, unions, and disadvantaged populations may halt some of the changes described above. And reactions in different regions will vary depending upon widely differing economic and political circumstances in the states.

The long-evident institutional ambivalence about governance and coordinating structures will likely intensify. In any meeting of system presidents with the chancellor, one or two entrepreneurial spirits seek more freedom from system constraints while the remainder prefer that their territorial boundaries be protected. Increasing deregulation and competition in higher education also lead to inevitable abuses in quality and pricing, which in turn lead to more legislative intrusion. In short, the scope and activities of regulatory structures will likely swing on a pendulum in response to continuing dilemmas in higher education.

Statewide coordination and governance issues—especially those relating to the equity of funding policies among partners in the system—are perennial in nature. But the world of state boards is likely to undergo significant change. Many state boards have now reached maturity, and with changing public attitudes they are likely to undergo significant change. Some will "reinvent" themselves; others will go out of existence. Those that do reinvent themselves will likely take a more indirect approach to the change agenda, one that creates the conditions under which public goals might be served by a constantly changing mix of providers and collaborators.

Rather than seeking the perfectly rational governance structure that has eluded them in the past, states will need to accept the more chaotic developments of a market-driven industry. Statewide governance changes in the past have seldom added much value; those of the future will need to prove that they make a difference in cost, quality, access, or price.

The higher education enterprise itself, moreover, is also likely to face significant change. The forces described in this chapter have serious implications for institutions of higher education, most notably greater competition. Porter (1980) explains the evolution of industries from growth to maturity to decline. Institutions in the "industry" of higher education are facing problems similar to firms in mature industries. For example, in industry a firm's self-perceptions and perceptions of the industry are deeply entrenched. As an industry matures, buyers' priorities begin to adjust, they become more knowledgeable consumers, and competitors respond to the new consumer demands. This often results in resentment and irrational reaction to new competitors. (For example, firms take the position

"We will not compete on price.") Entrenched firms often cling to "higher quality" as an excuse for not meeting the aggressive pricing and marketing moves of competitors (Porter, 1980, pp. 248–249). It is difficult to imagine any organizations more deeply rooted in tradition than institutions of higher education. Their self-perception assumes that competition exists primarily in peer institutions holding similar, traditional definitions of "quality." Furthermore, boundaries of competition are often reinforced by state boards that license new providers and define geographic service areas. But the future promises to challenge these long-standing and accepted practices. Telecommunications and distance education already have begun to render interstate and intrastate boundaries obsolete. Access to networked computers increasingly shifts control of learning to students who increasingly have new providers from which to chose. Competition is inevitable. Institutions of higher education will need to strategically assess which traditions to hold on to and which to reconsider in light of new industry conditions. It is not likely that traditional higher education institutions will disappear. But the industry, which already includes new providers and a different composition of consumers, looks very different than it did a mere thirty to forty years ago.

Institutions will seek protection from competition first by turning to legislators for protectionist legislation, but more constructively by turning to each other. The years ahead promise a constantly changing landscape of coalitions, partnerships, mergers, strategic alliances, and other ad hoc arrangements as institutions search for their market niche. The tolerance of states and public officials for this "creative chaos" will surely be tested. Some states will seek, probably unsuccessfully, to control through consolidation; some will seek to creatively "manage the competition"; a few may even enthusiastically embrace the new values of entrepreneurship. Few, however, will be left untouched. It should be an exciting ride.

Further Reading

Readers interested in the themes in this chapter may want to examine Armajani, Heydinger, and Hutchinson (1994) on entrepreneurial models for higher education delivery, Johnstone (1993) on student learning productivity, and MacTaggart (1996) on restructuring higher education governance systems.

References

Armajani, B., Heydinger, R. B., and Hutchinson, P. *A Model for the Reinvented Higher Education System*. Denver: State Higher Education Executive Officers, 1994.

Association of Governing Boards. *Ten Public Policy Issues for Higher Education in 1996*. (AGB Public Policy Paper Series No. 96–1). Washington, D.C.: Association of Governing Boards, 1996.

Bateman, M., and Elliott, R. W. "An Attempt to Implement Performance-Based Funding in Texas Higher Education: A Case Study." In R. M. Epper (ed.), *Focus on the Budget: Rethinking Current Practice*. Denver: State Higher Education Executive Officers and Education Commission of the States, 1994.

Berdahl, R. O. *Statewide Coordination of Higher Education*. Washington, D.C.: American Council on Education, 1971.

Blanco, C. D. *Doing More with Less: Approaches to Shortening Time to Degree*. Denver: State Higher Education Executive Officers, 1994.

Breneman, D. W. *A State of Emergency? Higher Education in California*. San Jose: California Higher Education Policy Center, 1995.

Callan, P. M. "Government and Higher Education." In A. Levine (ed.), *Higher Learning in America: 1980–2000*. Baltimore: John Hopkins University Press, 1993.

College Board. *Trends in Student Aid: 1985 to 1995*. Washington, D.C.: College Board, 1995.

Colorado General Assembly. *A Bill for an Act Concerning Five Specific Policy Areas for Additional Funding in Higher Education, House Bill 96–1088*. LLS No. 96–0362.01D. Denver, 1996.

Epper, R. M. *Coordination and Competition in Postsecondary Distance Education: A Comparative Case Study of Statewide Policies*. Unpublished dissertation, University of Denver, 1996.

Ewell, P. T. "Developing Statewide Performance Indicators for Higher Education: Policy Themes and Variations." In S. S. Ruppert (ed.), *Charting Higher Education Accountability: A Sourcebook on State-Level Performance Indicators*. Denver: Education Commission of the States, 1994.

Folger, J., and Jones, D. P. *Using Fiscal Policy to Achieve State Education Goals*. Denver: Education Commission of the States, 1993.

Glenny, L. A. *Autonomy of Public Colleges: The Challenge of Coordination*. New York: McGraw-Hill, 1959.

Glenny, L. A., Berdahl, R. O., Palola, E. G., and Paltridge, J. G. *Coordinating Higher Education for the '70s: Multi-campus and Statewide Guidelines for Practice*. Berkeley: Center for Research and Development in Higher Education, University of California, 1971a.

Glenny, L. A., and Hurst, J. "Current Statewide Planning Structures and Powers." In L. A. Glenny and G. B. Weathersby (eds.), *Statewide Planning for Postsecondary Education: Issues and Design*. Boulder: National Center for Higher Education Management Systems, 1971b.

Glenny, L. A., and Schmidtlein, F. A. "The Role of the State in the Governance of Higher Education." *Educational Evaluation and Policy Analysis*, 1983, *5*(2), 133–153.

Gold, S. D. "The Outlook for State Support of Higher Education." In R. E. Anderson and J. W. Meyerson (eds.), *Financial Planning Under Economic Uncertainty*. New Directions for Higher Education, no. 69. San Francisco: Jossey-Bass, 1990.

Graham, H. D. "Structure and Governance in American Higher Education: Historical and Comparative Analysis in State Policy." *Journal of Policy History*, 1989, *1*(1), 81–107.

Halstead, K. *State Profiles: Financing Public Higher Education 1978 to 1994*. Washington, D.C.: Research Associates of Washington, 1994.

Harvey, J., and Immerwahr, J. *The Fragile Coalition: Public Support for Higher Education in the 1990s*. Washington, D.C.: American Council on Education, 1995.

Hauptman, A. M., and Mingle, J. R. *Standard Setting and Financing in Postsecondary Education: Eight Recommendations for Change in Federal and State Policies*. Denver: State Higher Education Executive Officers, 1994.

Hines, E. R. *State Higher Education Appropriations: 1992–93.* Denver: State Higher Education Executive Officers, 1993.

Isaak, L. A. *Report on Streamlining of Major Campus and System Financial/Administrative Affairs Functions.* Bismarck: North Dakota University System, 1993.

Johnstone, D. B. *Learning Productivity: A New Imperative for American Higher Education.* Studies in Public Higher Education, No. 3. Albany: State University of New York, 1993.

Layzell, D. T., and Caruthers, J. K. "Performance Funding for Higher Education at the State Level." A paper presented at the 1995 annual meeting of the American Educational Finance Association, Savannah, Mar. 10, 1995.

Lively, K. "Florida's Governor Asks Higher-Education Officials to Prepare 'Privatization' Plan for University System." *Chronicle of Higher Education,* Sept. 22, 1993a, p. A28.

Lively, K. "Leaders of State Higher Education Agencies Face New Pressures." *Chronicle of Higher Education,* Sept. 29, 1993b, pp. A28–A29.

MacTaggart, T. J. (ed.). *Restructuring Higher Education: What Works and What Doesn't in Reorganizing Governing Systems.* San Francisco: Jossey-Bass, 1996.

Manegold, C. S. "Colleges Fear Law on Student Loans Means Meddling." *New York Times,* Jan. 12, 1994.

Marshall, R., and Tucker, M. *Thinking for a Living: Education and the Wealth of Nations.* New York: Basic Books, 1992.

McGuinness, A. C., Epper, R. M., and Arredondo, S. *State Postsecondary Education Structures Handbook, 1994.* Denver: Education Commission of the States, 1994.

Millard, R. M. "Power of State Coordinating Agencies." In P. Jedamus and M. W. Peterson (eds.), *Improving Academic Management: A Handbook of Planning and Institutional Research.* San Francisco: Jossey-Bass, 1981.

Millett, J. D. *Conflict in Higher Education: State Government Coordination Versus Institutional Independence.* San Francisco: Jossey-Bass, 1984.

Mingle, J. R. *Effective Statewide Coordination: What Is It?* Atlanta: Southern Regional Education Board, 1987.

Mingle, J. R. "The Public's Responsibility to Invest in Higher Education." Paper presented to The National Commission on Responsibilities for Financing Postsecondary Education, Washington, D.C., June 1992.

Mingle, J. R. *The Case for Coordinated Systems of Higher Education.* Denver: State Higher Education Executive Officers, 1995.

National Center on the Educational Quality of the Workforce. *The EQW National Employer Survey.* Philadelphia: University of Pennsylvania, 1995.

Ohio Board of Regents. *Toward the Year 2000: A Strategic Agenda for Higher Education.* Vol. 3. Columbus: Ohio Board of Regents, 1988.

Osborne, D., and Gaebler, T. *Reinventing Government: How the Entrepreneurial Spirit Is Transforming the Public Sector.* Reading, Mass.: Addison-Wesley, 1992.

Porter, M. E. *Competitive Strategy: Techniques for Analyzing Industries and Competitors.* New York: Free Press, 1980.

Rodriguez, E. M. *Building a Quality Workforce: An Agenda for Postsecondary Education.* Denver: State Higher Education Executive Officers, 1992.

Russell, A. B. *Faculty Workload: State and System Perspectives.* Denver: State Higher Education Executive Officers and Education Commission of the States, 1992.

Russell, A. B. *Advances in Statewide Higher Education Data Systems.* Denver: State Higher Education Executive Officers, 1995.

Snell, R. (ed.). *Financing State Government in the 1990s.* Denver: National Conference of State Legislatures and National Governors' Association, 1993.

Southern Regional Education Board. Commission for Educational Quality. *Changing States: Higher Education and the Public Good.* Atlanta: Southern Regional Education Board, 1994.

State Higher Education Executive Officers. [sheeo-academic@osshe.edu]. An electronic survey of academic officers on time-to-degree policies. February 1996.

Thompson, J. "Issues for the Nineties: An Analysis of 14 State Master Plans for Higher Education." Unpublished doctoral dissertation, Department of Education, University of North Texas, 1994.

Tolsma, B. *Education Network of Maine.* Presentation at the Minnesota Higher Education Coordinating Board's Alternative Delivery Conference, St. Paul, February 1995.

U.S. Congress. Senate. *Hearings before the Permanent Subcommittee on Investigations of the Committee on Governmental Affairs.* 101st Cong., 2nd Sess., Hearing 101–659, Feb. 20, 26, 1990. Washington, D.C.: GPO.

Wallace, T. P. "Public Higher Education Finance: The Dinosaur Age Persists." *Change,* July/August 1993, 56–63.

Western Cooperative for Educational Telecommunications. *Balancing Quality and Access: Reducing State Policy Barriers to Electronically Delivered Higher Education Programs.* Boulder: Western Interstate Commission for Higher Education, 1995.

Western Governors University Design Team. "Western Governors University: A Proposed Implementation Plan." Denver: Western Governors Association, June 1996.

CHAPTER FOUR

THE ROLE OF INTERMEDIARY ORGANIZATIONS

Elaine El-Khawas

Intermediary organizations are a distinctive type of formal organization, quite ubiquitous in American society even though the term itself is not in common use. These are the coordinating organizations that bring together otherwise separate entities. The local chamber of commerce and the county medical society are examples, as are national organizations such as the AFL-CIO, B'nai B'rith, and the National Association of Secondary School Principals. Trade associations and public-policy coalitions are other examples.

In higher education, intermediary organizations are both numerous and diverse. Some are the "presidents' clubs" that offer a forum for discussion among college, community college, and university presidents. Others, such as the Education Commission of the States or the Southern Regional Education Board, are independent agencies that serve the broad purposes of state governments by fostering resource sharing and collective action. Still others—accrediting agencies, for example—carry out monitoring and inspection roles that resemble governmental functions.

Although numerous, the intermediary organizations serving higher education have received relatively little attention in social science inquiry. Most analysis has focused on the structure and formal roles of such organizations (Bloland, 1985; Harcleroad, 1994). Occasionally, analysts have examined actions of intermediary organizations on public policy matters (King, 1975; Murray, 1976; Gladieux and Wolanin, 1976; Gladieux, Hauptman, and Knapp, 1994). These studies, framed in political-science concepts of power and negotiation, have viewed intermediary organizations in limited terms, primarily assessing their role as lobbyists, that is, as rational actors on public policy issues.

The literature has given little attention to the dynamics of intermediary organizations, whether in their internal conflicts and challenges or in the way they affect other actors. This is unfortunate because organizational theory could offer relevant insights, especially in terms of its focus on the adaptive capacities of organizations (Cameron and Whetton, 1983) and its appreciation of the significant role of external actors on organizational behavior. To date, however, organizational theorists in higher education have focused mainly on individual colleges and universities. There has not been good analytical assessment of the special roles that intermediary organizations have played or the ways that they have influenced either government or colleges and universities.

This chapter offers a framework for examining the role of intermediary organizations in higher education. The first section, "A Conceptual Perspective," discusses concepts pertinent to understanding intermediary organizations in higher education. It argues that the source of authority of these organizations and the nature of their mandate are critical defining variables that help explain how they try to influence their environment. These variables also help explain how some organizations have greater discretion than others in "constructing" their understanding of their priorities and imperatives (Tierney, 1987).

Certain types of intermediary organizations in American higher education and the challenges they face are discussed in the second section, "Current Challenges for Key Organizations." Section three suggests "Implications for University Planners" and administrators. It stresses that intermediary organizations may pose certain threats for university functioning, but on the whole they offer tremendous opportunities as well.

A Conceptual Perspective

While each intermediary organization in higher education has its own distinctive origins and often has evolved a special role, the general nature of intermediary organizations can also be assessed. In the first instance, they are forms of collective action to address the common interests or needs of a specific client group.

In the contemporary U.S. context, intermediary organizations in higher education often seem to be just an unexceptional part of the landscape. Yet, it is valuable to consider their general nature and other roles they could play, and to recognize that, as with other organizations, any intermediary organization may change over time, possibly being more or less effective in different circumstances.

One device for understanding the general role of intermediary organizations is to consider examples from other industrialized countries, not just the narrower context of the United States. The most salient difference is that in other countries intermediary or buffer organizations often are creatures of government; they have been established by, receive all funding from, or otherwise are closely aligned with government agencies. The Swedish National Board of Universities and Colleges, now defunct (Furstenbach, 1992), and the currently operating Higher Education Funding Council for England (El-Khawas and Massy, 1996) were both established by their governments as independent, or intermediary, agencies but with the mandate to carry out certain governmental functions: allocating and dispensing government funds to universities and providing other services specifically appropriate to higher education (for example, conduct of planning studies, and procedures for evaluating academic programs).

In the United States, on the other hand, intermediary organizations have most often emerged as special types of voluntary associations. Although differing among themselves in their origins and purposes, they share the characteristic of operating in a public arena, seeking to act as mediators between government and a client group.

Two key concepts offer a framework for understanding intermediary organizations: the source of authority and the scope of the organizational mandate. Each deserves some explanation.

Source of Authority

Intermediary organizations differ in their source of sponsorship or authority, most importantly according to whether or not they are closely aligned with government authorities or with universities (El-Khawas, 1992). A continuum of differences in authority should be recognized. As Figure 4.1 illustrates, an intermediary organization may occupy a particular place on this continuum ranging from "Aligned with Government" to "Aligned with Academe." However, Neave has noted that intermediary bodies rarely occupy a neutral position: "Either they are outposts of the university world . . . or they are the operational edge of government. . . ." (Neave, 1992, p. 11)

The experience in Europe, in Australia, and other countries outside of North America is found at the governmental end of the continuum. Intermediary organizations have been established by government; although sometimes given areas of autonomy, they derive their power and authority from government support. The University Grants Committee (UGC), which operated as a highly respected and prestigious intermediary organization in the United Kingdom, is the classic example. It was the model for similar structures in India, Hong Kong, and many

FIGURE 4.1. DIFFERENCES IN SOURCE OF AUTHORITY.

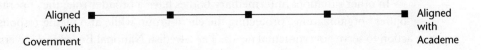

Aligned with Government ■━━━━━━■━━━━━━■━━━━━━■━━━━━━■ Aligned with Academe

other Commonwealth countries. The DFG (*Deutsche Forschungsgemeinschaft*, or German Research Agency) is another highly respected intermediary organization that operates with considerable autonomy in awarding research funding to academics in Germany (Muhlberg, 1992).

Based on a broadly comparative analysis, Neave has distinguished three types of intermediary bodies:

- "Primary" bodies, which have financial and allocative responsibilities and dispense governmental funds to colleges and universities under publicly set rules
- "Secondary" bodies, which perform functions of coordination and advice
- "Tertiary" bodies, which serve as arenas for debate and discussion (1992, pp. 10–11)

The first two categories, found most often in countries outside of North America, may have formal autonomy, but they still depend on government and therefore stand on the governmental end of the continuum. In contrast, the third category, more typical in the United States and Canada, is at the university end of the spectrum, depending crucially on university support for its legitimacy. The Pennsylvania Association of Colleges and Universities is an example; another, in Canada, is the Ontario Council of Universities.

In the United States, the demise of the Council on Postsecondary Accreditation (discussed later in this chapter) illustrates the principle that an organization's source of authority is its critical defining characteristic, more important than aspects of its operating style or the level of popularity an intermediary body appears to have. COPA ended not because of government action but because its members, who were on the academic end of the continuum, lost confidence in it.

Scope of Mandate

Sometimes intermediary organizations have a limited mandate, for example to provide necessary coordination or communication in order to translate the views of one group to the other. The *Wissenschaftrat* (or Science Council) in Germany plays this role; it prepares and issues periodic reports that make recommendations to government, but it does not have decision powers, nor can it establish policy.

In other situations, intermediary bodies have a broader role; they operate as "buffer" organizations, protecting the client group while also taking responsible action to serve governmental needs. The Swedish National Board of Universities and Colleges (Furstenbach, 1992) followed this pattern.

Categorizing American Organizations

American intermediary organizations can be arrayed in terms of this continuum, based on differences in their source of authority (see Figure 4.2). It must be recognized, at the outset, that state agencies (discussed in Chapter Three) are in many respects the functional equivalent of the European intermediary bodies that operate on the governmental end of the spectrum; they may have some autonomy but are primarily agents to carry out governmental purposes. Other state organizations have independent powers in specific areas but still derive their operating authority from the government; examples of such organizations are the independent agencies established to administer student financial assistance (such as the Pennsylvania Higher Education Assistance Authority).

Next on the continuum of Figure 4.2 are the regional compacts such as the Southern Regional Education Board. They were created by formal interstate agreements but given quite general mandates and substantial operating autonomy. To skip to the other end of the continuum, some organizations derive their formal authority entirely from colleges and universities. Consortia are examples, typically created for limited purposes by a specific number of colleges and universities. Institutionally based membership associations are another example of organizations aligned with academic institutions. As with consortia, they have entire institutions as members. Unlike consortia, the composition of the membership can change over time, even dramatically. Institutionally based organizations often play varied roles: convening meetings, providing member services (publications, research, workshops), and championing good practice. Many have a "representational" mandate, to speak to government agencies about the collective needs of higher education.

American accrediting agencies, both regional and specialized, are near the middle of the continuum of Figure 4.2. Compared to quality assurance agencies in other countries, American accrediting groups are independent and have considerable autonomy. Even in the United States, they straddle the divide between government and academe. Accrediting agencies are private organizations but they carry out governmentlike policing roles: monitoring, evaluating, and sanctioning illicit actions. Yet because their source of authority rests with academe, much of their activity is

FIGURE 4.2. AMERICAN INTERMEDIARY ORGANIZATIONS.

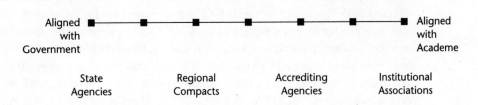

directed toward gaining the voluntary support and acceptance of the colleges and universities they evaluate. Thus, their decision-making commissions comprise university officials, and in acknowledgment of academic culture they introduce changes in their procedures only after lengthy periods of comment and discussion. Their explanatory materials emphasize their objectivity and devotion to broadly shared goals of educational excellence and program improvement.

In recent American policy debate, national and regional accrediting agencies are being cast primarily as agents of the public interest. Despite their origins in voluntary action by higher education institutions and despite protests by the agencies themselves, they have gradually taken on quasi-governmental mandates tied to their inspection and quality-assurance roles. Federal legislation in 1992 mandated a stronger policing role for regional and national accrediting groups. It included actions akin to an auditing function in the area of financial aid administration. Although this legislation was short-lived (given zero funding in early 1996, with legislative language introduced to terminate this mandate entirely), nevertheless it is indicative of a long-term push toward placing accreditation on the governmental side of the continuum.

The recent demise of the Council on Postsecondary Accreditation can be understood in terms of the tensions inherent in functioning between government and academe. COPA was created by the academic community in 1975, primarily as a coordination device within academe. It also accepted a narrow quasi-governmental responsibility: to inform the federal government about the legitimacy of individual accrediting agencies. In true "intermediary" style, however, it was also seen by accrediting agencies as responsible for protecting them from undue federal intervention. As the federal government steadily increased the importance and the specificity of the accrediting role in quality assurance, COPA's academic patrons judged it to be ineffective in protecting them. Passage of the 1992 Higher Education Adjustment Act—which set out the extensive reporting and auditing responsibilities for accrediting agencies—was seen as confirmation of this general perception.

Conversely, the establishment of COPA's successor organization, the Council for Higher Education Accreditation (CHEA), represents a repositioning of the national voice for accreditation. If COPA had moved too far away from colleges and their presidents, early signs are that CHEA will be strongly aligned with college and university presidents. Indeed, it was established only after winning support in an unprecedented nationwide balloting of college, community college, and university presidents. Over sixteen hundred presidents cast ballots, with 94 percent voting to support CHEA ("National Referendum Votes . . . ," 1996). An earlier attempt at creating a successor organization, to be called a Higher Education Accreditation Board, did not get off the ground largely because many felt that the design did not give a sufficient role to presidents.

Current Challenges for Key Organizations

The following pages offer brief profiles of four major types of intermediary organizations active in American higher education. Each type has an established role; each affects individual institutions in different ways. The discussion focuses on their distinctive operating styles and the challenges they face in the current policy environment.

As Neave has argued (1992), the issues facing intermediary organizations provide a barometer of the relationship between higher education and government. During stable times, such organizations operate routinely and appear to be fixed parts of the landscape. In more turbulent times, intermediary organizations can quickly become the focus of vigorous debate about their role and functioning. During the 1980s, for example, several European countries saw significant shifts in governmental positions toward higher education; it was also during this time that several intermediary organizations were either disbanded (Sweden) or consolidated and reorganized (United Kingdom).

The United States may be experiencing such turbulent times as well. National political debate has questioned the role of government and, especially, the role of government regulatory approaches. Privatization is much in vogue during the 1990s. Strong political winds are shifting governmental roles to the state level. These changes are likely to continue and may even accelerate as part of a long-term trend that has increased the scope and authority of state governments.

These trends shape the policy climate in which the four types of intermediary organizations operate. Their responses reflect differences in their sponsorship as well as in the roles they have established for themselves.

Regional Compacts

Four regional organizations currently serve higher education; each has been created by interstate agreements signed by governors and annually reaffirmed by state legislatures. The newest, the Midwest Higher Education Commission (MHEC), was established in 1991 among eight midwestern states. Others include the New England Board of Higher Education (NEBHE, established in 1955), the Southern Regional Education Board (SREB, 1948), and the Western Interstate Commission on Higher Education (WICHE, 1948). A comparable interstate compact established the Education Commission of the States (ECS) in 1966.

These are formally independent organizations that provide services to both institutions of higher education and to state officials having responsibilities related to higher education. (ECS and SREB direct their agendas to elementary and secondary education along with attention to higher education.) Half or more of their funding comes from annual payments by the states that formed the compacts. The remaining funds derive from foundation grants or special project funds awarded by their member states.

How do these organizations define their agendas? In part, they are guided by the advice of their governing bodies, usually an appointive commission of legislators, legislative aides, and other state officials. Governors are the commissioners for ECS, and they sometimes participate on regional commissions. These organizations have some flexibility to shape their own agendas and do so by understanding and adapting to their environment, recognizing special opportunities where they can contribute and monitoring changes in external circumstances that might threaten their role. Not surprisingly, the four regional compacts often overlap considerably in their services and special projects.

Two distinctive roles have emerged: first, offering policy-oriented advice, including leadership on issues that broadly affect all of the member states; and second, offering practical services that are based on rationales of efficiency through coordinated action. The latter traditionally have included data and information services as well as student exchange programs. Recently, each of the regional groups has also developed projects to help strengthen higher education's telecommunications capacity.

Such practical actions offer strength through resource sharing. Cost efficiencies result from combined buying power (for example, with MHEC's purchasing of interactive video equipment and services) and from avoiding expensive but duplicative specialty training (for example, in WICHE's exchange programs for nursing and veterinary sciences). Similarly, it is thought that greater effectiveness can be gained on policy matters by sustained, multistate pressure on a common agenda, as with SREB's push for educational improvement or NEBHE's push for regional economic development linked to higher education.

Although these organizations face no overt threats to their operations, their fate is inextricably caught up in the recent shift of political momentum from the federal level to the state level. This shift could increase the role of regional organizations, as support agencies for clusters of states. As states encounter new policy questions along with greater autonomy, they may seek new alliances and opportunities through regional cooperation. Recent experience in Western Europe, spurred by initiatives of the European Union, offers many illustrations that regional cooperation can accomplish purposes otherwise difficult for individual governments. At this point the prospect is unclear: are regional compacts part of the new solution, as devices for enhancing the newfound powers of state government? Or will they instead be seen as distant agencies unable to respond to specific state concerns?

Regional compacts may also be affected by reduced state funding for higher education and the trend toward deregulation. Will their unique services still be needed, and will their constituent states be able to support regional planning and development? Or will deregulation bring about a shift by the regional compacts, causing them to align themselves more closely with individual institutions or systems and champion their specific interests?

Some insights about the future role of regional compacts may be gained by watching developments related to the recent actions of the Western Governors Association to jointly develop a "virtual university." In the initial design stage, this collaborative approach to distance learning has relied heavily on expertise found in regional organizations, including WICHE and the governors' organization. As it develops, the virtual university could challenge the educational role of institutions in the region. However, early signs suggest that this ambitious concept will also need the active participation of many, if not all, universities and colleges in the region. For the long term, the roles of the various actors are still to be worked out.

Regional Accrediting Agencies. Throughout the last decade, regional accrediting agencies have been a focus of much public policy debate on higher education's responsibilities to society. They have been integrally involved with efforts toward greater institutional accountability.

In the late 1970s and early 1980s (Young and others, 1983), regional accrediting commissions broke from traditional review procedures focused almost entirely on capacity and process; they broadened their scope and called for performance indicators and other measures of institutional effectiveness. This change was consistent with their long-term role of evaluating and encouraging good educational practice, but it marked a change in operating style, a broadening of their mandate to include more specific forms of policing—which could lead to more rigorous evaluation by site teams and, possibly, more critical judgments than in the past. Regional accrediting agencies also endorsed and required institutional use of new approaches to student assessment; these were bold moves, often made in response to accountability pressures being voiced by state legislatures and governors. From the institutional perspective, accreditors had adopted a new role: they were now forcing quick action even though effective assessment methods and procedures had not yet been worked out.

The pressures on accrediting agencies to expand their role has continued in the 1990s. Some of these associations have been involved in efforts to press for greater racial, ethnic, and gender diversity. All have been pressed to emphasize both financial and educational accountability. Their responses, strategies, and actions have differed across the regions. Recently, they have been drawn collectively into the controversial federal debates about management oversight for financial aid funds.

In the perspective of this chapter, most of these recent actions arise from the efforts of regional accrediting agencies to respond to a changing environment by broadening their role and by aligning themselves more closely with governmental concerns. For decades, regional accrediting agencies restricted themselves to a narrow mandate involving periodic conduct of an external review geared more toward suggestions for improvement than to demanding inspection or harsh monitoring. Reporting requirements were kept to a minimum, and institutions were allowed considerable flexibility in shaping their reports and self-studies. This narrow mandate was broadly accepted by colleges and universities, who saw it as largely routine and uneventful. It also was accepted by government, at least in the sense that most governmental agencies recognized the authority of accrediting agencies and fully accepted the findings of accrediting reviews.

In the changed environment of the 1980s, when accountability pressures appeared in diverse and insistent forms, regional accrediting agencies expanded their traditional mandate but initially did so in ways that were consistent with the past. Nevertheless, their operating style changed. Regional accrediting commissions became more activist, setting deadlines and insisting on timetables. In effect, they began using the stick more than the carrot.

In the late 1990s, the prospect is that they will become still more activist. Regional accreditation has encountered new pressures, especially from government agencies, for greater uniformity across the regions in their standards and requirements. Agencies may also find that consumer demands will be heard more frequently and more stridently. Historically, the consumer's perspective has usually been expressed indirectly, perhaps through a legislator's specific questions or a journalist's critique. Individual complaints to accrediting agencies have been rare. Today, as tuition costs rise and the popular mood is more consumer-aware, accreditors and colleges should expect that concerns will be addressed to them more frequently. Criticisms of higher education that have appeared in the popular press recently could accelerate this trend.

A general issue can be raised: have the changes already made by regional accrediting agencies, in response to changes in their environment, moved them too far away from their constituents? In moving toward new governmental needs, did accrediting agencies step beyond the bounds of their long-accepted mandate? Several agencies have adopted so-called diversity standards, calling for appropriate institutional response to the changing demographics of student populations. The controversy over these diversity standards suggests that accrediting agencies exceeded the narrow mandate that many colleges and universities had accorded to regional agencies. Rather than deferring to individual campuses for defining what is good educational practice, the regional agencies that have adopted diversity standards were seen as defining a specific element of good practice. The fact that some, but not all, regional agencies adopted these standards suggested that some "arbitrariness" was involved.

Specialized Accrediting Agencies. Specialized accrediting agencies are a separate category of organization, engaged in monitoring and evaluation of higher education. Currently, fifty-eight agencies are recognized as accreditors of specific academic programs (Kitchens, 1995, pp. 642–646) that include professional fields (for example, law, business, engineering, architecture, social work, nursing, and other health-related professions) and a wide range of other subjects (journalism, dance, music, funeral direction, library science, public affairs, teacher education).

These organizations, established mainly between 1914 and 1975 (Harcleroad, 1994, pp. 208–209), are intended to foster quality educational practice through independent review and approval processes that, in broad outline, resemble those of regional accrediting agencies. Their specialized focus on a single field of study allows for greater scrutiny, however, including specification of appropriate curriculum content, faculty credentials, and faculty workload, and it permits them to set standards for assessing student accomplishment.

As external monitoring organizations, specialized accrediting agencies have continually faced tensions in trying to function between universities and government. From their origins in institutions or organizations representing their professional field, these agencies have seen their position evolve over the last few decades toward closer links with government entities. In many fields, state licensing requires that candidates for a license be graduates of accredited programs. In some fields, state reviews of academic programs are coordinated with specialized accrediting agencies, a link that appears to be growing (Wise, 1995). As an indirect effect of their role in protecting the public interest—especially relevant in health-related fields and other professions tied to public welfare and safety—many specialized agencies have developed quite detailed program standards.

As voluntary monitoring organizations, specialized accrediting agencies are often on the defensive. The accrediting process is criticized, sometimes for being too thorough (and therefore too costly in time and resources), while others call for greater uniformity of standards as a way to avoid uneven treatment of institutions. At times, accrediting is criticized for seeming to be unduly "clubby" or "protectionist," offering "special pleading" on behalf of its field's needs (Wegner, 1995) or on behalf of certain departments.

Sorting out the confusion of different positions in these debates can be difficult. This chapter's perspective suggests that some of the controversy arises from the general dilemma of trying to serve two masters. Governments expect monitoring and policing; institutions prefer advice and assistance. With respect to specialized accrediting agencies, however, the issue is more complex. It seems that conflicts arise over their role because they are trying to serve the needs of *three* masters: the government; the institutions that have programs in their specialty; and the needs of the profession, as articulated by one or more professional bodies. Criticism from institutions, for example, most often focuses on the specificity of standards. Yet, these standards were developed by professionals in the field based on their views of what constitutes good educational practice.

Most changes in the standards of specialized accrediting agencies probably are made because of changing professional consensus about good practice, a response to professional pressures that may be wholly separate from changing governmental expectations. This suggests that specialized accrediting agencies, at least in the current period, give their primary loyalty to the profession, not to institutions.

The standards and procedures of specialized agencies are likely to become more elaborated over time, precisely because they depend on the voluntary support of their professional membership. Procedural safeguards are important ways to show objectivity and fairness and thus to maintain the support of key constituents (Brennan, El-Khawas, and Shah, 1994). A state agency, in contrast, could develop standards and defend them on the basis of law and regulation. As independent agencies grounded in professional expertise, specialized agencies need to maintain the support of their professional members. Thus prospects for further tensions have roots in the structure of these agencies, that is, in the source of authority resting with the professions. A vitally important client—the institutions that operate programs in the specialty—has secondary status, even though those institutions control the resources and have the decision authority over the programs.

Institutionally Based Associations

This general category includes many associations, large and small, single-purpose and multipurpose. It includes national associations, their regional subunits (such as the Western Association of College and University Business Officers), as well as state and local associations (the Ohio Association of Colleges and Universities). These organizations have been established by college and university administrators to pursue a common agenda. Institutional consortia also are examples, often established for limited purposes (such as to offer combined purchasing power or collaborate on library resources). Other associations serve the ongoing needs of college financial officers, registrars, directors of campus bookstores, and other diverse professional areas of campus operations.

The activities of most of these associations are directed primarily toward institutions of higher education (for example, through advisory publications, conferences, and training workshops). Relatively few direct their activities toward government and take formal positions on issues of public policy. Those active on federal policy matters—here called representational associations—are the focus of the following remarks.

Representational associations active in the nation's capital include the six associations representing college and university presidents—the American Council on Education (ACE), the Association of American Universities (AAU), the National Association of Independent Colleges and Universities (NAICU), the National Association of State Universities and Land-Grant Colleges (NASULGC), the American Association of State Colleges and Universities (AASCU), and the American Association of Community Colleges (AACC)—as well as the association representing student financial aid administrators (NASFAA). These are classic intermediary organizations in the sense that they "stand between" the government and their constituents. They are distinctive, compared to organizations in Europe, because they are creatures of colleges and universities, based solidly at the academic end of the continuum. Indicative of this status is the fact that these associations rely on dues from institutional members for their core operations. In contrast, the rectors' councils in Germany and other European countries receive core funds from government.

Their role, nevertheless, is to bridge the gap between government and academe. Although their first loyalty is to their academic membership, it is also true that they rely on support and recognition from the government side. If they are to maintain an effective government-relations role, for example, they must have access to government. They must have sufficient credibility with government officials to be heard, as evidenced by invitations to offer testimony, opportunities to present analyses and policy alternatives and, also, instances of successful influence over government policy.

Pressures on these "representational" associations today arise from two long-term trends: the lessened importance of federal government activities to higher education, and the need for the Washington-based associations to coordinate their activities. The lessened federal role is due in part to the increasing role of state government, but it is also affected by other trends, including greater university links with business and industry, the diminished size of federal student assistance funding, and the prospect of reduced federal support in many areas of university interests. The federal role in higher education has always been narrow, limited largely to research support and student aid funding. However, recent changes have accelerated this trend and raised new questions about the role and importance of the Washington associations.

Coordination is a constant need among Washington-based associations. Federal policy issues arise in different settings, including the courts, various government agencies, and congressional committees. Different issues call for expertise of various types and have effects on different types of institutions. The Washington-based associations with public policy agendas have developed many mechanisms, formal and informal, for coordinating their activities. Their success varies, perhaps inevitably so when complex issues are at stake and many actors have different interests and views.

The effect of these two trends—less importance for federal policy and greater need for coordinated action—has been to increase the pressure on each association to demonstrate that it offers a unique resource for its membership. Thus the organizational imperatives of maintaining member loyalty have led to competition among the associations as well. Duplicative and competing services exist, although over time a division of labor often evolves.

Because these associations derive their authority and legitimacy from colleges, community colleges, and universities, the greatest threat they face is if their members no longer sense that they make a distinctive contribution. Some associations respond to this vulnerability by broadening their mandate, developing a variety of services that expand the reasons for institutional membership. Cook has described this imperative well, stressing the dual demands on these organizations (1995). For other associations—for example, the National Association of Independent Colleges and Universities—the organizational response was to focus on a narrower mission: the government-relations role.

Implications for University Planners

This review of some of the issues that intermediary organizations face offers a context for considering the role they may play in the future for institutions of higher education. From the perspective of university administrators, it seems evident that a multiplicity of external agencies will certainly continue to exist, and thus it will be necessary to develop a strategic view of which agencies are important and how they influence the university. Among the many external actors, are there some to be seen as threats, likely to constrain or complicate the university's own plans and actions? Are certain external agencies best thought of as allies, presenting opportunities to assist the university in pursuing its goals?

For most U.S. colleges and universities, whether public or independent, it is the actions of state-level agencies that are most consequential. Second in importance, perhaps, are the actions of accrediting agencies. The relative influence of other intermediary organizations varies widely, depending on specific issues and institutional circumstances.

In evaluating the strategic role of any of these external agencies, several key points should be emphasized. First, all of these organizations exist to allow for or to encourage collective action on higher education matters. Thus, their potential, whether for good or evil, lies in the value of collective institutional activity on any specific issue. University administrators should look beyond any short-term issues or aggravations felt with the work of these organizations if they are to adequately evaluate the way that each organization operates to serve a *collective* interest in higher education.

Secondly, the intermediary organizations that form an important part of any university's external environment can undergo significant change. They can be influenced to take on new roles or to pull back in others. And as the recent experience with COPA and now CHEA emphasizes, their role can be entirely recast under certain circumstances. University leaders should no longer assume that existing organizations and agencies are "just part of the landscape," immutable forces to contend with or work around if difficulties arise.

In fact, changes regularly take place on the associational landscape. COPA, now defunct, was created in 1975. Several specialized accrediting bodies were established only in the last two decades. There also have been many changes, over the last five to ten years, in the nature of state boards and oversight agencies in several states. Similarly, new private organizations have arisen during this time, for example, the National Association of Scholars and a new accrediting commission for the liberal arts. The Midwest Higher Education Consortium is another example, established only in 1991. Other organizations have either increased or decreased in their relative importance, although often without any explicit announcement of such change. Certainly too, existing organizations, especially among institutionally based associations, have undergone considerable internal change during the last decade.

For universities and colleges, then, an active stance is warranted. Significant change could be sought, especially among those intermediary organizations that have some flexibility in the scope of their mandate. Individual universities or, even better, groups of universities could ask an organization to develop a new project or expand its current activities to address new issues. Conversely, individual or collective action might be warranted to seek relief from the onerous activities of an intermediary organization. As another option, a group of university and college administrators could work together to form a new organization that would pursue common interests not now being met satisfactorily.

Among the intermediary organizations reviewed in this chapter, major directions of activity are well established and can be expected to continue. Yet along with universities and colleges, they also are actors in the broad social, political, and economic environment and must adapt to changing circumstances. New roles and relationships can certainly be considered.

New Roles for Regional Compacts

The relationship between individual universities and the regional compacts is quite amenable to influence. If universities wished to, they could press for different activities by the compacts. These organizations trace their origin to governmental agreements, which necessarily hold them accountable to state governments; however, their mandate is broad and subject to changing definitions. Almost any issue or activity could be proposed, requiring only that regional cooperation offer gains not attainable by individual action.

The current activities of the regional compacts generally do not pose any threats to universities and colleges. Most are designed to assist institutions, whether by offering gains through economies of scale or by offering services not otherwise available. Nevertheless, because their source of authority lies with state governments and because their agendas depend heavily on state officials, it is wise for university planners and administrators to stay informed about both the current and planned activities of the regional compacts. This is especially the case in a climate where much political momentum in the United States has shifted to the state level, possibly increasing the number of professional staff in various state offices and raising new interest in state-coordinated actions.

The policy-related role of regional compacts is especially ripe for monitoring, in light of the shifting political demands that seem to be moving toward the states. Thus far, most of the regional compacts have been quite limited in their activities to support policy debate and decisions within their member states, but there are several precedents for policy activism. University leaders may wish to participate directly in policy discussions organized by the regional compacts, or at least stay well informed about such policy discussions and the new directions that might emerge.

In fact, in an environment where state and federal governments are pressing for greater accountability by higher education institutions, the regional-compact organizations could well play a new role, as sources of objective advice on various approaches to accountability. Regional compacts thus might be sought out as relatively neutral third parties, uniquely able to host meetings of state officials and university administrators to sort out accountability issues and develop reasonable approaches. At times, the regional compacts might thus serve as counterweights to the authority of higher education agencies in a single state.

Looking to another regional role, institutional planners may find it useful to encourage regional agencies to expand their data and information services. This is a major area in which regional compacts could assist individual institutions in their regional area. These agencies could, for example, move toward an active role in regionwide planning for higher education. Comparative ratios and "peer" comparisons within a region may offer new insights about cost and financing questions. Regional compacts may be able to generate sophisticated demographic and employment projections on a regional basis, offering better insights than state-level or national data. Their regional perspective would allow the development of special information, for example, on interregional flows of labor or students.

New Roles for Regional Accrediting Agencies

University planners would be well advised to pay close attention to the activities of their regional accrediting agencies over the next few years. These organizations are sensing considerable threats to their existence, and their effectiveness has been challenged by many external groups, with accusations from the media, from outside critics, and from governmental officials as well. The agencies have responded by improving the accountability dimension of their work. Over the next few years, regional accrediting agencies are likely to give greater attention to the development of comparable standards across regions, to stronger enforcement of standards, and to better use of evidence that documents actual student outcomes.

It is possible that regional accrediting agencies will adopt a quasi-governmental role, monitoring and policing standards for public accountability while giving less emphasis to their role in encouraging institutional improvement. Because their source of authority derives from institutional support, however, they are also susceptible to influence by their members. In contrast, most European counterpart agencies—those charged with quality assurance and institutional review responsibilities—were established by government agencies and look to the government as they make operational decisions.

University administrators, as members of regional accrediting bodies, should be alert to ways to safeguard their long-term interests in the accrediting process.

Active participation in decision-making bodies is much needed over the next few years. Wherever necessary, university leaders should call on accrediting representatives to increase the opportunities for full debate and consideration of the important issues that need resolution.

With the prospect of an increasing accountability role, it is possible that regional accrediting agencies will need to increase their own staff capabilities in analysis and evaluation of data reporting. As accrediting procedures become more specific, definitional issues and data reporting requirements arise. Disclosure of graduation rates, for example, constitutes a desirable "outcome" measure, but there are complex issues to resolve in determining how such rates should best be calculated. These areas, not traditionally a strength of regional accrediting agencies, are especially appropriate for contributions by university officers with expertise in research analysis and planning. University involvement is both a responsible action, reinforcing the fact that accrediting agencies are membership organizations, and a useful action of self-protection, ensuring that decisions reflect important realities of college and university operations.

New Roles for Specialized Accrediting Agencies

A university perspective on its likely future relationships with specialized accrediting agencies must start from recognition that the basic relationships that now exist are likely to continue. Some institutions have continuing ties to only a few specialized agencies and have developed satisfactory working arrangements. Other institutions have negative experiences, feeling unduly constrained by requirements imposed by certain agencies with which they have ties.

As this chapter has suggested, some of the difficulties that institutional administrators have recently faced with the requirements of specialized accrediting agencies arise from the needs articulated by members of professional groups. Specific standards for each accrediting agency are developed with wide input from professionals related to the specialty area. It appears, in contrast, that operating needs and constraints felt by universities and colleges have not been given adequate consideration as standards and requirements are developed.

The immediate prospect is that specialized accrediting requirements will continue to be burdensome for many institutions of higher education. However, in recognition that universities and colleges can legitimately seek a stronger voice in agency decisions, it is appropriate for university administrators to consider alternative models, whether different standards and procedures or different ways in which the agencies and the universities jointly attempt to ensure that academic programs are of high quality. Groups of institutions might call for special review committees, for example, or might develop a framework of alternative review and evaluation procedures that could be debated within the appropriate professional bodies.

New Roles for Institutional Associations

Over the next few years, there is likely to be some redefinition of role among the associations that are institutionally based. Most have generally tried to offer two different roles: government representation, mainly with federal agencies and with the U.S. Congress; and constituent services, as found in publications, conferences, research, special studies and commissions, training opportunities, etc. Will the government representation role diminish, as federal budgets are reduced and state governments are given greater responsibility? Will the associations develop more "service" roles, although possibly competing with each other for such roles?

The current congressional push to downsize the federal government will undoubtedly affect the representational role of many Washington-based associations, but the actual impact is still unclear. For the short term, the representational associations have a very important role in staying alert to changes that will affect universities, identifying strategies for action, and coordinating effective steps to protect institutional interests. Adversity, it is sometimes said, creates a greater need for such association action. Over time, however, if the number of government programs decreases substantially, the salience of federal government activity could diminish, at least for some types of institutions.

The other services offered by the associations have been reviewed by special committees from time to time to ensure that they are not unduly duplicative of each other. If the associations give new emphasis to this service role, it may become pertinent for such a committee review to take place again. Yet because the institutional associations derive their authority wholly from the combined support of their membership, adjustments and changes can be made relatively easily and should not raise serious issues of duplicative or unresponsive service.

Conversely, there should be many situations in which the resources of the associations can assist universities and colleges. Information and research data can be obtained, often with comparisons based on similar institutions. Emerging problems can benefit from joint exploration through association-sponsored projects. Many association staff are highly knowledgeable about changing models of good practice and sources of expertise on specific questions.

Despite the complexity of acronyms and the abundance of newsletters and other materials issued by the current set of institutional associations, the core function for all of these associations remains clear: they have been established as coordinative bodies, to help institutions accomplish their common purposes. If the purposes now being served no longer speak to important needs, university administrators should be ready to take the initiative to propose new approaches more attuned to today's needs. Some administrators, for instance, may feel that most institutionally based associations, and especially those with "representation" roles in Washington, have given priority to relatively short-term planning needs and issues. An additional role might be proposed, in which associations would develop new projects and activities to assist institutions in adapting to rapidly changing conditions at a time when the cost of long-term decisions can be considerable. A core number of like-minded institutions could propose and help develop a new project, possibly one that offers training and experience with simulations and with building and evaluating alternative scenarios for campus action.

Concluding Comments

Undoubtedly, the external environment for U.S. universities and colleges will continue to be affected by the diverse array of intermediary organizations that play an increasingly significant role in higher education in the United States. The prospect is that actions of many of these organizations will complicate university planning. Accrediting agencies are especially likely to impose timetables and reporting requirements that feel burdensome. Other organizations have the potential role of protecting or assisting individual institutions. University administrators should nevertheless remain mindful of the core reality that most such agencies are subject to influence by universities and colleges, whether individually or collectively. Such organizations exist to coordinate action toward the common interest for all of higher education. University leaders can and should act to ensure that such broader purposes are served.

Further Reading

There is a quite limited analytic literature on intermediary organizations. A special issue of *Higher Education Policy* (volume 5, published in 1992), the quarterly journal of the International Association of Universities, offers one of the best sources for readers interested in analyses based on experience in various countries. Twenty-two articles focus on buffer or intermediary organizations in more than ten countries. Also relevant are several chapters in Altbach, Berdahl, and Gumport's edited collection on *Higher Education in American Society* (1994).

Descriptive materials can be found in publications issued by each of the associations covered in this chapter. The biweekly coverage in the *Times Higher Education Supplement* often describes new developments and controversies affecting intermediary organizations in England, Europe, and various nations in the British Commonwealth community.

References

Altbach, P. G., Berdahl, R. O., and Gumport, P. J. *Higher Education in American Society.* (3rd ed.) Amherst, N.Y.: Prometheus, 1994.

Bloland, H. G. *Associations in Action: The Washington, D.C., Higher Education Community.* ASHE-ERIC Higher Education Report No. 2. Washington, D.C.: Association for the Study of Higher Education, 1985.

Brennan, J., El-Khawas, E., and Shah, T. *Peer Review and Assessment of Higher Education Quality: An International Perspective.* Higher Education Report No. 3. London: Quality Support Centre, Open University, 1994.

Cameron, K. S., and Whetton, D. A. "Models of the Organizational Life Cycle: Applications to Higher Education." *Review of Higher Education,* 1983, *6*(4), 269–299.

Cook, C. "Higher Education and Its Washington Associations: Federal Relations as a Membership Incentive." Paper prepared for the 1995 annual meeting of the American Political Science Association, Chicago, Oct. 1995.

El-Khawas, E. "Are Buffer Organizations Doomed to Fail? Inevitable Dilemmas and Tensions." *Higher Education Policy,* 1992, *5*(3), 18–20.

El-Khawas, E., and Massy, W. F. "The British Experience." In W. F. Massy (ed.), *Resource Allocation in Higher Education.* Ann Arbor: University of Michigan Press, 1996.

Furstenbach, J. "When the Pyramids Crumble." *Higher Education Policy,* 1992, *5*(3), 55–58.

Gladieux, L. E., Hauptman, A. M., and Knapp, L. G. "The Federal Government and Higher Education." In P. G. Altbach, R. O. Berdahl, and P. J. Gumport (eds.), *Higher Education in American Society.* (3rd ed.) Amherst, N.Y.: Prometheus, 1994.

Gladieux, L. E., and Wolanin, T. R. *Congress and the Colleges.* Lexington, Mass.: Heath, 1976.

Harcleroad, F. F. "Other External Constituencies and Their Impact on Higher Education." In P. G. Altbach, R. O. Berdahl, and P. J. Gumport (eds.), *Higher Education in American Society.* (3rd ed.) Amherst, N.Y.: Prometheus, 1994.

King, L. R. *The Washington Lobbyists for Higher Education.* Lexington, Mass.: Heath, 1975.

Kitchens, M. (ed.). *Accredited Institutions of Higher Education, 1994–95.* Washington, D.C.: American Council on Education, 1995.

Muhlberg, C. "Is the Deutsche Forschungsgemeinschaft a 'Buffer Institution' for Research in Germany?" *Higher Education Policy,* 1992, *5*(3), 61–63.

Murray, M. A. "Defining the Higher Education Lobby." *Journal of Higher Education,* 1976, *47*(1), 79–92.

"National Referendum Votes to Establish Council for Higher Education Accreditation." *Higher Education and National Affairs,* May 27, 1996, p. 2.

Neave, G. "On Bodies Vile and Bodies Beautiful: The Role of 'Buffer' Institutions Between Universities and State." *Higher Education Policy,* 1992, *5*(3), 10–13.

Tierney, W. G. "Facts and Constructs: Defining Reality in Higher Education Organizations." *Review of Higher Education*, 1987, *11*(1), 61–73.

Wegner, J. W. "The Accreditation Debate: Thoughts on the AALS's 'Membership Review' Function." *The AALS Newsletter*, April 1995, no. 95–2, pp. 1–3.

Wise, A. E. "NCATE's Emphasis on Performance." *NCATE Newsletter*, 1995, *4*(3), 3–6.

Young, K. E., Chambers, C. M., Kells, H. R., and Associates. *Understanding Accreditation*. San Francisco: Jossey-Bass, 1983.

CHAPTER FIVE

EFFECTS OF COMPETITION ON DIVERSE INSTITUTIONAL CONTEXTS

David D. Dill

Planning in colleges and universities has often been seen as a function of the type of institution. Administrators and faculty members routinely argued that the external conditions of public institutions were so different from those of private institutions that planning must be designed for the particular conditions of the public sector. Alternatively, they argued that the internal traditions and organizations of institutions affected the implementation of planning and budgeting procedures. For example, the structure and culture of community colleges or liberal arts colleges were discovered to be measurably different from each other as well as from those of research universities. Thus knowledge and understanding of institutional cultures and structures were thought to be critical to the successful design and implementation of planning and budgeting processes in academic institutions.

Distinctions between the public and private sectors as well as between types of institutions will continue to be important for the management of colleges and universities, but increasing competition in the overall environment is making academic management and planning more, rather than less, similar across academic settings (Becher and Kogan, 1992; Cameron and Tschirhart, 1992; Clark, 1995; Slaughter and Leslie, 1997). Both public and private institutions need to develop means of increasing productivity and stimulating innovation. Both research universities and community colleges need to foster integration and coordination within and across increasingly diverse programs and units. These common social demands will be addressed in all types of institutions of higher education with recognizably similar techniques for organizing and implementing planning systems.

The following sections examine the implications of environmental changes on academic planning systems. The first section reviews the traditional research on structural and cultural differences between types of higher education institutions. Those measurable differences between colleges and universities have led to the prevailing view that different types of institutions required different forms of governance, management, and planning. The second section suggests how the changing environment is challenging all colleges and universities to adapt and change, leading to common approaches to planning. The third section reviews common patterns of planning in this new environment.

Critical Variables in the American System of Higher Education

One of the clear patterns in research on American higher education has been the observed variations in faculty behavior, academic governance, and management across different types of institutions (Baldridge, Curtis, Ecker, and Riley, 1978; Clark, 1987; Dill and Helm, 1988). This differentiation between academic institutions has generally been attributed to the nature of their environments (as in public control versus private flexibility), the nature of the professional task (such as variations in the quality of students and in the faculty's involvement in research), and institutional size and complexity (Dill and Helm, 1988). These variations have traditionally influenced the power and authority of presidents and deans, the degree of shared authority and consultation in academic decision making between central administrators and faculties, and the design of planning and budgeting processes. Shared authority, in which faculties and academic units were actively involved in strategic decision making, was most visible at research universities and elite liberal arts colleges. Collegial forms of planning and budgeting became less common as one descended down the pecking order, through public comprehensive colleges and less-selective private liberal arts colleges (especially sectarian institutions), and were least evident in community colleges and private junior colleges. As Clark (1987) observed in his research study of the American academic profession, "Interviews in institutions situated between the extremes of research universities and community colleges demonstrated that as one moves up the status hierarchy, one encounters more professional control, and as one moves down, one observes more administrative dominance and even autocracy" (p. 268).

The Nature of the Environment and Task Complexity

These acknowledged differences in institutions can be graphically represented. Using a modification of the Carnegie Classification of Colleges and Universities (Carnegie Foundation for the Advancement of Teaching, 1994), Figure 5.1 arrays the major types of colleges and universities according to their environment and their task complexity.

Two-year (associate of arts) colleges, almost two-thirds of which are publicly supported institutions, have traditionally operated in predictable funding and regulatory circumstances with a lower level of task complexity than other institutions. The relatively less complicated nature of the task was reflected in their single-level degree structure, lower average student SAT scores, limited numbers of faculty members with a Ph.D., and negligible proportion of faculty members engaged in research (Baldridge, Curtis, Ecker, and Riley, 1978).

Liberal arts (baccalaureate) colleges II, primarily private institutions, exist in an environment more competitive for student enrollment, and their task, while historically organized around a single, undergraduate liberal arts program, reflects a greater degree of complexity in faculty involvement in research as well as in student quality.

Comprehensive (master's) colleges and universities, again primarily public institutions, are partially sheltered from extreme competition for students by their public financial support, but their task is markedly more complex than liberal arts colleges, with postgraduate professional degrees and substantial commitments to academic research.

Liberal arts (baccalaureate) colleges I, 95 percent of which are private, are competitively engaged with doctorate-granting institutions in the pursuit of quality undergraduates and faculty members, and while their programs are essentially undergraduate and nonprofessionally oriented, their faculties conduct substantially more research than institutions positioned below them in Figure 5.1.

Finally, doctorate-granting universities, both public and private, are characterized by the greatest competition and task complexity. While public doctorate-granting universities have some protection from market forces by virtue of their state support (and are therefore ranked just below private doctorate-granting universities in competitiveness), both public and private universities are engaged in substantial competition for graduate students, faculty members, and grant and contract support to underwrite their research missions. Furthermore, both public and private universities have the most complex degree structures, ranging from undergraduate through postdoctoral programs, and they possess both the highest proportion of faculty members with Ph.D.s and the greatest faculty involvement in research.

FIGURE 5.1. ESTIMATED DISTRIBUTION OF CARNEGIE CLASSIFICATION INSTITUTIONS ON ENVIRONMENTAL UNCERTAINTY AND TASK COMPLEXITY AS OF 1990 (*n* = 2873).

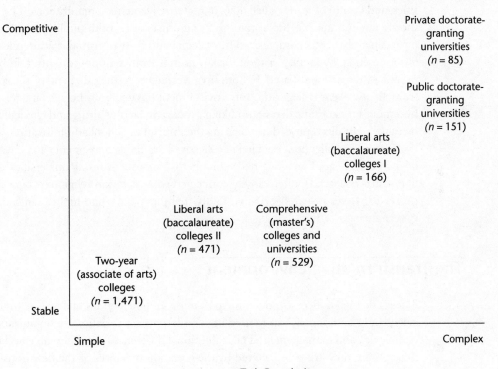

Source: Data from Carnegie Foundation for the Advancement of Teaching, 1994.

With some obvious adjustments, these categories of institutions can also be similarly ranked with regard to institutional size and structural differentiation (Baldridge, Curtis, Ecker, and Riley, 1978). Doctorate-granting universities are, on average, the largest and possess the greatest structural differentiation as reflected in their total number of departments, schools, research centers, and administrative units. Comprehensive colleges and universities are next, and while liberal arts colleges I are much smaller in faculty and student size, they have been surprisingly similar to the comprehensive institutions in number of departments and structural units, reflecting the complexity of their academic tasks. Finally, liberal arts colleges II and two-year colleges (with some notable exceptions among public community colleges, such as Miami-Dade) have historically possessed the least structural differentiation and specialization, with the smallest numbers of faculty members, students, academic departments, and structural units.

As noted earlier, this same hierarchy of institutions also reflects different *authority environments* (Clark, 1987) as embodied in the general understandings, ground rules, and frames of governance that characterize academic organizations. The authority environments of doctorate-granting universities, both public and private, have generally been characterized by collegial authority over major academic decision making, by faculty criteria for key administrative appointments, and by a process of department-based, bottom-up governance. At the other end of the spectrum, the two-year college authority environment has generally been characterized by a more bureaucratic decision-making process on faculty hiring and curriculum, by more centralized procedures bearing the imprint of school administration, and by contractual obligations detailed in collective bargaining agreements. In between, liberal arts colleges I are governed similarly to doctorate-granting universities, and liberal arts colleges II, often closely connected with sectarian religious groups and possessing fewer research-oriented faulty members, have had highly centralized governance procedures.

The Transformative Environment

The reader will notice how often the past tense and the conditional terms "historically" and "traditionally" were used in describing these variations in organization, complexity, and management. The institutional differences are observable and significant, but they are being altered by the common pressures of the new transformational environment. Confronted with rising expenditures and voter revolts over taxes, state governments are substantially cutting per-student support for higher education and experimenting with deregulation and privatization schemes for their public-sector colleges and universities (Slaughter and Leslie, 1997). One effect of these changes is to introduce greater uncertainty and competition among all colleges and universities, both public and private, for students, faculty members, and resources. Cuts in the federal budget, particularly in support for basic research and student financial aid, further increase the intensity of competition among all institutions for students and research support. In addition, the increasing complexity of society spawns internal organizational complexity in the form of new academic specializations and programs. The combination of competition and complexity creates new incentives for institutional innovation and program development as a means of appealing to student markets and potential research support in the private sector.

This transformative environment has already led to structural adjustments in all types of colleges and universities. Two-year colleges have rapidly evolved from institutions with a transfer-oriented function to comprehensive community colleges that must integrate an array of technical and quasi-professional programs serving adults, individuals seeking career renewal, college graduates desiring vocational preparation, workers in need of on-the-job training, and jointly enrolled high school students (Cohen and Brawer, 1996). Liberal arts colleges, particularly those not in the selective elite, have been rapidly broadening their curricula through the inclusion of undergraduate, professionally oriented programs as a means of attracting students (Zammuto, 1984). This shift in mission is reflected in the Carnegie classification's change from "liberal arts" colleges to "baccalaureate" colleges. The increasing competition among doctorate-granting universities for research funds has led to an explosion of organized research units (Geiger, 1990) designed to attract grant support, and to technology transfer units (Dill, 1995) designed to capitalize upon the institution's research discoveries.

Task complexity has also been influenced by the broadening of academic opportunity, which has led to a varied population of students, making the teaching function more intricate at research universities and community colleges alike (Nowotny, 1995). There is also evidence of the seepage of the research function into all classifications of institutions. Since the 1980s, with the singular exception of two-year colleges, the proportion of research time faculty members report has increased in all colleges and universities (Fairweather, 1995).

The net effect of these changes in the environment and responsibilities of colleges and universities is to increase uncertainty and competition as well as the complexity of their academic tasks. Those colleges and universities that historically have operated in more stable and simple conditions are confronted by increasing competition for students and resources and by more internal complexity in carrying out their tasks, while both private and public doctorate-granting universities are experiencing even greater environmental uncertainty and competition than in previous generations.

A predictable and early response to uncertainty of task and environment is increased centralization of decision making (Zammuto, 1986). Studies reveal that as competition, conflict, and demands for survival increase, the initial reaction of leaders is to make decision making more centralized and less participatory. Confronted with declining resources in the 1980s, many leaders tightened their grip on institutional budgeting procedures and developed hierarchical systems of goal setting and academic planning in which small numbers of administrators made decisions about program cuts, program closures, and the reallocation of resources. These changes in governance were most observable in those authority environments which had traditionally been more bureaucratic. However, faculty members in universities, state colleges, liberal arts colleges, and community colleges also perceived that control, power, and decision making were more closely held by administrators and that wide faculty involvement in important decisions about institutional governance was less common (Anderson, 1983).

But as noted above, uncertainty also breeds task complexity. As all colleges and universities responded to the educational needs of more varied student populations, as they developed market-oriented vocational and professional programs, as they expanded their research activity, and as they created entrepreneurial units to counter shrinking financial resources, internal program differentiation clashed with attempts to centralize organization and management. Uncertainty in the environment and in tasks creates a greater need for internal restructuring, program innovation, and quality improvement, which cannot be easily directed from the center. Thus, as in business corporations, colleges and universities need to reconcile demands for greater coordination with increasing demands for greater decentralization.

The effect of the transformative environment is that all colleges and universities must deal with increased competition, uncertainty, and complexity. As a consequence, the influence of factors such as public or private control, traditional patterns of authority, and local politics on the design of an institution's organization and management—at least in those colleges and universities which successfully adapt to the new environmental conditions—will likely diminish. The implementation of academic structure and management will always need to be sensitive to the specific needs and cultures of particular institutions, but in the new transformative context the organization and administration of all colleges and universities will require greater flexibility in decision making, more participation in governance, more integration on both the vertical and horizontal dimensions, and greater delegation of authority and responsibility to the appropriate strategic level (Cameron and Tschirhart, 1992). Much more collaboration among differentiated units will be needed.

The sections that follow explore specific examples of how the design of a college and university planning process can enhance institutional collaboration and integration.

Competitive Environments and Organizational Design

Academic organizations in transformative environments must develop improved mechanisms for communication and cooperation. Organizations in complex environments with high competition and technological dynamism adopt different forms of internal organization and management than those in stable environments. The contingency model of organizational design, developed in the 1970s by Lawrence and Lorsch (1986) and elaborated by others (Nadler, Gerstein, and

Shaw, 1992), provides a specific means for understanding the link between the nature of the environment and the internal organization and planning processes that are necessary for successful competition.

The Contingency Model

From a contingency perspective, the form of management and structure in effective organizations is contingent upon the core technology and nature of competition in the relevant industry (Lawrence and Lorsch, 1986). When the external environment is stable and the technology relatively certain (as was typical in community colleges during their early development), organizations are characterized by centralized, "mechanistic" structures, with a clear hierarchy of authority and specified rules and procedures. In contrast, rapidly changing environments and uncertain technologies, previously characteristic of research universities but now becoming more common in other postsecondary institutions, require organizations with more adaptive, free-flowing, "organic" structures. Horizontal as well as vertical communication and sufficient autonomy so that employees can "discover" their jobs rather than be assigned them are characteristic of an organic structure.

The design of organizational structure, management, and planning can be understood as a function of two complementary processes, *differentiation* and *integration* (Clark, 1995; Lawrence and Lorsch, 1986). As a task becomes more complex and uncertain—as in interdisciplinary teaching or research, or in support services for multicultural or multi-age students—organizations *differentiate* into highly specialized units. Each unit in the organization develops an expertise, a tightly focused perspective, and, often, distinguishing values. Obvious examples are the distinctive "cultures" of the academic disciplines and professions (Becher, 1989). However, without effective mechanisms for coordination, differentiation can lead to duplication and conflict, even in research universities.

Therefore organizations must also *integrate* the work of differentiated units. The importance of collaboration among units is intensified as competition forces organizations to increase the pace of innovation, improve quality, and lower costs. As the demand for productivity rises, effectively managed colleges and universities invest more time and resources in horizontal mechanisms of planning, coordination, and collaboration to improve cooperation between units. Integrating mechanisms require lateral and reciprocal forms of communication such as face-to-face hearings, liaison roles, strategic task forces, ad hoc teams, and the reorganization of management structures and departments (Galbraith, 1977). Effective organizations in transformative environments possess organizational structures with high levels of both differentiation and integration.

The "Network" Organization

Growing competition, complexity, and a faster pace of technological change increase the vulnerability of traditional bureaucratic or hierarchical organizations. Centralized structure and management systems are unable to adapt to the speed with which their core programs must change. Management and planning systems that help foster organizational restructuring are needed. Colleges and universities are therefore experimenting with a new form of structure, the network organization (Dill and Sporn, 1995).

A network provides a structure for relations among individuals or groups: a lateral pattern of exchange with reciprocal lines of communication (Powell, 1990). A network contrasts sharply with a hierarchical pattern of exchange, the latter with its reliance on vertical communication flowing mostly one way and filtered through administrators. Hierarchies limit the amount and frequency of information that can occur between parties. Competition and complexity create a demand for innovation and adaptation. In this context, individual faculty members need to participate in planning processes that enhance the opportunity for frequent, reliable exchanges of information. For example, faculty members and academic groups need to exchange knowledge and skills, experimental technologies and unique sources of data, perceptions of clients' needs, and suggestions for improving teaching and service. Networks, which encourage face-to-face and reciprocal communication, permit the exchange of "thick" information (Powell, 1990). Hierarchies also lack flexibility under conditions of uncertainty. Hierarchies assign value to an exchange, usually through compensation to an individual or group. But the value of academic exchange is not always known in advance and is not simple to quantify. Planning processes that encourage the formation of informal groups of faculty or staff around shared academic interests or administrative problems may produce vital new academic activities or managerial improvements. In conditions of uncertainty, therefore, network structures that encourage reciprocity, trust, and long-term commitment offer the best potential for adaptability and program innovation.

Networked organizations differ in architecture from hierarchically designed structures (Nohria and Ghoshal, 1994). Assets, knowledge, and competence are distributed throughout the institution and reside in multiple locations rather than being concentrated in the center or disbursed to basic units. Because some operating units interact with different environments and possess different kinds and degrees of resources, they play different roles within the organization. In planning new services or strategies, some units lead, while others play a supportive role. Integration is facilitated through shared values, strong but flexible planning and budgeting systems featuring horizontal communication, and common incentives.

Integrating Network Organizations Through Planning

The challenge in a network organization is how to provide autonomy to subsidiary units while still giving central administrators the capacity to encourage coherence, quality, and organizational adaptation. How can integration in such a complex system be achieved? Uncertainty in the institution's environment, including dramatic reductions in resources, often leads to misguided administrative action to establish control by centralizing planning and allocation. A college or university that wishes to respond to the challenges, however, must nurture independent development in its academic units and internal services. The dynamics of network organization aid in negotiating the conflict between independence and coordination (Bartlett and Ghoshal, 1989).

Within network organizations, coordination and cohesion are best achieved by planning processes that feature horizontal integration and shared values (Dill, 1982; Nohria and Ghoshal, 1994). Developing and publicly articulating a set of core values at the corporate level are the essential first steps in adapting colleges and universities to their new challenges (for a more extensive discussion of this process, see Chapter Nine). Articulation and communication of these values in the early stages of a planning process are critical tasks for the central administration. In a network organization, coordination through shared values permits subsidiary units the autonomy and independence necessary for the development of their capabilities.

Following the definition of core values, the planning process in a network organization must be designed as a means of fostering institutional adaptation and improvement through organizational processes that encourage integration at the unit and institutional level. If the process is not designed to promote collaboration, it cannot hope to effectively promote academic innovation, quality enhancement, and improved productivity. Thus the design of a planning process in a network organization must first consider those structural arrangements that will facilitate horizontal communication and coordination among related functional units, and vertical, reciprocal communication among academic leaders and strategic operating units. Second, the design must encourage individual units themselves to develop the collective capacity to adapt to changes in the environment brought about by increasing competition and complexity. Finally, the complexity, diversity, and decentralization of a network form of organization requires more broad-based forms of communication and information distribution to the overall academic community as a means of sustaining their support for the legitimacy of the planning process. In the context of academic planning, these design elements can be organized into four general categories (Dill, 1994):

- Designating and grouping related functions where necessary
- Encouraging reciprocal (down-up) communication and contact
- Promoting a planning capability within each strategic unit
- Increasing direct communication with the members of the larger academic community

Design Elements for Designating and Grouping Units

In colleges and universities with many different academic and administrative units, the design of a planning process can either lessen or increase adaptation, coordination, and organizational efficiency. Any planning process must designate the level at which units develop plans for review at higher levels. This is not a superficial design issue. If the unit designation is placed too low in the organization, for example at the department level, the authority of deans may be compromised, differentiation may increase, and the reviewers may be overwhelmed with information. If the unit designation is placed too high in the organization, for example at the level of a vice president, the planning process may lose the opportunity to stimulate innovation and institutional savings.

At one highly differentiated professional school, the planning process designated each program as a planning unit, regardless of size. As a result, all of the faculty were involved in developing unit plans, the unit plans were seldom coordinated, the review process was time consuming and cumbersome, and the experience increased differentiation and conflict. By contrast, a design that selects planning units with too broad a span of control may lead to the preparation of formulaic reports. An environment of strategic uncertainty and resource scarcity requires that responsibility and accountability for strategic choices be delegated to identifiable "micro-enterprise" units (Gerstein, 1992), where operating programs, technologies, and customers interact and where assessments of quality and cost can be made most effectively.

A related design element is the grouping of selected units in the planning process in order to promote collaboration and integration. Trow's (1983) case study of the review and reorganization of the biological sciences at the University of California at Berkeley is an instructive example of the importance of unit grouping as a mechanism of organizational adaptation and restructuring.

At Berkeley, as at other research universities, the biological science departments had traditionally been organized according to categories of living things: zoology, botany, bacteriology, and entomology. With the developments during this century in molecular theory, biochemistry, and advanced research technologies, biologists have turned to studying the underlying similarities in the composition of all living organisms. Newer departments of molecular genetics and cell biology subsequently emerged, which overlapped with the more traditional disciplines and crossed departmental boundaries. By the 1980s Berkeley had twenty different departments in the biological sciences located in five different schools, most with a full complement of faculty members investigating a similar range of "new" disciplines.

A national assessment of graduate programs revealed Berkeley's declining competitive status in a number of the biological disciplines. Many of the university's research and teaching laboratories in the biological sciences were in poor condition and in danger of becoming obsolete. Individual departments began having difficulty competing successfully for the best young faculty members. An external review committee reported that the lack of an effective means for coordination and interchange in the newer, interdisciplinary subject areas limited development in several emerging fields. In response, the central administration appointed an *ad hoc* faculty Internal Biological Sciences Review Committee to evaluate all biological programs and to propose a coordinated plan. The committee produced a set of priorities for funding research across existing departments; a plan for new, collaborative research facilities; and the establishment of interdepartmental "affinity groups" to promote communication and collaboration among the dispersed departments. Through the selective grouping of units, the biological sciences at Berkeley have gradually been reorganized, strengthened, and made more efficient. In the 1990s Berkeley has built upon this experience by developing a comprehensive planning process that focuses on the systematic restructuring of related academic disciplines and fields.

The general planning strategy of grouping units to promote adaptation and restructuring is applicable at all types of institutions and for both academic and administrative units. For example, units that share a similar technology (administrative and academic computing) or similar customers (admissions, financial aid, and registrar) or related academic expertise (management programs in education, health, and public administration) might be urged to develop plans in concert with each other.

Design Elements Encouraging Reciprocal (Down-Up) Communication

One predictable reaction to declining resources and increasing uncertainty is centralization of authority and top-down flow of information. However, most analysts argue that environmental changes require greater horizontal participation in decision making, and more reciprocal, down-up forms of communication (Cameron and Tschirhart, 1992; Lawrence and Lorsch, 1986).

At many colleges and universities, planning processes are initiated by a *call-to-plan* document, which is usually issued by the president or chief academic officer.

This document can be a critical instrument for stimulating reciprocal forms of discussion and debate. Departments, schools, and administrative units develop their strategies within directions articulated by university leaders (Dill and Helm, 1988). Institutional priorities rarely emerge spontaneously from committee meetings and discussions. They are first asserted by individual leaders; then they are criticized, modified, and reshaped through the reciprocal processes of communication and negotiation between academic leaders and institutional members (Starr, 1993).

Reciprocal communication is also incorporated into the planning process through the procedures used for reviewing unit plans and providing feedback. Plans may be reviewed incrementally or hierarchically. If incrementally, a typical sequence is to review the mission statement, then the unit's initial draft plan, and then the final planning document. This step-by-step process encourages socialization and adaptation. Plans can be reviewed hierarchically, by line administrators and/or by a committee or planning group composed of administrators, faculty members, students, and staff members, thereby promoting horizontal communication. Although expensive in terms of administrative time, many colleges and universities require, in addition to formal planning documents, scheduled presentations or hearings as part of their planning or budgeting process. This design feature promotes two-way communication between central administrators and unit heads. Presentations make it possible to solicit the views of other institutional constituents if the reviewing body is structured with that objective in mind.

While units are almost always required to submit written plans to a particular office by a particular date, not all planning calendars *also* stipulate that each unit will in turn receive a written response to its plan, from a particular person, by a particular date (Schmidtlein and Milton, 1989). By formally delineating the responsibilities of *all* participants in a planning process, a planning design can foster the reciprocal communication that is essential to achieving adaptation and integration in a complex, differentiated academic institution.

Design Elements Promoting Planning in Strategic Units

Encouraging the development of the units' capacity for planning is a major objective of a planning process in a network academic organization. The organization of most colleges and universities is analogous to a multidivisional firm operating many differentiated programs. Each of these programs—whether academic such as arts and sciences, engineering, and law, or administrative support programs such as information technology and technology transfer—involves different markets, technologies, and program components. The strategies for these diverse programs cannot be established centrally. Instead, each program must develop its own strategic choice-making process.

Each unit should develop a plan that represents the *collective* choice of the members of the unit. In order to emphasize the importance of the process, units may be asked to provide both their plans and a brief description of the procedures by which plans were developed. Units can be assisted by using external consultants, temporarily assigning an individual from a more experienced unit, or designating a faculty or staff member to assist with planning at the unit level.

A second means of assisting planning is by distributing data oriented toward the unit level. Many colleges and universities have developed standard unit data profiles or formats for their planning units (Dill, 1994). These centrally produced profiles provide trend information on academic and service unit budgets, personnel resources, and relevant activity indicators. Through these profiles, colleges and universities can develop a common information vocabulary, which can contribute to the integration of the institution. Institutions designing a comprehensive planning process can also benchmark a number of peer institutions and identify the types of planning data that have already proven useful to these organizations at the institutionwide as well as unit levels. By developing, disseminating, and refining these planning data as part of a comprehensive planning process, a more reflective, data-based process of choice making can be encouraged.

The format of the unit planning report can influence the extent to which planning is implemented at the strategic unit level. Some planning processes produce information for central decision makers to use in making decisions. If, however, one significant purpose of a comprehensive planning process is to delegate responsibility and accountability for strategic choice making to appropriate levels of an organization, then this should be reflected in the outline of the report. Unit planning reports might require formal assessments of the state of each school or administrative area with emphasis on program, financial, and managerial strengths and weaknesses. Unit plans could be required to identify linkages with other units, the human resource implications of the plans, measures that can be used to assess progress toward stated goals, and anticipated sources of funds.

The format of a unit planning report can help make a unit aware of its external environment and competition. Thus the planning outline used in Northwestern University's planning process requires both academic and administrative units to select the five top competitors in their fields, identify the reasons for their preeminence, rank the focus unit in relationship to these competitors, and articulate the unit's distinctive strengths (Dill, 1994). To promote accountability *within* strategic units, the emphasis in the requested planning document must be on encouraging the unit members to clarify their collective judgment regarding necessary strategic direction as well as requiring the unit itself to identify means of reallocating existing resources to achieve the changes advocated.

The design of planning processes in a competitive environment must foster choice making at different levels of academic organization. Increasing task complexity has led to an organizational differentiation that cannot be eliminated. Planning in these settings entails setting broad institutional direction, managing essential support services, and encouraging strategic choice at the appropriate unit level.

Design Elements Increasing Direct Communication

Hierarchical forms of communication can be ineffective in promoting commitment and continuity in a diverse and fluid academic community. Greater emphasis needs to be placed upon direct forms of communication, including open meetings, interim reports through campus newspapers, and direct mailing of planning and budgeting documents to individual members of the academic community.

A critical design element for promoting the sharing of information is the content of the president or chief academic officer's original call to plan. The call-to-plan document can establish a common culture of information, ideas, language, and norms; it can articulate the institutional criteria that will become the normative basis, at every level, for choices regarding priorities and budgetary allocations. The protocol typically includes (Dill, 1994):

- Core values or criteria to be employed in the planning process
- Shared perceptions of the institution's environment
- Recommended institutional priorities
- Planning assumptions on financial resources, enrollment, and/or space

A second means of promoting direct communication, as noted in the previous section on reciprocal processes, is by including faculty members, students, and staff along with central administrators, in the process of examining and reviewing unit plans (Dill and Helm, 1988).

Finally, as discussed earlier, communicating planning outcomes to the broader community can significantly influence the legitimacy of the planning process in a network organization. A number of colleges and universities distribute documents to all members of the academic community on a regular cycle. At some colleges and universities these documents include extensive discussion and analysis of all operating revenues and expenditures for the institution, including the proposed plans and budgets of all academic and administrative units. (A creative example is the *Operating Budget Guidelines* distributed annually at Stanford University.) Direct contact is needed to communicate institutional norms for planning, the data upon which decisions are made, and the strategic choices to be implemented.

Conclusion

While the precise form of organization and management for each college and university needs to be designed with sensitivity to the specific institution's mission and traditions, the network model of academic organization provides a useful metaphor for understanding the type of planning processes that may be needed for most colleges and universities in the new environment. The network form is not new to academia, but its application to the design of planning processes will require developing novel mechanisms for academic communication and collaboration. As Burton Clark (1995) recently observed, "Effective institutional leadership then means the recognition of the primacy of the professional clusters—the historians in their subdomain, the physicists and economists in theirs—and the construction of new tools for making those clusters more effective in research and teaching. Compared to the old style state-led segmental budgeting, this may necessitate a radical combination of lump-sum financing for the decentralization from university administration to basic units, with integration of the whole fashioned by new forms of dialogue, information tracking, and periodic full-scale review" (p. 166).

Properly designed, the process of planning is critical for achieving integration in highly differentiated academic organizations. By articulating the criteria by which collective decisions will be made, promoting consolidation among units where necessary, encouraging reciprocal communication and debate on unit plans, facilitating strategic planning within academic and service units, and increasing direct communication on these matters to all members of the academic community, a planning process can make a tangible contribution to the capacity of a college or university to adapt to uncertain and challenging conditions.

Further Reading

Readers seeking further information on the theme of this chapter should consult the following: Baldridge, Curtis, Ecker, and Riley (1978) and Clark (1987) on the empirical research describing differences in administration and organization among types of colleges and universities; Lawrence and Lorsch (1986) and Galbraith (1977) for the classic and still relevant arguments on the contingency model; Nadler, Gerstein, and Shaw (1992) for organizational design models derived primarily from business organizations; and Dill and Sporn (1995) for a more extensive discussion of the application of the network model to the organization of colleges and universities.

References

Anderson, R. E. *Finance and Effectiveness: A Study of College Environments.* Princeton: Educational Testing Service, 1983.

Baldridge, J. V., Curtis, D. V., Ecker, G. P., and Riley, G. L. *Policy Making and Effective Leadership.* San Francisco: Jossey-Bass, 1978.

Bartlett, C., and Ghoshal, S. *Managing Across Borders.* Boston: Harvard Business School Press, 1989.

Becher, T. *Academic Tribes and Territories: Intellectual Enquiry and the Cultures of Discipline.* Milton Keynes, England: Society for Research in Higher Education and Open University Press, 1989.

Becher, T., and Kogan, M. *Process and Structure in Higher Education.* (2nd ed.) London: Routledge, 1992.

Cameron, K., and Tschirhart, M. "Postindustrial Environments and Organizational Effectiveness in Colleges and Universities." *Journal of Higher Education,* 1992, *63*(1), 87–108.

Carnegie Foundation for the Advancement of Teaching. *A Classification of Institutions of Higher Education.* Princeton: Carnegie Foundation for the Advancement of Teaching, 1994.

Clark, B. R. *The Academic Life: Small Worlds, Different Worlds.* Princeton: Carnegie Foundation for the Advancement of Teaching, 1987.

Clark, B. R. "Complexity and Differentiation: The Deepening Problem of University Integration." In D. D. Dill and B. Sporn (eds.), *Emerging Patterns of Social Demand and University Reform: Through a Glass Darkly.* New York: Pergamon Press, 1995.

Cohen, A. M., and Brawer, F. B. *The American Community College.* (3rd ed.) San Francisco: Jossey-Bass, 1996.

Dill, D. D. "The Management of Academic Culture: Notes on the Management of Meaning and Social Integration." *Higher Education,* 1982, *11*(3), 303–320.

Dill, D. D. "Rethinking the Planning Process." *Planning for Higher Education,* 1994, *22*(2), 8–13.

Dill, D. D. "University-Industry Entrepreneurship: The Organization and Management of American University Technology Transfer Units." *Higher Education,* 1995, *29*(4), 369–384.

Dill, D. D., and Helm, K. P. "Faculty Participation in Strategic Policy Making." In J. Smart (ed.), *Higher Education: Handbook of Theory and Research.* Vol. 4. New York: Agathon Press, 1988.

Dill, D. D., and Sporn, B. "University 2001: What Will the University of the Twenty-First Century Look Like?" In D. D. Dill and B. Sporn (eds.), *Emerging Patterns of Social Demand and University Reform: Through a Glass Darkly.* New York: Pergamon Press, 1995.

Fairweather, J. *Faculty Work and Public Trust: Restoring the Value of Teaching and Public Service in Academic Life.* Boston: Allyn & Bacon, 1995.

Galbraith, J. R. *Organization Design.* Reading, Mass.: Addison-Wesley, 1977.

Geiger, R. L. "Organized Research Units: Their Role in the Development of University Research." *The Journal of Higher Education,* 1990, *61*(1), 1–19.

Gerstein, M. "From Machine Bureaucracies to Networked Organizations: An Architectural Journey." In D. Nadler, M. Gerstein, and R. Shaw (eds.), *Organizational Architecture: Designs for Changing Organizations.* San Francisco: Jossey-Bass, 1992.

Lawrence, P., and Lorsch, J. *Organization and Environment.* (2nd ed.) Boston: Harvard Business School Press, 1986.

Nadler, D., Gerstein, M., and Shaw R. (eds.) *Organizational Architecture: Designs for Changing Organizations.* San Francisco: Jossey-Bass, 1992.

Nohria, N., and Ghoshal, S. "Differentiated Fit and Shared Values: Alternatives for Managing Headquarters-Subsidiary Relations." *Strategic Management Journal,* 1994, *15*(6), 491–502.

Nowotny, H. "Mass Higher Education and Social Mobility: A Tenuous Link." In D. D. Dill and B. Sporn (eds.), *Emerging Patterns of Social Demand and University Reform: Through a Glass Darkly.* New York: Pergamon Press, 1995.

Powell, W. W. "Neither Market Nor Hierarchy: Network Forms of Organization." *Research in Organizational Behavior,* 1990, *12,* 295–336.

Schmidtlein, F. A., and Milton, T. H. "College and University Planning: Perspectives from a Nation-Wide Study." *Planning for Higher Education,* 1988–89, *17*(3), 1–20.

Slaughter, S., and Leslie, L. *Academic Capitalism: Politics, Policies, and the Entrepreneurial University.* Baltimore: Johns Hopkins Press, 1997.

Starr, S. F. "A President's Message to Planners." *Planning for Higher Education,* 1993, *22*(1), 16–22.

Trow, M. A. "Organizing the Biological Sciences at Berkeley." *Change,* 1983, *15*(8), 28–53.

Zammuto, R. F. "Are the Liberal Arts an Endangered Species?" *Journal of Higher Education,* 1984, *55*(2), 184–211.

Zammuto, R. F. "Managing Decline in American Higher Education." In J. Smart (ed.), *Higher Education: Handbook of Theory and Research.* Vol. 2. New York: Agathon Press, 1986.

CHAPTER SIX

PRINCIPLES FOR REDESIGNING INSTITUTIONS

Richard B. Heydinger

To thrive in the twenty-first century, higher education must guard against the smug attitude that in recent decades characterized General Motors, IBM, and the U.S. Post Office. GM did not believe that foreign competitors could ever produce a car that the American public would buy in great numbers. IBM knew that companies wanted large mainframe computers and so was blindsided by the wave of technological change and consumer needs that was set in motion by two youngsters building microcomputers in their garage. The Post Office turned a deaf ear to its customers, since the federal government provided a guaranteed source of funding and an exclusive franchise for its services. All of these dominant organizations convinced themselves that they could dictate the terms and conditions of their own evolution.

This chapter gazes into higher education's crystal ball and hypothesizes organizational adaptations that may occur as our industry evolves in the decades ahead. Some of the changes discussed in this chapter are well under way and

Note: The author is grateful to Michael O'Keefe and the McKnight Foundation for providing him with support to attend the 1995 Salzburg Seminar on "Higher Education: Institutional Structure for the Twenty-First Century." Olin Robinson, the Salzburg Seminar, and the W. K. Kellogg Foundation also assembled a wonderful group of colleagues, without whom many of the ideas contained in this paper would not have been developed.

accepted as part of the official future (Hawken, 1982) of higher education. Other alternatives may seem radical and implausible. We must keep IBM, GM, and the U.S. Post Office in mind, for it is impossible to believe that higher education will escape the fundamental changes under way in all other sectors of society.

Alternative Developments in the Twenty-First Century

Presented in this chapter are six clusters of developments that might redirect higher education as it journeys into the twenty-first century:

1. Advanced learning
2. Anywhere, anyplace learning
3. Instructional enterprises
4. Market makers
5. Learning agents
6. Virtual enterprises

This is an eclectic set of possibilities. They are not mutually exclusive, some are variations on the same theme, and some would actually work in competition with each other.

Advanced Learning

Perhaps the most pervasive change coming in the twenty-first century will be a whole new way of looking at "higher education." As we all know, the dominance of the traditional campus-based model comprising full-time students seventeen to twenty-two years old has long since disappeared. In the last twenty-five years, we have seen significant growth in enrollment options and a significant diversification of the student population. Yet history will show us that this trend is only in its formative stages; the most dramatic shifts lie ahead.

Under way today is a veritable revolution in how the public views the need for learning and training. As Davis and Botkin note, "The marketplace for learning is being redefined dramatically from K–12 [sic] to K–80, or lifetime learning, whose major segments are customers, employees, and students, in that order" (1994, p. 16). They argue that imparting knowledge will be a fundamental concern of product as well as service development. Increasingly, businesses are recognizing that investment in employee learning is a strategic advantage. In siting new offices, corporations frequently use the availability of quality higher education as a significant factor in their decisions. Thus higher education has changed from a peripheral concern of the twentieth century to an axial concern of the twenty-first century (Clark, 1984).

To remind ourselves of this fundamental shift, it is useful to change our terminology so that we embody this new outlook. We must change our orientation from one of higher education to that of "advanced learning." This new term is useful because it provides an implicit commentary on some of higher education's most fundamental assumptions. Advanced learning:

- Cares only that learning in fact takes place; it does not care how or where learning happens
- Views learning as assessed by outcomes, not whether people jump through the hoops of a predefined process
- Sees faculty as coaches working collaboratively with students toward the same objectives, not as cloistered monks whom students seek out to have wisdom imparted

Although to some readers these changes may seem only semantic, the organizations that embrace advanced learning will work differently and measure their success in much different ways than do today's higher education institutions.

Anywhere, Anyplace Learning

This development is familiar to all of us, for its introduction has taken place over the past few decades. Correspondence courses have been offered for many years. They have been augmented recently by radio and television delivery systems that take learning out to the student. Today the majority of master's degrees in engineering are earned by students who take their courses on-site, at their place of work. Yet we are still at a low point on this growth curve. The twenty-first century will witness the full force of this development. At least three basic forms are emerging.

Distance Learning. This approach encompasses the wide variety of options focused on taking course materials to students wherever they are located. Today these alternatives continue to expand rapidly. Recently the State of Maine established a university whose sole mode of instruction will be via satellite-transmitted TV signals.

In reality, the term *distance learning* reveals how mired we are in the past and how institution-centered rather than student-centered we remain. "Distant from what?" we might ask. Distant not from learning, of course, but from where the professors view the center of activity (Pruitt, 1995).

In distance education, most of the learning activity is homework with occasional work in class; whereas conventional education is mostly class work with occasional homework. In conventional education the faculty teaches; in distance education, the institution teaches through the processes it sets up. These processes are set up to carry out on a large scale instructional functions that the classroom faculty executes on a small scale (Guri-Rozenblit, 1993, p. 289). As this market continues to expand, a proliferation of specialty organizations focused on "distance" education will join such existing market players as the British Open University and the Mind Extension University and National Technological University in the United States.

Open Learning. Although frequently mentioned in the same breath with distance learning, open learning is a much different concept. Open learning puts the student squarely at the center of the equation in developing her or his learning plan. In contrast, distance learning may or may not permit students to be partners in developing their learning plans.

Similarly, open learning stands in contrast to the traditional faculty-driven curriculum model, which presents the students with a set of program options and gives them little freedom to determine their own learning activities. Like distance learning, open learning has continued to grow in recent decades, with alternatives such as the University Without Walls programs and Walden University. As momentum swings toward learner-driven education, these models should continue to proliferate.

The Virtual Classroom. Although not as well developed as distance and open learning, within this cluster of options the virtual classroom may be the largest growth area during the twenty-first century. Driven by a recognition that society offers powerful laboratories for the concepts being taught in the classroom, many programs will continue to expand their notion of the "classroom" to include off-campus activities. Students have long recognized this. When given an opportunity to redesign the curriculum, one of their most strongly held suggestions is to push back the boundaries of the classroom and extend them to all of society (Heydinger and Wallace, 1995).

The virtual classroom has another, now perhaps more commonplace, definition. It encompasses the range of possibilities offered us by the ubiquitous availability of telecommunications. As we all suspect, we have only begun to scratch the surface of possibilities. Geographically separate classrooms connected via a two-way television network are not even newsworthy anymore. Courses and degrees are available via the Internet with "classroom" discussion, paper submission, and instructor feedback all taking place in cyberspace. Today you can receive an

MBA, earn a baccalaureate in management information systems, and take engineering courses, all via "the Net."

As compression techniques continue to improve dramatically and bandwidth becomes a free good, advanced learning will take place wherever the learner is. At this point it is impossible to imagine, much less predict, what the virtual classroom of the future may encompass. It's as if we're standing in 1905, discussing the newfangled automobile, and are invited to envision the suburb and the drive-through lane at a fast-food restaurant.

Instructional Enterprises

As the boundaries of classrooms disappear, colleges and universities may become more horizontal organizations, with units or individuals collaborating across a number of campuses to offer services. This could easily spawn a whole new set of institutional arrangements and advanced learning options. Here are three possibilities.

Outsourcing Instruction. For a number of decades, outsourcing has been an acceptable alternative to higher education, but only within a limited set of functions (for example, food services, laundry, printing, and continuing education).

However, "sacred" ground was trod recently in Minnesota with an attempt to outsource an entire block of instruction with a single contract. The president of the six-campus, public Minnesota Technical College sought competing bids from accredited institutions in the state to deliver 232 sections of general education. Although his initiative failed because of pressure from a neighboring faculty union, outsourcing will be tried again by other institutions. It provides administrators with a cost-effective alternative that offers many degrees of freedom not available in traditional organizational arrangements. For example, the institution can specify the outcomes it expects, stipulate the conditions of teaching it desires (for example, office hours), and limit the length of institutional commitment to this resource.

Teaching Enterprises. Sometime in the twenty-first century, a group of faculty will come together and form their own teaching enterprise. Conceptually, this alternative is identical to the outsourcing model described above. The only difference is the locus of the initiative. These faculty may be organized around a discipline (for example, biology), a problem area (freshwater), a pedagogical style (personalized system of instruction), or a particular type of student (the hearing impaired). These individuals will package their expertise, curriculum materials, and computer software and market them to higher education institutions, high schools, corporations, and government agencies.

To increase their chances of success, these entrepreneurs will ask themselves what the customer needs. In this case, their customer will be the organization with whom they are contracting. Many technical and community colleges have begun a form of this through their customized training programs. However, if a teaching enterprise is truly an independent business venture, the result will be a set of innovative approaches that are not available in today's higher education bureaucracies.

Faculty with Agents. As some pundits have noted, higher education is one of the most sophisticated cottage industries ever established. When this perspective is coupled with the possibilities of the virtual classroom and teaching enterprises, it seems distinctly possible that "teaching stars" will emerge. These individuals will be the personalities most sought after for virtual classrooms and multimedia applications. It will then be a short evolutionary step for these stars to be represented by agents. Just as entertainers and sports personalities have agents, so too may a limited number of faculty. The skeptic is invited to consider George Gilder's assertion that "It's a sure thing that education will be a much bigger market than entertainment" (Gilder, 1995, p. 22).

Market Makers

This term is borrowed from economics, in which a market is defined as a forum that brings together willing sellers with wanting buyers. The possible developments in this cluster encompass some of the most potent forces for constructive change across traditional higher education.

Market makers are intermediary organizations that exist "between" sellers (higher education providers) and buyers (learners). They are prevalent in other industries, and we have come to expect their services. For example, the stock market is a highly developed intermediary that provides a forum for buyers and sellers to conduct their transactions. There are even spin-off intermediaries such as brokerage houses and investment newsletters. These market-making organizations facilitate market transactions so that they take place more effectively and efficiently.

As advanced learning continues to take on added importance, and as the learner is faced with a growing number of options, market-making organizations are likely to expand and become more prevalent in higher education. For example, the Council for Adult and Experiential Learning (CAEL) currently manages employee-learning and tuition-assistance programs for over one hundred thousand private- and public-sector employees. In this intermediary role, CAEL serves as a broker between employees (learners or buyers) and higher education providers (institutions or sellers).

Discussed below are two market-making organizations. One provides information to the consumer; the other offers an approach for banking funds to cover the costs of a student's education.

Learning Connection. This organization is most aptly described as a consumer information center on advanced learning options. No organization in higher education quite like it exists today, although pieces of the model are currently being developed.

The Learning Connection might offer three services. First, it would assist students in making choices about their advanced learning options. Today there are a small number of private entrepreneurs who on a fee-for-service basis assist high school students in selecting a college. Similarly, the Commission on Higher Education in Indiana offers a service that provides descriptive information about Indiana colleges and universities as well as the admissions and financial aid process.

Second, the Learning Connection might certify student outcomes. With employers becoming increasingly skeptical about the skills that degree students bring with them, a learning connection could offer baseline skill certification. The American College Testing service (ACT) is moving in this direction with the development of its Work Keys program in pilot centers around the country.

Third, the Learning Connection might also serve as a credit bank. To earn a baccalaureate degree, today's "average" student attends more than two institutions. This trend seems destined only to increase as learning opportunities become more diverse. Thus, it is easy to imagine a learning connection maintaining students' electronic portfolios, to summarize their advanced learning experiences and verify their level of skill certification. Both British Columbia and Minnesota are in various stages of developing a credit bank.

Learning Bank. The Learning Bank is a banking institution that focuses exclusively on helping students fund their advanced learning programs. The Learning Bank might be a unit of government or a private organization commissioned by the state. Each citizen might be given a learning account in the state's learning bank. Funds could be deposited from both public and private sources. For example, grandparents could put their zero coupon bond here for their grandchild's education. Parents might have tax incentives to save funds here for their children's education. And, most importantly, the state legislature could allocate its appropriation to the Learning Bank rather than give it directly to the institutions.

This approach radically alters the balance of power in today's higher education equation. Rather than public institutions receiving a significant portion of their operating funds from the state, institutions would have to earn their funds by attracting students to their campus and retaining them. Learners would have funds in their learning accounts that they could spend according to state guidelines. For example, state appropriations might be permitted to be spent only in public institutions. Alternatively, some states might decide to let their appropriations follow students to any accredited higher education institution within the state, whether it be public or private.

In considering a Learning Bank, we should make no assumptions about the nature of the financial aid policies or the level of support provided each student by the state. These approaches could be as a liberal or conservative as the state desires. The Learning Bank also does not negate the need or possibility of private financial aid programs.

The Learning Bank would be an efficient agent for implementing changes in higher education financing policies. To alter financial-aid policies, only the Learning Bank need change its computer programs rather than every institution scrambling to make these changes.

Both the Learning Connection and the Learning Bank would be new players in the higher education market. These two entities are built on the premise that giving students additional power would provide a more equitable marketplace than currently exists, thus improving the overall quality of higher education. Typically, when markets are out of balance, the highest-quality goods and services are not provided.

Learning Agents

This cluster of developments is built on an assumption that currently students have no advocates in the higher education process. It hypothesizes that a group of consumer-oriented services might appear, to support students as they attempt to take advantage of the overwhelming variety of advanced learning options.

Brokerage Houses. Advanced learning brokerage houses would bring together a diverse set of learning materials, people, and experiences to create a degree or certificate program. For their students, these brokers might create individualized degree programs from resources around the world. Already today, this possibility is probably more within our grasp than we recognize.

Brokers might draw together groups of students and negotiate quantity discounts with various learning providers. These brokers might negotiate payments with renowned faculty, in exchange for spending a certain amount of time on-line each week with brokerage students. Brokerage houses might certify learning for students and even guarantee them job placement.

Personal Learning Agents. Reports on the future of the information super-highway suggest that software robots are being developed that will travel the Internet looking for specified "items" for their owner. These items might easily include advanced learning options. Imagine that you decide to take one or two "courses" on the culture and history of Uruguay to prepare for an upcoming extended business stay in Montevideo. You also want to brush up on your spoken Spanish. You instruct your software robot to travel the Internet and gather both catalog and evaluative information for the advanced learning options on these topics. After reviewing these options, you instruct the robot, already programmed with your credit card information, to purchase selected items, enroll you, and download the necessary materials. Sounds far-fetched, but conceptually there are no known barriers.

Less futuristic but perhaps even more effective would be groups of individuals who would offer the same learning-agent services as the robots. We have examples in many other industries (travel agents, insurance brokers, stockbrokers). Shouldn't there be similar agents to assist students in traversing the highways of advanced learning?

Virtual Enterprises

As the above developments play out, it is easy to imagine the "unbundling" of today's monolithic higher education institutions into families of more focused enterprises. Each enterprise would be responsible to its own set of customers. Initially these enterprises might parallel the operating units of today's universities and colleges. For example, a university's computer center might become a free-standing enterprise; so might the library, the law school, or even the English department. There might be a facilities enterprise that would own and operate the campus buildings. Their incentives would be to find the best space for their customers, and to maximize the use of these valuable community resources that we call campuses.

In fact, enterprises have been a part of higher education for a long time. Continuing education units and research centers are typically run as enterprises. Their success in large measure is due to the alignment of their purposes with the needs of those they are serving. The attractiveness of the enterprise option is its flexibility and institutional accountability, two assets in higher education that are most in need of strengthening.

These enterprises could be either public or private. In public universities, the enterprises would most likely remain public, although it is easy to imagine a mix of public and private groups coming together to form a virtual public university. The purposes of the institution and the accountability for its outcomes would all be tightly held by a public body on the order of a higher education policy board (Armajani, Heydinger, and Hutchinson, 1994).

To some higher education traditionalists, these ideas may sound like a future gone mad. Traditionalists might envision a breakdown of the current order; in part, that is intended. They also might envision the disappearance of the campus as we know it today. That is not intended, nor need it be an outcome of this development. Enterprises or virtual enterprises (that is, collections of enterprises) are a content-free idea. They may be as conservative or as radical as one chooses. They may emphasize traditional higher education values or incorporate entirely new sets of values.

Eight Steps Toward Reinventing a Traditional Higher Education Institution

Many of the developments described above hypothesize the creation of new advanced learning entities. Certainly, creating a new entity from the ground up is one way to overcome the shortcomings of our contemporary models while taking advantage of the broad societal forces at work. As difficult as it may be to give birth to a new organization, transforming an existing one is probably even more difficult. Combine that with six hundred years of tradition and a pervasive academic culture that spans organizational boundaries, and you have the makings of a most daunting challenge. Yet we can offer some general advice to those who will rise to the challenge.

To oversimplify a complex topic, there are two distinct types of organizational change strategies: *outside-in* and *inside-out*. Outside-in strategies are given this name because the impetus for change comes from outside the organization, with it often being superimposed by another organization or governing body. Inside-out strategies are those in which the organization decides on its own that it must change and sets about to craft a strategy that will yield the desired results.

An example of an outside-in legislative strategy would be the awarding of educational vouchers to all higher education students in a state. A voucher might cover the full cost of attending a public institution. Public policy might permit eligible students to spend their voucher at any institution within the state, public or private. Supporters of this strategy argue that this introduction of additional competitive forces into the student matriculation process would cause significant changes in enrollment patterns that, in turn, would result in needed institutional restructuring.

Although there will not be further consideration of such external or outside-in strategies in this chapter, all evidence indicates that such "levers for change" will look increasingly attractive to state legislatures, particularly if they perceive institutions as unresponsive to the "real" higher education needs of their state.

Here are eight steps that can be taken for those seeking a reinvented higher education institution (reprinted by permission of The Public Strategies Group, Inc.):

1. Decide on the mix of service orientation and compliance responsibility.
2. Define the primary customers and get in touch with them.
3. Develop specific institutional outcome measures.
4. Make controls an asset.
5. Align organizational decision making.
6. Build in trust and responsibility at every turn.
7. Budget strategically.
8. Separate providers from producers.

All of these are inside-out approaches to change, or steps that institutions can themselves take. These steps have been developed through the experience of the Public Strategies Group in working with higher education institutions as well as a number of other public-sector organizations. The steps do not preclude any of the new models for delivering advanced learning that are outlined above, nor do the steps presume any type of institution (say, a large university or a small liberal arts college). Similarly, these reinvention steps are value-neutral and would be equally as effective for a church-related, campus-based college or a campus-free, external-degree graduate institution.

As the first step down the path of reinvention, a college or university must decide on the mix of *compliance* responsibility and *service* orientation that underlies the institution's educational philosophy. Compliance organizations are established to bring people into conformance with a set of rules or regulations that exist to serve the greater societal good. The true customers of compliance organizations are other than those being directly served. Prisons, licensing agencies, and revenue departments are examples of pure compliance organizations. These organizations have a "coercive" purpose underlying what they do (Hasenfeld and English, 1983).

Service organizations exist to provide services directly to those with whom they interact. The parks department, the department of transportation, and the department of human services are examples of governmental service organizations. These organizational units have a "normative" purpose, as they strive to meet or exceed the expectations of those they directly serve.

Most people would agree that higher education is not exclusively a compliance organization. Its purposes are not to coerce students into learning a certain way, or even into learning a prescribed curriculum. However, there is also a strong belief among many people working in colleges and universities that their mission is much different than the traditional service institution in which the customer (that is, for the instructional mission, the student) knows best. Often this argument centers on a confusion of who really is the customer. Is it the student? The parents? Is it future employers? Or is it really the community? Hasenfeld and English (1983) posit that there is a third type of organization, a *utilitarian* organization that is characterized by a mix of compliance and service orientations. Probably this mix of compliance and service orientations embodies the philosophy of most American higher education institutions.

These distinctions are highlighted because individuals involved in institutional restructuring must recognize these competing outlooks, bring them to the fore, and get some agreement on the mix of compliance and service orientations that make up the institution's philosophy. Without this, there will be an inherent and sometimes unidentifiable tension underlying important discussions of institutional direction and restructuring alternatives. The first step down the path of reinvention is to gain an understanding of this fundamental question. From it flows the resolution of many subsequent strategic choices.

The second step toward reinvention is to get everyone in the institution to identify their primary customer group(s) and then require them to get in touch with the group(s). If people reject the word *customer* as an acceptable concept for higher education, so be it. Any word is acceptable as long as it embodies the meaning: those whom you exist to serve. Inherent in this discussion is the fundamental concept that the purpose of any organization lies outside the organization, not within it. This can be a difficult debate for higher education institutions that view themselves as existing in part to serve faculty.

With resolution of the customer question, the institution should do whatever it can to promote or even require direct interaction between those producing services (faculty) and those consuming the services (students, employers). However, this is a time to listen to those being served—not a time for describing programs, marketing, or fundraising.

One way to get in touch with those being served is to establish "quality improvement audit" teams for each program, comprising employers, program alumni, faculty from peer institutions, and current students. QIA teams are similar to the advisory committees that are common for vocational and professional programs. However, there are some extremely important differences. These groups are not advisory; their recommendations should influence decision making. Also, a QIA team should not be brought together to have faculty present a canned presentation describing the academic program. Instead, QIA teams are assembled to assess the quality of a program as they view it from their own perspective. This is done by integrating data on program outcomes with their own firsthand experiences to form judgments about program effectiveness and needed changes.

There are many other ways to stay in touch with those you serve, such as customer surveys, suggestion boxes, focus groups, etc. For example, each quarter the president of a small church-related college asks that one student from each course section come to a meeting that he convenes. The sole purpose of this meeting is to give feedback directly to the president on complaints or compliments the students wish to voice. Within twenty-four hours of this meeting, the president distributes a memo to the entire college community that summarizes the issues presented by the class representatives and indicates the action that will be taken in response to each concern or criticism. This is a powerful example of staying in touch with those you serve while simultaneously sending them a message that you value their opinions.

The third step toward reinvention is to develop specific institutional outcome measures. As Osborne and Gaebler have said, "What gets measured gets done" (1992, p. 146). This truism is reflected in the research success of American higher education. Experience in many different settings, including education and human services, has shown that development of sensible outcomes can focus the organization on a set of meaningful accomplishments.

Because organizations exist to serve others, not themselves, it is "others" who should be engaged in formulating the outcomes. Faculty and administration should play a role in these discussions, but it is those being served who should be the ultimate judges of our success.

With a robust set of measures agreed upon, these outcomes should be pushed down through the organization. Outcomes should be regularly and systematically assessed. They should be reported and discussed widely. As Osborne and Gaebler say, "If you don't measure results, you can't tell success from failure" (1992, p. 147). Massy (1989) supports this point of view in his work on faculty productivity when he urges us to design a set of faculty productivity measures and then get them out on the table for faculty to discuss, even if only in the privacy of the departmental meeting.

The fourth step toward reinvention uses these outcomes to make controls a real asset, not a set of bureaucratic shibboleths that infuriate people. A reinvented organization holds people accountable for things that matter, not measures of process that question their professionalism. For example, a higher education board focused on outcomes would not be concerned about faculty office hours, travel expenses, teaching loads, or even *cost* per student. It would be concerned about which program is producing the most learning for the dollars invested.

Boards, administrators, deans, and department chairs must learn to let go of the controls that do not impact the outcomes they seek. Instead, people in the operating units should decide which controls they need to place on themselves for inputs and means. Then hold people accountable for delivering on outcomes. An important step toward reinvention is to loosen up the "means of production" while holding on tightly to quality control.

The fifth step toward reinvention is to align information, accountability, and organizational decision making. Today in higher education there is often misalignment. Consider, for example, that it is the academic counselors who typically have the most information about students and their needs, and the placement officers who have the most information about the needs of employers. Yet it is the faculty who make the curriculum decisions, while the administration and trustees are held accountable for the quality of education received.

In this situation, information, decision making, and accountability are spread across three groups. Successful organizations are those that have aligned or brought together these three factors in a single role. To bring about this alignment, a reinvented college places decision authority with those most in touch with the customer, not someone far up the hierarchy or someone working in a different part of the organization.

A powerful if not somewhat heretical tool for bringing this system into alignment would be to give all the funds, now allocated to departments for instruction, to an "instructional purchasing agent." This person or group would have the sole responsibility for purchasing curriculum. Essential in this approach is to ensure that the performance of the purchasing agent is judged solely on its success at ensuring that students have the education available to them that best serves their long-term interests.

The dean of a college of technology within a public Midwestern university brought this approach to life by designating one of his associate deans as the representative of the students in curriculum determination. He followed this up with the powerful step of allocating all instructional funds to this associate dean and telling her that she was in charge of purchasing curriculum for students. Academic departments then had to come to this associate dean and "sell" their curriculum. The dean observed that it was one of the fastest, most effective curriculum change strategies that he had ever been party to.

This is a dramatic example of bringing the forces of information accountability and decision making into alignment. Alignment not only yields increased effectiveness but typically significant cost savings, too.

The sixth step along the path of reinvention is to incorporate trust and responsibility into all decisions and organizational practices. Bureaucratic controls that carry the implicit message "we don't trust you" work against the organizational change necessary to create a reinvented, postbureaucratic college or university. For example, faculty signatures required on course registrations send the implicit message that you, the student, cannot be trusted to manage your own education or evaluate your own level of preparation for a course. It is doubly insulting when such a requirement is put in place and then departmental secretaries literally rubber stamp these signatures for anyone who stops by the departmental office.

One of the most significant steps we can take to usher in an era of change is to demonstrate to the people making up the organization that we trust them. It sends a powerful message that empowers people to take control of their own destiny. Higher education has been particularly unwilling to trust young people who can otherwise vote, drive, and even die for their country.

The seventh reinvention step focuses on the ever-important allocation of resources. To take this step, institutions must budget strategically. This should include allocation strategies that reward program success and accomplishment. Budgets should be viewed as investments in producing value and purchasing outcomes, not as the funding of costs. For example, even if total resources are down, resulting budgeting decisions can be much different if the process is viewed as working through the investment trade-offs that yield different outcomes produced rather than a process of determining which positions are to be cut.

The eighth step down the path of reinvention is powerful and straightforward, yet it is often seen as the most radical and hence the most difficult even to consider. It calls for a clear, organizational separation between *provider* and *producer*. Providers are responsible for ensuring that a service (that is, education) is available and effectively delivered. Producers are those who actually develop and deliver the service.

In today's educational governance system, boards of regents or trustees are held responsible for *both* providing and producing. In trying to serve both, neither responsibility is served as well as it might be if the responsibilities were separated.

Provision and production have been effectively divided in other public sectors. For example, public utility commissions are empowered only to ensure the provision of utility service. Airport commissions are responsible for ensuring the provision of effective air service. Imagine if these two bodies were also responsible for *producing* the service. Can there be any doubt that the quality of air service would be different today if the airport commission were also concerned about keeping "its" flights fully ticketed and maintaining airplanes, not just running the airport and encouraging carriers to provide service in their regions? It is not accidental that the lights go on in both poor neighborhoods and wealthy neighborhoods. We can thank the separation of producer from provider in the form of a public utilities commission for this.

Yet in higher education, we have combined responsibility for provision and production in the same governing entities. We could appoint a provider board of trustees whose sole responsibility would be to ensure that students had high-quality education available to them. If this board also had the power of the purse, they could purchase educational services from the most effective producer. A second board, the producer board, would be responsible for governing the institution(s), the producers. This latter group would be responsible for ensuring that faculty get paid, buildings were clean, and curricula were developed. In this scenario institutions would have to prove themselves to the provider board before they received funding. This separation of powers is one of the most powerful reinvention tools.

In these eight steps are embodied the design principles of reinvention. They may not work for all institutions; however, experience has shown that they are powerful levers for change.

Implications for Institutional Research and Planning

The challenge for this section is to fast-forward well into the twenty-first century and examine the implications of such developments for institutional research and planning. Given the rapid pace of change and the fundamental restructuring of higher education that may occur, it is difficult to be precise in these predictions.

As you sit in the twenty-first century chair of an executive officer or higher education planner, you may find that your life has changed in five important ways. First, your perspective will have to be much broader. Today's presidents can focus a telephoto lens on a cluster of peer institutions and make useful comparisons. Tomorrow's leadership and planning will require a wide angle lens that takes in a much broader array of organizations. Competition for advanced learning will be originating from a variety of organizations, such as cable television networks, corporate universities that offer graduate degree programs, and even photocopying stores that offer computer training. Although today's colleges and universities are in the higher education business, presidents and boards will come to understand that they are really in the advanced learning business. As competition broadens, these leaders will ask their support staff for analysis that goes well beyond the traditional higher education sector.

Second, competition in the advanced learning market will intensify dramatically. Most likely this competition will come from the for-profit world, which is characterized by a faster pace and a primary concern with market share. These new competitors within the advanced learning market have the potential to dramatically change the pace of decision making within higher education. If this occurs, the life of administrators will be more fast-paced, demanding, and hectic than ever.

Third, as the focus continues to shift toward the needs of those being served and away from the needs of those producing the education, planning will need to provide the analysis to facilitate that shift. Emphasis on the needs of students and employers will continue to grow. The effective advanced learning institution of the twenty-first century will understand its clientele far better than today. Many private higher education institutions have already made this shift in their admissions processes. Yet few institutions are examining their outcomes and those they serve in the detail that will be necessary to thrive throughout the twenty-first century.

Fourth, there will be increased calls for accountability and performance funding. Parents and students will be more demanding consumers as they compare a much wider variety of advanced learning options. Employers will be looking for demonstrable skills and measurable knowledge, not credentials.

Funders will want to know about the return on their investment. Tennessee has had sixteen years of experience with holding back a small portion of funds (in 1995 it was up to 5.45 percent) to reward higher education for performance that the legislature is seeking. Minnesota has a simple allocation scheme in place that awards $1 million to each system every time it meets one of five targets the legislature sees as desirable (for example, an increase in distance learning or an increase in the proportion of matriculants in the top 10 percent of their high school class). Ohio is developing a performance-based budgeting system, and Texas has had vigorous discussions about moving in this direction. Even though to date legislatures have lacked the political will to take dramatic steps in this direction, the forces coming together portend a significant move in this direction in the years ahead.

Any crystal ball for higher education is cloudy at best. Nevertheless, the twenty-first century has the potential to be a most exhilarating, challenging time for traditional higher education. The effective institution will ride these "sea changes" to their advantage and be willing to compete directly with the many new advanced learning organizations that are entering today's higher education market.

Further Reading

Readers interested in the general principles that guided the development of this chapter should consult Barzelay and Armajani (1992) and Osborne and Gaebler (1992). Those interested in a more detailed treatment of how these principles apply directly to redesigning a public higher education system should see Armajani, Heydinger, and Hutchinson (1994), or a parallel yet provocative redesign of higher education in Norris and Dolence (1995). Heydinger and Wallace (1995) offer a brief summary of student-oriented designs of advanced learning options.

For readers interested in expanding their knowledge about the rapidly changing context for learning, see Davis and Botkin (1994). On a strategic assessment of the challenges facing traditional higher education, see Massy (1989), "To Dance with Change" (1994), from the PEW Roundtable (published in the newsletter *Pol-*

icy Perspectives, Institute for Higher Education, 4200 Pine St., Philadelphia), and Heydinger and Simsek (1992).

Speculation on the impact that communications and computing technologies will have on learning is provided by Dyson (1995), Gilder (1995), Negroponte (1995), Perelman (1992), and Tofler (1994). For those wishing to stay abreast of emerging trends, *On the Horizon,* "the Environmental Scanning Publication for Educational Leaders" (Jossey-Bass, San Francisco), is a semimonthly publication offering its readers a regular digest of thought-provoking developments relating to education.

References

Armajani, B., Heydinger, R. B., and Hutchinson, P. *A Model for the Reinvented Higher Education System.* Monograph. State Policy and College Learning (SPCL) series. Denver: State Higher Education Executive Officers, 1994.

Barzelay, M., and Armajani, B. *Breaking Through Bureaucracy.* Berkeley: University of California Press, 1992.

Clark, B. R. "Conclusions." In B. R. Clark (ed.), *Perspectives on Higher Education.* Berkeley: University of California Press, 1984.

Davis, S., and Botkin, J. *The Monster Under the Bed.* New York: Simon & Schuster, 1994.

Dyson, E. "Intellectual Value." *Wired,* 1995, *3*(7), 136–184.

Gilder, G. "Focal Point on Convergence." *Educom Review,* Mar./Apr. 1995, pp. 20–23.

Guri-Rozenblit, S. "Differentiating Between Distance/Open Education Systems: Parameters for Comparison." *International Review of Education,* 1993, *39*(4), 287–306.

Hasenfeld, D., and English, J. *Human Service Organizations.* New York: Prentice-Hall, 1983.

Hawken, P., Ogilvy, J., and Schwartz, P. *Seven Tomorrows.* New York: Bantam, 1982.

Heydinger, R. B., and Wallace, J. "Students Create the College of the Future." *Wingspread Journal,* 1995, *17*(2), 13–15.

Heydinger, R., and Simsek, H. "An Agenda for Reshaping Faculty Productivity." Monograph. State Policy and College Learning (SPCL) series. Denver: State Higher Education Executive Officers, 1992.

Massy, W. F. "A Strategy for Productivity Improvement in College and University Departments." Paper presented at the Forum for Postsecondary Governance, Santa Fe, New Mexico, 1989.

Negroponte, N. *Being Digital.* New York: Knopf, 1995.

Norris, D. M., and Dolence, M. G. *Transforming Higher Education: A Vision of Learning in the Twenty-First Century.* Monograph. Ann Arbor: Society for College and University Planning, 1995.

Osborne, D., and Gaebler, T. *Reinventing Government.* Reading, Mass.: Addison-Wesley, 1992.

Perelman, L. *School's Out.* New York: Morrow, 1992.

Pruitt, G., president of Thomas Edison State University in Trenton, New Jersey. Comments made in a presentation to the Salzburg Seminar, April 4, 1995.

"To Dance with Change." *Policy Perspectives,* Apr. 1994, 5(3), entire issue.

Tofler, A., and Tofler, H. *Creating a New Civilization.* Atlanta: Turner, 1994.

PART TWO

REDIRECTING INSTITUTIONS THROUGH CONTEXTUAL PLANNING

The planning function and its varied processes, approaches, and techniques in higher and postsecondary institutions have been developed primarily over the past four decades. They largely reflect the changing demands on and challenges faced by the institutions themselves. Indeed, the emergence of the planning function is one of the significant organizational changes that have occurred as institutions of higher education have developed their own adaptive capacity to respond to an increasingly complex and changing environment.

Notions of long-range and strategic planning are now well-understood institutional planning strategies and approaches. They were, and continue to be, important ways in which institutions seek to compete in a system or industry of postsecondary institutions. Yet as we face the prospect of a redefinition of our industry to a postsecondary knowledge network or environment and the critical challenges reshaping both our industry and our institutions, new approaches to planning are emerging. Faced with the potential need to plan for redefining our industry and redirecting our institutional mission and our external network of relationships, it is also important to understand how we might reorganize and renew our institutional capacity—our structures, processes, and culture for supporting such redefinition and redirection.

The chapters in Part Two discuss the changes in our approach to planning and its relationship to the ongoing processes of institutional leadership and management with which a dynamic, change-oriented planning function interacts. The chapters address three common questions: (1) what is the latest perspective on the nature of planning and its relationship to our institutions' leadership, governance, and the management processes being addressed? (2) how can planning be used in redirecting our internal institutional structures, processes, and culture? and (3) what new approaches or developments are emerging that might be useful in future planning efforts?

Chapters Seven through Thirteen focus on the nature of planning and some of its central elements. Chapter Seven examines the emergence of a new conceptual approach to planning, contextual planning; the chapter contrasts it with long-range and strategic planning and identifies the elements of a contextual planning process. Chapter Eight reviews what we have learned about strategic planning and how to use it more successfully. Chapter Nine discusses a critical issue in both strategic and contextual planning: the nature of institutional vision and mission and how it can be used to focus institutional coherence when there are increasingly fragmenting forces working upon our institutions. Chapter Ten analyzes the changing perspectives on leadership that are essential to support planning. Chapter Eleven focuses on developments in how we think about the future and environmental forces, and about how we develop scenarios essential for creating new institutional vision and mission. Chapter Twelve identifies the critical problem of linking people to planning, the process of understanding and changing institutional culture as one plans for significant institutional changes. Chapter Thirteen addresses a practical organizational dilemma: how to organize an institution's planning function.

CHAPTER SEVEN

USING CONTEXTUAL PLANNING TO TRANSFORM INSTITUTIONS

Marvin W. Peterson

This chapter examines contextual planning, a new strategy for or approach to planning that may be more appropriate for a turbulent environment in which the character of the postsecondary system or industry is also in a state of flux. Chapter One discussed such an environment, in which the emergence of a postsecondary knowledge industry suggests the need to consider broad planning questions dealing with redefining that industry and the institution's role in it, redirecting institutional mission and external relationships, redesigning or reorganizing institutional structures and processes, and reforming or recreating a new academic culture.

Planning in an environment that addresses these questions needs to be *proactive,* attempting to shape as well as to understand the newly emerging postsecondary knowledge industry. Planning needs to have the potential to *transform* the institution in extensive and significant ways. Planning, therefore, needs to anticipate *macro change* approaches that are multilevel and designed to alter external relationships, change internal structures, and incorporate concern for reshaping individual roles and the institution's culture. Such a strategy, designed to guide our institutions into the twenty-first century, needs to be a *comprehensive* one, requiring *leadership* that is multidimensional, willing to take risks, and able to provide a consistent and committed effort.

Contextual planning is not seen as unrelated to or inconsistent with effective long-range or strategic planning approaches. Rather, it is seen as an extension of our understanding of planning necessitated by and related to the changing nature of our institutional environment and our system or industry. In presenting a contextual approach, this chapter first addresses the evolutionary nature of planning to suggest the relationship of long-range, strategic, and conceptual planning. These three approaches are then contrasted to clarify the nature of contextual planning and its relationship to the other two. A process view, identifying the elements of contextual planning, further provides insight into its nature and applicability. A brief case study shows how the approach is useful in understanding one institution's efforts to redirect its mission for the twenty-first century. Finally, a set of conditions for implementing contextual planning is discussed.

The Historical Evolution of Planning Approaches: A Contingency Model

As noted in Chapter One, planning for and by postsecondary institutions is largely a post-1950 phenomenon. As with many management functions in colleges and universities, the development of both the content focus of planning and approaches to planning have been sporadic, uneven, and highly varied. Regarding content, campus and facilities planning emerged earliest as a formal activity on many campuses in the 1950s, when enrollment demand exploded and the need for new and expanded campuses was pressing. Financial and resource planning became a visible concern in the late 1960s and early 1970s, when enrollment demand leveled and economic factors required a realistic assessment of the future. In the mid-1970s and early 1980s the emphasis shifted to enrollment forecasting and academic program planning, as both enrollment demand and financial resources remained constrained and institutional competition for scarce resources increased. Comprehensive or integrated planning, like academic planning, was occasionally implemented from the mid-1970s on, when continuing constraints required broader institutional attempts to become more efficient and effective. One analysis, using a contingency model, has suggested that these fragmented and varied patterns in the development of planning have largely been responses to the changing management pressures on institutions induced by changing environmental conditions (Peterson, 1986).

A similar contingency view of approaches to planning—the notion that the content and nature of planning are dependent on or responses to changes in the environment—provides a useful model for understanding the more general development of long-range, strategic, and contextual planning approaches. A brief history of the changing, post-World War II external conditions for higher and postsecondary education provides some perspective on their institutional impact on the evolution of organizational models, notions of institutional performance, and approaches to planning that have emerged. Of particular note is how the approach to planning reflects the changing character of the resource environment (availability of finances, demand for services, and degree of public support) and the changing definition of the higher or postsecondary industry, which reflects the primary focus of an institution's competitive milieu. Table 7.1 portrays a model suggesting how these approaches to planning are related to the condition of the institution's resource environment and its industry perspective.

1950–1975: Plans, Forecasting, and Long-Range Planning

Following World War II and extending through the 1960s, U.S. higher education experienced an unprecedented period of growth and expansion marked by strong government financial support, expanding enrollment demands, and very positive public support. Institutions defined other traditional higher educational institutions as their industry (see Chapter One). Competition for expanding student enrollments and financial resources was limited and usually focused within one's own institutional-type sector. During this period, the pressure on institutional management was to provide a sense of direction for their growing institution and to account for the expanding human, financial, and physical resources they were absorbing in order to maintain public support. Two internally oriented models of organization emerged in the literature; they emphasized the purposive nature of the institutions and helped us understand and manage these growing institutions. The first, the formal rational or bureaucratic organization (Stroup, 1966), focused on building rational structures to administer and develop mechanisms to account for growing resource flows and needs. The second, the collegial model, was also stressed; it reflected our notions of colleges and universities as self-contained communities of learners (Goodman, 1964), professionals (Clark, 1963), or constituents with a common community of interests (Millett, 1962). The focus of performance during this era was primarily on resources: the quantitative characteristics of students, faculty, programs, and facilities needed to justify financial resources. Planning emphasized developing formal institutional or campus master plans to justify resources and guide development; it began to rely on self-studies to document strengths and weaknesses for accreditation and to guide further development.

In the late 1960s, disruptions reflected student dissatisfaction with increasingly large, impersonal, professionalized, and formally structured institutions; the U.S. role in the Vietnam War; and the civil rights movement. In order to continue favorable environmental support, the pressure on institutional management was to maintain control on campus and to ensure greater access for minority students.

TABLE 7.1. A CONTINGENCY MODEL: ENVIRONMENTAL CONDITION, COMPETITIVE PERSPECTIVE, AND PLANNING APPROACH.

Condition of Environment	*Primary Competitive or Collaborative Perspective*		
Resource Availability, Enrollment Demand, Public Support	**Higher Education Industry**	**Postsecondary Education Industry**	**Postsecondary Knowledge Industry**
1950–1975: munificent, growing, supportive	Plans, forecasting, and long-range planning		
1975–1995: constrained, changing, neutral		Strategic planning	
1995 and beyond: limited, reordering, critical			Contextual planning

Colleges and universities began to be viewed both as open systems (Katz and Kahn, 1978) and as political organizations (Baldridge, 1971) made up of competing constituencies. In part to reassure public support and to strengthen higher education's image, an emphasis on performance that was based on peer judgment of reputational quality of graduate and professional education emerged in the form of American Council on Education (ACE)-sponsored studies (Cartter, 1966; Roose and Anderson, 1970). Planning became short-term and responsive. Contingency planning designed to deal with the underlying sources of discontent was common.

By the early 1970s, an economic recession and the end of the postwar baby boom demand forced an assessment of that reality on many campuses. Meanwhile state, federal, and other external agencies were demanding greater institutional accountability and becoming more sophisticated in collecting and analyzing data and asking tough management questions. Concurrently, the 1972 Higher Education Amendments shifted federal student aid distribution from institutions directly to the student. These changes focused institutional management on improving internal efficiency, seeking new student markets, and taking planning more seriously.

New organizational thinking emphasized comprehensive, information-based managerial models to inform decisions (Lawrence and Service, 1977) or else market-oriented models designed to identify and attract new students. Performance concerns began to shift to an emphasis on results—but primarily quantitative measures of productivity (outputs) or efficiency (indices of cost per unit, workload, etc). Planning now emphasized forecasting and the development of a long-range, continuous planning process in which assumptions, projections, and plans were constantly revised; planning began to emerge as a formal administrative position or task force on many campuses.

1975–1990: Strategic Planning

In the late 1970s and throughout the 1980s, continued economic constraints; new alternative demands for public funds; real decline in the number of traditional college-age students; and forecasts of significant changes in the economic, ethnic, and educational background of future college-age students painted a new picture of the industry and environment. Resources and enrollments would be a constraint on growth, demand was changing, and the public was clearly not as supportive. Following the 1972 Higher Education Amendments, proprietary institutions began competing with more traditional higher education institutions for students and funds in a new postsecondary industry. The management press was both to reduce, reallocate, and retrench (Mortimer and Tierney, 1979) and to become more effective. New organizational models stressed flexible, decentralized, organized anarchies (Cohen and March, 1974) or matrix models (Alpert, 1986). Colleges and universities were viewed not just as responsive institutions but as strategic organizations that could revise their priorities, change clientele and program mixes, and seek a strategic market niche within the postsecondary education industry. Performance based on results such as effectiveness or goal achievement began to be examined. By the late 1980s, criticism of both K–12 education (National Commission on Excellence in Education, 1983) and higher education (Study Group on the Condition of Excellence in American Higher Education, 1984) led some academic leaders and many public policy officials to ask for performance results reflecting student learning outcomes and to encourage the use of student and academic assessment. Strategic planning eclipsed long-range planning and became the primary focus of the 1980s (Keller, 1983).

As we entered the 1990s, two things were clear. First, our organizational and governance models, our performance criteria, and our approaches to planning are heavily influenced by external challenges. Second, the new models, criteria, and approaches do not supersede the earlier ones. Rather, they become part of a more complex picture of how we understand the organizational patterns and the governance, performance, and planning patterns in our institutions.

The 1990s and Beyond: Contextual Planning

In looking to the coming century and millennium, Chapter One portrays both our environment and our industry quite differently from those of previous decades. Changing societal conditions (new patterns of diversity, the telematics revolution, quality as learning and improvement, contribution to economic productivity, new postsecondary relearning markets, and globalization) all are seen to have extensive implications for both our postsecondary industry and our institutional environments. A postsecondary knowledge network or industry that includes many new types of organizations, focuses on the use of knowledge for learning, offers a potentially far more flexible technology for learning, and redefines our traditional working relationships from service provider to collaborator or competitor with these new types of organizations is likely to be highly competitive. The resource environment for traditional postsecondary institutions suggests that (1) financial resources will be increasingly limited as government's capacity to support—and student and parental ability to pay—continues to decline, (2) the demand for postsecondary learning services is being seriously reordered by new clientele, (3) new modes of delivery are emerging, and (4) the public perception of postsecondary education is becoming increasingly critical.

Reflecting these contextual changes in the industry and environment, new organizational models not surprisingly are already emerging. Notions of colleges and universities as conglomerate (Clark, 1995) and network (Dill and Sporn, 1995) organizations suggest institutions that are more complex combinations of units and embedded in new webs of interorganizational relationships. The notion of organizations as cultural entities (while not new) is also growing in popularity as the need to change traditional academic settings and the nature of academic work are being discussed. The challenges also suggest new performance criteria for our institutions: how they will redesign their external relationships, redefine their missions, deal with internal reorganization, and recreate or renew their institutional culture.

Amid efforts to deal with this more complex and competitive postsecondary knowledge industry and its highly turbulent environment, a new mode of planning has emerged: contextual planning. This approach is broader and more flexible than strategic planning and may be more useful in the face of a changing industry and turbulent resource environment. It is more holistic than strategic planning and deals with redesigning the *context*, both in the external environment and within the organization.

Contingency Revisited

This discussion has suggested that the approaches to planning are contingent on and reflect the changing complexity and competitiveness of the industry and the increasing turbulence in our institutional environment (Table 7.1). Clearly, the three approaches described in the next section are not mutually exclusive and do not replace one another. Indeed, forecasting and long-range planning processes are and will continue to be useful in a clearly defined sector of higher or post-secondary institutions with limited competition and in more favorable resource environments. Strategic planning, it is suggested, is appropriate for a clearly understood but more competitive postsecondary sector in which resources are more constrained but somewhat predictable. More importantly, the three approaches to planning may reinforce one another; forecasting and long-range planning can inform strategic planning, which in turn informs contextual planning. Or vice versa: contextual planning may lead to identifying parts of the institution whose subenvironments are more stable and offer the institution strategic advantage. We now turn to a discussion of the three approaches and an elaboration of contextual planning.

Three Planning Approaches: Elaborating Contextual Planning

Contextual planning may best be understood by contrasting it with long-range and strategic planning. Each planning approach is discussed here through definition and the primary planning question it addresses. The three are contrasted in terms of their *external and internal perspectives* (Tables 7.2 and 7.3). The external perspective examines dimensions related to their primary environmental assumption, the principal organization-environment dynamics, the institution's external strategy, and the nature of the planning process. The internal perspective examines dimensions related to the internal organizational planning focus, the assumed primary motivation mechanism emphasized, and assumptions about how to control member behavior.

Long-Range Planning

Long-range planning focuses on forecasting future resource flows and environmental trends or conditions, establishing institutional plans for that new reality, devising ways to get there and continually reassessing them (Kirschling and Huckfeldt, 1980; Wing, 1980). Long-range planning asks "What can we achieve in this

TABLE 7.2. EXTERNAL PERSPECTIVES OF THREE PLANNING APPROACHES.

Planning Approach	Environmental Assumption	Organization-Environment Dynamic	Institutional Strategy	Planning Process
Long-range planning; "responsive"	Predictable sectors and resource flows	Responsive, rational	Limited competition, adjust plans to reality	Assumptions, forecasts, and plans
Strategic planning; "adaptive"	Conflicting sectors and resource flows	Adaptive, judgmental	Postsecondary education competition, comparative advantage, "fit" or "niche"	Institutional mission, image, and resource strategies
Contextual planning; "proactive"	Complex but malleable	Proactive, intuitive	Cross-industry cooperation, coalition, or competition	Redefine institutional role, mission, and external relationships

environment?" and "How can we get there?" It is planning that is *responsive* to a predictably changing environment.

Long-range planning assumes the external environment controls what it is possible for the institution to achieve; that enrollment demands and resource flows are somewhat stable or changing in a manner that can be reasonably predicted; that there is limited competition from other institutions; and that institutional mission is largely defined in order that plans can be adjusted to external realities. Institutional planning relies on a rational or quasi-rational process to predict trends, develop plans, and devise a strategy for moving the institution ahead. Forecasts, environmental assumptions, and plans are the major focus.

Internally, long-range planning tends to view the institution as a formal organization. Attention is focused largely on clarifying institutional purpose, goals, policies, and procedures; on designing institutional process and programs to achieve them; and on allocating resources and monitoring performance according to them. Planning, even if participatory in style, is primarily designed to direct and control institutional behavior; it is focused on preaudits assessing the need for resources; and it assumes member behavior is constrained and can be directed to support the planned purposes.

TABLE 7.3. INTERNAL PERSPECTIVES OF
THREE PLANNING APPROACHES.

Planning Approach	Organizational Planning Focus	Motivation Mechanism	Mode of Control	Member Behavior
Long-Range planning	Purpose/policies, goals/objectives (formal organization)	Direction and control	Inputs, preaudit	Constrained behavior
Strategic planning	Program and resource allocation strategies (resources)	Guidance, review, and improvement	Outcomes assessment, postaudit	Flexible behavior
Contextual planning	Direction, values, process, and meaning (organizational culture)	Themes and visions	Sense of direction, involvement, and ownership	Empowered behavior

Strategic Planning

Strategic planning may use forecasting, but it relies more on "assessing the current and future environmental opportunities and threats, by examining the changing character of the environment and the patterns of competition within the industry, and on assessing the strengths and weaknesses of the institution in order to identify its comparative advantage, a strategic niche and appropriate strategies for competition effectively" (Peterson, 1980). Its focus is on asking "How can we modify the institution to be a more effective competitor within our environment and our industry?" It is *adaptive* planning in a clearly defined but competitive industry (Keller, 1983; Peterson, 1980; Mintzberg, 1994; Baldridge and Okimi, 1982; Schmidtlein and Milton, 1990).

While the assumption is that most of the environment is beyond the institution's capacity to control (or that some important elements of the environment are not predictable or may be in conflict), strategic planning does present both possible opportunities as well as threats; it suggests that adapting the institution's mission, purpose, and functions to the environment is desirable. It focuses on competing in a less predictable and more complex environment by understanding needs and demands, how other institutions are meeting or failing to meet them, and the strengths and weaknesses of your own institution in that competitive environment.

The intent of planning is to identify your institution's comparative advantage and the market niche it will attempt to fill. Developing an adaptive strategy places greater reliance on judgment about the appropriate strategy than does long-range planning. Planning focuses on modifying the institution's mission and purposes, developing a favorable "image," and designing a strategy to attract resources that ensures the institution can effectively compete in its market niche.

Internally, strategic planning acknowledges formal structure but tends to focus on the organization as a more loosely coupled pattern of structures, programs, and resources. Emphasis is placed on designing a strategy for allocating programs and resources in order to maintain the institution's comparative and competitive advantage. Implementation involves establishing goals to guide behavior and designing review processes to ensure goal achievement. Control shifts to a greater focus on results: assessments of outcomes, goal achievement, and other forms of postaudit review. Flexible member or unit behavior consistent with the strategy is encouraged so as to help the institution adapt to changing environmental and competitive forces.

Contextual Planning

Contextual planning is not a new concept to higher education (Cope, 1985; Chaffee, 1985). It may incorporate elements of long-range and strategic planning, but it is different in one basic way. It does not assume that environments are uncontrollable, that industries are permanent, or that institutions cannot change their basic mission, structure, and patterns of interorganizational relationship. Contextual planning is concerned with examining the changing nature of the institution's industry, identifying feasible new institutional roles and external relationships, and then attempting to shape both environmental conditions and institutional arrangements to become an effective competitor in a new industry. Contextual planning is a process that focuses on creating or shaping external contexts most favorable to our institution's mission, and on designing internal institutional contexts that allow members to contribute to the new institutional roles. It asks about the changing nature of our industry and how can we shape it, as well as our institution, to ensure viability. Contextual planning is *proactive*, seeking to both shape the industry and reshape the institution.

Contextual planning, then, begins with the assumption that the environment and the industry may be changing but they can be influenced. Relationships among existing industries beyond higher and postsecondary education are seen as interactive, complex, and changing—perhaps in unpredictable ways, but malleably. In order to compete in such an environment, contextual planning must be proactive. Contextual planning examines the nature of an industry and the forces that shape it in order to understand how the industry is being redefined and what new cross-industry organizational patterns or relationships are emerging. Consideration of new patterns of competition, coalition, or cooperation are a key part of the external strategy. Such planning involves intuitive choices as well as rational decisions or strategic judgments. The potential of contextual planning is not only in redefining an institution's industry and its own role in the industry but also in redesigning its mission and relationship to other organizations (including those in previously unrelated industries).

Internally, contextual planning may require redesigning or reorganizing an institution's primary academic functions, processes, and structures to meet a changed institutional role or mission. Since many faculty and staff chose to work in higher education because they value their work and what the institution stands for, contextual planning needs to focus on the academic and administrative culture of the institution and processes for changing that culture as well. Implementing an understanding of the redefined institutional external relationships, role and mission, and structural changes relies on providing visions and themes of what the institution will be like—what it will stand for and what it will mean to its members—to motivate them. Member control involves reforming behavior and values. It may rely on conveying the sense of direction of new institutional initiatives or a sense of urgency or importance, on using incentives or providing resources that members can use, and on creating opportunities for being involved and having a sense of ownership. Short of catastrophic changes such as threats to the institution's existence, value changes usually occur when members are empowered: fully involved in critical choices, provided incentives to participate, and assisted in learning to make the needed changes.

Thus contextual planning is an approach that does not fully replace long-range or strategic planning. But it is more holistic. It forces institutions to take a broader view of a postsecondary knowledge or learning industry and of an external environment for higher education that may include organizations from other previously unrelated industries. It seeks to examine how the larger environment and industry is changing and can be reshaped or influenced by the institution. It considers new role-and-mission options and new types of interinstitutional linkages. Then it tries to redesign or reorganize internal structures and processes appropriately and to establish or recreate an institutional culture that motivates and supports its members in responding to this new direction.

A Process View of Contextual Planning

Contextual planning is thus an approach to planning designed to respond to situations in which the nature of one's industry is in flux, significant questions about the role and mission of an institution may be raised, and extensive transformation in the institution is required. Figure 7.1 presents a framework for understanding contextual planning and seven process elements that seem to be reflected in this planning approach.

Contextual planning begins with an assessment of the changing conditions or challenges in the external environment, the changing nature of the postsecondary knowledge network or industry, and an assessment of the institution itself. In Chapter One, seven major challenges to the postsecondary industry and to our institutions are suggested. The changing nature of the postsecondary knowledge industry or network is also explored, as are the internal and external impacts on an institution. Nine characteristics of the emerging postsecondary knowledge industry are identified. The discussion in that chapter poses four critical planning issues for institutions that choose to adopt a contextual planning approach:

Redefinition: what is the nature of an emerging postsecondary knowledge industry, and what is our institution's role in it?

Redirection: how should our institution's mission change to reflect these new realities, and what external relationships with other organizations should we develop?

Redesign: how should we redesign or reorganize our academic functions, processes, or structures?

Renewal: How do we renew or recreate our academic workplace and institutional culture to accommodate these changes? Our preparation of future faculty?

Clearly, addressing these questions raises the potential of institutional transformation: significant changes in how institutions define the industry in which they compete, new or modified notions of institutional role and mission, potential competitive or collaborative relationships with new types of organizations, substantial redesign or revision of academic and administrative structures, functions and processes, and modifications of institutional culture. These are at least potential outcomes for a contextual planning process.

While contextual planning is only an emerging approach, the experience of several institutions that have attempted to plan for a changing industry suggests at least seven elements in the planning process to guide contextual planning.

Insight

In an industry in flux, it is critical to develop understanding, an informed insight into the dynamics of a shift from an industry of postsecondary institutions to a

FIGURE 7.1. FRAMEWORK FOR CONTEXTUAL PLANNING.

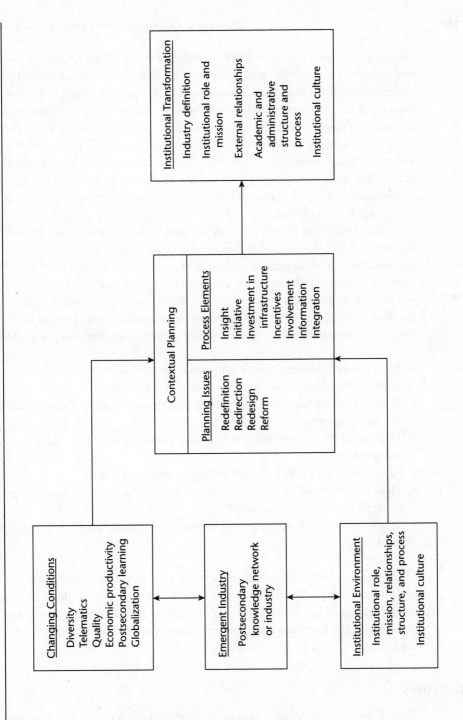

postsecondary knowledge industry. Unlike strategic planning, which seeks to find a strategic niche in an existing industry, the focus in contextual planning is on understanding the dynamics of a moving target: a rapidly changing industry whose form is still being shaped. Planners and executive officers need to become students of their own postsecondary industry as well as of related industries. In a sense, the focus shifts to trying to understand the changing nature of a vast network of information and knowledge, of postsecondary learners, and of the organizational players in this rapidly changing area within which formal postsecondary teaching and learning occur. The attempt is to gain a perspective on where the emerging knowledge industry is heading.

While traditional planning techniques such as forecasting, trend analysis, and scenario building may be useful, they need to be focused on the intersections of the postsecondary information, computing, telecommunications, and training and development industries. In doing so, it is useful to examine not only the challenges to our current postsecondary system or industry (diversity, telematics, quality, economic productivity, postsecondary relearning, and globalization) but also how those become forces reshaping the postsecondary industry identified in Chapter One:

- Who are the changing or emerging *consumers* (clientele) for postsecondary education? What are their learning needs and preferences?
- Who are our *suppliers* (sources of funds and employers of graduates), and how are they changing?
- Who are the *new competitors* entering our postsecondary educational service marketplace?
- Are *substitute services* increasingly available, and from where?
- How are *innovations* in the development and transmission of knowledge and learning changing our industry?
- Where and how is our *pattern* of *competition* changing, for both students and graduates?

If we focus both on the challenges to our existing postsecondary industry and on the emerging postsecondary knowledge industry, new and informed insights should emerge. They form the basis for defining this emerging industry and for determining the role the institution might take in attempting to shape the emerging industry or reshape the institution.

Initiatives

Beyond insight into the emerging postsecondary knowledge network or industry and the role an institution might play, it is important for the institution to examine its own strengths and weaknesses and to establish one or more initiatives. An *initiative* is a broad thrust or sense of direction that the institution intends to take that reflects its new role and may suggest a new mission or reinforce a current one. In a rapidly changing or emerging industry, it is important to identify such an initiative to prevent being left behind. Initiatives may be a "marketing niche," as in strategic planning, but usually they focus on a broader direction: confirming a new role or mission for the institution such as serving a very different clientele, developing a new capacity, preparing for a new set of competitive conditions, etc. It implies potentially substantial institutional change but lacks highly defined objectives or specific program and resource strategies. These may emerge later, designed to establish direction but not constrain efforts or activities directed to fulfilling the initiative.

Such an initiative serves in part as a "vision," a sense of direction for the institution and its constituents. In that sense, it is both a symbolic attempt to establish a cultural meaning and direction for the institution and a signal that efforts supporting the initiative will be encouraged and supported. As with all institutional planning, attempts to stimulate broad understanding of the insights about the changing industry and to gain support for the initiative are important practical planning concerns needing to be considered. However, the key element is that the initiative be perceived as viable and that a significant opportunity for members to participate in achieving it be available.

Investment in Infrastructure

One of the key differences between strategic planning and contextual planning is how programs are identified and resources are channeled to support planning efforts. Strategic planning usually relies on defining clear priorities, identifying specific programs, and developing supportive resource strategies to compete in a strategic niche. Contextual planning, however, assumes that in an industry in flux, many programmatic efforts are desirable. Some will be modifications of existing programs, but others will be new experimental or risk-taking ventures. It also assumes that in a postsecondary institution with a well-educated professional faculty and staff there will be numerous ideas of what works best in support of a given initiative—and that those will often be different in differing parts of the institution.

Under these assumptions, a critical feature of contextual planning is to invest resources in building an infrastructure that will serve and support groups in their development of ideas, efforts, and programs consistent with an initiative. These investments can include changes in academic or administrative structures or processes to support such initiatives or to remove barriers, development of new facilities, purchase of new equipment, addition of new technological capacity, development of new external ties and relationships, initiation of changes in hiring and staffing support, and so on.

The intent is to make critical, visible investments that support movement in the direction of the initiative. It is an investment in that it is some form of comprehensive, relatively long-term support, but it is also a symbol of institutional commitment. Making such investments requires prudent resource management to redeploy resources, or creative fundraising.

Incentives

Academic professionals are often far more likely to respond to incentives than to planned priorities and predefined programs. A key element in contextual planning is to provide incentives for various units and faculty and staff to engage in program development or redesign and in changes of their personal roles or behavior to support an initiative. Incentives for involvement can be targeted for institutionwide, unit, or individual support. They may be in the form of financial support, released time from other duties, or other forms of special developmental assistance.

Incentive can come in the often overlooked form of special recognition or rewards for outstanding proposals or successful efforts. Recognizing efforts in promotion reviews is another visible way to remove barriers and garner support. The key is to provide both substantive incentives and professional or psychological rewards. Increasing participation is the key to increasing the diversity of ideas, ensuring the success of the initiative, and gaining long-term support for it.

Involvement

While investing in appropriate infrastructure and providing incentives and rewards stimulates good ideas and potential participants in supporting an initiative, there is the danger that the initiative becomes the province of a few. In most instances contextual planning involves initiatives directed at the whole institution or large segments of it. To ensure a rich array of ideas and broad participation, it is important that the opportunities for involvement be widely available (Dill and Helm, 1988; Lawler, 1992). Investments should provide resources that are readily available, and incentives should be ample to support several worthwhile efforts. Similarly barriers to involvement, such as workload, institutional policies and procedures, or other things that restrict involvement, may need to be addressed.

Equally important is that those who wish to be involved—whether supported directly or on a voluntary basis—need to have the opportunity for improvement.

This involves recognition for trying something new, special training where necessary, and an opportunity to learn new skills and ways of doing things.

Information

An initiative even with wide-scale involvement can suffer if internal and external constituents lack information about or awareness of an initiative. Institutional support for major initiatives should include widely disseminated information about the reasons for and nature of the initiative, its significant investments and what they make available to faculty and staff, and the incentives for and patterns of involvement. Public recognition of success stories, new approaches, and new efforts is often gratifying to those involved.

While internal reports, newsletters, seminars, and other modes of institutional dissemination are useful in informing participants and other institutional members, external efforts should not be overlooked. Quite often, initiatives that reflect a new institutional role, mission, or mode of doing business are not readily perceived externally. Enhancing the institution's new initiative may involve changing its "image," which suggests emphasizing external coverage of the initiative via newspaper, TV, reports in professional journals, etc., as well.

Integration

A successful initiative will spawn many new ideas and efforts, a number of innovative projects, and some high-risk ventures. The intent is to better position the institution as the emergent or changing industry takes shape. Unlike strategic planning, there is less initial focus on clear program definition, tightly controlled resource guidelines, and intensive evaluation and review. Contextual planning, however, is not intended to support unending proliferation and fragmentation. Periodically, the array of activities supporting an initiative needs to be assessed. Successful efforts need to be reinforced. Similar ones may be merged to provide better focus. Some may be promising but need redirection or support. Others must be closed or folded back into ongoing activities.

The key is that contextual planning, which is designed to create new initiatives in an uncertain and rapidly changing environment, places a greater emphasis on stimulating movement than on carefully directing planning; the latter is only possible in a well-understood industry and environment. However, once the initiative is well under way, it has to be assessed and focused. The new structures, programs, and activities need to be integrated into the organization and managed as part of its ongoing efforts.

Once the initiative is successful, the institution will have substantially redirected key elements of its role and mission and established new external relationships; different internal patterns of structure and process will be emerging, and a new culture or change in academic workplace values will be in place to support this effort. At that time, as the shape of the industry and the pattern of competition becomes more settled, the new initiatives will at least partially transform the institution and its programs will become subject to a more strategic mode of planning. As the initiatives are evaluated and mature, they will need to be merged into the institutional pattern for managing its ongoing operations.

A Case Study: Technological Innovation

There are numerous examples of contextual planning, that is, redirecting an institution in the midst of industry change and environmental uncertainty. University medical schools are redesigned as hospital systems or HMOs as the health care industry is redefined. Small liberal arts colleges for traditional students become professionally oriented to serve older, part-time students in the growing training and development sector. Single-purpose colleges merge to become more comprehensive institutions serving a broader postsecondary market. However, a brief case study of a major research university's attempt to position itself in the emerging postsecondary knowledge industry may provide a useful explication of contextual planning.

Institutional Context

Throughout the 1980s, Major University, despite its national reputation and relative success, had struggled with constantly declining resources. Attempts at strategic planning and priority setting designed to facilitate institutional resource reduction and reallocation had failed to create an environment that supported cost-effectiveness. In the mid- to late 1980s, Academic Vice President Wellgood had introduced an institutionwide planning process to shift the university from a reactive to a more proactive stance and to view the external environment as challenging rather than threatening. The effort, which focused in part on reviewing essential themes and components of the university's mission, was successful in getting the strategic planning team (executive officers and faculty leaders) to focus on changes in the external environment. But no substantive plans or actions were forthcoming. A priority fund to support innovation, obtained by taxing existing unit allocations, was needed to cover other budget shortfalls. More draconian program reviews led to some downsizing of units but generated significant negative publicity, loss of morale in the affected units, resistance to program review in other areas facing similar action, and minimal savings.

Insight

In 1988, Wellgood, a nationally renowned scientist and successful academic administrator, was named president of the institution. However, before assuming office he was given a six-month sabbatical. During that time he traveled widely, visiting other university presidents, association heads, and foundation executives to gain perspective on what was happening in postsecondary education. He also engaged various groups around the university, exploring themes raised in the previous planning discussions and in his travels. These would provide the grist for his presidential inaugural address.

In that address, Wellgood stressed the need for a new paradigm in which Major University would interact with a constantly changing environment as it approached the twenty-first century. He described a university culture that relished, stimulated, and managed continuous change. He also stressed continuous renewal of the institution's role and mission and identified three distinct themes for the university. One of these emphasized establishing the university as a world leader in the use of information technology in the knowledge age. The address reflected a contextual perspective: the need to establish a planning capacity capable of both adapting to and modifying its environment, and to create an internal culture supporting change and a managerial capacity to manage it.

Initiative

The initiative focusing on information technology in an age of knowledge had been a topic of discussion during his term as academic vice president but was never clearly articulated until his inaugural address. The address was followed by intensive discussions with the faculty governing body, with the board of trustees in their annual retreat, and among executive officers and administrative groups; the discussions elicited general support for the implied direction and appropriate concern about its lack of specifics. Shortly thereafter, the president further clarified the initiative in a vision statement distributed widely on campus. This document reflected a summation of the earlier planning efforts, refinements during his pre-presidential sabbatical, and the early discussions.

Because Major University had a significant history in the development of mainframe computing, several professional schools were already embarking on efforts to stimulate computer use themselves. Since Wellgood's ideas had been discussed with various planning, executive, and faculty groups, the initiative was viewed as an appropriate one. Exactly what it meant and how the institution would change was not spelled out. However, earlier discussions about strategic priorities had always engendered disagreements and even conflict among the deans.

Investment in Infrastructure

At least three critical investment decisions provided support for this initiative. One involved a structural change. An executive officer was hired to spearhead the university's effort in information technology, and a universitywide Division of Information Technology (DIT) was initiated in 1990 to coordinate varied but fragmented academic and administrative computing efforts, the libraries' use of information technology, the transition from a mainframe to a microcomputing environment, and the university's nascent internal networking and external telecommunications linkages.

A second set of internal technological investments between 1990 and 1993 led to the development of one of the country's largest privately owned phone systems; the installation of a fiber optic cable system linking all offices, classrooms, and residence halls on campus; and the development of a campuswide set of computing sites completely equipped with fully networked computers. This network provided both phone and computer jacks in all offices and was capable of handling integrated data, sound, and video transmission. The phone system allowed access to all university information resources from any location.

A third set of externally directed technological investments during the same period linked the campus to a host of local, state, national, and international computer and information networks using the latest in information and telecommunications networks. These new relationships involved contracts, partnerships, and joint ventures with numerous computing, information technology, and telecommunications firms and government agencies.

In essence, the university invested heavily in new organizational structure, technology, and external relationships to provide support for this initiative. This occurred without a clearly defined strategic niche, clear purposes to be achieved, or an internal set of priorities or programs designed to succeed. Rather, it had invested in infrastructure designed to support faculty, academic, and administrative activities consistent with the initiative.

Incentives

Several incentive programs have been an integral part of the information technology initiative. An internal Presidential Initiative fund was established to provide over $1 million to stimulate innovative, interdisciplinary, and venturesome research in this area. The Division of Information Technology established special arrangements with computer firms to provide lower educational prices and discounts to faculty, students, and staff or to academic departments and administrative units to purchase computers and software. Other incentives included on-campus repair, maintenance, and upgrade services on equipment and a comprehensive program of regularly scheduled workshops, for free or at a nominal price. Deans were encouraged to seek development funds to support or to initiate joint efforts with computer, information, and telecommunications firms to obtain equipment to add to the network or new funding for educational and research efforts related to information technology.

Involvement

In addition to the various incentives that encouraged the purchase of computers and software and provided training to large numbers of faculty, students, and staff, several other internal and externally oriented activities have promoted involvement. For example, DIT staff assist units wanting to exchange information, computer services, and telecommuter courses using the institution's internal computing network or through its links to the external networks. Customized instructional services to assist faculty and entire units in designing and implementing new computer and telecommunications courses and programs have supported a variety of specialized applications. A program to train trainers and provide workshop materials assists units in becoming more self-sufficient.

The patterns of involvement are not only internally directed. One university program on information technology integration promotes research and development efforts that use technology to build partnerships between external sponsors and university researchers. DIT also works jointly with corporate and government partners to develop new applications of information technology. The university has also taken leadership in founding or participating in consortia with other universities to expand their educational and research capacity.

This pattern of fostering widespread opportunity for involvement by faculty, staff, and students in units throughout the university both internally and in expanded relationships with external groups has greatly enhanced the involvement in this initiative and broadened the base of understanding of what can be done in a technology-driven educational and research environment.

Information

Conscious efforts to disseminate information about information technology are ubiquitous. DIT produces a bimonthly publication available in hard copy and electronically, focusing only on major university activities and participants. A variety of large-scale workshops sponsored by DIT have provided participants with information for both beginners and advanced users. In cosponsorship with other schools and colleges, a variety of symposia have explored the future of computing, information, and telecommunications technology and the changing role of universities in the age of information. On a more informal basis, the university has supported the development of specialized user-groups on e-mail who are constantly exchanging information.

Externally, DIT has supported staff presentations at various professional postsecondary associations. The university's information technology initiative has also been the focus of articles in several national professional publications. This widespread use of information has made the information initiative common knowledge throughout the university, enhanced people's understanding of its potential in many areas, and provided visible recognition for interesting new activities and their developers. Information as well as incentives and opportunities for involvement are increasing support for the initiative.

Integration

The success and rapid expansion of the information technology initiative has necessitated better understanding of its size, nature, and cost; more focused strategic planning for the effort; and more effective management of an expensive and expanding infrastructure. Recently DIT has done a series of planning reports to begin examining the various services it provides and to track the patterns of use of the university's information network. A number of reports have attempted to examine the emerging organizational structure of the information technology initiative and its relationship with and use by various academic and administrative units. These reports have led to a reorganization of DIT, its staffing, and its support service relationship to various academic and administrative units. Studies of the costs of the information technology infrastructure and various DIT services have been undertaken. Procedures for budgetary allocations for them are being designed. Preliminary efforts to charge for services are being discussed. Deans now regularly review their units' educational technology initiatives and developments in their annual budget meetings with the academic vice president. The shape of a broad initiative reflecting an industry change and with the potential to transform the institution could not be clearly seen in advance; but with maturity the initiative has required attention to the elements of good organizational design to ensure it is well managed in the future.

Institutionalizing Information Technology Initiatives

To date, the information technology initiative has spawned a wide array of activities, approved substantial investments, encouraged a variety of incentives, supported numerous modes of involvement, publicized the effort widely, and begun the process of management integration. Clearly, careful organizational design, strategic planning, and more concern for managing for DIT is beginning to emerge. However, the success of an initiative designed to transform the institution using a contextual planning approach is whether or not it stimulates new initiatives that ensure a dynamic future in pursuing information technology in the age of knowledge. As this is written, three new initiatives using information and telecommunications technology are being launched. The first is an initial $40 million dollar investment in a new Media Union, which will combine a digitized library with links to other worldwide information sources and a facility that will provide opportunities for interdisciplinary groups of students and faculty to experiment with new modes of knowledge transmission using interactive computing, video, and telecommunications technology for learning without limits of time or location. The intent is to foster interdisciplinary efforts in which representatives from more than one school or college will create new teaching-learning modalities that can be transmitted anywhere.

A second initiative involves transforming a small school of library sciences into a school of information sciences. A new dean with a background in information and computer sciences, an infusion of new faculty, and an investment in advanced classroom technology are designing a school that will train information experts of the future and will become the core faculty in the university using modern telematics technology for teaching and learning.

Yet a third initiative involves creating a position of associate vice president for academic outreach to stimulate new external delivery modes for the university's intellectual resources, using the internal and external infrastructure that is now in place. Stay tuned!

Implementing Contextual Planning

Limited experience with contextual planning and a review of the process itself suggests several factors or conditions that are essential to implementing it successfully.

A Paradigm Shift: Perspective, Change, and Thinking

To successfully implement and guide a contextual planning process requires a paradigm shift for institutional leaders and planning participants in at least three dimensions: cross-industry knowledge perspective, change orientation, and contextual thinking. First, contextual planning focuses not on the dynamics of the postsecondary industry or a segment of it, but on the emergence of a developing yet ill-defined postsecondary knowledge industry. This focus involves examining and understanding the changes occurring in the current postsecondary industry. It also involves taking a cross-industry perspective to attempt to understand the dynamics of several related industries (computing, information resources, telecommunications, postsecondary training and development, and perhaps, entertainment) as they interact or overlap in creating this emerging postsecondary knowledge network or industry. The focus is on knowledge development, dissemination, and applications for a broad and diverse array of postsecondary learners in varied settings and by varied means.

Second, because contextual planning focuses on significant changes in the external environment and industry, suggests a proactive stance in shaping that industry, may involve redefining an institution's role and mission, and may result in major institutional redesign or reorganization, the dynamics of macro change at the industrywide and institutionwide levels take on a far more central focus. Traditionally, managing change in an existing institution is focused at the individual, program, or process level—a micro change focus. Even strategic planning or the current attention given to restructuring and reengineering tends to focus only on internal institutional changes that are limited in scope. The potential for and dynamics of significant macro change strategies need to be embraced and understood by institutional leaders and planners.

Finally, contextual planning requires contextual thinking: understanding one's external and internal environment and the dynamics between them more holistically. It means focusing on broad themes of environmental and industry change, on reexamining external relationships, on redefining an institution's role, on redesigning institutional structure, and on recreating or building culture. It requires identifying and articulating new directions and initiatives, understanding the infrastructure implications of a new initiative, and knowing how to use incentives to involve people and to provide information about the initiatives and the responses it engenders. In essence, it involves an emphasis on reshaping the external environment of one's institution and the internal design and function of the institution—reshaping internal and external contexts.

These shifts toward embracing a new industry perspective, focusing on change, and thinking contextually underscore the primary governance and planning challenge: getting the institution to focus externally on questions such as "How is the postsecondary industry being transformed by the emergence of a postsecondary knowledge industry?" "What role should our institution play in that shift?" and "How should it redefine its external relationships?" Internally, it involves addressing another question: "How to redesign or reorganize our basic educational and research processes and academic structures?" This requires understanding the institution's culture and traditions, its dominant patterns, its primary constituents and how to engage them in macro change strategies, and understanding how to recreate or reform the institution's academic culture.

New Models of Organization and Performance

Implicit in the discussion of contextual planning in an emerging industry is the need to think about new models of organization and new criteria for successful institutional performance. Our previous notions of colleges and universities as formal organizations (bureaucracies), collegial communities, political entities, or organized anarchies, while useful, may be replaced by some newer models. The institution as a "network" or "interorganizational network" is one such model. In the past, we have conceived of postsecondary institutions as part of state or multicampus systems or consortia. However, the notion of a postsecondary knowledge network or industry consisting of unbounded research linkages, postsecondary relearning enterprises, learning networks, economic development combines, or global institutions suggests a fluid network or interorganizational model, one allowing us to focus on boundary relationships, interorganizational structures, and the patterns of collaborative arrangements with other postsecondary and noneducational institutions.

Another model, a variant on the organized anarchy model, is the institution as "conglomerate" (Clark, 1995), a holding company of a variety of related postsecondary enterprises. While some large universities may already function in this way, pressures from environmental challenges to support new interdisciplinary research agendas, participate in economic development, extend postsecondary educational opportunity, and utilize new information technology all affect departments or schools differentially and suggest such a model. In a conglomerate model, the organizational intent is to develop a core identity for the institution; to design effective patterns of autonomy, coordination, and decentralization for autonomous units; and to balance the tendency to fragment the institution.

A final organizational model is not a new one but has reemerged in our discussions of contextual planning: the "organization as culture" (Clark, 1963; Tierney, 1990; Peterson and others, 1995). Contextual planning's focus on redefining the nature of our industry, on redirecting institutional roles, missions, and external relationships, and on redesigning or restructuring academic processes affects the basic pattern of academic work in teaching, learning, and research. Organizational culture, especially the beliefs faculty and staff hold about the institution, their work, and its meaning for them, is critical—both as a resistance to change and as a focus for cultural reform. Sensitivity to and management of organizational culture is an important concept in this new era.

New notions of institutional performance criteria also emerge in discussing contextual planning. While our past and current focus on resource acquisition, reputation, and results still deserves attention (noted in the introduction of this chapter), contextual planning suggests new, broader, and less clearly defined concepts related to successful redefinition of institutional role and mission, redirection of external relationships, redesign or restructuring of academic and administrative structures, and reform or re-creation of the academic workplace culture. Clearly, these are difficult performance concepts to operationalize and measure, but they reflect the success of a contextual planning process that results in extensive institutional change and transformation.

Macro Change

Colleges and universities have typically engaged in incremental or micro change strategies: changing individual faculty or administrative patterns, modifying programs or processes, changing policies and procedures, merging and separating units or occasionally closing them. One of the implications of contextual planning with its proactive focus on major challenges to an institution is the need to think in terms of engaging in more macro change efforts. Attempts to redefine institutional role and mission, redirect external relationships, redesign or reorganize academic structures, and reform culture all involve extensive and sometimes long-term change strategies. Indeed, one of the assumptions of a contextual planning process is that changes at these varying levels of the institution will be linked or integrated. While it is beyond the scope of this chapter to discuss macro change strategies, successful contextual planning involves developing such strategies to implement major institutional changes. The seven process elements of contextual planning reflect a change strategy that is extensive and longer-term, involves widespread participation, and seeks to promote structural, cultural, and behavioral change.

Contextual planning has an implicit multilevel, comprehensive strategy of change. The direction of change is broadly focused and offers most institutional units or members an opportunity to participate. The emphasis on changing infrastructure—developing the platform for or a capacity to move in a given direction—is a less-directive change strategy. The use of incentives, opportunity for involvement, and information is directed toward building support for the initiative and changing the institutional culture through people's participation. The deferral of management integration—more rational program designing, planning, resource allocation, and evaluation—is aimed at reducing barriers to change in an uncertain environment but does not obviate the need for such concerns once initiatives begin to stimulate change. Such a strategy, while comprehensive, is not always a comfortable one in limited resource environments or institutions with a history of formal planning and management approaches.

Assessment

The assessment of student learning, faculty and staff performance, academic programs, or administrative units—and even institutions—is now widely understood and practiced in postsecondary education. However, contextual planning suggests the need for several broader forms of assessment that are not currently done in most institutions. Externally, attempts to redefine one's industry require assessing the changes in the postsecondary industry and other industries related to the emerging postsecondary knowledge industry. Redirecting external relationships could involve a careful assessment of each potential interorganizational linkage and the implications of various organizational arrangements for that linkage. Redefining an institution's role and mission may involve assessing the competitive and/or collaborative implications of such a change. Internally, attempts at redesigning and restructuring should be the focus of both a predecision review of different alternatives as well as postdecision reviews of the changes adopted. A complex but equally important assessment related to institutional redesign involves attempts to assess both the institutional members' capacity and readiness for change and to monitor or assess changes in institutional culture. This broader focus on assessment of industry, institutional, and cultural patterns and changes could inform planners prior to action, support attempts at formative evaluation as changes are implemented, and ultimately serve to document the success of a contextual planning initiative over time.

Paradox: Change and Consistency, Conflict and Commitment

Contextual planning, with its emphasis on significant planning issues and potential for macro change, exaggerates a curious paradox. Major changes in postsecondary institutions are likely to lead to differing views, unclear choices, and conflict among constituents and with traditional institutional values or patterns of operation. Yet the changes engendered by contextual planning may affect large segments of the institution, require substantial resources, impact organizational culture, and be difficult to reverse. Such changes are only likely to succeed with long-term commitments and consistent efforts by institutional leaders over a long period of time. The reality is that avoiding conflicts may be less difficult in the short run but can invariably lead to the institution's failing either to introduce a major change or to implement it successfully. Although forcing constituents to address issues and choices can lead to intensive conflict, it can also lead to creative alternatives or new strategies. Such conflicts and uncertainties usually cannot be avoided, require leadership with the courage to address them, and may strengthen commitment in the long run.

Resources and Risk

Given the emphasis on macro change, investing in infrastructure to support broad initiatives, and providing incentives, contextual planning often requires the commitment of substantial resources—finances, personnel, facilities, and management credibility—to achieve the desired change. Such commitments assume the capacity to generate flexible resources and a willingness to risk their investment in implementing a planned initiative. Both creating flexible resources (often at the expense of supporting ongoing activities) and committing substantial resources to invest in infrastructure changes are risk decisions. Contextual planning requires a willingness to assess and face risks, view changes as investments, and make the changes with as much informed judgment as possible. But risk is a necessary concomitant of contextual planning that guides significant change in the institution.

Leadership: A Complex Process

Contextual planning suggests the need for multidimensional leadership. It requires leadership that has a broad and future-oriented perspective, understands complexity, is proactive, addresses conflicts, takes risks, and provides consistency and commitment in identifying and implementing changes. It requires leadership at many levels: developing external strategies, guiding internal redesign and restructuring, supporting cultural and individual change, and coordinating change strategies at these varying levels. Such leadership is likely to be the result of a team effort or of participation at differing levels, rather than the capacity of a single individual. Four forms or styles of leadership are appropriate for contextual planning (Bensimon, Neumann, and Birnbaum, 1989). "Transformational" leadership is useful in providing a vision and in identifying one or more initiatives that address the complexity of the changing environment and industry and provide a symbolic sense of direction that faculty and staff can understand and support. "Strategic" leadership clarifies new interinstitutional relationships and internal reorganizations and provides a rationale for or strategy for implementing those changes. "Managerial" leadership to realign programs, processes, policies, and resources during the period of change is particularly crucial. Finally, "interpretive" leadership that links major changes to what faculty and administrators do in their own roles and to what it means to them is important in reforming culture and ensuring the committed efforts of individuals. Providing and integrating such multiple levels and styles of leadership is the glue that holds a contextual planning process together, from initial discussion through implementation of new organizational patterns.

Summary

Contextual planning is an emerging approach to planning that supplements our earlier long-range and strategic approaches. Contextual planning differs in the breadth of its focus and its approach to guiding or steering significant institutional change. It is suggested that the three approaches to planning are contingent on the degree of turbulence in the environment and the changing nature of our industry. Only contextual planning takes into account the turbulence and complexity of the major challenges currently reshaping our institutions and our industry. The process elements of contextual planning have an implicit macro change strategy that links change at varying levels. Most importantly, contextual planning forces or assists institutions in addressing critical issues related to redefining the nature of our industry and an institution's role in it, redirecting our external relationships, redesigning academic processes and structures, and reforming or recreating our institutional culture. In an era of rapid change and complex challenges to our postsecondary institutions and industry, it is an important new approach to planning for the twenty-first century.

Further Reading

While the literature on planning in higher education is extensive, Peterson's early chapter "Analyzing Alternative Approaches to Planning" (1981) provides a broad overview and Norris and Poulton's *A Guide for New Planners* (1991) offers a more recent perspective for those new to the field. George Keller's *Academic Strategy* (1983) remains a classic on strategic planning, while a recent critical perspective is provided by Schmidtlein and Milton's report "College and University Planning: Perspectives from a Nation-Wide Study" (1989) and their edited volume on *Adapting Strategic Planning to Campus Realities* (1990). These and other recent critiques highlight the shortcomings of strategic planning and the need to place it in its institutional context. Dolence and Norris's volume on *Transforming Higher Education* (1995) highlights the need for planning to respond to a rapidly changing environment and use planning for introducing more radical institutional changes or transformations. Contextual planning as related in this chapter is an emergent model not widely discussed. Chaffee's early work on "The Concept of Strategy" (1985) and Cope's article on "A Contextual Model to Encompass the Strategic Planning Concept" (also 1985) both approached this broader perspective institutionally, while Cameron's chapter on "Organizational Adaptation and Higher

Education" (1989) provides a more extended or environmental perspective on adapting institutions to extensive environmental change.

References

Alpert, D. "Performance and Paralysis: The Organizational Context of the American Research University." *Journal of Higher Education,* 1986, *56*(3).

Baldridge, J. V. *Power and Conflict in the University.* New York: Wiley, 1971.

Baldridge, J. V., and Okimi, P. H. "Strategic Planning in Higher Education: New Tool—or New Gimmick?" *AAHE Bulletin,* 1982, *35*(2), 15–18.

Bensimon, E. M., Neumann, A., and Birnbaum, R. *Making Sense of Administrative Leadership: The "L" Word in Higher Education.* ASHE-ERIC Higher Education Report, no. 1. Washington, D.C.: School of Education and Human Development, George Washington University, 1989.

Cameron, K. S. "Organizational Adaptation and Higher Education." *Journal of Higher Education,* 1989, *59*(3).

Cartter, A. M. *An Assessment of Quality in Graduate Education.* Washington, D.C.: American Council on Education, 1966.

Chaffee, E. E. "The Concept of Strategy: From Business to Higher Education." In J. C. Smart (ed.), *Higher Education: Handbook of Theory and Research.* Vol. 1. New York: Agathon Press, 1985.

Clark, B. R. "Faculty Culture." In T. F. Lunsford (ed.), *The Study of Campus Cultures.* Boulder: Western Interstate Commission on Higher Education, 1963.

Clark, B. R. "Complexity and Differentiation: The Deepening Problem of University Integration." In D. D. Dill and B. Sporn (eds.), *Emerging Patterns of Social Demand and University Reform: Through a Glass Darkly.* New York: Pergamon Press, 1995.

Cohen, M. D., and March, J. G. *Leadership and Ambiguity: The American College President.* New York: McGraw-Hill, 1974.

Cope, R. G. "A Contextual Model to Encompass the Strategic Planning Concept: Introducing a Newer Paradigm." *Planning for Higher Education,* 1985, *13*(3), 13–20.

Dill, D. D., and Helm, K. P. "Faculty Participation in Strategic Policy Making." In J. C. Smart (ed.), *Higher Education: Handbook of Theory and Research.* Vol. 4. New York: Agathon Press, 1988.

Dill, D. D., and Sporn, B. "University 2001: What Will the University of the Twenty-First Century Look Like?" In D. D. Dill and B. Sporn (Eds.), *Emerging Patterns of Social Demand and University Reform: Through a Glass Darkly.* New York: Pergamon Press, 1995.

Dolence, M. G., and Norris, D. M. *Transforming Higher Education.* Ann Arbor, Mich.: Society for College and University Planning, 1995.

Goodman, P. *Community of Scholars.* New York: Random House, 1964.

Katz, D., and Kahn, R. L. *The Social Psychology of Organizing.* (2nd ed.) New York: Wiley, 1978.

Keller, G. *Academic Strategy: The Management Revolution in American Higher Education.* Baltimore, Md.: Johns Hopkins University Press, 1983.

Kirschling, W. R., and Huckfeldt, V. E. "Projecting Alternative Futures." In P. Jedamus and M. Peterson (eds.), *Improving Academic Management.* San Francisco: Jossey-Bass, 1980.

Lawler, III, E. E. *The Ultimate Advantage: Creating the High Involvement Organization*. San Francisco: Jossey-Bass, 1992.

Lawrence, G. B., and Service, A. L. (Eds.) *Quantitative Approaches to Higher Education Management: Potential, Limits, and Challenge*. AAHE-Eric Research Report, no. 4. Washington, D.C.: American Association of Higher Education, 1977.

Millett, J. D. *The Academic Community*. New York: McGraw-Hill, 1962.

Mintzberg, H. *The Rise and Fall of Strategic Planning: Reconceiving Roles for Planning, Plans, Planners*. New York: Free Press, 1994.

Mortimer, K. P., and Tierney, M. L. *The Three Rs of the Eighties: Reduction, Reallocation, and Retrenchment*. AAHE-ERIC Research Report, no. 4. Washington, D.C.: American Association for Higher Education, 1979.

National Commission on Excellence in Education. *A Nation at Risk*. Washington, D.C.: U.S. Department of Education, 1983.

Norris, D. M., and Poulton, N. L. *A Guide for New Planners*. Ann Arbor, Mich.: Society for College and University Planning, 1991.

Peterson, M. W. "Analyzing Alternative Approaches to Planning." In P. Jedamus, M. W. Peterson, and Associates (eds.), *Improving Academic Management: Handbook of Planning and Institutional Research*. San Francisco: Jossey Bass, 1980.

Peterson, M. W. "Continuity, Challenge, and Change: An Organizational Perspective on Planning Past and Future." *Planning for Higher Education*, 1986, *14*(3), 7–15.

Peterson, M. W., and others. *Total Quality Management in Higher Education: From Assessment to Improvement. An Annotated Bibliography*. Ann Arbor: University of Michigan, Center for the Study of Higher and Postsecondary Education, 1995.

Roose, K. D., and Anderson, C. J. *A Rating of Graduate Programs*. Washington, D.C.: American Council on Education, 1970.

Schmidtlein, F. A., and Milton, T. H. "College and University Planning: Perspectives from a Nation-Wide Study." *Planning for Higher Education*, 1988–89, *14*(2), 26–29.

Schmidtlein, F. A., and Milton, T. H. (eds.) *Adapting Strategic Planning to Campus Realities*. New Directions for Institutional Research, no. 67. San Francisco: Jossey-Bass, 1990.

Stroup, H. *Bureaucracy in Higher Education*. New York: Free Press, 1966.

Study Group on the Condition of Excellence in American Higher Education. *Involvement in Learning*. Washington, D.C.: National Institute of Education, 1984.

Tierney, W. G. *Assessing Academic Culture and Climate*. New Directions for Institutional Research, no. 70. San Francisco: Jossey-Bass, 1990.

Wing, P. "Forecasting Economic and Demographic Conditions." In P. Jedamus and M. Peterson (eds.), *Improving Academic Management*. San Francisco: Jossey-Bass, 1980.

CHAPTER EIGHT

EXAMINING WHAT WORKS IN STRATEGIC PLANNING

George Keller

Lately there has been a flurry of opinion that strategic planning doesn't work. One pair who conducted a study of kinds of campus planning wrote, "Many prescriptions in current planning literature are not consistent with the realities of campus decision processes," which they say have a hopelessly "political character" (Schmidtlein and Milton, 1988–89, p. 17). They also found "considerable cynicism among many participants" (Schmidtlein and Milton, 1991, p. 4). Another doctoral student argued that "The values of the academic culture generally are inconsistent with the underlying concepts of strategic planning" (Prinvale, 1991, p. 18).

A former MIT professor who made the idea of "reengineering" popular recently admitted that "50 to 70 percent of reengineering efforts were not successful" and added: "These failures are significant. They reflect a fundamental fact of reengineering: it is very, very difficult to do" (Hammer and Stanton, 1995, p. xiv). And organization scholar James March, who once glumly wrote that "The [college] president is a bit like the driver of a skidding automobile" and it is "a mistake for a college president to imagine that what he does in office affects significantly either the long-run position of the institution or his reputation as a president" (Cohen and March, 1974, p. 203), is even more disconsolate in his latest book: "It is hard to be confident that any decision process will yield decisions that can be unambiguously described as intelligent. . . . Such a catalog of despair might be seen as an invitation to abandon decision making" (March, 1994, p. 271).

One of Canada's best-known scholars of management, Henry Mintzberg, has written in an unusually ill-natured book that "The work of creating strategy cannot be programmed like that of shoveling coal" (Mintzberg, 1994, p. 303); he argues that good strategic actions are largely a matter of feel, intuition, artistry, and luck, with sharp analysis contributing very little to the synthetic moves of a successful strategist. Though he speaks almost entirely about corporate and government planning, Mintzberg argues that environment scans, competitive analysis, or appraisals of an institution's strengths and weaknesses seldom lead to strategic decisions and action. Mintzberg quotes a cantankerous college dean as saying "I see planning as an expanding bureaucracy, of very little assistance to me, but capable of creating structures of bullshit" (Mintzberg, 1994, p. 405).

What are we to make of these and similar expressions of pique and cynicism? Clearly, efforts at strategic planning and action in academe have not always been successful. But strategic planning efforts in any area of organization life have frequently failed. Change is never cheerfully embraced, and strategic initiatives require a difficult combination of thought, insight, daring, and persuasiveness that few persons possess.

As for strategic behavior interfering with the "realities" of politics in organizations, since when is politics real and other forms of action not? Besides, good strategic design and behavior always expects and accepts a considerable amount of political lobbying, turf protection, and alignments against the new. Those who allege that strategic thinking is alien to "academic culture" forget that strategic thinking is alien to just about every organization's culture, and to nearly every person's style of living. Like logic or art, strategic action is rare and difficult, but that does not make it impossible. What is needed is a sense of its intricacy and obstacles and some knowledge of what is likely to be most conducive to excellent strategic planning and management at colleges and universities.

The explosion of strategic thinking and initiatives in higher education has roots and reasons, despite what the skeptics contend. And it has lifted up dozens of U.S. colleges and universities, and saved others from decline.

Roots and Reasons

The spread of strategic planning and decision making has been one of the most remarkable developments of the past two decades in U.S. higher education. In the late 1970s only a few institutions, most notably Carnegie Mellon and Stanford, were experimenting with the process. Since then, perhaps as many as one-fourth of America's 2,160 four-year colleges and universities and several hundred two-year colleges may have attempted to realign or restructure themselves for the future.

Growth in the use of strategic planning instead of the older forms of long-range planning; five-year planning; or annual, incremental, minor adjustments is not surprising. With its roots in military thinking and action, political diplomacy, and modern business management, strategic planning is stimulated by the need to overcome an enemy or strong threats, or by a fierce desire to attain some difficult objective such as the U.S. presidency, personal fame, or organization prominence against tough competition. Until the mid-1970s, colleges and universities faced few serious enemies or threats. Growth was prevalent, financial support abundant, and public criticism nearly mute; and competition was trivial. Although some institutions ambitiously fought for new levels of quality and national reputation, most did not feel pressed to launch strategic initiatives.

But in the late 1970s, the United States entered a new era of massive and widespread social, economic, demographic, and technological change and new, international competition. Colleges and universities suddenly were confronted by the effects of America's declining birth rates since 1960, which would reduce the number of U.S. high school graduates by one-fourth between 1978 and 1996; by advanced technology such as personal computers, cassettes, satellite transmission, and the like; by the rapid dissolution of traditional family structures and community support groups; and by huge numbers of mainly Latino and Asian immigrants—an estimated 30 million between 1965 and 1995.

Institutions were also affected by growing crime and increased drug use, by the decline of most central cities and the rise of new "edge cities" and suburban business centers, and by the potentially lethal combination of higher education's escalating internal costs and a declining ability of families, states, and the federal government to pay for its alarming cost increases. In the 1990s, colleges and universities have faced numerous other threats to their stability, financial strength, and customary faculty behavior; and they began to face a growing number of harsh critics and public dissatisfaction. Today's environment is rife with discontinuities, new trends, and disturbing surprises (Keller, 1994).

The heart of strategic thinking is the creation of a set of initiatives allowing an army, a country, a corporation, or a university to maintain stability or win a new position amidst a blizzard of discontinuities, unprecedented threats, and surprising changes. Stratagems are really meant to deal with outside threats and competition. Many colleges in recent years have had little choice: either become more strategic or decline. The previous kinds of planning that were inner-directed, self-preoccupied, and incremental—those dust-gathering, growth-oriented, expensive wish lists called five-year plans—were no longer appropriate.

Instead of concentrating on the faculty's wants and growth, colleges had to start paying attention to serving the new variety and breed of students, the public's major concerns, their state's or region's needs, and their own runaway finances.

Especially finances. Since 1983, higher education costs have risen annually at nearly 40 percent above the rate of inflation. Between 1950 and 1995 the costs of higher education, in constant dollars of purchasing power, have *quadrupled.*

Universities have been forced to move away from complacency, self-satisfaction, and narcissism toward steps to cope with the turbulent outside environment that has been reducing enrollments, forcing financial cutbacks, and transforming pedagogy through new technology. They have had to become strategic. They have been pressed to rediscover good teaching and caring service to others, especially to their paying clienteles. They have had to become more efficient, productive, and businesslike. Each institution has had to search for and stress its comparative advantages (Keller, 1983).

Because the forms of strategic management were almost unknown in higher education, colleges had two main problems. One was to decide on their market niche, or the special array of educational services they would select to attract students, political and public supporters, and donors, in the competitive world of thirty-five hundred colleges and universities. The other was to invent a new process by which to make strategic decisions. Who should decide the future direction of the campus, its priorities, its academic emphases, the nature of its response to the new demographics, economics, and technology? How can a collegial institution of higher learning without a military or corporate hierarchy arrive at a plan of strategic action?

The past dozen years have been a period of extraordinary experimentation in academe with the process of strategy formulation and implementation. Traditional patterns of governance, faculty autonomy, loose financial controls, course proliferation and redundancies, and routine services to students have had to be altered. The role of the board of trustees or regents is being reexamined (Chait, 1995). Dozens of books and articles have been exploring the ingredients of academic leadership, the difficult art of piloting major institutional changes.

The early twentieth-century pattern of strong presidential management and institution-shaping by persons like James Burrill Angell, Frank Aydelotte, Nicholas Murray Butler, Charles Eliot, Daniel Coit Gilman, William Rainey Harper, and Andrew White has long since crumbled. As the nation's demand for trained intellect increased, faculty became the most powerful group on campus by the 1970s. Most professors detest the idea of stronger management, marketing, efficiency, and financial controls as well as institutional strategies that tend to confine the kind of academic growth. Also, many scholars are more loyal to their disciplines than to their campuses.

So academic institutions entered the 1980s and 1990s with an urgent need to change, to be better managed and more tightly focused, but without the structures to manage institutional change (Cole, Barber, and Graubard, 1994). In the words of a famous 1974 book, "The American college or university is a prototypic organized anarchy. It does not know what it is doing" (Cohen and March, 1974, p. 3). Strategic decision making was an attempt to lessen the near anarchy and *laissez-faire* economics of universities and to reengineer them so they could adapt to the radically new conditions of the 1990s and beyond.

Trial and Error

It is obligatory to recognize that during the past dozen years colleges and universities have been *inventing* the process whereby they reach rough agreement about how they should deal as whole institutions with the turbulent environment. Strategic decision making is new for academe. There are no accepted academic models; and military, political, and industrial models for strategy making are not easily transferrable.

Naturally, there have been clumsy efforts, nervous probes, and failures. Analysts such as Frank Schmidtlein of the University of Maryland have documented the less successful ventures (Schmidtlein and Milton, 1988–89), although such reports have often been flawed by a failure to distinguish between new-style, externally oriented strategic planning and old-style, internally driven, long-term or five-year planning. But there have been notable successes in strategic reengineering, too.

Take Carson-Newman College of Jefferson City, Tennessee, for example. In 1987 its president, Cordell Maddox, with trustee support, launched a strategic planning effort to improve enrollment, finances, and academic quality. With the aid of an outside consultant, the Baptist institution reorganized its many small departments into seven divisions; raised the quality of its entering students and the teaching of its faculty; established a Center of Baptist Studies, a Center of Appalachian Studies, and a Church Music Institute; appointed a young, dynamic provost; built a new field house of architectural distinction; and launched a $50 million capital funds drive. It emerged from obscurity to be listed in *U.S. New & World Report's 1995 Guide to Best Colleges* as among the South's better regional liberal arts colleges and the fourth "most efficient" in the region. By the turn of the century, Carson-Newman hopes to become the finest small Baptist college in America.

One can also point to successful strategic efforts at Centre College in Kentucky and Stevens Institute of Technology in New Jersey, at Duke, the University of Miami, and the University of Washington, at the University of Pennsylvania's Wharton School and its School of Nursing, at Virginia's George Mason University, Northwestern University, the University of Guelph in (Guelph) Canada, and the University of Maryland, to name a few. Northeastern, Tulane, and Syracuse universities are among those who pruned their budgets appreciatively and carried out some restructuring, as has the University of Calgary in (Calgary) Canada.

Each of these universities has approached the formulation of their strategy in a different manner. Some have had strong presidential or administrative direction. Others have relied heavily on faculty analysis and suggestions. Most have employed some combination of both. In a few cases, such as in Maryland, the state's Board of Regents forced its public colleges and universities to rationalize their diverse offerings, cut costs, and create a greater distinctiveness (Eaton, Miyares, and Robertson, 1995).

Strategic planning must respond to the local campus culture, decision-making traditions, the degree of urgency, and the administrative vision, political skill, and courage at each campus. Some colleges, especially state and community colleges, have faculty unions; most do not. Some, like Haverford or Oberlin, have powerful—often paralyzing—traditions of widespread involvement of all the stakeholders, including students and alumni, in policy decisions.

Thus there is no fixed protocol for academic strategic decision making, and even less similarity across institutions about how they implement and enforce the strategic changes agreed upon. Not only is strategic management too new to have settled on a proven set of procedures but also the colleges and universities across the United States are too varied in size, sponsorship, faculty behavior, endowment, kinds of students, and operating styles. Also, the literature on academic strategy making is skimpy, and empirical findings about successful strategies are nearly nonexistent.

Still, we can get glimpses of several ingredients and procedures that seem to be conducive to successful strategizing. How? One method is through personal involvement. (I have participated in one way or another in the strategic efforts of more than fifty educational institutions during the past dozen years.) Another is through conversations with other strategic experts, such as Robert Cope, Donald Norris, and Robert Shirley; and with strategic campus leaders, such as Richard Cyert, James Duderstadt, George Johnson, and Rebecca Stafford. Reading the best literature on the subject also helps.

Some Basic Ingredients

Probably the most important ingredient in successful strategic decision making is to have a determined senior-level champion of strategic change. It is usually the president, but it can be a vice president for academics or finance, or the chair of the board of trustees. This leader must be thoroughly committed to creation of a less anarchic and traditional institution and a more directed, focused, and contemporary portfolio of educational and research services. This senior champion must be persistent and results-oriented, and willing not only to initiate the planning process and define its expected outcomes and timetable but also to implement the chosen priorities with oversight, incentives, punishments, budget reallocations, and persuasive advocacy.

Numerous presidents and deans seem keen on having a strategic plan as an icon or showpiece but lose their nerve about implementing its priority actions. This lack of follow-through contributes to cynicism on the part of those who spent contentious time carving out some new directions and reallocations. Their previous suspicions that the strategic decisions might not be carried out by the administrative leaders and financed adequately are confirmed.

Where the president issues annual reports on the progress made in fulfilling the precepts of the plan, reallocates dollars in the annual budgets, and frequently and publicly praises those who are altering their traditional ways in the directions the plan suggested, the strategic initiatives are highly likely to move off paper and into the operational activities of the college. This usually takes several years. Strategic change comes about only if there is such a senior and determined person to champion real rather than cosmetic adaptation to new societal, financial, and competitive conditions—in short, a leader.

Along with the driving force of one or two such leaders, successful plans require a buy-in by other important institutional figures. Most of the deans, many department heads, and a majority of the most respected faculty need to be persuaded that the kinds of change and directions of change are reasonable though risky. They are the ones who will implement the planned changes, so their imaginative ideas and concurrence are necessary.

This buy-in is usually accomplished by selecting numerous campus leaders to participate in the task force that develops the strategic plan. The planning team should be a powerful one rather than a mere collection of delegates from the various internal constituencies and interest groups (Schuster, Smith, Corak, and Yamada, 1994). For the strategy group, the most forward-looking and institutionally committed of the campus influentials are likely to produce a wise set of new initiatives (Gonçalves, 1991–92).

The proposed initiatives of the small strategy group should be talked over with other groups of faculty, administrative heads, and student and alumni leaders, and with key political figures if the institution is a publicly supported one. Successful plans almost never emerge from below, from endless meetings by many people on campus. But neither can strategies succeed unless the small strategic planning team consults broadly before it publishes its final report and obtains skeptical assent from a majority of the significant persons at the institution.

Colleges or universities that seek "consensus," the utopian grail of campus faith, seldom succeed in getting either a bold strategy or consensus. Like America itself, most institutional populations have enormous differences of opinion and commitment. But rough agreement among and support from a majority of the deans, heads of academic departments, and major staff officials is vital for success.

Also vital is the disciplining or separation of those campus authorities who refuse to go along with the new strategic initiatives or who try to sabotage it. To permit a few key persons to flaunt their opposition to the strategy without negative consequences conveys to others that the leadership is not serious about the new course of action and that noncompliance is acceptable.

The Indispensable Element: Good Communication

Attention is a scarce resource. Most scholars lead busy lives and attempt to fulfill many obligations. Most persons on campus suffer from information overload and multiple demands upon their time and interests. So a major necessity for leaders trying to get college persons to focus on creating a new strategy and then changing their behavior is to capture their attention and hold it despite the unrelenting barrage of other claims. Good communication is essential for success in transforming an institution. James March has written (1994): "Decisions will be affected by the way decision makers attend (or fail to attend) to particular preferences, alternatives, and consequences. They will depend on the ecology of attention: who attends to what, and when. . . . Decisions happen the way they do, in large part, because of the way attention is allocated" (p. 24).

How the president frames the university's current situation and the urgency of institutional change is therefore a contributing factor to success (Kahneman and Tversky, 1984). The agenda for decision making needs to be carefully crafted to persuade preoccupied professors and staff that their attention to the scary matter of major strategic adaptations is crucial for the continued viability of the college or university.

The communication must be strong and continual, from the inception of planning through the several years of its implementation. At the beginning, the president, possibly joined by the vice presidents of academic affairs and of finance and by the chair of the board of trustees, needs to make a compelling case for the urgency of creating a strategic action plan. The threats to the college's current stability should be described in stark detail, and the new environment of higher education and of the particular campus should be graphically depicted, with statistics, trend data, and implications. A sense of urgency, seizing people's attention, must be communicated. "Make the status quo seem more dangerous than moving into the unknown," one analyst advises (Kotter, 1995, p. 62).

In explaining what he or she intends to do, the president needs to lay out a plan for the plan: how the institution will study the urgent situation, who will do it and by when, what outcomes he or she expects, and how consultation will take place. The mechanics of arriving at a strategic course of action to tackle the new conditions and perhaps take advantage of them, using the campus's competitive advantages, should be clearly understood. Faculty members and campus special-interest groups tend to be especially critical of the process of decision making; they may use arguments that the process was flawed or that they were not consulted adequately as an excuse for not becoming more strategic.

After the strategic planning task force arrives at some priority alterations and they are approved, the president, vice presidents, and deans should communicate relentlessly the new emphases and direction of the institution to the public, their faculty and staff colleagues, alumni, incoming students, and political and financial supporters. And as the new strategy unfolds, the campus executives should keep reporting, verbally and in print, how the new structures, priorities, and behaviors are bringing in new results. People must know the strategy is making a difference, that it is bearing additional fruit. Slowly, the campus culture will then change.

Four to Keep in Mind

Four other ingredients of success are worth mentioning. The point at which strategic discussions usually break down or stall is after the analyses are completed and the college's current situation is diagnosed and understood, and it is time to propose the new initiatives and priorities for the future. Here, minds are able but spirits are weak. On most campuses, creative intellect, entrepreneurship, and metapolitical behavior are not as strong as critical intellect, protection of prerogatives, and political wariness.

A variety of dodges may be tried to evade the responsibility and psychological pain of hard decisions, priorities, and novel structures and emphases: a vague set of goals or objectives; a laundry list of dozens of further explorations, recommitments, and new committees; numerous operational improvements instead of a few real strategic initiatives (Stafford, 1993). Faculty members especially have difficulties at this stage. Stanford's former president, Donald Kennedy, recently observed (1994, p. 95):

> University faculties have unwritten understandings, and one of them is that they usually criticize another's discipline only in private. In a recent round of harsh budget cuts at Stanford, we involved a group of distinguished faculty from all fields. . . . They frequently worried that we were cutting too much "across the board," and not singling out whole programs for elimination. Yet they could not develop a consensus on which programs should go. There was

private advice to us, of course, on what victim "the administration" might select—and in nearly every case the recommended deletion was a discipline far from the domain of the recommenders.

At this point in the process, the president, a bold dean, or a respected professor needs to prepare a detailed position paper with priorities and new ventures based on the data and deliberations up to this point and offer it as a draft of what probably should be done. The paper typically ignites some of the strategists into disagreements, turf struggles, and perhaps a firestorm of objections and skepticism. But the paper forces the planning group—and others—to invent their own initiatives and rank their own priorities, especially if the president and trustees insist on a real plan for strategic transformation and not another bland stew of goals. It moves the group from analysis to prescription.

In the 1990s, strategic planning increasingly is done in an atmosphere of financial austerity or reductions. This complicates reengineering because many on campus argue, "How can we move forward in new directions when we have to cut back people and programs?" This is a valid objection. But a financial crisis is frequently an opportunity for genuine changes. It allows colleges and universities to make the bold deletions they had little stomach for in more prosperous times, and it compels strategic action and priority setting because across-the-board pruning only weakens the entire institution.

However, a second important factor in success is trimming deeply enough and capturing some new money so that innovations can continue to occur as well as cutbacks. Morale is damaged when the prospect is for strategic cuts only and not for new ventures as well. Venture capital is not well understood as a necessity in academe, but it *is* indispensable. Everyone on campus needs to feel that the institution is still moving ahead even though it is being forced to trim in some areas.

A third ingredient for success is close attention to finances. Some strategic plans will blithely suggest new graduate programs and academic departments, massive increases in undergraduate scholarships and graduate fellowships, or several multimillion dollar renovations and new construction—with no consideration of where the resources will come from. Ignoring the financial realities of university life is one of the most common items of neglect in strategic thinking (Stafford, 1993). Costs in higher education have been rising faster than inflation since the early 1980s, while the ability of parents and the states to support these increases has been declining (Breneman, 1994).

So candor, thoroughness, and ingenuity about finances are vital for the creation of a successful strategy. Excellent strategic initiatives often elicit new financial contributions from graduates, foundations, corporations, and government agencies. Realism therefore needs to be softened by hopes that creative and forward-looking strategies will probably garner fresh support. But doing the financial projections is essential to ward off accusations by outsiders that academics live in a peculiar world of eleemosynary blather.

Also, the strategic initiatives and reallocations must be reflected in annual budget allocations. Unless money follows the new ideas, the strategic priorities will not get adequate support and the planning exercise will be perceived as a sham. For success, the budget process should always be amended to implement the strategic plan.

Fourth, success is best achieved if it proceeds on the basis of what social psychologist Karl Weick calls "small wins" (1984). A strategic transformation is a huge change in behavior, academic emphases, structure, rewards, finances, and campus culture. Such a change is intimidating, even menacing; and it is beyond most people's comprehension. What helps strategic transformation succeed is a series of small wins, or sequential, smaller renovations. If faculty, staff, and students see that the efforts in one area have resulted in positive gains, then they are more likely to tackle the next one or two priority actions. Confidence grows. Trying to do everything at once usually leads to frustration, crushing overwork, and lack of concentration. Small wins also allow for fine-tuning and adjustments to the strategy as it is being implemented. As Deborah Gladstein and James Brian Quinn (1985) write in one of the finest brief descriptions of successful strategic decision making: "Overall strategies typically emerge after a long process of realignment in both the formal and informal organizations and as individuals and opportunities present themselves. . . . In essence, a manager merely operates as an expert brewmaster, not like a master of a slaveship" (p. 213).

A Final Word

While these factors, and others, contribute to the success of strategic decision making and institutional change, there is one overriding element for a successful academic strategy: attention to the changing societal context.

Colleges and universities tend to be amazingly narcissistic, fixating on their own traditions, privileges, operations, and aspirations. They usually are relatively heedless about market forces and shifts in demography, the economy, competitors, and public preferences. Yale historian Jaroslav Pelikan notes that "One of the most besetting vices of the university, and yet at the same time one of its most charming characteristics, has always been its quaint tendency to look inward and ignore the context of the society within which it lives and without which it could not exist" (1992, p. 137).

But we live in a time of fundamental changes within the United States and in the world. To ignore those changes is perilous for all of society's institutions, but especially for institutions of higher learning, many of which are precariously financed and becoming more costly to run each year. Colleges and universities that have successful strategies are those that monitor the external environment in which they operate and respond strategically to important external developments—without sacrificing their essential values and procedures. Indeed, the difference between old-time, long-range planning and today's strategic planning is precisely an intimate, Darwinian attention to the external environment and its needs.

David Breneman, the noted education economist, former college president, and now dean of the University of Virginia's School of Education, said in a remarkable essay (1994): "It is vital that college and university leaders, trustees, state and federal policy officials, corporate and foundation officials, opinion leaders, and informal citizens engage in discussion, planning, and action consistent with the new reality. . . . Higher education is indeed entering a new era, in which the old assumptions that have guided action for several decades must be rethought" (p. 6).

Strategic decision making will become even more important in the decades ahead. It is helpful to learn which ingredients are most conducive to success.

Further Reading

I especially recommend *Strategic Planning for Public and Nonprofit Organizations* (Bryson, 1995); *Collegiate Culture and Leadership Strategies* (Chaffee and Tierney, 1988); *Opportunity from Strength: Strategic Planning Clarified* (Cope, 1987); *Innovation and Entrepreneurship* (Drucker, 1985); *Planning in Community Colleges* (Knoell, 1989); *Mintzberg on Management* (Mintzberg, 1989); *A Guide for New Planners* (Norris and Poulton, 1991); *Strategies for Change* (Quinn, 1980); *Making Decisions and Producing Action: The Two Faces of Strategy and Change* (Gladstein and Quinn, 1985); *Strategic and Operational Reform in Public Higher Education* (Shirley, 1994); *Sheep in Wolves' Clothing, or How Not to Do Strategic Planning* (Stafford, 1993); and *Institutional Revival: Case Histories* (Steeples, 1986). In Cole, Barber, and Graubard (1994), see especially four essays: Jonathan Cole's "Balancing Acts: Dilemmas of Choice Facing Research Universities," Donald Kennedy's "Making Choices in the Research University," Steven Muller's "Presidential Leadership," and Robert Rosenzweig's "Governing the Modern University."

References

Breneman, D. *Higher Education: On a Collision Course with New Realities.* Washington, D.C.: Association of Governing Boards, 1994.

Chait, R. *The New Activism of Corporate Boards and the Implications for Campus Governance.* Washington, D.C.: Association for Governing Boards, 1995.

Cohen, M., and March, J. *Leadership and Ambiguity.* New York: McGraw-Hill, 1974.

Cole, J., Barber, E., and Graubard, S. *The Research University in a Time of Discontent.* Baltimore: Johns Hopkins University Press, 1994.

Eaton, G., Miyares, J., and Robertson, R. "Statewide Planning During Declining State Support." *Planning for Higher Education,* 1995, *23*(4), 27–34.

Gladstein, D., and Quinn, J. B. "Making Decisions and Producing Action: The Two Faces of Strategy and Change." In J. Pennings (ed.), *Organizational Strategy and Change.* San Francisco: Jossey-Bass, 1985.

Gonçalves, K. "Those Persons Who Do Your Planning." *Planning for Higher Education,* 1991–92, *20*(2), 25–29.

Hammer, M., and Stanton, S. *The Reengineering Revolution: A Handbook.* New York: Harper Business, 1995.

Kahneman, D., and Tversky, A. "Choices, Values, and Frames." *American Psychologist,* 1984, *39*(4), 341–350.

Keller, G. *Academic Strategy: The Management Revolution in American Higher Education.* Baltimore: Johns Hopkins University Press, 1983.

Keller, G. "The Impact of Demographic and Social Changes on Higher Education and the Creation of Knowledge." In *Changes in the Context of Knowledge.* Occasional paper no. 26. New York: American Council of Learned Societies, 1994.

Kennedy, D. "Making Choices in the Research University." In J. Cole and others (eds.), *The Research University in a Time of Discontent.* Baltimore: Johns Hopkins University Press, 1994.

Kotter, J. "Leading Change: Why Transformation Efforts Fail." *Harvard Business Review,* Mar./Apr. 1995, 59–67.

March, J. *A Primer on Decision Making: How Decisions Happen.* New York: Free Press, 1994.

Mintzberg, H. *The Rise and Fall of Strategic Planning.* New York: Free Press, 1994.

Pelikan, J. *The Idea of the University: A Reexamination.* New Haven: Yale University Press, 1992.

Prinvale, J. "What Can We Believe? The Use of Strategic Planning in Colleges and Universities." Doctoral dissertation, School of Education, Stanford University, 1991.

Schmidtlein, F., and Milton, T. "College and University Planning: Perspectives from a Nation-Wide Study." *Planning for Higher Education,* 1988–89, *17*(3), 1–19.

Schmidtlein, F., and Milton, T. "Why Planning Often Fails and What Seems to Work." Paper delivered at the Society for College and University Planning Annual Conference, Seattle, July 16, 1991.

Schuster, J., Smith, D., Corak, K., and Yamada, M. *Strategic Governance: How to Make Big Decisions Better.* Phoenix: Oryx Press, 1994.

Stafford, R. "Sheep in Wolves' Clothing, or How Not to Do Strategic Planning." *Planning for Higher Education,* 1993, *22*(1), 55–59.

Weick, K. "Small Wins: Redefining the Scale of Social Problems." *American Psychologist,* 1984, *39*(1), 40–43.

CHAPTER NINE

FOCUSING INSTITUTIONAL MISSION TO PROVIDE COHERENCE AND INTEGRATION

David D. Dill

Guides for planning in contemporary organizations, including colleges and universities, routinely stress the importance of first clarifying an institution's central purpose or mission (Bryson, 1995). *Mission* in this context is generally understood as a statement of the institution's *raison d'être,* justification to the larger society for its existence. Formal mission statements are therefore often crafted with an institution's external constituents in mind, as public relations exercises designed to satisfy or entice external stakeholders and supporters. Perhaps for this reason the process of mission clarification in postsecondary institutions has often been viewed as a superficial and largely symbolic activity of public relations, rather than a meaningful component of an institution's planning process. Recent analyses of academic adaptation to the new environment of postsecondary education, however, suggest that clarification of the strategic focus of an institution is an essential task for sustaining a college or university (Clark, 1995). Mission understood as identifying the appropriate scale and scope of an institution, as well as articulating the community values by which an institution determines programs that are academically and economically viable, is essential to strategic reform in the current and future contexts.

It is one thing to assert the importance of mission clarification in the new postsecondary environment and another to suggest how this process relates to college and university planning. In the sections that follow, the nature and techniques of mission clarification are examined. First, the reasons for renewed attention to defining institutional mission are introduced. Second, since institutional missions in the public sector are shaped by the actions of state boards of higher education, the role of state agencies in mission clarification is briefly explored. Subsequent sections address mission clarification at the institutional level of planning in both public and private colleges and universities.

Mission, it is argued, is best conceived not as a prose statement of aspirations but as a collection of strategic decisions that influence the relationship between an institution and its environment. These strategic decisions encompass the scale and scope of an institution, its geographical service area, the type of students to be served, and what has come to be called the "core competencies" of an institution. Finally, the concept of mission has often been associated with a statement of the essential values of an institution. One of the most powerful contributions of mission clarification to institutional planning, therefore, is in the specification of those collective values or criteria that are applied by the community in determining an institution's priorities. In summary, by reconceptualizing the process of mission clarification, from one of influencing external publics to one of guiding institutional strategic choices, the vital contribution of mission definition to college and university planning can be better understood.

Everything in General and Nothing in Particular

In the early 1980s, as colleges and universities began to react to the first impacts of the new competitive environment of postsecondary education, many institutions engaged in what Richard Chait (1979) aptly termed "mission madness," a time-consuming development of vague and often meaningless mission statements. This early, somewhat cynical perspective on the use of mission statements as public relations tools was captured in "The Importance of Being General," a classic article by Gordon Davies (1986):

> [T]here are very good reasons not to define institutional missions, especially within state-supported systems of higher education. It is safer to talk about missions than to define them, politically more astute to avoid the confrontations that would be inevitable if mission statements were to be made more precise than they usually are. [p. 86]
>
> The scholarly literature about mission is dissociated from practice primarily because, except for the theorists, it is to no one's interest that missions be defined clearly. Institutions do not appear to engage in rigorous definition of their missions because the prevailing incentives are to do otherwise. The recruiting slogan of the U.S. Army, "Be all that you can be," is parodied in higher educa-

tion as "Get all that you can get." Do not get boxed in; remain flexible and alert to every opportunity. [p. 88]

Davies insightfully suggested that the root logic of careful mission definition ran directly counter to the entrepreneurial instincts of college and university leaders. When faced with decreasing resources in the 1970s and 1980s, these leaders understandably avoided the contentious internal reforms necessary to make their institutions economically viable and instead turned to any and all external opportunities as a means of increasing institutional revenues and prestige. Many private liberal arts colleges, confronted with declining enrollments, dropped their traditional focus on general education as they added vocational and quasi-professional programs in an attempt to attract paying students. Community colleges expanded from their early emphasis on a transfer and college-parallel mission to a complex mission combining transfer, vocational, adult and continuing, remedial and developmental education programs. Public comprehensive colleges sought to become research universities, adding doctoral programs and placing more emphasis on research and publication in faculty hiring and promotion criteria. Existing doctoral universities sought to become "world class universities" by recruiting prominent and expensive researchers and making sometimes risky investments in technology transfer and speculative economic development activities. By the mid-1990s, there was a frequently voiced concern in all institutions about articulating institutional mission in a more focused manner, to reduce both the scale and scope of academic programs and administrative activities, to state clear and explicit priorities for the future, and to reallocate funds to an institution's highest priorities (Brint and Karabel, 1989; Keohane, 1994; Shirley, 1994; Starr, 1993).

In a recent study of how public and private colleges and universities are responding to the more competitive postsecondary environment, Leslie and Fretwell's (1996) views on the importance of institutional missions offer a decided contrast to Davies' comments of a decade earlier:

The freedom to be whatever the imagination suggests is also the freedom to be nothing in particular. And this is the fear that haunts institutions that are stressed. Their leaders sense that they have perhaps squandered opportunities to make clear choices about their institutions' identity, focus, and distinctive qualities—and that it may be too late to make these choices.

We heard many times some variant of the complaint "we have become everything in general and nothing in particular." But crisis had forced *all* of the institutions we visited into thinking about choices. Some had made their choices, others were able to talk through the options that seemed reasonable, and ambivalence was clearly complicating the process for a few. For the most part, they all knew the value in differentiating themselves from other institutions—in defining their missions more clearly, in developing a distinctive identity, and in focusing their programs to serve a clearly identifiable market [p. 83].

The evidence from Leslie and Fretwell's and related field studies of institutions facing the new postsecondary environment (Parker, 1986) suggests that institutions with an expressly stated mission can better respond to conditions of decline. The significance of mission to successful adaptation by colleges and universities in the current competitive environment corresponds with recent survey research regarding correlates of effectiveness in four-year colleges. This research has discovered significant relationships between mission consistency—the degree to which programs and activities are in line with the stated mission—and various measures of institutional effectiveness, including measures of student development (Ewell, 1989; Fjortoft and Smart, 1994).

The reemergence of mission as an important factor in institutional planning is wholly consistent with predictions regarding the effects of the new environment. As the federal and state governments cut support for higher education, and as institutional funding becomes increasingly diversified with greater reliance by both public and private institutions on competitively awarded research support, private fundraising, and tuition and fees, success is determined less by political manipulation or public relations and more by merit and effective performance. In this new context, institutions must rethink their essential relationship to their environment, seeking ways to differentiate themselves from their competitive rivals, discovering the niches in which they seek to compete, and designing their academic and administrative programs to meet new societal demands. In this process of adaptation, mission definition and clarification and its relationship to institutional management take on new meaning.

Institutional Missions and State Systems: Governments Versus Markets

In the public sector of higher education, institutional mission is shaped by government policy, most directly by the planning activities of state boards of higher education, which determine the degrees to be awarded, the programs to be offered, and the clientele to be served. However, state efforts to limit program duplication, particularly in high-cost graduate and professional programs, and to increase the efficient use of state resources often fall victim to colleges or universities making an "end run" to the legislature or governor for favored treatment (McGuinness, Epper, and Arredondo, 1994). (Note that this behavior is not ex clusive to the state level nor to public institutions; compare the efforts of both private and public institutions to evade the rigors of competitive federal research funding by lobbying the federal congress for specially "earmarked" research appropriations.) Institutions in growing urban centers compete with traditional research universities, often located away from population concentrations, for graduate and professional programs, especially expensive engineering degrees. Institutions located in isolated rural areas press for programs for place-bound adults. Attempts by state boards to merge, consolidate, or close institutions in an effort to gain economies of scale or scope are often foiled by the political efforts of institutional stakeholders and by the electoral needs of politicians: "Elected officials may be intimidated by unnecessary duplication and the waste it causes, but they are successful because they say 'yes' far more often than they say 'no.' They need the maneuvering room the imprecision about institutional mission provides, and few can afford to say 'never' on any particular issue. So the drift toward curricular sameness is inexorable, a process that can be controlled to some extent but not halted" (Davies, 1986, p. 93).

In the face of these political realities, state boards often choose to delay or stall the process of program review in the hope that something will cause the pressure to subside. The academic program approval process at the state level has therefore been characterized as "highly political, indirect and situational" (Davies, 1986, p. 88). In the new postsecondary environment, however, the traditional process of mission clarification at the state level is undergoing change due to severe state budget constraints, growing public distrust in the efficiency of large state bureaucracies, and increasing concern about the accountability of public expenditures (McGuinness, Epper, and Arredondo, 1994).

One weakness of multicampus university systems is a failure to implement differentiated system policies on faculty promotion and tenure as well to differentiate incentives for teaching. Consequently, all institutions in a multicampus system inexorably drift toward the values of the research university, even those institutions with an undergraduate teaching mission. One state response to mission clarification has therefore been the use of "segmental consolidation," in which all institutions with a similar mission, such as community colleges, comprehensive universities, or doctoral-granting universities, are consolidated into separately organized institutional clusters for purposes of state coordination and planning (McGuinness, Epper, and Arredondo, 1994). Segmental consolidation helps to lessen the tendency of institutional drift toward a common mission.

During the 1990s the passive and reactive approach to institutional mission definition by state agencies of higher education has been replaced by a more aggressive accountability agenda, as governors and state legislators call upon state boards to be active forces for change. Therefore, a second approach to mission clarification at the state level is through the development of performance indicators and report cards that provide information to the public on institutional performance (Ewell, 1994). These performance indicators, unlike previously collected institutional data, are more focused on outcomes than inputs, and they permit and indeed encourage interinstitutional comparisons. Performance indicators are often defined for specific institutional sectors, for example, different performance indicators are used for four-year institutions and community colleges. Because these performance indicators are now being linked to incentive, competitive, or targeted funding (for example, funding directed toward technology transfer activities), the use of performance indicators has become a means of bringing institutions into conformance with their stated mission—supporting colleges and universities not for what they aspire to be, but for what they are.

The use of state consolidation and control as well as performance funding, however, has been criticized as inefficient and counter to current national economic policies promoting greater institutional autonomy and more reliance on market competition (Kerr and Gade, 1989). A number of states, such as New Jersey with its state colleges and Oregon with its university system, have moved to delegate greater personnel and financial autonomy to public colleges and universities, including the capacity to raise and retain tuition revenues. Within the new competitive context, as students pay for an increasing proportion of their tuition in the public sector, and as public institutions must compete with each other for sources of revenue, including performance-related state funding, there is the possibility that market forces may prove a more efficient instrument for promoting institutional differentiation than government regulations designed to define and enforce specific institutional missions. For market forces to be effective in promoting institutional differentiation, however, state regulation may need to place greater stress on the provision of relevant information (Romer, 1995). Massy (1994) has noted that the "incomparability myth," the notion that colleges and universities are unique institutions that cannot be easily compared with each other, has provided public institutions with monopoly power that they can use for economic exploitation. This connection between the ambiguity of institutional mission and exploitation was captured by Lang and Lopers-Sweetman (1991) in a subhead of their study of college and university mission statements, "Mission Statements as Smoke Screens for Opportunism" (p. 606). Even in competitive conditions, institutions may not achieve optimum levels of efficiency and effectiveness unless sufficient information exists to permit various customers (including governments) to make rational economic choices on educational quality. Toward this end, the systematic development of publicly available benchmark information (Massy, 1994) for various sectors of higher education may prove to be an additional market-based instrument for promoting mission differentiation in the competitive post-secondary environment.

A number of such benchmark data networks have already emerged among institutions competing for similar niches. For example, the American Association of Universities' Data Exchange shares benchmark information among leading public and private research universities, and the Higher Education Data Sharing organization collects and disseminates information among a number of smaller private institutions. The Association of Governing Boards of Universities and Colleges has also developed a collection of strategic indicators for institutional management that is now publicly available (Massy, 1994). It is possible that a project among the various state boards of higher education to develop and share comparable benchmark data on the performance of public institutions, codified according to the institutional classifications developed by the Carnegie Foundation for the Advancement of Teaching (1994)—doctorate-granting institutions, master's colleges and universities, baccalaureate colleges, associate of arts colleges, and specialized institutions—would be a means of encouraging public institutions to develop their plans and programs with reference to their real competition and with relevance to the strategic niche they must fill to be successful. Rather than attempting to control institutional missions through program approval and performance funding, state boards might thereby reinforce the increasing competitive market pressures that are encouraging institutions to succeed by identifying and filling strategic niches.

While new and more innovative policy instruments are needed at the state level to encourage differentiation in the missions of public institutions, the primary challenge to mission clarification remains in the planning processes of individual colleges and universities.

Mission Clarification I: Mission Statements Versus Strategic Decisions

Within colleges and universities, the principal attention to institutional mission has been in the construction of generally vacuous documents termed "mission statements." Warren Bryan Martin (1985) has captured the character of these statements: "The mission statement is the foundation on which the House of Intellect stands. And lofty are the utterances that express the importance of our college's mission. Indeed, they float like puffy clouds over our solidly positioned edifice. Broad is the applicability assigned these statements; so broad that they are thought to cover every contingency. Yet narrow is the gate to understanding them, and few there be that find it. No wonder, then, given the missions statement's depth and height, breadth and density, that it is so often ignored" (p. 40).

Several studies of college and university mission statements have confirmed that the contents of these documents are not only often vague and empty but also rarely used in the internal planning processes of colleges and universities (Lang and Lopers-Sweetman, 1991; Newsom and Hayes, 1990).

As noted, mission statements have most often served as proclamations of institutional aspiration. As such they are directed not internally but externally, toward legislators, donors, and those in a position to provide support for the institution's dreams. Davies (1986) reports that in some state systems such as Alabama and Virginia (and also in North Carolina), state boards have permitted public institutions to publish their statements of mission but have pointedly noted that they were written by the institution and not endorsed by the state board. In Virginia such statements are explicitly labeled by the state board as institutional "aspirations." In the rapid growth environment experienced by U.S. higher education after World War II, in which state subsidies for public colleges and universities and federal subsidies for research and student financial aid were readily available, this strategy of mission statements as proclamations of aspiration made good strategic sense. In the current competitive environment, mission statements that offer no guidance to internal planning are of little value.

Mission as Strategic Decisions

In their analysis of a sample of mission statements from public and private institutions in the southeast, Newsom and Hayes (1990) discovered that most institutions could not list any use of their statements. Although many of the institutions surveyed had rewritten their statements within the last five years, in the majority of cases this was in response to accreditation reviews rather than for any reason associated with institutional planning. When the institution's name was disguised, most of the colleges and universities could not be identified from their mission statements. Nonetheless, among that minority of mission statements which contained specific institutional purposes, Newsom and Hayes (1990, p. 30) discovered some systematic patterns (Table 9.1).

As noted in Table 9.1, with the exception of the geography dimension, where public college and universities have an incentive to be precise (concerning in-state students), public institutions are clearly less willing to define specific purposes in their mission statements than private institutions. This suggests first the market protection that state control has historically provided to public institutions in comparison to the competition confronted by private institutions. As the postsecondary

TABLE 9.1. PERCENT OF COLLEGES WHOSE MISSION STATEMENTS CONTAINED SPECIFIC PURPOSES.

Dimensions of Mission	Public	Private	Sectarian	Total
1. Target clientele: what constituencies does the college want to have?	30%	50%	19%	30%
2. Products: what outputs beyond general teaching, research, and service does the college intend?	31	42	31	33
3. Geography: what specific location will the college serve?	74	25	0	54
4. Commitment: what will be emphasized for survival or growth?	43	58	25	42
5. Philosophy: what are the college's specific beliefs, values, and philosophical priorities?	31	67	75	44
6. Self-definition: how does the institution view itself?	36	50	19	35
7. Public image: what reputation does the college wish to have among the public?	46	75	94	58

Source: Newsom, W., and Winston, C. R. "Are Mission Statements Worthwhile?" *Planning for Higher Education,* 1990, *19*(2), 28–30. Reprinted by permission of the Society for College and University Planning, 4251 Plymouth Road, Suite D, Ann Arbor, Mich. 48105-2785, Email <SCUP@UMICH.EDU> World Wide Web <http://www.umich.edu/~scup/>

system becomes more competitive for public and private institutions alike, we can expect public institutions to attempt to redefine their missions in dimensions similar to those of private institutions. Second, consistent with other analyses of institutional mission statements (Davies, 1986; Lang and Lopers-Sweetman, 1991), Newsom and Hayes (1990) suggest the importance of a statement that helps shape an institution's scale and capacity: target clientele (what constituencies—students—will the institution serve?), geography (in what geographic area?), commitment (with what mix of academic programs?), and philosophy (what values will be used to make programmatic choices?).

In a classic article on university strategic planning in the early 1980s, Shirley (1983) similarly argued that a college or university mission statement is best understood as a part of an institution's strategy, and that this strategy consists of a set of decisions that, once made, define the relationship of the total institution to its competitive environment. These decisions in turn give direction to and act as constraints upon administrative and operational activities. The set of decisions that Shirley suggests as a basis for the formation of an institutional strategy are similar to those previously identified in the mission statements of some colleges and universities: (1) the demographic characteristics of the student clientele (for example, full-time, part-time), (2) the geographic areas to be served by its various programs (international, national, state), (3) the mix of programs and services to be offered (such as the balance between undergraduate and graduate programs as well as between teaching, research, and service activities), and (4) the means by which the institution will seek to gain a differential or comparative advantage over its competitors (for example, by a programmatic focus on engineering and the sciences). These four strategic decisions are interrelated; the answers to all four help focus the activities of an institution and identify the particular niche (that is, the combination of geographic, economic, and programmatic opportunities) the institution will attempt to fill in the postsecondary system.

Leslie and Fretwell (1996) provide a number of examples of how contemporary colleges and universities are applying this strategic-decision logic in clarifying their institutional missions:

> Many public institutions serve commuting populations of low- and middle-income students, and most institutions develop at least one distinctive program or curricular identity that draws a certain kind of student. . . .
>
> Geography was important too; even the more nationally known universities understood that their market niches were geographically bounded. In some cases those boundaries were very close to the campus. "The traditional and current mission of [this institution] is to serve kids from ———— County [and its immediate environment]. . . ."
>
> Three of our site institutions defined their niches in terms of the opportunities they provide to minority students. Ethnically diverse Bloomfield College, which serves a predominantly urban population, offers programs that focus on preparing students to assume leadership roles in a multicultural society. . . . The University of Texas at El Paso orients its programs to the needs of the predominately Hispanic population it serves, focusing on preprofessional preparation for fields like health care and law, as well as other fields for which a regional need can be identified. And the population within Maricopa County Community College District's service area is also heavily Hispanic, so there is a need to teach classes in Spanish and a need for faculty who can appreciate the heritage and educational preparation of students from different ethnic and cultural backgrounds. . . .

One institution was struggling with the realization that its fiscal viability depended on undergraduate students, while its faculty were oriented toward graduate education and research. Recognizing that he had radically changed his own perspective, the provost acknowledged: "We can't afford to continue equal emphasis on the traditional trinity of teaching, research, and service. . . . Now we have agreed we are going to be a 'student-centered research university.'" [p. 84–86]

In addition to these examples of contemporary institutions confronting the new competitive environment, the opportunities and challenges now presented by academic programs offered internationally or by distance education further underscore the importance of carefully assessing the nature of student clientele and the geographic service area of an institution.

Scale and Scope

One obvious response to increased competition in the private sector is lowering unit costs. Thus many companies restructure or downsize in an attempt to gain economies of scale and better position themselves in their markets. The combination of increased competition and enrollment growth in the coming decades forces a similar evaluation on the part of higher education institutions. Recent research on the relative efficiency of colleges and universities suggests that economies of scale— generally understood as economies of size or quantity of output, and usually measured by total enrollment—are possible for many institutions. For example, reviewing sixty years of research on economies of scale, Brinkman and Leslie (1986) concluded that two-year colleges having one thousand to fifteen hundred students gained economies of scale in educational and general (E&G) expenditures of up to 25 percent over smaller institutions. Savings were somewhat larger for administrative expenses and operation and maintenance of the physical plant, and substantially less for instructional expenses. Four-year private colleges achieve similar savings in E&G expenditures at about the two-thousand-student range, and comprehensive private and public colleges at the three-to-four-thousand range. Particularly in four-year institutions, however, there is an interaction effect between institutional size and academic complexity. Institutions with a more narrowly focused or required academic program (St. Johns College in Annapolis, Maryland, with its required "Great Books" curriculum being the obvious example) will be better able to cope with the costs of small enrollment size. Conversely, four-year colleges at the suggested scale but with complex curricula will experience increasing cost pressure. While these total-enrollment guidelines may appear obvious, well over a third of U.S. colleges and universities lie below these recommended scale sizes (Carnegie Foundation for the Advancement of Teaching, 1994). This suggests that decisions regarding economies of scale will be an important strategic consideration for increasing numbers of colleges and universities in the competitive period ahead.

The research on economies of scale for doctoral-granting institutions, both public and private, is more complex because of the obvious interaction between scale and scope. Economies of scope occur when a complementarity between outputs simultaneously yields efficiencies, as in the joint production of doctoral education and contract research. Economies of scope are therefore highly relevant to strategic decisions regarding the appropriate size of an institution as well as the proper balance between undergraduate and graduate teaching, research and public service. Research universities are essentially multiproduct firms and can use activities in one sector such as graduate education to achieve economies in another sector such as undergraduate education.

Research on economies of scale for doctoral-granting universities has suggested that substantial economies exist for both the public and private sectors (Rhodes and Southwick, 1987; Cohn, Rhine, and Santos, 1989; de Groot, McMahon, and Volkwein, 1991). For example, Rhodes and Southwick (1987) suggest the least efficient size for a private university is below six thousand students, and for a public university it is in the range of six thousand to fourteen thousand. However, the multiproduct nature of research universities introduces the issue of economies of scope as a complicating factor. Universities that tend to specialize in only one area (such as graduate education) tend to have higher costs; both public and private universities that combine graduate education and research missions in a balanced way are more cost-effective. Thus a public university below the mean in graduate student enrollment should link growth in this activity to measurable improvement in research funding, and a university with above-average involvement in graduate education and research, such as the University of Chicago, should seek economies of scope by expanding its smaller-than-average undergraduate program. Furthermore, a university of below-average scale will likely become more cost-efficient through expansion only if growth occurs simultaneously in more than one area of its mission.

Core Competencies

As increasing competition forces institutions to differentiate themselves from their competitors, more colleges and universities are becoming more selective in their coverage of academic subjects and approaches to them. For example, among sixty-seven universities in France, sixteen are heavily multidisciplinary, ten are partly multidisciplinary, and forty-one were dominated by one or two areas of knowledge (Clark, 1995). The city of Grenoble possesses three separate universities: Grenoble I, a science and medicine university; Grenoble II, a social science university; and Grenoble III, a humanities university. Within the U.S. system of higher education the importance of selective excellence is reflected in the growth over the last twenty-five years of specialized institutions of higher education (Carnegie Foundation for the Advancement of Teaching, 1994). In 1970, institutions focusing on medical and other health professions, engineering and technology, business and management, art, music and design, and law represented 14.9 percent of all postsecondary institutions. By 1994, they represented 19.3 percent, the largest growth of any segment.

Within the corporate sector, one can observe the emergence of a comparable phenomenon, the attention to identifying "core competencies" (Prahalad and Hamel, 1990). In business, core competencies have come to be understood as corporatewide technologies and production skills that permit the company to adapt existing businesses to the competitive market and also use the competencies as a source of new products. As Lang and Lopers-Sweetman (1991) note, ". . . successful organizations—organizations that last—build on some central, declared skill or strength. They may branch out somewhat, but they maintain a basic stability because they stick very close to their central purpose. Diversification for its own sake, in areas where the organization may not have strengths, is folly. Adaptation must occur around the core" (p. 609).

In academic terms, core competence might be understood as a distinctive collection of disciplines or professional knowledge and skill within an institution. Carnegie Mellon University in Pittsburgh, for example, has identified the information sciences as a core competency, around which it can develop its science and social science fields and thus provide a comparative advantage for the entire institution. Core competence needn't be limited to subject fields, however. Stanford University has long held a comparative advantage over its private university competitors because of its unusual competence in academic planning and budgeting, which it developed in the 1970s, and which it has used to strengthen the overall institution and improve the planning and budgeting processes of strategic units within the institution. Similarly, Northwestern University has developed a core competency in the process of program review and is gaining a comparative advantage over its competitor institutions by systematically applying this competence to improve the quality and reputation of its academic and administrative programs.

The key insight to be drawn from the corporate concept of core competencies is not the specific skills or technologies that provide comparative advantage, but the importance of defining and developing a portfolio of competencies for the institution. If large universities in particular view themselves only as bundles of decentralized, disparate programs in which individual schools or departments control both resources and core technologies or competencies, the overall institution will have serious difficulty adapting and especially responding to opportunities for academic programs, service, and research. The new planning process of the University of California at Berkeley, for example, implicitly recognized the potential restrictions posed on the institution by the existing academic architecture of schools and colleges. Traditional departmental reviews and faculty recruitment plans had proved ineffective in comparing departments, disciplines, and programs within broad categories of the university, and in developing new fields from interdisciplinary efforts. In planning for its future, Berkeley created an Academic Planning Board for the university as a whole and identified ten core academic areas. These included traditional clusters of disciplines, but they also included as identified separate core competencies the biosciences; economics; and environmental, ecological, and earth sciences. In each academic area, advisory panels composed of faculty members from both inside and outside the university were formed and asked to make recommendations on priorities, opportunities for consolidation, and new fields for development. In seeking to define and strengthen its core academic areas, Berkeley is attempting to build the core competencies by which it will secure its future.

By shifting the concept of mission from statements of aspiration designed to attract external supporters to strategic decisions designed to clarify the nature of an institution's relationship to its environment—its clientele, its geographic service area, its scale and scope, and its core competencies—the critical contribution of mission to institutional planning becomes more obvious.

Mission Clarification II: Academic Values and Strategic Criteria

Discussions of college and university mission inevitably stress that such statements should include a set of commonly held values that will guide decisions on the shape of the institution and provide direction for the development of the institution as a whole (Martin, 1985; Lang and Lopers-Sweetman, 1991; Shirley, 1983). Inevitably, however, these value statements, to the extent that they exist, present "naive criteria" (Braybrooke and Lindblom, 1963) such as "academic excellence"—purposefully vague, singular goals that provide little or no guidance for the difficult strategic choices now confronting colleges and universities. Rather than invest the time and effort necessary to build agreement among members of the academic community on underlying values, which could serve as the basis for difficult choices, most college and university leaders have preferred to articulate vague generalizations that would not alienate various internal constituencies. Thus the principal problem in the development of effective strategic choice-making processes at most colleges and universities has not been the failure to implement planning and budgeting procedures, but the failure to develop *ex ante* criteria that can serve as an agreed-upon framework for making difficult choices among academic and administrative activities (Cole, 1994; Benjamin and others, 1993).

Among those institutions effectively adapting to the new postsecondary environment, efforts to clarify community values essential to strategic choice have played a prominent role (Dill, 1994; Leslie and Fretwell, 1996). For example, over the last twenty years, a number of public and private research universities—notably Michigan, Minnesota, Columbia, Princeton, and Stanford—invested substantial effort in developing criteria to inform strategic choice making at each institution (Shirley and Volkwein, 1978).

In the 1970s, the provost of Stanford University, confronted by a need to cut $16 million from the institution's operating budget, publicly outlined four criteria for starting or terminating a program and allocating resources: (1) academic importance, (2) student interest, (3) possibility for excellence in the program, and (4) funding potential (Chaffee, 1983). For more than ten years, there was consistent public evidence that these four criteria served as the basis for strategic choice making including the review and (re)allocation of operating budgets, the initiation of new programs, and the elimination of the Department of Architecture.

In the mid-1970s, the University of Michigan also confronted substantial revenue shortfalls because of major decreases in its state funding. Because of these cuts the university was forced to consider the possible reduction or discontinuance of academic programs. Consequently, the academic vice president, in association with a faculty appointed Budget Priorities Committee, developed criteria for making general-fund budget cuts. These criteria were formally adopted in 1979 by the University's Board of Regents as criteria for "program discontinuance" (University of Michigan, 1979). The criteria were (1) quality of the program, (2) centrality of the program to the mission of the administrative unit in which it is located and to the role of the university, (3) cost of the program relative to societal and student demand, (4) uniqueness of the program compared to those offered at other Michigan universities, (5) potential cost savings through reorganization, and (6) service value of the program to other units of the university. The criteria were then consistently utilized to make budgetary cuts in academic and administrative programs. In 1982, under a different vice president, these same criteria were again publicly articulated as a basis for decisions regarding a planned reallocation of $20 million of the university's budget.

In the early 1980s, the University of Minnesota learned that because of a projected state budget deficit it would have to cut $25.6 million from its budget by the end of the 1983 budget year. During the first planning year, prior to any decisions about budgetary cuts, the vice president for academic affairs and a leading faculty-student governance committee from the universitywide senate developed criteria that would be utilized by all units in recommending high and low program priorities. Six criteria were developed: (1) quality, (2) connectedness (the extent to which programs serve other departments and colleges), (3) integration (the extent to which programs effectively combine teaching, research, and service), (4) uniqueness, (5) demand (both student and societal), and (6) cost-effectiveness. The cuts were successfully implemented and the universitywide "ownership" of the guiding criteria was identified as an important contributing factor (Heydinger, 1982). Ten years later, these essential criteria were still being used at the University of Minnesota as a basis of program planning and resource allocation (Lewis and Kallsen, 1995).

In the early 1970s, as a result of comparable financial pressures to those affecting Stanford, Princeton University established a standing Committee on Priorities composed of faculty members, students, and administrators to advise the president of the university on the allocation of resources. The committee, which continues to be active at Princeton, was charged with making recommendations on matters affecting the annual budget, including broad priorities among possible expenditures, as well as matters affecting longer-range plans for resource allocation. Early in their deliberations, the committee recommended a series of criteria to serve as a basis for resource allocations at Princeton (Herring and others, 1979): (1) faculty and program quality, (2) number and quality of graduate students, (3) future of the field and national needs, (4) national program contribution, (5) comparative advantage or unique resources, (6) interaction and impact on other graduate programs, (7) interaction and impact on the undergraduate program, and (8) cost lines.

More recently, in the 1990s, Columbia University discovered that it must make strategic choices among its academic programs and activities if it is to survive as a major research university. In this process it made extremely difficult decisions to close two departments, linguistics and geography, and to close the School of Library Service. In the contentious debate over these decisions, Columbia articulated informal criteria for choice, which enabled the academic community to see the need to develop a more systematic framework for future strategic decisions. Under a joint faculty-administration effort, the following criteria were identified as a basis for choosing among "competing goods" (Cole, 1994): (1) centrality of the field to the university's mission and goals; (2) current state of the field, discipline, or specialty; (3) current academic excellence of the field at the university (whether its organizational shape be department, school, institute, or center); (4) projected vitality of the field over the next several decades; (5) relevance and contribution of the field to the undergraduate curriculum and to the training of graduate and professional students; (6) contribution to other fields, disciplines, and schools at the university; (7) additional investment required to improve significantly the quality of the department, school, or organizational structure; (8) sense in which the field meets important social needs; and (9) reversibility of the required commitment, such that the investment can be terminated or redirected if it yields less advancement of knowledge than anticipated.

Reviewing the initiation of planning processes at these five universities, it is clear that the definition of criteria to guide strategic choice making was an early and essential contributor to the successful efforts. These academic communities thereby collectively reestablished normative bonds that they could call upon in subsequent difficult choices. While the verbal expression of these criteria obviously reflected the specific traditions and language of each institution, there is a remarkable convergence among both public and private universities on the criteria perceived as essential for adaptation to the new postsecondary environment. Public universities, however, are more apt to include some regional or public-service component to their stated criteria, such as demand in the local region or uniqueness of the program in the state, while the leading private universities rely on more universalistic criteria, such as academic importance, national program contribution, and funding potential reflecting the national and international competition for financial resources, faculty members, and students.

Table 9.2 summarizes the generic criteria identified for strategic choice making at Michigan, Minnesota, Columbia, Princeton, and Stanford. These dimensions represent universal social values underlying the stated criteria: (1) the *quality* of the program or activity; (2) the *centrality* of the program or activity, that is, whether it is an essential condition of the enterprise; (3) the *demand* for the program or activity, on the part of students, other programs, and the larger society; (4) the *cost-effectiveness* or relative efficiency of the program or activity; and (5) the *comparative advantage* of the program or activity, that is, the extent to which it is a unique offering. The consistency of these basic values among the five institutions suggests that they could serve as the beginning for identification and clarification of strategic choice making criteria at any college university (Dill, 1994; Benjamin and

TABLE 9.2. STRATEGIC CHOICE CRITERIA AT SELECTED PUBLIC AND PRIVATE UNIVERSITIES.

Criterion	Michigan	Minnesota	Columbia	Princeton	Stanford
Quality	yes	yes	yes	yes	yes
Centrality	yes	no	yes	yes	yes
Demand	yes	yes	yes	yes	yes
Cost-effectiveness	yes	yes	yes	yes	yes
Comparative advantage	yes	yes	no	yes	no

others, 1993). Obviously, however, and consistent with the experience of these institutions, the means of expressing these criteria and the process for developing them must be sensitive to the culture and traditions of a particular institution.

Conclusion

College and university missions, when expressed as statements of institutional aspiration with naïve criteria, have proven to be of little worth in helping institutions cope with the competitive pressures of the new postsecondary environment. However, when mission is conceived as a set of strategic decisions governing the relationship of a college or university to its environment, and as a consensually developed set of strategic criteria grounded in the culture and traditions of a particular institution, then mission is central to the implementation of a successful planning and resource allocation process. Mission in this sense addresses the means by which a college or university defines the niche in which it will choose to compete and the social values by which it will shape its scale, scope, and core competencies.

Further Reading

Readers seeking further information on college and university missions should consult the following: Davies (1986) for an informative discussion of the reasons why institutional missions have generally been ineffective, particularly in the public sector; Bryson's (1995) *Guide* for discussion of the relationship between missions and strategic planning; Ewell (1994) and Romer (1995) for valuable discussions on state actions to shape institutional mission and performance in the public sector; Leslie and Fretwell (1996) for numerous informative case studies of mission definition among colleges and universities; Shirley's (1983) outline of the strategic decisions that should form the core of any mission statement; definition by Prahalad and Hamel (1990) of the concept of core competencies in the business sector; and Benjamin and others (1993) and Shirley and Volkwein (1978) for greater detail on the application of strategic criteria in the planning process.

References

Benjamin, R., and others. *The Redesign of Governance in Higher Education.* Santa Monica, Calif.: Rand, 1993.

Braybrooke, D., and Lindblom, C. E. *A Strategy of Decision.* New York: Free Press, 1963.

Brinkman P. T., and Leslie, L. L. "Economies of Scale in Higher Education: Sixty Years of Research." *The Review of Higher Education,* 1986, *10*(1), 1–28.

Brint, S., and Karabel, J. *The Diverted Dream.* New York: Oxford University Press, 1989.

Bryson, J. M. *Strategic Planning for Public and Nonprofit Organizations: A Guide to Strengthening and Sustaining Organizational Achievement.* (Rev. ed.) San Francisco: Jossey-Bass, 1995.

Carnegie Foundation for the Advancement of Teaching. *A Classification of Institutions of Higher Education.* Princeton: Carnegie Foundation for the Advancement of Teaching, 1994.

Chaffee, E. E. "The Role of Rationality in University Budgeting." *Research in Higher Education,* 1983, *19*(4), 387–406.

Chait, R. "Mission Madness Strikes Our Colleges." *Chronicle of Higher Education,* 1979, *18*(36), 36.

Clark, B. R. "Complexity and Differentiation: The Deepening Problem of University Integration." In D. D. Dill and B. Sporn (eds.), *Emerging Patterns of Social Demand and University Reform: Through a Glass Darkly.* New York: Pergamon Press, 1995.

Cohn, E., Rhine, S. L. W., and Santos, M. C. "Institutions of Higher Education as Multi-Product Firms: Economies of Scale and Scope." *The Review of Economics and Statistics,* 1989, *71*(2), 284–290.

Cole, J. R. "Balancing Acts: Dilemmas of Choice Facing Research Universities." In J. R. Cole, E. G. Barber, and S. R. Graubard (eds.), *The Research University in a Time of Discontent.* Baltimore: Johns Hopkins University Press, 1994.

Davies, G. K. "The Importance of Being General: Philosophy, Politics, and Institutional Mission Statements." In *Higher Education: Handbook of Theory and Research.* Vol. 2. New York: Agathon Press, 1986.

de Groot, H., McMahon, W. W., and Volkwein, J. F. "The Cost Structure of American Research Universities." *The Review of Economics and Statistics,* 1991, *73*(3), 424–431.

Dill, D. D. "Rethinking the Planning Process." *Planning for Higher Education,* 1994, *22*(2), 8–13.

Ewell, P. T. "Institutional Characteristics and Faculty/Administrator Perceptions of Outcomes." *Research in Higher Education,* 1989, *30*(2), 113–136.

Ewell, P. T. "Developing Statewide Performance Indicators for Higher Education: Policy Themes and Variations." In S. R. Ruppert (ed.), *Charting Higher Education Accountability: A Sourcebook on State-Level Performance Indicators.* Denver: Education Commission of the States, 1994.

Fjortoft, N., and Smart, J. C. "Enhancing Organizational Effectiveness: The Importance of Culture Type and Mission Agreement." *Higher Education,* 1994, *27*(4), 429–447.

Herring, C. P., and others. *Budgeting and Resource Allocation at Princeton University: Report of a Demonstration Project Supported by the Ford Foundation.* Vol. 2. Princeton: Princeton University Press, 1979.

Heydinger, R. B. *Using Program Priorities to Make Retrenchment Decisions: The Case of the University of Minnesota.* Atlanta: Southern Regional Education Board, 1982.

Keohane, N. O. "The Mission of the Research University." In J. R. Cole, E. G. Barber, and S. R. Graubard (eds.), *The Research University in a Time of Discontent.* Baltimore: Johns Hopkins University Press, 1994.

Kerr, C., and Gade, M. *The Guardians: Boards of Trustees of American Colleges and Universities: What They Do and How Well They Do It.* Washington, D.C.: Association of Governing Boards of Colleges and Universities, 1989.

Lang, D. W., and Lopers-Sweetman, R. "The Role of Statements of Institutional Purpose." *Research in Higher Education,* 1991, *32*(6), 599–624.

Leslie, D. W., and Fretwell, E. K. *Wise Moves in Hard Times: Creating and Managing Resilient Colleges and Universities.* San Francisco: Jossey-Bass, 1996.

Lewis, D. R., and Kallsen, L. A. "Multiattribute Evaluations: An Aid in Reallocation Decisions in Higher Education." *The Review of Higher Education,* 1995, *18*(4), 437–466.

Martin, W. B. "Mission: A Statement of Identity and Direction." In J. S. Green and A. Levine (eds.), *Opportunity in Adversity: How Colleges Can Succeed in Hard Times.* San Francisco: Jossey-Bass, 1985.

Massy, W. F. "Measuring Performance: How Colleges and Universities Can Set Meaningful Goals and Be Accountable." In J. W. Meyerson and W. F. Massy (eds.), *Measuring Institutional Performance in Higher Education.* Princeton: Peterson's, 1994.

McGuinness, Jr., A. C., Epper, R. M., and Arredondo, S. *State Postsecondary Education Structures Handbook.* Denver: Education Commission of the States, 1994.

Newsom W., and Hayes, C. R. "Are Mission Statements Worthwhile?" *Planning for Higher Education,* 1990, *19*(2), 28–30.

Parker, B. "Agreement of Mission and Institutional Responses to Decline." *Research in Higher Education,* 1986, *25*(2), 164–181.

Prahalad C. K., and Hamel, G. "The Core Competencies of the Corporation." *Harvard Business Review,* 1990, *68*(3), 79–91.

Rhodes, E. L., and Southwick, Jr., L. "Determinants of Efficiency in Public and Private Universities." Paper presented at the SPEA-EUR/RUL Conference, Rotterdam-Leiden, The Netherlands, June 1987.

Romer, R. *Making Quality Count in Undergraduate Education.* Denver: Education Commission of the States, 1995.

Shirley, R. C. "Identifying the Levels of Strategy for a College or University." *Long Range Planning,* 1983, *16*(3), 92–98.

Shirley, R. C. *Strategic and Operational Reform in Public Higher Education: A Mandate for Change.* AGB Occasional Paper no. 21. Washington, D.C.: Association of Governing Boards of Colleges and Universities, 1994.

Shirley, R. C., and Volkwein, J. F. "Establishing Academic Program Priorities." *Journal of Higher Education,* 1978, *49*(5), 472–489.

Starr, S. F. "A President's Message to Planners." *Planning for Higher Education,* 1993, *22*(1), 16–22.

University of Michigan. *Regents Meeting of October.* Ann Arbor: University of Michigan, 1979.

CHAPTER TEN

ENHANCING THE LEADERSHIP FACTOR IN PLANNING

Anna Neumann and R. Sam Larson

As several chapters in this volume show, institutions of higher education are far more likely to be influenced by a variety of national and global changes than they have been in the past, and institutional administrators and planners need to be prepared to respond. More importantly, administrators and planners are expected to converse with policy makers and others outside the higher education enterprise in shaping social issues that extend far beyond the campus. They have the opportunity to participate in the construction of societywide understanding of crucial issues facing this nation and the world—issues not specifically about higher education but to which higher educators may be asked to speak.

Thus, in the future top-level college and university administrators may need to be more significant social actors than they have been in the past. The ability to work externally is important for future leaders in higher education, but a crucial caveat follows: while assuming responsibilities externally, college and university administrators and planners remain the *official leaders of the internal enterprise*. They need to be active and creative members of their external environment— thereby shaping it—while remaining at the center of institutional life. Though administrators and planners must continue to look and act in outward directions, their leadership responsibilities draw them inward, for example as they strive to connect the work of faculty within their institutions to significant dynamics outside. Effective leadership, now and in the future, cannot be merely activity on the outside, just as it cannot be merely activity on the inside; good leadership is likely to be more integrated—in fact, blurring traditional internal and external divisions (Neumann and Bensimon, 1990). One of the challenges of higher education administration and planning in the future will be how to make this complex internal-external leadership work—how to think, talk, and act within institutions so as to accomplish important tasks outside. Just as important will be how to think, talk, and act outside institutions so as to maintain intellectual and cultural meaning within.

College and university administrators and planners, as social actors, need to be adept at interacting with other high-placed social actors, including heads of state, political figures, and directors of corporations and government agencies. But this external activity cannot be the be-all and end-all of college and university leadership, for top-level administrators and planners themselves are rarely the primary academic contributors to substantive social and economic change. Rather, the primary academic contributors to such change are the members of the enterprises they lead, in particular the faculties that remain at the core of those institutions. Thus, as future college and university administrators become increasingly involved in their external environments, they will need to become increasingly involved in their internal environments, seeking substantive expertise that addresses external contingencies—but shapes them as well.

This chapter presents several new or "revised" leadership concepts in relation to the internal life of colleges and universities engaged in a rapidly changing external world. It also considers the implications of these revisions for institutional planning. With this dual purpose in mind, we define *leadership* as the creation of ways of knowing and thinking about problems, issues, questions, concerns, places, and people—in brief, about campus reality itself. But leadership also refers to the creation of ways of knowing and thinking about issues that exceed the bounds of campus life, for example, aspects of local, national, and international environments to which campus members may relate professionally. Moreover, this definition of leadership applies as much to how campus insiders (faculty, students, staff) understand diverse internal and external realities as it does to how outsiders (trustees, alumni, legislators, and community members) understand them.

This definition of leadership implies that people both inside and outside institutions are able to know any aspect of campus and noncampus life in multiple ways. Typically, we commit ourselves to a few "comfortable" ways of knowing, perhaps just one (Neumann, 1995a). Leaders, however, induce people to expand narrow perspectives on the world. They themselves strive to engage in a form of learning that amounts to continual rethinking, and they encourage the same in others (Smircich and Morgan, 1982; Morgan, 1986). In addition, leaders, as we view them, take few aspects of institutional life for granted, no matter how established and accepted; they inspire thinking that exceeds current or established views (Smircich and Morgan, 1982). Our view of leadership resonates with an image of good teaching: a leader as a teacher striving to understand what and how others know, and encouraging them to experiment with alternative ways of knowing (Cohen and Barnes, 1993; Neumann, 1995b). We view planning as encouraging and joining in this approach to leadership. We also view planning as the creating of structures and opportunities that enhance the efforts of people both within and outside institutions to know and learn about their worlds (institutional and otherwise) in ways that exceed established knowledge.

In the following sections, we discuss traditional leadership and planning concepts that require rethinking, in light of dramatic external and (concomitantly) internal changes in higher education: the open-systems view of organization, hierarchy as a mode of organizing, and the linearity of administrative logic.

Rethinking the "Open Systems View"

Colleges and universities have long been construed as open systems, as loosely unified collectivities largely separated from their external environments. However, a variety of external agents may enter the open system (Kast and Rosenzweig, 1985; Katz and Kahn, 1978; Scott, 1992). Desirable entrants include students, state revenues, monetary contributions, new faculty, and other "human resources," and diverse forms of public support. Less desirable entrants include state and federal regulations, public demands and expectations, and accountability measures. From the perspective of the open system, the college or university is dependent upon and interactive with the external environment (the economy, culture, society generally), which contains other organizations such as resource suppliers, regulators, competitors, and peers (Kast and Rosenzweig, 1985).

Over the years, college and university leaders have consistently been admonished to be more "open" in the spirit of the open system, that is, more attentive and responsive to the external world. They have been asked to revise their institutions' missions in light of external needs. They have been urged to reform their institutions to be of greater service to industry, community, state populations, and society in general. But because institutional leaders work with people who think and learn, they must also do something else: they must come to grips with *the more personal, internally driven values and aspirations that lie within their institutions and within the lives of the people in them,* even when these do not connect well with environmental imperatives. Thus, contemporary leaders are faced with the challenge of how to cultivate in-house conversations that exceed and challenge the open-systems idea *at the same time* that they cultivate other conversations aligning with the open-systems view. It is likely, for example, that faculty, students, and staff may have projects in mind that are intellectually and personally valuable to them but which they cannot easily (or immediately) articulate, develop, or justify in terms of externally directed, open systems. Institutional leaders who do not acknowledge and support internal sources of value and meaning such as these create as great a threat to their institution's survival—that is, to its spiritual and intellectual survival—as do leaders who fail to acknowledge the values and meanings of outsiders who provide the "resources" that the open-system requires so as to thrive in more material ways.

In a revised view of organization and leadership, open-systems discourse, oriented outwardly and adaptively and often with service to others in mind, exists side by side with another discourse. This second discourse looks inward to personal values and individual meanings in addition to the more externally oriented open-systems considerations. In this paradoxical imagery of organization, leaders purposefully foster opportunities for both discourses to grow together. Leaders crossing these dual conversational tracks—one directed out, the other in—listen with care to both, striving to learn from both.

Considerations for Institutional Planning

How might planning facilitate the rethinking and operation of a college or university that responds to external forces (as the open system does) at the same time that it responds to the personal values and meanings of those in the institution? This is a challenging question when (as often happens) the two aims are not compatible—and in particular when they clash. What happens, for example, when external groups call for the reduction or elimination of academic programs (in the spirit of the open system) while internal groups voice their disapproval for such efforts (in the spirit of living up to personal and institutional values)? What happens when market forces and academic commitments collide? In the language of leadership, a president, dean, or planner seeking to learn from the strengths of two or more divergent discourses might *purposefully* foster both.

In such cases, it is important to consider that the academic world, as currently constructed, requires communities of divergent discourse, even when such divergence leads to open disagreement and conflict. What should be avoided in planning and related administrative efforts is a stance favoring a single-minded view that stifles the disciplined growth of certain lines of thought in favor of others (Bensimon and Neumann, 1993). Some colleges have, in the past, favored more internally oriented views, wishing to remain true to their values even at the risk of losing vital material resources. Others—a growing number now—have favored more externally oriented views, attending to market demands at the expense of personal and institutional values. Though these points of view may appear radically different from each other, neither on its own ensures institutional survival (Chaffee, 1985). Both views matter, even when they conflict with each other. Planners seeking to encourage the growth of both views (and to learn from them) might do well not to force difficult connections until the time seems ripe for thoughtful conversation between people with different views. Until then, a planner might wish to view divergent organizational discourses as special locales within which she, perhaps like an attentive stranger, may learn about the thinking, knowing, and learning of the institution's people, diverse as they may be.

However, simple divisions, as between people whose thinking is inwardly directed and others whose thinking is more outwardly directed, are illusory. For example, individuals subscribing to an internally oriented, academic community (as opposed to representing one that is more externally market-oriented) will themselves be divided deeply about the nature of their scholarly commitments. Individuals subscribing to a more externally oriented view will also differ in what this means and how to proceed in the development of an external orientation (Martin, 1992). Given this reality of institutional life and faculty cultures, leaders and planners may need to support and foster the growth of multiple academic subcommunities, that is, to encourage a range of diverse discourses constructed in thoughtful and disciplined ways within the larger community of scholars. Leaders and planners seeking to learn from diverse subcommunities such as these need first to support the development of these subcommunities, and second to spend time in them, learning what they have to offer, what meanings their members construct in the name of learning, scholarship, and academic organization (Tierney, 1993).

Rethinking Hierarchy

Among the most steadfast ideas in higher education is hierarchy: stratification (by responsibility, authority, ability, seniority, etc.) of the persons working in colleges and universities (Bensimon and Neumann, 1993). Hierarchy shows itself in the administrative structuring of college and university life and in the professional configuration of faculties (see Bensimon, Neumann, and Birnbaum, 1989, for a review). In administration, organizational charts—explicit or assumed—represent a president and vice presidents, or a chancellor and vice chancellors, holding power and authority over deans who in turn oversee department chairs who in their turn are presented as coordinating departments. This represents the bureaucratic hierarchy of the institution. Among the faculty, stratification occurs through professional rank, seniority (that is, time in institution or profession), graduate or undergraduate teaching assignments, research or teaching designations, and a variety of other sorting schemes. This represents the professional hierarchy of the institution. Every institution has its unique hierarchical configurations, some quite obvious and others more subtle (for additional perspectives, see Etzioni, 1964).

What do conceptions of hierarchy imply for leadership? Whether bureaucratic or professional, they typically view leadership as reflecting the power, abilities, and contributions of people in *upper-level strata* (Bensimon, Neumann, and Birnbaum, 1989). Thus, in considering the relationship between a president and vice presidents, hierarchy typically attributes leadership to the president. In considering the relationship between senior and junior faculty, hierarchy attributes leadership to professors in senior positions. Recent efforts to revise leadership in higher education show that this traditional intertwining of hierarchy and leadership is problematic (Bensimon and Neumann, 1993). If we define leadership as the act of conceptualizing alternative ways of thinking about our organizations (Smircich and Morgan, 1982), it is conceivable that at least on some occasions professors and instructors (whose daily work is thinking and coming to know) may be better "leaders" than those who are hierarchically above them in administration. Similarly, newcomers to the faculty (for example, junior faculty) may, by virtue of their newness, be able to suggest fresher ways of thinking through problems and challenges than those hierarchically above them. In sum, the understandings of people lower in the hierarchy may be as insightful as the understandings of people at higher levels, and conversations between them might yield even greater insight.

A hard look at hierarchy also indicates the need to think about it broadly. Though intended to provide rational order and stability, hierarchy may, by virtue of its stratifying qualities, engender *political* activity stemming from people's desires to climb ladders of prestige and power. The power plays associated with hierarchy may result in a highly chaotic, if not anarchic, structure (Cohen and March, 1974). Finally, the stratification created by hierarchy separates groups of people at one level from other groups of people at other levels. This creates distances in communication that need to be bridged.

Considerations for Institutional Planning

This revised view of hierarchy in higher education raises interesting and important issues for planners. For one, faculty members may provide leadership to administrators. Professors who remain intellectually active and explore alternative perspectives in their work may turn their creativity, at least briefly, onto institutional challenges. Professors whose work connects them to life beyond the campus may "bring home" diverse perspectives for illuminating local concerns. For example, an academic scientist who advises a large pharmaceutical company about research and development activities may bring particular insights back to his lab and institution, as may a sociologist who collaborates with sociologists at other universities, a political scientist who analyzes federal legislation, or an anthropologist who studies and participates in the efforts of local community groups.

Leadership, especially for planning, need not be limited to senior or accomplished professors. It may come, as well, from new or junior members of the faculty, from secretaries and staff, and from students whose experiences in departments, programs, and institutes can shed light on troublesome situations. This point has been advocated by earlier leadership and planning models that promote participation, but it is all too often overlooked.

Emerging critiques of hierarchy as the conceptual backbone of academic leadership go even further, especially so if we define leadership as the creating of new or different views and understandings of academic realities. Consider the case of faculty who create portions of the external environment to which their own institution's top-level leaders and others are expected to respond. For example, the professor who contributes to a foundation's efforts to rethink its research agenda and formulate its RFPs to which others in the university respond, shapes future university efforts in this area. The professor who advises a national agency that monitors university activities in a particular scientific domain in effect contributes to the protocol for such activities at the institutional level. The professor who serves as an expert witness in a medical, biotechnical, or affirmative-action case sets precedents for how related issues will be treated in the future, with implications for institutional operations. These are professors who, by virtue of their substantive expertise, shape aspects of the external environment to which their institution responds.

This is a point to be kept in mind by administrators and planners with responsibilities for responding to changes "out there," for it suggests that *administrators' own leadership may be framed by the very individuals they seek to lead within their institutions.* A related point is that traditional theory places administrators and planners at the cognitive center of organizational activity (Katz and Kahn, 1978). The "mindwork" of organizations—for example, planning and environmental scanning—is portrayed as occurring in administration (Bensimon and Neumann, 1993). An alternative perspective suggests that much organizationally related mindwork may be occurring among the faculty, a point that administrators may wish to consider.

It is possible, then, to envision certain individuals working at "lower" levels of the institutional hierarchy as leaders, and those who work at "higher" levels as thoughtful followers—or better yet, as "learners" of what the alternative leaders have to offer. Leadership can emanate from below as well as from above. Planners seeking to connect meaningfully to leadership—as advisors or as leaders—might do well to converse as intently with people who do *not* possess the formal role responsibilities or power of institutional leaders as with those who do.

Rethinking Linearity

The image of leadership that has dominated higher education administration has traditionally been rational and linear (Bensimon, Neumann, and Birnbaum, 1989; Chaffee, 1983, 1985). For example, traditional leadership models portray thinking as preceding action; the implication is that acting without advance thinking—that is, without advance planning—is senseless if not wasteful (Bolman and Deal, 1991; Scott, 1992). What the linear image leaves out is a view of leaders thinking and learning not only before they act but *while* they act (Schön, 1983). Linearity in the classic sense overlooks the possibility that action may lead to thoughts *and plans* that emerge during the very course of action or afterward in reflection (Birnbaum, 1988). This insight has reshaped many traditional leadership notions in higher education. It suggests, for example, that leaders' "visions" for their institutions may emerge *in the very course* of institutional events and activities, in fact, growing from them rather than directing them linearly.

Emerging theory also shows that linear approaches to leadership that situate thought before action miss opportunities for learning in yet another way. A president who walks into an institution committed to a new idea (or a new vision) and who hopes to use that idea to direct institutional activity may neglect ideas (and visions) that *reside already* in current activity. To induce meaningful change, this president should try to learn and absorb existent ideas and encourage their reshaping from inside, as an "insider" (Bensimon, 1990). Another way to say this is that the president has to learn the "operative plan" (whether articulated or not) before initiating conversations about how that plan might be altered. And it is conceivable that once inside, the president will come to believe that certain aspects of the operative plan simply should not or cannot change (see Neumann, 1995a).

But of what use is this kind of leadership? If leadership only follows current organizational activity, how will change ever occur? Isn't a bold new vision required for real change? Recent developments in leadership theory suggest several responses to these questions. First, in and of themselves leaders cannot redirect institutions because institutions are cultures. Cultures are not easily changed since this requires changes in what people know and how they learn about their organizational worlds. Institutions as cultures may even resist directive, bureaucratic change (Birnbaum 1988; Cohen and March, 1974; Martin, 1992). Second, in considering change, leaders must join their institutions and "work them" from inside—that is, as cultural insiders—before they can begin to think about possible redirection (Bensimon 1990). And third, organizational change entails individuals' learning (and relearning) as opposed to the redrawing of organizational charts or the redirecting of institutional activity from the outside in (Neumann, 1995a,

1995b). Meaningful institutional change is likely to take both thought and time, for it involves changes in what people know and how they know it. That is, it involves deep-level learning.

Considerations for Institutional Planning

The linearity associated with traditional conceptions of leadership parallels the linearity that has traditionally driven college and university administrative processes, including planning (Chaffee, 1983). Campus plans (whether called strategic, long-range, or something else) typically consist of a vision articulated by a president or chancellor, followed by goals and objectives designed to achieve the vision. Actions are expected to flow from the goals and objectives that frame them. Thus planning, in the classic sense, is linear by virtue of its sequencing of thought and action. More developed planning models offset the constraining features of this linearity by including feedback loops whereby the consequences of actions inform and alter preset goals and objectives (see discussions by Keller, 1983; Norris and Poulton, 1991; Peterson, 1980).

However, such feedback loops are often limited conceptually and practically. Conceptually, feedback helps us assess whether we did what we intended to do. If feedback indicates that we did not meet our goal, then we try again, or we alter the goal and related objectives. All too often, however, we do not question the assumptions and understandings on which our plans are based; we assume them to be "given." Thus, though our actions, evaluated upon completion, may lead us to new and revised plans, they rarely lead us to reconsider how we understand our campus and our world. But in addition to this conceptual problem, feedback loops may be flawed in a more practical sense. For example, planners may neglect to use feedback mechanisms even when these are readily available. Or if they do use them, they may fail to seek out negative feedback (for example, disagreement or failure), giving attention instead to those actions that support leaders' or planners' own preferences or that represent "good news" (Birnbaum, 1988).

A revised view presents planning as a process of institutionwide conversation and interpretation. In this imagery, an organic, naturally emerging institutional conversation replaces a static, linearly deduced institutional plan. Rather than actions flowing smoothly from preset vision and goals (the linear view), vision emerges inductively in bits and pieces, from actions examined closely in conversations that flow in fits and starts, often anything but smoothly. The image of the linearity of an initial abstract plan converted into concrete and systematic action is replaced by an alternative image: people in conversation with each other about what they are doing or what they have done, and learning in the very moments of talking together, or in reflection after action. In the traditional imagery of planning, thought precedes action, and there is relatively little talk. A planner guides this process of conversion from thought to action, from abstraction to concrete accomplishment, from the plan of the past to the action of the future. In the revised image of planning as conversation, action begins, and talk and thought emerge as action continues. A planner strives to convene the conversation and to keep it alive, helping to bridge talk and thought, action and reflection, occurring in the present moment even though about the past and with hopes for the future.

In this view, the institutional planner assumes the role of interpreter, first for the president about campus members' ways of life and the concerns of external stakeholders, and second for a variety of campus members about the president's wishes and intentions, questions and puzzlements, concerns and hopes. Having a planner who acts as interpreter may be particularly important to a new president just joining her or his institution and seeking to understand established campus cultures (Bensimon, 1990). But the planner-as-interpreter is just as important to long-time faculty who seek to understand the entering president as an important new member of the campus community (Neumann, 1995a). The planner-as-interpreter might point out to a new president those features of the cultural landscape that this president may not yet be able to see. For example, if a particular community values a certain type of teaching (for example, a school that uses case-based teaching, community service, or work-study) or a certain form of communication (speaking personally rather than writing formal memos), the president needs to know this and to frame her actions with this in mind. But the planner must also be prepared to act in reverse: to explain to college members what the president hopes for, what she sees and cannot (yet) see, or what she questions. This is an image of the planner helping members of the college community understand their leadership, and at the same time helping people in leadership positions understand how life in their college flows and why. It is from such understanding that vision may emerge.

Conclusion

In this chapter we have considered recent revisions of several core ideas about leadership in higher education, and we have explored the implications for institutional planning. These new images of leadership and planning portray leaders and planners as actively involved in the co-creation of meaning with insiders and outsiders relative to issues both inside and outside the institution (Bensimon and Neumann, 1993; Peterson, 1985). They also portray colleges and universities as human settings within which individuals think, know, and learn alone and together. The job of leaders and planners is to facilitate such "mindwork" *throughout* the institution.

What are the implications of this revised conception for how university planners work? And how might we move beyond current habits and constructions to the revised view that we present? We can begin by thinking of the planner as a conduit for ongoing conversations between the president and other institutional members, and importantly among institutional members themselves, especially those not in formal leadership positions. A planner may maintain such dialogues through formal means, for example, by sharing planning documents and planning questions with a variety of campus members (Dill, 1993–94) and by carefully attending to how people respond to what they read and hear about planning. Similar opportunities may be generated by convening focus groups, lunchtime conversations, or task forces and advisory boards, or simply by the planner being available for informal talks.

What is important in such forums is that conversation, in the best sense of the term, be maintained—that all participants have opportunities to talk, that people try genuinely to understand what others are thinking and what they have to say, that all try to listen, that all be open to question and exploration. But the idea of "conversation" must also permeate space and time, for conversation refers to far more than typical meetings, assemblies, or simply hallway talk. Planners might see themselves as fostering conversations among institutional actors who never see each other and who may not know each other, by bringing the ideas of some to others, and by relaying questions and thoughts across the boundaries of campus time and space. The best and most helpful "conversations" may occur as planners make the thoughts of some people available to the thinking—in which term we include questioning and extension—of others and share the results of such thinking with all. In the future, leaders and planners may rely more heavily on conversation that seeks out thought in action and that encourages learning.

A major challenge, then, for leaders and planners in coming decades is likely to be how to enhance, support, and sustain this kind of learning among people in the university and beyond it, and how to avoid disruptive intrusions on such learning. Leadership and planning, viewed as key internal institutional processes concerned with people's learning, have significant power to shape the effects of college on the world beyond college.

Further Reading

Readers interested in further consideration of relationships between leadership and planning may wish to see Chaffee (1985) and Bensimon and Neumann (1995a) on conceptions of planning and strategic management; Bensimon and Neumann (1993) and Bensimon, Neumann, and Birnbaum (1989) on administrative and faculty leadership; and Birnbaum (1988) on collegiate organization.

References

Bensimon, E. M. "The New President and Understanding the Campus as a Culture." In W. G. Tierney (ed.), *Assessing Academic Climates and Cultures.* New Directions for Institutional Research, no. 68. San Francisco: Jossey-Bass, 1990.

Bensimon, E. M., and Neumann, A. *Redesigning Collegiate Leadership: Teams and Teamwork in Higher Education.* Baltimore: Johns Hopkins University Press, 1993.

Bensimon, E. M., Neumann, A., and Birnbaum, R. *Making Sense of Administrative Leadership: The "L" Word in Higher Education.* ASHE-ERIC Higher Education Report No. 1. Washington, D.C.: School of Education and Human Development, George Washington University, 1989.

Birnbaum, R. *How Colleges Work: The Cybernetics of Academic Organization and Leadership.* San Francisco: Jossey-Bass, 1988.

Bolman, L. G., and Deal, T. E. *Reframing Organizations: Artistry, Choice, and Leadership.* San Francisco: Jossey-Bass, 1991.

Chaffee, E. E. "The Role of Rationality in University Budgeting." *Research in Higher Education,* 1983, *19*(4), 387–406.

Chaffee, E. E. "Three Models of Strategy." *The Academy of Management Review,* 1985, *10*(1), 89–98.

Cohen, D. K., and Barnes, C. A. "Pedagogy and Policy." In D. K. Cohen, M. W. McLaughlin, and J. E. Talbert (eds.), *Teaching for Understanding: Challenges for Policy and Practice.* San Francisco: Jossey-Bass, 1993.

Cohen, M. D., and March, J. G. *Leadership and Ambiguity: The American College Presidency.* New York: McGraw-Hill, 1974.

Dill, D. "Rethinking the Planning Process." *Planning for Higher Education,* Winter 1993–94, *22*, 8–12.

Etzioni, A. *Modern Organizations.* Englewood Cliffs, N.J.: Prentice Hall, 1964.

Kast, F. E., and Rosenzweig, J. E. *Organization and Management: A Systems and Contingency Approach.* (4th ed.) New York: McGraw-Hill, 1985.

Katz, D., and Kahn, R. L. *The Social Psychology of Organizations.* (2nd ed.) New York: Wiley, 1978.

Keller, G. *Academic Strategy: The Management Revolution in American Higher Education.* Baltimore: Johns Hopkins University Press, 1983.

Martin, J. *Cultures in Organizations: Three Perspectives.* New York: Oxford University Press, 1992.

Morgan, G. *Images of Organization.* Newbury Park, Calif.: Sage, 1986.

Neumann, A. "Context, Cognition, and Culture: A Case Analysis of Collegiate Leadership and Cultural Change." *American Educational Research Journal,* Summer 1995a.

Neumann, A. "On the Making of Hard Times and Good Times: The Social Construction of Resource Stress." *Journal of Higher Education,* 1995b, *66*(1), 3–31.

Neumann, A., and Bensimon, E. M. "Constructing the Presidency: College Presidents' Images of Their Leadership Roles: A Comparative Study." *Journal of Higher Education,* 1990, *61*(6), 678–701.

Norris, D. M., and Poulton, N. L. *A Guide for New Planners.* Ann Arbor, Mich.: Society for College and University Planning, 1991.

Peterson, M. W. "Analyzing Alternative Approaches to Planning." In P. Jedamus, M. W. Peterson, and Associates (eds.), *Improving Academic Management.* San Francisco: Jossey-Bass,
1980.

Peterson, M. W. "Emerging Developments in Postsecondary Organization Theory and Research: Fragmentation or Integration." *Educational Researchers,* 1985, *14*(3), 5–12.

Schön, D. A. *The Reflective Practitioner.* New York: Basic Books, 1983.

Scott, W. R. *Organizations: Rational, Natural, and Open Systems.* (3rd ed.) Englewood Cliffs, New
Jersey: Prentice Hall, 1992.

Smircich, L., and Morgan, G. "Leadership: The Management of Meaning." *Journal of Applied Behavioral Science,* 1982, *18*(3), 257–273.

Tierney, W. G. *Building Communities of Differences: Higher Education in the Twenty-First Century.* New
York: Bergin and Garvey, 1993.

CHAPTER ELEVEN

ANALYZING ENVIRONMENTS AND DEVELOPING SCENARIOS FOR UNCERTAIN TIMES

James L. Morrison and Ian Wilson

College and university leaders are being bombarded by tumultuous forces for change as we go into the twenty-first century: virtual classrooms, global communications, global economies, telecourses, distance learning, corporate classrooms, increased competition among social agencies for scarce resources, pressure for institutional mergers, statewide program review, and so on. It is no exaggeration to say that, in total, these forces hold the potential for a radical rethinking of the mission, structure, curriculum, student body, and stakeholder relations of virtually every college and university.

In order to plan effectively in this environment, college and university leaders must be able to anticipate the impact of new developments on their institutions and curricular programs. Efficient contextual planning in uncertain times depends on obtaining accurate and continuous intelligence about changes in the institution's external environment.

Environmental analysis has evolved slowly over the past forty years. Originally, in the 1950s, planning in most organizations was largely a budgetary, internally oriented effort. As the need for greater attention to the external environment became apparent in the 1960s, careful monitoring of current trends was added to the planning schedule. Then, as turbulence and surprises proliferated, monitoring was supplemented by "scanning" in an effort to provide an "early warning system" of trends-yet-to-come. Finally, as the limitations of forecasting became more and more apparent during the 1970s and 1980s, and as organizational leaders saw the need to consider the possibility of alternative futures, we saw the emergence of scenario-based planning.

This chapter describes and illustrates a three-pronged environmental analysis effort to obtain strategic intelligence: scanning, monitoring, and scenarios. Scenarios provide comprehensive, internally consistent, long-term perspectives on the future as a framework for strategic thinking as well as for the scanning and monitoring operations. The terms *scanning* and *monitoring* are often used interchangeably, but they have separate and distinct natures and functions. Scanning is focused mainly on the future (what may happen); monitoring, on the past and present (what has happened or is happening). Scanning is largely unfocused, taking in a 360 degree horizon; monitoring is highly focused. Scanning identifies early warning signals of new trends that might become important; monitoring tracks developments in trends of known importance. The information generated by scanning and monitoring is essential in developing scenarios that provide the context for organizational decision making.

Since implementation of environmental analysis involves the commitment of institutional resources, in this chapter we go into detail describing how you can develop an environmental analysis capacity in your institution. We conclude with a brief discussion of readings that elaborate this topic.

Scanning and Monitoring the External Environment

Conceptually, the external environment can be subdivided into three components: the *market* environment, the *industry* environment, and the *macroenvironment*. The market environment refers to customers (for example, students and potential students, parents of students and of potential students, political leaders, employers and potential employers of students, professional associations of faculty and administrators). This environment is specific to a particular institution. Thus, although the market environments of a community college and a research university within ten miles of each other may overlap, they also differ.

The industry environment comprises all enterprises associated with higher education. At this level, trends such as the number of institutions that require entering students to own computers or the percentage of faculty members using multimedia materials in their classes affect all institutions, although the effect of these factors varies depending upon the type of institution (research or comprehensive, two- or four-year).

The macroenvironment focuses on changes in the social, technological, economic, environmental, and political (STEEP) sectors that could affect colleges and universities directly or indirectly. These sectors are interrelated. Changes in one sector at any level (local, national, global) may lead to changes in another. A war in the Middle East may cause the price of oil to increase, thus stimulating a recession, which in turn results in budget cuts. Technological developments in California that enable the conversion of wind power to low-cost energy may be introduced worldwide, thereby reducing the costs of fossil fuel energy, with concomitant economic ramifications. Thus developments in the macroenvironment can affect developments in the market and industrial environments. This point underscores the necessity of scanning the macroenvironment as well as the market and industrial environments if we want to pick up the early signals of change that may affect our institutions.

Environmental Scanning

The use of environmental scanning as a tool for contextual planning in higher education has been described by Morrison (1985, 1987, 1992), illustrated by survey reports of Friedel, Coker, and Blong (1991) and Pritchett (1990), and analyzed by Hearn and Heydinger (1985) and Hearn, Clugston, and Heydinger (1993).

The purpose of environmental scanning is to serve as an early warning system by alerting institutional leaders to potentially significant external developments in their early stages. The earlier the warning, the more lead time we have to plan for the implications of these changes. Consequently, the scope of environmental scanning is broad, a full-circle sweep to pick up any signal of change in the external environment.

Environmental Monitoring

Monitoring follows scanning. Every possible change or potential shift in the macroenvironment cannot be given equal attention. We select items by defining topics or ideas that are incorporated in "the interesting future—the period in which major policy options adopted now could probably have significant effect" (Renfro and Morrison, 1983, p. 5). We collect data on the critical trends and potential events in the interesting future so that changes in their status can be detected.

The purpose of monitoring is to ascertain the past and possible future directions of these trends, or to enable us to estimate the strength of indicators of potential events. Scanning provides us with critical trends and potential events. Monitoring entails using trend descriptors or potential event indicators as key words in a systematic search to obtain information about them. Thus, when monitoring, we seek information containing forecasts and speculations about the implications of trends and events identified in scanning for colleges and universities.

Establishing an Environmental Scanning/Monitoring Process

Establishing a continuous scanning/monitoring system to create strategic intelligence requires effort and resources. Simpson, McGinty, and Morrison (1990), in describing how the University of Georgia's Center for Continuing Education established their system, note that at least a half-time professional with support staff was necessary for that organization. The professional staff person is responsible for identifying information resources, maintaining the scanning files (electronic and paper copy), training scanners and abstractors, and maintaining the structure to process information into strategic intelligence for the institution. This section provides guidelines on what these tasks require.

Identifying Information Resources. The important criteria for information selection are diversity and assurance that all dimensions of each STEEP sector are covered. Information can be obtained from a variety of sources: newspapers, magazines, journals, TV and radio programs, conferences, and from knowledgeable individuals in personal information networks.

Microenvironmental Scanning Resources. In order to ensure that we are adequately scanning the macroenvironment, we must identify specific information resources for each STEEP category, locally through globally. Although Morrison (1992) has compiled a comprehensive list of information sources organized by category for the macroenvironment, the following scanning publications are particularly useful when initiating a scanning system.

The Wilkinson Group publishes a monthly scanning newsletter, called *Happenings,* for nonprofit organizations (Wilkinson Group, 2319 Sierra Highlands Drive, Reno, NV 89523 [702–747–5995]). The World Future Society (7910 Woodmont Avenue, Suite 450, Bethesda, MD 20814 [301–656–8274]) publishes *Future Survey,* a monthly abstract of books, articles, and reports containing forecasts, trends, and ideas about the future. The Global Network publishes *John Naisbitt's Trend Letter* (1101 30th St., NW, Suite 130, Washington, DC 20007 [202–337–5960]). The *Kiplinger Washington Letter* office is at 1729 H St., NW, Washington, DC 20006 (202–887–6400). Jossey-Bass publishes *On the Horizon,* which focuses exclusively on education (kindergarten through postgraduate, including continuing education). In addition, the *Horizon Home Page* (URL address: http://sunsite.unc.edu/horizon) contains (1) a futures-planning database of articles on trends and events submitted for consideration in the print publication; (2) the archive of *Horizon List,* an Internet listserv on which these articles are distributed and discussed; and (3) a link to a variety of information databases in all of the STEEP sectors, called *The Education On-Ramp.* Exhibit 11.1 contains the addresses of these Web-accessible sources.

Perhaps one of the most useful information resources is your own network of friends and colleagues within the institution and in the profession. You can phone a colleague at another institution and get information quickly. Or you can post your question in two Internet newsletters, published by the Association for Institutional Research (AIR) and the Society for College and University Planning. (To receive AIR's electronic newsletter, contact air@mailer.fsu.edu; for SCUP, contact scup_office@um.cc.umich.)

Using Electronic Databases. There are a number of electronic databases that contain up-to-date descriptions of articles (by title, and many times by abstract) available on a subscription basis. *ABI Inform, ERIC, PAIS, Dialogue,* and *BRS* contain hundreds of databases specializing in all areas. Undoubtedly, your library already subscribes to these databases and database services. These resources are amenable to monitoring (that is, to retrieving information about critical trends and potential events that you and the planning team have identified earlier in the scanning process). In addition, there are a number of listservs on the Internet that contain discussions about potential events and emerging trends (see Exhibit 11.2).

Maintaining the Scanning Files. Scanning files are usually both electronic and hard copy. It is faster and easier to maintain files electronically, which are accessible twenty-four hours a day across campus through local networking systems. Moreover, an electronic system allows scanners and abstractors to enter their information into the system directly, although it is usually a good idea for the person in charge of the system to exercise responsibility for formatting and editing.

We encourage the practice of backing up electronic files with hard copy of information sources (e.g., newspaper articles) as well as abstracts of these sources. Hard-copy files can be maintained in the office of the professional staff person responsible for the scanning/monitoring system, or even in the library in a vertical file under the care of a professional information scientist.

Training Scanners and Abstractors. It is important to recruit and train faculty members, key administrators, and members of the board of trustees as well as planning committee members to serve as scanners and abstracters. Heterogeneity of backgrounds, experience, and perspectives guards against parochial viewpoints and provides assurance that the scanning/monitoring system includes people who read a variety of materials across the STEEP sectors.

An effective way to recruit scanners is to hold a one-day workshop focused on potential developments in the external environment that can affect the future of the

EXHIBIT 11.1. WEB ACCESSIBLE INFORMATION
SOURCES IN THE STEEP SECTORS.

Social Sector

Digest of Education Statistics <http://www.ed.gov/NCES/pubs/D95>

- Change <http://www.educ.kent.edu/CHANGE>
- Distance Education Clearinghouse <http://www.uwex.edu/disted/home.html>
- EDUCOM <http://educom.edu/>
- HEPROC: Higher Education Resources <http://rrpubs.com/heproc>
- Institute of Higher Education <http://nervm.nerdc.ufl.edu/the2000>
- League for Innovation in the Community College <http://www.league.org/>
- Technology and Higher Education Statistics, Surveys, and Reports <http://www.iat.unc.edu/library/liblinks/ed-stats.html>
- Times Higher Education Supplement <http://www.timeshigher.newsint.co.uk>

Technology Sector

- CAUSE, the Association for Managing and Using Information Resources in Higher Education <http://www.colorado.edu/>
- EdTech <http://h-net.msu.edu/~edweb>
- The Future of Networking Technologies for Learning <http://www.ed.gov/Technology/Futures/index.html>
- From Now On: The Educational Technology Journal <http://www.pacifi-crim.net/~mckenzie/>
- Internet Resources: a newsletter aimed at the higher education community <http://www.hw.ac.uk/libWWW/irn/irn.html>
- The Network Observer <http://communication.ucsd.edu/pagre/tno.html> TNO is a free on-line newsletter about networks and democracy.
- The Office of Technology Assessment of the Congress of the United States <http://www.ota.gov>.
- Technology and Higher Education Statistics, Surveys, and Reports <http://www.iat.unc.edu/library/liblinks/ed-stats.html>

Environmental Sector

- Ecological Economics <http://csf.colorado.edu/ecol-econ>
- EE-Link: Environmental Education <http://www.nceet.snre.umich.edu/>
- The Environmental Education Network <http:envirolink.org/enviroed/>
- Technology for a Sustainable Future <http://gnet.together.org/tsf/toc.html>
- Environmental Protection Agency <http://www.epa.gov/>

Economic Sector

- Brave New Work World <http://www.newwork.com>
- Economic Education Web <http://ecedweb.unomaha.edu/>
- The Economist <http://www.economist.com/>
- Futurework <http://csf.colorado.edu/futurework/>
- International Political Economy <http://csf.Colorado.EDU/mail/ipe/>
- The Wall Street Journal <http://update.wsj.com>

Political Sector

- CNN Politics Page <http://www.cnn.com/POLITICS/index.html>
- Digital Future Coalition <http://home.worldweb.net/dfc/>
- Education Policy Analysis Archives <http://seamonkey.ed.asu.edu/epaa/>
- IANWeb <http://www.pitt.edu/~ian/ianres.html> from The International Affairs Network
- International Political Economy <http://csf.Colorado.EDU/mail/ipe/>

institution. Ask participants to identify critical trends, potential events, and emerging issues. These exercises allow participants to bring their individual knowledge to the discussion, thus initiating the development of an event-and-trend set that you can use to construct the scanning/monitoring taxonomy. Identifying critical trends and potential events, and discussing their implications for the future of the organization, generates both agreement that this activity merits inclusion in institutional planning and enthusiasm for being part of the scanning/monitoring process. Exhibit 11.3 contains a sample instructional handout for such a workshop. It also illustrates the general concepts and logic essential for conducting an external analysis.

Morrison (1992) suggested that scanners and abstracters be instructed as follows.

- Seek information about signals of change in the STEEP categories (social, technological, economic, environmental, political), on the local, regional, national, and global levels. Examine information sources for movement in relevant variables (such as number of institutions requiring computers of entering students, or percentage increase in the number of students with e-mail accounts). What change is already taking place? Is the movement upward or downward? What are the projections? What are the incipient or emerging trends? That is, what combinations of data points—past trends, events, precursors—suggest and support the beginnings or early stages of a possible trend? What external events, policies, or regulatory actions would affect the projections?

EXHIBIT 11.2. LISTSERVS IN THE STEEP SECTORS.

To subscribe to a listserv, send a message to the listserv (or listproc). Do not put anything in the subject field. In the message field, type "subscribe" (without the quotes), the name of the list, and then your name. Do not type a period after your name. For example, to subscribe to the Academy for Global Communication and Education list, type the following message to listproc@hawaii.edu:

SUBSCRIBE ACE-L (YOURFIRSTNAME) (YOURLASTNAME)

Social

Academy for Global Communication and Education (ACE-L; listproc@hawaii.edu). The purpose of this listserv is to develop global classrooms and to encourage collaborative global-local educational projects and experiences. It may thus be considered as a mutual exploitation society of kindred spirits to promote global learning.

American Association for Higher Education (AAHESGIT; listproc@list.cren.net). This moderated list focuses on the problems/issues/methods of incorporating technology in teaching.

Institute for Academic Technology (iatforum; listserv@unc.edu) focuses on the use of technology in instruction.

World Wide Web in Education (wwwedu; listserv@k12.cnidr.org) is a list for teachers, academics, Web designers, students, and concerned citizens to voice their opinions and suggestions on how to better develop the Web as a pedagogical instrument.

Technological

Edupage (edupage; listproc@educom.unc.edu), a summary of news items on information technology, is provided three times each week as a service by Educom, a Washington, D.C.-based consortium of leading colleges and universities seeking to transform education through the use of information technology.

Innovation (innovation; innovation-request@NewsScancom) offers a weekly summary of trends, strategies, and innovations in business and technology. This listserv requires a $15 subscription (but gives a six-week trial).

The Red Rock Eater News Service (RRE; rre-request@weber.ucsd.edu) is a mailing list focusing on topics relating to the social and political aspects of computing and networking.

The FASTnet list (FASTnet; majordomo@igc.apc.org) is intended primarily for addressing issues in U.S. science and technology politics that cross-cut or transcend the concerns of groups that are organized to address a single substantive area (such as telecommunications policy, environmental racism, defense conversion, biotechnology, health research, workplace issues, etc.).

Economic

Futurework (futurework; listserv@csf.colorado.edu), focuses "on the new realities created by economic globalization and technological change."

Environmental

Environment, Technology, and Society (envtecsoc; listproc@csf.colorado.edu) was established by the Environment and Technology Section of the American Sociological Association.

Political

The Politics of Science and Technology (pol-sci-tech; majordomo@igc.apc.org) is oriented toward discussing and advancing democratic politics of science and technology anywhere in the world.

Public Opinion Research (por@listserv.unc.edu; listserv@unc.edu) is an on-line discussion list for academics and professionals interested in public opinion research. This list focuses on brief postings of recent poll results, announcements of research projects, and methodological and substantive queries.

• Look for signals of potential events on the horizon. For example, the number of courses offered on the World Wide Web may portend a major change in how teaching will be conducted in higher education.

• Look for forecasts by experts. Are we moving toward a sustainable world (as argued by Brown, Flavin, and Postel, 1991), a world where attention is focused on energy efficiency, reusing and recycling materials, protecting biological and environmental bases, feeding and stabilizing the world population)? Or are we moving toward a world where commercial telecommunications firms dominate the schooling function (as argued by Perelman, 1991)? What are the implications of such forecasts for your institution?

EXHIBIT 11.3. EXTERNAL ANALYSIS WORKSHOP HANDOUT.

Event Exercise

Identify Potential Events.   The first exercise is to identify potential events that could affect the future of the institution if they occurred. Events are unambiguous and confirmable. When they occur, the future is different. Event identification and analysis is critical in strategic planning.

It is important that an event statement be unambiguous; otherwise, it is not helpful in the planning process because (1) it is unclear what may be meant by the statement (that is, different people may understand the statement differently) and (2) we have no clear target that allows us to derive implications and action steps. For example, consider the following event statement: *There will be significant changes in political, social, and economic systems in the United States.* Each person on a planning team may agree with this statement but may also interpret it differently. It would be far more useful in analysis to have statements like *In the next election, the political right gains control of Congress.* Or *Minorities become the majority in ten states.* Or *The European Community incorporates Eastern Europe in a free trade zone.* The latter statements are concrete and unambiguous, and signal significant change that could impact the institution.

Another point. We should not include an impact statement in the event statement. Consider the following event statement: *Passage of welfare and immigration reform will negatively impact higher education.* First, we need to specify each welfare reform idea and each immigration reform idea as an event. Second, it may well be that an event can have both a positive and a negative impact. For example, there may be signals that within five years 30 percent of college and university courses will use multimedia technologies in instruction. This event could have both positive and negative consequences on the institution. If, for example, the faculty are not currently oriented to using multimedia technology, the event may adversely affect the competitive position of the institution. On the other hand, distributing the signals of this event in a newsletter to the faculty may bring about an awareness of what is happening and assist in developing a desire to upgrade their set of teaching skills.

Select the Most Critical Events.   The second exercise is to select those events that may have the most impact on the institution in the next decade. We use paste-on dots for this exercise. Group members are given five dots to indicate their selection. Voting criteria are as follows:

- Vote for five of the most critical events for the future of the institution that have some probability of occurrence within the next decade. Do not be concerned about the event having high or low probability; be concerned only about the severity of the impact (positive or negative).

- Do not put more than one dot on one event statement.
- Put all dots by the beginning of the event statement (so that we can quickly see the frequency distribution of dots).

Identify Signals. The third exercise is to identify the signals that your top two events (as indicated by the frequency distribution of votes from the critical-events exercise above) could occur.

Derive Implications. The fourth exercise is to take one of your top two events and derive the implications of that event for the college. In other words, assume that this event occurs. What would happen to the institution as a result of its occurrence?

Develop Recommendations. The final exercise is to develop recommendations as to what institutional leaders should do *now* in anticipation of this event occurring. Again, do not be concerned about the probability of occurrence of the event. Let's see what recommendations you invent, and then examine the recommendations to see if they make sense to implement regardless of whether the event occurs or not. One outcome is the creation of plans that we could not have conceived without going through the process, but that, when we examine the plans, make sense to begin implementing now.

Trend Exercise

Trends. Trends are estimations/measurements of social, technological, economic, environmental, and political characteristics over time. They are gradual and long-term. Trend information may be used to describe the future, identify emerging issues, and project future events. Trend statements should be clearly stated and concise, and contain only one idea. Examples of trend statements are:

- The number of computers with voice recognition software sold in the United States
- The number of U.S. colleges and universities requiring computers of entering freshmen
- The number of students 18–21 applying for admission to U.S. colleges and universities

Identify Critical Trends. Trends define the context within which organizations function. Therefore, it is important to identify critical trends, particularly those that are emerging, forecast their future direction, derive their implications for effective planning, and construct plans to take advantage of the opportunities they offer, or ameliorate their consequences if they may negatively impact the institution. In trend identification, it is important to look widely in the social, technological, economic, environmental, and political (STEEP) sectors locally, regionally, nationally, and internationally.

Prioritize Trends.   Each planning team member has five "dots." The criterion for voting is to select the five most critical trends. Put a dot on the left-hand side of each trend statement (so that we can see the frequency distribution easily). Remember: one dot per trend.

Develop Implications.   Select one trend and derive the implications of that trend for the institution. When the discussion is exhausted, we then proceed to the bottom line of the exercise: what should the institution do in light of the implications of the trend?

- Look for indirect effects. A particular item might not have direct implications for your institution, but it could nevertheless be included as a variable for monitoring or for further analysis as it might affect you through second- or third-order effects. For example, the development of the North American Free Trade Agreement in response to the free-trade agreement among the European Community portends either free-trade zones with tariffs between them or international free trade. If the latter occurs, there will be tremendous shifting of capital and labor (severalfold amplification of the "giant sucking sound" Ross Perot described before the NAFTA treaty). The effect on postsecondary education would be indirect and in response to the need for immediate retraining of people for jobs in new or greatly expanding industries.

- Remember that scanning is an art form; guidelines on how to do it are necessarily few. There are no hard-and-fast rules leading to correct interpretation of information nor to correct interpretation of an issue or change. Keep in mind that your institution has a variety of stakeholders (faculty, administrators, staff, parents, legislators, community leaders); try to view information that you receive vis-à-vis implications from their point of view. The data do not speak by themselves. Your skills, abilities, experience, and judgment are critical in breathing life into and interpreting the meaning of the data. View yourself as an artist "to mold and shape material into a coherent whole; to present a vision; to help others imagine and reflect" (Neufeld, 1985, p. 44).

• Write abstracts. Abstracts assist the scanning/monitoring process because they provide a brief summary about a potential development so that other members of the scanning/monitoring team do not have to read the entire source; abstracts provide members of the team with preliminary thoughts as to how this potential development could affect the institution.

When preparing abstracts, write the lead sentence in response to these questions: "If I had only a few minutes to describe this article to a friend, what would I say? What is the most important idea or event that indicates change?" Your response to these questions should be one paragraph. Include statistical data where possible. And include a statement of the implications of the emerging trend or potential development for the institution. The summary-and-implications section of the abstract should be one typed page at most.

The resulting abstracts and the general experience of key institutional decision makers in identifying critical emerging trends and potential events constitute the major input for the third component of external analysis: developing scenarios.

Scenarios as a Planning Tool

Scenarios can play a critical role in environmental analysis systems. They are particularly appropriate to colleges and universities, given the consensus-building decision-making processes and the new uncertainties in those institutions' environment. When combined with environmental scanning and monitoring, scenarios provide college and university leaders with the long-term perspectives and recognition of alternative possible futures that they need to inform planning—and thinking and action—in uncertain times.

These leaders, responsible for organizational planning, immediately and instinctively turn to some sort of forecast of the future as a starting point. Why? Because we have all been educated to believe that if we are to make decisions about the future of an organization, we must first know what the organization's future will be like.

On the face if it, that is a reasonable proposition. Yet in reality we are asking for the impossible: certainty and predictability in an uncertain world. The further out on the horizon of forecasting we go, the more unreasonable is the demand. But, even for the shorter term the expectation of precision is a snare and a delusion.

The future is, in a profound sense, unknowable. But not everything is uncertain; some things are relatively predictable. We can do a respectable job of "sensing" the basic dynamics of the future and the alternative courses they might take.

Building on this foundation, scenarios steer us on a middle course between a misguided reliance on prediction and a despairing belief that we can do nothing to envision the future and therefore cannot shape our future.

Scenario-Based Planning

The term *scenario,* taken from the world of theater and film, refers to a brief synopsis of the plot of a play or movie. In a planning context, scenarios can be described as "stories of possible futures that the institution might encounter." Scenarios are graphic and dynamic, revealing an evolving future. They are holistic, combining social, technological, economic, environmental, and political (STEEP) trends and events, the qualitative as well as the quantitative. They focus our attention on potential contingencies and discontinuities, thereby stimulating us to think more creatively and productively about the future.

By basing decisions on alternative futures, and by testing planned actions against the different conditions these scenarios present, we are better able to prepare for uncertainty and ensure that our decisions are as resilient and flexible as possible to deal with contingencies that we might otherwise deem unthinkable.

One way to develop scenarios is to turn the job over to a brilliant futurist or to an imaginative planner to sketch out alternative possible futures that our planning should consider. The fundamental problem with this approach, however appealing it might be, is that the decision makers—those who will ultimately use the scenarios—do not "own" them. The scenarios remain forever the product of someone else's thinking, and so they lack the credibility necessary for them to be the basis for action.

To deal with this problem, SRI International developed an approach that (1) is a structured blending of rationality and intuition and (2) relies on decision makers themselves to develop their own scenarios. Its process is tight enough to give organization and logic to scenario development, but loose enough to encourage creativity and imagination.

The methodology involves a relatively straightforward six-step process (Figure 11.1) with two important elements. The first is what we term the *decision focus* of the scenarios. The starting point for the process is not a generalized future of the world but the very specific decision(s) that confront the organization. The point here is that the scenarios should be designed specifically to help us make those decisions. The range of decisions that scenarios can address is quite broad, from an immediate, pressing decision (a major investment in a new building or computer system, for instance) to broader, longer-range concerns such as the strategic posture of the university or long-term prospects for certain curricular areas. Regardless, the choices to be illuminated give scenarios their focus; they are where scenario efforts begin and end.

FIGURE 11.1. SCENARIO PLANNING MODEL.

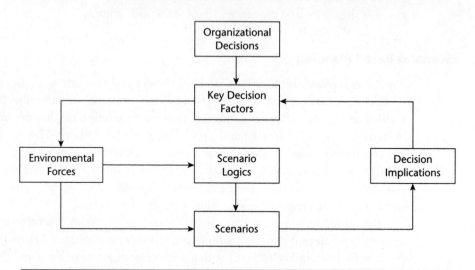

Source: Reprinted by permission of SRI International.

The other key element is the *scenario logic.* This gives scenarios a kind of organizing principle or logical structure. The logic of a scenario comes from a theory, assumption, or belief about change. Each distinct scenario logic is an argument about the future, a different interpretation of the uncertainties in the underlying forces that leads to a different view of the future.

A scenario process that stresses focus and logics is adaptable to many different applications, and it fits relatively well with other forecasting and planning approaches often taken by colleges and universities. David Hornfischer (1995) described how the Berklee College of Music used this process to assist in the development of its strategic plan. In the following section, we describe the scenario process the college used and include excerpts from the Berklee experience to illustrate the outcomes at each of the six steps of the process.

A Sample Scenario Process: Berklee College of Music

Step 1: Identify and Analyze the Organizational Issues That Provide the Decision Focus. Clarifying the decision focus of the whole process is the first task. It is doubly important. In the first place, it reminds us that scenarios are not an end in themselves; they are a means to help us make better strategic decisions. Second, the decision focus effectively grounds the scenarios in specific planning needs. A tight focus prevents the scenarios from drifting into broad generalizations about the future of society or the global economy, thereby clouding their implications for any particular institution.

The decisions that form the scenario focus tend to be strategic rather than tactical in nature for the simple reason that scenarios deal more with longer-term trends and uncertainties (often with a five-to-ten-year time horizon) rather than shorter-term developments. Virtually any decision or area of strategic concern in which external factors are complex, changing, and uncertain can be appropriate for treatment by scenarios. A university might, for instance, be trying to develop a long-term strategic vision for itself. Or it might be confronted with major capital allocation decisions in which the main concern is the long-term need for, and viability of, expansion plans. A current issue is the need to assess the impact of information and communications technology on curriculum, student-teacher relationships, and the location of education ("Is the 'virtual university' a realistic prospect?"). Given the inherent uncertainties in the conditions surrounding such decisions, the use of scenarios to explore alternative futures in which the results of a decision might be played out makes a great deal of sense.

As a general rule, the narrower the scope of the decision or strategy, the easier scenario construction and interpretation will be. Developing scenarios for broader strategic concerns (for example, the long-range positioning of a university vis-à-vis distance learning) is substantially more difficult than for a straightforward investment decision.

The Berklee College of Music began its scenario development process by defining its decision focus: what is the future of enrollment at Berklee? This question was chosen because as a relatively young institution its long-term financial stability is dependent on maintenance of a stable enrollment.

A word of caution. While clarifying this strategic focus is critical for a successful project, it is important to note that this is not the time for strategizing. That comes later, in the final step of the process. Decision makers, particularly senior administrators, have a natural impatience with analysis and want to cut to the chase. However, this otherwise praiseworthy bias toward action must, for the moment, be held in check so that the context for action (that is, the scenarios) can first be established.

Step 2: Specify the Key Decision Factors. Having thought through the strategic decision(s) we want to make, we need then to examine the key decision factors (Figure 11.1). In simple language, these are the key factors we would like to know about the future in order to make our decision. Granted that we cannot actually know the future, it would still be helpful to have some "fix" on the future course and "value" (or range of values) for these factors. Decision factors for an anticipated major expansion of manufacturing facilities, for example, might include market size, growth, and volatility; competing products or substitutes resulting from new technology; long-range economic conditions and price trends; future government regulations; capital availability and cost; technology availability and capacity. For a college or university, the relevant factors are more likely to be social values and priorities, demographics of the potential student pool, governments' education policies, changing workforce skill requirements, financial concerns, and so on.

In the Berklee case, the key factors affecting future enrollment levels were identified as student costs (tuition and aid availability), the state of the world economy, the relevance and quality of Berklee's program, increased competition for students, and marketing programs.

The important thing to note about decision factors is that they normally relate to external, largely uncontrollable conditions. The Berklee case is an exception in that only two factors, the world economy and competition, are external; the remainder are internal factors under Berklee's control. As a general rule, however, scenarios are best thought of as descriptions of alternative external futures; and the key decision factors normally relate to conditions in an organization's environment. This is not, of course, to suggest that the more controllable internal factors such as an organization's strengths and weaknesses, culture, and organization are unimportant and irrelevant to the decision. Of course, they are important. But because they are controllable, decisions about them belong more appropriately in the strategizing phase than the scenario-development phase of the planning cycle. Scenarios, we should remember, are designed to give us insights into the sort of market and competitive environment, the social and political climate, the technological conditions that we may have to deal with. Then, and only then, should we make our decisions about what we should do.

Step 3: Identify and Analyze the Key Environmental Forces. The next step is to identify the external forces that determine the future course and value of our key decision factors. Here we may benefit from the environmental scanning/monitoring system described earlier, ensuring that we scan for signals of change in the task, industry, and macroenvironment.

The objective is to start building a good conceptual model of the relevant environment, one that is as complete as possible, including all the critical trends and forces, and that maps out the key cause-and-effect relationships among these forces.

The next step is to get a clear picture of future prospects for these environmental forces: what the major trends and uncertainties are, how the forces are interrelated, which are most important in determining the key decision factors, and which best represent underlying or driving forces for significant change in the future. In practice, these analyses are less complex than they might seem; the basic thrust of analysis here should move quickly to focus on the few most important forces. Here, a review of the abstracts collected in the scanning process informs our discussion of (1) the current direction of the most critical forces today, that is, current trends and the reasons for them; (2) their future prospects, that is, how much, in what ways, and how fast these trends might change in the future; and (3) their relevance to the decision focus, that is, the direction and magnitude of their impact on the future course of the key decision factors.

At this stage we need to do some sorting out of these forces, recognizing that they are not all equally important or equally uncertain. Clearly, our assessment should try to differentiate between trends and developments that we believe to be relatively predictable and those about which we have some feeling of uncertainty. For instance, while the typical scenario process is likely to identify a total of fifty or so relevant external forces, the number of key drivers of an organization's environment is certainly significantly fewer. And, while uncertainty is a prevailing condition of the external environment, not everything is uncertain. Indeed, some key trends such as demographics may be considered virtually predetermined elements of the future; the potential students ten years hence, for example, are already born, so their number is already known.

In our planning and decision making, we need to be very clear about what is important and what is truly uncertain, and why. To be systematic in this sorting-out process, we can use an impact/uncertainty matrix (Figure 11.2). With a simple high-medium-low scoring system, we can position each of these forces on the matrix in terms of (1) the level of its impact on the key decision factors (obviously, all the forces are presumed to have some impact, but some are more important than others) and (2) the degree of uncertainty we feel about the direction, pace, or fact of its future course.

As a result of this sorting out, we can focus our attention—and the search for scenario logics that comes in the next step of the process—on two quadrants of the matrix. The high impact/low uncertainty forces, those in the top left cells, are (we think!) the relative certainties in our future for which our planning must prepare. The high impact/high uncertainty forces (those in the upper right quadrant are the potential shapers of entirely different futures (scenarios), ones for which our planning *should* prepare.

In Berklee's case, their scenario team focused on seven key driving forces that would, they felt, affect the future course of their key decision factors, and hence the outcome of their decision issue. Two of these driving forces were essentially economic in nature: the state of the global economy in general and the level of national spending on education. Two others related to the state of Berklee's market

FIGURE 11.2. PROBABILITY IMPACT—UNCERTAINTY MATRIX.

	High	High Impact/ Low Uncertainty		High Impact/ High Uncertainty
Level of Impact	Medium			
	Low	Low Impact/ Low Uncertainty		Low Impact/ High Uncertainty
		Low	Medium	High

Degree of Uncertainty

Source: Reprinted with permission from the authors and the World Future Society.

and competition: the state of the music industry and its products (including record and instrument sales) and the changing nature of music literacy. Two were demographic forces: the size and character of the future student population and changing faculty demographics. The seventh driving force was Berklee's ability to impact its environment and shape its own future.

Step 4: Establish the Scenario Logics. This step is the heart of the scenario development process: establishing a logical rationale and structure for the scenarios we select to develop. It is that stage in the process where intuition/insight/creativity plays the greatest role. Theoretically at least, it would be possible to develop scenarios around all the high impact/high uncertainty forces identified in the previous step. Practically, however, this would result in an unwieldy process and an impossibly large number of scenarios. Even if the sorting-out process in Step 3 reduced the number of critical forces to, say, fifteen or twenty, taking all the permutations and combinations of the alternative outcomes of these forces would produce an astronomically high number of scenarios, far more than the human mind could encompass and any planning system could utilize. As a practical matter, we must recognize that even those executives who are prepared to venture beyond single-point forecasting balk at having to deal with more than three, or at most four, alternative scenarios in their strategic thinking and decision making.

So the central challenge in this step is to develop a structure that will produce a manageable number of scenarios—and do so logically. *Scenario logics* are a response to this challenge. The term, however, clearly stands in need of definition if we are to understand, and act on, its premise. In this regard, it is more helpful to think in terms of an operational (rather than a dictionary) definition of the term. We can, for instance, think of scenario logics as being the organizing principles around which the scenarios are structured. They focus on the critical external uncertainties for the organization and present alternative "theories of the way the world might work" along each of these axes of uncertainty. For example, economic growth will be "driven by expanding trade" or "hobbled by increasing protectionism"; competition in our markets will be "marked by growing consolidation" or "restructured by the entry of new players." They are logical in the sense that a persuasive and rational case can be made for each of the contradictory outcomes; indeed, it is often the case that our disagreements about the future are the very source of these logics.

Berklee organized their scenarios around a four-quadrant structure (see Figure 11.3) built on two axes of uncertainty: the overall strength of the U.S. and global economies and the demand for musical education. Each has alternative logics describing and explaining radically different outcomes.

Step 5: Select and Elaborate the Scenarios. In determining how many scenarios to elaborate, we should remember a basic dictum: develop the minimum number of scenarios needed to bound the "envelope of uncertainty." This number is usually three or four. The objective is not to cover the whole envelope of our uncertainty with a multiplicity of slightly varying futures, but rather to push the boundaries of plausibility using a limited number of starkly different scenarios.

In Berklee's case, their structure led to the identification of four different scenarios. This, the planners considered, was a manageable and useful number, so all the resulting scenarios were developed and further elaborated. However, what happens if we end up with a structure consisting of, say, three axes of uncertainty, giving rise to eight $(2 \times 2 \times 2)$ derivative scenarios? Some selection is clearly needed if we are not to overwhelm the decision makers who must use them. Once again we need a combination of intuition and rationality to guide our selection. It is helpful to use five criteria at this point.

1. The selected scenarios must be *plausible,* that is, they must fall within the limits of what logic says might happen—regardless of our judgments as to probability.
2. They should be *structurally different,* that is, not so close to one another that they become simply variations of a base case.

FIGURE 11.3. BERKLEE SCENARIO STRUCTURE.

A Return to Economic Growth

	Back Bay to Bombay	Competitive Pressures	
High Demand for Berklee Education			Low Demand for Berklee Education
	Berklee, Inc.	Dazed and Confused	

A Faltering U.S./Global Economy

Source: Reprinted by permission of Jossey-Bass Publishers.

3. They must be *internally consistent,* that is, the combination of logics in a scenario must not have any built-in inconsistency that would undermine the credibility of the scenario.
4. They should have *"decision-making utility,"* that is, each scenario, and all the scenarios as a set should contribute specific insights into the future that bear on the decision focus we have selected.
5. The scenarios should *challenge the organization's* conventional wisdom about the future.

Using these criteria, it is usually possible, within a short period, to winnow the eight candidate scenarios down to the requisite three or four. Some of the possibilities may be eliminated because their combination of logics is thought to be implausible or inconsistent; others, because they would not present any significantly different insights to the decision makers; still others, because they do not push the envelope far enough.

Once the scenarios have been selected, they then have to be elaborated. At this point, all they have by way of description is a combination of two (or three) driving logics (e.g., in the Berklee case, "Back to Bombay" is driven by strong economic growth and high demand for musical education). There are many ways to elaborate the description of scenarios, but there are three important features.

1.   A highly descriptive title: short enough to be memorable but descriptive enough to convey the essence of what is happening in the scenario. After people

have had the scenarios described to them, they should find each title to be a memorable encapsulation of the scenario. One warning: avoid such terms as *best case, worst case, high growth, low growth.* Such terms say nothing about why it might be the *best* case (from whose point of view?), or *why* the growth is high or low. They tend to favor making snap judgments about the scenario; they work against provoking decision makers to examine the scenario conditions and their consequences, seriously and thoroughly.

2.   Compelling "story lines." Remember: scenarios are not descriptions of end points (how big will our market be in 2005?) but rather narratives of how events might unfold between now and then, given the dynamics (logics) we have assigned to that particular scenario. In simple terms, a scenario should tell a story; that story should be dramatic, compelling, logical, and plausible.

3.   A table of comparative descriptions. This provides planners and decision makers with details along specific dimensions, a sort of line-item description that details what might happen to each key trend or factor in each scenario. In theory, this table might include every one of the macro- and microenvironmental forces that were identified in Step 3; but in practical terms it is usually advisable to prune this list to the more important forces. It is difficult to get from such a table an overview of what is happening in each case; that is the role of the story line. But the table does provide the detailed back-up material—the flesh on the skeleton—that gives the scenarios their nuance and texture.

These three features can always be embellished with charts, graphs, and other visual material to help bring the scenarios to life. The guiding principle in determining the extent of this elaboration is, as always, the requirement of the decision focus: provide as much detail as is needed to help executives make the decision, and no more.

Berklee named and described the four scenarios as follows:

1.   "Back to Bombay" (high demand/strong economy). This is the good-news scenario in which a rising economic tide coupled with strong demand for a Berklee education allows the school to expand and become a truly global musical college. A backdrop of solid economic growth of over 3 percent paves the way for a second Clinton term with a renewed sense of community and public purpose. The music business rides the economic tide; in combination with increased diversity of music styles, Berklee's contemporary/technology-based curriculum is ever more appealing to potential students from around the world.

2. "Competitive pressures" (low demand/strong economy). Here the economy is also strong, but pressures from other schools as well as noninstitutional (perhaps Internet-based) competition created by new technologies diminish the attractiveness of a formal and expensive degree to a more business-aware student.

3. "Berklee Inc." (High demand/weak economy). While interest in a Berklee education remains strong because of its contemporary curriculum, economic pressures make the cost even more burdensome. The impact of a weak U.S. economy growing at less than 2 percent is felt across the globe. The U.S. government, overwhelmed by social and economic issues, reduces its commitment to student aid programs. Berklee is forced to increase scholarship budgets and to seek greater corporate support.

4. "Dazed and confused" (low demand/weak economy). This is the disaster story, where a faltering economy combined with the continuing diminishment of school music programs and a slumping music industry put increased pressures on Berklee's enrollment.

These brief encapsulations do not do justice to the texture and level of detail in Berklee's full scenario story lines. In this case, as in others, the logical structure of the scenarios is intended to provide a framework for the human imagination to engage in what-if thinking, explore the future, and speculate in detail about the consequences of trends and actions.

Step 6: Interpret the Scenarios for Their Decision Implications. This is the stage at which we close the loop, linking back to the decision focus of the first step and starting to turn scenarios into strategy. This is our repeated reminder that scenarios are a tool, a means to an end, not an end in themselves.

Strategy, of course, requires far more than scenarios in its development: strategic vision, goals and objectives, competitive analysis, assessment of core competencies, for instance. But this final step in the scenario process can develop some initial and valuable strategic insights.

How to produce these insights is, again, a matter of discretion; but there are certain approaches that should be considered. Most obviously, we can examine the scenarios in detail to determine the opportunities and threats that each poses for our organization. Then two questions suggest themselves. First, which opportunities and threats are common to all (or nearly all) the scenarios? These are the ones on which presumably our strategic thinking should be focused. The second question is: how well prepared are we (or can we be) to seize those opportunities and obviate (or minimize) the threats? The answers to these questions provide an initial assessment of the core competencies that the organization needs if it is to succeed in the conditions portrayed in the scenarios. Bringing together the answers to these two questions suggests some discrete strategy options (though not yet an integrated strategy) that deserve more disciplined analysis.

A second possible approach is to use the scenarios as test beds for assessing the resilience and vulnerability of the organization's current strategy. This exercise can be as straightforward as a judgmental assessment by the executive team as to how well (or badly) the strategy plays out in each scenario. A start would be to go through an opportunities/threats assessment (as above) and then use this assessment to address a second set of questions: are we satisfied with the resilience of our current strategy, its flexibility to deal with different possible conditions? Are there things we could do to improve its resilience? And, importantly, are there contingency plans we should put in place to help us move in a different direction, if that is necessary?

The planners at Berklee used their scenarios and discussion of their implications to develop a shared vision and a resilient strategy for their institution. The vision, "Creative Musicianship for a Changing World," provides for increased student diversity and for the continuing introduction of new technologies and teaching methodologies into the curriculum. It commits Berklee to strengthening its participatory and collegial culture, and to expanding access to secondary collaboratives, postsecondary consortia, international music education, and relationships to the music industry.

Conclusion

Environmental analysis is an essential step in issues identification and management, in developing strategy and vision (see Chapters Eight and Nine), in organizational learning (Chapter Twelve), and in contingency planning (see Chapter Five).

Developing a comprehensive environmental scanning/monitoring process to feed scenario planning is expensive in that members of the academic enterprise are heavily occupied with day-to-day problems and may see the time spent in external analysis as taking away time from handling immediate problems. This is particularly true for senior members who have the responsibility for organizational decision making. Noal Capon (1987) and Henry Mintzberg (1994) have noted that one of the weaknesses of external analyses in corporate strategic planning is that often senior decision makers are not involved in making the analyses; consequently, the results of the analyses lack validity. However, if senior leaders are involved with scanning, monitoring, and scenario development, the analyses have organizational validity and usefulness. And in turbulent times, not expending the resources—including the time of senior leaders—to anticipate developments that can affect the future of the institution is foolhardy.

Further Reading

For more about scanning and monitoring, see Fahey and Narayanan (1986) for an excellent overview of these processes as used in the corporate world, and Hearn and Heydinger (1985), Morrison (1992), and Simpson, McGinty, and Morrison (1990) as they are used in higher education. Peter Schwartz (1991) and Pierre Wack's articles in the *Harvard Business Review* (1985a, 1985b) provide insightful and valuable overviews of the use of scenarios in planning. Wilson puts external analysis in the perspective of strategic planning (1994) and strategic visioning (1992).

References

Brown, L. R., Flavin, C., and Postel, S. *How to Shape an Environmentally Sustainable Globe*. New York: Norton, 1991.

Capon, N. *Corporate Strategic Planning*. New York: Columbia University Press, 1987.

Fahey, L., and Narayanan, V. K. *Macroenvironmental Analysis for Strategic Management*. St. Paul: West, 1986.

Friedel, J. N., Coker, D. R., and Blong, J. T. "A Survey of Environmental Scanning in U.S. Technical and Community Colleges." Paper presented at the meeting of the Association for Institutional Research, San Francisco, May 1991.

Hearn, J. C., Clugston, R. M., and Heydinger, R. B. "Five Years of Strategic Environmental Assessment Efforts at a Research University: A Case Study of Organizational Innovation." *Innovative Higher Education*, 1993, *18*(1), 7–36.

Hearn, J. C., and Heydinger, R. B. "Scanning the External Environment of a University: Objectives, Constraints, and Possibilities." *Journal of Higher Education*, 1985, *56*(4), 419–445.

Hornfischer, D. "Sing a Song of Scenarios: Using Scenario Planning." *On the Horizon*, 1995, *3*(5), 13–15.

Mintzberg, H. *The Rise and Fall of Strategic Planning: Reconceiving Roles for Planning, Plans, and Planners*. New York: Free Press, 1994.

Morrison, J. L. "Establishing an Environmental Scanning Process." In R. Davis (ed.), *Leadership and Institutional Renewal*. New Directions for Higher Education, no. 49. San Francisco: Jossey-Bass, 1985.

Morrison, J. L. "Establishing an Environmental Scanning System to Augment College and University Planning." *Planning in Higher Education*. 1987, *15*, 7–22.

Morrison, J. L. "Environmental Scanning." In M. A. Whitely, J. D. Porter, and R. H. Fenske (eds.), *The Primer for Institutional Research*. Tallahassee, Fla.: Association for Institutional Research, 1992.

Neufeld, W. P. "Environmental Scanning: Its Use in Forecasting Emerging Trends and Issues in Organizations." *Futures Research Quarterly*, 1985, *1*(3), 39–52.

Perelman, L. *Schools Out! Hyperlearning, the New Technology and the End of Education*. New York: Morrow, 1991.

Pritchett, M. S. "Environmental Scanning in Support of Planning and Decision Making: Case Studies at Selected Institutions of Higher Education." Paper presented at the annual meeting of the Association for Institutional Research, Louisville, Ky., May 1990.

Renfro, W. L., and Morrison, J. L. "The Scanning Process: Getting Started." In J. L. Morrison, W. L. Renfro, and W. I. Boucher (eds.), *Applying Methods and Techniques of Futures Research*. New Directions for Institutional Research, no. 39. San Francisco: Jossey-Bass, 1983.

Simpson, E., McGinty, D., and Morrison, J. L. "Environmental Scanning at the Georgia Center for Continuing Education: A Progress Report." In D. M. Johnson (ed.), *A Handbook for Professional Development in Continuing Higher Education*. Washington, D.C.: National University Continuing Education Association, 1990.

Schwartz, P. *The Art of the Long View*. New York: Doubleday, 1991.

Wack, P. "Scenarios: Uncharted Waters Ahead." *Harvard Business Review*, 1985a, *63*(5), 73–89.

Wack, P. "Scenarios: Shooting the Rapids." *Harvard Business Review*, 1985b, *63*(6), 139–150.

Wilson, I. "Realizing the Power of Strategic Vision." *Long Range Planning*, 1992, *25*(5), 18–28.

Wilson, I. "Strategic Planning Isn't Dead—It Changed." *Long Range Planning*, 1994, *27*(4), 12–24.

CHAPTER TWELVE

CREATING AND CHANGING INSTITUTIONAL CULTURES

Ellen Earle Chaffee and Sarah Williams Jacobson

Long ago, planning may have fit a stereotype: an executive function involving very few people, conducted in private, recorded on paper, and implemented through orders making their way down the chain of command. But in institutions of higher learning, attempts at long-range planning of that sort produced the infamous, forgotten dust-catchers on the president's bookshelf, ignored by nearly everyone. The stereotypical approach simply could not work in higher education, whether it worked elsewhere or not. Executive ownership, command, and hierarchy have not been part of our culture in modern times. Put another way, and admittedly oversimplifying the point, one might say that the score was Culture 1, Planning 0.

Understanding and dealing with the complex dynamics of culture and planning is the focus of this chapter. We begin with a description of culture and planning in the context of higher education institutions, followed by a closer look at these dynamics from the perspective of theory and research. We conclude with some suggestions for administrators to enhance planning through cultural change.

Cultures and Planning in Higher Education Institutions

For at least two decades, collegiate organizations have eschewed the historic approach to planning. A brief flirtation with management by objectives in the 1960s might have been the capstone experience in bureaucratic planning. But culture won again. By the late 1970s, those responsible for planning in higher education institutions began to recognize that emerging models of strategic planning offered a better fit. Brainstorming, seeking input, simplifying, revising, and other elements of strategic planning capitalized on existing elements of collegiate culture. As more people became involved, ownership and commitment spread. More people on campuses saw the big picture and were able to recognize and act on unforeseen opportunities. A new literature arose, defining alternative planning processes and shifting the emphasis from the document to the process and discussion that produced it. The time frame for planning was becoming shortened, which meant more frequent planning and thus more involvement and flexibility.

Although its forms and details are by no means uniform, a strategic, process-oriented approach to planning has now lasted nearly two decades in higher education. One reason for this is that strategic planning recognizes the organizational environment, which began to provide some harsh lessons for colleges and universities that were retaining an ivory tower mentality. Another is its flexibility: it can accommodate ever-increasing rates of change in both organizations and their environments. A third important reason for the durability of strategic planning is that it requires high levels of participation and analysis, thus capitalizing on some key features of the cultures in most higher education institutions.

If one test of an effective plan is that the organization acts upon it, then there is a lesson in this scan of history: the planning process that is inconsistent with organizational culture is doomed to fail. The dynamics of collegiate cultures sometimes present particularly difficult challenges to effective planning, so the durability of strategic planning is noteworthy. Nevertheless, the demands of the environment have continued to exceed our capacity to respond. As the pace of change and demands for accountability continue to rise and resources become ever scarcer, the need may now be less for a new planning model and more for some important changes in organizational culture itself in order to facilitate effective planning: becoming more receptive and responsive to the lessons generated by strategic planning about the environment and about organizational experience. Colleges and universities need to develop a culture that values organizational learning, continuous improvement, and change.

Organizational culture is the dominant pattern of basic assumptions and shared meaning that shapes what participants see and do. An organization may have subcultures, and these may complement or contradict one another. We say *subcultures* plural both to recognize the diversity of cultures among institutions of higher education and to signify different cultures within each such institution.

Some cultural features occur across institutions of higher learning. For example, certain elements are common to nearly all collegiate cultures: high levels of faculty autonomy, both individually and collectively; an expectation of intellectual integrity; and respect for the scientific method of inquiry. Capitalizing on these elements of culture, collegiate planning must involve and inform the faculty, be realistic and truthful, and build on analyses and documentation.

But collegiate cultures also differ from one another. This is easy to recognize in different institutional types. For example, research universities tend to emphasize faculty commitment to their disciplines, while community colleges tend to emphasize faculty commitment to teaching and learning. True, all faculty have strong disciplinary orientations, and nearly all faculty are substantially committed to teaching and learning. Nevertheless, one might expect a plan in a research university to aspire to national prominence in its academic disciplines, using the results of empirical studies to identify effective strategies to accomplish this. On the other hand, the plan of a community college might be more likely to focus on transfer or placement of graduates, using the results of investigations into the expectations of receiving institutions or employers to identify needed improvements. Therefore, while the techniques and process of effective strategic planning might be shared across the diversity of institutional cultures, the products obviously vary.

At this general level, the cultural foundations of higher education institutions are so fundamental and pervasive that planners typically take them for granted. This is understandable, but it is not always wise. For example, inattention to such implicit assumptions may account for the long delay between public insistence on improving the quality of undergraduate education and the emergence of a teaching emphasis in the strategic plans of major universities. Meanwhile, public concern mounts, and public confidence in higher education is eroded.

Another cultural dynamic is also both widely recognized and perhaps inadequately addressed in planning: each collegiate institution encompasses important and sometimes sharply divergent subcultures (as we discuss next). Planners may not always need to accommodate each of the diverse cultures in the planning process. For routine or project-oriented planning purposes, for example, it may be most important first to identify, understand, and work through the dominant culture, and second to pay attention to diverse subcultures when laying out expectations for the planning process or in the plan itself.

However, the most substantial planning issues at the institutional level are hardly routine in today's environment. Increasingly, leaders are exhorted to "transform" their institutions—essentially, to turn them into something new. While planning is necessary for transformation, it is insufficient to accomplish that. The magnitude of the task calls for the development of a new, shared vision of what the institution wishes to become. Successfully developing and cultivating that vision inevitably involves creating a new, transcendent culture. Leaders must engage widespread participation in and commitment to the new vision; doing so requires them to work through the existing culture(s). Defining and cultivating a shared vision have therefore become integral parts of the planning process.

Increasing attention to the importance of vision in the last decade or so may be a response not only to the need to find common ground among diverse subcultures but also to the need to transform the institutional culture itself. As described in Chapter One, numerous external pressures, rapid and dramatic changes in technology affecting teaching and research, scarce resources, and a consumer orientation among students make clinging to the ivy an increasingly untenable strategy. This is a perilous situation for an enterprise that finds its identity at least as much in upholding tradition as in plowing new ground.

What most institutions need to do is develop a shared culture that values and seeks change in ways that affirm fundamental commitments while letting go of their trappings. For example, tenure may or may not be the only secure way to protect academic freedom, and the classroom may not be the best learning environment for some objectives. Clinging to tenure or the classroom per se is unnecessary and counterproductive. Any method or cultural artifact that warrants such tenacity will rise to superiority throughout the planning debate; the debate, however, needs to be on principle, not tactics. Affirming the centrality of academic freedom, learning, inquiry, and scholarship can permit institutional leaders to capitalize on existing cultural strengths even as they assist the culture in the search for new approaches and assumptions that better accommodate new realities.

Planning is the establishment of a readiness to act, throughout the organization, on the basis of a shared understanding of the organization's desired future (its vision), maintaining awareness of both the organization and its environment. While a written plan is essential, this definition requires more. Organizational actors must share a reasonably consistent view of a desired future and its implications for their actions. In a dynamic environment, such as that presently encountered by colleges and universities, the institution with participants who accept the vision, understand institutional strengths and weaknesses, and know the environmental threats and opportunities will be ready to act on multiple, emergent, and decentralized initiatives. Effective planning, therefore, requires an organizational culture that is receptive to a shared vision, willing to understand both the organization and environment, and trusting.

Institutions with diverse subcultures need a shared vision to unite people and coordinate action, but their very diversity makes this difficult to achieve. For example, administrators may seek high enrollment, efficiency, or accountability, while faculty may seek smaller classes, more travel funds, and fewer committees. These sets of goals are not necessarily mutually exclusive, but they illustrate fundamental differences in language and thought between the two subcultures. Before they can share a vision, they need to find shared goals and language.

Willingness to understand the organization and environment is a similarly challenging requirement. The administration is usually willing to deal at the institutional level and to work at the interface between the institution and its environment, but the faculty tends to prefer to leave those concerns to the administrators. This may work out well for all, if the faculty can accept the conclusions and action plans that administrators draw from understanding the organization and environment. If the faculty cannot, they resist the plan.

Accepting such administrative conclusions illustrates one of the benefits of trust between different groups. Not everyone can participate in formulating plans, and those who do not participate need to trust the results. Otherwise, they will actively resist the plan or decline to act in ways that would support the plan. Similarly, planners cannot be everywhere, and they typically cannot order compliance in many important sectors of the institution, so they need to trust others to carry out the plans.

With this overview of some important relationships between culture and planning, we turn now to theory and research on these two topics. The final section contains recommendations for action.

Defining Institutional Culture(s)

We adopt as a starting point for our review a definition of culture proposed by Schein: "Culture can [now] be defined as (a) a pattern of basic assumptions (b) invented, discovered, or developed by a given group (c) as it learns to cope with its problems of external adaptation and internal integration, (d) that has worked well enough to be considered valid and, therefore (e) is taught to new members as the (f) correct way to perceive, think, and feel in relation to those problems" (1990, p. 111).

Within this general definition, manifestations of a group's culture exist on at least four levels: core assumptions, basic values, norms of behavior, and artifacts (Hunt, 1991, p. 227). At the deepest level, important assumptions, generally unexamined and often taken for granted, form a core. While it is often supposed that these assumptions or "mindsets" (Reger, Mullane, Gustafson, and DeMarie, 1994) are universally shared within a group externally identified as a unit, this is often not the case. For example, there may be widely divergent assumptions among faculty in a given institution, or even a department, concerning what it means to "teach" and what it means to "learn." However, interchange within a group concerning underlying assumptions seldom takes place; in fact, the individual holders of such assumptions seldom think about or examine them. Yet they form the basis of all perceptions, feelings, values, norms, and behavior, the second and third layers of culture.

While greater recognition and conversation occur at the second and third levels of culture—the "this is the way things are done around here" levels—it is highly possible that persons espousing similar values or behaving in apparently similar ways may in fact hold quite different underlying assumptions. This renders conversation problematic. To use the previous example, faculty may converse around the value of "quality instruction" assuming that all share underlying assumptions about the nature of that quality when in reality they do not.

Finally, at the most superficial level, artifacts of various kinds and importance develop around deeper cultural values and assumptions. Such artifacts range from the way a group's work site looks and feels, to stories, myths, and jokes, to policies and formal processes. Diverse forms, methods, and processes of institutional planning are cultural artifacts of a very important kind. Artifacts act in powerful ways to hold a group's culture together as well as to reinforce and perpetuate it. To return to our faculty example, teaching evaluations, awards, tenure, and promotion serve to perpetuate the cultural mindsets, values, and behaviors of some faculty while effectively silencing others.

Groups that share a common history and have been relatively stable over a period of time tend to have "strong" cultures, in that the underlying assumptions, values, and reinforcing artifacts are widely shared by most participants. In fact, acceptance of a new member by the group depends upon an individual's successful socialization within it. Therefore, entrants to group cultures, no matter their relative formal authority, will have a difficult time in attempting to change them. Attempts to sway the culture at the level of artifact will have little effect unless some means are found to alter their deeper foundations. When challenged, groups tend to defend their cultural convictions mightily.

Finally, it is important to note that the deep foundations of culture, as well as the layers built around it, are not always rational or even self-protective. Participants bring to the organization unexamined psychological and cognitive baggage drawn from the wider culture of origin (Hofstede, 1980) as well as individually conducted lives. Under threat, these patterns of behavior may be triggered and accentuated, leading participants in a given cultural group to act in seemingly irrational or pathological ways characterized by defensiveness, anger, emotional outbursts, and psychological withdrawal (Bridges, 1991).

This chapter advocates a transformational kind of planning, meaning that planning itself is an instrument through which organizations and their cultures can change and grow. Such transformational planning depends upon the cooperation and psychological investment of important cultural constituencies within a given institution of higher learning. Therefore, it is important to examine the nature of the most important subcultures operating within it. To attempt transformational planning (at the level of cultural artifact) without an understanding of the underlying values and deeper assumptions of those cultures, and the ways in which they may be oppositional, is a project sure to produce conflict and perhaps doomed to failure. Successful transformational planning efforts depend upon both a clear recognition of cultural flash points and the development of inclusive strategies designed to mitigate them.

Institutional Culture(s) in Academic Settings

While at one time it may have been possible to speak of a unitary culture (Morgan, 1989) as characterizing institutions of higher learning in the United States, this is clearly no longer the case (Bergquist, 1992; Kuh and Whitt, 1988; Schoenfeld, 1994). In fact, these authors point to the existence of a number of overlapping, sometimes internally conflicted, cultures composed of administrators, faculty, students, and staff. However, while admittedly oversimplified, for purposes of the argument we present here we consider only the two identifiable subcultures that are generally most involved with institutional planning: one variously labeled the *collegial (or community of scholars or faculty)* culture, and the *administrative, managerial, or corporate community* culture (Schoenfeld, 1994).

The Collegial or Faculty Culture

To consider the collegial culture as a monolith is a considerable simplification. Schoenfeld notes, for example, that "anyone who has ever sat on a campus promotion-and-tenure committee knows of the differences in standpoints among the natural and physical sciences, the social studies, the humanities and fine arts, and the professional schools, not to mention between 'extension' and 'residence' professors" (1994, p. 29). Kuh and Whitt (1988) indicate that collegial culture is actually segmented in at least four ways: disciplinary, professional, institutional, and a national system of higher education. Beyond obvious disciplinary differences, faculty in large research institutions share concerns that differ considerably from those in small private colleges or those focused on a teaching mission. While it is inappropriate to oversimplify faculty culture as universal, it is nonetheless possible to identify certain elements that transcend disciplinary, professional, and institutional boundaries.

At the deepest assumptive level, members of the collegiate culture share the belief that the overarching purpose of the academy lies in the production and dissemination of knowledge as bounded by disciplinary affiliation, and as determined and defined within and by those disciplines. Even when cooperative ventures are developed across disciplinary boundaries, it is with the authority of an expert that representatives from given disciplines contribute. Consistent with this belief, the most important heroes within the collegial culture are those individuals who have contributed, and are contributing, most significantly to its knowledge base. Students are seen preferably as potential converts to disciplinary membership but, at the least, as a ready audience for its tenets. Ultimate meaning within the collegial culture, therefore, lies in disciplinary rather than institutional connection. Consideration turns inward, toward issues of the ongoing life of the discipline or organization, rather than outward toward consideration of impinging constituencies.

Because ultimate institutional meaning is found in the dissemination of knowledge, those doing the disseminating are viewed in the collegiate culture as being those who should hold greatest power within the institution. Thus, the idea is advanced that faculty governance should appropriately prevail in all important institutional decision making. Such decision making is taken very seriously, generally involves respectful solicitation of input from all disciplinary constituencies, and creates opportunities for sometimes endless public discourse and dialogue. Decision making serves a ceremonial as well as instrumental function; the ultimate goal is rarely efficiency. Consistent with this decision-making modality, effective faculty leadership is "conceived as the voice of the professional community, linking the college's academic core to the different and separate organizational and administrative contexts within which it is embedded" (Neumann, 1991, p. 54).

Notions of faculty governance and leadership are today often supported by an expanded interpretation of academic freedom that in the past focused on the right to teach and do research without interference: to include freedom from administrative direction, interference, and "oppression" in all matters. The dual icons of faculty governance and academic freedom are supported by the collegial culture's most important artifacts—tenure and promotion—which reinforce an underlying and historic respect for intellectual hierarchy.

It is important to remember that the collegial culture has evolved over a very long period of time and that some of its members often implicitly view their professional mission as having a nearly sacred quality (Bergquist, 1992). Individuals are drawn to a faculty career based on intellectual interest and talent. They are socialized in protracted graduate education to see the world in particular ways. The more successful an individual's academic career, the more likely it is that the person will wear disciplinary blinders. Therefore, the more prestigious the university, the more likely it is that collegial culture will be "strong" and seemingly intransigent to those who would change it. Change may also be difficult in less prestigious settings, where faculty efforts to prove their worth in the disciplinary community may lead to defensiveness, overreaction, and heightened devotion to protecting the discipline from perceived outside threat.

The Administrative Culture

In earlier periods, members of academic administration were drawn primarily from within the ranks of faculty, often as the pinnacle of an individual career. Kuh and Whitt (1988) describe the evolution in the 1960s and 1970s of a cadre of academic administrators of a different stripe. Often trained specifically in administrative skills without ever holding a faculty position, possessing quite different interests and duties, belonging to separate national organizations, gaining and creating knowledge in journals specifically geared to their interests, these administrators have developed a unique professional identity over time (Schoenfeld, 1994), one distinct enough to be viewed as a culture.

Charged with the overall maintenance, growth, and all too often survival of the organization, the administrative culture finds ultimate meaning in work directed toward organizational goals and purposes. Since such accountability is seen as constituting ultimate meaning, a high value has been placed on fiscal responsibility, management process, effective supervision, and planning—all directed toward meeting the self-identified needs of key clients and constituencies. The administrative culture has often adopted currents of management thought in the private sector. Thus, a discourse acknowledging the importance of various "stakeholders" to the institution (students, faculty, citizens, employers, funding agencies), "markets," "contributions to margin," "customers," "total quality management," and "strategic planning" has become common in universities of all sizes and types. These management techniques are important artifacts of the administrative culture and also provide a common language and assumptive base.

Success and potential career progression for members of the administrative culture are determined by the degree to which administrators are successful in achieving goals of the organization and furthering its purposes. A high value is therefore placed on the efficient and effective use of resources such as time, money, and personnel. Demographic shifts, declining student populations, and an increasingly skeptical public outside academe have had the effect of increasing competitive pressure on the administrative culture, thus reinforcing those values.

As boundary spanners, members of the administrative culture direct their worldview and energy outward toward the various constituencies to which it must respond. Faculty, though important, are seen as but one of many (often competing) voices. The job of faculty is seen as revolving around "the core functions of instruction and scholarship" (Neumann, 1991), while organizational matters are the purview of administrative decision making. Even where formal criteria for faculty evaluation reflect traditional views emphasizing contributions to disciplinary knowledge and the number of publications, members of the administrative culture tend to evaluate the overall quality of faculty work by the degree to which it is purposely and creatively responsive to the values and demands of various organizational stakeholders such as students, parents, employers, and funding agencies.

Oppositional Cultures: Implications for Planning

Bensimon argues that "administrators have been socialized into viewing their campuses as if they were a cohesive whole" (1992, p. 6). Within such a view, the planning process should be a simple matter of determining the shared vision and goals of the organization based on input from relevant constituencies, developing a strategy for reaching them, and then just "doing it." However, administrative planning strategies developed without recognition of deeply embedded cultural differences have sometimes had the effect of creating dissension, discord, and power struggles on already embattled campuses. Robert Birnbaum (1992) reports that, based on his synthesis of faculty opinion surveys, as many as 64 percent of presidents or chancellors lack the professional confidence and support of their faculties. Often such dissension is reduced to the level of name-calling, with each side trying to out vilify the other. The result may be paralysis, even though this is the very outcome all organizational actors must avoid.

That this situation is occurring at a time when higher education enjoys reduced public and governmental confidence and is coming under increased threat renders it a problem of the greatest seriousness. Few people outside academic circles care much to understand the cultural gulfs that divide faculty and administration. They only care that institutions of higher learning do a more effective job of what they do while living within a budget. This demands a high level of agreement in the strategic planning process between faculty and administration, agreement that can never be reached unless underlying cultural mindsets are examined and understood. This does not mean, however, that confrontation among people is required or will ever be productive. To the contrary, the goal is to understand differing cultural mindsets sufficiently well, and to craft the planning process with such finesse in accordance with that understanding, that all can work together for organizational transformation. Further, organizational transformation of the magnitude we are suggesting here necessarily involves engaging the energy and input of all organizational members—staff, students, and external stakeholders, as well as faculty and administrators—in order to be effective.

Transforming Institutions: Culture and Planning

Any number of approaches to institutional planning can be successful. There is no one right way, and what works in one place will not work in another. For institutions that seek major transformations, however, planners must use their planning process as an important tool for change, not only in institutional activity but also in institutional culture.

People and cultures may not resist change itself so much as they resist being changed. That is, a change process whereby someone dictates the change is less effective than one in which change occurs as a byproduct of efforts to achieve a desired outcome. Everyone knows that the carrot is better than the stick. Administrators, whose culture often supports a rational approach to problems, must resist a natural tendency to operate directly on people and culture. They need to take a more complex, although still rational, approach.

The learning organization that continuously improves to meet the needs of a fast-paced, changing environment requires a culture that supports shared vision, a willingness to understand the organization and its environment, and trust. The planning process can enhance these three elements without requiring a unitary culture. The good news is that administrators need not adopt the collegial culture, nor faculty adopt the administrative culture. Research universities and community colleges need not have the same culture; indeed, they ought not. What members of each institution need to do is incorporate throughout their planning processes various methods of fostering a shared cultural value on continuous improvement in meeting the needs of the people the institution serves.

One general tenet for planners is to capitalize on useful elements of the existing cultures, especially those that exist across a subculture. Another is to be very explicit and deliberate in defining the desired organizational transformation and using or developing supportive cultural dynamics, building them into all planning-related activities. For example, we know of one institution where the leadership wishes to focus the attention of all on the need to achieve certain results such as increased student retention. The emphasis on measuring results is consistent with the rationality of both the administrative and the collegial subcultures. Identifying a limited set of key results and publicly monitoring progress lends specificity to the vision and helps motivate change in the desired directions. These thoughts lead to some specific suggestions for administrators.

Enhance the Use of Rational Decision Making

Administrative rationality is echoed in the faculty's appreciation for the scientific method and the primacy of knowledge as the foundation for thought and action; it thus provides a solid bridge between the two subcultures. Administrators can enhance the effectiveness of rational planning processes in at least three ways.

First, communicate planning-related information widely, often, and in diverse ways. In particular, share information about the organization and its environment. Although most faculty and staff do not require the extensive knowledge in this area that administrators do, many take an interest in concise, targeted information that pertains to their priorities. For example, admissions staff in a traditional college may know full well that the number of high school graduates is projected to decline in the service area yet fail to appreciate the implications of that fact for institutional strategy. Furthermore, the faculty may not know it. Faculty may also be unaware of how dependent their departments are on traditional students, or how their actions and decisions affect a student's decision to attend. Neither faculty nor admissions staff may be aware that numerous federal employees in the region need to upgrade their educational qualifications to comply with new mandates; that fact may be known only to the secretary whose spouse is a federal employee. Without her input, knowledge important to the institution's future is lost.

Do not assume that issuing a report satisfies the need for communication. Bring oral, written, and visual information into meetings, speeches, and newsletters. Bring in guest speakers to make key points that pertain to them. In discussion, actively inquire into the information base that leads people to reach different conclusions. Many disagreements can be resolved with facts and data, and this simple method is too often overlooked.

Second, be open to new ideas, open with sensitive information, and open in dealing with problems. None of this is easy or natural, but it fits a rational culture. We tend to think that our ideas are right, that some things are better left confidential, and that problems can be dealt with in private. From time to time, yielding to those tendencies is productive and wise. However, yielding to them may generate fear, defensiveness, and mistrust no matter how compelling the reasons for confidentiality. When openness is the norm, even to the extent of taking sensible risks in sharing information or problems, cross-cultural trust and communication can grow.

A third way to use rationality as a basis for change is to perform new kinds of analyses. For example, most institutional data are based on academic terms or years, with organizational units as the focus. In addition, an institution might produce analyses that take individual students as the unit of analysis, tracking their experiences over a relatively long time, perhaps to identify causes for dropping out, correlates of success in school or later life, or patterns of course taking. Systematic studies of graduate placement experiences or employer satisfaction are already reasonably common, but their results may or may not be applied systematically in the planning process.

Build on Existing Foundations

If the change effort fails to acknowledge and affirm existing assets, resistance will kill it. One of the most powerful saboteurs of a new direction is failure to give recognition to initiatives already under way that can help achieve the organization's vision. Those involved in such initiatives may resent being told to do what they are already doing, or they may simply wonder what new action is desired. On the other hand, providing such recognition, perhaps soliciting active assistance from those involved, makes the new direction more familiar, clarifies it by giving a concrete illustration, and creates instant allies for change.

One of the most pervasive norms in higher education is consultation. Few administrators would promulgate a plan developed by an elite few in private. However, it is all too easy to miss opportunities to capitalize on the consultation process to enhance organizational transformation. Such opportunities include using faculty disciplinary expertise in the planning process, which both enhances the quality of the product and engages the faculty member in institutional issues on the basis of his or her other—sometimes primary—priorities. On occasion, planners may underutilize existing structures as well, for example by establishing an ad hoc group when an existing one is suited to the task and may have a rich history of working together that would enhance its productivity. For example, the faculty senate or executive committee might join with the staff leadership group when the planning process requires a representative faculty/staff group.

Another potentially valuable enhancement to consultation is to involve new people in the discussion. For example, by including students, admissions personnel, and employers of graduates in the planning process, institutions enable the faculty and administration to hear the voice of the customer directly. Planning committee members are far more easily persuaded by that voice than by administrative exhortations. A faculty member who happens to take an interest in institutional research might be a creative adjunct member of the planning staff. We know of two campuses that benefited considerably from using planning facilitators from nearby businesses for their vision development processes.

Often the most powerful and readily accepted shared vision contains strong elements of tradition or past practice. Personnel in a small college that has for decades taken pride in its personal service to students might feel threatened by an impending tide of instructional technologies, but a vision that lodges the new in a clear sense of how technologies can free faculty and staff to provide ever more intensive personal and individualized service could become the magnet for enthusiastic transformation.

Lead for Involvement and Ownership

Virtually every organization is better equipped for contemporary challenges if it increases the extent to which each participant is involved in and feels a sense of ownership for organizational issues and planning. Collegiate cultures, lacking many of the directive tools of other kinds of enterprises and buffeted by the rapidly changing currents of diverse stakeholders, are particularly dependent on each person's having the capacity to recognize a significant event and take appropriate action on it. In research universities, faculty involvement may be high, but their ownership of institutional concerns may be low. In most colleges and universities, staff involvement and ownership need to be substantially higher.

The most obvious solution is to have numerous or large committees with diverse representation. But planners can do more. Presenting such groups with well-crafted questions is both consistent with some of the subculture (especially among faculty) and also more effective than asking for comments on proposed answers. When these questions call for judgments rather than information, responding with another question to help committee members probe for their own answers can also increase a sense of ownership. Often, using tools such as brainstorming, affinity diagrams, and consensograms (see, for example, GOAL/QPC, 1995) capitalizes on the wisdom of each member of the group efficiently and effectively.

Planners might assist planning teams in conducting their own surveys or focus groups, rather than reading the results of those conducted by someone else. This suggests expanding to maximum limits the role of planning staff as supporters for the planning activities of others, even to the point of collecting and analyzing data. It is also useful to have trained group facilitators, as well as analysts and visionaries, among the planning staff.

Many of the suggestions in this section may seem to require additional time, compared to traditional practice; some of them certainly do. However, when the tools available for group planning are properly applied, they can actually save a great deal of time. For example, committees have been known to spend hours debating the finer points, when a quick consensogram would have revealed that they were in strong agreement on the essential point. Many participants have been known to raise the same point ad nauseam because they did not feel heard or appreciated early in the discussion, when starting with some team-building activities would have prevented that feeling altogether. Many discussions have groped and floundered because participants did not start with a brainstorming period to get all of the issues laid out for systematic attention.

Even when a more involving, hands-on approach does take more time, the payoff can be immeasurably large. To return to a previous example, a secretary who is involved and feels some ownership in the future of the institution can mean the difference between knowing about a potential new clientele or not. We know of a custodian who recognized when his father-in-law, a state senator, had given him significant information, and who felt both able and motivated to pass the information to the university president. The payoff for taking the time can be an institution with many participants acting as environmental sensors, idea generators, and virtually spontaneous purveyors of institutional strategies in ways that central administration could never have imagined or planned for.

Summary and Conclusion

Those who lead planning activities often operate in an administrative subculture that systematically fails to provide adequate recognition to the power of the cultures in which planning occurs. If they pay attention to those cultures and seek to understand them, planners are in a position to improve both the plan and its implementation. Moreover, if they help to establish an institutional culture with a shared vision, a willingness to understand the organization and its environment, and trust, they gain access to the efforts and enthusiasm of all participants in transforming the institution. In effect, planning and implementation become part of daily life.

Planners need not make dramatic changes in their planning processes in order to accomplish greater cultural compatibility and change. Substantial gains are available through new and expanded modes of communication within the planning process, if planners consciously build on existing cross-cultural themes and existing foundations, and if they solicit widespread involvement and ownership in shaping the institution's future.

Further Reading

To gain a perspective on the meaning of culture and its diverse forms in organizations, see Bridges (1991), Hofstede (1980), Morgan (1989), and Schein (1990). Bergquist (1992), Kuh and Whitt (1988), Peterson and Spencer (1993), and Schoenfeld (1994) consider cultures specifically as they appear in colleges and universities. Bergquist (1992) and Chaffee and Tierney (1988) provide discussions that relate to the intersection of planning and culture.

References

Bensimon, E. M. "Feminist Thought as a Source of Critique and Reconceptualization of Multiculturalism in Higher Education." Paper presented at the annual National Conference on Racial and Ethnic Relations in American Higher Education, San Francisco, June 1992.

Bergquist, W. H. *The Four Cultures of the Academy.* San Francisco: Jossey-Bass, 1992.

Birnbaum, R. "Will You Love Me in December As You Do in May?" *Journal of Higher Education,* 1992, *63*(1), 1–25.

Bridges, W. *Managing Transitions: Making the Most of Change.* Reading, Mass.: Addison-Wesley, 1991.

Chaffee, E. E., and Tierney, W. G. *Collegiate Culture and Leadership Strategies.* New York: Macmillan, 1988.

GOAL/QPC. *Memory Jogger Plus.* Methuen, Mass.: GOAL/QPC, 1995.

Hofstede, G. *Culture's Consequences.* Thousand Oaks, Calif.: Sage, 1980.

Hunt, J. G. *Leadership: A New Synthesis.* Newbury Park, Calif.: Sage, 1991.

Kuh, G. D., and Whitt, E. J. *The Invisible Tapestry: Culture in American Colleges and Universities.* ASHE-ERIC Higher Education Report No. 1. Washington, D.C.: George Washington University, 1988.

Morgan, G. *Images of Organization.* Thousand Oaks, Calif.: Sage, 1989.

Neumann, A. "Defining Good Faculty Leadership." *NEA Higher Education Journal,* 1991, *7*(1), 45–60.

Peterson, M. W., and Spencer, M. G. "Qualitative and Quantitative Approaches to Academic Quality: Do They Tell Us the Same Thing?" In J. Smart (ed.), *Higher Education: Handbook of Theory and Research,* Vol. 9. New York: Agathon Press, 1993.

Reger, R., Mullane, J. V., Gustafson, L. T., and DeMarie, S. M. "Creating Earthquakes to Change Organizational Mindsets." *The Academy of Management Executive,* 1994, *8*(4), 31–46.

Schein, E. H. "Organizational Culture." *American Psychologist,* 1990, *45*(2), 109–119.

Schoenfeld, C. "Campus Cultures in Conflict." *CUPA Journal,* Winter 1994, pp. 29–33.

CHAPTER THIRTEEN

ORGANIZING THE ELEMENTS OF PLANNING

Raymond M. Haas

For many—some would say most—institutions of higher education, the history of planning has had a pendulumlike quality, its movements in and out of favor often being associated with changes in the external environment or in the presidential leadership of the institution. It follows, therefore, that the question of how planning should be organized probably has been asked more often in colleges, universities, and community colleges than similar queries about other activities of those institutions. But no matter how many times a planning function is reorganized, the organizational components remain relatively few in number: a planner, a planning director, a planning office, and a planning committee. For many institutions, because of perceived affinities among managerial functions and/or economies of scale, organizational questions related to planning may also involve the institutional research function and other decision support activities.

Note: The author gratefully acknowledges the contribution of the additional readings section of this chapter by Christina Morell, a candidate for the Ph.D. degree in higher education administration at the Center for the Study of Higher Education in the Curry School of Education at the University of Virginia.

The Planner

Whether in the literature of business administration, public administration, or education administration, one finds a fairly standard description of the role of the administrator: to plan, to organize, to motivate, and to evaluate. The planners in any institution, therefore, are the managers or administrators. Moreover, with the generally decentralized structure and the highly participatory style of management that tends to prevail in institutions of higher education, it seems likely that far more persons have administrative roles (and therefore some planning responsibilities) in those settings per capita as compared to other types of institutions.

While "responsibility for planning" is listed among the prescribed duties of many persons in a college, university, or community college, as in the corporate and government worlds the chief executive of an organization bears the principal responsibility for planning the future of the entire organization.

In carrying out institutional planning responsibilities, a president or chancellor can choose to act alone or, either formally or informally, to involve others. Again, within the culture of collegiality that pervades higher education, few chief executive officers overtly take the autocratic route to planning. This being the case, and since chief executive officers typically designate a group of senior officers of the institution as a "cabinet," and since that group generally deliberates over an agenda of significant institutional issues, it is recommended that consideration be given to involving the cabinet in the task of institutionwide planning and to giving it a separate name, for example *planning committee,* for those occasions when it is meeting for that purpose.

Consideration also should be given to augmenting a cabinet's membership when it meets as a planning committee, to include representatives of important constituencies and/or "wise persons" from the community at large. In order to preserve the principle that the managers are solely responsible for planning, some institutions do not augment the membership of the cabinet, instead adopting a two-tiered approach and naming a panel of constituency-based advisors and/or wise persons to counsel the planning committee in the execution of its planning responsibilities.

"What's in a name?" Shakespeare asked in *Romeo and Juliet.* As regards the titling of groups involved in institutional planning so-called, the answer could readily be "plenty." It is prudent to choose a group's name carefully and to be sure that its title describes, as precisely as possible, what it is that the group will be doing. For instance, in the two-tiered approach the wise-person/constituency-based group should not be called a planning committee if it serves solely as an *advisory* group, even if the advice it is giving is on matters related to the plans of the institution. Managers tend to know that one of their jobs is to plan; and when groups made up of non-managers have the word *planning* in their title, they tend to be viewed by the planners, if only subliminally, as unwarranted competitors for that role. Similarly, groups made up of nonmanagers that carry *planning* in their title may understandably feel that they are "responsible" for planning.

A special note must be made about the importance of the culture of the particular academic community in which planning is being done. In a choice between the dictates of campus culture and textbook approaches to management, chief executive officers should tend to defer to the dictates of culture while making their case for any changes that may tend to clarify and simplify matters—within whatever norms that same culture may wish to have observed regarding the introduction of change.

The Planning Director/Facilitator

Perhaps nowhere does terminology get more in the way of clarity in planning than in the use of the title *planner* to designate the person whose task is generally defined as being to design an institutional planning process, to equip the "real" planners for the institution with the tools necessary to complete their jobs, and to monitor the execution of the planning process to see that planning actually gets done. If the managers of the institution are the planners, then the person usually called the planner is really the planning director or, perhaps more precisely, the planning facilitator.

It is significant that the Society for College and University Planning (SCUP) is not titled the Society for College and University *Planners*. The planning directors/facilitators who constitute a significant portion of the society's membership realize that they are not planners in the precise meaning of the word; rather, they are advocates for the use of planning within the higher education setting, the campus experts on planning processes, and the persons most knowledgeable about the informational and other tools used by planners. Indeed, it is a widely accepted aphorism among SCUP members that persons holding the position of planner in higher education are not the persons who are responsible for doing the planning. If explaining a mistitled name for a profession is so common that it has achieved the status of an aphorism, it may be time to consider changing the name of the profession.

Again, one might ask, "What's in a name?" The dilemma caused by the term *planner* is that some persons who assume the role of planning director or planning facilitator under the title *planner* tend to promote a personal agenda for the future of their institutions. In order to have credibility in their roles, planning directors/facilitators should be agenda-less when it comes to the future of their institutions. Their goal should be to put in place a planning process that is sufficiently acceptable to the members of the academic community it serves so that the process actually validates the substance of the plan. This is no mean task precisely because colleges, universities, and community colleges have a weak history of codifying and institutionalizing their planning processes. As a result, the most vulnerable facets of institutional plans historically have been the processes by which they were prepared. If members of the academic community wish to cast doubt upon a plan, the most significant questions they could ask have nothing to do with the contents of the plan. They are "How was the plan prepared?" and "Who took part in the planning process?" To repeat, the goal of the planning director or planning facilitator should be to lead the academic community in putting in place a planning process that is sufficiently acceptable to the members of the community it serves that the process actually validates the substance of the plan. In other words, the community should come to support the plan at least in part because it was prepared in such a highly acceptable manner.

The qualifications required to be a successful planning director/facilitator are the same as those required for directors or facilitators of managerial functions of any type, and more (except that, in higher education, the returns tend to be higher for "facilitating" than for "directing"). It is for this reason (and also because *director* may suggest more of a sense of personal rather than communal ownership of the process) that this author recommends—even in the face of established practice to the contrary—the use of the title *planning facilitator* in the field of higher education.

Planning facilitators generally are highly skilled in mediation and, in support of that skill, very knowledgeable of their industry and of the stakeholders in that industry. In higher education, those stakeholders may include the institution's faculty, staff, prospective and actual students, trustees, parents, donors, grantors, elected and appointed public officials, trade unions and their members, and those who hire the institution's graduates or accept them for advanced study.

Planning facilitators also must be knowledgeable concerning the various approaches to planning and the planning processes that have been used in institutions of higher education, business, and government. For some time, planning persons in higher education have been borrowing tools from the workshops of managers in business and government, not always with enduring success. In the history of managerial toolmaking, implements that have stood the test of time tend to be those most adapted to the setting in which they were used. Since the business and government settings are different from those in colleges, universities, and community colleges, borrowed tools must be used with care. Much of the problem in this regard has come from the fact that the plans of corporations are called to judgment more frequently (once a quarter) and based on fewer (generally, one) and more precisely measured indicators of effectiveness (generally, earnings per share) than are the plans of institutions of higher education. Therefore, while planning tools developed in other settings—for example, TQM, zero-based budgeting, strategic planning, management by objectives, and so on—may be useful in higher education, they should be modified to the needs of the educational setting in which they are used.

The Planning Office

Reporting Lines

There is an old adage in affairs related to administration that structure should follow function; like many statements of its genre, this adage generally represents good advice. If a planning office is managed by a planning director/facilitator and if the function of the planning director/facilitator is to assist managers (but especially the president) in the execution of their planning responsibilities, then it follows that the planning director/facilitator should report directly to the president. This can be handled in a variety of ways. At one of the public technological universities in the United States, the planning office is headed by a vice president for strategic planning who reports to the president. At another American institution, a public university that is part of a large system with its own planning office, the planning function is headed by an executive assistant to the president, who reports to the president.

Where the decision is made that institutionwide planning will not come under the direct supervision of the president, it is generally recommended that the office report to the chief academic officer, because academic affairs comprise the *raison d'être* of the institution and it is typically in academic affairs that the principal issues and the most significant resources (the ones affected by institutional plans) generally reside. Admittedly, this advice sounds like that parody of the Golden Rule, "He who has the gold makes the rules." Where the vice presidents work well together as a team, it seems desirable, as the author has recommended in an earlier work (Jedamus and Peterson, 1980), to have the planning function report to the office of the vice president for administration or its equivalent, thus leaving the academic officers more time to devote to academic leadership.

In some cases, institutionwide planning is best served by appointing the person who is most qualified by training or interest to serve as the reporting line for the planning function. At a medical university with which the author has worked, for instance, that person happens to be a dean and thus is leading the development of the planning function at the institution.

Whether a planning office reports directly to the president or not, and no matter how far down inside the organizational structure the planning office is placed, it is important that its leader attend the meetings of the president's cabinet whenever that group meets in its capacity as the planning committee for the institution. The planning director/facilitator need not be an active participant in these meetings, but it is important that the person in that role have the opportunity at least to watch the planning process in action, especially if the process is to be continuously adapted to the needs of the institution.

Activities Assigned to the Planning Office

Aside from the question of its reporting line, attention also must be given to the composition of activities constituting the portfolio of the planning office. Interesting things have been happening in that arena. As mentioned earlier, colleges and universities are wont to experiment with management tools that have their origins in business or public administration. And since there is some credence to the proposition that administration is administration no matter what the setting in which it is practiced, the work of colleges and universities in that regard is laudable. The dilemma develops, however, over the practice of some colleges and universities, when they have borrowed managerial tools from the business or public sector, to give those management tools the organizational stature of an "office." Thus there are offices for total quality management, offices for transformation, offices for reengineering, offices for assessment, offices for restructuring, offices for continuous improvement, and so on.

The alternate approach to creating a separate office for each management tool is to lump the responsibilities for all significant managerial tools in one office and thus save on overhead expenses. In many cases, the planning office has become the institutional "managerial tool crib" of our colleges and universities. This decision makes sense to some degree because planning was one of the earliest management tools to be set aside as a separate office, and it can be argued that the management skills and style required to be a "tool manager" are approximately the same irrespective of the specific tool or number of tools involved, that is, freedom from an agenda, mediation, process orientation, and knowledge of stakeholders. Therefore, as institutions of higher education have recently accelerated acceptance of a wide variety of managerial tools from the private and public sectors, there has been a concomitant expansion of the portfolio ordinarily assigned to planning offices. Nowhere does this situation (perhaps a trend) show up more clearly than in the position titles and office titles that have appeared in employment advertisements: director of institutional effectiveness and planning, office of academic planning and assessment, and so on.

Institutional Research and Planning Analysis. The activity most frequently merged with those of a planning office (or vice versa) is institutional research. This arrangement generally makes a great deal of sense, if only because both research and planning are managerial tools, or, in the case of a small institution, the work to be done in both planning and institutional research may not require the efforts of more than one or a few professionals. But there are even more important reasons for considering this approach. They have to do with symbiosis and synergy.

In the corporate world, marketing research does not have a life of its own. Indeed, marketing research is at its best when it is inextricably tied in a symbiotic relationship to the needs of the marketing plan. A marketing plan is generally thought to consist of situation analysis, definition of mission and goals, opportunity analysis, selection of a target market, prescription of strategies and tactics, scheduling of implementation, and the evaluation of results versus the plan. And marketing research departments focus on gathering information to support decision making in every aspect of the marketing plan. Moreover, it is in this symbiotic or mutually supportive relationship between planning and research that synergistic results are most likely to occur: plans suggest the need for useful research and useful research suggests the type and substance of the plan to be made. Similarly, when planning and institutional research are combined in a single office in higher education, the attention of institutional research personnel is far more likely to be on analysis of proposed plans and in development of planning data and other planning aids for the planners than it is on preparation of reports required by outside agencies—a function that in offices of institutional research often consumes an enormous number of the available hours.

While far less typical, it may be more conducive to symbiosis and synergy, and just as consistent with administrative theory and practice, to merge in one office the planning, budgeting, institutional research, and internal audit functions. A possible benefit of this approach is that it might increase the probability of the managerial rather than the accounting aspects of budgeting being emphasized, that operations auditing as compared to compliance auditing might come to the fore, and that decision support in all these areas might become the principal focus of institutional research (see Haas in Jedamus and Peterson, 1980).

Information Resource Management. The relationship of planning offices (especially those including the institutional research function) to the information resource management function presents a dilemma for many institutions, one related to the question of ownership of data and data files. As the author has proposed in a previous work (Jedamus and Peterson, 1980), it makes good sense to keep institutional research separate from record keeping and information resource management generally, and to place the responsibility for data collection and data file maintenance on the administrative offices that have the greatest need for the data and are in most direct contact with its source. For instance, the registrar should be responsible for student records and for reports required from those records. The role of institution research in relation to the registrar is to expedite report preparation by administrative offices so that those reports are ready in a timely manner, and to coordinate the collation of data as produced by several offices to ensure the consistency and relevance of summary reports. The persistent tension this particular separation of assignments produces revolves around the fact that the administrative offices charged with accounting for a particular resource—money, faculty, students, staff, space, and so on—typically have needs different from the institutional research office in terms of the timeliness, accuracy, and relevance of the data being kept. It is this persistent tension that often leads to directors of institutional research and planning facilitators' being named as important contributors to institutional policy related to information technology and information resource management.

Planning Committees

In the collegial traditions of higher education, it seems that nothing is more traditional in planning than the appointment of a planning committee. Indeed, whether or not the chief executive officer or the chief academic officer appoints a planning committee, it is likely that some faculty group such as a senate or union will. Moreover, it is not uncommon for there to be a planning committee on campus even in the absence of a planning office or a planning director/facilitator; even when the use of either a planning office or a planning director/facilitator or both is contemplated, it is not uncommon for a planning committee to be appointed first. In the evolution of administrative forms related to planning on college, university, and community college campuses, committees seem to have arrived first and to have the greatest comparative capacity to endure.

No matter how a campus may constitute its planning activities, the most critical elements related to the use of a planning committee are (1) the charge, (2) the reporting line, and (3) the membership. In all these things, the existing culture of the campus is likely to be a more powerful force in determining what works than logic or management theory. However, it is also in the shaping of a planning committee's charge, its reporting line, and its composition that significant paradigm shifts have been the means by which major historic impasses related to planning were broken.

The Charge to a Planning Committee

If one accepts the hypothesis that the responsibility for planning rests with the managers or administrators of an institution of higher education, then the aphorism that planning directors are not responsible for planning can be extended to read "and what have traditionally been called planning committees should not be responsible for planning, either." Nowhere is this logic violated more frequently than in the assignment of a name to a group of nonmanagerial participants in planning and in the formulation of its charge.

It only makes sense that if one is appointed to a planning committee, one would expect to have some responsibility for making the plans for the institution. Moreover, these expectations are typically reinforced by the charge to the committee and more specifically by the list of tasks to be completed, which might include such assignments as academic and nonacademic program review and the setting of program priorities for the institution. Unfortunately, assignments of these types immediately cause the administrators charged with planning to feel (perhaps only subliminally) that their planning responsibilities have been usurped and assigned to a committee. In the deliberations and jockeying for position that often follow, planning committees are generally at a disadvantage principally because their members are not charged to make decisions related to resource allocation, and because they are perceived to be working part-time and temporarily on an activity of seemingly undemonstrated permanence.

All of the above leads to a suggested paradigm shift that, as mentioned earlier, in the author's experience has sometimes been the means by which impasses caused by the traditional, conflict-producing charge can be resolved. It is suggested that planning committees as we know them be abolished and, in their place, there be appointed on each campus a group whose title would be something like the "advisory committee on planning processes." Its charge would be to advise the planning director/facilitator regarding the design of a planning process, the design of the tools to be used by the institution's planners in carrying out their assignments, and his or her role in monitoring the execution of the planning processes to see that planning actually gets done and that the plans are then used to inform the institution's decisions related to priority setting and resource allocation.

The rationale for this proposal is threefold. It avoids apparent and real conflict in assignments where the members of a committee and a set of administrators both perceive that the other has been charged with the task of institutional planning. Second, it sets a constituency-based group to work on the task of overcoming the vulnerability of plans in the higher education setting regarding the process by which they were prepared. The third major argument for this approach is that by resolving questions relating to planning processes in advance, the institution's attention tends to be focused on planning issues rather than on how it is that those plans were produced and by whom.

One of the goals of an advisory committee on planning processes should be to help create a planning process that, because of its acceptance by the community, not only reduces the vulnerability of the plan to attacks based on process but in the best of all worlds actually validates the substance of the plan. Moreover, it does not seem unreasonable to expect members of the advisory committee on planning processes, if they feel that they have helped design an acceptable planning process, each then to accept responsibility for mobilizing his or her constituent group in support of that planning process.

The second goal of an advisory committee on planning processes has to do with helping the planning facilitator equip the planners for the institution with the tools necessary to complete their jobs. The major issues associated with decision-support systems and other data-based planning tools are typically related to the timeliness, accuracy, and relevancy of the data being used. As in the case of the planning process, it is an excellent use of a constituent-based committee to get issues of this type resolved in advance so that they are not permitted to distract the institution from the substantive matters related to its future. Again, a legitimate assignment for each member of the committee is that he or she deliver that constituent group's support for the data standards and definitions agreed to by the committee.

The third goal of the advisory committee on planning processes requires the support of the chief executive officer, more than in the case of the other two. In order to monitor the execution of the planning process and to see that planning gets done, members of the committee must be provided with access to vantage points that permit their judgments on this topic to be made. A member or members of the advisory committee on planning processes should be invited to observe the meetings of the president's cabinet when it sits as the planning body for the institution. In addition, the president should agree to describe to the committee the perceived consonance between the institution's plan and the major institutional decisions that are to be informed by the plan.

The substantial level of communications between the chief executive officer and the advisory committee on planning processes can enable members of that group to be witnesses to the community regarding the viability of the institution's plans and planning processes. Implicit in all that has been said about the charge to the planning facilitator and the charge to the members of the advisory committee on planning processes is that the latter are the persons most responsible for teaching the members of their institutional community about its planning processes, the plans produced through the use of those processes, and how those plans are being used to inform decisions related to priority setting and resource allocation. The absence of just such a plan for frequent and comprehensive intra-institutional instruction related to its plans and planning processes is one of the leading causes of the pendulumlike history of planning processes in institutions of higher education alluded to in the opening remarks of this chapter.

The Reporting Line for a Planning Committee

In the traditional approach to planning on campuses, the planning committee is generally responsible to the chief executive officer or the chief academic officer, depending on who appoints its members and prescribes its charge. When an advisory committee gives counsel about process, it is recommended that the group report to the planning facilitator and that it see its role as helping with the charge given to that position, that is, designing a planning process, equipping managers with the tools necessary to do planning, and monitoring the execution of the planning process to see that planning actually gets done.

Many colleges and universities have historically charged a separate group to do facilities planning for the institution. Those groups, often called master planning committees, provide another illustration of how planning committees are frequently mistitled. One would hardly argue in an academic community that the plan for facilities is the institution's "master plan." This approach to organizing the planning activities of a college only serves to fragment any comprehensive consideration of an institution's future. It is recommended that institutions err on the side of integrating their planning by charging a single group with all *planning* for all resources and another single group for *advising* about planning processes for all resources. Of course, as various topics are joined in a planning process, different persons can be brought into the system as needed, so long as they are qualified to assist.

Composition (Membership) of the Planning Committee

There are really three different functions potentially to be performed by committees, so a decision needs to be made as to whether to use three different committees or, for the sake of simplicity, to combine the functions into a lesser number. The functions to be performed are to plan, provide constituency-based advice on the plan, and provide constituency-based advice on the design and implementation of a planning process.

The responsibility for planning for an institution belongs to the administrators or managers within the institution, with principal responsibility for the task being held by the chief executive officer. If a CEO adopts a team approach to top management and involves the members of a cabinetlike body in group decision making related to the preparation of plans, then when the group meets for that purpose it is in effect the planning committee for the institution. When a cabinet meets as the planning committee, some institutions augment its membership of vice presidents, assistants to the president, and so on, to include representatives of the faculty, staff, or student body in the decision-making process.

The second situation is one wherein a group is appointed to give advice about institutional plans to the president's cabinet when it sits in its role as a planning committee. Considerable confusion has been caused on American campuses when such groups are called planning committees where in fact their function has been to provide *advice* to the president's cabinet in acting as the planning body for the institution. It may sound mundane, but groups of the type described should be called something like the advisory committee to the planning committee or the advisory committee to the president on institutional plans. Most often, advisory committees include members of each of the groups usually represented on constituency-based committees on the campus. In addition to representatives of the faculty, staff, and student body, such groups could include members of the alumni, major donors, and/or community officials. If one wishes to convey the point that planning is a routine and enduring activity, it may be important symbolically to observe very strictly any institutional norms for representation and not do anything that might insinuate that planning is an atypical activity deserving atypical patterns of representation.

Should the planning director/facilitator feel the need for a group to provide advice and assistance on the design and implementation of planning processes, for the sake of clarity that group should be called something like the advisory committee on planning processes. Because the purpose of having committees of this type is to avoid attacks on the plan based on issues related to process, it is imperative that the members be chosen as representatives of constituent groups. As a practical matter, any group should be represented whose failure to endorse the planning process could result in the institution's being incapable of using the plan as the basis for setting priorities and making resource-allocation decisions.

Some institutions eschew the use of group representatives on planning advisory committees and opt instead for the wise-person approach. That is, advisors are chosen based on their particular expertise regarding the issues facing the institution and the task to be performed by the committee rather than on the basis of their group affiliations.

The question of committee size is directly related to the philosophy of membership selection. The author has worked with wise-person committees having as few as nine members and constituency-based committees with as many as forty. There is, of course, the option to appoint persons to serve on more than one committee, or, as is more often done, to combine the two advisory functions (process and substance) into the charge for one committee. When the latter is done, it is very important that the two facets of the committee's work be clearly understood by all involved.

Planning as a Function Versus Planning as a Process

To this point, the discussion of organizing the elements of the planning function (a planner, a planning director/facilitator, a planning office, and a planning committee or committees) has focused on the institutional structure required to operate the planning function. Let us turn now to focus on the question of how institutions of higher education design, organize, and operate their planning processes in order to best accomplish the results they desire to achieve through the operation of those processes.

From the point of view of the chief executive officer, the first step in the planning process should be to designate the planning director/facilitator. The desired attributes for persons filling this role were described earlier; in brief, the planning director/facilitator should be credible among his or her colleagues and have such a "penchant for processes" that he or she is viewed as being neutral regarding the substantive issues with which the planning process deals. At this point, the CEO, aided by the planning director/facilitator (perhaps in consultation with knowledgeable members of the board of trustees), should tentatively outline the roles felt to be appropriate for himself or herself, the cabinet, the planning director/facilitator, and the planning committee or committees. Once this *dramatis personae* of planning participants has been completed, it is time to work within the rubrics and culture of the institution to name, charge, and designate the members of the planning committee(s).

After all the roles have been assigned, the participants in the planning process should prepare and reach agreement on (1) a schedule for designing a planning process for the institution, (2) a schedule for developing a plan for the institution using the process designed in Step 1, and (3) a schedule for using the plan to inform designated resource-allocation decisions. It is surprising, given the allegiance professed to the proposition that planning is useless unless it affects the allocation of resources, how infrequently a plan identifies in detail the specific regular or episodic resource-allocation decisions that will be informed by the contents of the plan. This latter exercise is important also because by specifying the decisions to be informed by the plan one also achieves insights as to the issues that need to be joined and the types of information that need to be provided in the plan if it actually is to be used as a guide in a resource-allocation process.

In general, the component parts of a strategic plan are the situation analysis, including planning assumptions and forecasts; the mission or role of the institution in society; the vision and/or the goals the institution hopes to achieve while carrying out that role; the strategies that guide the selection of tactics; and the tactics (or specific actions) the institution executes in order to achieve those goals, along with a timetable for doing so. The plan may also state the means the institution will use *ex post* to evaluate the plan and its execution. The schedule for designing a planning process (Step 1) specifies (tentatively) the time that is required, by which participants, to decide on which of the components from this list the institution will incorporate in its plan and through what process or processes they will be developed.

It is also in this early stage that a schedule should be prepared to describe the time line to be followed (and by whom) in actually preparing and gaining institutionally appropriate approvals for each of the specified components of the plan.

Schedules are, of course, sequential approximations of how long it takes to execute a series of tasks. In this case, the acid test of each schedule is whether or not the plan can be prepared, approved, and disseminated in time for its intended use in informing specified decisions, the deadline or deadlines for which should be widely broadcast and well known.

It is unquestionably true that planning is a political process. Nowhere is this truth more palpable than in designating the participants in each stage of the planning process. Moreover, it is true that the level of political activity is directly correlated with the community's perceptions that the processes that are being designed and the plans that are being made actually affect the allocation of resources. Therefore, not only must the planning schedules be viewed as ever-changing, sequential approximations of tasks to be performed, but they also should be understood to be ever-changing approximations regarding the roster of participants in each step of the planning process. In other words, people opt in and out of the planning process as they continually estimate its importance to the future of the institution and to their particular role in the institution.

Organizing the Planning Function to Address Future Academic Challenges

Part Four of this book examines strategies of planning that are called for in dealing with some specific academic challenges that all institutions now face or will face as they enter the twenty-first century. The contemporary challenges include multiculturalism and diversity, telematics, academic restructuring, faculty renewal, quality, economic development, and higher education as a global postsecondary industry.

If structure should follow function, then since these issues inexorably affect the functions of teaching, research, and service in our institutions of higher education, so too will whatever functional changes they engender inexorably affect the "structures" and "processes" by which institutions carry out their planning. Indeed, in the case of multiculturalism and diversity it could be argued that many institutions were able to effect changes in structure involving new paradigms for multicultural representation in planning long before they were able to effect comparable changes in their student body, curriculum, the teaching-learning process, scholarship, and faculty. It is difficult to generalize, but just the reverse seems true regarding telematics, wherein some institutions were able to make enormous strides in enhancing certain academic functions through global telecommunications, widely distributed information resources, and more sophisticated computing and analytic capacity long before similar resources were brought to bear on modernizing planning processes and structures.

Faculty development and economic development are, in effect, contemporary issues with which contemporary plans must deal. It is possible that current planning structures and processes are sufficiently adaptable to handle a wide variety of ever-changing, significant issues without themselves undergoing change. But at a minimum, as topical issues change consideration should be given to revising an institution's rubrics for determining patterns of representation. That is, as issues change, the definition of the relevant constituencies that should be represented in a planning process may also change.

Just as in industry, restructuring in higher education represents a mixed bag of efforts and results. For some, *restructuring* has been a buzzword that has merely replaced the worn-out buzzwords *reorganization* and *retrenchment*. The most significant attempts at restructuring in industry have occurred because of the insightful development of transforming ideas related to either products and/or markets. For instance, it was the transforming concept that its competitors were not other airlines but people driving their own cars that caused—indeed, required—one of America's leading airlines to adopt a structure and administrative processes that were different from those of other airlines. In other words, standard industry practice just would not work in the face of the new concept. Therefore, it could be argued that institutions undergoing so-called restructuring in the absence of a concomitant plan that transforms the conceptualization of their products and/or markets may simply be rearranging the pieces (reorganizing, changing job assignments, or eliminating personnel) without an enduring imperative induced by genuine conceptual change.

It is the absence of such an imperative that in the past enabled institutions (after having tried restructuring) to lapse back into various inefficiencies, whose symptoms are higher unit cost, bureaucratic delays, and deteriorated customer service. Somewhat similar statements apply to the commitment of some institutions of higher education to programs involving Total Quality Management and Continuous Quality Improvement. If not associated with transforming concepts principally related to customer service, they tend to amount to no more than the application of traditional industrial engineering techniques to the most amenable administrative processes.

As an example of potential restructuring being driven by the enduring imperative of a possible transforming conceptual change, there are nations whose educational systems are based on the model of the university as a place where students who have been admitted are, in effect, graded and weeded out. In this system, the quality of an institution is judged in part on the basis of its attrition rate, that is, high-quality institutions have high failure rates and vice versa. Should any of the institutions following this model change to an approach that conceives of the university as being responsible for developing each admitted student to his or her potential, then there would need to be a radical restructuring of course offerings, examinations, student services, and so on. The former structures and processes would simply not work in the face of the revised conceptualization of the "function" of the institution.

As a postscript to this discussion, it is possible that the notion of a global postsecondary knowledge industry (as used by the editors of this book) has the power to be a transforming concept for many institutions of higher education in the United States, just as the notion of a global marketplace has enabled the transformation of many American corporations. If so, one possible result could be the necessary redesign of many administrative structures and processes currently used in American higher education, not the least of which would be those related to planning.

Some Closing Thoughts

The issues that are related to organizing the planning *function* are closely tied to the issues related to organizing the planning *process*. It is for this reason that institutions should find it instructive to view planning both as a function to be performed and as a process to be followed, with the goal being to understand and scrutinize in detail those institution-specific points at which the organizational issues related to function and those related to process tend to intersect.

Finally, institutions of higher education need to embrace for their own use one of the basic principles on which they were founded, namely that concepts are teachable and people are educable. With all the controversy that surrounds the introduction of a potentially successful planning process (people tend to ignore planning processes seeming to have little effect on the future of their institution), it is amazing how little attention individual "educational" institutions pay to the need to teach planning to their various constituents who are called upon to help design, operate, and use their planning processes. If education is a life-long venture, surely educational institutions should incorporate into their planning processes a formal and scheduled educational program on planning that lasts for at least the life of the plan.

Further Reading

In "Wise Moves in Hard Times: Creating and Managing Resilient Colleges and Universities," Leslie and Fretwell (1996) provide a detailed account of the planning experiences of thirteen colleges and universities and their attempts to respond to fiscal challenges affecting their mission and objectives. "Strategic Governance: How to Make Big Decisions Better," by Schuster, Smith, Corak, and Yamada (1994), focuses on the need for colleges and universities to integrate more effectively their planning processes with their governance patterns as a means of facilitating institutional responses to changing societal demands. H. Mintzberg, in "The Rise and Fall of Strategic Planning: Reconceiving Roles for Planning, Plans, Planners" (1994) examines the relationship between planning and strategy in order to expose the factors that typically impede the use of strategic plans. Finally, two *New Directions for Institutional Research* monographs, both published by Jossey-Bass in 1990, also are especially relevant to the concepts addressed in this chapter. In "Assessing Academic Climates and Cultures," W. G. Tierney examines the way culture and climate influence the decision-making processes and objectives of a college or university; and F. A. Schmidtlein and T. H. Milton, in "Adapting Strategic Planning to Campus Realities" (1990), examine the range of approaches available to higher education institutions in their attempts to anticipate and adjust to the demands of a changing environment.

References

Leslie, D. W., and Fretwell, E. K. *Wise Moves in Hard Times: Creating and Managing Resilient Colleges and Universities.* San Francisco: Jossey-Bass, 1996.

Jedamus, P., Peterson, M. W., and Associates. *Improving Academic Management: A Handbook of Planning and Institutional Research.* San Francisco: Jossey-Bass, 1980.

Mintzberg, H. *The Rise and Fall of Strategic Planning: Reconceiving Roles for Planning, Plans, Planners.* New York: Free Press, 1994.

Schmidtlein, F. A., and Milton, T. H. *Adapting Strategic Planning to Campus Realities.* New Directions for Institutional Research, no. 67. San Francisco: Jossey-Bass, 1990.

Schuster, J. H., Smith, D. G., Corak, K. A., and Yamada, M. M. *Strategic Governance: How to Make Big Decisions Better.* Phoenix: Oryx Press, 1994.

Tierney, W. G. *Assessing Academic Climates and Cultures.* New Directions for Institutional Research, no. 68. San Francisco: Jossey-Bass, 1990.

PART THREE

REORGANIZING MANAGEMENT SUPPORT FOR PLANNING

Planning for a changing environment requires redefining the external context and substantially redirecting the internal institutional context. This cannot be done in isolation. As an institutional function that guides change in such a dynamic period, planning needs to be supported by other management processes. And those processes, themselves, need to be reorganized or revised to reflect the new planning realities and challenges.

Chapters Fourteen through Twenty focus on a number of ongoing institutional management processes and issues that are critical either to support the planning process or to implement its resulting decisions. Chapter Fourteen focuses on the rapidly changing area of information and decision-support systems, which can provide an increasingly rich array of intelligence for planning in an information-rich era. Chapter Fifteen examines the link between planning, budgeting, resource management, and resource reallocation and strengthening institutional competitiveness as well as efforts to redirect the institution. Chapter Sixteen discusses relatively recent attempts to relate resource acquisition—particularly institutional fundraising and development efforts—to the institutional planning process. Chapter Seventeen reviews current thinking and innovations about the changing nature of institutional facilities as a major planned investment in a more dynamic, information-rich, technology-based, and technology-distributed learning environment. Chapters Eighteen and Nineteen focus on two processes central to academic planning and the ever-increasing demands for accountability: (1) using program review and evaluation to support planned change and (2) using assessment to improve planning and, thereby, strengthen the academic performance of students, faculty, programs, and institutions. Finally, Chapter Twenty discusses the nature and application of policy analysis to inform critical planning discussions and strategic choices.

CHAPTER FOURTEEN

EXPANDING INFORMATION AND DECISION-SUPPORT SYSTEMS

Dennis P. Jones

As noted in the introductory chapter to this volume, the context within which the planning function is being performed in higher education is becoming more complex and less predictable. For most institutions, both the size and nature of student demand are becoming more variable. Performance expectations—as expressed by all external clients—are rising and being stated in more explicit, and frequently more narrowly defined, ways. The explosion in educational technology and telecommunications creates enormous opportunities for innovation and change in teaching and learning activities, and in how that information can be stored and used in support of planning and management functions. However, this same technology has created conditions under which many more providers—both inside and outside the established academy—can offer instruction to students in any given location. Coupled with the actions of the western governors to create a "virtual university" that would award credentials as well as promote delivery of instruction through use of technology, this heightened capacity promises to significantly change the higher education landscape in the coming decades. And while the external environment is becoming more chaotic, there is less and less margin for error in institutional decision making; years of tight budgets and more precise budgeting practices have long since removed the cushion in most institutions.

The unforgiving nature of the decision-making environment creates an understandable demand from college administrators for information that can reduce some of the uncertainty. Interestingly, the same set of environmental forces creates a demand for more, and different, information on the part of external constituents as well. There is behavioral evidence that more state governments are seeking to define their relationships with higher education institutions through market mechanisms rather than solely through control and regulatory devices. (Witness, for example, the rising popularity of incentive and performance funding schemes.) State and federal agencies are also assuming a responsibility in the marketplace on behalf of students, recognizing that the free-market system works only to the extent that consumers are fully informed about the existence, and consequences, of available choices. With this in mind, it may well be that a feature of future decision-support systems is the extent to which they not only are *about* the external environment but represent the interests of the external environment as well.

The impact of technology must be noted again at this juncture. It is not only a major factor that must be considered in institutional planning; advances in computing and other technologies provide those responsible for the planning function with much more powerful tools than were previously available. This technology allows analysts the luxury of creating and effectively using much larger databases than were feasible just a few years ago. They can build databases with more records; more importantly, they can accommodate more data elements per record. As a result, fewer data are lost between the point of original collection and the creation of the analytical database. This capacity has a downside in that it largely removes the need for discipline in the creation of databases; everything can get entered, without prior judgment about use and utility.

Technology is also becoming less and less expensive, allowing more and more capacity to be widely distributed within the institution. The tools that go with this capacity are also becoming cheaper and much more powerful. Available tools allow users to retrieve data in almost any conceivable combination and to display the results in whatever formats best suit the needs of the user, all without the requirement of considerable technical expertise.

Finally, technology has opened the door to almost limitless supplies of data and information that originate and reside at sites external to the campus. Data about demographics, employment, the economy, and many other factors that must be considered in the planning process are now available on CD-ROM and, increasingly, on the Internet. The latest research findings and ideas about the use of these data are available electronically as well. And when all else fails, electronic bulletin boards allow planners and analysts to ask questions of, and seek help from, colleagues around the globe.

The changes mentioned here are combining to overwhelm most institutions, which are not planning for the significant reforms that will allow them to align comfortably with emerging realities. Rather, they are seeking ways to continue business as usual—within the reality of increased demands and constrained resources. In addition, few are harnessing the power of the available technology to help themselves in meeting these challenges. Most institutions are awash in data but have very limited capacity to convert those data to information that supports planning. It is true that off-the-shelf tools allow users to shift the focus from the technology of building databases and retrieving data to use of data, that is, to analysis, interpretation, and the search for meaning. But most institutions have not made that leap. Although the technology also allows decentralization of data use and analysis, large numbers of institutions are still stuck in a mindset that funnels access to data through offices of institutional research or planning. In those places where the capacity to access data has been widely dispersed, the operational failure to enforce a standard data architecture and to ensure that users have access to the same data has often created more problems than the technical capacity has resolved.

This brief overview paints a bleak picture of the increasingly chaotic environment in which higher education institutions are functioning, and of the institutions' capacity to support a planning function attuned to the forces within that environment. Creating and using the decision-support systems (DSS, or DS systems) that are most helpful in this evolving environment require a considerable change in the state of the art at most institutions. This chapter describes the ways in which decision-support systems have to change in order to help decision makers function effectively in the future. It starts with a description of the different perspectives—the needs of those different kinds of decision makers—that must be reflected in the design of DSS. Then the chapter describes the changes in current capacity and thinking that are required to serve the needs of internal and external decision makers, respectively. Throughout, the emphasis is on the contents and conceptual structures of the DSS rather than the technology or technologies through which decision-support systems are implemented. This focus reflects the author's observations that these are the areas in greatest need of attention.

The Matter of Perspective

At the most basic level, a decision-support system can be viewed as the capacity to compile and store appropriate pieces of data and to retrieve and organize these data (to transform data into information) in such a way that they (1) help a particular user or type of user (2) address a particular problem or issue. Thus, in thinking about the design and development of a decision-support system, the central question is "for whom?" Once this question is answered, subsequent questions about the kinds of problems or issues to which the system must be responsive become more readily apparent.

Because this chapter deals with decision support for planning (as opposed to operating) decisions, the answer to the central question is "for those individuals—presidents, vice presidents, board members, and administrators and faculty serving on institutionwide committees—who are engaged in making the strategic decisions about the future of the institution." Decision makers at this level deal with issues that are broad in scope, are often poorly defined, and do not recur on a regular basis. These characteristics have major implications for the design of DSS. Specifically, the systems must contain a broad array of data that can be accessed and used very flexibly. (Excluded are almost all applications of "expert systems," which have the most to offer in applying decision rules based on experts' judgments to operating decisions that must be made on a frequently recurring basis.)

By focusing on only these internal audiences, however, the developers of DSS run the risk of perpetuating a solely provider-driven perspective on critical issues and possible responses to them. Thus, they serve to reinforce the status quo. If there is any merit to the argument that changing demands and constrained resources force institutions to change in significant ways in order to be successful, then decision-support systems that congeal thinking around business as usual do a real disservice.

As an antidote to such hardening of the conceptual arteries, it is suggested that DSS be designed with a set of external users in mind, *regardless of whether or not these external users actually have access to it*. The design issue is not one of access; rather, access is one of the perspectives reflected in the design. It has often been said that there has been no significant change in higher education absent an impetus from external forces. Given that market mechanisms are one of the means through which these external forces are most likely to bear upon colleges and universities, it is increasingly important that institutions understand their current (and potential future) position in that marketplace. There is perhaps no better way to accomplish this particular objective than by creating conditions under which institutional planners and decision makers can see the institution through the lenses of external clients of (that is to say, investors in) the enterprise. Consider the simple diagram presented in Figure 14.1.

From the perspective of someone situated within the institution (at point A), the view is of currently enrolled students (at point B), the competitors for potential students (other providers), and the existing set of relationships with state government and other external constituents. The student sees not only the institution at point A but the whole array of potential service providers, and a quite different set of relationships with state government. Decision makers at the state level necessarily see the demand expressed by all students as well as the full array of providers available to respond to that demand. This diagram also calls at-

FIGURE 14.1. PERSPECTIVES ON THE HIGHER EDUCATION SYSTEM.

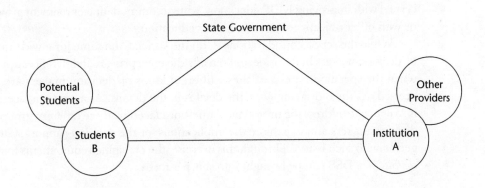

tention to the fact that the relationships among the entities, not just the characteristics of the entities themselves, are the important considerations in the planning process.

If institutional decision makers could put themselves in the shoes of critical external constituents—students, the state, employers, graduate/transfer institutions—and create the capacity to inform the kinds of judgments these constituents routinely make, they would be in a much stronger position to make sound judgments within their own sphere of responsibility. From this point of departure, it is possible to deal more systematically with the kinds of information that will be required to support the planning function in colleges and universities in the difficult years ahead.

Planning as a Change Process

Planning is essentially a change process. As such, it requires explicit attention to:

- The "reality check": an honest appraisal of current conditions within the institution and in the external environment
- A determination of the desirable (or most likely) future conditions, along with an assessment of the extent to which external forces allow (or, indeed, require) the institution to move in these directions
- The kinds of steps necessary to move from the current position to the desired future condition

These generic steps apply as well to students selecting a college; to employers investing in workplace training or applied research; and to state governments concerned with improving K–12 education, with accommodating enrollment growth, or with other objectives involving higher education.

While the set of considerations is, on the surface, the same for a wide range of decision makers both inside and outside the enterprise, real differences appear when the specific interests of these different kinds of decision makers are addressed. As the old saying goes, the devil is in the details. As a consequence, it is instructive to address the prototypical questions faced by these different groups of decision makers and to explore the implications for the decision-support systems germane to such issues. Through this exercise, the changing requirements for the *contents* of a DSS can be brought into sharper focus.

Intra-Institutional Planning Decisions

In the final analysis, strategic planning within a college or university typically revolves around decisions about:

- Clientele: the different student bodies and other groups (types of employers and so on) that are the intended audiences and beneficiaries of the institution's programs and services
- Program: the array of programs and services to be offered
- Comparative advantage: characteristics of the institution and the ways it does business that are particularly attractive to clients and that distinguish it from competitors
- Asset structure: the creation and ongoing maintenance of the assets needed in order for the institution to fulfill its mission (including attention to human and programmatic assets as well as physical assets such as buildings, equipment, and library books)
- Mission: the statement of institutional purpose and uniqueness that encapsulates consideration of clientele, programs, and comparative advantage

These are the decision areas given most consideration in existing decision-support systems. A more in-depth review of these systems, however, usually reveals some serious gaps and design flaws. Among the major problems are:

- Missing data, more often than not occasioned by adopting a singular, internal perspective on any given issue.

- Failure to focus on the relationships. Either the necessary data to examine relationships are missing (for example, data about competitors or about underlying populations from which students are drawn) or the variables that allow the links to be made easily are absent.
- Failure to allow for appropriate disaggregations. Most analyses proceed from a general observation to more detailed investigations conducted in order to seek explanations for an observed phenomenon. Ewell (1995) labels the process "thinking in layers." Again, what is required is to include variables that allow the necessary disaggregations to be made.
- Inability to flag discrepancies. As noted previously, technology allows the user to "warehouse" almost limitless supplies of data. Often, the more data that are available, the more difficult it is to find meaning within them. Thus, DS systems have to be designed (using comparative statistics, trend data, and so on) to draw attention to conditions needing further analytic attention. Too frequently, information systems contain only cross-sectional, descriptive data that are insufficient for the task of flagging key changes or discrepancies.

Some of the typical problem areas, organized under the headings of the key strategic planning decisions, are noted in the following paragraphs.

Clientele

Data about clientele are rapidly becoming one of the stronger elements of the decision-support capacity at most institutions. Most institutions have a long-standing ability to provide descriptive, cross-sectional data about applicants and enrolled students. Spurred by student right-to-know legislation and by actions of state agencies and accrediting bodies, the capacity to conduct longitudinal, cohort-based student tracking studies has expanded rapidly in recent years. Even so, important gaps remain. To some extent, these gaps arise from a failure to capture the necessary data elements about current students. Ewell, Parker, and Jones (1988) indicate the array of data about existing clientele required to support the planning function:

- Demographic: student characteristics as well as data about the underlying populations from which they are drawn
- Educational background
- Enrollment status
- Student goals and objectives (included as part of enrollment status in the document cited)

- Term-by-term tracking data, including academic activity, academic performance, and remediation status
- Follow-up data that indicate students' involvement with other institutions of higher education and employers

Within this array, the data most frequently missing deal with outcomes, particularly those arising from sources outside the institution—from alumni and employers, for example. In addition, the data about prior academic history are likely to undergo substantial change in the next decade. Typically, these data reflect students' experiences at traditional educational institutions: high schools, colleges, and universities. Increasingly, however, students are receiving formal education in the workplace and having their learning recognized in the form of certifications that are widely accepted and utilized by employers. The Certified Network Engineer (CNE) and related certifications bestowed by Novell, Inc., are prime examples. Acceptance of such experiences and the competencies attained as legitimate components of prior academic history is likely to be increasingly important to clients of higher education and therefore to higher education institutions as well.

Missing in most institutional data systems are data about student goals and expectations. Historically, it has been assumed that students enroll in an institution to obtain a degree or certificate at that institution. A recent study (Adelman, 1996) found, however, that more than 60 percent of the students who began their studies in 1982 and received bachelor's degrees by 1995 attended two or more institutions; this proportion was up from about one-third a decade earlier (Adelman, 1996). In addition, many students who "drop out" before receiving a degree do so because they have fulfilled their objectives. In an increasingly market-driven environment with very mobile participants, most institutions will find it necessary to acquire and utilize data about student goals. Further, the fact that goals change means that these data have to be updated at least annually.

A larger gap, however, is failure to systematically acquire data on clients other than current students. Absence of data about employers is particularly notable. It is rare that data gathered through continuing education activities undertaken for employers or data found in business offices as a result of corporate tuition assistance programs find their way into planning databases. Even more rare is conscientious compilation of data about place of employment for current students. At a time when most students work and when workplace-based learning is increasingly important, failure to compile data that would allow an institution to identify the existing, student-created networks is especially problematic.

Another weak spot is failure to compile data about *potential* students. Most institutions do a reasonably good job of compiling data about recent high school graduates. Missing in most, however, is systematic attention to demographic data that would allow projection of part-time student enrollments—for example, Bureau of the Census data about numbers of twenty-five to forty-four-year-olds in the service area who have educational attainment levels that would qualify them for the institution's programs or employment data (from the State Occupational Information Coordinating Committee—SOICC—or other local sources) that would provide information on markets for continuing professional education. This weak spot reflects less an absence of available data than a failure to tap the rich array of data regularly collected by state and federal agencies. To make these data more readily available, agencies such as the Bureau of the Census and the Bureau of Labor Statistics are making basic data available on their Web sites.

Interestingly, some of the more important gaps arise out of analytic rather than database shortcomings; the data are there, but they are not utilized to full advantage. It is not uncommon, for example, to find situations in which longitudinal data are used in calculating retention or attrition rates, but the more extensive analyses are not being performed that would indicate characteristics of students who are not being successful at the institution. More common are circumstances in which data about important student activities or experiences—often experiences such as counseling or tutoring explicitly designed to help ensure academic success—are either not gathered at all or are gathered but not integrated into the longitudinal database. It is typical to find situations in which data about students' involvement with various support services are captured somewhere in the institution but never used in the analyses that explore the absence (or presence) of student success. Equally common are instances in which investment of student aid funds is not investigated for its impact on student retention and success. This is one of the rare instances in which data and the technology to use it are widely available but use of that capacity falls far short of its potential. Perhaps this is because analyses of longitudinal student data arise in response to external pressures; analysts develop a compliance mentality early on. In that environment, it is typical that analysts devise "hard wired" responses—COBOL programs that generate the required annual data report as a production run in the computer center—rather than flexible tools that allow successive disaggregation of data for use internally in the institution. Perhaps this is because the techniques have not been widely used for a sufficient period of time to yield a body of conventional wisdom about productive avenues for investigation. Whatever the reason, efforts that could ensure that the power of this capacity is brought to bear on key academic policy issues—the structure of the curricula, admissions policies, the availability of academic support services, and so on—are a requirement of decision-support systems designed to meet the needs of the coming decade.

Programs

Data about programs and services offered also are often incomplete because of the singular, provider perspective from which they have traditionally been developed. This provider perspective has led to the ready availability of certain kinds of data at most institutions, including those about:

- Levels of activity: student credit hours produced in instructional programs, revenues from research and contract training programs, and numbers of clients served in the various student service programs.
- Resources consumed: expenditures in various budget categories and, much less frequently, the full-time equivalents (FTEs) of various kinds of personnel utilized in the program.
- Outputs: numbers of degrees granted in instructional programs; numbers of books, journal articles, or creative works produced under the aegis of research and scholarly works programs; and reports and other products as a consequence of service program activities. With regard to the outputs of research and service programs, it is typical that the basic data are collected in individual personnel files but not entered into a planning database that would make the data available to decision makers in aggregate, trend form.

Most of these data are simply descriptive of a single dimension of the program.

Missing in this program-specific catalog of data are those simple data of program *counts* that would provide managerial insight into program proliferation and the changing mix of programs and services. This applies not only to instructional programs but to research, public service, and student service activities as well. It is instructive, for example, to compile trend data on such measures as the number of organizational units engaged in direct provision of student support services or on the number of programs in which degrees were granted relative to the size of the student body. These data are even more useful when placed in a comparative context. Data about numbers of fields in which degrees are granted are available through the Integrated Postsecondary Education Data System (IPEDS) maintained by the National Center for Education Statistics (NCES). Data about numbers of service programs require special studies or involvement in consortial programs such as the American Association of Universities' (AAU's) Data Exchange. It is likewise instructive to compile data that reveal trends in the distribution of personnel effort across the primary academic functions of instruction, research, and service. As with program outputs, this is an area in which data are typically available on an individual basis (usually in personnel folders) but where the analyses and aggregations that shed light on departmental, collegewide, or institutional trends are seldom performed.

To be truly effective, the DSS of the future has to contain not only data about costs and productivity of programs but about the clients for these programs (reflecting the fact that institutions serve numerous client groups and student subgroups) and the extent to which client needs have been satisfied. That is, there has to be an emphasis on the relationships between clients and programs, not just on program descriptors. From this perspective, it is important that a DSS be capable of providing information about:

- The characteristics of students who are attracted to each of the institution's programs. Recognizing that almost all institutions serve multiple student bodies (described in terms of such characteristics as age, academic preparation, academic objectives, full-timeness of study, and so on), it is critical that data be readily available indicating the characteristics of the clientele for the various academic programs and support services. This need extends to employers and other clients beyond the student (for example, understanding the characteristics of clients for research and service activities of various units within the institution).
- The nature of the interactions of students with the program: the order in which they experience the curriculum, presence of work experiences (internships, coops, and so on), the degree to which they experience "good practice" and utilization of support services.
- The consequences of this involvement, the outcomes associated with participation. Information about employment and subsequent postsecondary education activities is high in importance; however, other data should also be considered. Among the candidates are data that reflect student satisfaction with their academic experience and those that reflect students' self-assessments of things they learned well along with areas in which their education was deficient.

In short, it is important that the DSS of the future be at least as focused on the primary clients of higher education—the students, employers, and others served by the enterprise—as on the ways in which institutions go about providing those services.

Comparative Advantage

In an environment in which almost all institutions must compete actively for students, it is not enough to simply understand the characteristics of enrolled students;

it is also important to understand insofar as is possible *why* students enroll and why other clients are attracted to the institution. Some of this can be determined by analyses of data about:

- Characteristics of students who enroll vis-à-vis those of students who are accepted but don't enroll
- Characteristics of competitors to which institutions lose significant numbers of accepted students
- Characteristics of competing institutions to (and from) which students transfer
- Students' stated reasons for selecting the institution

The results of such analyses frequently yield answers indicating that key factors are location, price, and program availability. Often, however, the results of such analyses are inconclusive. In such instances, it is necessary to dig deeper, into issues of institutional culture and image. This almost always means collecting data through means of surveys. Among the possibilities of off-the-shelf surveys are:

- The Institutional Goals Inventory (IGI) of the ETS, which asks internal stakeholders questions about institutional goals in an "is/should be" format.
- The National Center for Higher Education Management Systems' (NCHEMS) Institutional Performance Survey (IPS), which asks these same internal stakeholders a wide variety of questions about institutional functioning and culture.
- The Cooperative Institutional Research Program (CIRP) survey, which collects data about prior experiences, priorities, and values from incoming freshmen. Since this survey is nationally normed, it provides a basis for understanding those dimensions along which a particular institution's incoming class is significantly different from the norm.
- The College Student Experiences Questionnaire (CSEQ), which collects data on student activities and the levels of time and effort they are investing in their own education.

Using locally designed surveys, it is possible to gather "image" data about the institution and its primary competitors, for example by asking respondents to provide (or select from) a list of adjectives they would use to describe each institution.

These data reflect the importance of "market research" in a market-driven world. In such an environment, having data that help delineate a market niche and understand areas in which the institution is strongly attuned to (or in conflict with) client preferences is critically important. It is a type of data that, increasingly, institutions ignore at their peril.

Assets

Finally, from an intra-institutional perspective, the DDS designed with future decisions in mind has to be much more capable of supporting decisions about institutional assets and their creation, maintenance, and utilization. In this context, the concept of *assets* is used in the broadest sense, to include human (faculty, staff, and student body) and programmatic (investment in curricula) assets as well as buildings and equipment. In each case there is a need for data, as follows.

General Descriptive Data. Central to data about assets are those items that serve to characterize the amount and nature of the various assets available to an institution: square feet of facilities of various room use classifications; FTE of employees of various classifications, gender, age, ethnicity, and educational attainment; number of volumes of books and other materials in the library; and so on. These are commonly collected data, and it is unlikely that the DSS of the future will require substantially different kinds or amounts of data than would be suggested by current good practice. The one likely exception is educational technology, where future requirements will certainly demand more thorough attention to the kinds and amounts of technology in place within the institution.

Acquisition Costs. With regard to buildings and equipment, these costs are relatively easy to establish and the data are usually readily available. The notion of an "acquisition cost" for human assets, however, is a foreign concept. As a result, the appropriate data are seldom developed—and if they are, they are seldom compiled in a way that makes them useful for management purposes. For clarity, the acquisition cost of a faculty member would include not only base compensation but the costs of any inducements offered to attract the individual to the campus. For a superstar researcher, such inducements may be numerous, including equipping a laboratory, providing graduate students, guaranteeing summer salary, and a reduced teaching load. At the other end of the spectrum, such costs may include nothing more than partial reimbursement for moving expenses and a personal computer. The acquisition costs of a student body are the costs of student financial aid (or the amounts of forgone income arising from price discounts) required to recruit a student body of the required size and characteristics. Similarly, the acquisition (development) costs of curricula are seldom calculated. Occasionally, special projects are created for the purpose of revising some portion of the curriculum. At best, such projects reflect but a fraction of the total investment in curricula. The major part of the investment is in faculty time devoted to curricular improvement, the costs of which are seldom if ever calculated. Historically, this failure has not been critical. However, as more and more courses or course modules are developed elsewhere and made available through licensing and other arrangements, information about these development costs takes on increasing importance. In the absence of such information, there is no comparative data upon which to base the make-or-buy decision.

Maintenance Costs. While inclusion of acquisition cost information in DSS design is currently spotty, data about the costs of maintaining institutions' assets are almost uniformly absent from such systems. This deficiency must be overcome in DS systems designed to serve the emerging needs of higher education executives. In some cases the requirements are obvious; annual depreciation costs of buildings and equipment along with expenditures on building renewal and renovation and equipment replacement are key components. Equally important, but almost never included, are data about annual expenditures on faculty and staff development and on improvements to curricula. The former is particularly important. Faculty and staff are the key assets of almost all colleges and universities. Yet almost no overt and conscious attention is given to the ongoing maintenance of those assets. This substantial hole must be plugged in the DSS of the future.

Utilization of Assets. Again, most current DS systems have adequate data about utilization of some institutional assets; data about room assignments and classroom utilization are generally available as are data about program majors and course enrollments (the equivalent of program utilization data). Again, the major deficiency utilization of data is in dealing with the utilization of human assets. Most DS systems make no provision for centrally capturing data about assignment of personnel to different institutional functions (instruction, research, student services, administration) or for the aggregation of these data in ways that allow decision makers to ascertain trends in allocation of human resources to various functions. An additional need is now emerging: the need for data about allocation of faculty effort to various activities within the instruction function. As technology becomes an increasingly important component of the teaching/learning environment, the role of faculty inevitably changes, with more emphasis being placed on development of curricular materials and on helping students interact with that material, and less on transmittal of information. As this transformation occurs, it becomes increasingly important that institutional administrators be able to track the amount of effort—and therefore money—being devoted to key instructional activities: curricular planning and design, development (and maintenance) of materials, transmittal of information, mediating students' interactions with these materials and information, and evaluating learning outcomes. These needs create requirements for entirely new elements of a DSS.

Further Guidelines. For more details about facilities asset data, readers are referred to National Center for Education Statistics (1994); for human asset data to National Center for Education Statistics (forthcoming). There are no similar guides for data about equipment and programmatic assets.

Mission

An institution's mission is reflected in the clients it serves, the services it offers, and the values and characteristics (the elements of comparative advantage) that it cultivates. Therefore, if a DSS contains data appropriate to these other domains, data necessary for review of institutional mission are included as well.

Information Defined by External Perspectives

In addition to those items of information defined by internal decision-making requirements, the DSS of the future is likely have to include information that reflects the needs of important external constituents—data not only *about* these constituents, but *for* them. To some extent this information is determined by the decision-making requirements of these external audiences, and to some extent by the accountability requirements imposed by these audiences. In the end, however, this information is required by an institutional obligation to understand the perspectives of these key constituents, to monitor how well the institution is performing in the eyes of these constituents, and to take steps to improve that performance. Focus groups conducted with representatives of these external constituents reveal that they have substantially different needs and expectations (see Education Commission of the States, 1995; and Ewell and Jones, 1994). The design of the DSS of the future should be informed by an explicit understanding of these different perspectives.

Students

Students represent a key constituency for all institutions of higher education. From an institutional perspective, these individuals make one overriding decision: whether to attend a particular college or university. In making that decision, the prospective student seeks answers to some very basic questions (Education Commission of the States, 1995; Ewell and Jones, 1994; and Ewell and Jones, 1996):

- Will I have access to the academic programs and courses I want and the resources and support services I need if I attend this institution?

- What's the likelihood of success for a student like me—similar in socioeconomic status, academic preparation, and so on—at this particular institution?
- What happens to students who are successful in the programs in which I am especially interested? What kinds of jobs do they get? What kinds of graduate programs are they accepted into?
- With what aspects of their collegiate experience have students like me been most satisfied? Least satisfied?

Developing answers to these questions requires data from four different sources, all of which are necessary to provide information needed by institutional decision makers. The key difference is the way the data are organized and presented for use by student decision makers. First, there is a need for data selected from the internal record systems of the institution, information about access to core courses (were students closed out in the registration process?), majors (how many were admitted, how many denied admission?), small classes (what proportion of freshmen have at least two classes small enough for effective, active learning?), senior faculty (what proportion of lower-division student credit hours are taught by full-time faculty?), and support services (what proportion of applicants for child care services are denied, and what level of academic support services will be encountered?). Second, there are data gleaned from institutional records and organized in a longitudinal fashion. For this purpose, the required data are those demographic and academic history variables that allow characterization of "students like me," along with data about academic experiences (courses taken, performance in those courses, and support services utilized). The bottom line is the measures of student persistence, retention, and attrition. Third, there are data that can be gathered most easily through use of course evaluation forms, data about the incidence of written assignments and group work, hours per week of study time required in the core courses, and so on. Fourth and finally, there are data gathered through use of alumni surveys, data about job placement, subsequent educational activities, and areas of particular satisfaction and dissatisfaction.

These data, gathered to address the key questions of prospective students, are of enormous importance to institutional planners and academic administrators. For an institution to be successful in the long run, a part of the planning process almost necessarily must focus on efforts to see the institution through the eyes of prospective clients and to rectify shortcomings identified through the use of these data. At this juncture, it is interesting to note that student right-to-know, the impetus for most institutions' enhancing their ability to conduct longitudinal analyses of student data, led many institutions to violate good practice in using the methodology in support of internal decision making. The law encourages a focus on a single retention number, rather than separate numbers of each student subpopulation; it did not encourage inclusion of explanatory variables; and it ignored consideration of follow-up data.

An intriguing, related question is whether and how these data are made available to those prospective students on whose behalf they were ostensibly derived. Feasibility is no longer at issue. Technology allows these data to be made available to such potential users. In at least one state, discussions are progressing on using the Internet and the World Wide Web as a vehicle for interactively soliciting student profile information and then delivering institutional performance information for the group of previously enrolled students meeting that profile. This would be a substantial step in the provision of consumer information—and an enormous threat to at least some institutions.

Employers

In the main, employers view institutional accountability along a single dimension: are students who graduate from the institution prepared to enter the workforce as fully functioning, effective members? In some regards, their expectations may be impossibly high; almost all employers require their employees to have specialized knowledge and skills that can be learned only on the job. For the most part, however, they ask reasonable questions:

- Have graduates had experiences that acquaint them with the realities of the world of work: internships, co-ops, and so on?
- Do they possess high levels of important skills? Can they communicate well? Are they good problem solvers? Do they function effectively as members of a team?
- Have they learned the basic content of their major field of study?

The first of these questions can be addressed by easily acquired descriptive information. The last can be answered by references to the kinds of data normally compiled on student transcripts. It is on the second question that higher education institutions almost uniformly stub their toes. They have neither clear statements of expectation nor relevant measures of performance, whether devised as internal assessments or designed to systematically reflect employer (or subsequent college) judgments as to level of preparation on an array of critical skills. While there are numerous avenues available for acquisition of such data, credibility of the data (and of the institution) is enhanced when follow-up data are collected from employers or institutions to which students transfer and the judgments of outsiders are made an important part of assessment.

It can be anticipated that the data developed to serve the needs of employers, data about levels of competence in various knowledge and skill areas acquired by college graduates, represent one of the largest departures from current practice in design of a DSS. Their preferences, if colleges and universities accommodate them, change the coin of the realm from credit hours to levels of competence. This is another area in which data gathered in response to the needs of an external client can be an invaluable planning and decision-making tool for academics.

State Policy Makers

In many respects, state political leaders have the same set of interests as potential students and employers. After all, these institutional clients are the policy makers' political constituents. Failure to serve these constituents is, more often than not, duly noted. In addition to interests that are congruent with those of major constituents, however, state policy makers have agendas that are uniquely theirs. Each state, implicitly or explicitly, has a "public agenda," a set of issues that has captured the imagination and attention of these policy makers. These issues vary greatly from state to state but frequently include such items as reform of the K–12 system of education, diversification of the state's economic base, protection or improvement of the environment and the state's quality of life, and changing the way the state is dealing with a variety of social problems. The question for the state's system of higher education is "What are you doing that contributes to the solution of these priority statewide issues?" Successful planning requires not only that institutional administrators have a clear understanding of this agenda but that information be available that helps them monitor their institution's contribution to the attainment of that agenda.

Additional External Data

The kinds of data suggested so far as being central to support planning in the coming decades are largely under the control of institutions; they are derived from institutional record systems or can be compiled by institutions by asking questions of their primary constituents. There is, however, another set of data that may well prove essential to the planning process and that is much more difficult to compile: data about the extent to which competition is arising from noninstitutional providers of postsecondary instruction.

Technology, and people's access to it, has evolved to the point where it now promises to provide the primary method of access to certain kinds of education for an increasingly large number of individuals. Technologically delivered education is particularly attractive to individuals whom colleges and universities have typically labeled as their nontraditional students. To some extent, technology (particularly computer-based technology) will expand the market for postsecondary education. It is particularly effective at delivering "just in time" education, assistance in learning a narrowly defined skill or acquiring a particular piece of knowledge that has particular import to the learner at a given point in time. In this format, technology expands access to large numbers of individuals who would not enroll in a semester-long college course to acquire this information. In other instances, however, technology provides direct competition for clients and services that have historically been within the purview of institutions of higher education. Employers are becoming less and less dependent on local colleges and universities to deliver specialized instruction at the workplace. Much instruction of this sort can now come as easily from across the globe as across town. Similarly, more and more instruction is available through the Internet on terms that meet the requirements of individual learners.

This emerging capacity suggests the critical importance of institutions' monitoring the changing size and nature of their nontraditional and corporate client base. In addition, it is increasingly important to ask questions of these clients that have heretofore gone unasked. Specifically, institutions need to begin systematic gathering of "intelligence" about the other providers of instruction being tapped by their clients. As time goes on, it may be important to commission special studies (conducted by telephone polling firms or other such entities) that will help decision makers better understand the extent and nature of the competition being provided through alternative providers.

Summary

The decision support systems that support planning for the twenty-first century have many features in common with those currently in place. However, even the best of the current DS systems have to be expanded to include new or additional data on a variety of topics. Among these are:

- The costs of acquiring/developing and maintaining the key assets of the institution. The need for expansion is particularly acute with regard to human assets and curricula.
- The utilization of these assets. Again, the new elements focus on human assets and the allocation of effort to both functions and instructional activities.
- Performance of the institution as measured in terms that reflect the needs and priorities of key external constituents: prospective students, employers, and state policy makers among others. The major refinements in this arena

are information about competencies achieved by students and more systematic information about students' educational, employment, and civic activities after leaving college (along with external judgments concerning their level of preparation for these activities).

- The nature and extent of competition arising from noninstitutional sources of instructional programming.

None of these represents an insurmountable problem. The skill with which these data are compiled and presented to institutional decision makers, however, undoubtedly affects the quality of future planning exercises—and the ability of many institutions to meet the challenges of the coming decades.

Further Reading

The literature on decision support systems is extensive. Some of the better conceptual articles have been written by Gorry and Scott Morton (see, for example, Morton and Morton, 1989). Because this field is changing so rapidly, however, the literature on the applications of these ideas quickly becomes outdated. Some of the best information is found on World Wide Web sites and through Internet discussion lists that deal with decision support systems or, increasingly, under the nomenclature *executive support systems* (ESS).

References

Adelman, C. "Nothing Ever Stays the Same—Or Does It? Curriculum, Grading, and Attendance Patterns, 1972–1993." Paper presented at the AAHE Conference on Assessment and Quality, Washington, D.C., June 1996.

Education Commission of the States. *Making Quality Count in Undergraduate Education.* Denver: Education Commission of the States, 1995.

Ewell, P. T. (ed.). *Student Tracking: New Techniques, New Demands.* New Directions for Institutional Research, no. 87. San Francisco: Jossey-Bass, 1995.

Ewell, P. T., and Jones, D. P. "Pointing the Way: Indicators as Policy Tools in Higher Education." In S. Ruppert (ed.), *Charting Higher Education Accountability: A Sourcebook on State-Level Performance Indicators.* Denver: Education Commission of the States, 1994.

Ewell, P. T., and Jones, D. P. *Indicators of "Good Practice" in Undergraduate Education: A Handbook for Development and Implementation.* Boulder, Colo.: National Center for Higher Education Management Systems, 1996.

Ewell, P. T., Parker, R., and Jones, D. P. *Establishing a Longitudinal Student Tracking System: An Implementation Handbook.* Boulder, Colo.: National Center for Higher Education Management Systems, 1988.

Morton, G., and Morton, S. "A Framework for Management Information Systems." *Sloan Management Review,* Spring 1989.

National Center for Education Statistics. *Handbook on Human Resources: Recordkeeping and Analysis.* Washington, D.C.: U.S. Department of Education, forthcoming.

National Center for Education Statistics. *Postsecondary Education Facilities Inventory and Classification Manual (Revised and Reprinted 1994).* Washington, D.C.: U.S. Department of Education, 1994.

CHAPTER FIFTEEN

CHANGING FISCAL STRATEGIES
FOR PLANNING

Paul T. Brinkman and Anthony W. Morgan

"Long ago, when people wished to discern the shape of things to come, they looked to the stars; today they look at the budget" (Caiden, 1988, p. 42). Today, most analysts of planning and budgeting, at least in the nonprofit sector, assume or advocate a comprehensive, sequential, and rational linking between these two managerial activities. Plans, be they strategic or otherwise, are developed and budgets become the mechanisms for their implementation. In this chapter, we examine this traditional and sometimes normative view, particularly in light of the theme and assumptions of this book.

Most discussions of budgeting focus almost exclusively on the expenditure side of the equation: how expenditure authorizations are allocated to institutions or to units within institutions. Historically, private colleges and universities have been more dependent and therefore more acutely aware of what might be called "revenue markets," including the sensitivities associated with higher tuition levels and donor satisfaction and the connections between those sensitivities or constraints and expenditures. Diversification of revenue sources and increasing competition for revenues in the public sector, however, have made the links between revenue sources and allocation of resources more critical for everyone in higher education. We have therefore paid more attention in what follows to the revenue side of budgeting and the dynamics of planning and budgeting for resources secured in different revenue markets.

Finally, we examine two methods of allocating resources, known as performance budgeting and responsibility center budgeting, against the framework of higher education's need to maintain public trust, its reliance on multiple revenue sources, and its financial future. In the latter context, we also weigh the possibility that colleges and universities might eventually behave more like for-profit than not-for-profit organizations. Our focus is planning and budgeting at the institutional level. We deal with the perspectives of both the central administration within an institution and those of academic and administrative units.

Context

We believe the following developments are likely to occur and have significant impact on planning and budgeting.

Assumptions

1. Many institutions will face a decline in real resources per student (Brinkman and Morgan, 1995).
2. Technology will become ever more pervasive in virtually all higher education endeavors, introduce new levels of competition both from within higher education and from new educational providers, and complicate costing and pricing.
3. The production, control, and management of information will become increasingly important in most organizations.
4. New and expanding markets, such as distance education, will provide opportunities and forces for change.
5. The push for accountability will increase rather than abate.

In short, we envision a fast-moving environment of shifting competition and changing opportunities. Combined with a relatively difficult resource situation, tolerance for error is diminished. Conditions favor the fast and surefooted.

Budgetary Context

Facing that environment is a higher education enterprise whose budgetary practices and characteristics are in some ways less than ideal, given what needs to be done. The salient features are these:

1. The default fiscal strategy for most higher education institutions and their operating units is to increase revenues rather than reduce costs.

2. Most higher education institutions are in multiple "businesses" with different financial objectives and operating within different markets.

3. Most higher education institutions have multiple revenue sources; these sources differ with respect to acquisition and spending rules.

4. Institutions differ significantly from one another in the share of revenue coming from particular sources, as do their individual operating units.

5. Particularly in the academic area, budgetary structures do not always match up well with planning structures. The chemistry department or the office of undergraduate education, for example, may both be planning nodes, but typically the latter is not a budget center. Plans and budgets can also be out of step in a temporal sense.

6. Higher education budgets have multiple purposes. Short-run goals often collide with long-term goals.

7. Higher education budgets tend to be an inertial force; the typical budgeting process is such that anything more than incremental change is likely to meet resistance.

Elements of a Fiscal Strategy

In what follows, we specify in a normative fashion the elements of a fiscal strategy that need to be present no matter how planning and budgeting are organized and developed.

Resource Acquisition

A fiscal strategy includes responses, explicit or implicit, to certain questions. Is the institution committed to revenue maximization? In balancing the budget, will revenue enhancement normally be the first option, or will it be a second option after expenditure reduction? Will revenue be pursued wherever there are possibilities, or only selectively according to a plan or set of principles?

However these questions are answered, most institutions and their business units would probably agree with the following goals for revenue acquisition: (1) ensure marginal revenue growth, (2) ensure predictable and stable revenue, and (3) find revenues that are flexible in how they can be deployed. Organizations need to develop new revenue sources and expand existing ones in order to meet legitimate organizational needs and keep key constituents happy. The absence of reasonable predictability (as evidenced by planning and budgeting in poor countries) causes enormous problems for both planning and budgeting. Unrestricted revenues are highly prized because they can be used to address a range of needs.

Resource Allocation

A fiscal strategy contains the objectives and the rules for allocating resources. The strategy indicates, first and foremost, the basis upon which allocations are to be made. (Often, this is equivalent to how "need" is to be determined.) Second, budget centers need to be established, as do rules governing how their debts and surpluses are handled. Finally, a procedure for allocation, such as zero-based budgeting, must be specified. Whatever the procedure, the fiscal strategy must include provision for how various short-term and long-term allocation goals are addressed.

Without resource allocation, essentially nothing can happen. Making something happen involves two short-term objectives: (1) meet immediate production and support costs, and (2) impose efficiency. From a longer-term perspective, other objectives must also be addressed: (1) preserve organizational assets, (2) invest in the future, and (3) deploy resources strategically.

Arguably, all of these things that the acquisition and allocation processes ought to do in conjunction with various plans should be incorporated in any institution's overall fiscal strategy. Ideally, all of these objectives would be addressed openly and in an integrated way.

Other Dimensions

Assumptions of declining real resources and emerging competitive forces give impetus to several other important dimensions of planning and budgeting as they generate a fiscal strategy: reallocation, incentives, the links between planning and budgeting, and maintaining political support. Strictly speaking, reallocation of resources is just a type of allocation, but experienced practitioners know the difference between distributive and redistributive politics (Morgan, 1992). Conditions of fiscal stringency combined with rapid change increase the need to bring reallocation strategies front and center. Any fiscal strategy, and especially any serious reallocation effort, must be formulated with explicit incentives as part of the design (Berg, 1985) unless an institution is prepared to operate in a highly centralized, top-down manner. A fiscal strategy flows out of the intersection of plans and budgets. Explicit attention to that fact should be included within the fiscal strategy itself: how the intersection is managed, who has responsibility for its occurrence, check points, and so on. Finally, fiscal strategies that ignore political realities are likely to be short-lived, especially in difficult times.

With these additional dimensions, it is obvious to us that a fiscal strategy is and should be woven deeply into the fabric of institutional management. Simplistic approaches, such as "we want to do X; can we afford it?" won't do. This becomes even more evident as we examine the issues and strategy options below.

Issues and Strategies

We focus on three tasks: maintaining trust in a trust market, managing in the context of multiple revenue sources, and dealing with financial stringency and reallocation. While concerned about a range of planning and budgeting issues, we pay special attention to the extent to which performance budgeting (PB) and responsibility center budgeting (RCB) are likely to be helpful platforms for handling these tasks. In the former approach to budgeting, resource allocations to operating units are linked in some manner to specific levels of performance by those units, such as test scores on a licensure examination (for details, see Ashworth, 1994). In the RCB approach, budget responsibility is highly decentralized, as some or all large operating units, such as a college within a university, are given responsibility for managing all of their own finances. They are assigned revenue, including that from tuition, and must use that revenue to cover their full costs (for details, see Zemsky, Porter, and Odel, 1978; Whalen, 1991).

Maintaining Trust in a Trust Market

Operating in a trust market is a critical ingredient of the environment for higher education institutions. A trust market is characterized by asymmetry of information: the seller knows more about the product or service being sold than does the buyer. For example, few buyers of higher education services truly understand the economics of the enterprise or the qualitative nuances within an academic discipline or an undergraduate education.

In a trust market, business depends on the trust the buyers have in the integrity of the sellers. If the level of trust deteriorates, buyers may at some point refuse to make transactions. It deteriorates if buyers feel they are being taken advantage of, or if they feel that the sellers are not behaving appropriately.

For some time, as Winston (1992) has argued, higher education has been drawing down on what once was a large reservoir of trust. The drawdown has been due to many specific developments and episodes: the rash of criticism of the academy (some of it coming from inside), concerns about workload, salaries that seem high when compared to those of high-profile public figures, occasional but highly publicized instances of scientific fraud committed by university researchers, the overdone aspects of college athletics, the indirect-cost recovery debacle, student loan defaults, the breakdown of consensus on accreditation, and so on. Many of these problems are rooted in higher education's revenue-maximizing behavior, which has intensified since Bowen (1980), among others, called attention to it more than a decade ago. Other problems are rooted in choices about resource utilization, choices that often reflect the private interests of faculty and administrators (James, 1990) or lust for prestige (Garvin, 1980) rather than the interests of constituents.

One such constituent, the federal government, has been showing signs of diminishing trust. The hearings on indirect-cost recovery rates were an example. The message implicit in student right-to-know legislation is quite clear. State governments have also been growing uneasy, as the accountability movement demonstrates. States are interested in reducing the asymmetry of information; they would not be if trust levels remained high. Students have been less vocal, perhaps, but they have been voting with their feet—or at least that is one way of interpreting the increased market share enjoyed by community colleges.

Higher education institutions are facing a dilemma. They are thoroughly accustomed to revenue maximization and setting their own priorities as first principles of fiscal strategy. Yet both behaviors threaten the trust various constituents place in our enterprise. At some point, loss of trust engendered by revenue maximizing results in a net loss in revenue—a classic bind. Similarly, efforts to dictate product and service mix may eventually result in a decline in the demand for those products and services.

There is an obvious need, then, to address these problems. Institutions must learn to focus less on revenue acquisition and more on cost containment. They must better understand their own operations and both the primary and secondary effects of their choices. They must be more forthcoming about their activities and align their priorities with those of their constituents.

A deteriorating trust market and the actions required to reverse the situation indicate a need to strengthen the linkage between planning and budgeting. Planning structures should provide the appropriate venue for consideration of possible second- and third-order effects of alternative fiscal strategies. The loss of trust is just such an effect. No one set out to accomplish that deliberately. Similarly, planning activities should as a matter of course orchestrate the analysis of priorities for both internal consistency and agreement with constituent needs and interests.

From the latter perspective, it would seem that either PB or RCB is likely to be preferable to incremental budgeting. Implementation details are important, of course, but PB in particular has some clear advantages in a trust market.

First, performance budgeting cannot be implemented without serious consideration being given to the range of performances that will be rewarded or supported and to the powerful incentives created by those decisions. Those considerations can and should lead backwards, as it were, to how the institution and its programs are supported, which in turn can and should lead to a discussion about constituents and their interests. Second, if the agreed-upon performance indicators happen to include those favored by constituents, the institution has an obvious basis on which to build and maintain trust. If valued performance goes in some other direction, the institution at least has an evident, visible problem with which to contend. Higher education got into some of its trust problems gradually and in an unplanned way. There is value in bringing priorities and consequences into sharper focus.

We think these advantages of PB could be achieved even if the institution did not quantify the relationship between specific measures of performance and the allocation of resources. Indeed, our preference would be to include performance as an important basis for allocation decisions but not, as a rule, to quantify the relationship because of the imperfect nature of most measures and the difficulty of integrating multiple measures in any mechanical way. Ashworth (1994) and Lasher and Greene (1993) provide helpful assessments of the strengths and weaknesses of PB, albeit in the context of funding institutions and not internal allocation.

Managing Multiple Revenue Sources

From a comparative financing perspective, American colleges and universities are the envy of the world. Historically, higher education institutions in most other nations have received an overwhelming share of their support from a national government and are in turn subject directly and singly to its political and economic vicissitudes. These nations have looked at the diversity of sources of funding available to American colleges and universities as providing some measure of financial stability and alternative avenues for revenue growth. When government funding growth is nonexistent or slow, tuition and private funds might provide a counterbalancing effect. Even the existence of two or three different governments (federal, state, and local) contributing to the support of public institutions is viewed as a stabilizing force, both politically and economically. Not surprisingly, more nations, including several in Europe, are moving away from single-source funding of higher education.

The reality of living with multiple sources of revenue reveals, however, the two edges of this mighty sword. The existence of these multiple streams of revenue substantially undermines simplistic models of planning and budgeting. Most discussions and models of planning and budgeting simplify either by assuming a single revenue source (in the form of an overall bottom line) or focusing on projected differential growth rates as a basis for scenario planning. Yet each revenue source operates in its own "revenue market" that imposes criteria and constraints for acquisition and use of funds. All revenues are not, therefore, interchangeable; nor can they be deployed at will for priorities derived through careful, institutional academic planning. Capital campaigns, for example, are often disillusioning to faculty when they finally confront the reality of a donor-driven philanthropic revenue market. In addition to the constraints and conditions imposed by these various revenue markets, the very existence of multiple streams complicates integrating plans and budgets, particularly at the level of the central administration.

Responsibility Center Budgeting. The existence and growth of multiple sources of revenue, some of which goes directly to units or even individuals within institutions, combined with the complexity of managing from the central administrative level often provide the impetus for RCB, or at least substantial budgetary independence. Substantial independence of subsidiary budgetary units, whether in a formal RCB system or not, poses new challenges to administrators accustomed to traditional paradigms of central planning and budgeting. Institutions operating primarily on a single source of revenue, such as tuition, can of course adopt RCB, but the existence of other significant sources and the experience of attracting and controlling those resources at the unit level whets the appetite of units for more and greater autonomy over both revenues and expenditures. As a rule, then, diversity of revenue sources pushes planning and budgeting responsibilities out from the center, although the extent of this depends on the mix and significance of multiple revenue sources.

RCB is a system whereby all or part of the tuition reflected in enrollments, along with sponsored research and other revenues, is returned to units in proportion to what the unit "earns." In theory, the unit controls its own pricing policy and is responsible for all, or nearly all of its costs (Berg, 1985). Surpluses and deficits are the responsibility of the unit. Additionally, in most RCB systems, the central administration of an institution oversees a taxing or subvention system where some activities such as libraries, judged to be valued but outside of proper market forces, are subsidized. Other central services, such as computing or printing, often operate on a charge-back system and must compete with outside vendors.

Just as there is a strong case to be made for PB in a trust market, there are persuasive arguments in favor of RCB in the context of multiple revenue markets and rapidly changing market conditions. The incentive structure created under RCB, for example, is designed with defined responsibility centers as the units of analysis and is intended to force decisions about efficiency and effectiveness of programs to that unit level—close to the action where managers' knowledge of market supply and demand forces is greatest. Although cost consciousness is something academics are not renowned for, it is therefore thrust upon academic and support units, who must operate within what their respective revenue markets produce. Priority setting, regarded by some as the heart of planning, should become very explicit and be debated within the unit.

RCB has been in operation for many years at such well-known private universities as Harvard, Pennsylvania, and Southern California. A newly adopted RCB in a portion of Indiana's public sector (Whalen, 1991) was recently evaluated by Robbins and Rooney (1995). They cite as RCB strengths operational-level flexibility, multiyear planning, information-rich discussions, more explicit and operative incentives, and greater understanding of planning and budgeting.

Any system also has its weaknesses, or at least tendencies that may not well serve certain organizational goals. RCB engenders entrepreneurism—a virtue and a potential vice. The search for revenue can be intense and may lure units far afield from a focused academic mission. Revenue maximization may also overpower concerns for educational quality. Additionally, there are an interrelated set of organizational issues that arise out of RCB with its centrifugal forces. Reimbursement and subvention rates are examples of the administrative pricing complexities with which administrators must deal. Complex subventions involving multifactor taxing and/or subsidization formulas are not only difficult to develop but often contain unintended incentives to which operating units respond. Competing courses may proliferate as a means of securing tuition funds, and professional schools may provide a larger proportion of general education classes than desirable because of favorable course reimbursement rates.

The need for more information and management at the unit level also raises a question of total administrative costs. As units add more development staff, accountants, and managers, and as faculty spend more time on administrative activities, what happens to total institutional administrative costs?

The Role of the Center. RCB, or even just significant levels of revenue flowing directly to units within an institution, raises questions about the role of the central administration, or center, in planning and budgeting for these flows and their uses. For example, if a public medical school derives 10–15 percent of its revenues from the state and competes successfully in revenue markets for research and clinical income, what is the role of the center?

Since much of higher education's legacy for planning and budgeting devolves from the corporate business world (Chaffee, 1985), it is instructive to learn from the debates over the role of the corporate center and its various business units. Large, diversified corporations must operate with two levels of strategy: (1) corporate, to determine which businesses the corporation should be in and how the corporate center should manage those businesses; and (2) business unit, which concentrates on how to operate competitively within the particular market of that business (Porter, 1987). Porter's premise is that diversified companies do not compete, but their constituent business units do. Successful corporate strategy must therefore grow out of and reinforce business-unit competitive strategy. Business-unit strategy or planning, commensurate with RCB strategy in a higher education context, is where the action is and where information about markets and decisions about investments should be made.

How comparable are colleges and universities to diversified corporations and corporate/business-unit strategies? Certainly there is substantial variation by institution, but some do fit this model. Many large universities, four-year colleges, and community colleges run highly diverse "businesses" that operate in very competitive markets. Clark Kerr's term "the multiversity" captures the reality of multiple and diverse activities all sharing a common heating plant. But there are also some significant differences between the collegiate and corporate worlds. One of the most striking is the undergraduate core. A university chemistry department competes nationally for research revenues that flow directly to the department; it also competes in its own graduate student market, complete with competitive stipends. But chemistry departments are an integral part of many undergraduate majors and also contribute to general education programs. No one business unit captures this market for general education or for undergraduate education as a whole.

Another important conceptual issue for linking planning and budgeting in colleges and universities is determining the best level or organizational unit of analysis. Porter's theory defines "strategic business units" as those businesses within a diversified corporation that operate within a defined competitive market of their own. In matters of research and graduate studies, as well as the major itself, the discipline rather than the college is probably the most common parallel to a strategic business unit in the private sector. The exception is professional schools or colleges, where there may not be sufficiently well-defined disciplinary divisions. In other functional areas such as contract instruction, for example, the most appropriate unit may well depend on the size and configuration of the particular institution.

The most suitable level or unit of analysis on which to build a financial strategy therefore varies by type of institution, function, and even institutional context or culture. Thinking through this unit-of-analysis issue raises questions as to the role of the college level, within a university, as well as the central administration in planning and budgeting. If, as Porter's theory implicitly suggests, the department is the fundamental strategic business unit for colleges and universities, what value does the dean or vice-presidential level add?

Fueled by increasingly diverse and independent revenue sources, the natural centrifugal forces within institutions are posing major challenges to traditional models of planning and budgeting, which have focused on the primary role of the central administration while the role of constituent units is appropriate participation in central decision processes. What we are seeing is a redefinition of roles and questions being raised as to continuity of leadership and level of management expertise at the strategic business unit or disciplinary level.

Unintended Consequences. Having access to multiple revenue sources can provide stability. During the 1980s and early 1990s, for example, increases in public-sector tuition made up for some of the decreases or slow growth in state support. But stability thus achieved can be costly. Those same increases in tuition contributed to the loss of trust in higher education.

Paradoxically, dependence on multiple sources of revenue can also reduce stability and the institution's control over its own destiny. For example, growth in clinical-practice income allowed medical schools to expand their activities at relatively little direct cost to state government or students. Now, changes in health care threaten that revenue source and pose a very serious problem for medical schools. Institutions that tenure or promote faculty on the basis of extramural funding (Lederman and Mooney, 1995) may be climbing out on a similar limb.

Revenue maximization in conjunction with multiple revenue sources means that institutions are at risk of drifting from their moorings by any number of revenue-related developments. A change in direction that may accompany a change in revenue shares is not necessarily bad, but it might well be if the change in direction is a second-order, unplanned effect rather than an intended outcome—as is usually the case.

Dealing with Financial Stringency and Reallocation

In an environment of declining real resources, productivity gains are critical if institutions are to avoid stagnation and decline. Such gains can be realized either through changes in production functions or through reallocation of resources to higher-value programs and services (growth by substitution).

A prolonged period of financial stringency affects planning and budgeting and underlying fiscal strategies. For example, Massy (1994) hypothesizes that as financial stress increases, nonprofit institutions are likely to behave more like for-profit institutions.

What might that hypothetical response mean in the mid-1990s? We can get a good idea of the implications of such a change from the following strategies, delineated in a recent annual report to investors by a for-profit firm:

- Evaluate each business based on best-practice standards of quality, cost, revenue growth, and profitability
- Invest in high-growth businesses
- Streamline day-to-day processes
- Invest in technology
- Leverage economies of scale
- Improve responsiveness to clients
- Segment markets in new ways
- Allocate resources in a focused way
- Hold expenses at current levels or cut them if planned revenues don't materialize
- Expand high-growth businesses
- Divest businesses that are not producing adequate returns or are no longer central to the more focused strategic direction (Shipley, 1995, pp. 2–3)

Are not-for-profit colleges and universities willing and able to conduct themselves in this manner? Most critical in this regard are the prospects for marginal analysis, which is fundamental to the strategies listed above, and for reallocation, which is often an important way of responding to the results of marginal analysis and indispensable in the absence of significant revenue growth.

Both are problematic for higher education. Making them key elements of a fiscal strategy requires a transformation in planning and budgeting. Marginal analysis entails a complex calculus of marginal revenues, costs, and values. Done in the manner of a for-profit firm, it requires agreement on a surrogate for "profitability" and on appropriate ways of determining whether "returns" are "adequate." Better ways of assessing quality and marginal cost would have to be found, too. How many institutions currently have the knowledge to support these calculations? In short, it is difficult to be sanguine about the prospects for the agreements and the additional knowledge required to support marginal analysis. However, it is conceivable that institutions could benefit by thinking in marginal terms and applying the principles of marginal analysis as best they can even in the face of inadequate information. For example, an academic department can profitably address alternative uses of faculty time, fundamentally a marginal analysis, without measuring precisely either costs or benefits.

Significant reallocation is infrequent, if not rare, in most higher education institutions. The long dependency on increased revenues has created a psychological disposition against reallocation. It is hard to imagine a program that does not have a constituency (either within or outside of the institution) who will resist reallocation when it threatens their interests. Reallocation is further complicated by the diversity of revenues at most institutions. Legal constraints embedded in some revenues can be an impediment to reallocation.

It is apparent, then, that marginal analysis and reallocation, so appropriate in theory, are tough sells in practice. They are tough sells, both cognitively and politically. But times are hard, and therefore what model should be pursued? Should institutions design for, and get tough with, more definitive central planning? Should they conclude that central planning and budgeting will not work and decentralize to something like RCB? Or should they develop a strategy of mixed models? We offer some suggestions in the next section, "Linking Planning and Budgeting."

Some form of PB could be helpful in promoting reallocation, assuming it were possible to reach agreement on the types of performance to be included and the ways in which they are measured. Once in place, these agreements constitute at least one basis for comparing programs at the margin. In addition, if the strategy includes, for example, a tax on all units to create an allocation pool, differential performance over time brings about reallocation "naturally"; the larger the magnitude of the tax rate and the differentials, the more extensive the reallocation. If performance measures are driven by planning goals or planning strategies derive from an analysis of critical issues, this approach to budgeting can support both reallocation and better links between planning and budgeting.

The capability to reallocate resources is, of course, a virtual necessity. The fast-moving higher education environment requires that resources be at least somewhat mobile. Changes in political priorities, technology, competitors, and so on damage and can overwhelm institutions that are locked into spending patterns from another era.

Subventions, while they sometimes entail nothing more than moving resources from the strong to the weak, may also be a shift of resources to areas such as a liberal arts core or a program in theology that are central to the mission of an institution, if not its *raison d'être*. Like reallocation, then, the capability to undertake subventions in an acceptable manner is a critical component of a good budget system.

Paradoxically, as financial stringency deepens the need for marginal analysis and for reallocation increases, so does the political difficulty of implementing a substantial reallocation tax. Any approach of this type almost certainly establishes powerful incentives that have to be thought out in advance, lest they do serious harm.

In the responsibility center approach to budgeting, it seems that the implicit if not explicit message to the business units is to behave in a for-profit mode. The units are pushed toward marginal analysis, or at least toward comparing the relative value of their various programs and activities in some manner (for example, see Jacquin, 1994). Financial stringency makes this comparative analysis all the more urgent. Conceivably, units could make allocation decisions that would be detrimental to institutional goals or institutionwide responsibilities. For example, various departments could participate too heavily or too little in general education, thus unbalancing it with respect to disciplinary representation.

The central administration can tax business units to create a reallocation pool or use its subventions to bring about reallocation. The reallocation itself can be based on an institutional-level strategic plan. With respect to avoiding the payment of economic rents to business units or otherwise getting effective and efficient use of allocated resources, the center faces an asymmetry of information not unlike that faced by funders outside the institution in a trust market.

Linking Planning and Budgeting

We have attempted to show how the ground rules have been evolving for higher education planning and budgeting. If the loss of trust in higher education is to be stemmed and even reversed, if institutions are to come to grips with their complex revenue structures, and if they are to cope with long-term financial stringency, then new links between planning and budgeting need to be formed. It isn't that the general goals of planning and budgeting have changed, but the road maps are undergoing some important revisions. Old solutions are not as appropriate as they once were. In particular, strategists must probe a little deeper to get at second- and third-order effects. When they do so, the linkage between planning and budgeting becomes a little easier to bring about.

Nonetheless the linkage between planning and budgeting has proven difficult to achieve (Schmidtlein, 1989–90). Planners need to take the initiative if the track record is to improve. We suggest the following strategies to increase the odds of successfully linking planning and budgeting.

Our most basic strategy might be described as selective and opportunistic rather than comprehensive. While some observers would recommend the latter approach, we think it runs the risk of collapsing under its own weight and of requiring busy people to engage in activities that may not always be meaningful. We think a more modest and explicitly opportunistic approach has a greater chance of success at most institutions. Some suggestions follow for finding situations and issues in which the links between planning and budgeting should be most easily forged. Schmidtlein (1989–90) provides a systematic analysis of the prospects for those links in relation to classical approaches to resources allocation such as formula budgeting.

Perhaps the most obvious way to start the search for opportunities is to look for issues where resource allocation can scarcely be done at all without fairly explicit planning. A good example is an effort to develop a long-term strategy for library funding within the framework of the future shape of the library. The information required to support such an effort greatly exceeds what is readily available to budget analysts and line officers. Planners are, or should be, adept at developing information, especially from sources outside the institution. They can bring that to the table along with the perspective that fundamental, long-term questions about the library can only be addressed within the broader framework of institutional mission and programmatic direction.

A similar strategy is to look for emerging issues where the terrain is unfamiliar, or where comparative analysis is helpful (for example, see Middaugh, 1995–96), or where much of the impact is in the future. For example, technology-based distance education seems to be an especially appropriate issue for forging links between planning and budgeting. This is an area where planners can use their environmental scanning skills and whatever skills they might have in bringing together a wide range of ideas and people. It is also an area where revenues options are likely to be quite complex, in terms both of sources and shifts from one-time to base and back again. Immediate and long-term costs for investment and development are important issues, as are long-term maintenance and replacement costs. In short, numerous fiscal and strategic issues arise that are appropriately addressed in a planning mode. An externally imposed need for a major reallocation of resources can be a good opportunity to link plans and budgets. Planning in one form or another, but particularly strategic planning, may generate interest in reallocation, or reallocation needs and opportunities may surface for other reasons. In any case, a thoughtful approach to reallocation requires knowledge that exceeds what is required to budget for day-to-day operations.

Planners need to find or develop tools and techniques that can be useful to the budget process. For example, given the revenue complexities and the allocation challenges discussed above, long-run scenarios make sense; they have been used successfully in the private sector (Shoemaker, 1995). They can increase the chances of realizing the long-run goals of maintaining assets, investing wisely, and offering the right products and services. They can also focus discussions on these goals and, if used in conjunction with a simulation model, provide a quantitative perspective on relationships among long- and short-term goals. Scenarios can serve as a platform for discussing higher education's production technologies. Production technologies and production preferences are at stake when an institution attempts to better align itself with constituent interests. Those technologies and preferences and the effects of changing them (or their mix) are part of what is typically addressed in simulation models. (The classic treatment of this type of modeling is in Hopkins and Massy, 1981; a straightforward application can be found in Lovrinic, DeHayes, and Althoff, 1993; and Kundey and Taylor, 1994, provide evidence that budget officers are unlikely to use these tools on their own.)

Finally, linkages between planning and budgeting can sometimes be enhanced by altering what is expected of ongoing planning and evaluation activities. The goal is to force into the open questions that invite the linkage, or in other words, to shape the agenda such that planning and budgeting questions of comparable gravity rise in close proximity to one another. Consider, for example, the typical program review. What if the review has to include a recommendation that the program should grow (however defined), stay the same, or shrink (command fewer resources)? This shifts the ground from what tends to be mostly a tactical discussion ("Are we doing things right?") to a strategic discussion of the extent to which the institution should be engaged in this effort. The appropriate fiscal issues are also likely to arise if substantial resources are going to be needed or are made available for other purposes.

Speculations

The experience of many institutions in dealing with continuing economic pressures gives them an experiential base for dealing with future conditions. Whether that base includes fundamental changes in planning and budgeting patterns is critical to the institutional cultural changes that lie ahead.

While economic pressures affect institutions quite differently, a second development probably has an even broader impact. The long-promised and anticipated technology revolution looms, but will it ever come? Futurists of the fifties predicted educational technology changes that never happened. The core processes of higher education instruction have remained basically the same for centuries, with some allowance for larger class sizes and modest doses of electronic mediation. Current and projected information technology has the potential for far more fundamental change in those production processes. How seriously should this potential be taken? Should sizeable institutional investments in new technologies and people, far beyond what has been made to date, be made in an effort to get ahead of the curve in anticipation of whole new levels of reconfiguration and competition? Or should institutional leaders, remembering the past, wait and see? It seems to us that for most institutions the risks of an overly cautious approach run much higher than before and therefore compel institutions to engage in new levels of planning for change. Will an institutional culture of caution allow such change in the absence of immediate and compelling external pressures?

A third line of speculation, closely related to this discussion of change, concerns organizations of the future. Charles Handy (1994), a leading management and organizational writer, argues that federalist organizations are best suited to deal with change. The line operating units of organizations, or the federal components that are close to markets and customers, must be given sufficient latitude to operate while the organizational center must focus and limit its efforts to (1) overall system planning, (2) central banking, and (3) designing and monitoring decision processes. If the traditional tendency of the organizational center to overcontrol is allowed, adaptation to changing markets may be hampered.

Organizations, including colleges and universities, must also ask tough questions about their traditional structures. Which administrative offices add value to the organization? Does the dean level of administration add value if the strategic business unit is really the discipline complimented by interdisciplinary programs such as general education? Will the forces of change in the future, reflected primarily through constituents and economic markets, be met by our traditional organizational structures? Or would a movement toward RCB at the departmental level only reinforce disciplinary myopia and power?

While these questions may appear to have more to do with academic governance than planning and budgeting, they are hardly independent. We have discussed two ideal types of planning and budgeting: a more centralized, plan-based model exemplified in performance budgeting and a more decentralized, market model in responsibility center budgeting. While some institutions advocate one or the other, we do not expect to see radical moves to either extreme, but rather mixed models dependent upon both the institutional type and the function within institutions. Massy (1994) argues for a mixed, or hybrid, approach in his concept of "value responsibility budgeting," which combines key elements of incremental, performance, and responsibility center budgeting. While we like the concept, we are less sanguine than he is about the universal applicability of the full hybrid approach across institutions and functions. It makes sense to us, for example, to develop the core of the undergraduate experience, general education, using primarily a plan-based model. Other functions, ranging from research and graduate programs to delivery of contractual instruction, seem suitable candidates for more market-based models. A mix-and-match design of planning and budgeting systems is perhaps the greatest challenge facing those entrusted with developing fiscal strategies for the decades ahead. It is certainly one of the core functions of the organizational center and one that has profound long-term impact.

Further Reading

Readers interested in the themes in this chapter might want to examine Meisinger and Dubeck (1994) on the fundamentals of budgeting and financial reporting; Lasher and Greene (1993) on the strengths and weaknesses of various approaches to budgeting; Morgan (1984) on the conceptual roots of various budgeting strategies; Berg (1985) on budget incentives; Massy (1994) on performance, responsibility center, and value responsibility budgeting; Ashworth (1994) on performance budgeting (at the state level); Whalen (1991) on responsibility center budgeting; and Hyatt (1993) on strategic restructuring in the context of linking planning and budgeting.

References

Ashworth, K. H. "Performance-Based Funding in Higher Education." *Change,* Nov.-Dec. 1994, pp. 8–15.

Berg, D. J. "Getting Individual and Organizational Goals to Match." In D. J. Berg and G. M. Skogley (eds.), *Making the Budget Process Work.* New Directions for Higher Education, no. 52. San Francisco: Jossey-Bass, 1985.

Bowen H. R. *The Costs of Higher Education.* San Francisco: Jossey-Bass, 1980.

Brinkman, P. T., and Morgan, A. W. "The Future of Higher Education Finance." In T. Sanford (ed.), *Institutional Research in the Next Century.* New Directions for Institutional Research, no. 85. San Francisco: Jossey-Bass, 1995.

Caiden, N. "Shaping Things to Come: Super Budgeters as Heroes (and Heroines) in the Late-Twentieth Century." In I. S. Rubin (ed.), *New Directions in Budget Theory.* Albany: State University of New York Press, 1988.

Chaffee, E. E. "The Concept of Strategy: From Business to Higher Education." In J. C. Smart (ed.), *Higher Education: Handbook of Theory and Research.* Vol. 1. New York: Agathon Press, 1985.

Garvin, D. *The Economics of University Behavior.* New York: Academic Press, 1980.

Handy, C. *The Age of Paradox.* Boston: Harvard Business School Press, 1994.

Hopkins, D. S. P., and Massy, W. F. *Planning Models for Colleges and Universities.* Stanford, Calif.: Stanford University Press, 1981.

Hyatt, J. A. "Strategic Restructuring: A Case Study." In W. E. Vandament and D. P. Jones, (eds.), *Financial Management: Progress and Challenges.* New Directions for Higher Education, no. 83. San Francisco: Jossey-Bass, 1993.

Jacquin, J. C. "Revenue and Expense Analysis: An Alternative Method for Analyzing University Operations." *NACUBO Business Officer,* 1994, *28*(3), 41–47.

James, E. "Decision Processes and Priorities in Higher Education." In S. A. Hoenack and E. L. Collins (eds.), *The Economics of American Universities.* Albany: State University of New York Press, 1990.

Kundey, G. E., and Taylor, E. P. "The Financial Officer's Toolbox: Do Financial Officers Use Available Methods and Tools?" *NACUBO Business Officer,* 1994, *27*(11), 29–32.

Lasher, W. F., and Greene, D. L. "College and University Budgeting: What Do We Know? What Do We Need to Know?" In J. C. Smart (ed.), *Higher Education: Handbook of Theory and Research.* Vol. 9. New York: Agathon Press, 1993.

Lederman, D., and Mooney, C. J. "Lifting the Cloak of Secrecy from Tenure." *Chronicle of Higher Education,* Apr. 14, 1995, pp. A16–A18.

Lovrinic, J. G., DeHayes, D. W., and Althoff, E. J. "Developing an Economic Model: How One Midwestern University Is Approaching Cost Control." *NACUBO Business Officer,* 1993, *27*(1), 34–38.

Massy, W. F. *Resource Allocation Reform in Higher Education.* Washington, D.C.: National Association of College and University Business Officers, 1994.

Meisinger, R. J., and Dubeck, L. W. *College and University Budgeting.* (2nd ed.) Washington, D.C.: National Association of College and University Business Officers, 1994.

Middaugh, M. "Closing in on Faculty Productivity Measures." *Planning for Higher Education,* 1995–96, *24*(2), 1–12.

Morgan, A. W. "The New Strategies: Roots, Context, and Overview." In L. L. Leslie (ed.), *Responding to New Realities in Funding.* New Directions for Institutional Research, no. 43. San Francisco: Jossey-Bass, 1984.

Morgan, A. W. "The Politics and Policies of Selective Funding." *Review of Higher Education,* 1992, *15*(3), 289–306.

Porter, M. E. "From Competitive Advantage to Corporate Strategy." *Harvard Business Review,* 1987, *63,* 43–59.

Robbins, D. L., Sr., and Rooney, P. M. "Responsibility Center Management: An Assessment of RCM at IUPUI." *NACUBO Business Officer,* 1995, *28*(9), 44–48.

Schmidtlein, F. A. "Why Linking Budgets to Plans Has Proven Difficult in Higher Education." *Planning for Higher Education,* 1989–90, *18*(2), 9–23.

Shipley, W. V. "Chairman's Letter." In *1994 Annual Report.* New York: Chemical Bank, 1995.

Shoemaker, P. J. H. "Scenario Planning: A Tool for Strategic Thinking." *Sloan Management Review,* Winter 1995, *36,* 25–40.

Whalen, E. L. *Responsibility Center Budgeting.* Bloomington and Indianapolis: Indiana University Press, 1991.

Winston, G. C. "Hostility, Maximization, and the Public Trust." *Change,* 1992, *24*(4), 20–27.

Zemsky, R., Porter, R., and Odel, L. P. "Decentralized Planning Responsibility." *Educational Record,* 1978, *59,* 229–253.

CHAPTER SIXTEEN

LINKING FUNDRAISING AND DEVELOPMENT WITH PLANNING

Bruce A. Loessin

Financial resource development in American higher education is changing, and as always clues to the future are available through a look at the recent past. In the late 1970s and 1980s, philanthropy experienced a time of considerable optimism. The latter decade, in particular, saw a nationwide expansion of fund raising programs (Worth, 1993). Total giving to America's charities substantially increased, and higher education shared in this escalation of charitable intentions (Kaplan, 1995). The financial opportunities for higher education were further fueled by the continuing erosion of the "ivory tower" concept of American higher education. The membrane separating the academy from the external community became increasingly permeable, and the new college-community relationship settled most visibly in the fundraising area. Nowhere else in the university context could external representatives so easily be attached as in the fundraising organization. Volunteers by the thousands met in institutional settings, hearing about academic plans and scholarly needs. Committee assignments abounded, and the academy became in many instances the favorite meeting place for community-oriented individuals.

This breach of traditional academic boundaries needed, as all social movements do, a host organization to structure activities for the new community involvement. Thus evolved the modern American capital campaign. While capital drives have proliferated throughout the American nonprofit setting, the major forces for the concept still are centered at American colleges and universities. The most significant development techniques and applications, and the most impressive goals, still emerge from higher education. Billion-dollar targets have become commonplace. The sophistication of such efforts spins off applications used by other nonprofit organizations in the same way NASA technologies are applied to everyday American consumer products.

The Capital Campaign Context

During the 1980s, the modern university capital campaign transformed itself into a complex combination of high technology, social recognition, and art form. What started out years ago as a basic volunteer organization driven by committees eventually yielded highly sophisticated approaches in such arenas as direct mail and computer-assisted telemarketing. The most advanced techniques for mass marketing are in regular use today throughout higher education. Development systems for keeping track of donors have spawned a plethora of competing high technology firms. Formerly, alumni and friends would meet in focus groups to review who had money. They still meet, but now it is often to peruse lists conceived from advanced techniques in electronic screening and Internet-oriented financial information.

Simultaneously, the visibility of multimillion dollar campaigns attracted the best talent available to present the case in a fashion appropriate to the size of these operations. The results have been more spectacular than any other issue in history associated with university affairs. College and university campaigns now field literature costing hundreds of thousands of dollars and compete with Fortune 500 companies for awards in graphic design. Commonplace are capital campaign special events, which define the field for quality—and occasionally for opulence. Generations ago, college officials would have been shocked at the cost of such affairs. But from the 1980s on, expensive campaign kickoff and celebration events have become accepted milestones in most campaigns.

Most importantly, the external social and political life of communities has now infused the academic environment. The glitter and size of the campaigns attracts influential people and dignitaries, who act as emissaries from the social life outside the academy. Networking and personal recognition have become preoccupations for those involved in university campaigns. The depth of this infusion of social recognition is evident in the fact that aspiring social and political leaders vie for roles in the most prominent capital campaigns on both a local and national level. The capital campaign has become a vehicle for the most rapid ascent to prominence in the community or constituency.

All of this excitement in the 1980s led to what will probably always be viewed as the heyday for education resource development. The growth in fund expectations was precipitous, and income to higher education increased. (For some historical comparisons, see Murawski, 1996.) While all of this was transpiring, another subtle change took place, with no notice among the public and little internally. For decades, capital resources raised by higher education were referred to as "the margin of excellence." The implication was that the funds raised were "extra" to an institution's basic mission. The money was for new programs, qualitative attainment, and desirable physical improvements. But funds raised in higher education were increasingly related to the ongoing mission of the institution. Somewhere in the 1980s, monies switched from providing an extra margin to being completely essential to survival. This change produced an inevitable effect on attitudes toward development activities; namely, fundraising became less enjoyable and more pressure packed. Private financial resource acquisition became a serious preoccupation at many institutions where these pursuits had formerly been occasional or casual.

The Effect on Professional Development

This historic change in the environment of resource development was mirrored in the nature of the institutional development profession. Fundraising personnel over the years had been an eclectic group, often pursuing their careers in a variety of fashions depending on the nature of their educational institutions. Institutional loyalty and personal gregariousness were often the most highly valued characteristics of development officers, and there was limited instruction available in the fundraising field. There was little consistency or standardization as well.

Professional institutional advancement work changed with the increased sophistication of the megacampaign process, and with the much larger size of the funds being raised. When the raised funds are central to the survival of an institution, it is understandable that no one wants amateurs in charge. The pressure mounts, and the fundraising endeavor evolves into a virtually new occupation characterized by high technology techniques, organizational management skills, promotional expertise, investment savvy, and strong career advancement motivation. There were important positive outgrowths from this evolution. Fundraising attracted higher quality executives interested in the increasingly high pay. Academic programs sprouted new curricula featuring issues relating to fundraising. National organizations blossomed to hold conferences and provide training designed to increase the sophistication of the entire fundraising community. The opportunity to tap into what seemed an ever-expandable pool of resources also stirred entrepreneurial spirits. Creativity and new ideas were endemic in the growth of the development profession in the 1980s.

All of this excitement in the 1970s and 1980s led to some very desirable outcomes. Volunteerism from outside the educational setting increased, as people became educated about and involved with academic life. Operating revenue increased at an opportune time, allowing institutions to navigate troubled financial waters vis-à-vis the economy and limited public funds on the state and national levels. Endowments burgeoned, anchoring a future of secure income, particularly for America's most prestigious colleges and universities. The American philanthropic heritage of private support for nonprofit education was reinvigorated and reached new heights. The resource development profession became more organized, better trained, and more professionally managed.

The Changing Agenda

Perhaps it is true that all trends must eventually end, or at least change. The fundraising growth of the 1970s and 1980s has shown noticeable moderation in the 1990s. While 1994 was a generous year, possibly due to a strong stock market, charitable giving to higher education only rose 3.2 percent in 1995, the lowest increase since 1987. In constant 1995 dollars, this accounts for only a .03 percent change. The Council for Advancement and Education notes that since 1990, support for higher education has grown 9.9 percent in constant dollars. Individual giving has not increased at a desirable rate for most charities. Higher education is particularly vulnerable to the trends in corporate giving because of research relationships in science, engineering, and medicine. Corporate giving to higher education, adjusted for inflation, has increased just 1.4 percent over the last ten years. (For a discussion and tables on higher education giving, see Council for Aid to Education, 1995.)

In the meantime, modest improvements are compounded by the fact that there has never been a time in which higher education needs private funding more than now (Hancock and McCormick, 1996). Colleges and universities are caught in a number of dangerous trends. Federal funding is increasingly endangered as officials work on balancing the budget and reducing the deficit. Many states already face declining revenue available for higher education. Double-digit percentages of tuition increase, once the most dependable cash resource for colleges, have exceeded the threshold of intolerance for students and parents. Worse yet, nonprofit organizations outside the educational arena are proliferating in America, and their financial needs are expanding. These organizations are very competitive for funds and are unusually aggressive because their survival is at stake—often on an annual basis. The conclusion: there is little more money available and substantially increased need for scarce resources.

The considerable expectations of the 1970s and 1980s have changed considerably. What happened here? What can we learn from past experience about what will transpire through the end of the nineties and the first decade of the twenty-first century? The first lessons, as always, are in history. In this case, the seeds of the presently sobering circumstances were always present in higher education capital campaigns.

A Diminishing Presence

The format of the higher education capital campaign, no matter how successful, has always had characteristics that foreshadowed its possible decline as the only appropriate long-term financial vehicle for the academy. (For a reprise of material in this section, see Ryan, 1995.)

1.   Capital drives are not appropriately geared to an institution's regular budgets, planning, or academic process. In discussing "Emerging Themes in Nonprofit Leadership and Management," Dennis Young put it this way: " . . . nonprofit organizations do not yet seem to have taken the implementation of sophisticated management and governance practices completely to heart" (Young and others, 1993). Because capital campaigns are "one-shot" by nature, their underpinnings are self-contained and rarely connected to the university's budget process in a sophisticated long-range pattern. University budget preparation during a capital campaign is usually conducted separately and sometimes without cross-referencing of the impact made by campaign revenue.

2.   Capital campaigns often do not put sequential stress on clearly established academic priorities. In many cases, it is the availability of funds from donors that dominates the pace of a campaign, rather than the necessity of specific contributions in moving the institution forward most effectively. The driving force in a campaign is the financial goal, and funds are sought to reach that end. The result is that money often comes into a university where it is least needed, further widening rather than closing the gap between the rich and poor academic units. At major universities, a disproportionate share of the funds raised is for medical purposes. While the funds for medicine are certainly needed, the results blur the comparative lack of response for the other academic units. This has often created disillusionment for faculty members who read about big campaign numbers but don't see the results for their own departments.

3.   Capital campaigns produce "gear up, gear down" cycles, which can be destructive to the consistency of an institution's operation. Colleges rapidly build up staff, increase travel budgets, import new computer technology, and deploy

volumes of promotional literature during the upswing of a campaign format. Budgets increase substantially in a short period. Often, as a campaign concludes, the opposite occurs. Budgets recede quickly, with little time for enough preparation for orderly retreat.

It is hard to imagine that the best decisions are being made in the often chaotic buildup for campaign readiness. It is self-evident that rapid staff acquisition by nature introduces new people who do not know the university well and do not know the volunteers and alumni at all. One can only imagine what would happen if a college pursued a similar course with an academic department. Essentially, the erratic cycles of capital campaigns are antithetical to the deliberate and purposeful lifestyle of the American academy.

4.   Capital campaign cycles can negatively affect the regularity of healthy constituency development. Often large numbers of volunteers and alumni are rushed into action in the heat of a campaign. Focus groups, rating sessions, campaign committees, and special events abound. But when the campaign ends, much less contact follows; sometimes years go by before a college renews a relationship with a constituent. Contact may reemerge through new people representing the university at the advent of yet another campaign. The impression is that the university contacts alumni and friends only in the search for resources, and not from a desire for a lasting association. This phenomenon is connected to the observable recent decline in volunteer leadership.

5.   Capital campaign cycles can be disruptive to loyalty and morale in the university and its circle of friends. Institutional development offices find some disruption at the end of a capital campaign, whether the effort was successful or not. Staff members face diminishing responsibilities—or even job loss—no matter whether they personally did a good job or whether the campaign made its goal. Volunteers who work with university officials involved in campaigns are aware of the problems being created by artificial downsizing and often feel caught in the middle of internal issues; in the end they may be left with little or no support once the money has been collected.

6.   Capital campaigns can be innately wasteful and expensive, even if managed well. The staffing up and gearing down consumes executive time. Resources are burned up in searches and interviewing. The new campaign personnel need a learning-curve adjustment period, and then there is downtime as people seek new jobs at a new campaign at a different institution.

In addition, campaign paraphernalia has become inappropriately costly. A video can cost $50,000 or more, and the slick literature that is a trademark of most campaigns is now a hefty budget item in itself. Special events have become particularly onerous, with dinner costs skyrocketing in recent years.

A New Paradigm

Higher education resource development is evolving into a new format for the first part of the twenty-first century. The major tenet of this new era is the regularization of fund development practices into the everyday life and process of the academy. Fundraising practices that once were, and often still are, associated only with the conduct of capital campaigns will become as standard in colleges and universities as billings for tuition or publication of course schedules. Capital drives should diminish substantially in number and length. Eventually, one might hope that capital drives will only appear as they were originally intended: an occasionally implemented special reaction to a singular set of circumstances.

These changing times are going to be difficult for colleges in general and for the institutional advancement profession in particular. For a generation, the capital campaign was the ready answer for almost any question raised about resource development. When issues first emerged about the efficiency and appropriateness of these efforts, reactions were defensive.

Nevertheless, the changing of the times is inexorable. Credible sources are publicly calling for a shift in the campaign-dominated higher education environment. The key to developing this new paradigm is institutional planning. Colleges and universities can make the inevitable happen more quickly and with less disruption by actively planning a changed model for raising private revenue. There are a number of major issues that are woven into the college fabric to complete this mission.

Integrating the Institutional Development Program with the Financial Management System

In many instances, colleges have quite sophisticated development and finance systems. The problem is that rarely are they connected at vital points. If fundraising necessities were integrated with academic priority development, the resulting analysis would strongly affect the outcome of many of the institution's decisions. (For a thorough discussion of these issues, see Nahm and Zemsky, 1993.) In the present context, academic program decisions are often made without appropriate consideration for the funds that can or must be privately contributed to guarantee a program's success.

A hard look at integrated data tells the appropriate officers whether they can rely on a steady private income stream for a program. Certainly in some instances, lack of private funding leads an institution to downsize or even eliminate an academic or administrative unit. However, the most overlooked issue is that many opportunities exist in which funds are available and can be sought to bolster or save a financially strapped department. An astute budget analysis that includes fund development priorities can serve as a road map for the officials in charge of institutional advancement. Often fundraising goals are very broad-gauged; this is particularly true in a capital campaign format. Changing the budget-building exercise to include fundraising dimensions allows for much more specific targets for the fund development program.

This whole budget unification process will result in major changes in all institutions, but it has an accelerated impact on the larger, more diversified universities where the institutional budget preparation takes place on many decentralized levels. At a major research university, the integration of fundraising opportunities and expectations with budget priorities is replayed at the level of every major college, school, department, center, or institute. This leads to even greater program specialty for the fundraising plan, particularly at private universities where there is a high percentage of privately raised dollars in the operating budget.

Program Planning for Private Resource Development

Budgets for the institutional advancement program should be strategically built on maximizing fund income possibilities for the institution, not on a capital campaign superstructure (Loessin and Duronio, 1990). Careful planning entails the use of peer-group benchmarking in order to decide an institution's potential. The most dangerous element in less sophisticated capital campaign budgeting is the drive toward incremental thinking—each campaign has to be bigger and bring in more money—when the real question should be how many dollars can be raised by an institution if it takes full advantage of its opportunities (Brittingham and Pezzullo, 1990). If this planning approach is followed, some institutions will find that they have dramatically underestimated their fundraising potential for years, in spite of running what they thought were successful fund drives (Loessin and Duronio, 1990).

Peer-group benchmarking sounds formidable, but it can actually be done with a modest effort. Data can usually be found at the Council for Financial Aid in Education, which reveals the basic giving patterns of colleges and universities. The idea is to pick several other institutions that share similar size and characteristics with your own operations and compare income streams over a period of years. It is best to look at average income over a period of time rather than concentrating on any one year, where there may be aberrant low or high results. Most often, this data can also be broken down into categories such as corporate, foundation, and individual giving. This information shows where a development program is weak or strong compared to similar institutions, and it leads to changes that bolster specific inadequate areas in the fundraising program.

While basic peer comparisons can yield important clues for building and repairing the fundraising structure, larger and more complex institutions should be engaged in far more sophisticated analysis. Comparative income streams should be analyzed not only on an institutionwide level but in the decentralized units as well. Professional and graduate schools should have their own peer comparisons, and the results should be reviewed on both the graduate and undergraduate level. To ensure precision, the peer groups for the individual academic units should be individually selected; they are likely to vary somewhat from the institutions chosen for overall university comparisons. Further valuable research can be done by analyzing other factors that affect the income stream and therefore either accelerate or contain fundraising outcomes. For example, what is the economic growth in a certain region, and how diverse is the industrial base? These factors influence the corporate income stream at each of the institutions being compared.

Diversifying Resource Dollar Goals: Set Them by Academic Priority, Not Size

If funds were raised for the most important purposes and the true mission of colleges and universities, it is probable that smaller goals would result in larger impact (Poderis, 1996, particularly chapter three). Planning could allow university officials to decide where and how much money has to be raised to add real value to the institution. This strategy demands that the fundraising program stick to a plan for academic progress. These high-impact dollars reduce the overly broad appeal of many campaigns. This approach ends many of the contributions that actually cost the college money and drain resources by demanding attention, staff time, and program support money for activities that are not the highest priority and sometimes are not even in the organization's best interests (Hancock and Mc-Cormick, 1996). If the well-planned, high-impact fundraising program succeeds, academia will soon be hearing about individual academic accomplishments resulting from donations, rather than new and bigger dollar goals.

The capital campaign system is also overly oriented to individual donor satisfaction. Therefore, campaign commitments have become more and more earmarked, sometimes with excruciating precision, by donors who have a particular social or education interest. These readily accepted restrictions are sometimes costly and distracting to the institution, which must administer the details of the agreement and often add its own money to the project to make it work appropriately. Colleges have many named chairs, projects, programs, institutes, and centers that are underfunded and draining money from the central academic mission.

College officials and advancement officers should plan and implement programs to alert alumni and friends of the importance of the high-priority academic programs to the institution's health and future. Donors also should be encouraged to understand and enjoy present, rather than ever-new, academic programs. Capital campaigns have dangerously sold almost all new issues to the donor public, thus adding another layer of administrative bureaucracy and underfunded programming. Even buildings that have the cost of construction covered are a problem. Often the institution has not planned and budgeted appropriately for administrative costs, furniture, equipment, and maintenance. All this is left to future generations, who may find that their institution is ill-prepared to carry the financial load.

Educating Donors to Make High-Priority Choices

The university should educate donors to tilt more funds in the direction of a program because it is a high priority; otherwise, aspirations of the program must be altered or downsized. These are hard decisions, but a tough planning process can put them on the table. In private research universities, the private income stream can contribute 20 percent or more of the operating budget. Clearly, the very size of these numbers dictates a more scientific approach to financially linking private income with academic decision making.

Donors are much more educable about institutional priorities than is commonly imagined. Givers have not been as sensitive to colleges' greatest needs because too little has been done to make a case for what constitutes future institutional success. Most donors give because they have an institution's best interest at heart; documents can be prepared that relate philanthropy to the long-range vision of the educational program. Presidents of all colleges can become well versed on these materials and use them in private conversation with the largest donors. These major givers are the source of much of the income from fund development programs and will be most susceptible to a data-based presentation about the future well-being of the institution.

To better inform the donor community at an institution, there must be (1) more volunteer involvement and (2) preliminary education of the primary officials who meet the donor community. Distributing literature on university plans or writing an article in the university magazine is not enough. College officials must go an extra step to personally brief individuals and groups of donors and ask for their input. By this involvement, an institution secures an appropriate network of volunteers who are vouching for institutional priorities. To keep this network alive, university officials must also take the often neglected road of thoroughly involving the deans, finance officers, and communications officials who interface with the donor community. The drive to focus on priorities is a campaign in its own right and needs a separate and distinct plan of action. If accomplished on schedule, it can produce a climate of opinion that brings donated dollars to the institution's most urgent needs.

Planning Resource Development as a Universitywide Responsibility: Involve the Academic Leadership

When fundraising becomes engaged with academic process, the gulf presently separating academicians from campaign staff lessens considerably. Faculty leadership should be engaged in setting policy and establishing budgeting goals. Faculty should participate in resource development on a regular basis. Faculty involvement is probably the major missing ingredient in capital campaign fundraising. If faculty play a part in capital resource planning, they will inspire a considerable wave of new and untapped resources.

The faculty have several key characteristics that can be useful in planning successful resources development:

- Faculty are the ones who must field the funded programs. Donors should be introduced to the people who are in fact the real authorities in the area being considered for a donation.
- Faculty often are the people closest to the alumni, who feel akin to their field of the study and to the faculty who taught them.
- Faculty research anchors the institution's relationship to many corporations and foundations.
- Faculty have on the whole greater longevity at an institution. Connecting donors and volunteers with faculty is a mission with a good chance of producing the long-term relationships that are in the best interest of the academy.

Times are changing for the now venerable capital campaign, in its time a highly successful vehicle for the financial support of higher education. A new model of volunteering and fundraising is evolving that stresses regularizing advancement programming and more closely integrating it with other systems in support of the academic mission. Institutions can and should engage in planning intended to hasten this process. Capital campaigns have significant innate flaws that are exacerbated by the financial needs and conditions surrounding today's academy. In order to produce more academic revenue without significant waste and disruption, institutions should move quickly to implement institutional development programs that are fully integrated with the life of the institution, and that exhibit consistent, intense, and comprehensive activity.

Further Reading

More about the recent state of fundraising can be found in Worth (1993) and Young and Associates (1993). For more specific information on advancement planning and positioning, turn to Duronio and Loessin (1991) and Dunn (1986). A good account of the fundraising professional environment is in Carbone (1987), and specifics on the president's role are comprehensively covered by Fisher and Quehl (1989).

References

Brittingham, B. E., and Pezzullo, T. R. *The Campus Green: Fund Raising in Higher Education.* (ASHE-ERIC Higher Education Report No. 1). Washington, D.C.: George Washington University, 1990.

Carbone, R. F. *Fund Raisers of Academe.* College Park, Md.: Clearinghouse for Research on Fund Raising, 1987.

Council for Aid to Education. *Voluntary Support of Education 1995,* pp. 6, 15.

Dunn, J. A., Jr. *Enhancing the Management of Fundraising.* San Francisco: Jossey-Bass, 1986.

Duronio, M. A., and Loessin, B. A. *Effective Fund Raising in Higher Education.* San Francisco: Jossey-Bass, 1991.

Hancock, L., and McCormick, J. "What to Chop." *Newsweek,* Apr. 29, 1996, p. 59.

Fisher, J. L., and Quehl, G. H. *The President and Fund Raising.* New York: Macmillan, 1989.

Kaplan, A. (ed.). *Giving USA.* New York: American Association of Fund-Raising Council Trust for Philanthropy, 1995.

Loessin, B. A., and Duronio, M. A. "The Role of Planning in Successful Fund Raising in Ten Higher Education Institutions." *Planning in Higher Education,* 1990, *18*(3), 45–56.

Morganthau, T., and Nayyar, S. "Those Scary College Costs." *Newsweek,* Apr. 29, 1996, pp. 52–56.

Murawski, J. "A Banner Year for Giving." *Chronicle of Philanthropy,* 1996, *8*(16), 1, 27–30.

Nahm, R., and Zemsky, R. "The Role of Institutional Planning in Fund Raising." *Educational Fund Raising,* 1993, pp. 57–68.

Poderis, T. *It's a Great Day to Fund-Raise!* Cleveland: FundAmerica Press, 1996.

Ryan, E. "Taming the Campaign Extravaganza." *Currents,* 1995, *21*(10), 12–16.

Worth, M. J. *Educational Fundraising: Principles and Practice.* Phoenix: Oryx Press, 1993.

Young, D. R., Hollister, R. M., Hodgkinson, V. A., and Associates. *Governing, Leading, and Managing Nonprofit Organizations.* San Francisco: Jossey-Bass, 1993.

CHAPTER SEVENTEEN

ADAPTING FACILITIES FOR
NEW TECHNOLOGY AND LEARNERS

Ira Fink

Higher education in the United States has always been both labor-intensive and facilities-intensive. Facilities provide the space on campus in which instruction and research take place; with the nature of these activities rapidly changing, our campus facilities must change as well.

The early history of higher education in the United States was often one where administrative, instructional, and residential facilities were housed in a single building. As higher education matured and its curriculum was further defined, specialized and stand-alone facilities were developed for administration, instruction, recreation, and housing, each a separate function of the university campus.

This growth and diversification of higher education facilities has continued almost unabated for the past 150 years. The result has been the construction of three billion square feet of buildings on campus and another one billion square feet of on-campus student housing, much of it built following World War II. The value of these facilities now approaches $400 billion. The amount of money needed to bring these facilities back to good condition, also known as the deferred-maintenance backlog, has been pegged by some authors to total 20 percent of the current capital investment in higher education, or $60–$80 billion. These trends mean that in the face of a rapidly changing technological environment, higher education is shackled with a large and aging instructional and research facilities base that served it well in the latter half of the twentieth century but is less likely to do so into the next century, particularly beyond the early decades. This is important because higher education is faced with a need not only to maintain its existing facilities but also to add or renovate facilities so as to accommodate new and changing approaches to teaching or research that did not exist as recently as a decade ago.

Describing the needs and planning for facilities at this period in university development is a daunting task. For the past decade, campus facility issues have focused on the large deferred-maintenance backlog; ten years from now we will likely see the emergence of campuses tailored to an even more technologically capable student population than is the case today. Writing about these changes at the present is difficult because of the unresolved institutional political and economic trade-offs that need to be made between funding new technology and reducing the deferred-maintenance backlog. In the foreseeable future, funds will be insufficient to do both.

The current facilities thesis is simply stated: technological advances in the delivery of education need to be accommodated in both existing and new facilities. There are, however, as noted in earlier chapters, also substantial demographic, social, organizational, and economic changes occurring in American society that, when linked with technological advances, are changing both the "face" and the place of the American campus.

Three themes in campus facilities planning for the twenty-first century will have an impact on the nature of our campuses and our facility response.

First, although the face of the campus, in terms of students, faculty, and staff, lags behind the nation in terms of its demographic and social make-up, it nonetheless will change significantly. The increasingly diverse student population is likely to choose to coordinate their time on campus with both their class schedule and their employment schedule, thus extending the campus beyond its present boundaries to sites within closer proximity to the student populations.

Campuses have historically met societal needs and societal changes in higher education demand through changes in facilities. The large growth in enrollments as a result of the baby boom following World War II resulted in the construction of hundreds of millions of dollars of facilities on new and rapidly expanding campuses across the United States. The need to house the throngs of new students saw campuses building thousands of residence halls and apartment spaces. In the space age, campuses constructed science and engineering facilities to meet student demand. Large increases in nontraditional, or adult, students resulted in campuses starting courses earlier in the day and staying open later, providing instruction in sites distant from the main campus, and providing administrative and student services in renovated and storefront facilities to meet the needs of the adult learners.

The changing face of higher education through the turn of the century and beyond again is likely to result in facilities change on our campuses; these physical changes are hard to gauge. Some of the social changes may result simply from campuses building facilities such as student recreation centers to position themselves more competitively for students; other campuses may build cultural facilities, such as museums and performing arts centers to bring the community on to campus; while others are now realigning academic departments and research units as advances in biology and biological sciences become increasingly more important.

Second, the rapid advancement already occurring in the use of information technology on campus will continue at its dizzying pace. One result is that campuses are likely to become distinguishable by the degree to which they incorporate information technology into their facility futures. Technology has already influenced how institutions work, and it will continue to do so. Those institutions which do not or cannot afford to embrace technology are likely to remain fixed in the past of "teaching by telling." Those that embrace technology are becoming part of the "global village."

Third, as higher education changes from a teacher-centered focus to a learner-centered focus, libraries are becoming gateways, classrooms are becoming centers of interactive communication, and education is becoming an anytime, anyplace activity. Individual campuses are leading the way in one or more efforts at revising how students are taught and faculty teach. As a result, facilities must accommodate the emerging necessity for groups of students to work together.

Because higher education program changes have occurred slowly, the facilities in place on many four-year campuses served their populations well for most of the twentieth century. Because of the migration toward more interdisciplinary programs, toward programs geared to lifelong learning, and to the integration of technology in our daily activities, many of our higher education facilities are now programmatically as well as physically obsolete as we enter the twenty-first century.

The Changing Face of the Campus

U.S. Population Projections

In 1950, the U.S. population totaled 152 million persons. By the year 2000, the population is expected to reach 276 million, a growth of 124 million. By the year 2050, the population could increase to 392 million (Day, 1993). This is more than a 40 percent increase from the projected year 2000 population, and a 260 percent increase over 1950.

Fastest Growing Groups

The fastest growing age group in the U.S. population is aged forty-five to fifty-four; it will increase 44 percent between 1990 and 2000. The thirty-five to forty-four-year-old group will grow 12 percent, while the twenty-five to thirty-four-year-old group will decline by 28 percent. With the decline in the twenty-five to thirty-four age group comes a decline in nontraditional enrollments.

Because of lower U.S. birth rates in the 1970s and 1980s, the size of the peak U.S. college-age population—which was achieved in 1980—will not be reached again until around the year 2010. Census projections made in 1986, prior to the recent large wave of immigration to the United States, show the eighteen to twenty-four-year-old age group remaining relatively constant at approximately 25 million through the middle of the next century. However, 1993 census projections, which account for almost one million more immigrants to the United States each year, show that the effect of immigration increases in the eighteen to twenty-four-year-old age group consistently through the middle of the twenty-first century.

Forty percent of the new immigrants to the United States are from Asia, and another 40 percent from Latin and Central America. This level of immigration, coupled with four million or more births per year in the past five years, will greatly impact higher education after the turn of the century.

Ethnic Shifts

Throughout our nation's history, the bulk of its citizens were of European ancestry; they were largely responsible for our Anglo-American traditions, particularly in higher education. That population base is gradually changing, through both immigration from Asia and Latin America and a low birth rate among the non-Hispanic white population.

The non-Hispanic white segment of the U.S. population will steadily decline from three-quarters of the total in 1990 to slightly above one-half by the year 2050. This shift results from projections that the non-Hispanic white population will be only 12 million larger in 2050 than the 194 million it is today while the U.S. population will grow by 129 million (Day, 1993). Thus, a net of only one in ten persons added to the population by the year 2050 will be non-Hispanic white.

During this same time, to the year 2050, the U.S. black population is projected nearly to double to 56 million, from its 1993 size of 31 million. After 2012, on a net basis, more blacks will be added to the U.S. population each year than non-Hispanic whites.

The fastest growing race/ethnic group (with the highest rate of increase) is the Asian and Pacific Islander population, with annual U.S. growth rates that may exceed four percent in the 1990s. The Asian population is expected to grow from eight million in 1993 to thirty-eight million in 2050.

The race/ethnic group adding the largest number of persons is that of Hispanic origin. After 1996, the Hispanic population is projected to add more persons to the U.S. population every year than will any other race or ethnic group. In 1993, the U.S. population of Hispanic origin totaled twenty-five million; it is projected to nearly triple to eighty-eight million persons in the year 2050.

Not all of these changes will occur equally across the United States. In California, by the year 2000 the non-Hispanic white population will have already declined to a level just slightly above one-half of the state's total population. Thus, the nation's demography in the year 2050 will look like California's population of the year 2000. By the year 2040, it is projected that California's population will be one-third white, with approximately one-half of the state's population being of Hispanic origin.

In 1995, in four states, Hawaii, California, New Mexico, and Mississippi, along with the District of Columbia, 50 percent or more of the high school graduates were from minority backgrounds. In ten other states, between 30 and 50 percent of the high school graduates were minorities, and in fourteen other states figures ranged between 15 and 30 percent. The largest increase in minority high school graduates continues to occur in coastal states. Since, on average, more than 80 percent of students attend a college or university in their state of home residence, institutions need to increase minority enrollment or else face enrollment declines.

There are other indicators of the changing face of the campus. For example, the number of eighteen and nineteen-year-olds is projected to increase gradually through the year 2010 and then decline for a decade before increasing once again. Non-Hispanic whites aged eighteen to nineteen will increase to the peak year of 2010, before declining for a decade. This age group will remain level for thirty years and decline again to the year 2050. At no time after 2010 is the number of non-Hispanic white eighteen- and nineteen-year-olds projected to exceed the level of 2010. As a result, we will begin to see marked changes in our freshman classes after the end of the current decade. And unless Hispanic participation rates in higher education increase, the biggest change will be a decline in freshman enrollments nationally beginning around the year 2010. The face of campuses will change continuously as our minority populations on campus increase. Coupled with these increases will be issues of multiculturalism, which may or may not impact facilities depending upon how they are addressed in the larger society and the specific cultural values and needs of ethnic groups at individual campuses.

Stated another way, the census projections are that through 2030 our nation will increase by a total of approximately fifteen million persons aged nineteen or younger, who, on balance, will be non-white. In other words, the non-Hispanic white population nineteen or younger will peak in size in the year 2000. It is declining in relationship to all persons of the same age; in 1993, 69 percent of the U.S. population aged nineteen or younger was non-Hispanic white, but this will decrease to 50 percent by the year 2030. As our majority population base declines, campuses need to concentrate on serving a considerably more diverse population, both for their own interests and for society's interests. This change is already occurring. For example, in California, at UC Berkeley, UCLA, and UC Irvine, the freshman classes no longer have a majority population; each freshman class is more than 40 percent of Asian ancestry.

This major change in the ethnicity of our nation, and in turn of our campuses, is likely to have an impact on higher education facilities, as has all societal change in the United States. The nature of the effect on facilities remains an open question. It could be that certain campuses will have a surplus of space because their enrollments are declining, while at the same time others need more space because they attract a minority population that outpaces the shrinking non-Hispanic white population on campus. It is too early to measure the facilities impact of the changing face of our campuses.

Higher Education Facilities and the Information Age

Trends Already Occurring in the Information Age

Some authors have indicated that we are at the end of both a century and an era regarding higher education. This is particularly troubling because higher education is slow to entertain notions of change, especially those involving underlying cultural assumptions about faculty roles and the nature of student learning (West and Daigle, 1993). Today we are seeing a shift in the fundamental structure and nature of our society. A postindustrial, knowledge-based society is evolving rapidly, just as a century ago the industrial revolution transformed an agrarian society (Duderstadt, 1992). To serve this knowledge-based society, our campus facilities need to both anticipate and accommodate rapidly changing advances in telecommunications (voice), personal computing (data), and multimedia (video).

The Two-Stage Process of Advancement in Information Technology

We are at the beginning of a two-stage process of advancement in information technology on campus. The first stage, which has been going on since the 1980s on many campuses, creates the electronic campus and links higher education information sources. If our institutional excursions into this use of information technology did not advance any further, higher education would be well positioned because to date we have managed to bring our text-based methods of "teaching by telling" into the electronic age. Current use of information technology does not drastically change how our campuses look or function. At Northwest Missouri State (Rickman and Hubbard, 1992), student rooms, faculty offices, and administrative offices are electronically connected to one another; at the University of Notre Dame, the new DeBartolo Hall contains eighty-four state-of-the-art networked classrooms. While this trend is to continue well into the early twenty-first century, it may not be forward-thinking enough.

The second stage of advancement in information technology is on the horizon. While its timing is more difficult to predict, it will have the larger impact on our campuses, transforming our education delivery systems from teacher-focused to learner-based. This change will be accomplished in conjunction with institutions outside of the academy. Examples are the Institute for Academic Technology, a partnership of IBM and the University of North Carolina begun in 1989, and the selected campuses chosen to be New Media Centers in a program sponsored by Apple Computer, Sony Electronics, Adobe Systems, and others.

As one author has stated, "The learning revolution is not yet here. Its tools are being assembled; it requires creative minds to master and apply them" (Coombs, 1992, p. 3).

Proliferation of New Information Outlets

New information outlets have a considerable facilities impact and serve to differentiate the first and second stages of this new age of information technology. Publishers, utilities, regional coalitions, and collectives may begin to deliver information faster, cheaper, and more conveniently to our students and faculty than do our current institutions (Katz, 1992).

In other words, technology is creating not only new products but new markets, and just as importantly new providers. As indicated in a position paper by the Pew Charitable Trusts, "What telemarketing and phone banks did for catalog sales, what QVC did for home shopping, what ATMs did for banking, the information highway is about to do for distance learning and higher education" (*Policy Perspectives*, 1994, p. 3A). At some point, higher education will begin to move away from its supplier-driven model of facilities and campuses and move forward to a demand-driven model, which requires faster adaptation to societal needs and has the potential to diminish the importance of the campus as a center.

The newly forming communications, media, cable, and networking conglomerates could become a major source of providing higher education and related services in the future. They may become the providers to our high school graduates who do not go on to college, as well as to those who do. And they can offer these services unencumbered by the expense of campus-bound education. They offer services wherever there is a cable-connected TV set or a computer capable of handling interactive multimedia processing or being connected to the Internet.

Assuming higher education demand becomes profitable to these new organizations, they may be better positioned to offer services nationally and internationally than are the 3,400 disparate and almost single-purpose colleges and universities across the United States. There is significant money to be made in controlling the electronic networks and the programming they deliver (*Policy Perspectives*, 1994) or these organizations would not be currently shelling out billions of dollars to position themselves. Colleges and universities are largely unaware of and therefore unprepared for this new competition (*Policy Perspectives*, 1994). Higher education's historical reliance on government and private donations for facilities funding will need to be accelerated so that our teaching facilities can match the demand. This need for technologically advanced facilities could be simply interior renovation of programmatically or functionally obsolete facilities on campus while maintaining their existing architectural significance on the campus.

The first stage has already seen the gradual development of large-scale distance learning programs, such as the Open University in England and the National Technical University in the United States. The second stage in the transformation will also take place gradually and incrementally, as has the first. It will reach maturity when, as William Graves writes in his article "The Silicon Scholar," "Teachers will be transformed from lecturers to coaches, students transformed from passive recipients to active participants, and serial text enlivened by interactivity and the possibilities of the graphical multi-media screen: these are the immediate educational horizons" (Graves, 1993, p. 127).

While colleges and universities possess the intellectual capital to compete in the emerging market for information services, too often they lack the leadership or incentive to adapt or the resources to move forward (*Policy Perspectives*, 1994). Higher education's usual reaction to external forces has not been a sense of urgency but rather an impulse to resist, to counter the need for change, and to stand on the prerogatives of process (*Policy Perspectives*, 1994). People ferociously resist relinquishing what power they have, and teachers are notoriously conservative about education (Coombs, 1992).

Campus-Bound Students

The campus as a location developed out of the necessity to centrally locate intellectual resources. In our not-so-distant past, books could be used only by a few people at a time, were hard to copy, and were fragile. Thus, it made sense to concentrate them in just a few places, where they could be stored, protected, and shared. As places with the library at the center, campuses allowed each student to interact with a wide range of academic resources (Erhmann, 1992). This "campus-bound" ideal of education through the past to the present, and perhaps somewhat into the future, has had many consequences for the ways in which education is organized, funded, and accredited (Erhmann, 1992). It has also had a major impact on the development of largely single-purpose facilities on campus, identified by both a name (X Hall or Y Center) and a function (business school, chemistry building, English department).

What is becoming important about the new information technology is not its hardware or its software, but its disrespect for boundaries—all of them, including academic or campus boundaries (Ward, 1994). This change also begins to affect the types of facilities in which we work and teach. In effect, we already see off-campus students using on-campus resources, and on-campus students using off-campus resources. As advances in technology continue, the campus as a place diminishes in significance as the locus of knowledge.

Information Technology Strategic Plans

To accomplish the changes outlined above, there is a need for information technology strategic plans on each campus. These plans eventually become more important than facilities plans, because the future use of technology will diminish our need for permanent, single-purpose, campus facilities whose site selection drives many current planning efforts. When campuses ultimately become centers for storage, retrieval, transfer, and management of knowledge, the role of the campus as a locus of educational activity will be greatly reduced, if not totally redundant (Lucier, 1992).

Implications of Change on Building Types

Teaching by Telling

As higher education changes from a teacher-centered focus to a learner-centered focus, libraries become gateways, in forms we have not yet conceived. Classrooms currently viewed as the center of instruction need to change to adapt to newer interactive technologies. Perhaps even campus parking issues can be solved by telecommuting or distance education.

Historically, as the curricula and offerings of higher education have multiplied, so have its buildings. Each discipline or department sought its own separate home for offices, classroom space, and laboratories. All of these places have been geared to the centuries-old traditional method of instruction: a scholar or faculty member in the front of the room facing his or her charge of dutiful students.

While the introduction of television was supposed to impact the teaching and learning processes forever, it turned out to be less powerful than first imagined; the print, lecture, and classroom culture continued (West and Daigle, 1993). The result was the continuation of campuses composed of separate or separated buildings. As Paul Venable Turner describes in his award-winning book *Campus: An American Planning Tradition,* American campuses are composed of buildings set in parklike settings (Turner, 1984).

With today's mass market for electronic information, a transformation is under way (Katz, 1992). As computer hardware and software costs decline, as personal computing capabilities increase, and as campuses install technology infrastructure, impediments to the use of technology decrease; however, the new methods of interaction and communication require more flexible facilities.

Information Networks as a Campus Utility

At the forefront of this change is the construction on campuses of new utility infrastructures for communications technologies (Neff, 1994). Whereas in the past, campus growth was limited by utility or transportation systems, today's limits to growth are more technology-based. As a result, we need to change the nature of our capital funding for information technology from a one-time, nondepreciated expense, such as buildings, to a continuous, updatable operating expense to match the relatively short life of contemporary telecommunications and computing.

The University of California, San Diego (UCSD), for example, has 160 miles of fiber optic cabling on its campus. It has both its own educational TV station and educational cable TV station. Students who live in UCSD "smart dorms" can access the on-campus networks and the entire University of California library system. This same capability exists for students, faculty, or staff who live off-campus.

To compete for the best students and the best scholars, up-to-date technology is required and the cost of obsolescence must be built into our budgets for technology. The University of Washington, for example, allocates about one million dollars each year for its network computer upgrades. Other campuses spend five to seven dollars per square foot to equip their rooms with technological capabilities.

With each step toward network information, whether for e-mail, Internet connectivity, or database access, there is a continuous rise in the service expectations of our constituents (Katz, 1992). With each new generation of equipment and programs, our constituents expect faster services. This demand results in higher costs, both initially and over time.

The Library

Historically, the library has been a storehouse (Katz, 1992). The library of the future is a gateway (Hawkins, 1994); it is about access and knowledge management as opposed to ownership (Hawkins, 1994).

According to a 1993 report from the Research Libraries Group, by the year 2000 research libraries must become more adept at providing information and becoming managers of knowledge. At the same time they must be affordable, requiring no increase in the share of resources spent, and with no increase in square feet of space (Dougherty and Hughes, 1993). This is important because it is estimated that collections at public university libraries double in size every sixteen years, every twenty-two years at prestigious private universities (Cummings and others, 1992).

Whereas the library of the past concentrated on having information stored "just in case," the future library has information "just in time" (Neff, 1994, p. 44). In becoming an electronic learning center (Elmore, 1992), it will be capable of providing information "just for you."

Classrooms

The university of the twenty-first century could be localized in space and time. Or it could involve people throughout their lifetimes, wherever they be on this planet or beyond (Duderstadt, 1992). It is more than conceivable that lifestyles in academia and elsewhere will become increasingly nomadic, with people living and traveling where they wish, taking their work and social relationships with them (Duderstadt, 1992) or being educated where they wish, by whom they wish.

The personal computer has moved the locus of power from the teacher to the learner (Coombs, 1992). As a result, the classroom of the future will be where the student, as opposed to the teacher, is located (Neff, 1994). Our classrooms will be our desktop or laptop computers.

At the second stage in our information technology future, the role of the campus as a place where teaching occurs is diminished, except for specialized instruction facilities such as those for laboratory sciences.

If we want successfully to integrate technology into the curriculum, we need to transform how educational programs are conducted and provide appropriately designed facilities. We need to teach our faculty to be facilitators and guides, as well as lecturers and teachers. We will design new learning experiences and show our teachers how to teach by providing students with access to technology and tools.

In the future, students will become more dynamically involved in access to information, able to create and manipulate multimedia information, whether text-, audio-, or video-based. To achieve this type of future, higher education must create facilities that provide a more flexible learning environment (Coombs, 1992). This covers a long continuum, ranging from text-based to the virtual classroom. We will develop hybrid learning environments, some place-based and others not (including the virtual classroom). In the future we are not bound to a campus, a building, a room, a time of day, or season of the year.

Learning Styles

We are already beginning to understand that there are different kinds of learning styles and many ways to teach. Today, teachers have so many more active options than in the not-so-distant past, when our teaching methods were more passive. Our ability to become interactive with computers and networks, using the World Wide Web, facilitates a learning revolution.

In the second stage of information technology, the burden is still on the teacher, but this time it is to create a learning environment for students that is dependent upon subject matter but independent of location.

Our distance education programs, which are currently text-based, need to change substantially as they become interactive. Project DELTA (Direct Enhancement of Learning through Technology Assistance and Alternatives) is the effort by California State University to create a statewide distance education program to address the burgeoning enrollment needs in California over the next decade and beyond. The Western Governors' University is an effort to provide educational access to place-bound students in rural, often isolated areas, and to assist in providing retraining services to workers in metropolitan areas with large labor forces. We need to develop these and many other high-technology learning environments to meet future demand for higher education.

At some point, we will begin to think about and create distributed learning environments. The students of the future, using a graphical user interface at their computers or at kiosks, will have access to their courses, their grades, the activities on campus, the library, and other information sources, from any place of campus residence or anywhere on the globe. It is education on demand, including education at home. Pieces of this technology are already in place at campuses such as Carnegie Mellon University and Case Western Reserve.

Technology Will Change the Way an Institution Works

In short, technology changes the way an institution works. When this occurs, we have less emphasis on bringing people to campus. We have different ways of reaching people in an information-rich environment. We reexamine how our facilities support this change, and update those that can support our new activities. We may even begin to discard facilities that are no longer needed.

Historically, campuses have looked at communication and instruction in isolation. Distance education, even that which is video-based, still replicates face-to-face instruction from lecturer to learner.

In our future, instruction on campuses needs to distinguish among communication behaviors based upon communication types. The desire to get together as a class will still exist, but in forms different than today's.

At some time in the twenty-first century, the kind of text-based communication through the computer to which we are currently accustomed will give way to multimedia. This requires that we learn more about our learners and train our teachers more thoroughly.

In this changing environment, it is important to distinguish between providing the electronic tool and incorporating the tool into what students, faculty, and staff do each day. It is no longer simply sufficient to have a fiber optic backbone on campus, or a computer on every desktop. It is important to integrate technology resources into what campuses do daily.

Critical Factors for Successful Facilities Planning

There are a number of critical factors for successful facility planning in this rapidly changing technological environment.

Strategic Planning

First, there is a need to reach a collaborative agreement as to where the campus is headed regarding the use of electronic technology in teaching and research. This agreement could come about through developing a strategic plan that identifies campus needs and interests.

In the first stage of the advancement of information technology, campuses provided a backbone of fiber cable connecting buildings and eventually offices, classrooms, and libraries, all at a relatively modest cost. In the second stage, campuses are now developing specialized instructional spaces in buildings, including interactive multimedia and distance learning capabilities. These technologies are expensive in terms of necessary room size, equipment, electrical and heating, and ventilating and air conditioning requirements for the buildings in which they are located.

Organizational Planning

To implement the electronic technology systems, new organizational structures are often required. These changes can result in the merger of campus libraries, academic facilities, computing facilities, telecommunication facilities, and media services.

By necessity, change in organizational structure transforms facilities. The facilities implication of organization structural change could be as small as relocation of offices, or as large as creation of entire buildings housing one or more units with contemporary information technology. For example, campuses such as the University of Washington are renovating science facilities into computer centers.

Visionary Person

A third critical factor for success is to find a visionary person to direct the technology facilities planning effort. This person is one who believes more strongly than most in how information technology can assist the campus. Information technology visionaries are found in the library, in media centers, or in administration. Their visions quite often result in facility changes ranging from a specialized room to an entire building where the technology is housed and can be made accessible.

Shared Vision

A fourth factor for success is that the vision should be shared; it has to be accepted by faculty and students as well as by the administration and the governing body. Achieving a shared vision is no small task, since each of us sees the future differently. It is also no small task since new or renovated technology-laden facilities are considerably more expensive to plan, build, operate, and maintain. Whereas a few years ago computer centers were hidden in basements, today they are visible parts of the campus.

It is important to visualize facilities not only for the function they serve but also as comfortable gathering places on campus. In short, our facilities future is likely to be both high-tech and high-touch. Technology does not prevent facilities from having a feeling of openness, from being comfortable and convenient places for group interaction, and from giving attention to individual needs.

Consider, for example, a library with a dual facility role: as a place to read and study as well as an electronic gateway to the world of information beyond the campus. It is important not to overlook the need for people places in our information technology-rich buildings and throughout the campus.

Technology Planning

Once the direction is focused, the fifth important factor is to complete an inventory of information technology resources already existing on campus and the facilities in which they are located. This backbone information network is to be considered as one more campus utility, just like water, gas, electricity, sanitation, and storm drainage.

One feature of the new technology-rich teaching environments is that they require more square feet per teaching station, to accommodate hardware such as computers and monitors. This new teaching environment also requires support facilities in the form of control rooms, equipment rooms, cable closets, and raised-floor machinery rooms.

At some point in our campus development, students, faculty, and staff expect the technology utility to be ubiquitous and available when needed. The facilities implications include the initial infrastructure and equipment costs, and the question from whose budget these funds come. We are seeing a gradual shift in information technology expenses, away from central computing and library activities toward decentralized departmental expenditures.

It is also important to budget for the significant maintenance and upkeep once the systems are in place. Adding the information technology equipment (for example, built-in audio/visual capabilities) can double the cost of a room; its continued maintenance can average 20 percent of initial cost per year.

Network Infrastructure

The sixth important factor is recognition that a network or backbone infrastructure is a necessary and required condition. As institutions migrate toward making each staff office an individual campus workstation, and as these workstations are linked to central campus networks, the network becomes the gateway to resources throughout the campus, the country, and the world. The network is supplementing the faculty and the library as a repository of knowledge.

Planning the network requires communication infrastructure rights-of-way to be created across the campus and within buildings. With voice, data, and video, it is important to think how these services are brought into and administered throughout buildings. It is also important to include an appropriate level of voice, data, and video connectivity in every classroom, laboratory, office, and library space. Each connection further drives up the cost of renovation or new construction. If the connectivity cannot be afforded, then cable trays and conduit need to be included within the floors, walls, and ceilings of our buildings to support its future installation.

Financial Planning

Success requires a means to pay for the technology and its supporting space and facilities. Campuses now contend with a whole new set of issues as we think about how to provide and pay for the utility infrastructure and facility improvements necessary to accommodate new information technology hardware and software, while at the same time reducing the deferred-maintenance backlog. For example, in some instances, buildings that are programmatically obsolete for science or engineering are renovated as computer-assisted learning environments.

Some campuses are already beginning to charge "technology fees" to students in the same way that we have historically charged laboratory fees and activity fees. Coupled with cost allocation is the need to be able to document the cost of these technology delivery systems to the campus, or the added cost to a building project, including upgraded power and HVAC systems. Campus architects have to add one more line item to their facility project cost data sheets to separate and identify the cost of incorporating technology into the facilities. Given new demands for up-to-date instruction and research space, architects must also choose whether to maintain obsolete buildings or start anew.

Capital Planning

Financial planning brings up the eighth critical factor: developing a long-term capital plan.

Capital planning for information technology is very complicated. In many cases, we are superimposing the technology infrastructure upon existing campus development, which generally means we need to consider the entire campus as whole and at one time. When we enter existing buildings to add the cable or conduit infrastructure, we incur the cost of asbestos abatement, the absence of identified pathways, and the prospect of how to maintain future flexibility in the facilities.

Both new and old buildings are required, with a variety of dedicated space for technology systems and staff workplaces. These needs add new cost to projects. A system of entry rooms and cable closets can increase the square footage of a building by 1 percent; constructing specialized computer-laden instructional environments can double the square footage of space per student station and thus double the cost; providing TV production and editing studios can result in rooms three times as costly as typical classrooms.

Keeping Systems Current

Ninth, it is important to recognize that all the pieces of technology, including facilities and equipment, have a short life. It is crucial to keep the network running and stay abreast of equipment change.

With each new generation of equipment, campuses have found, equipment prices come down, systems requirements increase, and user expectations go up. Many schools have been sadly mistaken in believing that adding technology is a one-time cost, or even a method of cost saving. Not only is there an initial capital facility and infrastructure investment; there is also a significant annual cost in maintaining the system. New technology is conceivably as costly to higher education as reducing deferred maintenance on current facilities, perhaps $60–$80 billion nationally. At a time when campuses have a tremendous deferred-maintenance backlog to overcome, they now must compete for limited funds to add more technological capability to the buildings.

Training Services (and Facilities)

Tenth, education and training services are needed. These services are necessary for both people who are unfamiliar with technology and those wanting to learn more.

With training comes the need for training facilities. We are now seeing the development on campuses of special training areas to help users learn how to use the computers and how to put together a presentation. "Computer commons," such as the one at Arizona State University, are a new building type. Space is also needed to fix and store equipment. Campuses are short of classrooms, because of the need for technologically advanced teaching space, and also because much existing classroom space has been converted to free-time, drop-in computer rooms.

Describing specific buildings incorporating new technologies, or pieces of buildings, brings up many related concerns. How does a campus determine how much and what type of space is needed? The planning standards and space guidelines used by many public universities are no longer appropriate; they are based on space needs of earlier generations of students and faculty. Finding appropriate standards or guidelines for technologically advanced buildings is still a major need; who will lead this important facilities planning effort?

Technology Standards and Dedicated Space in Each Building

An eleventh important planning factor is that dedicated space in each building is needed to accommodate the technology infrastructure. We must establish the level of service (cable trays, conduits, outlets, and power for the equipment) for electronic technology throughout the campus and within buildings for voice, data, and video. Thus, two new important factors in any building projects are (1) identifying the infrastructure pathways and (2) determining the typology of spaces within a building to serve the technology infrastructure.

Some campuses, such as the University of Washington, have well-established standards for incorporating the new technologies in every new facility project. These standards cover the "entrance" rooms to buildings, the communications rooms and risers within the building, the cable tray and horizontal distribution system, and communications outlets, station conduit, and typical room designs within each facility.

The university requires a dedicated, single-purpose entrance room on the lower floor of each new building. This is the point at which the campus fiber optic network enters the building to join the riser system. The riser system is a series of vertically stacked, dedicated closets or communication rooms, one above the other, on each floor. There is one communication room of approximately 110 square feet per 10,000 square feet of floor area. The closets are in turn connected to cable trays, normally beneath the ceiling. They serve as the horizontal right of way for cable and wiring to each room.

At Washington State University, one of every fifty student residence hall rooms was permanently displaced for use as utility closets for the technology infrastructure, as part of a campuswide project to wire the campus. This resulted in both one-time and recurring loss of revenue-providing rental housing.

In conclusion, it is important for campuses to establish a hierarchy of dedicated rooms and spaces within each building to serve the needed technology infrastructure.

The Future

As indicated at the outset, campuses continue to experiment with technology—in small-scale, technology-laden projects involving single-purpose buildings and single-purpose rooms, because there is not enough money to be comprehensive and the information technology is still evolving.

In the future of facilities, it is simply not enough to have a computer sitting on one's desk. The user has to introduce himself or herself to the potential of the tool, and that suggests a need to provide time and facilities for learning and acceptance.

The areas of slowest incorporation of technology are training for faculty and staff as well as students, and the specialized facilities needed for training. Changing the faculty culture is important as that culture currently does not reward teaching to the extent that it rewards research. Many faculty who are tenured and motivated to experiment with changing instructional technology may not see any incentives for their efforts. A pilot training project for fourteen faculty and support staff at the University of Washington cost approximately $1,000 per person. At Notre Dame University, the campus provided stipends of $1,000 each to twenty-five faculty to learn to use new technologies in teaching when DeBartolo Hall was opened (*Changing the Process of Teaching and Learning*, 1994).

Another major area of needed research is the electronic classroom, which is still being defined. Electronic classrooms continue to adapt, change, and be upgraded as campuses move from teacher-based to learner-based environments.

While we concentrate on providing the electronic tools, we still have to consider what is needed to make good places of teaching and learning. There are predictions of a sixfold increase in the speed of personal computers by the end of this decade. Think what that will do to computer requirements on campus. With the technologies and equipment all changing, it is important for campus design professionals to visualize where their campus will be in a few years. Meanwhile the familiar uses continue to evolve, at a dizzying pace.

Clearly, we can no longer talk about the future of campus facilities, whether it be for a new building or a renovation project, without talking about technology. Technology simply permeates every aspect of the campus.

In conclusion, the future will bring:

1. The need for continued experimentation (including case-study technology and facility projects) on every campus.
2. The need for evaluating these separate technology and facility planning efforts; along with evaluation, a discussion of what works and what doesn't; and dissemination of this knowledge.
3. The need to fund continuously the use of technology on campus not as a means of cost saving but as a means of enhancing education and learning.
4. The need to measure the long-term impact of information technology on the campus as a physical place, perhaps to redefine the campus in the process.
5. The need to continue moving forward with exploration of new facility types and new methods of education delivery, lest higher education lose out to better-funded suppliers, such as phone companies, cable companies, and media conglomerates.
6. Lastly, the need to bring together those on campus who can provide the facility planning knowledge and leadership, to take the bold steps required for incorporating new information technology into the everyday activities of the campus.

Further Reading

Much of the higher education literature about facilities is geared to looking at the past and trying to figure out how to make the facilities last into the future. This is true of most writings concerned with deferred maintenance and facilities upkeep and repair. It is difficult to locate publications that are proactive regarding facilities needs for the changing campus, in terms of both enrollment changes and technology changes. The quarterly publication of the Society for College and University Planning, *Planning for Higher Education,* generally has two or more relevant articles per issue on the topic of facilities planning. *Facilities Manager,* the quarterly publication of the Association of Physical Plant Administrators (APPA) and periodic APPA monographs address topical issues about management and upkeep of the campus physical plant.

U.S. Census publications (for example, Day, 1993) provide the best insight into the coming higher education population through their projections of population change by age and ethnicity. By contrast, the projections of future enrollments by the U.S. Department of Education are less useful because they do not account for or include significant shifts in ethnicity occurring in the population.

Good sources of information about changes in information technology in higher education are the bimonthlies *EDUCOM Review* and *Cause/Effect.* For a wonderful insight into the effect of changes in information technology on faculty, see the University of Notre Dame's publication *Changing the Process of Teaching and Learning* (1994). A good source on the relationship between changes in pedagogy and the cost of information technology over a wide range of pedagogy can be found in Bates (1995). The best current collection of information about technology-rich learning environments is Stuebing (1994). For those interested in global education and virtual reality, the work of Tiffin and Rajasingham (1995) is worth reading.

A good source of references on traditional and electronic classrooms can be found in Fink (1995). The most complete source book on campus planning and facility development is also by Fink (1994). The Project Kaleidoscope handbook (*Structures for Science,* 1995) is an excellent reference for both science facilities and campus facility planning in general.

References

Bates, A. W. *Technology, Open Learning, and Distance Education.* New York: Routledge, 1995.
Changing the Process of Teaching and Learning: Essays by Notre Dame Faculty. South Bend, Ind.: University of Notre Dame, 1994.

Coombs, N. "Teaching in the Information Age." *EDUCOM Review,* 1992, *27*(2), 28–31.

Cummings, A. M. (ed.). *University Libraries and Scholarly Communication. A Study Prepared for the Andrew W. Mellon Foundation.* Washington, D.C.: Association of Research Libraries, 1992.

Day, J. C. "Population Projections of the United States, by Age, Sex, Race, and Hispanic Origin: 1993 to 2050." *Current Population Reports,* P25–1104. Washington, D.C.: Government Printing Office, 1993.

Dougherty, R. M., and Hughes, C. *Preferred Library Futures II: Charting the Paths.* Mountain View, Calif.: Research Libraries Group, 1993.

Duderstadt, J. J. "An Information Highway to the Future." *EDUCOM Review,* 1992, *27*(5), 36–41.

Elmore, G. C. "Integrated Technologies: An Approach to Establishing Multimedia Applications for Learning." *EDUCOM Review,* 1992, *27*(1), 20–26.

Erhmann, S. C. "Challenging the Ideal of Campus-Bound Education." *EDUCOM Review,* 1992, *27*(2), 24–27.

Fink, I. *Campus Planning and Facility Development: A Comprehensive Bibliography.* (2nd ed.) Berkeley, Calif.: Ira Fink and Associates, 1994.

Fink, I. *Electronic Campus, Electronic Classroom, Electronic Library: An Annotated Bibliography.* Berkeley, Calif.: Ira Fink and Associates, 1995.

Graves, W. H. "The Silicon Scholar." In E. E. Dennis and C. L. LaMay (eds.), *Higher Education in the Information Age.* New Brunswick, N.J.: Transaction, 1993.

Hawkins, B. L. "Planning for the National Electronic Library." *EDUCOM Review,* 1994, *29*(3), 19–29.

Katz, R. N. "Financing New Information Access Paradigms, or Why Academic Information Managers Need Cost Models." *Cause/Effect,* 1992, *15*(2), 6–12.

Lucier, R. E. "Towards a Knowledge Management Environment: A Strategic Framework." *EDUCOM Review,* 1992, *27*(6), 24–31.

Neff, R. K. "Campus Nets for the Nineties." *EDUCOM Review,* 1994, *29*(2), 41–44.

Policy Perspectives, no. 5(3), sect. A. Philadelphia: Pew Higher Education Roundtable, Pew Charitable Trusts, 1994.

Rickman, J. T., and Hubbard, D. L. *The Electronic Campus.* Maryville, Mo.: Prescott, 1992.

Structures for Science: A Handbook for Planning Facilities for Undergraduate Natural Science Communities. Washington, D.C.: Project Kaleidoscope, 1995.

Stuebing, S. *Campus Classroom Connections. Building with Information Technology: A Case Study Guide of Higher Education Facilities.* Newark: New Jersey Institute of Technology, 1994.

Tiffin, J., and Rajasingham, L. *In Search of the Virtual Class: Education in an Information Society.* New York: Routledge, 1995.

Turner, P. V. *Campus: An American Planning Tradition.* Cambridge, Mass.: Architectural History Foundation/MIT Press, 1984.

Ward, D. "Technology and the Changing Boundaries of Higher Education." *EDUCOM Review,* 1994, *29*(1), 23–27.

West, T., and Daigle, S. "Higher Education in the Information Age: Project DELTA." *EDUCOM Review,* 1993, *28*(4), 31–34.

CHAPTER EIGHTEEN

PLANNING CHANGE THROUGH PROGRAM REVIEW

Lisa A. Mets

I once attended a management seminar for managers, at which seminar participants were asked to complete a personality questionnaire to help them understand their management styles. One of the questions asked something like, "When you arrive in a new city, do you prefer (a) to view a map before venturing out of your hotel, or (b) never mind the map, you'll find your way around?"

I think the difference in management style has something to do with one's need for information. Some individuals prefer to collect as much information as possible about the unknown before they act, while others are comfortable acting and using information as it comes to them along the way.

Engaging in change is similar in many ways to charting a course in a new city. Change managers have at least two options: (1) determine their destination and plot a course that will take them there, or (2) explore the terrain and see where it takes them. In other words, they may plan change or they may benefit from serendipity. Depending on a number of circumstances, the end result may or may not be the same.

Program review is widely practiced as an evaluation process in higher education. However, it is increasingly becoming known that program review can serve as an effective mechanism for introducing and sustaining continued planned change efforts in a university's planning and management functions. Thus, program review can be a management tool to help guide a unit, an institution, and a system through a well-mapped, planned change process. It can also provide opportunities for serendipitous change. This chapter explores the relationship between program review and planned change so administrators may consider using program review to help them redefine their institutions, redirect their missions, reorganize their programs, and renew the academic workplace.

Planned Change

The focus of this chapter is on *planned* change. To illuminate the concept: "Planned organizational change refers to a set of activities and processes designed to change individuals, groups, and organization structure and processes. The key word is 'planned.' There is some a priori theory and methods that are brought to bear on some target (individual attitudes, organizational processes) in order to reach some goal (humanization of the work place, organizational efficiency). . . . Planned organizational change emphasizes managerial choice" (Goodman and Kurke, 1982, p. 4).

Other kinds of change that are often discussed in management and higher education include "transformational change" (Cameron and Ulrich, 1986; St. John, 1991) and "frame-breaking change" (Hermon-Taylor, 1985). According to Cameron and Ulrich, transformations differ from other types of change: *"Transformation* implies a metamorphosis or a substitution of one state or system for another, so that a qualitatively different condition is present. *Transformation* implies a change *of systems, not just a change in* systems. . . . Other types of changes may suggest merely a variation on a theme or an evolution from one condition to another" (1986, pp. 1–2).

Frame-breaking changes are dramatic changes in an organization's strategy accompanied by a need for the organization to change its internal behavior. They may even cause an organization to reverse direction. The greater the strategic change, the greater the need for internal reassessment. Hermon-Taylor (1985) explains: "While the threshold between acceptable and frame-breaking change cannot be expressly defined and will vary from one organization to another, depending upon its size, its degree of bureaucracy, its leadership, and a host of other variables, it is possible to observe that some degree of change will run into internal obstacles that are too severe to be overcome. Unfortunately, this threshold of permissible change is often below what is required to ensure the long-term health or even survival of the organization" (p. 388).

Planned change received a great deal of attention in the 1960s and early 1970s. Two major volumes contributed significantly to our understanding of the planned change process. Bennis, Benne, Chin, and Corey (1976) compiled the perspectives of those who approached "deliberate change" through theories of social, interpersonal, and personal dynamics; Baldridge and Deal (1975) collected the views of those with sociological perspectives on change in educational organizations. A scholar and practitioner of planned change, Robert Nordvall (1987) provides an excellent review of models of planned change in higher education and suggests useful readings on the topic. As he points out, "Discussions of the planning process usually center upon how an institution can respond in an organized way to the shifting demands of its external and internal environments. The emphasis is upon determining wise responses, not upon carrying them out. Although it often discusses the diagnosis of organizational problems, the literature of planned change, in contrast, primarily emphasizes the process of the acceptance and implementation of new ideas" (p. 304).

Nordvall identifies six theoretical models of planned change in higher education:

1. *Research, development, and diffusion (rational planning):* the key feature of this model is to convince people to change by means of rational arguments based on research and development.
2. *Social interaction:* Focusing more on diffusion, this approach concentrates on making sure the arguments are targeted to the persons in the organization who are the most likely to adopt new ideas.
3. *Problem solving:* not premised on implementing change through rational arguments, this model concentrates on improvements in communications, trust, and individual and peer group relations within the organization as key elements.
4. *Political:* built less on better communications and increased trust, this model stresses the use of influence and power to affect the actions of key individuals within the organization.
5. *Linkage:* building on the others, this model underscores the importance of linking those interested in change both to sources outside the institution and to persons with similar interests inside the institution.
6. *Adaptive development:* also building on the other models, this one encourages adaptation of outside developments to the local context.

Although these models provide useful insight into the planned change process in institutions of higher education, Nordvall aptly notes that the search for a unified theory to explain how change occurs in all organizational contexts may be in vain. "Even if such a theory could be created," he says, "it is doubtful that it could provide detailed steps to guide all change efforts. At best, such a theory could provide a list of factors that have been proven critical in a broad range of change activities" (1987, p. 309). Nevertheless, Nordvall suggests that institutional experiences endorse the following guidelines for planned change:

1. Change cannot simply be ordered by top administrators. "Their role, at best, can be to establish procedures that facilitate change and to respond thoughtfully to change proposals made to them" (1987, p. 309).
2. Successful programs of change should be based on institutional research for proper analysis of the problem to be addressed.
3. Change occurs only if the need for it is perceived by both a broad group and some people with authority to implement the change.
4. Change requires ongoing implementation. Support for the change must be sustained even after it is instituted.

Strategy

To achieve planned change, one needs to keep in mind the concept of *strategy*. Cope (1978) was among the first to write about strategy in higher education. His definition of strategy is similar to those evident in the management literature:

> The intended meaning of strategy is extended here to encompass an institution's choice of goals, the plans for achieving these goals, and the deployment of resources to attain these goals. Strategy is the pattern of objectives, purposes, or goals and major policies and plans for achieving these goals stated in such a way as to define what the college or university is or is to become. Strategic policy planning results in: (1) the determination of the basic long-range goals of the institution, (2) the adoption of courses of action, and (3) the allocation of resources necessary for reaching these goals—all being integrated and unseparable. (1978, pp. 8–9)

George Keller's *Academic Strategy* (1983) introduced the concept of higher education strategy on a broad scale to the higher education community. His framework for the formulation of strategy comprises six elements: (1) traditions, values, and aspirations; (2) academic and financial strengths and weaknesses; (3) leadership abilities and priorities; (4) threats and opportunities in the environment; (5) market preferences, perceptions, and directions; and (6) the competitive situation. As Keller summarized it: "In short, you need to know what your college or university can or cannot do, and what it wants to do. Then you need to discern what it might do, and should do. Last, you need to decide what it will do. Your academic strategy, at least its more rational components, should exude from this compound of internal and external considerations" (p. 153).

Based on her analysis of the business literature, Ellen Earle Chaffee (1985) concludes, "Strategy tends to require an advance plan, the resources necessary to implement this plan, and an ability to remain alert to signs that modifications may be required" (p. 134). However, the business concept of strategy needs to be modified for the higher education setting. Chaffee finds that "a great deal of persuasion and negotiation will be inevitable in establishing an organizational strategy. Because strategy cannot be mandated from the top to the extent that it can in business, such changes become difficult" (p. 137).

Chaffee's analysis (1985) of the business literature on strategy reveals three models:

1. *Linear strategy:* "the determination of the basic long-term goals of an enterprise, and the adoption of courses of action and the allocation of resources necessary for carrying out these goals" (Chandler, cited in Chaffee, p. 140).
2. *Adaptive strategy:* "the development of a viable match between the opportunities and risks present in the external environment and the organization's capabilities and resources for exploiting these opportunities" (Hofer, cited in Chaffee, p. 142).
3. *Interpretive strategy:* "orienting metaphors or frames of reference that allow the organization and its environment to be understood by organizational stakeholders . . . stakeholders are motivated to believe and to act in ways that are expected to produce favorable results for the organization" (Chaffee, p. 145).

Chaffee's analysis of the higher education literature on strategy reveals that most of the work expresses the adaptive model of strategy. For example, authors have focused on institutional adaptation, keeping the organization in step with a changing environment, and achieving a good fit between organizational activity and environmental demand. Higher education topics such as organizational goals, rational planning, program review, master planning, and forecasting relate to linear strategy. Interpretive strategy is reflected in analyses emphasizing tradition, politics, myths, missions, values, and relationships.

Models of the Change Process

An early model of planned change was expressed by Lippitt in 1973. It was designed for consultants and external change agents. The critical phases in his model of planned change include (1) diagnosis of the problem, (2) assessment of the client's motivation and capacity for change, (3) assessment of the change agent's motivation and resources, (4) selecting progressive change objectives, (5) choosing the appropriate role for the consultant as change agent, (6) maintenance of change, and (7) termination of a helping relationship (Lippitt, Langseth, and Mossop, 1985).

Hermon-Taylor (1985) provides a model of the change process based on three stages in the process (diagnosis, formulation, and execution) and two frames of reference (strategic and organizational). The strategic frame helps the organization decide what it *should* do, and the organizational frame shows the organization what it *can* do.

Lorange's (1985) four stages of the change process are (1) sensitizing the organization to the needs for strategic change, (2) identifying critical blockages to strategic change (political, myopic, and resource blockages), (3) strategic problem solving (team versus individuals, top-down versus bottom-up, and manipulation versus confrontation), and (4) securing the implementation effort (assigning responsibilities for change and monitoring, managing key stakeholders, and managing the strategic system and evolution of strategic processes). The literature contains other models of change based on researchers' organizational experiences (Garvin, 1988; Kanter, 1983, 1989; Kanter, Stein, and Jick, 1992; Lippitt, Langseth, and Mossop, 1985; Peters and Austin, 1985; Peters and Waterman, 1982; and Waterman, 1987).

Organizational Change and Organizational Learning

There is an emerging reconceptualization of organizational change that emphasizes individual learning as the core process in organizational change. Organizational change itself is viewed as organizational learning. As reported in *Fortune* magazine, "Forget your tired old ideas about leadership. The most successful corporation of the 1990s will be something called a learning organization" (Senge, 1990, p. 4).

In his comprehensive review of the literature on organizational learning, Huber (1990) cites some of the definitions that have emerged in the literature. For example, according to Argyris and Schön, "Organizational learning refers to experience-based improvements in organizational task performance, and is decomposable into the improvement in performance of individual decision-makers whose learning comes to be encoded in organizational maps, memories, and programs" (cited in Huber, p. 2). Fiol and Lyles state that "Organizational learning means the process of improving actions through better knowledge and understanding" (cited in Huber, p. 2). As Bennis and Nanus suggest, "Organizational learning is the way the corporation increases its survival potential by increasing its readiness to cope with new changes and opportunities" (cited in Huber, p. 2). Huber himself concludes: "An entity learns if, as a result of processing information, it increased the range of its potential behaviors . . . an organization has learned if any of its units has acquired knowledge that it recognizes as potentially useful to the organization" (pp. 3–4).

Argyris and Schön (1981) distinguish among three levels of learning. Single-loop is the simplest and implies a change of action that does not violate a preestablished norm of effectiveness. The second, double-loop learning, leads to a change in the norms defining effective behavior. The third, deutero learning, stands for a higher level of learning whereby the organization is able to reflect on its ability to learn and to influence it. Normann (1985) links these three levels of learning to the concept of strategy: single-loop learning would correspond to operating decisions within a given framework, double-loop learning to single strategic actions, and deutero learning to strategic management (p. 223).

Senge (1990) describes a learning organization as "a place where people are continually discovering how they create their reality. And how they can change it" (p. 13). Learning organizations are possible because "deep down, we are all learners" (p. 4); and organizations "learn only through individuals who learn" (p. 140). Based on his experience with learning organizations, Senge predicts that learning organizations will, increasingly, be "localized" organizations, "extending the maximum degree of authority and power as far from the 'top' or corporate center as possible. . . . Localness means unleashing people's commitment by giving them the freedom to act, to try out their own ideas and be responsible for producing results" (Senge, 1990, pp. 287–288).

The literature is filled with prescriptions for organizational change, some within the framework of organizational learning (for example, see Dolence and Norris, 1995, for a framework for transforming higher education based on organizational learning). Translating a strategic idea into action may be achieved by a combination of many different means. Table 18.1 illustrates the "conditions" that Normann (1985) and the "disciplines" that Senge (1990) prescribe for organizational learning leading to organizational change.

Implementation of Change Strategies

As Cope (1978) stated, "Strategy has two equally-important aspects: formulation and implementation" (p. 10). Williams (1975) suggested, "The question of implementation is one of the most fundamental of all the issues facing a large-scale organization. In its most general form, an inquiry about implementation seeks to determine whether an organization can bring together people and material in a cohesive organizational unit and motivate them in such a way as to carry out the organization's stated objectives" (p. 554).

Williams suggested that implementation of change strategies rests on both the administrative and technical skills or capacity of the organization, and political

TABLE 18.1. COMPONENTS OF LEARNING ORGANIZATIONS.

Conditions to Achieve Change (Normann, 1985)	Required "Disciplines" for Learning (Senge, 1990)
Direction: A desired state or motivating vision	Systems thinking: A conceptual framework to make patterns clearer
Power: To back up the strategy and mobilize resources	Personal mastery: Discipline of continually clarifying and deepening personal vision
Strong driving forces: Personal ambitions or crisis	Mental models: Deeply ingrained assumptions, generalizations, or images that influence how we understand the world and take action
Cognitive ability: To analyze the situation and invent action strategies and structural arrangements	Team learning: Producing extraordinary results; starts with dialogue; teams are the fundamental learning unit in modern organizations
Leadership: To make the change credible and attractive to the organization	Building shared vision: When there is genuine vision, people excel and learn because they want to

Sources: Normann, R. "Developing Capabilities for Organizational Learning." In J. M. Pennings and Associates, *Organizational Strategy and Change.* San Francisco: Jossey-Bass, 1985; and Senge, P. M. *The Fifth Discipline: The Art and Practice of the Learning Organization.* New York: Doubleday, 1990.

feasibility. Cameron and Ulrich (1986) outlined five steps that leaders need to follow to implement transformational change: (1) create readiness for change, (2) overcome resistance, (3) articulate a vision, (4) generate commitment, and (5) institutionalize implementation. Peters, Waterman, and Phillips developed a framework of organizational aspects that influence organization change. In their Seven-S Framework, Peters and Waterman (1982) contend that transformational leaders need to manage *strategy, structure, systems, style, staff, skills,* and *shared values.* Waterman (1987) linked the Seven-S Framework to a Seven-C Framework comprising *capability, culture, chance and information, causes and commitment, control, crisis points,* and *communication.*

Organizational Characteristics Influencing Change

Traditional ideas of organizational change are grounded in theories of rational systems. To manage change in a rational system "is to find goals and/or means that can be evaluated easily and to which the participants can commit themselves. It is assumed that if relevant information is gathered to define the problem properly and if the resistance of recalcitrant parties is overcome, then a decision can be made that will correct any problems. In this view, a fairly stable group of decision makers who agree on goals and technology is managing change" (Berger, cited in Weick, 1982, p. 376).

Weick suggests that those ideas may need to be altered when they are "fitted to one distinctive property of open systems, loose coupling among their elements" (1982, p. 375). This suggestion is particularly relevant when one adheres to Weick's analysis of educational organizations as loosely coupled systems (Weick, 1976). The preoccupation with rational systems has been replaced by ideas about organizations as natural systems and open systems. The image of organizations as open systems contains assumptions that differ substantially from rational assumptions: "The open systems view of organizational structure stresses the complexity and variability of the individual components—both individual participants and subgroups—as well as the looseness of connections among them. Parts are viewed as capable of semiautonomous action; many parts are viewed, at best, [as] loosely coupled to other parts. Further, in human organizations, the system is multicephalous: many heads are present to receive information, make decisions, direct performance. . . . Coordination and control become problematic. . . . Open systems . . . shifts [sic] attention from structure to process" (Scott, cited in Weick, 1982, pp. 376–377).

Weick suggests that the choice of targets for change and the success of change efforts is affected by the pattern of tight coupling within elements and loose coupling between elements in the organization. He finds that change in loosely coupled systems is "continuous rather than episodic, small scale rather than large, [improvisational] rather than planned, accommodative rather than constrained, and local rather than cosmopolitan" (Weick, 1982, pp. 390–391).

Hermon-Taylor (1985) provides four models of change based on an organization's management style (authoritarian or participative) and its reasoning process (judgmental or analytical): (1) the *control-driven* model, where authoritarian managerial styles combine with judgmental reasoning and lead to a highly control-oriented model of change; (2) the *logic-driven* model, in which some authoritarian companies try to counteract the negative effects of the tension between strategic planning and the budget and planning process by making strategy development as analytical as possible; (3) the *collegial* model, whereby a participative management style is combined with a judgmental decision approach, such that people of good judgment achieve a reasoned consensus that guides the subsequent actions of the participants; and (4) the *informed-consensus* model, which combines a participative-analytical approach to strategic decision making; it is informed by logic and seeks to engage the cooperation of those charged with implementation.

Summary

Planned change is distinct from other kinds of changes. When we are engaged in planned change efforts, we are engaged in persuasion and empowerment. Individuals need to be persuaded to adopt the change(s); and once they are persuaded, they need to be empowered to implement the change(s).

The discussion above illustrates that planned change can be viewed through many lenses; yet there are many shared elements among the various perspectives. Scholars of planned change in higher education and in other organizational settings identify common motivating factors in planned change efforts. To engage in planned change efforts, participants may be motivated by information and reason (research, development, and diffusion model; rational model; control-driven model; logic-driven model; informed-consensus model), by collegiality (social-interaction model, problem-solving model, linkage model, and collegial model), and by special interest (political model). These elements common among the various models likely lead to successful implementation of planned change efforts: (1) persuasive and credible evidence that there is a need for change, (2) an agreement that the change is desired, (3) a broad base of participation by members throughout the organization in the change process, (4) the technical and resource means to achieve the change, (5) a capacity for organizational learning and problem solving, (6) ongoing communication throughout the change process, and (7) leadership to facilitate and sustain the change process.

There is increasing evidence that a well-designed program review process can facilitate planned change efforts. The program review process can be designed to effectively manage the motivation of participants in planned change and produce the same elements that are necessary for successful planned change. The following discussion provides an overview of program review and an example of an effective program review process that is facilitating an institution's planned change efforts.

Program Review

Program review is the distinctive name given to program evaluation in higher education (Barak, 1987). Starting in the 1970s, the literature on program review has evolved from anecdotal experiences with program review to more extensive commentary based on systematic observation and research. Comprehensive reviews of the literature are provided by Barak (1987) and Mets (1995a). Program review as a process has been pervasive in American institutions of higher education since the 1970s. Today, it is becoming more widely adopted by institutions and ministries of education in other countries, including Canada, Norway, and the Netherlands.

Barak (1982) found that 82 percent of responding colleges and universities and most higher education boards have some form of program review. Barak and Breier (1990) found that institutions and higher education boards are motivated by at least one of four objectives: to improve programs; to aid selection, certification, or accountability; to increase awareness or to sell a program's importance; or to exercise authority. In the late 1970s and early 1980s, program review became a major management tool for making strategic choices during times of fiscal constraint. This seems to be true of many institutions today. It appears equally likely today that institutions engage in program review to respond to demands for increased accountability or to improve quality.

The rich literature on program review provides good advice on how to design and implement an effective program review process. Conrad and Wilson (1985), Feasley (1980), and Gardner (1977) provide frameworks for program evaluation. Barak (1982), Barak and Breier (1990), Conrad and Wilson (1985), Cranton and Legge (1978), Craven (1980), and Wilson (1982) suggest how to design and conduct a program review. Barak (1982), Breier (1986), Mets (1995b), and Wroblewski (1995) provide research reports of institutional experiences with program review. Hoey (1995a) and Eaton and Miyares (1995) provide accounts of program review experiences in community colleges and in a university system. Few authors have explored the link between program review, planning, budgeting, assessment, and change (Arns and Poland, 1980; Barak, 1986; Barak and Sweeney, 1995; and Kells, 1980).

Elements of a Program Review Process

For those unfamiliar with program review and how it can be effectively linked to a university's planned change efforts, the program review process at Northwestern University (Office of the Vice President for Administration and Planning, 1989) provides a comprehensive model well worth examination and consideration. Northwestern's program review process was designed to stimulate planning and change. Program review findings are frequently consulted by management, and program review results are regularly considered in unit and institutional budget planning and priority setting. It is a model that has been in place more than a decade, and variations of it have been adapted to other institutional settings. Research on some of the outcomes of Northwestern's program review process and factors contributing to the implementation of program review recommendations is discussed in Mets (1995b). Because the process at Northwestern University is similar to that in many other institutions, I describe it briefly below as an illustrative example.

Northwestern's program review process is designed on a six-year cycle. It is continuous and part of an ongoing planning process. The first cycle began a decade ago and is described below. As the institution approached its second cycle, the program review process was streamlined. The first cycle required significantly more effort on the part of units to provide important baseline information. The second cycle builds on the outcomes of the first process. There are seven components of the program review process.

Program Review Council. In this first component, the university president appoints faculty and administrators to serve on the program review council. Members of the council chair subcommittees appointed to review individual units. The number of council members equals the number of units scheduled for review. Members serve rotating terms.

Program Review Council Subcommittee. A subcommittee usually consists of three members: two from units unrelated to the one under review and one from a related unit. Each subcommittee reviews the unit's self-study and the reports of the external reviewers; meets with members of the unit and related units, key administrators, and the external reviewers; and writes a report incorporating its findings from these sources and recommendations. The report becomes the basis on which all subsequent program review decisions are made.

Departmental Self-Study. In spring of the year before it is to be reviewed, the unit is notified and told that it should prepare a self-study. In the self-study, the unit identifies its strengths and weaknesses and proposes a plan for improvement. The unit provides multiple sources of evidence of its effectiveness and productivity.

External Reviewers. The unit proposes names of external reviewers, who are brought to campus for typically a two-day visit in the spring of the year of review. Administration and the unit reach agreement on who is to be invited. External reviewers meet with members of the unit and related units, administrators, and students and staff as appropriate. The reviewers write evaluative reports with recommendations.

Administrative Meetings. A series of meetings is held following the completion of the subcommittee's report and the review of the report by the program review council. The program review council subcommittee meets with the president and other key administrative officers to present its findings and recommendations. Based on this report, initial agreements and commitments are developed regarding recommendations. The president and key administrative officers meet with the dean or vice president in charge of the unit, and agreements and commitments are articulated. Key administrative officers (without the president) meet with the dean or vice president and unit head to discuss agreements and commitments. The dean or vice president and unit head meet with the unit to communicate agreements and commitments as to the implementation of program review recommendations.

Annual Updates. Each year, deans and vice presidents are asked to share unit progress with the vice president for administration and planning. This progress is then communicated to the program review council and the university trustees.

Two-Year and Four-Year Follow-Up Reports. Units submit follow-up reports to central administration, relaying progress in implementing program review recommendations. Central administration reviews unit progress and reevaluates priorities and commitments.

Northwestern's process is noteworthy because it incorporates many of the elements of planned change, strategy, and implementation that were discussed in the preceding section. It is a rational or logic-driven model in that the acquisition and utilization of information is a key element. It draws on the social-interaction model in that broad participation throughout the institution in all aspects of the process is essential for success. Because the program review process is designed to stimulate program improvement, it has elements of the problem-solving model. Communication and trust are the kingpins of the process. It has elements of an authoritarian model in that central and unit leadership have the power and resources—and use them in support of the outcomes of the process. The process assumes that it is healthy to promote the institution as a loosely coupled system by granting units some autonomy to set their goals and objectives, flexibility in management, and resources they manage themselves to achieve their ends.

Critical Factors for Success

The literature and research by Barak and Sweeney (1995), Mets (1995a, 1995b), Hoey (1995a), Wroblewski (1995), and Eaton and Miyares (1995) identify at least three critical factors for the successful use of program review results that lead to planned change: leadership, communication, and integration of program review with other institutional processes.

Leadership. It cannot be emphasized enough that leadership may be the most important factor to ensure the implementation of program review results. Leadership emanates from many sources within the institution, everywhere from the unit on up to the president. Throughout the first cycle, Northwestern's president played a central role in program review. He met with each and every program review council subcommittee and facilitated all subsequent meetings with deans and vice presidents. His executive cabinet consulted program review findings in budget planning activities and when considering institutional priorities. The president's participation in the process was more than symbolic, and the effect of his participation was far-reaching.

However, power is distributed differentially among the positions, particularly with regard to resource allocation and reallocation. Program review is a process that has resource implications. Leaders at all levels within the institution, but particularly at the unit level, need to be empowered with adequate resources to implement recommendations. Lacking resources, unit leaders and others may become disenfranchised from the change process through program review.

Communication. Communication is often cited as the second leading factor in successful program review. Like a rational systems model, program review assumes that good communication of credible information results in desired change. Given that program review processes systematically collect comprehensive information about units from a number of sources and through varying methodologies, the information tends to be viewed in a credible light. Northwestern's process for collecting information enhanced the credibility of the process and confidence in its results. Internal subcommittees and external reviewers provided corroborating evidence to unit self-perception.

However, because of the exhaustive nature of program review, greater demands are placed on the institution for enhanced communication mechanisms. Communication failures in program review are frequently attributed to top or central administrators, who may neglect to keep units informed of administrative priorities, commitments, and actions following program review. Successful implementation of program review recommendations requires a sustained dialogue between administrators and members of the reviewed units. If communication diminishes following program review, inertia may take over. Mets (1995b) has suggested that program review recommendations, like plans (Schmidtlein and Milton, 1988–89), may have a half-life of two years unless there is sustained communication and attention. At Northwestern, enhanced communication between administrators, faculty, staff, and other constituents was an explicit goal in the design of the process. Annual meetings, biennial reports, and reference to program review in budget planning and other management meetings reinforced good communication throughout all levels of the university.

Integration of Program Review with Budget, Planning, and Assessment Processes. One of the attractive features of program review is its ability to be linked with other regular management functions. Program review need not be an add-on activity within the institution. This process *is* budgeting, planning, and assessment. The results of program review can guide all other decision making within the institution, particularly that related to setting priorities and allocating or reallocating resources in order to achieve planned change. At Northwestern, there were no parallel or shadow budget or strategic planning processes that provided outcomes like those of the program review process. Program review provided the information for budget planning, unit and institutional goal setting, and strategies for institutional improvement.

Concluding Comments

As we approach the new millennium, there seems to be an innate desire that old ways of operating be replaced with new ways of doing things. There is anticipation that well-worn tools will become ineffective. This chapter has sought to show that a relatively old, familiar process—program review—need not be discarded from an institution's management repertoire. In fact, its effectiveness and value as an effective mechanism for guiding an institution through planned change may be enhanced in the new millennium. Program review has limitations; they are mentioned below. But those limitations do not diminish an institution's capacity to achieve planned change.

In the preface to this book, the editors postulate that today's challenges may call for a revolutionary change in many of our institutions, requiring redefinition of what we are, redirection of our institutional missions, reorganization of educational programs, and renewal of the academic workplace. What contributions can program review make?

Revolutionary Change

Whether we call it "revolutionary," "transformational," or "frame-breaking" change, program review is an unlikely process to take an institution from where it is today to something revolutionary tomorrow. At the least, program review results in incremental change (Hoey, 1995a); at best, it can lead to modest innovation in programs. This is unlikely to be something inherent about the program review process itself; rather, it seems to be a function of higher education as a loosely coupled system.

Redefinition

Redefinition is an intellectual activity. Helping institutions and units redefine themselves is a strength of program review. No other formal process within an institution invites administrators, faculty, and staff to become so intimate with their colleagues. The individual learning and consequent organizational learning that takes place through the program review process strengthens the institution's ability to effect change.

Redirection in Mission

Sound program review processes demand an examination or reexamination of a unit's mission and external relationships. The contribution to redirecting a unit's mission is a second strength of the program review process. However, it is unlikely that program review will lead a unit to a redirected mission far afield. Because program review tends to result in incremental change, redirected missions tend to be conservative in nature.

Reorganization

Program review processes can have the exciting outcome of recommendations to reorganize a unit's or the institution's educational programs. Participants in a well-designed program review process are asked to look beyond the unit for ways to optimize or maximize a unit's performance. Unfortunately, institutional barriers frequently prevent units from reorganizing themselves across unit boundaries. Disciplinary differences and labor market forces are often cited as barriers to effective reorganization. Program review can identify the need for structural change, but it cannot effect it.

Renewal

Executed well, program review can be an invigorating experience for the unit and the institution; it can significantly contribute to a spirit of renewal. Program review's success in this regard relates to the notion that there is a threshold beyond which resistant individuals will tolerate no change. Frame-breaking change takes individuals beyond this threshold and therefore leads to a spirit of resistance rather than renewal. Identifying the unit's and institution's threshold for change is a surmountable challenge within the program review process that can engender a spirit of vigor and renewal.

Final Thoughts

Program review is a familiar mechanism within higher education, but can it help institutions deal with the unfamiliar and take us to the unknown? Is program review a process that appeals to the person who reaches for a map in a new city, or to someone who prefers adventure rather than a charted course?

I believe program review can appeal to both personalities. Program review results in a map. Institutions have information about the educational terrain and knowledge about their resources, and they have an idea of where they want to go. However, the results are temporal. Higher education's rapidly changing context may force redirection at any moment. With its cyclical process and the natural half-life of plans, program review may be the best institutional process to help institutions keep turning sharp corners when needed. Indeed, program review can help an institution redefine itself. It all depends on where you start, where you find yourself, and where you may start again. . . . Hopefully, you won't end up where you started from.

Further Reading

For good discussions of the program review process, see Barak (1982, 1986) and Barak and Breier (1990). Hoey (1995b) provides an interesting conceptual framework for understanding how the results of program review are utilized. Because so many aspects of the program review process are similar to concepts of strategic planning and change, consider Bolman and Deal (1991), Mintzberg (1989), and Tichy (1983) for aspects of the change process that illuminate understanding when dealing with program review.

References

Argyris, C., and Schön, D. A. *Organizational Learning.* Reading, Mass.: Addison-Wesley, 1981.

Arns, R. G., and Poland, W. "Changing the University Through Program Review." *Journal of Higher Education,* 1980, *51*(3), 268–284.

Baldridge, J. V., and Deal, T. E. *Managing Change in Educational Organizations.* Berkeley, Calif.: McCutchan, 1975.

Barak, R. J. *Program Review in Higher Education: Within and Without.* Boulder, Colo.: National Center for Higher Education Management Systems, 1982.

Barak, R. J. *The Role of Program Review in Strategic Planning.* AIR Professional File, no. 26. Tallahassee, Fla.: Association for Institutional Research, 1986.

Barak, R. J. "Program Planning, Development, and Evaluation." In M. W. Peterson and L.

A. Mets (eds.), *Key Resources on Higher Education Governance, Management, and Leadership*. San Francisco: Jossey-Bass, 1987.

Barak, R. J., and Breier, B. E. *Successful Program Review: A Practical Guide to Evaluating Programs in Academic Settings*. San Francisco: Jossey-Bass, 1990.

Barak, R. J., and Mets, L. A. *Using Academic Program Review*. New Directions for Institutional Research, no. 86. San Francisco: Jossey-Bass, 1995.

Barak, R. J., and Sweeney, J. D. "Academic Program Review in Planning, Budgeting, and Assessment." In R. J. Barak and L. A. Mets, *Using Academic Program Review*. New Directions for Institutional Research, no. 86. San Francisco: Jossey-Bass, 1995.

Bennis, W. G., Benne, K. D., Chin, R., and Corey, K. E. *The Planning of Change*. (3rd ed.) Austin, Tex.: Holt, Rinehart and Winston, 1976.

Bolman, L. G., and Deal, T. E. *Reframing Organizations: Artistry, Choice, and Leadership*. San Francisco: Jossey-Bass, 1991.

Breier, B. E. "Program Review Policy in Intent, Implementation, and Experience: A Case Study." Lawrence: University of Kansas. *DAI* 47/2, 430A (University Microfilms no. 8608379), 1986.

Cameron, K., and Ulrich, D. O. "Transformational Leadership in Colleges and Universities." In J. C. Smart (ed.), *Higher Education: Handbook of Theory and Research*. Vol. 2. New York: Agathon Press, 1986.

Chaffee, E. E. "The Concept of Strategy: From Business to Higher Education." In J. C. Smart (ed.), *Higher Education: Handbook of Theory and Research*. Vol. 1. New York: Agathon Press, 1985.

Conrad, C. F., and Wilson, R. F. *Academic Program Reviews: Institutional Approaches, Expectations, and Controversies*. ASHE-ERIC Higher Education Report, no. 5. Washington, D.C.: Association for the Study of Higher Education, 1985.

Cope, R. G. *Strategic Policy Planning: A Guide for College and University Administrators*. Littleton, Colo.: Ireland Educational, 1978.

Cranton, P. A., and Legge, L. H. "Program Evaluation in Higher Education." *Journal of Higher Education*, 1978, *49*(5), 464–471.

Craven, E. C. (ed.). *Academic Program Evaluation*. New Directions for Institutional Research, no. 27. San Francisco: Jossey-Bass, 1980.

Dolence, J. G., and Norris, D. M. *Transforming Higher Education: A Vision for Learning in the 21st Century*. Ann Arbor, Mich.: Society for College and University Planning, 1995.

Eaton, G. M., and Miyares, J. "Integrating Program Review in Planning and Budgeting: A Systemwide Perspective." In R. J. Barak and L. A. Mets, *Using Academic Program Review*. New Directions for Institutional Research, no. 86. San Francisco: Jossey-Bass, 1995.

Feasley, C. E. *Program Evaluation*. AAHE-ERIC/Higher Education Research Report, no. 2. Washington, D.C.: American Association for Higher Education, 1980.

Gardner, D. E. "Five Evaluation Frameworks: Implications for Decision Making in Higher Education." *Journal of Higher Education*, 1977, *48*(5), 571–593.

Garvin, D. A. *Managing Quality: The Strategic and Competitive Edge*. New York: Free Press, 1988.

Goodman, P. S., and Kurke, L. B. "Studies of Change in Organizations: A Status Report." In P. S. Goodman and Associates, *Change in Organizations*. San Francisco: Jossey-Bass, 1982.

Hermon-Taylor, R. J. "Finding New Ways of Overcoming Resistance to Change." In J. M. Pennings and Associates, *Organizational Strategy and Change*. San Francisco: Jossey-Bass, 1985.

Hoey, J. J., IV. "Impact of Program Review on Community Colleges." In R. J. Barak and L.

A. Mets, *Using Academic Program Review.* New Directions for Institutional Research, no. 86. San Francisco: Jossey-Bass, 1995a.

Hoey, J. J., IV. "Organizational Factors in Program Review." In R. J. Barak and L. A. Mets, *Using Academic Program Review.* New Directions for Institutional Research, no. 86. San Francisco: Jossey-Bass, 1995b.

Huber, G. P. *Organizational Learning: An Examination of the Contributing Processes and the Literatures.* Unpublished manuscript, University of Texas at Austin, 1990.

Kanter, R. M. *The Change Masters: Innovation and Entrepreneurship in the American Corporation.* New York: Simon & Schuster, 1983.

Kanter, R. M. *When Giants Learn to Dance.* New York: Simon & Schuster, 1989.

Kanter, R. M., Stein, B. A., and Jick, T. D. *The Challenge of Organizational Change: How Companies Experience It and Leaders Guide It.* New York: Free Press, 1992.

Keller, G. *Academic Strategy: The Management Revolution in Higher Education.* Baltimore, Md.: Johns Hopkins University Press, 1983.

Kells, H. R. "The Purposes and Legacy of Effective Self-Study Processes: Enhancing the Study-Planning Cycle." *Journal of Higher Education,* 1980, *51*(4), 438–447.

Lippitt, G. L., Langseth, P., and Mossop, J. *Implementing Organizational Change: A Practical Guide to Managing Change Efforts.* San Francisco: Jossey-Bass, 1985.

Lorange, P. "Strengthening Organizational Capacity to Execute Strategic Change." In J. M. Pennings and Associates, *Organizational Strategy and Change.* San Francisco: Jossey-Bass, 1985.

Mets, L. A. "Lessons Learned from Program Review Experiences." In R. J. Barak and L. A. Mets, *Using Academic Program Review.* New Directions for Institutional Research, no. 86. San Francisco: Jossey-Bass, 1995a.

Mets, L. A. "Program Review in Academic Departments." In R. J. Barak and L. A. Mets, *Using Academic Program Review.* New Directions for Institutional Research, no. 86. San Francisco: Jossey-Bass, 1995b.

Mintzberg, H. *Mintzberg on Management: Inside our Strange World of Organizations.* New York: Free Press, 1989.

Nordvall, R. C. "Innovation, Planned Change, and Transformation Strategies." In M. W. Peterson and L. A. Mets (eds.), *Key Resources on Higher Education Governance, Management, and Leadership: A Guide to the Literature.* San Francisco: Jossey-Bass, 1987.

Normann, R. "Developing Capabilities for Organizational Learning." In J. M. Pennings and Associates, *Organizational Strategy and Change.* San Francisco: Jossey-Bass, 1985.

Office of the Vice President for Administration and Planning. *Academic and Administrative Program Review Procedures.* Evanston, Ill.: Northwestern University, 1989.

Peters, T. J., and Austin, N. *A Passion for Excellence: The Leadership Difference.* New York: Warner Books, 1985.

Peters, T. J., and Waterman, R. H., Jr. *In Search of Excellence: Lessons from America's Best-Run Companies.* New York: Harper & Row, 1982.

Schmidtlein, F. A., and Milton, T. H. "College and University Planning: Perspectives from a Nation-Wide Study." *Planning for Higher Education,* 1988–89, *17*(3), 1–19.

Senge, P. M. *The Fifth Discipline: The Art and Practice of the Learning Organization.* New York: Doubleday, 1990.

St. John, E. P. "The Transformation of Private Liberal Arts Colleges." *Review of Higher Education,* 1991, *15*(1), 83–106.

Tichy, Noel M. *Managing Strategic Change: Technical, Political, and Cultural Dynamics.* New York: Wiley, 1983.

Waterman, R. H., Jr. *The Renewal Factor: How the Best Get and Keep the Competitive Edge.* New York: Bantam Books, 1987.

Weick, K. E. "Educational Organizations as Loosely Coupled Systems." *Administrative Science Quarterly,* 1976, *21,* 1–19.

Weick, K. E. "Management of Organizational Change Among Loosely Coupled Elements." In P. S. Goodman and Associates, *Change in Organizations.* San Francisco: Jossey-Bass, 1982.

Williams, W. "Implementation Analysis and Assessment." *Policy Analysis,* 1975, *1*(3), 531–566.

Wilson, R. F. *Designing Academic Program Reviews.* New Directions for Higher Education, no. 37. San Francisco: Jossey-Bass, 1982.

Wroblewski, E. "New Directions for Academic Program Review at a Private, Comprehensive College." In R. J. Barak and L. A. Mets, *Using Academic Program Review.* New Directions for Institutional Research, no. 86. San Francisco: Jossey-Bass, 1995.

CHAPTER NINETEEN

STRENGTHENING ASSESSMENT FOR ACADEMIC QUALITY IMPROVEMENT

Peter T. Ewell

Since its emergence as a widespread topic of national discussion in higher education some fifteen years ago, assessment has been inextricably linked with accountability. Throughout this period, explicit external demands for information about results constituted the initial reason why the majority of colleges and universities got into the assessment business. The perceived need to satisfy constituencies like state governments and accreditors also decisively colored the assessment approaches actually adopted, who got involved in assessment efforts on campuses, and the manner in which assessment results were used (Ewell, 1993a).

As is often the case, this outcome was neither what policy makers intended nor what assessment's pioneers envisioned. But the academic administrators responsible for this result were responding rationally to some real environmental conditions. On the one hand, the very existence of assessment as an external mandate meant that faculty could disengage; added to the apprehension naturally associated with any evaluation was an understandable belief that assessment was an administrative, not an academic, problem. As a result, faculty all too often felt assessment to be something that administrators should "take care of" without involving them. More significantly in this period, no real incentives for grassroots engagement were present. The 1980s, in retrospect, were a decade of relative resource abundance for higher education, and while investments in innovation occurred (and could be afforded), few real changes in academic structure and pedagogy were perceived as necessary. Like parallel "reforms" in general education, assessment became widespread but marginal: few institutions remained unaffected, but deep engagement was rare.

The fiscal and management conditions of the 1990s, in contrast, have transformed the terms of engagement. Significant fiscal shortfalls are for the first time forcing institutions to seriously examine past practices in delivering undergraduate instruction. This conversation is fueled equally by emerging technologies that promise more for less but that may also fundamentally alter the way teaching and learning occurs. At the same time, accountability has become sharper and is increasingly tied to resource allocation. In all aspects of government, "entitlements" are being replaced by contracts for specific performance—with performance defined less by the providers themselves than by client needs and expectations. This combination has decisively shaped the context for assessment. The paramount current need is to reposition assessment as a tool for academic management—effectively "recycling" methods and information designed initially to meet external demands.

A principal challenge implied by this shift is transforming the mind-set of assessment from one dominated by end-point checking on goal achievement to one that emphasizes continuous, low-level monitoring of instructional processes and their interconnections. As a consequence, a main purpose of this chapter is to explore how this fundamental and needed transformation has evolved, shaped by both external conditions and the development of assessment technology itself. A second challenge is more formidable: to find better ways to systematically embed the results of assessment into academic planning and budgeting—especially where fundamental changes are contemplated. The second section of the chapter, therefore, examines some specific ways in which assessment practices can become integral to academic decision making for the future. In both discussions, moreover, a single theme is apparent: to be useful in the new millennium, assessment practices not only must examine "value added" but must themselves add value. And only the approaches that meet this condition can and should be maintained.

An Evolving Environment for Assessment

Three factors have influenced assessment's development over the past decade and, for better or worse, decisively shaped the tools and techniques now available. Accountability requirements—chiefly on the part of state governments, but increasingly including accrediting bodies as well—created an initial "market" for assessment and strongly affected the kinds of instruments and techniques that institutions developed and deployed. Changing fiscal conditions have also had a significant part to play, reflected both in the affordability of complex assessment approaches and the fiscal parameters governing institutional responses to assessment findings. Finally, considerable technical evolution occurred as institutions gained experience with designing and implementing new methods. Because the interactions among these forces are complex, a full understanding of each is important to recognize assessment's emerging potential.

The Demand for Assessment: The Accountability Dimension

Campus assessment practice has always reflected shifting alignments between internal and external demands. The roots of the movement were both campus-centered and radical: its early proponents advanced assessment not just as a means to gather information but as a point of entry for engaging the far broader topics of curricular reform and learner-centered pedagogy that also became prominent in the eighties.

As a result, original calls for assessment were always embedded in a wider change agenda (for example, Association of American Colleges, 1985; National Institute of Education, 1984). More importantly, recognizing the way change actually happens on college and university campuses, these approaches strongly emphasized visible faculty engagement and the development of diverse, campus-centered efforts. External interest, in contrast, resulted initially from an earlier political engagement with K–12 education. Here, "assessment" referenced a far different paradigm of change, one founded upon the visible establishment and maintenance of clear (and often centralized) standards for common student achievement (National Governors' Association, 1986).

The first interaction of these potentially conflicting agendas was benign (Ewell, 1994). Higher education leaders in most states were able to convince public officials that decentralized assessment approaches—consistent with the internal reform agenda just emerging—were both internally feasible and could simultaneously serve public purposes. Partly this was because, differently from K–12, few specific complaints about the performance of colleges and universities had arisen; higher education's "accountability problem" was therefore one of establishing public confidence in its own regulatory processes more than attaining particular standards. In part it was also because more basic goals were aligned. Many states in the mid-eighties were investing heavily in the "quality" of their public higher education systems—often in the form of addition-to-base incentive grant programs—and the assessment-for-improvement agenda of internal reform appeared highly compatible with these initiatives. Indeed, dollars provided to institutions through such mechanisms were often invested deliberately in upgrading campus-level assessment capacity in this period, usually in conjunction with other pedagogical or curricular changes.

Consistent with these developments, by 1990 over two-thirds of the states had resolved the question of assessment policy by adopting a campus-centered approach, allowing each institution to develop its own statements of expected outcomes and its own means to gather evidence of their achievement (Ewell, Finney, and Lenth, 1990). Stimulated in part by new Department of Education regulations, all six regional accreditation organizations implemented similar policies, requiring the development of local assessment programs by private as well as public institutions. The result was a pattern of institutional response demonstrated markedly in national surveys. The proportion of institutions reporting engagement in assessment rose significantly in the period 1988–1995 from 55 percent to 94 percent, while the percentage of those indicating that assessment had a real programmatic or curricular impact almost doubled from 40 percent to 76 percent; at the same time, almost half of those responding to the same survey in 1995 indicated that attention to assessment had for the most part "resulted in new reporting requirements," and two-thirds remained skeptical about misuse of results by external agencies (El-Khawas, 1995). External initiatives promoting campus-centered assessment had clearly been successful in heightening institutional attention and capacity. But simple engagement in "assessment activities" provided insufficient impetus for serious self-reflection and renewal.

Beginning about 1990, however, the accountability agenda began to change. On the one hand, significant economic downturns in many states strongly stimulated traditional concerns about academic efficiency in much the same manner as they had two decades earlier (McGuinness, 1994). With "outcomes" now a legitimate topic of discussion, however, policy makers could comfortably raise issues of performance along with cost, and they began to do so with considerable regularity. At the same time, doubts began growing about the ability of decentralized, noncomparable data-gathering approaches to effectively discharge public accountability functions (Ewell, 1991a). The result for many states was increasing separation of the "improvement" and "accountability" components of assessment policy. Few abandoned the campus-centered assessment mandates established earlier, but fifteen states had by 1995 implemented additional "performance indicator" systems using common measures (Ruppert, 1994). In stark contrast to the institution-centered approaches emphasized throughout the eighties, the explicit intent of such systems was to compare institutional performances—often for purposes of funding as well as public reporting (Ewell, 1994).

Accompanying this trend was an important additional change in perspective. Institution-centered assessment not only allowed a diversity of evidence-gathering approaches but it also emphasized the achievement of internally established academic goals. More and more, as the nineties progressed, state governments began emphasizing higher education's role in addressing larger societal or client-driven goals (Ewell and Jones, 1993; McGuinness, 1994). As a result, emerging state indicator systems often went beyond institution-posed outcomes to include measures of employer and student satisfaction. An equally prominent theme in state policy discussions of quality were issues of protecting consumers, and of providing higher education's clients with adequate information on the basis of which to make informed customer choices (Education Commission of the States, 1995). In the period 1992–1995, moreover, a major new champion of consumer-based accountability emerged in the form of the federal government. Reacting specifically to charges of fraud and abuse with respect to federal financial aid funds, the 1992 Reauthorization of the Higher Education Act incorporated highly prescriptive new regulations governing state and accrediting-body review, several of which addressed institutional outcomes. Though substantially rolled back by Congress in 1995, these regulations did succeed in highlighting consumer issues as a continuing part of the accountability equation, whether discharged by states or by accrediting bodies.

Taken together, these changes in the accountability context have a number of implications. First, institutional capacity to engage in assessment has become a major condition of doing business. Not only is outcomes information routinely required for public reporting by many external authorities, but the prudent institution will also want the ability to reanalyze, interpret, or refute claims about its performance that will increasingly be used to make high-stakes decisions. Second, as this implies, the basic character of public funding is shifting markedly from a mode based on "subsidizing operations" to one founded on "paying for performance" (Ewell, 1991a). In this context, information about outcomes, whatever its character, increasingly drives resource allocation. Consistent with the implied "market mechanism" of performance-based allocation, moreover, institutions need to become far more responsive to concerns about performance on the part of individual clients. Partly this is because of market pressures and increasing dependence on tuition revenues. At least as prominently, it results from growing public pressures for better consumer information.

The Demand for Assessment: The Productivity Dimension

Changing accountability and market conditions such as these mean that assessment information has an increasingly direct bearing on critical institutional revenue streams. Perhaps more significant, however, is assessment's emerging relevance in helping institutions cut costs and improve instructional productivity. When assessment first emerged, this was less a concern. Both accountability and improvement rested far more visibly on a rhetoric of quality than on one of efficiency. By the early nineties, however, higher education's fiscal environment had changed decisively. Most states experienced significant economic downturns, which together with growing taxpayer resistance meant significant cutbacks in public allocation.

For public higher education, these effects were amplified by a structural condition of state budgeting: allocations to colleges and universities in most states represented virtually the only discretionary dollars available to balance state budgets after taking into account mandated (or politically untouchable) expenditures in such areas as health care, corrections, or K–12 education. Faced with these conditions, public higher education experienced an unprecedented two-year downturn in real expenditures in 1990–1992, with some states suffering cumulative cuts of over 20 percent (Hines, 1994). While tuition increases could make up some lost ground, it was clear to all but a few institutions by the mid-1990s that attention to expenditures would be required.

Significant pressures on institutional budgets, moreover, generally arose in a context where simple cutbacks were precluded. On the one hand, a now-prominent accountability agenda meant that quality could not be simply "traded-off" against cost; externally, it was clear that explicit assessment would remain in place and that institutions would be held responsible for continuing to attain quality objectives. And it was equally clear that student access could not be denied; indeed, many states expected substantial increases in the numbers of students their postsecondary systems would be required to serve. The resulting pressure on institutions to hold down expenditures while maintaining quality and increasing output yielded multiple responses.

An initial manifestation (certainly the most visible) of this new set of conditions was a wave of institutional attempts to implement Total Quality Management (TQM), a family of approaches drawn from business and industry (for example, Seymour, 1991; Sherr and Teeter, 1991). Applied first to administrative functions, colleges and universities did occasionally succeed in duplicating industry's claim to simultaneously improve productivity and cut costs. But efforts to extend this application to academic functions often encountered precisely the same kinds of intellectual objections based on the alien language and inappropriate conceptualization earlier experienced by the more "psychometric" approaches to assessment (Ewell, 1993b). As a result, initial attempts to "restructure" academic functions tended to follow a different logic. Virtually every aspect of this response, however, had a potentially significant link to assessment.

A first level of response involved cutting "nonproductive" programs. Like parallel efforts in the late 1970s, the principal criteria used here were low enrollment and degree productivity. But newly available assessment results also had a part to play in many cases, especially if these were already incorporated into established program review procedures (Miller, forthcoming). Somewhat deeper "academic restructuring" efforts often involved a more critical examination of curricular requirements (Zemsky, Massy, and Oedel, 1993). At the most basic level, this commonly resulted in reducing the number of credits needed to complete a degree, or finding ways to accelerate student progress by means of advanced placement or continuous attendance (McGuinness and Ewell, 1994). More sophisticated curricular restructuring efforts entailed delving more deeply into course sequences and requirements in order to identify instances where greater coherence could be achieved. In both kinds of restructuring, assessment has become increasingly relevant, both to identify those students who can in fact be "accelerated" and to determine the effects of such changes on eventual outcomes.

Probably the most visible restructuring efforts, however, have emphasized the application of new technology to instructional delivery, a process seen by both academic administrators and state officials as the principal "magic bullet" needed to slay the productivity dragon (Resmer, Mingle, and Oblinger, 1995). Embodied in such mechanisms as interactive video for distance delivery and computer-assisted, self-paced hypertext modules intended to be embedded in regular coursework, the application of such technologies raises fundamental questions of pedagogical impact that at some point beg to be evaluated. At the same time, the very structure of such mechanisms—especially where they require independent student demonstration of mastery at their own pace—requires that the assessment of competency be built into curricular designs from the outset (Stanford Forum on Higher Education Futures, 1995).

The Changing Face of Assessment Practice

As these many contextual shifts took place, the technical practice of assessment was changing as well. By the mid-1990s, based on a decade of experience, institutional administrators had many approaches from which to choose and had accumulated considerable experience in how to deploy them. While this technical evolution unfolded in relative isolation from trends in the higher education environment, its direction yielded instruments and approaches that were far more suited to meeting the challenges posed by environmental change than the techniques available when assessment first emerged.

A first path of development saw assessment approaches becoming increasingly comprehensive. While assessment was visibly labeled an "outcomes" movement, its advocates argued from the beginning that information on inputs and educational environments would be required in equal measure if assessment results were to be of any real utility (Astin, 1991). Most institutions that actually engaged in assessment throughout the eighties learned this lesson empirically. A common pattern was to begin with end-point measures—often using standardized tests alone—followed by an interest in collecting data about student experiences, perceptions, and course-taking patterns after finding end-point results essentially uninterpretable (Ewell, 1991b). In what quickly became best practice, other institutions adopted a longitudinal approach from the outset by identifying a cohort of entering students and collecting data on outcomes and experiences systematically as they progressed (Katchadourian and Boli, 1985; Kellams, 1989). While few colleges and universities were ready to make the heavy investments needed to underwrite large-scale longitudinal studies, most institutional assessment programs had by the mid-nineties abandoned the exclusive use of isolated, one-shot investigations of outcomes.

Growing comprehensiveness also implied paying greater attention to examining curricular and environmental interconnections. As institutions began seriously investigating learning outcomes, they also began discovering that the curriculum as actually delivered, or as behaviorally experienced by students, often varied significantly from its original design. Such discoveries were frequently the real payoff of increasingly popular "portfolio" assessment designs, because examining samples of actual student work often revealed more about what students were taught and assigned than about the amount of learning taking place (Ewell, 1996). Other institutions began specifically using assessment techniques to examine the functioning of particular course sequences, and the ways in which individual courses acted in concert to reinforce identified core skills (Farmer, 1988; Harris and Baggett, 1992). A final theme centered on the student's own contribution to the learning process. Here, assessments of student goals (and how they change), use of time, involvement (Astin, 1992), and "quality of effort" in using available academic resources (Pace, 1984) became paramount.

A second significant evolution was toward a more "naturalistic" approach to assessment. Following classic principles of program evaluation, early assessment practice was deliberately set apart from instructional settings. The use of specially constructed evidence-gathering techniques (prominently including standardized tests) was consciously fostered, both to increase external credibility and because such approaches were thought to increase measurement precision (Ewell, 1989). As a practical matter, however, the use of obtrusive, purpose-built assessments encountered numerous difficulties. Students rarely saw participation as directly beneficial to their studies, and participation rates and levels of motivation remained a problem. At the same time, despite their methodological rigor, faculty often found the results of such exercises to be difficult to apply to their own instructional settings and circumstances. These escalating implementation difficulties, coupled with a growing impetus to render assessment methods more authentic in order to overcome institutional resistance, helped move many institutions toward less obtrusive approaches (Banta, 1988).

A first opportunity, many institutions discovered, was to take better advantage of existing points of contact with students. After systematically inventorying how they collected data from students, colleges and universities often found that many points of contact already existed but that these opportunities were organizationally dispersed and often duplicative in content (Ewell and Lisensky, 1988). This discovery in itself often led to short-term savings in data-collection costs. But at the same time, institutions often learned that existing instruments and opportunities could be more fully exploited. Prominent examples of the application of this logic were entering-student orientation and testing programs that could be expanded to gather additional information about student academic goals or perceived strengths and weaknesses, end-of-course instructor evaluation questionnaires that might contain additional items on student effort and behaviors, and upper-level student writing assessments that could be reoriented to examine disciplinary content in general education.

The ultimate existing point of contact, of course, was the classroom itself. As a result, assessment practitioners began experimenting with ways in which valid, generalizable information about student performance could be gathered using intact curricular and classroom settings (Warren, 1988). Probably the most straightforward such methods involved resurrecting "old" curricular practices, including such devices as upper-level writing exercises, capstone courses, or senior comprehensive examinations. In addition to being individually scored, the results of such exercises could be aggregated to yield information about how particular groups of students were performing. In applied fields such as health, business, engineering, or the fine and performing arts, such constructions were often natural because complex multitrait performance ratings were already being used to grade individual students; all that remained was to examine patterns of strength and weakness across students to convert them into assessments.

Conceptually similar but more sophisticated were "course-embedded" assessment approaches, in which selected examination questions were carefully constructed to yield data on both the mastery of course content and the development of more general skills such as critical thinking and the ability to make appropriate connections among different disciplines. Using "secondary reading" techniques guided by explicit scoring rubrics, such approaches allowed faculty to use naturally occurring examination settings to collectively examine selected areas of common interest without compromising student motivation or their own instructional goals (Erwin, 1991; Ewell, 1991b). Approaches such as these were often especially suited for investigating more intractable curricular domains such as general education.

Even more attractive to many institutions were approaches based on existing student products. At the most basic level, previously graded samples of individual student work could be aggregated and their common strengths and weaknesses

determined. Such approaches were often especially useful in examining course sequences, where an analysis of the specific errors students make in later work can
be used directly in the improvement of prerequisite course delivery. More com-
pellingly, portfolios of student work could be compiled, either over time for individual students to document growth or cross-sectionally across different student
types to examine patterns of variation (Black, 1993). Assessment approaches based
on work samples had many advantages. Because students completed the work for
other purposes, there were no obvious motivational problems, and faculty could
not quarrel with the authenticity of the data on which assessment conclusions were
based. But unless clear guidelines on size and purpose were established, institutions also found the use of portfolios awkward and time-consuming. In many cases,
as noted earlier, their utility was as much to document the kinds of assignments
students were given as assessing how much learning had taken place.

Whether purposely constructed or based on a secondary reading of existing
student products, naturalistic assessment techniques of this kind represented attempts to address the fact that conventional grading approaches yielded little usable data about collective performance. A final and more radical step in this path
of evolutionary development, therefore, involved changing grading and classroom
pedagogical procedures directly. For many professional or occupational programs,
this step was already partially accomplished. The assessment of individual students against clear, observable, criterion-based competency levels was common,
and using such measures to assign grades as well as to determine patterns of aggregate performance was natural. In other fields, however, changes of this kind
required a major shift of culture. Nevertheless, experiments with alternative grading methods based on primary trait scoring, core scoring, or other mastery-based
approaches steadily grew as it became clear that the ends of assessment and
pedagogy could be served simultaneously (Walvoord and others, 1995). Coupled
with both of these developments was a growing "classroom assessment" movement (Angelo and Cross, 1993) that allowed faculty to gain immediately useful
feedback about classroom-level perceptions and behaviors. Though deliberately
intended for use "in private" by individual instructors, widespread familiarity with
such techniques had by the mid-nineties done much to legitimize assessment for
line faculty.

In colleges and universities with relatively long histories of assessment, changes
in context and practice gradually changed the role of the process within the institution. On the one hand, they began dropping assessment approaches that simply cost money without informing internal curricular development; seen from the
outset as a "tax on the enterprise," such initiatives were maintained only so long
as they were explicitly required for accountability by external bodies. As assessment techniques became increasingly authentic and instructionally embedded,

moreover, faculty began more and more to rediscover their original merits as elements of curricular design. Capstone courses, senior seminars, and major-field comprehensive examinations—once a central feature of undergraduate curricula but largely abandoned in the late 1960s and early 1970s—began reemerging in large numbers not just as vehicles for assessment but because they made good pedagogical sense. At the same time, faculty experience with constructing formal assessment devices made them better test-builders in their own classes. Developments such as these had little directly to do with assessment's role as an information system grafted onto delivery; instead they occurred because at such institutions assessment had gradually become an indistinguishable part of curricular and faculty development.

Connecting Assessment Information to Instructional Redirection and Renewal

The argument of the preceding section is clear. On the one hand, the conditions that originally gave rise to a formal assessment movement in higher education some fifteen years ago have changed decisively. The demands now placed on higher education by its environments are not just political but also economic. Cost containment requires restructured approaches to instructional delivery that need information about relative performance in a measure at least equal to that associated exclusively with accountability. At the same time, assessment technique has evolved to the point that it is potentially optimized to provide precisely the kinds of information needed to respond to these conditions. Ironically, to fulfill this new potential, assessment as a distinct and visible activity needs to be increasingly deemphasized. Instead, its principal focus must be placed on making information about academic effectiveness—drawn from whatever source—an integral part of academic planning and pedagogical design.

For the practicing academic administrator, three implications are apparent. First, information drawn from assessment is crucial to designing and operating the kinds of restructured forms of instructional delivery that will be increasingly present in the new millennium; making effective use of them, however, demands new ways of thinking about how evaluative information should be collected and deployed. Second, at the programmatic and institutional levels, assessment activities are becoming increasingly integral to academic planning, both to set priorities among programs and to ensure that program delivery is appropriately aligned with the needs of increasingly salient and vocal external clients. Finally, how assessment as an institutional activity is organized and administered has to change, and some particular implementation syndromes avoided. Only with these conditions met can assessment information and procedures be effectively "recycled" to meet emerging institutional challenges.

Assessment in a Restructured Curriculum

As noted, both new economic realities and the growing possibilities of effective technology-based instructional delivery systems are driving an unprecedented level of curricular experiment. While many of the alternatives posed are simple, others involve a significant deconstruction of the traditional instructional paradigm. Among the most prominent are time-shortened course sequences that place a premium on interconnection, self-paced (and often technology-intensive) courses in which students can proceed at their own pace or test out of requirements if they can demonstrate previously acquired mastery, and asynchronous or hypertext modes of delivery in which students can choose their own paths through complex bodies of material (Twigg, 1995). Within this environment, assessment is increasingly assuming two roles. First, it is needed summatively to help determine the degree to which such alternative delivery formats—presumably less costly— can in fact deliver learning gains equivalent to those associated with more traditional forms. More importantly, because alternative forms are increasingly competency-based, effective assessment mechanisms are needed for them to operate at all.

A first manifestation of assessment's role in this new instructional environment is relatively traditional: helping to clarify goals and to actively guide the development of new curricular designs. The creation of alternative delivery mechanisms, especially those based on technology, by its very nature requires faculty to return to first principles. In an environment in which real-time, sequential coverage of equivalent blocks of content cannot be assumed as a building block, the primary foundation available for guiding curriculum or course design is intended outcomes. Often, however, the intended outcomes for the courses that alternative formats are intended to replace are not clear. Still murkier are those particular elements of current practice that are most effective and therefore ought to be preserved. And completely unknown are the possible adverse and unanticipated consequences for both learning and implementation that the widespread adoption of restructured curricula may entail. In all three areas, assessment techniques can play a relatively traditional evaluative role: helping to determine far more precisely which aspects of current delivery should remain unaltered and which might be effectively supplemented or replaced by more efficient alternatives.

A second major area of application is assessment's potential role in assuring greater connectivity. Consistent with key tenets of general education reform of the mid-eighties, curricular restructuring often rests heavily on the assurance that discrete instructional experiences, whether they be course-based or nontraditional, fit together effectively to yield a coherent whole (Gaff, 1983). At the macro level, this implies the need to examine student learning outcomes that are the joint products of many discrete experiences—not all of which may have contributed equally (or at all) to the final result. Assessment can play a familiar evaluation role in this environment, especially if it is built into naturally occurring capstone experiences that require comprehensive demonstrations of mastery. But it must also transcend this role in being able to further demonstrate the relative contributions of different factors to the joint product in question. Here it may be particularly important to couple comprehensive assessment results with detailed data on student background, experiences, and investments in order to determine which paths and patterns appear to work best. Especially useful in this latter task may be measures of student involvement and commitment (Pace, 1984) and of detailed course-taking behavior (Ratcliff, 1987). Related are overall measures of curricular structure and the incidence of instructional "good practice" that can be used in concert with outcomes measures to help monitor the actual alignment of instructional delivery with intended outcomes and established curricular designs (Ewell, 1996; Ewell and Jones, 1996).

A more direct implication of connectivity is more consistent with emerging quality management themes. Here the principal focus of concern is course sequences and, more particularly, the degree to which students are obtaining required prerequisite skills and are able to deploy these skills effectively in subsequent courses after what may be substantial lapses of time or significant changes in context. Assessment's role in this environment is far more focused, resting primarily on the development of embedded measures of essential prerequisite skills for use as pretests in subsequent courses that require such skills (Farmer, 1988), and/or analyzing the specific types of errors of fact or application that students make in subsequent coursework (Harris and Baggett, 1992). A reciprocal role is designing in-course exercises in basic courses that contextually anchor required skills in the specific kinds of applications that students face later—or, indeed, may already be facing in the courses that they are taking simultaneously. Important areas of contextual application here are written communication and quantitative analysis (most prominently, calculus and statistics). An important caveat in all such cases is that embedded assessments be constructed as much to detect patterns of strength and weakness as to provide feedback to individual students. This implies not only careful attention to design but also the development of active dissemination networks for sharing results among the faculty of associated courses and across disciplines (Baugher, 1992).

A third and final major area of application is more basic: to actively certify or credential student mastery. So long as the predominant paradigm of instructional delivery was the term-based course in which all students progressed simultaneously through a given body of material, the award of credit based primarily on "seat time" remained reasonable. As self-paced or multipath progressional alternatives continue to emerge, however, there is substantial pressure on keeping the traditional time- and content-based Carnegie unit as the principal unit of academic accounting.

Not surprisingly under these circumstances, the leading candidate for its replacement is assessed competence in some form. A simple illustration is the growing salience of advanced placement and credit-by-examination mechanisms in time-shortened degree programs, allowing students to place out of coursework whose basic curricular intention they have already attained (Miller, forthcoming). More sophisticated examples can be seen in technology-intensive self-paced course modules in such prerequisite fields as math and statistics or the introductory sciences, and in professional fields such as health care. Here the application of technology allows complex assessments of mastery to be built directly into the delivery of instruction at multiple points. This means first of all that individual students can be certified as they arrive independently at particular levels of proficiency, providing the asynchronous equivalent of traditional midterm and final examinations. Second of all, this means that all interactions and student responses can be recorded in a computer-based medium of instruction; however, it also means that revealing analyses can be undertaken of the different paths students choose and the specific difficulties that they encounter.

This emerging role of assessment in directly credentialing student achievement is also apparent in interinstitutional settings. Among networks of colleges and universities, assessed competency first provides an efficient potential alternative to increasingly cumbersome course-by-course articulation arrangements in determining the academic standing of entering transfer students. In parallel, the growing use of authentic assessment approaches to certify achievement in secondary schools has led several states to experiment with proficiency-based standards for collegiate admission (Rodriguez 1995).

All three of these implications, if realized, have assessment at the center of instructional design. Rather than being applied to instruction as a periodic means of checking on its effectiveness, assessment technology is engineered directly into the fabric of teaching and learning, to help perform standard academic functions of managing placement and awarding credit. But because the needed assessments can be designed to generate group results as well, the resulting architecture can also provide information useful for continuously monitoring instructional delivery and guiding improvement. Arguably, however, it is no longer assessment, but a regular form of academic management information.

Assessment and Academic Planning

Assessment's role in planning and administration in this emerging environment is tending toward a similar path. Increasingly, information about performance is not separate from other forms but is becoming incorporated into regularly established channels and procedures. One aspect of this development is internal, visible in such familiar processes as curricular oversight and academic program review. A second is external, manifested in the mechanisms institutions use to demonstrate their effectiveness to external clients and publics.

Within the first realm, assessment's role is largely to help inform increasingly salient decisions about program priorities. One term of this equation is, of course, determining which programs to cut or deemphasize. Traditionally, such decisions have been made largely on the grounds of efficiency, reflected in such measures as enrollments, degrees produced, and credits generated. Increasingly, however, this existing array of program performance indicators is being supplemented with available outcomes data that include graduation rates, occupational placement rates, or rates of passage in established licensure or certification procedures. This is in part simply because such data are more plentiful, having been stimulated largely by external reporting requirements. Partly, however, it reflects an emerging consensus that results as well as costs must be counted in determining overall productivity. Internal academic program review mechanisms show similar trends. Like accreditation self-studies, most institutional program review guidelines have always included questions about quality, but these were generally addressed in terms of resources rather than results. Again as a result of a decade of external mandates (both from states and from professional accreditation bodies), more and more institutions are including formal assessment requirements in such processes (Barak, 1991).

The increasing use of performance indicators as an integral part of priority setting begs a number of important questions, however. First, outcomes measures are by nature less precise than those reflecting resources and investments. This means that major abuses can occur if observed differences in program performances are not substantial. Following TQM principles of statistical quality control, this problem has led a number of institutions to establish clear statistical benchmarks to flag aberrant outcomes. Similarly, most institutions using such procedures rely on trend data of at least three years to help control for unusual circumstances or for naturally occurring statistical variation. More significantly, determining that the performance of a given program is low on an assessment measure of any kind does not in itself determine an investment decision. As with more traditional measures of efficiency, a prior determination must also be made about the relevance of the program to the institution's overall mission and goals to determine if the proper response to underperformance is additional investment, disinvestment, or phaseout (Keller, 1983).

Assessment also has a growing role to play in future program planning as new instructional delivery modes are contemplated and as institutions attempt to respond to changing client needs. Many, for example, are facing significant decisions about the acquisition of new technology with little real information about the instructional payoffs that might result from what are often significant up-front investments. As noted earlier, systematic information about the relative performance of different modes of instructional delivery for different kinds of students can be invaluable in making such decisions. At the same time, the specific needs of such key clientele groups as employers are both increasingly salient and shifting rapidly. As a result, program-level assessments that regularly monitor the performance of former students in the workplace and, where appropriate, that involve employers and professionals directly in the institution's own assessment procedures are particularly relevant.

Turning to assessment's role in external communication, several additional dimensions are apparent. Greater reporting on performance, of course, is now integral to accountability for both public and private institutions. At the same time, this function now encompasses more than just accountability because it may directly influence institutional revenue through tuition and service. In turn, the particular messages sent need to reflect internal academic planning, as new market conditions require institutions to actually follow through on promises made. In this environment, two metaphors for external communication are relevant and depend heavily on the deployment of information drawn from assessment. One, directed specifically at potential funders, is "return on investment," which highlights specific ways in which the institution's resources are deployed in order to gain particular valued returns. Its model is a corporate stockholder's report, containing on the one hand a "balance sheet" that presents the condition of the institution's core assets (faculty, resources, facilities, programs, etc.) as well as any investments made to renew and develop these critical resources, and on the other hand a "profit and loss statement" that notes the specific expenditures made and the kinds of aggregate outcomes resulting from these expenditures. Documents prepared on these lines are far more focused on results than are traditional institutional annual reports; they have already been promulgated effectively by several types of institutions.

A second relevant metaphor for guiding external communication is based explicitly on "customer service." Here the intended audience is individual students and their parents, who increasingly face an explicit and difficult set of choices. Modeled specifically on popular consumer-rating guides, reports of this kind seek to answer two quite different student-centered questions. One, an outcomes question, concerns the specific types of skills, jobs, and results that can be reliably associated with attendance. The second is an experience question, addressing the particular kinds of services and educational encounters, such as contact with faculty, small classes, appropriate advising, and responsive administrative procedures, that students can reliably expect to receive. Both types of reporting, moreover, require not only aggregate reporting but also the ability to break down assessment results for different kinds of potential students (Education Commission of the States, 1995).

In short, emerging market conditions for most colleges and universities are rapidly erasing boundaries between internal and external concerns. Academic planning requires that institutions know far more about what specific constituencies want in terms of educational products and experiences. At the same time, it requires that programs be internally aligned to actually deliver these outcomes and services once they are advertised as available. Information about results drawn from regularly established sources is increasingly requisite for discharging both functions.

Administering Assessment: Some Syndromes to Avoid

A final area of concern in this new operating environment is assessment's organization and administration. Accountability-centered assessment required clear central direction but often remained marginal to decision making. Assessment in a restructured environment, in contrast, must be integral to (and in many ways indistinguishable from) regular processes of communication and review. In particular, academic administrators should avoid a number of identifiable implementation syndromes that have repeatedly plagued institutions in the past.

The first syndrome is administrative isolation, which tends to occur particularly when professional assessment offices are created without explicit roles beyond external reporting. On the one hand, this means that those responsible for gathering and interpreting such information need to be deliberately included in discussions about academic direction setting and investment, much as budget directors and institutional researchers also should be. On the other hand, it means ensuring that the assessment function is built into the institution's regular academic planning process through appropriate committees or review bodies with an ongoing assignment. All too often, for example, the faculty-staff committees responsible for assessment see their job only as establishing a program, not developing and communicating its implications on an ongoing basis.

A second common syndrome is attempting to do too much assessment—a situation ironically caused in part by the compliance mentality associated with external mandates. If assessment is seen principally as a set of requirements to be met rather than findings to be used, it is natural to assume that all such responses are equivalent. Assessment in a restructured environment, in contrast, demands that major investments be made only in assessing areas of ongoing central importance or where specific information is needed to inform a particular decision. Consistent with this need, the best practice is increasingly to operate assessment on two levels (investing some resources in the development of a consistent base of information intended for overall monitoring of program delivery, usually in the form of indicators) and reserving remaining resources for periodic investigations in depth that are related to specific investment decisions.

A third difficulty is excessive methodological purity: attempting to impose on decision-related information the kinds of measurement criteria generally reserved for publishable research. Because assessment practitioners are often trained professionally as social scientists, standards based on statistical significance or standard tests of validity and reliability are automatically imposed in the absence of other criteria. But to be useful in a decision context, different benchmarks are required. Specifically needed instead are criteria drawn from the decision sciences that test the sensitivity of decisions to variations in obtained results (Ackoff, 1962). If sufficiently robust, in such contexts, even imprecise results can be of use.

A related fourth difficulty is excessive rigidity in planning and carrying out assessment activities. Again, this is partly a carryover of excessive research orientation. The classic evaluation methodologies upon which early assessment approaches were based emphasized established principles of scientific research, including clear hypotheses and carefully specified quasi-experimental designs. By their very nature, these required isolation from the mainstream of academic activity. Current good practice, in contrast, requires embedding multiple assessment opportunities in existing delivery and constantly reformulating goals and hypotheses based on the emerging data. Rather than summative testing of effectiveness against fixed objectives, the appropriate metaphor is one of continuously monitoring and adjusting both targets and delivery.

A final common problem is missed opportunities for discussing assessment results. Few institutions currently possess ready-made opportunities to collectively interpret what is happening in their curricula. Rather than one-way reporting, assessment is at its best when its results provide a basis for collective discussions of this kind, and such opportunities must be deliberately created. Retreats or workshops centered on specific, collectively recognized problems of importance to the community (such as first-year retention of minority students, for example) or sessions that regularly examine the institution's progress in attaining collectively agreed-upon plans can be of particular value in this regard.

Into the Future

Future developments in assessment are likely to continue the many trends noted in this chapter. The political context for higher education and its constrained fiscal consequences promise to continue indefinitely. Accountability based on performance—both to funding authorities and to paying customers who will likely bear an increasing share of the financial burden of attendance—is well established and shows no signs of abatement. Partly because of these forces, and partly because of expanding technological possibilities, restructuring will also continue to accelerate whether institutions choose to engage in it as a conscious activity or not. Where they do, assessment continues to be a key factor in determining the most fruitful paths to take. Where they do not, assessment becomes increasingly salient anyway, as a vital and unavoidable building block for establishing and operating alternative modes of instructional delivery.

Meanwhile, assessment practice continues to evolve toward greater authenticity, further erasing remaining boundaries between outcomes data and other forms of academic management information. At the same time, assessment techniques themselves increasingly reflect the impact of new technologies. Computer-based and computer-adaptive testing approaches that allow both shortened testing time and dispersed, time-independent assessment administration eliminate many of the drawbacks associated with large-scale summative examinations. More importantly, new instructional media increasingly allow designed assessments to be engineered directly into instructional material that can provide both individual feedback and group-level results. And as these trends continue, distinctions between assessment and grading continue to erode.

For academic administrators, these developments promise both better information about effectiveness and increased demands to manage complexity. Thankfully, if past trends continue, these two will occur in equal measure.

Further Reading

Readers interested in obtaining a more in-depth treatment of assessment policy and the continuing development of performance indicators at the state level are referred especially to Ruppert (1994), Ewell and Jones (1993, 1994), Ewell (1993a), and Gaither (1995). Comprehensive discussions of the use of performance indicators at the institutional and state levels are in Gaither, Nedwick, and Neal (1995) and Ewell and Jones (1996). For an excellent example of the development and impact of assessment programs on a wide variety of college campuses, see Banta and Associates (1993), as well as Banta, Lund, Black, and Oblander (1996). After almost five years, the most comprehensive current reviews of assessment practice at the collegiate level remain Erwin (1991) and Ewell (1991b). Finally, a good ongoing source of information is the bimonthly newsletter *Assessment Update*, published by Jossey-Bass.

References

Ackoff, R. L. (with Gupta, S. K., and Minas, J. S.). *Scientific Method: Optimizing Applied Research Decisions.* New York: Wiley, 1962.

Angelo, T. A., and Cross, K. P. *Classroom Assessment Techniques: A Handbook for College Teachers.* San Francisco: Jossey-Bass, 1993.

Association of American Colleges. *Integrity in the College Curriculum: A Report to the Academic Community.* Washington, D.C.: Association of American Colleges, 1985.

Astin, A. W. *Assessment for Excellence: The Philosophy and Practice of Assessment and Evaluation in Higher Education.* New York: ACE/Macmillan, 1991.

Astin, A. W. *What Matters in College?: Four Critical Years Revisited.* San Francisco: Jossey-Bass, 1992.

Banta, T. W. (ed.). *Implementing Outcomes Assessment: Promise and Perils.* New Directions for Institutional Research, no. 59. San Francisco: Jossey-Bass, 1988.

Banta, T. W., Lund, J. P., Black, K. E., and Oblander, F. W. *Assessment in Practice: Putting Principles to Work on College Campuses.* San Francisco: Jossey-Bass, 1996.

Banta, T. W., and Associates. *Making a Difference: Outcomes of a Decade of Assessment in Higher Education.* San Francisco: Jossey-Bass, 1993.

Barak, R. J. "Assessment: A Train on Its Own Track or a Major Element of a Supertrain?" In *Assessment Update*, 1991, *3*(4), 7–8.

Baugher, K. *Learn: Student Quality Team Manual.* Birmingham, Ala.: Samford University, 1992.

Black, L. C. "Portfolio Assessment." In T. W. Banta (ed.), *Making a Difference: Outcomes of a Decade of Assessment in Higher Education.* San Francisco: Jossey-Bass, 1993.

Education Commission of the States. *Making Quality Count in Undergraduate Education.* Denver: Education Commission of the States, 1995.

El-Khawas, E. *Campus Trends 1995.* Washington, D.C.: American Council on Education, 1995.

Erwin, T. D. *Assessing Student Learning and Development.* San Francisco: Jossey-Bass, 1991.

Ewell, P. T. "Hearts and Minds: Some Reflections on the Ideologies of Assessment." In *Three Presentations from the Fourth National Conference on Assessment in Higher Education.* Washington, D.C.: American Association of Higher Education, 1989.

Ewell, P. T. "Assessment and Public Accountability: Back to the Future." *Change*, 1991a, *23*(6), 12–17.

Ewell, P. T. "To Capture the Ineffable: New Forms of Assessment in Higher Education." In G. Grant (ed.), *Review of Research in Education*, 17. Washington, D.C.: American Educational Research Association, 1991b.

Ewell, P. T. "The Role of States and Accreditors in Shaping Assessment Practice." In T. W. Banta and Associates, *Making A Difference: Outcomes of a Decade of Assessment in Higher Education*. San Francisco: Jossey-Bass, 1993a.

Ewell, P. T. "Total Quality and Academic Practice: The Idea We've Been Waiting for?" *Change*, 1993b, *25*(3), 49–55.

Ewell, P. T. "Developing Statewide Performance Indicators for Higher Education: Policy Themes and Variations." In S. Ruppert (ed.), *Charting Higher Education Accountability: A Sourcebook on State-Level Performance Indicators*. Denver: Education Commission of the States, 1994.

Ewell, P. T. "Indicators of Curricular Quality Within and Across Institutions." In J. W. Gaff and J. L. Ratcliff (eds.), *Handbook of the Undergraduate Curriculum*. San Francisco: Jossey-Bass, 1996.

Ewell, P. T., Finney, J. T., and Lenth, C. "Filling in the Mosaic: The Emerging Pattern of State-Based Assessment." *AAHE Bulletin*, 1990, *1*, 3–5.

Ewell, P. T., and Jones, D. P. *The Effect of State Policy on Undergraduate Education*. Denver: Education Commission of the States, 1993.

Ewell, P. T., and Jones, D. P. "Pointing the Way: Indicators as Policy Tools in Higher Education." In S. Ruppert (ed.), *Charting Higher Education Accountability: A Sourcebook on State-Level Performance Indicators*. Denver: Education Commission of the States, 1994.

Ewell, P. T., and Jones, D. P. *Indicators of "Good Practice" in Undergraduate Education: A Handbook for Development and Implementation*. Boulder, Colo.: National Center for Higher Education Management Systems (NCHEMS), 1996.

Ewell, P. T., and Lisensky, R. P. *Assessing Institutional Effectiveness: Redirecting the Self-Study Process*. Washington, D.C.: Consortium for the Advancement of Private Higher Education, 1988.

Farmer, D. W. *Enhancing Student Learning: Emphasizing Essential Competencies in Academic Programs*. Wilkes-Barre, Pa.: Kings College, 1988.

Gaff, J. *General Education Today: A Critical Analysis of Controversies, Practices, and Reforms*. San Francisco: Jossey-Bass, 1983.

Gaither, G. H. (ed.). *Assessing Performance in an Age of Accountability: Case Studies*. New Directions for Higher Education, no. 91. San Francisco: Jossey-Bass, 1995.

Gaither, G. H., Nedwick, B., and Neal, J. *Measuring Up: The Promises and Pitfalls of Performance Indicators in Higher Education*. ASHE-ERIC Higher Education Reports. Washington, D.C.: ASHE-ERIC Clearinghouse/the George Washington University, 1995.

Harris, J. W., and Baggett, J. M. (eds.). *Quality Quest in the Academic Process*. Birmingham, Ala.: Samford University, 1992.

Hines, E. R. *State Higher Education Appropriations 1993–94*. Denver: State Higher Education Executive Officers (SHEEO), 1994.

Katchadourian, H. A., and Boli, J. *Careerism and Intellectualism Among College Students*. San Francisco: Jossey-Bass, 1985.

Kellams, S. A. *University of Virginia Longitudinal Study of Undergraduate Education*. Charlottesville, Va.: Office of the Provost, University of Virginia, 1989.

Keller, G. *Academic Strategy: The Management Revolution in American Higher Education*. Baltimore, Md.: Johns Hopkins University Press, 1983.

McGuinness, A. C., Jr. *A Framework for Evaluating State Policy Roles in Improving Undergraduate Education.* Denver: Education Commission of the States, 1994.

McGuinness, A. C., Jr., and Ewell, P. T. "Improving Productivity and Quality in Higher Education." *AGB Priorities*, 1994, *2*.

Miller, M. A. (ed.). *Restructuring Higher Education: Lessons from a State.* New York: ACE Macmillan, forthcoming.

National Governors' Association. *Time for Results: The Governors' 1991 Report on Education.* Washington, D.C.: National Governors' Association, 1986.

National Institute of Education. *Involvement in Learning: Realizing the Potential of American Higher Education.* Report of the Study Group on the Conditions of Excellence in American Higher Education. Washington, D.C.: GPO, 1984.

Pace, C. R. *Measuring the Quality of Student Experiences: An Account of the Development and Use of the College Student Experiences Questionnaire.* Los Angeles: Higher Education Research Institute, University of California, Los Angeles, 1984.

Ratcliff, J. L. *The Effect of Differential Coursework Patterns on General Learned Abilities of College Students: Application of the Model to an Historical Database of Student Transcripts. (Task 3 Report).* U.S. Department of Education, Office of Institutional Research and Improvement, Contract No. OERI-R-86-0016. Ames: Iowa State University, College of Education, 1987.

Resmer, M., Mingle, J. R., and Oblinger, D. G. *Computers for All Students: A Strategy for Universal Access to Informational Resources.* Denver: State Higher Education Executive Officers (SHEEO), 1995.

Rodriguez, E. M. *College Admission Requirements: A New Role for States.* Denver: State Higher Education Executive Officers (SHEEO), 1995.

Ruppert, S. S. *Charting Higher Education Accountability: A Sourcebook on State-Level Performance Indicators.* Denver: Education Commission of the States, 1994.

Seymour, D. T. *On Q: Causing Quality in Higher Education.* New York: ACE/Macmillan, 1991.

Sherr, L. A., and Teeter, D. J. (eds.). *Total Quality Management in Higher Education.* New Directions for Institutional Research, no. 71. San Francisco: Jossey-Bass, 1991.

Stanford Forum on Higher Education Futures. *Leveraged Learning: Technology's Role in Restructuring Higher Education.* Proceedings of the Technology and Restructuring Roundtable. Stanford, Calif.: Stanford Forum on Higher Education Futures, 1995.

Twigg, C. A. *The Need for a National Learning Infrastructure.* Boulder, Colo.: EDUCOM, 1995.

Walvoord, B. E., Anderson, V. J., Breihan, J. R., McCarthy, L. P., Robison, S. M., and Sherman, A. K. "Making Graded Tests and Assignments Serve Contemporary Needs for Assessment." In T. W. Banta, J. P. Lund, K. E. Black, and F. W. Oberlander (eds.), *Assessment in Practice.* San Francisco: Jossey-Bass, 1995.

Warren, J. "Cognitive Measures in Assessing Learning." In T. W. Banta (ed.), *Implementing Outcomes Assessment: Promise and Perils.* New Directions for Institutional Research, no. 59. San Francisco: Jossey-Bass, 1988.

Zemsky, R., Massy, W. F., and Oedel, P. "On Reversing the Ratchet." *Change*, 1993, *25*(3), 56–62.

CHAPTER TWENTY

USING POLICY ANALYSIS
FOR STRATEGIC CHOICES

Frans van Vught

The policy sciences are approaching middle age. Since its birth after World War II, the policy approach in the social sciences has created its own history, with claims concerning solutions for problems and doubts regarding the effectiveness of these solutions (Merton and Lerner, 1951). During the more than four decades of the history of the policy sciences, the term *policy analysis* has become the general indication of a relatively new perspective in the social sciences for combining scientific rigor with practical problem solving.

In this chapter, I use this term to discuss professional decision-support activities for higher education institutions. *Policy analysis* refers to the various activities that can be undertaken by higher education institutions to understand, influence, evaluate, and design their policies.

In the following sections, first the concept is explored. Both the scientific base of policy analysis and its professional character are characterized. Next, two crucial functions of policy analysis for higher education institutions are distinguished. Finally, four broad categories of policy analysis activities for higher education institutions are presented.

The general orientation of this chapter is strategic. Policy analysis is understood as a set of professional support activities to help top administrators of higher education institutions find and formulate strategic choices.

What Is Policy Analysis?

According to one of the earliest programmatic formulations of this perspective, Lerner and Lasswell's classic *The Policy Sciences* (1951), policy analysis is a science both *of* and *for* policy making. Policy analysis should describe and explain the processes and outcomes of policies, but it should also prescribe and recommend the contents of effective policies and the instruments to be used to solve practical problems. Policy analysis is analysis both *of* and *for* policy (Ham and Hill, 1984).

This point of view appears to have become dominant in the policy sciences. Many authors argue that the professional character of policy analysis is found in the combination of scientific rigor and practical advice, more specifically in use of the results of scientific analysis for practical problem solving. Williams (1971) points out that policy analysis is a means to synthesize information (including research) to produce a format for policy decisions. Quade (1976) argues that policy analysis seeks to help a decision maker make a better choice than would otherwise be made. According to Dunn (1981), policy analysis uses multiple methods of inquiry and argument to produce and transform policy-relevant information that may be utilized in solving problems.

On the one hand, policy analysis apparently is assumed to be rooted in scientific analysis. Policies by definition are based on knowledge, especially on one or more causal hypotheses about how means have an impact on ends. Policy analysis should be organized so that this knowledge can be produced, even though it is heavily heterogeneous and spread over several social science disciplines (Lane, 1993). In this sense, the main methods of policy analysis are indeed "no different from those associated with social science and the scientific method in general" (Nagel and Neef, 1979, p. 221).

On the other hand, policy analysis intends to combine its scientific orientation with practical advice for effective manipulation of the real world, however modest and cautious such advice may be. Policy analysis, from this point of view, is a craft, "an activity creating problems that can be solved. Every policy is fashioned of tension between resources and objectives, planning and politics, skepticism and dogma. Solving problems involves temporarily resolving these tensions" (Wildavsky, 1979, p. 17). The wish to offer practical advice implies an orientation toward defining a problem that is worth solving from a social perspective and capable of being solved with the resources at hand. Policy analysis, in this sense, is "the art of the possible" (Weimer and Vining, 1992, p. 215).

However, the combination of scientific analysis and the wish to offer practical advice makes policy analysis vulnerable. Emphasis on scientific analysis draws policy analysis into the realm of the basic research methods of the social sciences, leaving little room for practical problem solving. Alternatively, because of the wish to help decision makers, the practical orientation tends to downplay the objectives of the pursuit for truth and the need to understand social reality. The two dimensions appear to be at odds with one another.

But professional policy analysis cannot escape the task of finding a way to resolve the tension between scientific rigor and practical problem solving. To some authors, this implies a demarcation between scientific research and policy analysis. Quade, for instance, sees the tasks of scientific research in explanation and prediction, while policy analysis should be concerned with the manipulation of reality even if this may have to be accomplished without a full understanding of the underlying phenomena (Quade, 1976). Others underline the importance of understanding the causes and consequences of policy and define policy analysis first and foremost as a "happy marriage between basic and applied research" (Hoffenbert, 1990, p. 142).

I take the latter position. If policy analysis wants to have a place in academe, its recommendations have to be based on theoretical foundations and empirical tests. The conditions of limited resources and the circumstances of a specific policy problem may be highly relevant when formulating practical advice. But what matters even more are the hypotheses about the relationships between ends and means, and the scientific solidity of these hypotheses (Lane, 1993). Without a base in scientific research, policy analysis cannot be more than guesswork.

The Scientific Base of Policy Analysis

Policy analysis needs to have a base in scientific research. What does this base look like?

It is my opinion that effective policy analysis should be grounded in the empirical-analytical approach to social science research. To be able to characterize the scientific base of policy analysis, I now briefly sketch this approach.

Let me first emphasize that the empirical-analytical approach to social science research should not be confused with an uncritical imitation by social scientists of what sometimes are supposed to be the distinctive characteristics of the natural sciences. Such an imitation would, as Medawar rightly points out, lead to an "unnatural" scientific attitude characterized by wrongful belief "that measurement and numeration are intrinsically praiseworthy activities"; by equally wrongful belief that "facts are prior to ideas and that a sufficiently voluminous compilation of facts can be processed by a calculus of discovery in such a way as to yield general principles"; and by uncritical "faith in the efficiency of statistical formulae . . . the use of which is in itself interpreted as a mark of scientific manhood" (Medawar, 1984, p. 167).

The empirical-analytical approach to social science research has little to do with such an "unnatural" scientific attitude, although the critics of this approach sometimes seem to think so. These critics incorrectly claim that the empirical-analytical approach is "positivistic" and "reductionistic," implicitly assuming that this approach indeed is a simple imitation of some of the methods of the natural sciences. Moreover, they show little understanding of the philosophical and epistemological underpinnings of the natural sciences. As I indicate below, this critique misjudges the leading principles of the empirical-analytical approach to social science research.

What, then, are these leading principles? The first principle concerns the obligation to design theories properly. Theories are the vehicles by which we try to grasp the complexity of the world around us. When designing theories, we reduce the complexity of reality. We assume certain regularities and we omit what we judge to be irrelevant; this allows us to formulate our assumptions. As Popper has stated, in this sense designing theories can be characterized as "the art of systematic over-simplification, the art of discerning what we may with advantage omit" (Popper, 1982, p. 44).

A crucial quality of the theories we use to try to understand reality is that these theories should be falsifiable. A theory that is not falsifiable does not provide information simply because, although it may always be in accordance with the facts, it does not indicate when it may be supposed to hold and when not. The statement "It will rain or not rain here tomorrow" may be correct, but it cannot be refuted and it does not give us information. Theoretical statements that cannot be incorrect when confronted with reality do not help us to understand reality.

Another quality of our theories concerns their internal consistency. Theories should be so designed that one cannot deduce from them both a statement about reality *and* the negation of that statement. To refer again to Popper: "A consistent system . . . divides the set of all possible statements into two: those which it contradicts and those with which it is compatible. (Among the latter are the conclusions which can be derived from it.) This is why consistency is the most general requirement for a system, whether empirical or nonempirical, if it is to be of any use at all" (Popper, 1974, p. 92).

The requirement to design theories that are internally consistent holds for all theoretical systems, whether they are normative, mathematical, or empirical. For empirical theories, moreover, another requirement is of extreme importance: the requirement to design theories that also are externally consistent. This requirement implies that statements about observable phenomena that can be deduced from theories should not contradict the observation. When such contradictions are found (and cannot be removed), the theoretical system from which the statements are deduced is refuted and must be replaced by another, better theory.

These considerations indicate the second principle of the empirical-analytical approach to social science research. This principle includes acceptance of a falsificationist attitude to the study of social phenomena: when a theory is found to be externally inconsistent, it is judged to be falsified, and we should try to replace it with another theory.

The first two principles allow us to formulate two further principles on how to proceed when doing social science research. As was indicated before, a theory that accords with the facts but does not specify when it is and is not supposed to hold is not informative. Such a theory is said to have an empirical content of "zero": it is not possible to deduce from it one single statement that could be confronted with statements about observed phenomena. Along the same lines, it should be self-evident that the more a theory excludes (that is, the more statements about observed phenomena that are not "allowed" by the theory), the better the theory is (that is, the more the theory says about the world around us). Such a theory is said to have a larger empirical content.

The third principle is that social science researchers should try to design internally and externally consistent theoretical systems that have as large an empirical content as possible. Social science researchers should strive to formulate theories of which the class of possible falsifiers is as large as possible.

The fourth principle can be directly related to the third. In their striving to formulate theories with a large empirical content, social scientists should try to deduce from these theories strictly universal hypotheses that can be confronted with reality. These universal hypotheses should be derived from a consistent theory that should also specify under what conditions the hypotheses are supposed to hold. Universal hypotheses are far more interesting than singular or "particular" hypotheses, exactly because the class of possible falsifiers is much larger when universal statements are used.

Together the four principles of the empirical-analytical approach to social science research indicate that empirical theories are the best mechanisms we have to try to understand reality. Because empirical theories are formulated as internally and externally consistent systems of universal statements, and because they are designed in such a way that their empirical content is as large as possible, we may expect that these empirical theories offer us the best possible intellectual grasp of the world around us. Thus, if we want to try to solve problems in our environment, we should try to make use of these theories.

The Professional Character of Policy Analysis

Most authors in the field of policy sciences claim that policy analysis is a professional activity. For instance, in their well-known textbook Weimer and Vining emphasize that the product of policy analysis is advice and that as a professional activity policy analysis is client-oriented (Meltsner, 1990; Weimer and Vining, 1992).

The wish to offer client-oriented advice implies that policy analysis should be able to translate scientific knowledge into professional expertise. Professional policy analysis in this sense is application of knowledge under specific policy conditions.

According to Schein (1973), professional expertise has three components: first, an underlying discipline or basic science component upon which practical advice rests or from which it is developed; second, an applied science or engineering component from which many of the day-to-day diagnostic procedures and problem solutions are derived; and third, a skills and attitudinal component that concerns the actual performance of the client, using the underlying basic and applied knowledge (Schein, 1973). The knowledge base of a profession is to be found in basic science, or at least in a scientific body of knowledge about the field with which the profession is concerned. Without such a scientific base, professions cannot claim to be more than arbitrary approaches to specific aspects of reality. Without a scientific base, professions lack the legitimacy to impose their solutions upon the practical problems they want to address.

As mentioned previously, scientific knowledge has to be understood as the collection of empirical theories that are formulated as internally and externally consistent systems of universal statements with as large an empirical content as possible. A profession based on such a collection of theories has at its disposal a general body of knowledge, which is formulated in universal terms. Professionals can apply this *general* knowledge to *specific* and concrete circumstances. Professionals apply general principles (standardized knowledge) to concrete problems (Moore, 1970).

This interpretation of professional expertise seems to worry policy analysts. Social science appears to be unable to offer a definite base for the professional expertise of policy analysts. It has been pointed out by several authors that the social sciences have little more to offer than an "enlightenment function" (Weiss, 1977) and that the likelihood of success for policy analysis cannot be found in the social sciences knowledge base (Lindblom and Cohen, 1979).

This argument actually has an important and fundamental epistemological base. Even if in the social sciences we had a large number of relevant empirical theories at our disposal, these theories could not offer us a *final* argument on how to act in a specific practical context. Empirical theories provide us with mechanisms to understand reality. However, such an understanding is reached by assuming certain regularities about reality and leaving out many other aspects. Designing theories is indeed the art of "systematic over-simplification." As Popper has said, we could never predict the creation of a work such as Mozart's G-minor Symphony, however well we study Mozart's brain, paper, pen, and environment. Our theories are simplifications of an endless complex reality, and they can only be mutually compared. Moreover, they are attempts to try to find the truth by testing what is not true. But truth remains an ideal. Even if we could reach it, we would not know it (Popper, 1982).

Consequently, policy analysts have to look for other ways to ground their professional expertise. And they have done so. Several authors have suggested that values should play an important role in policy analysis (Fischer, 1985) and that the various stakeholders should be incorporated in policy processes (DeLeon, 1988).

Presently, the more or less generally accepted position regarding the professional base of policy analysis seems to be that, given the social sciences cannot offer a definite foundation for professional expertise, analysts have to accept the values and objectives of their clients as a major point of reference, while at the same time acknowledging that this client-orientedness should not restrain them from incorporating the interests of other actors in the analysis. "By looking at consequences of policies beyond those that affect the client, the analyst is implicitly placing a value on the welfare of others. Good policy analysis takes a comprehensive view of consequences and social values" (Weimer and Vining, 1992, p. 2). The professional character of policy analysis thus is a combination of two general principles. There is the need to look for as good a knowledge base as possible by applying the principles of the empirical-analytical approach to social science research. Without a base in scientific research, policy analysis runs the risk of slipping into guesswork. On the other hand, there is acceptance of the importance of exploring and evaluating the values of the various actors involved. As Wildavsky has put it, policy analysis is the art and craft of balancing social interaction against intellectual cogitation. "Policy analysis is about calculation and culture: What combination of social interaction and intellectual cogitation . . . leads us to figure out what we should want to do and how to do it? . . . Analysis teaches us not only to get what we want, because that may be unobtainable or undesirable, but what we ought to want compared to what others are to give us in return for what we are prepared to give them" (Wildavsky, 1993, p. 18).

Policy Analysis in Higher Education

In higher education, the influence and application of policy analysis so far appear to be rather limited. Based on his overview of the relevant literature in this field, Fincher calls the state of policy analysis in higher education "promising but not highly sophisticated" (Fincher, 1987, p. 285). Gill and Saunders indicate that although policy analysis has been taught for many years in graduate schools of business administration, public affairs, and management, its place in the higher education curriculum is rather recent (Gill and Saunders, 1992).

Higher education administrators (at the levels both of higher education systems and of universities and colleges) apparently are unaware (or perhaps not convinced) of the potential benefits of policy analysis. Fincher suggests that in higher education, public policies are often perceived as "something that happens to an institution," while the policies of the institutions themselves are regarded as "an unquestioned necessity or the lesser of several evils" (Fincher, 1987, p. 285).

Nevertheless, policy analysis can be highly relevant in the context of higher education. It can help higher education administrators and planners not only get a better understanding of the characteristics and consequences of the policies in their field but also find out which decisions and actions might be considered to influence these policies according to their own objectives and criteria.

Many authors have discussed and analyzed decision-making processes in higher education institutions, and various "models" have been suggested (Baldridge, Curtis, Ecker, and Riley, 1978; Chaffee, 1983; Hardy, Langley, Mintzberg, and Rose, 1983; Bess, 1988; Birnbaum, 1988). For our purposes it is important to underline the so-called "political model of decision-making" (Baldridge, 1971). This model assumes that organizations are pluralistic and divided into various interests, subunits, and subcultures. Each unit makes efforts to influence overall organizational decisions, trying to maximize its own interests. In the political model of decision making, organizational decisions are the result of negotiations and bargaining among administrators and groups with different interests and perspectives. The differences between the various groups and units give rise to political processes of coalition building and exertion of pressure on decision makers. Individuals and groups come together and interact by forming coalitions, bargaining, compromising, and reaching agreements they believe are to their advantage. They articulate their interests in many different ways, bringing pressure on the organizational decision-making processes from any number of angles and using their power whenever it is available (Baldridge, Curtis, Ecker, and Riley, 1978).

But these "political arenas" are not found only *within* higher education institutions. Colleges and universities also operate in various political arenas in their environment. They deal with various actors beyond their immediate boundaries. Potential students, alumni, research contractors, local communities, state systems, governing bodies, legislators, and donors are all related to higher education institutions. The institutions try to influence the decisions to be reached with all these external actors in ways that are believed to be most advantageous for them. Also in their environment, higher education institutions are confronted with various networks of actors having different interests and perspectives. Institutions must position themselves in these networks; they have to find ways to reach outcomes and decisions that are acceptable to them; and they have to form coalitions and exert pressure, just as various subunits do within the institution.

If we accept these conditions within higher education institutions and in their environment, then what could be the function of policy analysis for higher education institutions? It is twofold. Policy analysis can provide a better understanding of the environment of a higher education institution, especially of the policies to be found in that environment. It can also offer a vehicle or medium for conscious design and adoption of the institution's own policies. I call these two functions respectively the *external* and *internal* dimensions of policy analysis in higher education. The following sections address these two dimensions separately.

The External Dimension. The external dimension of policy analysis in higher education refers to understanding and (if judged to be worthwhile) influencing the *policy networks* of which a specific university or college is part. The external dimension requires an understanding of the institution's relevant policy environment and its position in that environment. It especially requires an analysis of the various actors (including the institution itself), their objectives, and their interrelationships in the networks in which policies are formed and implemented.

During the past two decades, policy networks have attracted growing attention in the policy sciences. Generally speaking, policy networks can be defined as social systems in which actors develop patterns of interaction and communication that show some permanence and that are directed at policy problems and policy programs. Generally speaking, there are two important characteristics of policy networks: multiformity and interdependence. Multiformity refers to involvement of a relatively large number of different actors. The actors in a policy network may differ in type (individuals, organizations, collective bodies) and base of representation. Additionally, the actors in a policy network may show differences in terms of goals, resources, visions, and interests. Interdependence refers to the reasons why the various actors participate in a policy network. In principle, two such reasons can be distinguished. First, actors may possess or control resources relevant to the realization of goals by other actors in the field. Second, realization of specific goals by one actor may have positive or negative consequences for other actors, which implies that cooperation, conflict, or bargaining processes between actors may take place. Usually, policy networks show a mix of symbiotic and competitive interdependence.

Similar to many other policy fields, higher education policy networks are the arenas where actors meet and communicate in order to discuss issues, find solutions, reach decisions, and implement agreements. In my country, the Netherlands, the higher education policy network consists of various officials of the Ministry of Education, Science, and Culture; representatives of the universities and colleges (the Association of Cooperating Universities and the Council for Higher Vocational Education); and representatives of student organizations and employers' organizations. These actors regularly meet in both formal and informal settings, which allows them to discuss their various interests and explore fruitful compromises.

Higher education policy networks offer individual actors opportunities (as well as constraints) to influence the overall policies of a higher education system. These networks create the conditions for communication and negotiation regarding choices that are made. An understanding of these arenas and of the opportunities and constraints they offer may be highly valuable for an individual higher education institution.

The external dimension of policy analysis addresses exactly these arenas, as well as the opportunities and constraints they offer from the perspective of a specific university or college. The function of the external dimension of policy analysis is to analyze the relevant policy networks in which the institution participates and to suggest possible strategies to influence the outcomes of these networks.

The Internal Dimension. The internal dimension of policy analysis refers to the design and adoption of institutional policies. Similar to policies that are shaped in the (external) policy networks, institutional policies are the results of the processes of communication and interaction between various (internal) actors. As was noted earlier, within institutions a large number of relatively autonomous actors exist, all of whom may have different goals, resources, visions, and interests. Also within institutions, networks can be distinguished in which decisions are reached regarding institutional policies. It is in these (internal) policy networks that institutional policies are shaped. As in external policy networks, so also in internal networks: designing policies and getting them adopted is as much a process of communication and interaction as it is a process of intellectual cogitation.

The recent literature on policy design underscores this point of view. In this literature, policy design and policy adoption are conceptualized as both an intellectual and a social process. The so-called "decomposition approach" to design (Simon, 1969) is presently being combined with "discourse" and "negotiation" approaches (Schön, 1983; Bucciarelli, 1994; White, 1994). Designing policies is a matter of formulating objectives, analyzing constraints, and decomposing problems into solvable subproblems. But it also is a matter of negotiating different interests, of interactive reflection-in-action, and of reaching agreements. Designing policies is analysis *and* interaction, calculation *and* culture.

The internal dimension of policy analysis focuses on the process of policy design and policy adoption. It intends to clarify and stimulate this process by offering conceptualizations and instruments for design and adoption in internal networks. It suggests mechanisms for communication and interaction; it offers tools to come to conclusions; it provides techniques to perform specific studies.

The function of the internal dimension of policy analysis is to analyze the benefits and the costs of alternative strategic choices for the various actors within the
institution and to contribute to a process in which these strategic choices can eventually be made.

Conducting Policy Analysis for Higher Education Institutions

This section offers a brief sketch of some concepts and approaches that can be
used when performing policy analyses for higher education institutions. This sketch
is based on the point of view that policy analysis is client-driven (Weimer and Vining, 1992) and that the most important clients for higher education policy analysts
are the top administrators of higher education institutions. According to Kerr
(1982 p. 36), a university president is many things: "he is leader, educator, creator,
initiator, wielder of power, pump; he also is officeholder, caretaker, inheritor, con-
sensusseeker, persuader, bottle-neck. But he is mostly a mediator. The first task
of the mediator is peace . . . peace within the student body, the faculty, the trustees;
and peace between and among them." I would like to add to this list that the president also is the promotor of the university's interests in the outside world. In
this sense, he is an internal and an external mediator.

Policy analysts try to assist university presidents (and their administrative colleagues) by offering them advice on opportunities and threats, and by exploring
possible outcomes of alternative sets of decisions and actions. Policy analysts study
(internal and external) arenas, diagnose problems, design solutions, and assess ways
for implementing these solutions.

There is not a clear and dominant recipe for all these professional activities,
except for the general heuristics that policy analysts need to keep their client's
interests and position in mind, and that they will find it useful to gather and organize information throughout the various activities undertaken. There is no simple, linear procedure an analyst can follow. The semirationalistic procedure, in
which the solution follows the diagnosis and is followed by implementation, hardly
appears to be applicable in practice. Rather, policy analysis is an iterative process
in which each step forces reconsideration of the previous ones until decisions have
to be made.

In the remaining part of this section, four crucial elements of policy analysis are briefly discussed. This is not the place to present the relevant concepts, approaches, and techniques in full detail. References to the literature are provided
as opportunities for further study.

Exploring Policy Networks. In the preceding sections, it is argued that the external and the internal dimensions of policy analysis focus our attention on "multi-

actor perspectives." The external dimension is said to refer to analysis of the external policy arenas to which a higher education institution belongs. The internal dimension is assumed to relate to design and adoption of institutional policies in the context of communication and interaction between internal actors.

Policy analysis can be helpful in exploring both these external and internal policy networks. It can offer an understanding of the various actors as well as of their perspectives and interests; by doing so, it can provide insight into the options institutional leaders may have at their disposal to promote the institution's interests and reach favorable and legitimized decisions.

A fruitful foundation for analysis of both external and internal policy networks is found in some specific social science theories. Specifically, the *social exchange theory*, as developed by Emerson, and the *resource-dependence theory* of Pfeffer and Salancik provide policy analysts with potentially powerful explanations of the structures and dynamics of external and internal policy networks.

In social exchange theory, emphasis is on the concept of dependency. Actor A is dependent on actor B whenever he strives for goals whose achievement can be facilitated by B. According to Emerson (1962), social relations consist of mutual dependencies, which implies that actors A and B can, to a certain extent, influence or control the relationship. Social exchange theory suggests that two critical factors determine the dependency of one actor on the other: the importance of the resources and the availability of alternative resources. The importance of specific resources is related to the actor's motivations and objectives, which in turn depend upon the context in which the actor finds herself. A higher education institution confronted with decreasing enrollments looks differently at the option to have a new program authorized than does an institution that has too many applicants for the positions in its programs. The availability of alternative resources (including alternative suppliers of needed resources) allows an actor to be less dependent on the actor controlling (access to) a specific set of resources. If a university is able to bring in large sums of money by means of contract research, it is less interested in decreased enrollment numbers than when its financial status depends heavily on the number of students. Emerson suggests that actors can follow several strategies when confronted with dependencies. An actor can withdraw from a relationship, or try to establish relationships with one or more new actors (network extension), or form a coalition with other actors in order to try to decrease certain dependencies, or offer more of her own resources to the actor upon whom she is dependent (status giving) (Emerson, 1972a; Emerson, 1972b; Cook, Emerson, Gilmore, and Yamagishi, 1983). These strategies suggest that the actual behavior of actors depends on the characteristics of the specific situation. For our purposes, this implies that a thorough study of the various actors (and of their mutual dependencies) in an (external or internal) policy network is extremely important. Social exchange theory offers us a set of concepts to undertake such a study.

Resource dependence theory is related to social exchange theory and also offers an interesting and valuable conceptual framework. This theory suggests that any social actor needs to interact with other actors in his environment in order to reach his goals. By definition therefore, any actor becomes dependent on other actors; only through interaction with others can an actor achieve her objectives, however powerful she may be. Social interactions are crucial mechanisms for an actor when she wants to acquire the resources needed to reach her objectives (Pfeffer and Salancik, 1978). A higher education institution depends upon the financial resources from tuition fees and research contracts and therefore needs to interact with potential students and contractors.

The literature on resource dependency suggests several categories of relevant resources: money and authority (Benson, 1975); products and services, operating funds, personnel, and information (Aldrich, 1972); and human activity, power influence, reputation, knowledge, and money (Aldrich, 1979). All these resources may be of importance for an actor to reach his goals, and all these resources are potentially controllable by other actors. Like social exchange theory, resource dependence stresses the concept of mutual dependencies of actors in exchange relationships. And like social exchange theory, resource dependence theory points at the same two factors, importance of resources and availability of alternative resources. In addition, the resource dependence approach emphasizes the importance of the extent to which an actor has discretion over the allocation and use of resources. Pfeffer and Salancik mention several bases for control: resource possession, control over access to a resource, actual use of (and control over the use of) a resource, and the ability to regulate and enforce regulations regarding possession, allocation, and use of resources. They argue that given the differences in these bases for control (and accepting the idea of mutual dependencies), organizational actors can either adapt themselves by seeking alternative resources or diversification or else try to affect their dependence on other actors (Pfeffer and Salancik, 1978).

Social science theories such as resource dependency and social exchange are powerful conceptual frameworks for analyzing the external policy networks to which an institution belongs, as well as for studying the policy-making processes within an institution. These theories offer us possibilities to judge the positions of the various actors involved, as well as their mutual dependencies and strategic behavior. By doing so, they allow us to see opportunities and threats, find ways to influence agenda-setting processes, form effective coalitions (both internally and externally), and suggest potentially successful decision-making procedures for the adoption of policies.

Diagnosing Problems. Several authors argue that diagnosing the problem is the crucial step in any policy analysis (see, for instance, Gill and Saunders, 1992; and Weimer and Vining, 1992). *Diagnosing the problem* refers to the process in which a client's problem is specified. The two basic activities for analysis here are understanding the problem and choosing relevant goals and constraints.

Understanding the problem implies first of all listening to the client. Clients tend to describe problems in terms of undesirable conditions for one or more organizations or groups. A university president may, for instance, formulate a problem in terms of negative effects for students, or decreasing prestige of the institution as a whole. More often than not, these conditions are symptoms rather than underlying causes. It is the analyst's task to assess the symptoms and provide an explanation of how they arise (Weimer and Vining, 1992).

To do so, policy analysts need to locate empirical data to put the symptoms into perspective. The data should present an image of the urgency and magnitude of the problem, and they should allow for a description of the development over time.

The crucial step in understanding the problem is modeling it, that is, identifying and describing the potential causal relationships that might explain and specify the problem. Modeling the problem requires being explicit, preferably explaining it with a theory from the empirical-analytical approach to social science research. As was argued before, empirically tested theories are the best mechanisms we have to understand reality. They offer us internally and externally consistent explanations of parts of reality and hence provide us with powerful means to understand and specify problems.

Policy analysts in higher education have to keep in mind that internal and external contexts make their work different from the public policy contexts of federal, state, and local governments in which policy analysis is most often applied. The internal higher education context is dominated by "a culture that includes faculty governance, autonomy and academic freedom" (Gill and Saunders, 1992; see also Weick, 1976; and Clark 1983). The external context shows a large number of actors who all have potential impacts on an institution and to whom the institution needs to show its potential benefits as well as its accountability.

Many social science theories may be used to model a problem in higher education contexts. As a matter of fact, the professional expertise of a higher education policy analyst to a large extent is determined by her knowledge of the social science literature, especially of the empirically tested, causal theories in this literature. As an example, let me briefly point at the *innovation theories* that have been developed over several decades in the social sciences.

In order to explore the state of the art with respect to our understanding of the relationships between governmental policy models and innovation processes in higher education institutions, van Vught (1994) identified two broad categories of innovation studies. One category is formed by the organizational variables related to success of innovations, and the other by the characteristics of successful innovation processes. The first category includes the principal organizational variables that have appeared to influence the success or failure of innovation processes in organizations. In this category are such factors as the level of centralization in organizational decision making, the level of formalization (by means of rules and codifications), the level of stratification (between top and bottom ranks of the organization), and the level of complexity (in terms of specialization and professionalization). The second category refers to the characteristics of the innovations themselves that appear to determine their success or failure. This category includes factors such as the compatibility of a new idea (the degree to which the idea is perceived to be consistent with the existing values of the majority of the relevant actors) and the profitability of a new idea (the degree to which an innovation is perceived by a majority of actors as being better than the idea it supersedes). Both these categories of studies offer relevant theoretical insights into the innovative capacities of higher education institutions (van Vught, 1994). For policy analysts, they provide a number of potentially relevant causal models when a problem is located in the realm of institutional innovation processes. By assessing the applicability of these and similar theories, the analyst discerns which theoretical model allows specification of the initial problem statement.

A special element of this aspect of policy analysis is identifying the "policy variables," that is, the variables that can be manipulated by one or more actors involved in order to find solutions for the problem. Here the task of the analyst is to point out the factors on which the client should focus his attention. The manipulable variables should of course be included as relevant causal factors in the model. And there should be ample empirical evidence that their manipulation leads to observable changes in the dependent variables that specify the conditions of the problem.

The second basic activity related to diagnosing problems is choosing relevant goals and constraints. According to Weimer and Vining (1992), this is probably the most difficult step in any policy analysis. Choosing goals and constraints requires analysts to be normative and to decide and argue what should be wanted in order to solve the problem. It thus implies understanding of the relevant values related to the problem, not only the values of the client but also those of other stakeholders and constituencies. This is the step where the professional base of policy analysis should be reflected in a careful and comprehensive exploration and evaluation of the values of the various actors involved. Policy analysts should make an inventory of the values, however vague they may appear. They should also try to formulate the goals that can be deduced from the values and to specify the possible trade-offs between these goals. Specifying the constraints focuses attention on limitations that have to be accepted. In this sense, constraints are simply goals that must be satisfied, whether they are budgetary, legal, administrative, political, or a matter of social custom.

The activity of choosing goals and constraints may be assisted by specifying *indifference curves,* a technique that allows the analyst to illustrate a combination of preferences giving the same level of utility to a specific decision maker (Stokey and Zeckhauser, 1978; see Chapter Three of that work). However, we have to keep in mind that choosing goals and constraints is first and foremost a matter of daring to be overt and normative about values, and of dealing with multiplicities and conflicts among goals.

Finding Solutions. Finding solutions for specified problems is another broad category of activities in policy analysis. Here the crucial basic activities are crafting of policy alternatives and *ex ante* evaluation of their impacts.

Crafting policy alternatives refers to formulating consistent sets of decisions and actions to be used by the client in order to attack the problem. Weimer and Vining suggest that crafting policy alternatives is basically a creative process, "one area of policy analysis in which you should stretch your imagination. Much of the intellectual fun of policy analysis arises in trying to come up with creative alternatives. Be brave" (1992, p. 226).

However, it should also be kept in mind that crafting alternatives is a way of working with the theories that were used for modeling the problem. Policy alternatives can be regarded as alternative chains of hypotheses in which (causal) cause-effect relationships are reformulated as (teleological) means-ends relationships. In the process of crafting policy alternatives, emphasis is put on the manipulable variables that were identified as empirically relevant causes explaining (part of) the problem. These manipulable variables become potentially relevant means for reaching desirable goals. If several manipulable variables are identified, these can be organized into alternative sets of teleological relationships, leading to alternative policies.

As was mentioned before, the literature on policy design offers several general approaches that may be followed in crafting policy alternatives. The decomposition approach suggests that finding solutions is a matter of describing a problem in terms of smaller subproblems that can be addressed by the technique of *linear programming* (Wagner, 1975). Other approaches emphasize the importance of communication and negotiation in design processes.

Some specific techniques that may be applied for crafting policy alternatives are *analysis of interconnected decision areas* (AIDA) and *morphological analysis.* In AIDA, each relevant decision area is specified by formulating the alternative options for each decision. Next, the relationships between the various options are explored in a so-called "option graph" by indicating (with "option bars") the combinations of options that are judged to be unacceptable. Finally, "dominance analysis" eliminates the alternatives that offer no advantage over others (Roberts, 1974). Morphological analysis is a way to decompose a problem by formulating for each parameter (of which several should be distinguished) a number of variations that either can or cannot be combined into consistent sets (Wilson and Zwicky, 1967).

A special technique that has proven to be relevant in crafting policy alternatives is *backward mapping*. Backward mapping is a way to "think backwards," from policy implementation to policy design. It focuses our attention on the conditions that the policy would like to establish and asks which interventions could be effective in creating these conditions and which decisions, actions, and resources are needed to support these interventions (Elmore, 1980).

Ex ante evaluation of policy alternatives is probably the best-known element of policy analysis. This activity predicts and values the impacts of policy alternatives and compares them across specified criteria.

Predictions of the impacts for each policy alternative should be based on the theories applied when modeling the problem. The theories offer general hypotheses of causes and effects. The model used to diagnose the problem specifies the conditions judged to be relevant under the circumstances in which analysis is performed. Predictions are thus based both in general social science theories and in the practical conditions that are related to the specific policy problem.

A crucial aspect of *ex ante* evaluation is specifying the criteria to be used in evaluating the desirability of the policy alternatives. Criteria are operationalizations of either objectives or constraints; they should, of course, reflect the goals and constraints that were chosen during diagnosis of the problem. Examples of criteria in the context of higher education are quality of a program, cost per student, uniqueness of a program, and percentage of unemployment among a program's graduates. Criteria should provide a basis for measuring progress towards a goal or acceptance of a constraint. As operationalizations (either quantitative or qualitative), they have a considerable influence on the outcomes of the evaluation.

The actual evaluations are usually done by means of well-known *ex ante* evaluation techniques (benefit-cost analysis, cost-effectiveness analysis, and multicriteria techniques). In *benefit-cost analysis,* all the predicted impacts are reduced to a common, financial unit of impact, after which that alternative is chosen which generates the largest net benefit. In *cost-effectiveness analysis,* the objective is either to find the alternative that produces the desirable outcome at the lowest costs (cost minimization) or to find the alternative that, given a fixed level of costs, provides the most desirable outcome (effectiveness maximization). *Multicriteria techniques,* of which there are several variations, produce an overview of the impacts of all alternatives by standardizing and ranking the criteria (Stokey and Zeckhauser, 1978; Weimer and Vining, 1992).

The result of *ex ante* evaluation is comparison of the policy alternatives across the criteria. In a simple case, there is either one clearly dominant criterion or a policy alternative that clearly scores best on all criteria. In many cases, however, trade-offs among criteria have to be made explicit in order to allow the client to compare the relative priorities of the alternatives for each criterion.

Facilitating Implementation. Facilitating implementation is the art of thinking strategically about implementation of the preferred policy. In the policy sciences, a specialized literature has been developed in which implementation processes are the prime focus of attention (for an overview, see Calista, 1994). To policy analysts, this literature offers some suggestions to try to secure the success of policy implementation.

Following Bardach (1977), an implementation process can be seen as an assembly process in which all the efforts of the actors involved may have an impact on the actual outcomes of the implementation. Deciding on a policy certainly is not sufficient to guarantee the compliance of the actors who are involved in implementing it. If these actors view the policy as contrary to their interests, they may very well avoid full compliance "through tokenism, delay, or even blatant resistance" (Weimer and Vining, 1992, p. 329).

From the perspective of policy analysis, it is worthwhile to pay attention to potential implementation problems by analyzing the motivations and resources of the relevant implementors. Here, again, social exchange and resource dependence theories may be helpful in studying and predicting the behavior of social actors. Moreover, these theories may be helpful in writing *scenarios*, anticipating problems that might occur during implementation of the various policy alternatives. Writing implementation scenarios thus becomes a technique of *forward mapping* (as opposed to backward mapping). This technique may be helpful as a method of discovering potential implementation problems and evaluating policy alternatives in terms of their implementation aspects (Bardach, 1977).

Epilogue

The policies of a higher education institution are the prime reflections of the strategic choices the institution wants to make. The policies of an institution truly are the results of the often long and complicated processes of strategic decision making in which many institutions nowadays are involved. The policies of a higher education institution are intended to contribute to reaching the objectives the institution has set for itself and to realizing the conditions that the institution judges to be important.

Policy analysis intends to support the institution's activities regarding strategic decision making. By offering various conceptualizations, approaches, and techniques, policy analysis intends to clarify contexts and processes. Policy analysis contributes to exploration of both external and internal policy networks, provides a perspective on diagnosis of policy problems, helps to find and evaluate alternative solutions for these problems, and tries to facilitate implementation of the preferred policy alternative.

Policy analysis is client-oriented. In higher education institutions, the clients are primarily the "mediators, initiators and gladiators" (Kerr, 1982, pp. 37–41) who occupy positions of university presidency. According to Kerr (1994), the coming decades will bring both greater need for academic leadership and more difficult circumstances for realizing such leadership. Policy analysis will be there to support the future leaders of our higher education institutions.

Further Reading

Readers interested in policy analysis in general might want to examine Lane (1993), Weimer and Vining (1992), and Wildavsky (1993). Also useful are Dunn (1981), Ham and Hill (1984), Hoffenbert (1990), Nagel and Neef (1979), Quade (1976), and Stokey and Zeckhauser (1978). The fundamentals of the scientific base of policy analysis are found in Medawar (1984), Popper (1974), and Popper (1982). For the professional character of policy analysis, see DeLeon (1988), Fischer (1985), and Meltsner (1990). Use of policy analysis in higher education is discussed in Fincher (1987) and Gill and Saunders (1992).

For more specific reading, examine Emerson (1972a and 1972b) on social exchange theory; Aldrich (1979), Benson (1975), and Pfeffer and Salancik (1978) on resource dependence theory; Simon (1969), Schön (1983), Bucciarelli (1994), and White (1994) on policy design; Elmore (1980) on backward mapping; and Calista (1994) on policy implementation.

References

Aldrich, H. E. "An Organization-Environment Perspective on Cooperation and Conflict in Manpower Training Systems." In A. Negandhi (ed.), *Conflict and Power in Complex Organizations.* Kent, Ohio: Center for Business and Economics Research, 1972.

Aldrich, H. E. *Organizations and Environments.* Englewood Cliffs, N.J.: Prentice Hall, 1979.

Baldridge, J. V. *Power and Conflict in the University.* New York: Wiley, 1971.

Baldridge, J. V., Curtis, D. V., Ecker G. P., and Riley, G. L. *Policy Making and Effective Leadership.* San Francisco: Jossey-Bass, 1978.

Bardach, E. *The Implementation Game: What Happens after a Bill Becomes Law.* Cambridge, Mass.: MIT Press, 1977.

Benson, J. K. "The Interorganizational Network as a Political Economy." *Administrative Science Quarterly,* 1975, *20*(2), 229–249.

Bess, J. L. *Collegiality and Bureaucracy in the Modern University: the Influence of Information and Power on Decision Making Structures.* New York: Teachers College Press, 1988.

Birnbaum, R. *How Colleges Work: the Cybernetics of Academic Organization and Leadership.* San Francisco: Jossey-Bass, 1988.

Bucciarelli, L. J. *Designing Engineers.* Cambridge, Mass.: MIT Press, 1994.

Calista, D. J. "Policy Implementation." In S. S. Nagel (ed.), *Encyclopedia of Policy Studies.* (2nd ed.) New York: Dekker, 1994.

Chaffee, E. E. *Rational Decision Making in Higher Education.* Boulder, Colo.: National Center for Higher Education Management Systems, 1983.

Clark, B. R. *The Higher Education System.* Berkeley: University of California Press, 1983.

Cook, K. S., Emerson, R. M., Gilmore, M. R., and Yamagishi, T. "The Distribution of Power in Exchange Networks." *American Journal of Sociology,* 1983, *89*, 275–305.

DeLeon, P. *Advice and Consent: the Development of the Policy Sciences.* New York: Russell Sage Foundation, 1988.

Dunn, N. *Public Policy Analysis.* Englewood Cliffs, N.J.: Prentice Hall, 1981.

Elmore, R. "Backward Mapping: Implementation Research and Policy Decisions." *Political Science Quarterly,* 1980, *94*(4), 601–616.

Emerson, R. M. "Power-Dependence Relations." *American Sociological Review,* 1962, *27,* 31–41.

Emerson, R. M. "Exchange Theory, Part I: A Psychological Basis for Social Exchange." In J. Berger, M. Zelditch, and B. Anderson (eds.), *Sociological Theories in Progress.* Vol 2. Boston: Houghton-Mifflin, 1972a.

Emerson, R. M. "Exchange Theory, Part II: Exchange Relations and Networks." In J. Berger, M. Zelditch, and B. Anderson (eds.), *Sociological Theories in Progress.* Vol. 2. Boston: Houghton-Mifflin, 1972b.

Fincher, C. "Policy Analysis and Institutional Research." In M. W. Peterson and L. A. Mets (eds.), *Key Resources on Higher Education Governance, Management, and Leadership.* San Francisco: Jossey-Bass, 1987.

Fischer, F. "Critical Evaluation of Public Policy." In J. Forrester (ed.), *Critical Theory and Public Life.* Cambridge, Mass.: MIT Press, 1985.

Gill, J. I., and Saunders, L. (eds). *Developing Effective Policy Analysis in Higher Education.* San Francisco: Jossey-Bass, 1992.

Ham, C., and Hill, M. *The Policy Process in the Modern Capitalist State.* Brighton, England: Wheatsheaf, 1984.

Hardy, C., Langley, A., Mintzberg, H., and Rose, J. "Strategy Formation in the University Setting." *Review of Higher Education,* 1983, *6*(4), 407–433.

Hoffenbert, R. L. *The Reach and Grasp of Policy Analysis.* Tuscaloosa: University of Alabama Press, 1990.

Kerr, C. *The Uses of the University.* Cambridge, Mass.: Harvard University Press, 1982. (Originally published 1963)

Kerr, C. *Troubled Times for American Higher Education: The 1990s and Beyond.* Albany: State University of New York Press, 1994.

Lane, J. E. *The Public Sector: Concepts, Models, and Approaches.* London: Sage, 1993.

Lerner, D., and Lasswell, H. (eds.). *The Policy Sciences.* Stanford: Stanford University Press, 1951.

Lindblom, C. E., and Cohen, D. K. *Usable Knowledge.* New Haven: Yale University Press, 1979.

Medawar, P. *Pluto's Republic.* Oxford: Oxford University Press, 1984. (Originally published 1958)

Meltsner, A. J. *Rules for Rulers: the Politics of Advice.* Philadelphia: Temple University Press, 1990.

Merton, R. S., and Lerner, D. "Social Scientists and Research Policy." In D. Lerner and H. Lasswell (eds.), *The Policy Sciences.* Stanford: Stanford University Press, 1951.

Moore, W. *The Professions.* New York: Russell Sage Foundation, 1970.

Nagel, S. S., and Neef, M. *Policy Analysis in Social Science Research.* Thousand Oaks, Calif.: Sage, 1979.

Pfeffer, J., and Salancik, G. R. *The External Control of Organizations: A Resource Dependence Perspective.* New York: Harper & Row, 1978.

Popper, K. R. *The Logic of Scientific Discovery.* London: Hutchinson, 1974. (Originally published 1959)

Popper, K. R. *The Open Universe: An Argument for Indeterminism, from the Postscript to the Logic of Scientific Discovery.* (W. W. Bartley III, ed.) London: Hutchinson, 1982.

Quade, E. S. *Analysis for Public Decisions.* New York: Elsevier, 1976.

Roberts, M. *An Introduction to Town Planning Techniques.* London: Hutchinson, 1974.

Schein, E. H. *Professional Education.* New York: McGraw-Hill, 1973.

Schön, D. A. *The Reflective Practitioner: How Professionals Think in Action.* New York: Basic Books, 1983.

Simon, H. A. *The Sciences of the Artificial.* Cambridge, Mass.: MIT Press, 1969.

Stokey, E., and Zeckhauser, R. *A Primer for Policy Analysis.* New York: Norton, 1978.

van Vught, F. A. "Policy Models and Policy Instruments in Higher Education: The Effects of Governmental Policy Making on the Innovative Behavior of Higher Education Institutions." In J. C. Smart (ed.), *Higher Education: Handbook of Theory and Research.* Vol. 10. New York: Agathon Press, 1994.

Wagner, H. M. *Principles of Operations Research.* London: Prentice Hall, 1975.

Weick, K. E. "Educational Organizations as Loosely Coupled Systems." *Administrative Science Quarterly,* 1976, *21*(1), 1–19.

Weimer, D. L., and Vining, A. R. *Policy Analysis: Concepts and Practice.* (2nd ed.) Englewood Cliffs, N.J.: Prentice Hall, 1992.

Weiss, C. H. (ed.). *Using Social Research in Public Policy.* Lexington, Mass.: Heath, 1977.

White, L. G. "Policy Analysis as Discourse." *Journal of Policy Analysis and Management,* 1994, *13*(3), 506–526.

Wildavsky, A. A. *Speaking Truth to Power: The Art and Craft of Policy Analysis.* New Brunswick, N.J.: Transaction, 1993. (Originally published 1979)

Williams, W. *Social Policy Research and Analysis.* New York: Elsevier, 1971.

Wilson, A. G., and Zwicky, F. *Morphological Research.* New York: Springer, 1967.

PART FOUR

RENEWING INSTITUTIONS AND PLANNING FOR ACADEMIC CHALLENGES

Part One discussed the changing postsecondary environment—the changes in our state and federal agencies and intermediary organizations for postsecondary education—that requires redefining our perspective on our industry and on our approach to planning in the twenty-first century. Part Two examined how two approaches to planning, particular planning elements, and the relationship of the planning function to institutional leadership and culture need to be revised to help redirect our institutions as they face the twenty-first century. Part Three examined how a variety of management functions need to be reorganized to support planning for redirection of our institutions. However, institutional planning does not focus just on a generic environment, nor do institutions just revise their planning approach and reorganize their management processes to make planning more effective. More often, planning addresses how institutions can or should deal with the major academic challenges affecting them. Chapter One identified six major challenges that virtually all postsecondary institutions need to plan for as we approach the twenty-first century. These challenges and their implications for academic structure and faculty work life are the focus of Part Four.

In examining these challenges to postsecondary institutions, the chapters in Part Four attempt to more clearly understand the challenges and how institutions might plan to address them. Specifically, each chapter addresses these three questions: (1) what is the nature of this challenge and how does it impact the postsecondary institution? (2) what are different planning strategies and planned approaches for dealing with the challenge? (3) what are likely future developments in this area of which planners need to be aware?

Chapter Twenty-One examines how institutions can respond to the increased press for multiculturalism and new perspectives on diversity. Chapter Twenty-Two is concerned with how institutions systematically plan for the rapid changes in information technology that affect academic and administrative processes in our institutions. Chapter Twenty-Three addresses the complex issue of restructuring academic processes to respond to new clientele, educational needs, and delivery technologies. In Chapter Twenty-Four, the author examines the implications of the new environment for faculty roles and the nature of academic life and discuss strategies for recruiting and developing faculty and for recreating a new academic workplace culture. Chapter Twenty-Five explores how institutions can plan for the omnipresent concern for improving both academic and institutional quality in a time of constrained resources, increased competition, and change. Chapter Twenty-Six analyzes how institutions can respond to new roles and new external demands that contribute to our societal concern for enhanced economic development. Finally, Chapter Twenty-Seven reviews the expanding globalization of academic life and scholarly work and the need to plan for this challenge.

CHAPTER TWENTY-ONE

ACHIEVING THE GOALS OF MULTICULTURALISM AND DIVERSITY

Sylvia Hurtado and Eric L. Dey

Institutions committed to achieving the goals of multiculturalism and creating diverse work and educational environments have learned that the task is much more complex than was originally envisioned. Over the past three decades, institutional responses to major social movements and government policies to promote social equity in higher education have largely consisted of changes in institutional policies and addition of campus programs to accommodate diverse students and faculty. However, institutional responses have shown great variation in the extent to which new programs and diversity goals were central to the operation of the institution (Peterson and others, 1978). Many institutions seem to have favored those changes that would allow them to operate in the same manner without affecting the majority of campus priorities and academic programs.

The task is more complex now because institutions have discovered that fundamental changes are necessary in how they approach their goals for achieving diversity and multiculturalism. Some institutions that have not transformed themselves have found it difficult to attract diverse students and faculty, whereas those campuses that significantly increased the number of women and members of various racial/ethnic groups have found other kinds of transformations inevitable. Increased representation of traditionally underrepresented groups has ushered in new constituencies, and consequently many more changes than some campuses were perhaps prepared to undertake. Diversified student enrollments, for example, led to campus protests that resulted in the establishment of ethnic and women's studies, minority student organizations, specific academic and cultural support programs, and multicultural programming (Treviño, 1992; Muñoz, 1989; Peterson and others, 1978). These changes, in turn, required a diverse faculty and staff.

Without planning, many of these kinds of changes were initially brought about by the interplay between institutional resistance and campus activism. But programs born out of conflict become part of the regular budgeting, evaluation, and planning process in short order. Moreover, the legacy of campus resistance and conflict must also be taken into account in planning new approaches to creating a diverse, multicultural campus environment. Therefore, institutions have had to consider the political history of current initiatives in examining their current array of approaches towards meeting diversity goals; they have had to rethink resistance to change in planning new initiatives; and they have also had to reach out to new communities or sectors for assistance in planning for the future as a multicultural campus.

Another issue that makes the task of accomplishing goals for multiculturalism more complex rests primarily with how campuses have come to define diversity and multiculturalism in terms of policies that affect practice. Concerns regarding the inclusion of new groups often focused on dualistic notions of diversity. Issues were discussed and goals devised focusing on the inclusion of one group, African Americans or women for example, in contrast to the majority. However, the social movements and legislation of the 1960s and 1970s also highlighted the plight of American Indians, Asian Americans, and Latinos, groups that all came to be included among college goals for diversity. Other groups that have faced discrimination, such as gay/lesbian and disabled constituents, also seek and receive support as part of the campus's expanding definition of multiculturalism. This expanded definition is partly a result of the demographic, economic, legislative, and sociopolitical influences on various campus contexts. Not only are there more groups to consider, with their unique needs, but we must also understand the nature of external pressures that support their inclusion and consider the groups as part of the campus community when determining how to implement diversity goals. However, each campus must come to terms with its definition of a diverse or multicultural environment that is consistent with the institution's mission because it will affect program plans and campus goals. Moreover, there are many approaches to accomplishing goals that are consistent with a campus's definition of diversity.

In this chapter we address three forces that influence institutions in achieving the goals of multiculturalism and diversity. We address those challenges that institutions face that are due primarily to changes in the external environment or larger social context, challenges that exert pressures on institutions to clarify their goals for diversity. Next, we address different institutional strategies, recognizing competing goals and priorities, and approaches that institutions have used in meeting the challenge of diversifying a campus. Finally, we discuss some of the promising developments that present new opportunities for college and university planners in the area of creating diverse learning and work environments. We conclude with the notion that fundamental institutional change needs to occur if institutions are to achieve their goals of multiculturalism and diversity.

Contexts That Present New Challenges to Meeting Diversity Goals

Historically, pressures external to the institution have served as the impetus for the initial development of diversity goals. As we move into the next millennium, aspects of the current context continue to present pressure for progress as well as introduce new challenges in meeting diversity goals. Demographic and economic imperatives, various legal initiatives designed to remedy or challenge discrimination, and the political context for planning development are all aspects of an institution's external environment that require clarification of goals for diversity. Although for different reasons, each of these contexts may exert pressures on the institution to consider how diversity goals are central to the educational mission of the institution.

Demographic and Economic Imperatives

By the year 2000, most new jobs in the economy will require a postsecondary education, and women and racial/ethnic minorities will compose a majority of the workforce (Justiz, 1994). It is projected that by 2010 one out of every three Americans will be Latino, African American, Asian American, or American Indian. This projection, however, does not reflect the rapid growth of racial/ethnic populations, which are fast becoming the majority in various states. Because the demographic and economic imperative is consistent with higher education's central mission to replenish the workforce, institutions may plan to educate a diverse student body in order to ensure that more college graduates have the appropriate technical and human relations skills that are sure to be useful in the future. We face a society that will consist of diverse work and educational environments, making it ever more important to provide all students with the skills necessary for success in an increasingly diverse world. In short, this diversity needs to be reflected in the student body, faculty and staff, approaches to teaching, and research in higher education.

At the same time that the numbers of diverse students have increased in higher education, however, there are widening attainment gaps among various racial/ethnic groups. For example, the gap in the college participation rate between white and African American high school graduates has doubled since the 1970s (Carter and Wilson, 1993). These disparities in higher education are almost certain to result in the perpetuation of different economic futures for these groups, which in turn will have a direct impact on state economies where the disparities among groups are the greatest. This creates pressure for institutions of higher education to take proactive steps in establishing diversity goals that build teacher training and assist in the development of urban schools, develop comprehensive outreach programs, and create new strategies to increase college access opportunities and student retention through the educational pipeline.

Many institutions have devised specific programs and services to address these issues (Mintz, 1993), but the demographic and economic pressures for tangible institutional progress are even greater. Some institutions of higher education directly benefit by effectively recruiting in diverse student markets, and many have already successfully offset declines in the enrollment of their traditional students. Perhaps more importantly, public and private businesses largely depend on higher education institutions to produce a diverse, college-educated workforce that can respond to an expanding and diverse clientele. Thus, the achievement of diversity goals becomes economically important to both the institution and the communities it seeks to serve.

Furthermore, a growing body of scholarship reveals that diverse work environments can be more organizationally effective and result in economic advantage. For example, research literature on organizations suggests that heterogeneous work teams promote creativity and innovation, improved problem solving and decision making, organizational flexibility, and tolerance for ambiguity (Cox, 1993). To avoid potential misunderstandings, conflict, and excessive time consumed with decision making, work groups must be managed so as to "maximize the potential benefits of diversity" (p. 39). In the business literature, the goal of managing diversity is to maximize "the ability of all employees to contribute to organizational goals and to achieve their full potential unhindered by group identity" such as race/ethnicity, sex, or age (p. 11). These findings suggest that organizational effectiveness can be enhanced by higher education leaders who understand and know how to maximize the benefits of a diverse student, faculty, and staff for the institution. For example, diverse planning committees are essential to resolve problems that hinder progress toward diversity goals as well as other key institutional goals that require joint problem solving and decision making. This may be particularly important when institutional goals require clarification in preparation and planning for anticipated budget constraints. In sum, demographic and economic imperatives provide pressures and, depending on institutional responses, new opportunities for institutions to achieve diversity goals.

Legal Initiatives

Legislation, executive orders, and court-ordered mandates have undoubtedly created immediate pressures for diversifying higher education in the past; they are likely to continue to challenge institutions in the future. While some groups included in a campus's definition of diversity are the target of many state and federal legal initiatives (women, racial/ethnic minorities, and disabled students), it is important to note that there exists no legal mandate for other groups as well as controversy regarding their status as a "protected class." For example, in the case of gay/lesbian students, faculty, and staff, individual institutional policy determines the extent to which those who continue to be the target of discrimination are to be included in statements prohibiting discrimination, are entitled to receive "spouse" benefits, or are to be offered specific services or academic programs as part of the institutional definition of diversity or multiculturalism (Kardia, 1996). Therefore, the influence of legal initiatives or mandates may vary depending on the target group, the stated mission of the institution, and/or legal conditions of the campus (public or private control) that obligate them to plan responses to such pressures. Thus, campuses may be compelled to engage in diversity planning, particularly when a court or agency finds evidence of discrimination, but at the same time can participate voluntarily in determining how to achieve fairness and equity for its constituents.

Both private and public campuses that receive federal funding are compelled to adhere to policies and practices of nondiscrimination according to Section 504 of the Rehabilitation Act of 1973, the 1990 Americans with Disabilities Act, Title VI of the Civil Rights Act of 1964, and subsequent executive orders, which all prohibit discrimination on the basis of disability, race, color, religion, sex, or national origin. However, simply evaluating and revising policies to be nondiscriminatory is not sufficient for campuses where past discrimination or current vestiges of discrimination are evident. These legal initiatives suggest that campuses are expected to provide reasonable accommodations for disabled employees and students and act affirmatively to provide opportunities for individuals from underrepresented groups. Some public institutions have been reviewed and will be influenced by new court-ordered mandates to proactively address educational opportunity and diversification of the faculty, staff, and student body.

For example, the Supreme Court heard *U.S. v. Fordice,* a significant case with regard to higher education desegregation in the state of Mississippi that has implications for eighteen other states with histories of segregated systems of higher education. The Court's 1992 decision confirmed that the decision to rule out "separate but equal" education in the 1954 case, *Brown v. Board of Education,* applies to public higher education. The Court maintained that there is evidence of a continuing legacy of segregation that currently has discriminatory effects in higher education; vestiges of segregation must be eliminated systemwide; "race-neutral" policies were not sufficient remedies for persistent inequality; and that remedies (proposed plans and goals) to correct inequities should be consistent with sound educational practices (Southern Education Foundation, 1995). Furthermore, a recent report from the Panel on Educational Opportunity and Postsecondary Desegregation examined institutions in twelve states and reported that none could demonstrate an acceptable level of progress in desegregation (Southern Education Foundation, 1995). These events suggest that renewed efforts towards meeting diversity goals are necessary in public higher education. The future of both predominantly white and predominantly black or Hispanic institutions in particular states depends on how statewide planning for diversity proceeds under these new conditions. Resolving the stratified system of institutional resources, academic programs, access, and admissions so as to ensure greater opportunity for African Americans and Latinos in these states requires clear goals and strategies to link desegregation with sound educational practice.

While the courts have deferred to educators to devise appropriate educational strategies to remedy unequal educational opportunities, they have not been silent on educational methods that may be linked with discriminatory practice. For example, in striking down the all-male admissions policy at Virginia Military Institute (VMI) in 1996, the Supreme Court justices noted that they did not contest the educational benefits of a single-sex education. Instead, they objected to the deliberate exclusion of women from an educational opportunity for which there was no equal. In addition, the justices commented on the adversative method of educational training designed to create physical rigor and mental stress to achieve the character traits necessary for a military career. While VMI suggested such an educational method may be unsuitable for women, the justices stated that it was not proven to be suitable for most men, nor was there sufficient evidence to suggest that it is "pedagogically beneficial" or more effective than other training methods (*Chronicle of Higher Education,* 1996). The VMI case clearly illustrated how service to a specific student population is linked with notions embedded in the curriculum that, in turn, are believed to achieve an institution's mission. In the coming years, VMI will no doubt reexamine its pedagogical practices to meet its mission of educating both men and women to serve the nation in military careers.

At the same time that there are legal initiatives to urge institutions forward in achieving diversity, there have been legal challenges to the approaches taken by some institutions. *Regents of the University of California v. Bakke* contested racial preferences in admissions and *Podberesky v. Kirwan* contested the same in the awarding of college scholarships; both cases addressed common strategies institutions have pursued toward student diversity goals. While the institutions lost both these challenges, the cases raised important points regarding institutional goal setting in relation to achieving diversity. First, the use of racial preferences to achieve diversity goals is subject to a stringent standard of judicial review, meaning that the program must serve a "compelling interest" or goal for the institution and be narrowly tailored to the achievement of that goal. Thus, institutions must clarify their goals and carefully design strategies to meet these goals. Second, racial preferences can be used in college admissions and in awarding scholarships as acceptable strategies for achieving diversity where there is evidence of past discrimination, present effects or conditions at the institution attributable to such a history, and/or where diversity is articulated as a desired educational policy (Bazluke, 1995). Those campuses denying their history of discrimination, taking little interest in documenting the problems of inequity on campus, and not embracing diversity as having an important educational function are not likely to withstand legal challenges—nor are they likely to achieve diversity goals. Third, the *Bakke* case actually supported institutional autonomy in the area of policy commitments to diversity by affirming the right of institutions to select their student body and include race as a factor (but not the sole determinant) in admissions if it is intended to serve an educational purpose. Thus, even with the threat of legal challenges, campuses retain significant autonomy in achieving diversity goals that are consistent with sound educational practice and are part of a well-articulated plan.

Political Context

Despite legal affirmation for institutional autonomy in the area of diversity commitments, it should be noted that some of the legal challenges reflect a political context that has the potential to hinder the achievement of diversity goals. Proactive approaches taken by institutions toward meeting diversity goals have encountered a backlash of resistance in some states and on particular campuses in the mid-1990s. Opposition to affirmative action has been motivated by politics and fueled by a general misconception of institutional practice. On a broad level, "affirmative action describes those practices that attempt to correct past or present discrimination and prevent future occurrences of discrimination" (Garcia, forthcoming). As a strategy, affirmative action is intended to meet the spirit of Title VI and subsequent executive orders in terms of attempting to increase the representation of previously excluded groups in settings that receive federal funding. This is why the use of institutional autonomy to reject affirmative action practices, as in the 1995 University of California Regents' decision, was an unusual event. It raised the question regarding whether the regents understood the rationale for the university's approach to achieving diversity, or whether they were unduly influenced by a Republican governor who hoped to make opposition to affirmative action a political issue in a preliminary campaign for the U.S. presidency. The regents have placed great faith in their institutions to devise new approaches to achieve diversity that will be economically necessary for educating an increasingly diverse state population, with a shrinking budget and with some risk of review for federal compliance. Some suggest that the affirmative action controversy emerged in a political context whereby state rights are being reasserted over federal control, economic uncertainties exist, and demographic and social transformations question predominant values. In such uncertain times, campuses must clarify their goals for diversity, communicate their goals and practices to the public, and articulate their vision of the multicultural environments they would like to achieve.

The Educational Imperative for Achieving Diversity Goals

While these external factors may exert some pressure on institutions to develop, clarify, or renew efforts toward diversity goals, it is the educational imperative that must take precedence in campus decisions and planning for diversity. That is, colleges must proactively pursue diversity goals because it makes good educational sense. Many campuses today have come to recognize diversity as an educational policy, which is a philosophy and goal consistent with the overall educational objectives of the institution. Until recently, however, there was relatively little empirical research to understand how diversity functioned as an educational policy. Research on college students and their educational environments now reveals that progress toward institutional diversity goals can have an impact on students' educational experiences. In a national longitudinal study of college students and faculty at their respective institutions, results revealed that an institutional emphasis on diversity goals was significantly associated with increased levels of cultural awareness and commitment to promoting racial understanding among students after four years of college (Astin, 1993). Approaches to integrating knowledge regarding diversity into the academic program also have an impact. Undergraduates attending institutions that had adopted an ethnic studies or Third World course requirement in the general education program, during the mid- to late 1980s, showed positive outcomes. Students tended to be more satisfied with instruction and their overall undergraduate experience, had higher levels of trust in the college administration, and perceived a distinct emphasis on multiculturalism on their campus. It is important to note that the study contained statistical controls for entering student characteristics and extensive environmental measures to rule out alternative explanations for these findings. Thus, in a rigorous test of the overall educational impact of college on students, a strong institutional emphasis on diversity goals shows consistently positive effects on students' undergraduate experiences and outcomes (Astin, 1993).

Although one institutional approach has been to introduce a few courses on women, racial/ethnic groups, or non-Western cultures to meet requirements in the general education program, many campuses have taken a more integrative approach to the curriculum. Linking data on faculty classroom practices with national data on student learning outcomes, we examined the potential effects of the integration of readings on women and minorities within the content of courses (Hurtado and Dey, 1993). We found a relatively strong and consistent effect of faculty teaching practices that have integrated race and gender issues into coursework on a variety of general education outcomes, including students' self-reported increases in critical thinking, writing skills, preparation for graduate school, academic self-confidence, and acceptance of people from different backgrounds, as well as activism and scholarship orientations among student personality traits. It may be that such curricular innovation heightens student awareness and knowledge of particular groups in American society and increases criticism of the status quo, thereby establishing an avenue for critical thinking among students. Integrating readings about race/ethnicity and gender also have a potentially self-affirming effect on students who are representative of the increasing proportion of women and students from different racial/ethnic groups in colleges and universities. These students may be more likely to "see themselves" in the curriculum, which could increase their self-confidence while also increasing all students' understanding of others who face problems in progress and attainment in society.

Research also supports the development of a diverse community, in terms of increased numerical representation of various groups, to achieve specific educational goals for all students. Specifically, campuses with high proportions of white students provide limited opportunities for interaction across race/ethnicity and limit student learning experiences with diverse groups in society (Hurtado, Dey, and Treviño, 1992). In environments that lack a diverse workforce or population, underrepresented groups are regarded as symbols rather than as individuals, or "tokens." Tokenism contributes to heightened visibility of the underrepresented group, exaggeration of group differences, and the distortion of the individuals' images to fit existing stereotypes (Kanter, 1977). Furthermore, the lack of interracial contact clearly influences students' views toward others as well as support for campus initiatives. One study found that white students who had the least social interaction with someone of a different background were less likely to hold positive attitudes toward multiculturalism on campus. The authors conclude: "In order to prepare students as participants in a more heterogeneous college environment, and as citizens in a global community, program planners and administrators need to recognize deficiencies in cultural sensitivity and build on the multicultural awareness that students do have" (Globetti, Globetti, Brown, and Smith, 1993, p. 218). Thus, the educational imperative suggests the importance of a diverse community and educational programming that improves social interaction, eliminates stereotypes, and enhances educational outcomes for undergraduates. It suggests a multifaceted approach to achieving a multicultural environment and strategies for change, which are addressed in the next section.

Institutional Strategies for Achieving Diversity

Planning and implementing change is always a complex undertaking within colleges and universities. In the case of pursuing goals related to diversity and multiculturalism, the process is especially challenging and complex. In this section, we discuss different considerations that need to be addressed when planning change related to diversity and multiculturalism, including appropriate goal setting, general planning concerns, and principles for action and assessment.

Identifying Goals

An important consideration in planning to implement strategies related to diversity and multiculturalism is to carefully consider and define realistic goals for the initiative. Given the complex nature of diversity issues, there are a number of intertwined topics that could legitimately—and simultaneously—serve as a focal point for diversity initiatives. These range from recruiting more diverse faculty and student body to infusing diversity into the institution's educational mission.

Most goals associated with diversity initiatives can be linked with a particular aspect of a campus's climate for diversity. It is increasingly recognized that the campus climate for diversity is inherently multidimensional (Hurtado, 1994; Hurtado, Milem, Allen, and Clayton-Pederson, 1995). A multidimensional approach is important because campuses must first be able to understand the dimensions of the problem that a relatively poor climate may present before embarking on efforts to improve it. Central to the multidimensional conceptualization of the campus climate for diversity is the notion that students are educated in distinctly racial contexts. These contexts in higher education are produced by an institution's *historical legacy of inclusion or exclusion* of various racial/ethnic groups, its *structural diversity* in terms of numerical representation of various racial/ethnic groups, the *psychological climate* that includes perceptions and attitudes between and among groups, and a *behavioral climate* dimension that is characterized by intergroup relations on campus.

A college's historical legacy of exclusion of various racial and ethnic groups can continue to determine the prevailing climate and influence current practices (Hurtado, 1994; Peterson and others, 1978; Richardson and Skinner, 1991). Institutional case studies have shown that an institution's historical context influences its climate for diversity, wherein success in creating a supportive climate is dependent upon early institutional responses to the entrance of diverse students (including commitment to affirmative action, institutional intent for minority specific programs, and attention to the psychological climate and intergroup relations on campus once substantial numbers of students of color are admitted). An institution's ability to assess and articulate its history with genuine honesty is the first step in identifying areas for supporting the development and implementation of various goals. Some campuses may use evidence of their historical legacy of exclusion as a rationale for diversity goals, while others have examined their history to find evidence in founding documents that support diversity goals as a cornerstone of institutional purpose. In referring to Stanford University founders' spirit of equality, President Gerhard Casper stated, "we would be betraying the Founders if we disregarded their stated concern about [their desire to resist] the 'tendency to the stratification of society'" (1995). Thus, the historical legacy of inclusion or exclusion can serve as an important starting point in identifying diversity goals.

An institution's structural diversity refers primarily to the numerical representation of various racial/ethnic and gender groups. The tendency of most institutions is to focus on increasing the numerical representation of various student and faculty groups, often in response to affirmative action goals and plans for desegregation. Increasing the structural diversity of an institution is an important first step toward improving the climate for diversity. Environments with highly skewed distributions of socially and culturally different people alter the dynamics of social interaction and attitudes towards others (Kanter, 1977). In addition, a proactive stance in increasing the representation of various racial/ethnic groups conveys a message that an institution highly values the development and maintenance of a multicultural environment. African American, Chicano, and white students attending institutions with high African American and Latino enrollments were most likely to believe that their institution had a strong commitment to diversity (Hurtado, 1990). Thus, by increasing their racial/ethnic enrollments, campuses can significantly improve the college experiences of historically underrepresented groups. Moreover, attaining a diverse student body and hiring a diverse faculty result in significantly more opportunities for all students to learn how to deal with others from various cultural backgrounds in their postcollege years. Those campuses that have achieved some degree of success in increasing the numerical representation of various groups, however, may focus on developing further goals related to the development of a functioning multicultural environment.

The psychological dimension of the climate for diversity involves an individual's view of group relations, institutional responses to diversity, perceptions of discrimination or racial conflict, and attitudes held toward others from diverse backgrounds. These perceptions are important elements of how students and faculty experience the institution, and they help shape expectations along with future interactions. From this perspective, then, all viewpoints are valid and are to some extent a product of the institution's environment. Developing goals to improve the psychological climate may involve assessment of perceptions of the work and learning environment to assist in identifying problem areas. Goals include such strategies as curricular innovations to increase knowledge of diverse groups, co-curricular programming designed to promote dialogue among groups where myths and stereotypes can be debunked, and workshops for staff where communication can be improved among groups and perceived conflict between groups can be converted into common goals for the institution.

Campuses have also been concerned with reports of racial incidents, the level of social interaction among different racial/ethnic groups, and sexual harassment on campus. The behavioral dimension of the climate consists of actual reports of general social interaction, interaction between and among individuals from different backgrounds, and the nature of intergroup relations on campus. Campuses have established reporting and disciplinary procedures to resolve some aspects of student, faculty, and staff behavior that have been deemed unacceptable in a community respectful of differences among individuals. Beyond the more serious forms of intergroup conflict, setting goals in the area of behavior is difficult because each individual derives identity and value from his or her social interactions. However, contact with someone from a different racial/ethnic group, or different sexual orientation, under conditions of relatively equal status reduces fear and prejudice among individuals (Allport, 1954; Kardia, 1996). Because student involvement plays a central role in the successful education of students, including promotion of cognitive and affective student outcomes, the behavioral environment is important not only with respect to the campus climate for diversity but also for promoting educational outcomes. This suggests that the campus can identify goals to increase student interaction with diverse groups outside the classroom and encourage pedagogical techniques that enhance interaction across diverse groups within classrooms; both strategies not only diminish social boundaries but also enhance the forms of engagement that lead to successful achievement of student educational goals. Programs that increase contact between faculty and diverse groups of students, and between student groups representing different campus communities, serve the dual purpose of improving the climate for diversity and enhancing students' educational experiences.

It is important to note that these dimensions of the climate for diversity are not discrete but are connected with each other. For example, the historical vestiges of segregation have an impact on an institution's ability to improve its racial/ethnic student enrollments, and such underrepresentation of specific groups may also contribute to stereotypical attitudes among individuals within the learning and work environment. Many change efforts focus on only one element of the climate—the most common ones being the need to increase the structural diversity of the institution, and recruiting students and faculty of color—although more comprehensive approaches are now being tried in order to take into account the dynamics of all these important interrelated elements of the climate (for example, the University of Michigan's "Michigan Mandate"). More generally, it has been argued that reciprocal and dynamic relationships exist between students, faculty, and their institutions (Dey and Hurtado, 1995). This means that in practice, pursuing one goal—say, diversifying the student body—will naturally tend to create pressure to pursue others, such as transforming the curriculum. Thus, efforts designed to focus on a single aspect of the climate likely generate pressures to address multiple facets of the campus climate for diversity.

Finally, in addition to considering the primary goals of the diversity initiative, it is important to consider the degree to which these initiatives relate to other campus goals. Institutional goals and priorities outside the precise domain of diversity and multiculturalism may be consistent with and serve to reinforce diversity planning, or they may be in conflict and forced to compete for attention and scarce resources. However, "success in integrating diversity planning and institutional planning is significantly affected by an institution's level of understanding of the relationship between initiatives to enhance diversity and its traditional mission" (Stewart, 1991, p.161). Planning for diversity goals and programming initiatives should be linked and consistent with overall goals for the campus and should be discussed along with general planning and programming efforts.

Planning for Change

There is an extensive literature on change within higher education settings, but much of the work focuses on understanding more "familiar curricular or structural change efforts" (Hyer, 1985, p. 283) rather than changes that might be seen by some as controversial. The more traditional models of institutional change have limited applicability in producing useful insights for those interested in achieving the goals of diversity and multiculturalism, but it is useful to review models of change derived from research on similar kinds of innovations within higher education. These include works focusing on cultural diversity (Stewart, 1991), legislative initiatives related to college athletics (Newcombe and Conrad, 1981) and affirmative action (Hyer, 1985), and integration of women's perspectives into the curriculum (Schuster and Van Dyne, 1984).

At the outset, it should be recognized that there are a number of stages in a campus's journey to becoming a multicultural institution; planning and change efforts need to be aligned with different stages of an institution's awareness of multicultural issues. These stages have been described as monocultural, nondiscriminatory, and multicultural (Stewart, 1991; Foster and others, 1988; and Richardson, 1989). A monocultural institution in this schema is one in which there is a lack of recognition on the part of institutional actors concerning the need to serve new populations. In the nondiscriminatory stage, there is limited recognition of the need to recognize and serve new populations. The orientation is toward making relatively minor adjustments to existing structures and policies as opposed to fundamentally rethinking institutional processes relative to diversity. In the multicultural stage, institutions have achieved a consensus about the need to serve new populations, and participants see this as a goal throughout the institution as opposed to something imposed by institutional leaders.

A number of important differences in planning, budgeting, and evaluative processes can be identified within this framework of institutional awareness. Summarized in Table 21.1, they point to a need to find a balance between an institution's stage of awareness and planning processes as the institution moves toward the multicultural stage. In striving to become a multicultural institution, the institution needs to seriously engage in a number of transformative tasks and develop effective policies to guide this transformation.

To begin the transformative process, the need to diversify the faculty and student body has to be recognized and given the highest priority by leaders at all levels of the institution (Hill, 1991). A good deal of research has indicated that development and implementation of policies similar to those used to achieve diversity and multicultural goals are greatly facilitated (or hindered) by leadership practices and institutional structures (Newcombe and Conrad, 1981; Hyer, 1985). Second, institutions need to create conditions whereby members of the institutional community who represent different cultures have respectful conversations with representatives of other cultures in order to complete their everyday activities (Hill, 1991). By structuring conditions that promote positive cross-cultural communications, institutions can help routinize interaction norms that otherwise lead to isolation. Third, involving broad-based participation in diversity planning and creating greater institutional involvement in the achievement of diversity goals is also a key strategy for success. In this way, diversity goals are not relegated for

TABLE 21.1. INSTITUTIONAL MULTICULTURAL AWARENESS AND PROCESSES RELATED TO PLANNING.

Stages of Awareness	Institutional Processes
Monocultural	Planning: None; denial of need to serve new populations Budgeting: No special funding available Evaluation: None
Nondiscriminatory	Planning: Top-down, temporary committee structures Budgeting: Exclusive reliance on special funding sources Evaluation: Ad hoc
Multicultural	Planning: Multiple approaches, coordinated planning activities Budgeting: Planned and coordinated funding strategies Evaluation: Systematic and comprehensive

Source: Adapted from Stewart (1991).

implementation in one unit on campus, but planning and implementation of diversity goals become aspects of many operating units on campus with coordinated oversight at the highest levels of institutional governance.

Another important aspect of goals of diversity and multiculturalism is monitoring how well these goals are being achieved. The need for effective and responsive assessment and evaluation systems is important since it can provide useful information for allocating resources and building support for programs (Hurtado, Milem, Allen, and Clayton-Pederson, 1995; Symonette, 1995). Thus, in planning new initiatives or in reviewing the success of existing initiatives, it is important to develop evaluation components that can be used in future decision making or reports to funding agencies that have provided incentive monies to achieve diversity goals. In a recent report of Ford Foundation-sponsored diversity initiatives, an external evaluation team noted how rarely such evaluations were planned at the initial stages of new projects (Musil, 1995).

Principles for Action

In order to move from models of change to strategies for action, it is important to acknowledge the complexities inherent in such efforts. Given the complex interrelationships surrounding these topics, it is important to develop a comprehensive approach to bring about change that focuses on the multidimensional nature of the campus climate. The multidimensional framework is an important tool for planners because it provides a conceptual handle for organizing various dimensions of that climate. As noted above, most campuses tend to focus on only one element: the goal of increasing the numbers of racial/ethnic students and/or faculty on campus. Although this is an important area for institutional effort, the framework underscores the notion that other elements of the climate also require attention and constitute key areas for focusing diversity efforts.

A number of general principles for improving the campus climate for diversity can be summarized:

- Emphasize the campus climate for diversity as an institutional priority
- Assess the current state of the campus climate for diversity
- Develop and implement a plan for constructive change
- Monitor the effectiveness of the plan in promoting positive change (adapted from Hurtado, Milem, Allen, and Clayton-Pederson, 1995)

These principles were derived from an extensive review of the higher education research literature and explicitly acknowledge the multidimensional nature of the campus climate for diversity. Thus, in addition to focusing on the basic question of structural diversity, the principles emphasize the need to consider the attitudinal and behavioral characteristics that shape the institution's climate. These latter dimensions of the institutional climate are an important consideration because they help characterize how particular groups of individuals on campus "feel" about, and relate with, one another.

The first principle suggests that to have real credence, the goal of an improved campus climate for diversity must be affirmed as an institutional priority. Beyond merely stating that diversity is important, campus leaders must be able to understand, believe, and articulate the ways in which diversity serves the larger goals of the academy. Campus leadership also needs to recognize and advocate the inseparable tie between diversity and academic excellence, without diminishing one or the other. Colleges and universities play a key role in educating leaders who are called to serve in an increasingly multicultural future. Unless the goal of creating a diverse learning environment is viewed as an integral component and a necessity in achieving academic excellence, the goal is likely to be considered separate from (and contrary to) the goals of the institution and therefore be devalued.

Another important principle is the need to assess the current campus climate for diversity in order to understand the dimensions of any problems. To do this, institutional actors need to engage in a deliberate, self-conscious process of self-appraisal. Such assessments provide baseline information on the current state of affairs regarding the campus climate for diversity. In most instances, this self-study process is formal, perhaps requiring the creation of commissions or committees charged with examining the structural diversity, psychological climate, behavioral patterns in campus departments, procedures, and informal social settings. In addition to gathering data on the climate from institutional records and survey instruments, the campus communities should also be encouraged to engage in less formal activities such as group discussions and examination of prevailing attitudes of individuals on campus. The end goal of these formal and informal self-appraisal activities is to systematically educate the campus and devise policies that address the factors that facilitate or block efforts to achieve an improved campus climate for diversity. Unfortunately, many campuses engage in diversity-related assessments without broad-based institutional investment in the next steps, nor with a clear idea of how they might utilize such information.

Campuses should move beyond the self-appraisal process to action. The third principle focuses on the need to develop and implement a plan designed to promote constructive change. This is the place where most efforts to achieve institutional change flounder, since it goes well beyond simply identifying goals. As a rule, academics excel at researching and describing problems but are not as facile in developing practical plans to systematically address such problems. In contrast, administrators interested in quick fixes may consider add-on types of solutions to diversity dilemmas without sufficient study of the complexity of the dilemma. A commonly encountered barrier takes the form of efforts to develop and execute plans without the benefit of guidance provided by empirical data. In this instance, plans that include specific goals, timetables, areas of responsibility, and practical activities, informed by empirical study of the problem, can be developed and implemented. A comprehensive plan of action should encourage both administrators and faculty to rethink existing structures and practices as they work toward meeting their mission of educating a diverse and multicultural student body.

Finally, procedural changes and programmatic initiatives need to be tracked to ensure that the desired effects are achieved. As suggested above, data from such evaluations provide an excellent source of guidance for making required modifications. Evaluation data are essential in making informed choices about how best to allocate scarce resources between competing programs. Moreover, the reports that flow from ongoing evaluation efforts can help keep the campus engaged in and informed about the institution's efforts to change. By keeping the issue before the campus community, a forum is created whereby success can be celebrated and shortcomings can be identified and corrected. Perhaps more importantly, successes in the areas of developing a supportive climate for diversity can engender public support for institutional initiatives and have the effect of attracting more students, faculty, and staff who wish to be affiliated with such a learning and work environment.

Assessing Current Status and Future Progress

In evaluating and assessing an institution's progress toward its goal with respect to diversity and multiculturalism, a number of research approaches can be productively employed. Data that could be used as part of a larger assessment and evaluation effort are shown in Table 21.2. These data are from a national study of college teaching faculty conducted in 1993 (Dey, Ramirez, Korn, and Astin, 1993); they show faculty ratings of the degree to which they believe their institutions emphasize a number of different priorities.

The results show that as a priority, faculty rate creating a diverse multicultural campus environment as being about average in importance at their institutions, with about half of the remaining priorities rating higher and half lower. The results in Table 21.2 are also interesting in that they show how creating a diverse multicultural campus environment is not antithetical to many of the other goals rated by the faculty. Although it is not surprising that the multicultural environment goal is most strongly associated with other kinds of diversity goals (that is, recruiting more minority students and faculty), it is interesting to note that it is also moderately correlated with the goal of promoting the intellectual development of students, which is the priority most commonly recognized by faculty. This insight reflects the notion that diversity is consistent with the general educational mission at most institutions, and it underscores the need to examine the relationship of diversity goals to other institutional priorities.

Although the table shows aggregated data from 308 institutions from across the country, this kind of information could be used in a number of ways by individual institutions. For example, an institution's priority structure could be compared with responses from institutions across the country and with peer institutions participating in similar faculty assessments through surveys administered on campuses. Institutions can also develop their own surveys to assess how students, faculty, or staff view diversity goals in relation to other institutional priorities.

In evaluating an institution's progress toward diversity and multicultural goals, planners should not limit themselves to a single approach. In addition to the kinds of surveys we have described, options for collecting information include focus groups, archival and document analyses, and observations of campus life. The key here is not to seek out the single best approach to collecting these kinds of information, but to be eclectic in seeking methods that help portray the changing complexities associated with diversity and multiculturalism on college campuses. Whatever method of assessment is chosen should also ensure that multiple perspectives from the campus are represented, including individuals who play different roles on campus (faculty, students, staff) as well as members of multiple campus communities that may be based on race, gender, disability, or field of study.

TABLE 21.2. ASSESSING INSTITUTIONAL PRIORITIES
FROM THE FACULTY PERSPECTIVE.

	Average Rating	Correlation with Multicultural Environment Measure	Rank of Rating	Rank of Correlation
Promote the intellectual development of students	3.29	.30	1	4
Increase/maintain institutional prestige	2.85	.10	2	–
Help students examine personal values	2.75	–.04	3	–
Develop community among students and faculty	2.60	.21	4	6
Enhance institution's national image	2.58	.20	5	7
Create diverse multicultural campus environment	*2.52*		6	
Develop leadership ability among students	2.50	–.01	7	–
Recruit more minority students	2.49	.79	8	1
Increase minority representation among the faculty	2.33	.77	9	2
Increase women's representation among the faculty	2.29	.66	10	3
Facilitate student involvement in community service	2.27	.03	11	–
Help students to bring about change in American society	2.11	.23	12	5
Hire faculty "stars"	1.69	.07	13	–

Note: Institutional priorities rated by institutional faculty on a scale from 1 ("Not a priority") to 4 ("Highest priority") and then averaged at each institution. Nonsignificant correlations ($p>.05$) are indicated by – in the far right column, which shows the rank of the correlation.

Source: Survey of undergraduate teaching faculty at 308 colleges and universities (Dey, Ramirez, Korn, and Astin, 1993).

Regardless of the methodologies employed to accomplish the task, assessments can also be conducted longitudinally in order to evaluate how an institution's changing priorities are viewed over time by students, faculty, or staff and how widely they are adopted by all constituents within the institution. Regular institutional audits regarding diversity are encouraged as part of assessing progress toward goals, understanding areas of institutional problems, and further aligning diversity goals with educational objectives (Smith, 1989). These audits may monitor race/ethnicity and gender differences in student access and progress, faculty/staff hiring and promotion, and the changing climate for diversity to capture attitudes, institutionalization of diversity goals, and aspects of campus relations.

Building Diversity into Quality Programs, and Building Quality into Diversity Programs

One of the most common goals of most institutions is to ensure a quality undergraduate education. Increasingly, diversity issues are being viewed as central to this goal. Most accreditation agencies appear to be moving in the direction of incorporating standards for achieving diversity in reviews of the quality of colleges and universities, although there was some initial controversy in the matter. The Middle States Association of Colleges and Universities was reviewed in 1991 for its approach to promoting diversity on college campuses by then Secretary of Education Lamar Alexander. Although the secretary questioned the appropriateness of reviewing the diversity of a college as a criterion of quality, more campuses are viewing diversity criteria as central to improving the quality of undergraduate education. For example, the Academic Senate for the California Community Colleges developed criteria to be used as the basis for accreditation reviews by the Western Association of Schools and Colleges. Among the criteria to be used in evaluating the quality of a community college are the extent to which faculty had received training in pedagogy, training in working with a multicultural student body, and the diversity among the faculty and staff that serve a diverse student body (Academic Senate for California Community Colleges, 1990). Thus, in some circles, institutional excellence is consonant with achieving diversity goals. If this trend continues for diversity to remain part of the criteria in evaluating the quality of the undergraduate experience, more campuses will have to explore ways to build diversity into quality programs and build quality into diversity programs.

Research universities can build diversity into quality programs by encouraging development of new knowledge regarding diverse groups and encouraging "problem-based" learning regarding issues of social inequality. This is often achieved through recruiting talented women and minority faculty and students to strong departments and programs, establishing postdoctoral programs to attract talented women and minorities in particular departments, and encouraging cross-disciplinary research and curricular innovations that introduce diverse perspectives on topics within courses. Many campuses provide incentives for departments to build diversity into quality programs in the form of cost sharing of faculty positions and competition for internal grants on curriculum innovation and research in specific areas. Foundations and other external funding agencies have also provided significant grants to improve diversity in quality programs with the proviso that such innovations or improvements be integrated into the institution's budget and planning process over time.

Building quality into diversity programs takes a similar commitment. Perhaps because of the political beginnings of some of the academic and co-curricular programs designed to meet the needs of a diverse student body, many of these retain marginal status at institutions with regard to budget, planning, and the perception of their contribution to the overall mission of the institution. For example, although some institutions provide little support for programs for students of color (black student unions, minority peer support programs, etc.), research has shown that students participating in such minority-related services actually interact more with faculty and are more likely to also use other general support services on campus (Gilliard, 1996). This suggests that minority-related programs apparently increase student involvement and engagement on campus, a key element to the improvement of student outcomes. Although some institutions have marginalized women's studies and ethnic studies programs, several campuses have recognized the opportunities these programs present because they encourage cross-disciplinary work and focus on important social problems that are consistent with the objectives of the institution. Several campuses have moved their women's studies and ethnic studies programs from marginal to premier status by attracting prominent women or faculty of color to these programs and developing research institutes. These institutions have become well known for these programs and institutes, which continue to attract diverse students and faculty who wish to learn and work in environments known for excellence with regard to diversity issues. Diverse students and faculty cannot be assisted by marginal programs, or programs that are allowed to languish. Campuses need to examine the problems and potential for existing diversity-related curricular and co-curricular programs to determine how to best achieve a quality undergraduate education. Such improvements can be made so long as institutions are mindful of the political history and old sensitivities tied to initial institutional resistance to diversity, and so long as they give considerable thought to how diversity programs can become central to the institutional mission.

Collaborative Arrangements for Implementing Systemic Change

Linking quality and diversity throughout the institution, however, may require systemic change. Many believe that there are simply not enough students and faculty who are academically prepared to create a diversified campus community. Although we establish in this chapter that diversity and excellence need not be in conflict when meeting campus goals, we do not want to underestimate the extent to which educational experiences can preclude opportunities for students from segregated, low-income environments to attend particular types of colleges. Comprehensive planning calls for multiple and creative approaches to overcoming this hurdle to achieve a multicultural learning environment in higher education.

A key element of this approach is to develop an increasing number of collaborative arrangements across educational sectors that include K–12 schools and colleges, two-year and four-year institutions, graduate institutions and specialized colleges, and links with business or community organizations. For example, under the aegis of the National Center for Urban Partnerships (NCUP), multisector collaboration teams in sixteen cities are working toward reducing the barriers to educational progress among students in urban areas. With strategic planning grants available from the Ford Foundation until the year 2000, NCUP has brought teams together to share information regarding creation of programs, evaluation of student progress, and the difficulties in creating systemic change in efforts to increase baccalaureate attainments. These collaboration teams include decision makers from each sector who are expected to honestly address problems in urban education, and who have the authority to commit to changes and negotiate agreements that lower important organizational barriers to promoting student success. The focus is on joint problem solving, with each "partner" offering what its institution can best contribute in terms of resources for solving the key educational problems in their community.

In another example, several four-year and graduate institutions have entered into collaborative agreements with institutions that serve special populations (historically black colleges and tribal colleges) in order to increase the number of African American and American Indian students in their academic programs. These arrangements allow for sharing of diversity and academic resources among institutions.

Both of these collaborative approaches not only pursue the goal of increasing the number of degree attainments among various racial/ethnic groups but also include programs to address the key problem of student underpreparation, which poses major barriers for students from low-income and racial/ethnic communities. However, until programs that result from such collaborations are widely adopted or institutionalized, the energy and commitment required for sustaining this work should not be underestimated. Many more institutions of higher education can be involved in creating systemic change, by developing collaborative arrangements across sectors or linking with existing ones, in order to share resources and lower organizational barriers that will ultimately benefit a greater number of institutions and diverse groups of students. This is an approach that has gained favor among state policy makers who support collaborations because they view them as a way to save money (Hawthorne and Zusman, 1992). In short, such collaborations allow institutions to meet the important institutional goals of improving student progress and achieving diversity.

Conclusion

The challenges to higher education with respect to diversity continue to increase into the foreseeable future. Demographic and economic imperatives in combination with changes in the political and legal context require institutions to transform themselves in ways that place diversity goals at the center of the institution's educational mission. Although changes of this sort may be more complex to implement than other types of planned change efforts, the changing context of higher education demands that colleges and universities rise to the challenge.

To foster the necessary transformations, a number of principles need to be adopted by institutions: (1) education must be student-centered, or responsive to the needs of students; (2) education must be accountable and performance-driven, with a clear vision of goals and monitoring of progress; and (3) approaches must be comprehensive (Southern Education Foundation, 1995). These principles, developed as part of efforts to desegregate higher education systems, incorporate many of the key themes in achieving the goals of diversity and multiculturalism we have presented here.

When education is student-centered and the educational development of students is a value communicated throughout the institution, diversity goals are pursued as part of a well-articulated plan to improve undergraduate education. Achievement of diversity goals is seen as accomplishing an educational objective that results in important undergraduate outcomes, including positive student views of the quality of life at the institution, increased critical thinking, acceptance of different perspectives and people from different backgrounds, and other skills that serve students in diverse work and learning environments in society. Institutions maintain a great deal of autonomy in pursuing diversity commitments that are consistent with the overall educational objectives of the institution.

If institutions are to remain accountable to their constituents, both educational objectives and diversity goals require clarification and monitoring. External and internal contexts call for the establishment of clear goals in order to meet demographic and economic pressures, meet legal obligations and withstand legal challenges, and articulate to the public a clear vision of the multicultural environments campuses would like to achieve regardless of the political climate. Much of the goal setting has to do with the institutional definition of diversity, whereby the institution clarifies those whom it intends to serve, as well as an approach that may include attention to the historical legacy of the institution, structural diversity, the psychological climate, or the behavioral dimension of the environment. Once goals and plans are in place, a systematic form of assessment or institutional audit is a useful way of monitoring progress on an institutional level. However, if educational objectives are to be regarded as consistent with diversity goals, assessment of diversity should be monitored along with the assessment of educational objectives. Such coordinated goal setting, planning, program initiatives, and assessment of progress ensure that both diversity and excellence in education are viewed and acted upon as activities central to the educational mission of the institution.

Finally, diversity goal setting, planning, and programming must be comprehensive to attain the goals of creating a multicultural environment. Institutions of higher education do not function in isolated environments. They are dependent on K–12 education to provide prepared students; public and private organizations depend on higher education to replenish the workforce; and institutions in turn are dependent on the overall economy. Comprehensive approaches and strategic planning may require that each sector of education be linked, with higher education institutions assisting in creating a seamless web from kindergarten through postsecondary education so as to improve the diversity of students earning baccalaureate and advanced degrees. This attention to external linkages can be complemented by comprehensive diversity programs within the institution. Taken together, these approaches suggest that successfully achieving diversity and multicultural goals is dependent on diminishing the amount of conflict among institutional priorities so that these goals are central to institutional operation and functioning. Most campuses have yet to attain this ideal state, but many institutions that are committed to achieving the goals of diversity and multiculturalism have embarked on a journey that will transform their environments.

Further Reading

Further reading on specific institutional strategies for achieving the goals of diversity and multiculturalism is in various reports issued by the Association of American Colleges and Universities, including lessons learned from various diversity initiatives in *Diversity in Higher Education: A Work in Progress* (Musil, 1995) and reports on curriculum transformation produced through their project on American Commitments: Diversity, Democracy, and Liberal Learning. Various resources and contacts for specific campus initiatives are documented by the American Council of Education's Office of Minorities in Higher Education. Campuses may find useful that office's resource book *Sources: Diversity Initiatives in Higher Education* (Mintz, 1993) as well as its more recent publications. Overviews of research on diversity issues that are linked with institutional practice are documented in Daryl Smith's two references, *The Challenge of Diversity: Involvement or Alienation in the Academy* (Smith, 1989) and *The Impact of Diversity on Students* (AACU Report), or *The Climate for Racial/Ethnic Diversity in Higher Education Institutions* by Sylvia Hurtado, Jeffrey Milem, Walter Allen, and Alma Clayton-Pederson. In addition to sending delegates to annual conferences on diversity issues, campuses may wish to discuss planning for diversity on the Internet listserv DIVERSE, sponsored by the AACU.

References

Academic Senate for California Community Colleges. *Accreditation: Evaluating the Collective Faculty.* Sacramento: Academic Senate for California Community Colleges, 1990.

Allport, G. W. *The Nature of Prejudice.* Reading, Mass.: Addison-Wesley, 1954.

Astin, A. W. *What Matters in College? Four Critical Years Revisited.* San Francisco: Jossey-Bass, 1993.

Bazluke, F. "Affirmative Action at the Crossroads: Legal Parameters Governing Racial Preferences in College Admissions and Financial Aid Programs." Paper presented at the University of Vermont Division of Continuing Education, Fifth Annual Legal Issues Conference, October 1995.

Carter, D. J., and Wilson, R. *Minorities in Higher Education: American Council on Education Eleventh Annual Status Report.* Washington, D.C.: American Council on Education, 1993.

Casper, G. "Statement on Affirmative Action at Stanford University," released on the World Wide Web [portfolio.stanford.edu:ad/Id 105149]. University Communications, Stanford University, Oct. 4, 1995.

Chronicle of Higher Education, July 5, 1996, pp. A27–A32.

Cox, T., Jr. *Cultural Diversity in Organizations: Theory, Research, and Practice.* San Francisco: Berrett-Koehler, 1993.

Dey, E. L., and Hurtado, S. "College Impact, Student Impact: A Reconsideration of the Role of Students Within American Higher Education." *Higher Education,* 1995, *30,* 207–223.

Dey, E. L., Ramirez, C. E., Korn, W. S., and Astin, A. W. *The American College Teacher: National Norms for the 1992–93 HERI Faculty Survey.* Los Angeles: Higher Education Research Institute, 1993.

Foster, B., Jackson, G., Cross, W. E., Jackson, B., and Hardiman, R. "Workforce Diversity and Business." *Training and Development Journal,* 1988, *42*(4), 38–41.

Garcia, M. (ed.). *Affirmative Action's Testament of Hope: Strategies for a New Era.* Albany: State University of New York Press, forthcoming.

Gilliard, M. *Racial Climate and Institutional Support Factors Affecting Success in Predominantly White Institutions: An Examination of African American and White Student Experiences.* Doctoral dissertation, University of Michigan, Ann Arbor, 1996.

Globetti, E. C., Globetti, G., Brown, C. L., and Smith, R. E. "Social Interaction and Multiculturalism." *NASPA Journal,* 1993, *30*(2), 209–218.

Hawthorne, E. M., and Zusman, A. "The Role of State Departments of Education in School/College Collaborations." *Journal of Higher Education,* 1992, *63*(4), 418–440.

Hill, P. J. "Multiculturalism: The Crucial Philosophical and Organizational Issues." *Change,* July/Aug. 1991, 38–47.

Hurtado, S. *Campus Racial Climates and Educational Outcomes.* Doctoral dissertation, University of California, Los Angeles. Ann Arbor: University Microfilms International, No. 9111328, 1990.

Hurtado, S. "The Institutional Climate for Talented Latino Students." *Research in Higher Education,* 1994, *35*(1), 21–41.

Hurtado, S., and Dey, E. L. "Promoting General Education Outcomes." Paper presented at the annual forum of the Association for Institutional Research (AIR), Chicago, May 1993.

Hurtado, S., Dey, E. L., and Treviño, J. G. "Exclusion or Self-Segregation? Interaction Across Racial/Ethnic Groups on Campus." Paper presented at the annual meeting of the American Educational Research Association (AERA), New Orleans, Apr. 1992.

Hurtado, S., Milem, J., Allen, W. A., and Clayton-Pederson, A. "The Climate for Racial/Ethnic Diversity in Higher Education Institutions: A Preliminary Report from the Common Destiny Alliance." Paper presented at the annual One Third of a Nation Conference, American Council on Education, Kansas City, Mo., Oct. 1995.

Hyer, P. B. "Affirmative Action for Women Faculty: Case Studies of Three Successful Institutions." *Journal of Higher Education,* 1985, *56*(3), 282–299.

Justiz, M. J. "Demographic Trends and the Challenges to American Higher Education." In M. J. Justiz, R. Wilson, and L. G. Bjork (eds.), *Minorities in Higher Education.* Phoenix: ACE/Oryx Press, 1994.

Kanter, R. M. "Some Effects of Proportions on Group Life: Skewed Sex Ratios and Responses to Token Women." *American Journal of Sociology,* 1977, *82*(5), 965–989.

Kardia, D. B. *Diversity's Closet: Student Attitudes Toward Lesbians, Gay Men, and Bisexual People in a Multicultural University.* Doctoral dissertation, University of Michigan, Ann Arbor, 1996.

Mintz, S. D. (ed.). *Sources: Diversity Initiatives in Higher Education.* Washington, D.C.: Office of Minorities in Higher Education, American Council on Education, 1993.

Muñoz, C., Jr. *Youth, Identity, Power: The Chicano Movement.* New York: Verso, 1989.

Musil, C. M. *Diversity in Higher Education: A Work in Progress.* Washington, D.C.: Association of American Colleges and Universities, 1995.

Newcombe, J. P., and Conrad, C. F. "A Theory of Mandated Academic Change." *Journal of Higher Education,* 1981, *52*, 555–557.

Peterson, M. W., Blackburn, R. T., Gamson, Z. T., Arce, C. H., Davenport, R. W., and Mingle, J. R. *Black Students on White Campuses: The Impacts of Increased Black Enrollments.* Ann Arbor: Institute for Social Research, 1978.

Richardson, R. C. *Institutional Climate and Minority Achievement.* Denver: Education Commission of the States, 1989.

Richardson, R. C., and Skinner, E. F. *Achieving Quality and Diversity: Universities in a Multicultural Society.* New York: American Council on Education/Macmillan, 1991.

Schuster, M. R., and Van Dyne, S. R. "Placing Women in the Liberal Arts: Stages of Curriculum Transformation." *Harvard Educational Review,* 1984, *54*(4), 413–428.

Smith, D. G. *The Challenge of Diversity: Involvement or Alienation in the Academy?* ASHE ERIC Report no. 5. Washington, D.C.: George Washington University, 1989.

Southern Education Foundation. *Redeeming the American Promise: Report of the Panel on Educational Opportunity and Postsecondary Desegregation.* Atlanta: Southern Education Foundation, 1995.

Stewart, J. B. "Planning for Cultural Diversity: A Case Study." In H. E. Cheatham (ed.), *Cultural Pluralism on Campus.* Washington, D.C.: American College Personnel Association, 1991.

Symonette, H. *University of Wisconsin System Design for Diversity Evaluation Initiatives.* Madison: University of Wisconsin Office of Multicultural Affairs, 1995.

Treviño, J. G. *Participation in Ethnic/Racial Student Organizations.* Doctoral dissertation, University of California, Los Angeles, 1992.

CHAPTER TWENTY-TWO

INFUSING INFORMATION TECHNOLOGY INTO THE ACADEMIC PROCESS

William H. Graves, Robert G. Henshaw,
John L. Oberlin, and Anne S. Parker

Information technology (IT) is identified in Chapter One as both a force for change and an enabler of change in higher education. Rising institutional expenditures for IT suggest a mission-critical role for technology. But most colleges and universities, regardless of size and funding context, are simply spending more on IT while scrambling to understand how to fit IT into the overall planning frameworks that guide their institutional futures. Linking IT strategically to mission is largely an unmet challenge. Nor has IT significantly replaced or reduced costs. IT generally has remained an increasing cost, one that is exacerbating the mounting pressure to contain overall institutional costs.

Recent reports from within the academy have recognized this impasse, while suggesting that IT can nevertheless fuel a major and necessary academic transformation. For example, the Pew Higher Education Roundtable (1994) recently released a report offering this argument:

> The changes most important to higher education are those that are external to it. What is new is the use of societal demand—in the American context, market forces—to reshape the academy. The danger is that colleges and universities have become less relevant to society precisely because they have yet to understand the new demands being placed on them. . . . [Americans need] real assurances that shifting economic and political fortunes will not place a higher education beyond their grasp. . . . It is precisely that promise that is

being imbedded in the new electronic superhighway—which may turn out to be the most powerful external challenge facing higher education, and the one the academy is least prepared to understand [p. 1A].

The growing societal expectation, then, is for *affordable relevance* and *affordable flexibility*. Society expects higher education to link its curricula, research agendas, and public service offerings more relevantly to social and economic needs. Society also expects higher education to become more flexible in its course and degree offerings in order to meet new educational needs. Rapid changes in the discipline areas of knowledge, along with rapid growth in the volume of the overall knowledge base, are fueling a growing emphasis on lifelong learning. Moreover, not all students are interested in a residential learning experience. Many consumers of instruction have tightly focused, self-selected learning objectives. This is especially the case with so-called nontraditional and life-long learners, who may have legitimate educational needs neither relevant to nor easily accommodated by the time-and-place constraints of traditional campus-based study or the time constraints of multiple-year degree offerings.

IT can help meet these expectations of relevance and flexibility. Linked to the Internet and based on open Internet standards, an *institutional intranet* of ubiquitous, easily accessible central and departmental communication, computation, and information resources can provide:

- A globally connected, robust digital communications environment to enhance the reach, timeliness, and effectiveness of human communication in every aspect of instruction, research, public service, and institutional management
- A *learning* infrastructure with attendant services to increase the quality of student and faculty academic work and to increase access to academic resources and credit-bearing instruction beyond the boundaries of the traditional classroom, lab, and library
- An information infrastructure and related services to enable an institution to streamline its management and public relations functions by redesigning their underlying processes

By deploying IT as a strategic investment, higher education could become a growth industry again! But growth industries attract competition. Moreover, new technologies offer commercial providers cost-effective means to deliver education and training products, along with a variety of advanced medical services and other services, to the home and the workplace. The commercial shape of the National Information Infrastructure (NII) is already visible in the growth of the Internet in the commercial world and in the growing number of homes with personal computers connected to the Internet. Higher education must learn, as industry has, to customize its services to meet rapidly changing needs with flexible, modular services. IT is the key.

It will indeed be ironic if we in higher education, who pioneered the Internet, fail to adapt our academic and administrative programs and structures to take advantage of its opportunities for institutional and collective productivity. So long as we bolt IT onto existing administrative and academic programs, we continue to add to overall costs without addressing concerns about relevance, flexibility, and cost containment. Instead, we must deploy IT to craft new, user-friendly, and more efficient administrative processes and new models of instruction that can increase enrollments without additional faculty labor, foster a high quality of learning, and maintain student satisfaction. Above all, we must remember that the heft of higher education's costs lies in instructional programs, mostly in instructional personnel. If we are to contain operating costs per student, whether paid from private or public coffers, then IT must be deployed to ensure that prevailing investments in instructional personnel and programs produce higher levels of instructional productivity.

Whether focused on instruction or institutional management, IT is cost-effective only if underlying models and processes are rethought and restructured. There is a rich literature on "reengineering" management processes, which draws mostly on recent experiences in the corporate sector. But the road map for restructuring instruction is incomplete, largely because the shift from the traditional contact-hour-lecture model of instruction to technology-mediated models is relatively uncharted territory. For that reason, we focus our observations about restructuring primarily on instruction, hoping to reveal the essential features of the trip ahead. This requires understanding (1) the difficulties inherent in linking new technologies with traditional instructional models, (2) the barriers to faculty adoption of new technologies in instruction, (3) strategies for managing support for IT, (4) financial strategies for navigating the transition, and (5) planning strategies for infusing IT into the institutional fabric.

Linking Instruction and Information Technology

To link IT and instruction wisely, we must understand (1) the present shortcomings of the prevailing instructional model, (2) the different characteristics of various instructional technologies, and (3) possible institutional strategies for transforming instruction. The challenge is to create new instructional models that synthesize this understanding so as to maximize the benefits of the time faculty spend with students in an economically viable way.

The contact hour prescribes the current instructional model, and human contact between mentor (instructor) and student is certainly valued in most learning communities. But few would argue that the contact-hour lecture is the best mechanism for such contact. Instead, the lecture too often represents a trade-off, a way to deliver knowledge while ensuring some contact between an instructor and students. The two parties are grouped together to produce a return on an institutional investment in a classroom teaching infrastructure and a semester-based or quarter-based currency of certification. Many academic executives, having managed mandated efficiencies by trading off a more Socratic faculty-student interaction against a contact-hour instructional infrastructure, now face the proverbial rock and hard place. Any further attempts to optimize the productivity of instructional investments within today's labor-intensive contact-hour paradigm by increasing class sizes or course loads are likely to compromise quality beyond a point acceptable to either the public or the professorate. Tinkering with an instructional model that is already buckling under increasing demands for productivity and accountability is a risk, not a plan.

Information technology has three primary manifestations in today's contact-hour environment: (1) interactive video networks deployed for distance education, (2) the personal computer as a stand-alone medium for learning (courseware, simulations, case studies, modeling, etc.), and (3) the personal computer connected to the Internet (or various commercial networks) to deliver instructional materials and foster communication between instructors and students. To avoid unwise investments in IT, it is helpful to be aware of the differences inherent in these three instructional technology frameworks. Management literature is rich with how-not-to examples of businesses investing in technologies inconsistently with their organizational goals. The point is not to pit one technology against another but to cast light on how to match technology with educational goals.

The first observation is that while bolting a technology onto the contact-hour model of instruction may enhance the quality of learning or extend the reach of instruction, it typically does so at additional cost. For example, courseware or other software available to students in computer labs may improve the quality of a traditional contact-hour course, but it brings added cost to the institution. Not even the deployment of interactive video networks for distance education, heralded by some as the future of higher education, can resolve the economic quality/quantity trade-off inherent in the contact-hour model. Video networks can increase access to education while requiring less capital investment than new bricks and mortar entail, but the contact-hour course delivered from any distance is still labor-intensive.

Although there can be strong justification, socioeconomic or educational, for overlaying technology on the prevailing industrial-age model of instruction, today's imperative for change obliges us also to think about utilizing the flexibility inherent in technology to discover new, *affordable* models of instruction that remove constraints not just of place but also of time. For example, computer networks (data networks) remove constraints of place while supporting real-time communication; unlike interactive video networks, they also remove constraints of time. The primary difference between data and video networking, moreover, is not video itself. After all, we can capture, store, and retrieve video in digital form across computer networks (one form of "video on demand"). The critical difference is that a real-time video network, as typically deployed for distance education, is not only time-dependent but also highly mediated. The space, equipment, personnel, and other resources needed for a teleclass or teleconference are scarce and must be negotiated and scheduled, and the required time-dependent interconnections must be managed by a technician.

In contrast, a student at a computer connected to the Internet can have access any time to any available Internet resource, and this access is mediated by computers without additional human intervention. Also, the underlying economics of data and real-time video networks are quite different. The incremental cost of adding one more node to an interactive video network is approximately the same high cost of an original node. In contrast, the institutional intranet required to participate meaningfully in the Internet community requires a large capital investment, but the incremental cost of adding one more node to it is relatively low: the cost of a personal computer and its support. Overall, data networks scale much more readily than do (real-time) video networks.

These characteristics of interactive video networks and data networks (Internet) argue for utilizing the former when real-time interaction is necessary or when a societal need justifies their expense, while deploying the latter more ubiquitously for asynchronous and real-time communication and for the delivery of shared instructional resources. Indeed, an institutional intranet (campus data network) developed around Internet standards can readily be connected to the Internet, and thereby to other institutions' intranets. This amplifies an institution's investment many times over and is at the heart of the collaborative possibilities inherent in the Internet. In contrast, it is not always possible to connect one institution's interactive video network to another's. There are neither standards nor a nationwide fabric of interconnection points to ensure sharing.

All of this means that an institutional intranet, which is obviously at the heart of any plan to reengineer administrative processes, can be also the key to restructuring instruction. Business and industry have historically pursued alternative instructional models in their education and training programs more aggressively than higher education (Apps, 1988). The time is right for higher education to experiment strategically with alternative models of instruction that draw on the Internet's communication technologies, information resources, and capacity to deliver interactive learning applications. The opportunity is to increase access to instruction, enhance the quality of students' learning, and reap a better overall return on investments in instruction.

Nonnetworked interactive learning applications have enjoyed a niche role in higher education for many years and have been demonstrated to improve the quality of students' learning. But stand-alone solutions do not provide a foundation for new instructional models. While "the network is the computer" may already be an overused phrase, it underscores a fundamental shift in the way information technologies are being used. The ability to share resources over an electronic network compresses time and tears down geographic barriers, allowing users to manipulate information almost infinitely. It is the network that enables the evolution of new learning paradigms.

The phrase *distributed instruction* implies a shift from today's institution-centered model of education to a society-centered model. It also captures the extended possibilities noted above and not implied today by the phrase *distance education*. Ultimately, accessibility to the global information infrastructure (the Internet) allows higher education to look at its services in a new context, which need not be from a strictly competitive perspective. The roles of academic institutions as both consumers of services and providers of services can be redefined. The individual institution need not be the sole owner of knowledge and talent in an environment in which resources can be shared (for a fee or not). Institutions can work together to provide "learning on demand" while retaining the valuable competitive institutional distinctions that guide and certify an individual's higher education. To create such an environment, the academy must confront its biases for the present model of service delivery and establish a solid course for navigating the transition between instructional paradigms.

There are four primary strategies for navigating this transition:

1. Focus on a major and costly educational problem within the institution or within a consortium of institutions—basic math skills, for example. There is lesser risk in trying new approaches to major problems that have resisted solution, and gains in such highly visible areas of the curriculum can seed innovation elsewhere.
2. Focus on those schools or departments that are ready to take leadership positions. Many professional schools and departments, such as business and the health-related academic units, understand the need to deploy IT in their outreach and continuing education programs.
3. Focus on the institutional continuing education service unit. These groups have understood the value of alternative instructional models for years. But many

are isolated from the institutional mainstream, so there is a danger that an investment in this direction might not pay off for the overall institution.

4. Focus on those instructors who are willing to try IT-based innovation. This has been tried at many institutions, and, as we note in more detail in the next section, it can result in *ad hoc*, individual successes. However, this approach seldom leads to overall institutional transformation.

Whatever strategy is deployed, key institutional players, long vested in established instructional models, need incentives to help develop effective alternatives. IT provides new leverage for higher education's most important asset: its intellectual capital, the faculty. Higher education must learn how the new technologies can enhance the social contract between learner, mentor, and institution. How can the bond between a faculty member and a student be strengthened while utilizing disintermediating information technologies to increase instructional productivity? Which aspects of learning can be best mediated directly by the faculty, and which can be mediated indirectly by interactive technologies? The challenge is not simply to open the eyes of participating faculty to new technologies and methodologies; faculty must be mobilized to redefine their profession in a rapidly changing world.

These transitions are not easy. Technologists alone cannot lead the way, as they did in creating the Internet. The development of a new learning infrastructure depends heavily on the willingness of faculty to embrace the transforming potential of IT, rather than perceiving it merely as a new window on an old instructional paradigm.

Integrating Technology

An understanding of the factors underlying the infusion of technologies serves academic institutions well as they seek to create environments in which the benefits of IT investments can be maximized. The following analysis shows why simply demonstrating the advantages of technology in an instructional environment is no guarantee of success. Asking questions such as "What kinds of technological knowledge are most common?" and "What major instructional problems are important to the institution and the discipline?" yields projects that are compatible with the institutional environment and therefore likely to yield the greatest return for the investment.

An analysis of two typical campus-based scenarios drawn from the authors' experience provides insights into the factors undergirding transformative practice. The first case is an award-winning mathematics software application designed to improve calculus problem-solving skills. The faculty member who created the application made the software diskettes readily available in the lab. Students practiced working problems and reported that the software helped. The instructor agreed and encouraged students by including a reference to the software in the course syllabus and by frequent reminders throughout the semester. Three years later, the computers were connected to a network, but a network-compatible version of the software was not purchased, and the software is no longer available.

Another institution uses a software package to facilitate writing in a foreign language. At first, students used the word processor and built-in language dictionary. Gradually, the instructor tailored assignments to the vocabulary and themes in the grammar aid and phrase guide. Over time, the faculty member restructured the introductory course to employ writing as an integral teaching strategy. With the aid of the software, students could begin writing after only a few weeks of introductory classes and continue throughout the course. Two years later, the computers were upgraded and attached to a network, and the latest networked version of the software was purchased. Instructors now employ a new network tracking system to monitor students' writing behaviors, analyze the log files, and advise students on how to improve their writing strategies.

Both innovations were put into routine use and provided some ongoing value; but why did one continue to improve the teaching process while the other did not? The answer, in part, lies in the concept of *infusion*, the degree to which an innovation becomes embedded in the individual's or organization's activities. The more deeply infused, the more the value of the innovation is realized (Zmud and Apple, 1992).

In the calculus example, the software was bolted onto existing practice. Even though it became routine and was a useful addition, its value as an integral part of instruction was deemed insufficient to merit continued use when expenses rose (the revamping of the lab). Members of an organization do not generally place a high value on innovations that retain a separate identity from the usual business of the organization, whether a single software package or a multimillion-dollar center (Curry, 1992). In the language scenario, however, the software was fully incorporated into the course, and the course and the introductory language curriculum were in turn shaped by the software. The instructor tailored assignments to the software's features and offered new advising services, enabled by information provided through the tracking system. If the software were to be discontinued, instructional objectives could not be met. The relative advantage and the value of the software increased over time by increasing the level of infusion.

The language scenario exhibits three levels of infusion: extended use, integrative use, and emergent use (Saga, 1993). The simplest level of infusion, extended use, means the adopter uses the innovation for more than the original purpose. More features of the technology are used to accomplish more tasks. Students use the software's topics and grammar tools in addition to the original dictionary and word-processing capabilities. Extending the software's use to other courses is another example.

The immediate benefits of extended use are likely to be decreased cost per task and increased efficiency in performing the new tasks. An important additional benefit is increased learning about the technology, which takes place through the new uses and potentially leads to greater levels of infusion.

Integrative use or innovation, the second level of infusion, means using the technology to establish or enhance work flow linkages among a set of work tasks. Essentially this means doing the same tasks in new ways (a frequent objective of total quality management programs). Integrative use yields efficiency gains with perhaps some increase in effectiveness. It requires a higher level of understanding of the tasks (why, rather than how) as well as the technology's features. In the language example, student writing is followed by instructor editing and correction of spelling, grammar, and vocabulary errors. As the students and instructors grow familiar with the software, students assume responsibility for correcting these mechanical errors and instructors review more substantive aspects of the writing.

The final stage, emergent use, or transformation, means using the technology to accomplish work tasks that were not feasible or recognized before the technology was applied to the work system. It reflects a change in the processes and strategies used to meet goals. The activities undertaken by the individual or unit change as the technology is fully incorporated into the fabric of work. On a large scale, this is equivalent to the somewhat overworked term *reengineering*. This level of integration produces the maximum benefit from technology investments. It is also the most complex, requiring a strategic understanding of core work processes and technology.

In the language scenario, the faculty members fully incorporate the language software into the instructional process. The software's features and its use are compatible with the objective to make writing a central activity in the program of instruction. In turn, instructors change the instructional process to accommodate the capabilities of the software. At that point in their coursework, students are unable to complete writing assignments without the software. By introducing previously unavailable information about a student's writing strategies, the tracking system changes the nature of faculty-student discourse about writing.

The calculus example, like many other instructional innovations undertaken on a much larger scale, failed to make a significant difference in the instructional process. To understand why infusion fails, three of the components in Saga's model (1993) are particularly worthy of further discussion here: management support, the organizational knowledge required to apply the technology in new and different ways, and IT maturity.

Most higher learning institutions have a very different organizational structure than businesses do. The former have both professional and bureaucratic characteristics and are often highly decentralized—an organization type Mintzberg (1979) characterizes as a professional bureaucracy. In a professional bureaucracy, the profession, not the institution, carries more weight in determining professional standing. While this is most obvious for research universities, the concept of management support in all institutions of higher education must be considered in two dimensions, the institution and the discipline.

Management support is most likely if IT is used to solve problems the institution and the discipline consider important. Perceptions of management support for technology use may also include rewards and recognition for what is traditionally an independent faculty activity. Diffusion theory tells us peer (institutional or discipline) approval, recognition, and rewards are more likely to be important for the large percentage who adopt an innovation later than for the innovators and early adopters (Rogers, 1983).

Infusion also requires organizational knowledge, an understanding of the procedures, processes, and contexts of the task at hand along with an understanding of the technology. For instructional innovations, this implies understanding both the subject matter and the learning processes. Technologist-led strategies for introducing technology in the past have tended to focus exclusively on improving the faculty's understanding of it. Faculty members are expert in content areas, but many know little about pedagogy. Institutional and professional rewards for research, or content expertise, and the difficulty in assessing instruction exacerbate the problem. To reconceptualize an educational task, a faculty member must know not only the subject matter but also something about learning: why particular strategies are appropriate and successful. He or she must not focus solely on the inputs, the content, but also on the learner outcomes and the processes necessary to achieve those results.

The third factor, IT maturity, includes two particularly key aspects: infrastructure development and diffusion of the underlying technology. Many large instructional workstation grant projects in the early 1980s provided examples of why infrastructure development is a critical factor in a failure to achieve infusion. These projects offered powerful examples of how technology could enhance teaching and learning, but they were not continued or were heavily modified when the grant funding ended (Hazen and Parker, 1989). The human, financial, and technical infrastructure that would provide continued support simply did not exist. Though the original investment was significant, the infrastructure at that time did not include funding for replacing equipment and software, nor did it include important technological underpinnings such as the pervasive high-speed interinstitutional networks needed for scholarly, discipline-based communication. In addition, much of the early work resulted in custom programmed software, and the ability to provide ongoing program maintenance did not exist.

Another important aspect of IT maturity is the need for a certain level of diffusion, or spread, of the underlying technology. Infrastructure is often developed in response to the spread of an innovation and in turn leads to further support. Widespread use also promotes a general understanding and acceptance of what technology can do.

Everett Rogers's theory (1983) of the diffusion of innovations offers an explanation for why instructional IT applications have not spread. The theory explains the process of adoption and spread of innovations through a social system. Groups of individual adopters exhibit certain typical, and very different, characteristics based on when they adopt the innovation. Rogers labels the first group to adopt as the innovators. Early adopters follow next, then early majority, late majority, and finally laggards, a group very reluctant to adopt an innovation if at all.

Many, if not most, of the technology initiatives of the past decade have been targeted to the innovators and early adopters. Equipment and software grants are a strategy attractive to those few but offer little in the way of the security, stability, and peer approval valued by the later adoption groups (Geoghegan, 1994). These later groups require different support strategies. They are much more risk-averse, are less tolerant of problems, and have different needs. Even a very gradual approach to technology infusion is likely to fail if there are no plans to support use, maintenance, and upgrading of the technology over time.

Management Strategies

To facilitate far-reaching changes in how faculty think about and utilize technology, it is necessary to recognize that support requirements vary among individuals, departments, and institutions. What management strategies are necessary to bring about these changes? While solutions must be crafted to suit specific environments, several general principles can be derived from the preceding analyses.

- *Academic versus administrative.* IT by nature is neither academic nor administrative; it is pervasive in its reach, serving all aspects of the institution's mission and operations. The new technologies are now strategic tools: enablers of totally new academic and administrative models. The officer with responsibility for central IT must be perceived as neutral, without bias toward either academic or administrative priorities but with knowledge of and a firm commitment to both.
- *Distributed support.* Later adopters require assistance by others more closely allied to their discipline. For large institutions, this means a distributed support

structure, with individuals housed within schools and units reporting to the unit, a central organization, or both. For smaller schools, the need may be met by discipline-area specialists within a central organization. These individuals serve as information conduits, guides, and interpreters.

- *Specialized support.* The diversity of knowledge required for infusion implies a need for technology and pedagogy specialists to support the work of the content experts, the faculty. These are pan-institutional or "regional" skills, most efficiently provided by central, or large discipline-area, organizations.

- *Institutional support.* Institutional legitimacy for faculty use of technology and investment in technology infrastructure must derive from vision and priorities conveyed by central academic leadership.

- *Central coordination.* Infrastructure and information technology diffusion cannot be managed or sustained by either local organizations or multiple central organizations. Infusion of technology into instruction requires significant resources, planning, coordination, and priority setting to provide the robust foundation upon which other specialists and individual efforts may build.

The increasing complexity and pervasive utilization of IT on campuses has led many academic institutions to shift from a focus on technology to a broader focus on people, services, and information along with the technology. With the expanded focus, there has been a requisite involvement in meeting institutional goals, as well as a shift in reporting levels, from at least three levels below the president (twenty years ago) to the highest decision-making levels on campus. At the same time, these forces support consolidation of the various central IT organizations into a single unit. The rationale behind these two organizational shifts is elaborated in the following paragraphs.

The University of North Carolina at Chapel Hill's recent reaccreditation report (Task Force on Educational Support Services, 1994) indicated that as "centralized" computing services become obsolete the need for "central" management becomes more acute. It suggested that management decide on priorities, assign responsibilities, avoid unproductive competition and needless duplication, achieve economies of scale where possible, and encourage appropriate change.

The demand for IT and its support is rising, both at the central and the unit levels. For this reason and others, such as the geographical distribution of various IT support units, there may be no immediate cost savings in moving to a unified management structure for central support units. But unifying the management of our central units is the best mechanism for avoiding duplicative efforts and for seeking long-term economies and productivity gains. Creating distributed institutional information repositories and digital archives, and moving toward wireless communication, for example, requires a managed team effort to avoid the costs of duplication and multiple standards. The benefits of unified management are more fully realized as existing boundaries drawn along the division of labor within our institutions are made obsolete by network-facilitated resource sharing (Ward, 1994).

Today's technologies are rapidly changing and offer many different options. A rapid-response process for adjudicating technical issues is needed to keep pace with technical changes and ensure institutionwide standards. This should be the responsibility of one central officer, not many. In some institutions, it is the president's responsibility by extension. It should, however, be the responsibility of an IT professional. The units should be able to turn to one central office to coordinate their IT planning efforts and to seek assistance in implementing their plans—designing and installing networks, for example. Otherwise, isolated units will tend to bolt technology onto old, familiar models in their domains of interest.

Almost all units require IT support, and it is critical that a proper balance between central and unit-level investments be achieved. Central investments should provide leverage for unit-level investments, but this happens only if there is an inclusive mechanism for IT planning. Planning for change also entails coming to grips with the downside of success: a seemingly insatiable demand for IT resources.

Financing the IT Investment

A sound plan for IT infrastructure and academic change must recognize the bottom line by connecting to the institutional budget in a way that reflects the true costs of technology infusion. This requires involvement of the senior administration—the chief executive, academic, financial, and planning officers—along with trustees and other politically important supporters. No technical or pedagogical problem involved is any more daunting than the bottom line. The technology revolution does not come cheap. Until the business case is quantified and verified, the promise of using information technologies to realize anticipated benefits remains just that: a promise.

The first step is to understand that the total value of IT is greater than the sum of its parts. To the extent that it functions in aggregate like an ecosystem, much of its value grows exponentially as its richness is increased. For example, the value of a departmental e-mail system is greatly enhanced if the entire campus community is also on the network. The value of technology investments may be best described as a continuous step function; the challenge for planners is to target the specific level of functionality desired and identify the minimum investments needed to produce those quantum returns.

There is no practical or predictable limit to the demand for IT. The record of academic institutions is littered with examples of technology at every level—

desktop PCs, departmental servers, campus networks, and shared regional super-computers—that have become functionally obsolete long before their hardware stopped working. The reason for this is simple: successful implementation almost always creates new demand and expectations that grow exponentially. Consider, for example, the implementation of a marginally effective e-mail system or networking environment on campus. Initially, the service is not utilized fully, but history shows that once a system becomes functionally viable there is an explosion in the number of users and the level of usage. The result is an increase in demand and an increase in total cost as more equipment is needed and better support and training become an imperative. Emerging technologies almost certainly repeat this pattern. For this reason, capacity analysis is increasingly a waste of time for long-term planning. The challenge is instead to accept exponential growth in demand for technology as a given and work to develop financial and management strategies to address it.

Computing systems have never been cheaper; the price of computing is halved no less often than every three years. Even so, the total cost of owning and using that technology appears to be rising. More sophisticated systems require more technical support, more training, more peripherals, and more time. The *price* of technology is what one pays to purchase it. The *cost* of technology includes the price as well as all the other expenses associated with owning and operating it.

Investing in IT involves more than just cost considerations. For instance, assessing the business case for central systems versus distributed computing environments is not solely a cost issue, nor is it a value issue. It is instead a cost/benefit issue. In the most extreme case, it seems safe to predict that central computing will prevail over distributed computing by using strict total-cost analysis. The problem is that technology should not be considered just as an expense. It is an investment in both the goals of the institution as well as the individuals charged with advancing them. No dean or department head would fill a faculty vacancy based solely on the fact that one applicant might be less expensive than another. It would be equally ridiculous to make investment decisions for technology based solely on cost. The challenge for planners is to know the cost/benefit trade-offs so that the best possible decisions can be made. Stated differently, the financial decision should not be based on minimizing cost, but instead on maximizing the net return of the investment.

The economics of IT are distinct from other capital assets with which finance and business professionals are trained to deal. For example, we can compare the financial economics of buying a computer to that of buying a truck. If the physical plant purchases a $25,000 truck with an expected life of five years, it has a capital cost of $5,000 per year. At the end of five years, the truck will be replaced by a new truck that will cost more but still be functionally identical. One way to help make this investment yield a higher return is to invest more in maintenance and to amortize the cost over more years. Computers, on the other hand, are very different. For example, if the physics department purchases a $25,000 computer and amortizes the expense over five years it also costs $5,000 per year. The difference comes when considering the economics of replacing this machine. The physics department is able to spend significantly less on a replacement computer and still receive a new computer that is orders of magnitude superior to the one it is replacing. This changes the equation fundamentally.

Given the superior performance of the replacement machine, its lower cost, and the anticipated increased demand, the whole premise of evaluating this investment like that of the truck seems silly. In fact, a strong argument can be made to turn the model on its ear. Increasing the amortization period for technology investments may actually make the investment decision worse. Instead of buying the biggest computer necessary to do the job for the next five years, a compelling argument would be to consider buying the smallest computer that would do the job for the next three years. The question is, would the physics department be better off buying a $25,000 computer for five years, or a $15,000 computer and replacing it after three years? It seems obvious that the second case is superior. It has the same annual cost, but the department gets the benefit of replacing it with a superior machine for less money after only three years instead of five. In cases where this is true, the rule of thumb for making computer purchases is to adopt a life-cycle model where you buy as little as possible and keep it for as short a time as possible.

If the cost/benefit outcome for IT is improving, it is inevitable that institutions will spend an increasing proportion of their budgets on it. Any organization in a competitive environment is forced over time to invest its money in areas where the return is greatest. In the case of IT, where it pays to invest today, it will pay even greater dividends to invest more tomorrow. Higher education has to spend more money on IT simply because it yields a greater benefit.

The paradox of planning for IT is dealing with the rate of change. In times of rapid architectural and technical change, when the need for a viable plan is greatest, the tendency is to abandon planning because of the belief that the changing environment makes planning impossible. While planning in this environment is difficult, it is not impossible. For starters, if the one thing that is known with certainty is that the technology will change, then the one thing that must be planned for is change. This is the first tenet of the financial game plan: to plan for change. Any financial strategy that makes change difficult or slow is likely to suboptimize, or even undermine, the investments that are dependent on it.

The second tenet is to tell the whole truth and nothing but the truth. The value of IT is increasing, demand appears unlimited, and prices are declining, but total costs are rising. There are very big benefits, but there will also be big expenses. This is likely the most misunderstood and misrepresented aspect of the future of IT. It costs a lot today and will cost even more in the future. Institutions must plan to spend more money on IT if they are to maximize its benefits. Superior strategies focus on architectures and implementations that build synergy and avoid redundancy. In this sense they offer opportunities for cost avoidance, but not cost reduction.

The third tenet is to position the financial problem within the institution at the appropriate level. Central computing authorities need to collaborate with their departmental counterparts to make the case for IT, but only the senior administration is actually able to solve the related financial problems. Campuses need support and understanding at these senior levels before they can proceed. If funding levels remain steady or if there is downsizing, financial pressures become more acute. At any rate, the case for IT is that it is a long-run investment in the competitive standing and productivity of the institution. It does not compete with personnel. It is a necessary investment in human potential as well as a part of the university's benefit package.

The decision to invest in educational technologies is often restrained by using either conventional methods of capital investment analysis or no analysis at all. When a formal analysis is done, the value of technology is almost always underestimated because of a hesitancy to include anything but the most directly obvious benefits. Higher education needs to expand its level of sophistication when making these decisions. A logical start would be to consider the above-stated tenets of strategic cost analysis of technological investments in order to better understand both the total value and financial impact of these investments (Shank and Govindarajan, 1992).

Shank and Govindarajan argue that traditional methods of financial analysis need to be extended to a more holistic assessment that includes three strategic considerations. The first is *value-chain analysis,* where the value chain for an organization is the sequence of value-creating activities from basic raw materials from service suppliers to the ultimate end-use product/service delivered to consumers. If the student is both raw material and finished product, the value chain includes content delivery, mentoring, advising, and a host of other academic activities and resources that contribute to the student's "higher education." The second strategic consideration is *cost-driver analysis,* where the emphasis is on understanding the structural cost drivers that relate to an organization's explicit strategic choices regarding economic structure scale, service complexity, scope of operations, or experience. In this analysis, technology investments represent structural choices about how to compete and deliver services. The last is *competitive-advantage analysis.* In the strategic cost management paradigm, understanding the implications of how the firm chooses to compete is critically important. In this case, the strategic choice is usually between low cost or product differentiation. For higher education, these are the variables that differentiate one institution from another and that determine the "street value" of an institution's graduates, its research, and its public services.

Does IT pay? If it does, where is the biggest pay-off? Again, a logical target of applying IT is in the teaching and learning process, which represents a significant portion of the operating budget of academic institutions. If 80 percent of the operating budget lies in these activities, even large investments in IT have the potential to be cost-effective. However, the long-term pay-off can only be maximized if the investments made are consistent with an institution's well-planned overall goals.

Planning for Information Technology

Information technologies are rarely integrated successfully without some substantial structural changes in the campus culture and operating environment (Gilbert and Green, 1995). Institutions that continue to resist these structural changes will not realize significant benefits from the new technologies. Obstacles are certain to emerge during this transformation; this suggests a gradual process that is closely tied to the planning function. Each institution must reevaluate its vision on new terms, questioning even the most fundamental aspects of its structure and mission in the context of technology-driven opportunity. This is more likely to happen if a broadly knowledgeable IT professional with academic credentials and administrative experience manages all central technology support offices and is a party to the senior councils in which directions are determined. The need is for a chief technology strategist, rather than a chief technologist. Without such a management and advisory presence, many IT-enabled opportunities for constructive change and new forms of excellence may pass without notice.

In addition to the participation of an institutional technology officer, IT planning should have three primary components:

1. A long-term strategic framework for prioritizing and funding those uses of technology which are most strategic to the institution's mission
2. A continuously evolving IT architecture (in analogy with a standards-based building code) and a more specific and tactical technology blueprint (a central implementation of the architecture) to guide purchase of information technologies and provision of attendant technology services at all levels of the institution
3. A collaborative process for ensuring that the strategic framework informs the IT architecture and the technology blueprint

In other words, technology planning is not solely about developing a plan for managing and utilizing centrally purchased technologies. Much of the responsibility for technology planning lies outside the central technology organization(s). The strategic framework, for example, must be developed, funded, and monitored in collaboration with the leadership of mission-critical academic and administrative units. Even the IT architecture and the central technology blueprint itself must have the confidence of, and therefore input from, any independent technology support organizations. These include a range of mission-critical units, such as the libraries, the schools and colleges in a large institution, and various administrative offices.

An institutional technology officer can facilitate an attempt to link technology as a tool to issues and initiatives strategic to the institution's future: new instructional models, new student services models, and new business process models, for example. But only the chief executive and academic officers can ensure the involvement of academic and administrative leaders in identifying institutionally strategic needs and the funding to meet them. In this regard, there are many mechanisms for connecting IT spending and implementation to mission, but the key is to create a mechanism to provide a sounding board for IT priorities and to advise the institutional technology officer on how to structure a collaborative process that takes into account mission-critical issues and needs while identifying the financial resources required to meet those needs.

The institutional technology officer also must give IT leaders from across the campus a voice in designing the IT architecture and implementing the technology blueprint. In addition to convening this group of technologists and creating a strategic mechanism for connecting the technologists' planning to mission-critical needs and directions, organizing customer focus sessions can be useful when they are constituted and convened as needed to address a range of specific service and application areas.

It is important to understand that the central technology blueprint has to be constantly adjusted, both in its scale to keep pace with unprecedented and often unpredictable demand and in its implementation to keep pace with changes in technology. The institution's technology environment is going to be in constant evolution for the foreseeable future, exacerbating the need to ensure the participation of decision makers from mission-critical academic and administrative units in formulating the strategic framework for deploying technology.

As we describe it, IT planning is almost tantamount to institutional planning. Consider the issues that we raise or imply throughout this chapter. For example, how should the center of campus be configured to serve the future goals of the institution? Which students need to be on campus, to what extent, and when? Can anytime-anywhere Internet communications increase the frequency and quality of faculty/student contact and decrease dependence on the rigid, labor-intensive contact hour and thus on the classroom? Consider the emergence of new educational service providers and their impact on the institution's mission-critical competencies. Will commercially delivered courses and on-demand learning enabled by digital technologies allow some institutions of higher learning to concentrate on the synthesizing aspects of general education? Will some academic institutions move away from instruction in basic skills by insisting on externally certified competence in these skills as a condition of admission? IT planning raises all of these issues if such planning is connected to mission, as it should be.

Underlying assumptions about the future of our institutions must be challenged through comprehensive planning and proactive leadership. Institutions of higher learning that awaken too late to the need for a new model on which to base delivery of instructional services will be in trouble. The development and adoption of new instructional models is not painless, and it does not happen overnight. Most academic executives are aware that the problems facing their institutions do not beg short-term solutions, but few have seriously challenged the culture of traditional instruction. While higher education leaders hesitate to act as partners to create a national educational fabric, viable alternatives to the present model of institution-based education are presenting themselves, and higher education as an institution may be hard-pressed to compete.

Conclusion

The limitations of the contact-hour model of instruction are becoming evident just as IT is emerging as a dominant change agent throughout our society. Many in higher education complain that the pressures brought to bear by the simultaneous rise of these two forces may be too much for higher education to contend with. We believe that the timing could not be more fortuitous for higher education, and that IT is the foundation on which new models of education service delivery are to be built.

Transition between paradigms is not easy. IT investments undermine efforts to contain costs in the short term, and strong leadership is needed to overcome cultural, political, and technical obstacles that present themselves along the way. On the other hand, the forces eroding the underpinnings of our old models are not to be turned back. In an environment where change is inevitable, those institutions which manage change most effectively will position themselves most favorably for the future.

Further Reading

Robert Heterick (1993) sounded an important call to connect IT to instruction; his work ultimately led to EDUCOM's National Learning Infrastructure Initiative (NLII). The conceptual framework for the NLII was first outlined by Graves (1993, 1994) and then fully articulated by Twigg (1994a, 1994b, 1994c). The NLII was launched in late 1994; Oblinger and Maruyama (1996) have described the essence of the collective thinking that is shaping it as a national movement.

A wealth of information on higher education technology management and organizational issues can be found in the publications of higher education's IT management professional association, CAUSE. These include CAUSE/EFFECT, a practitioner's journal, and publications cosponsored with other associations such as the HEIRAlliance Executive Strategies Series (1992–1995). Oberlin has two articles (1996a, 1996b) that expose many of the legacy misunderstandings about IT investments. The Gartner Group, Inc., is an excellent source of information on the true cost of owning and maintaining information technology environments (Gartner Group, 1993). John K. Shank and Vijay Govindarajan have written on the concept of strategic cost management (1993). Michael J. Earl and David F. Feeney (1994) have an excellent article on the strategic role of chief information officers.

References

Apps, J. W. *Higher Education in a Learning Society.* San Francisco: Jossey-Bass, 1988.

Curry, B. K. *Instituting Enduring Innovations.* ASHE-ERIC Higher Education Report. George Washington University, 1992.

Earl, M., and Feeney, D. F. "Is Your CIO Adding Value?" *Sloan Management Review,* 1994, *35*(3), 11–20.

Gartner Group. "Total Cost of Ownership." *Management Strategies: PC Cost/Benefit and Payback Analysis,* 1993, 36.

Geoghegan, W. H. "Stuck at the Barricades: Can Information Technology Really Enter the Mainstream of Teaching and Learning?" *AAHE Bulletin,* 1994, *47*(1), 13–16.

Gilbert, S. W., and Green, K. C. "Great Expectations: Content, Communications, Productivity, and the Role of Information Technology in Higher Education." *Change,* 1995, *27*(2), 8–18.

Graves, W. H. "Educational Ecosystem of Information and Computation: Medium and Message." *EDUCOM Review,* 1993, *28*(5), 7–12. http://ike.engr.washington.edu/iat/director/graves.html

Graves, W. H. "Toward a National Learning Infrastructure." *EDUCOM Review,* 1994, *29*(2), 32–37. http://www.educom.edu/educom.review/review.94/mar.apr/graves_article

Hazen, M., and Parker, A. S. "Instructional Computing at the University of North Carolina at Chapel Hill." In W. H. Graves (ed.), *Computing Across the Curriculum: Academic Perspectives.* Reading, Mass.: Addison-Wesley, 1989.

HEIRAlliance Executive Strategies Series. Boulder, Colo.: CAUSE, 1992–1995.

Heterick, R. C., Jr. *Reengineering Teaching and Learning in Higher Education: Sheltered Groves, Camelot, Windmills, and Malls.* CAUSE Professional Paper Series, no. 10. Boulder, Colo.: CAUSE, 1993. http://cause-www.colorado.edu/information-resources/ir-library/abstracts/pub3010.html

Mintzberg, H. *The Structuring of Organizations.* Englewood Cliffs, N.J.: Prentice Hall, 1979.

Oberlin J. "The Financial Mythology of Information Technology: Developing a New Game Plan." *CAUSE/EFFECT,* 1996a, *19*(2), 10–17.

Oberlin, J. "The Financial Mythology of Information Technology: The New Economics." *CAUSE/EFFECT,* 1996b, *19*(1), 21–29.

Oblinger, D. G., and Maruyama, M. K. "Transforming Instruction in Preparation for a High Bandwidth NII." *Monterey Conference Proceedings: September 1995. Higher Education and the NII: From Vision to Reality.* 1996, Washington, D.C.: EDUCOM.

Pew Higher Education Roundtable. "To Dance with Change." *Policy Perspectives,* 1994, *5*(3), 1A–12A.

Rogers, E. M. *Diffusion of Innovations.* New York: Free Press, 1983.

Saga, V. "The Nature and Determinants of IT Infusion." Dissertation proposal, Department of Information and Management Sciences, Florida State University, 1993.

Shank, J. K., and Govindarajan, V. "Strategic Cost Analysis of Technological Investments." *Sloan Management Review,* 1992, *34*(1), 39–51.

Shank, J. K., and Govindarajan, V. *Strategic Cost Management: The New Tool for Competitive Advantage.* New York: Free Press, 1993.

Task Force on Educational Support Services. "Final Draft Report." University Reaccreditation Office, University of North Carolina at Chapel Hill, 1994.

Twigg, C. A. "The Changing Definition of Learning." *EDUCOM Review,* 1994a, *29*(4), 23–25. http://www.educom.edu/educom.review/review.94/jul.aug/Twigg_Article

Twigg, C. A. "Navigating the Transition." *EDUCOM Review,* 1994b, *29*(6), 20–24. http://www.educom.edu/educom.review/review.94/nov.dec/twigg

Twigg, C. A. "The Need for a National Learning Infrastructure." *EDUCOM Review,* 1994c, *29*(5), 16–20. http://www.educom.edu/educom.review/review.94/sept.oct/Twigg_Article

Ward, D. "Technology and the Changing Boundaries of Higher Education." *Educom Review,* 1994, *29*(1), 24–27.

Zmud, R., and Apple, E. "Measuring Technology Incorporation/Infusion." *Journal of Product Innovation Management,* 1992, *9*(2), 148–155.

CHAPTER TWENTY-THREE

RESTRUCTURING THE ACADEMIC ENVIRONMENT

Patricia J. Gumport and Brian Pusser

This chapter addresses contemporary challenges facing managers of the higher education enterprise in a period of fiscal constraint with attendant demands for cost containment and accountability. While dramatic in impact, the challenges are not unprecedented. Over the past fifty years, university planners have played a central role in campus adaptation to shifting environmental demands at a number of critical junctures. That environmental demands have often been a force shaping the structure and policy of higher education does not mean that those demands have been consistent or predictable. Contextual demands over the last half century have ranged from calls for a dramatic expansion of enrollments and sponsored research activities to mandated retrenchment and program consolidation.

The approaches adopted by university planners have varied depending upon the nature of the demands. Familiar examples include managing enrollment shifts in the 1970s (Cheit, 1973), strategic planning for an uncertain resource environment in the 1980s (Hearn, 1988), and retrenchment initiatives in response to a changing economy in the 1990s (Hanson and Meyerson, 1990; Cole, 1993; Massy, 1993). Despite the range of contextual factors and demands, managerial imperatives for university adaptation have generally conveyed a sense of urgency, particularly in response to demands to limit or actually contract growth. Contemporary initiatives designed to position higher education institutions for life after retrenchment represent the latest draw from a familiar array of initiatives that attempt to reallocate resources according to the most current administrative perceptions of political economic priorities.

This chapter examines those planning deliberations that have most recently emerged under the name "academic restructuring." Our focus is on research universities, although the restructuring initiatives we discuss are applicable to, and have powerful consequences for, each segment of the postsecondary system. We examine the literature, and the proposals that address how universities should best respond to emerging challenges.

In essence, observers argue that the current pace of environmental change, resource constraints, market demands, and technological developments present unprecedented challenges for research universities. The emerging premise is that postsecondary institutions must now consider the redesign of core academic structures and processes. Demands for academic restructuring grow out of a postretrenchment context that assumes significant administrative cuts have already been made. We suggest later in this chapter that universities must move beyond administrative cuts, to rethinking the nature of administrative work in the postretrenchment environment (Barley, 1996).

Given the urgency of the contemporary calls for academic restructuring, it is useful to put the contemporary context in historical perspective. Just as this is not the first time observers and stakeholders have called for urgent reform in higher education, it is also not the first time such calls have been driven by the perception of financial constraints. Nor are such corollary contemporary rationales for reform as increased competition, changing demographics, and dire enrollment forecasts particularly novel. What is arguably new is the convergence of so many of these contextual demands at one time. As a result, the contemporary environment in which research universities operate has become extremely turbulent (Cameron and Tschirhart, 1992; Dill, 1993–94; Dill and Sporn, 1995a), and the word *restructuring* has become, in many arenas of education, a magic incantation (Tyack, 1990).

One of the planning issues we address in this chapter concerns whether initial university responses to fiscal constraint have contributed to the environmental turbulence universities face today. At the end of the last decade, university managers began to forestall the impact of fiscal constraints, particularly declines in state appropriations for higher education, through ad hoc planning (Gumport, 1993), tuition increases (Griswold and Marine, 1996), and cost-plus pricing and budget discipline (Zemsky and Massy, 1990; Pew Higher Education Roundtable, 1993a). Initial institutional responses to declines in external revenue sources at once delayed the full impact of revenue shifts while at the same time generating additional stress. The short-term solutions of raising tuition and ad hoc cost cutting contributed to increasing conflict with state legislatures and created additional political economic pressure on the institutions, as in the cases of Virginia and California (Breneman, 1995). Given accelerating calls for institutional restructuring and increased legislative intervention in higher education policy and planning, the issue of university autonomy moves to the fore. Without a careful approach to demands for restructuring, postsecondary institutions of all types are in danger of losing control of the transformations that must be made in response to increasing environmental demands (Pew Higher Education Roundtable, 1993b, 1993c).

Our analysis of the emerging literature on academic restructuring reveals a shift in the conceptualization of higher education institutions. Environmental demands have shifted from asking the university to do what it does for less money to asking the university to change what it does. The contemporary question is not whether higher education can continue business-as-usual given increased environmental turmoil; rather, the question is what sort of universities will emerge from adaptation to these inexorable demands.

In the first section of this chapter, we describe the factors that have led to the current planning challenges. Second, we sketch the demands for change. Third, we examine the nature of emerging restructuring initiatives, particularly those proposals drawn from management literature on organizational redesign, and their implications for core academic processes. Finally, we suggest what makes such academic restructuring problematic, particularly the limitations on applying a corporate analogy to academic purposes and processes.

Historical Antecedents

In the past century, higher education has been transformed by a relatively steady expansion of functions and structures, resulting in markedly increased enrollments and research capability. While there are many perspectives on what drives adaptation of complex organizations (Powell and Friedkin, 1987), in this chapter we focus on differentiation and adaptation driven by environmental demands (Pfeffer and Salancik, 1978). By taking this perspective, we are able to examine a variety of managerial initiatives ranging from adaptation for facilitating expansion to retrenchment for times of fiscal constraint.

Decades of university growth in the post–World War II era have been driven in part by what Burton Clark describes as the accretion of environmental demands for complexity: "With each passing decade a modern or modernizing system of higher education is expected and inspired to do more for other portions of society, organized and unorganized, from strengthening the economy and invigorating government to developing individual talents and personalities and aiding the pursuit of happiness. We also ask that this sector of society do more in its own behalf in fulfilling such grand and expanding missions as conserving the cultural heritage and producing knowledge. This steady accretion of realistic expectations cannot be stopped, let alone reversed" (Clark, 1993, p. 263).

Clark's characterization enables us to account for two levels of historical developments: change at the national system level (the expansion of institutions into diverse segments with differentiated missions) and change at the campus level (the expansion of missions to take on more functions, with the ensuing elaboration of complex structures). California provides a useful case of the complexity proposition. Higher education in California grew as part of an overall expansion fueled by the GI Bill (Kerr, 1987). The state system was formally segmented by the Master Plan for Higher Education in 1960 into three tiers: the University of California system, the California State University system, and the state community college system. Over time, each segment adapted its mission to do more, with the original land-grant University of California at Berkeley developing into a type of complex institution that Clark Kerr later characterized as the "multiversity" (1994, 1963). At both system and campus levels, the adaptation to complexity entailed budgetary growth; administrative growth; and expansion of enrollments, academic programs, and research activities. Given the relatively steady expansion of resources for higher education in California, few university administrators faced the formidable task of setting priorities under fiscal constraint (Gumport and Pusser, 1995).

The adaptive capacity of a higher education system and the structural elaboration of higher education organizations must be accounted for with reference to not only what changes but how and by whom. Two classic concepts from sociological theory enable us to understand the nature of those adaptive processes: differentiation and authority. With regard to differentiation, over time an organization's units are expected to divide into smaller, functional units of academic specialization (Durkheim, 1933; Blau, 1970). A parallel trend is said to occur with regard to personnel, where positions and work responsibilities proliferate. How the expanding enterprise is to be coordinated, and by whom, varies depending on how authority is institutionalized and formalized in rules (Weber, 1947; Zhou, 1993). Accompanying the structural differentiation in an organizational hierarchy is a social differentiation among groups and among positions based on resources, prestige, and power (Blau, 1973). The integration of these parts into a whole is presumably to be ensured by structural and procedural interdependence, as well as by professional and administrative authority (Clark, 1983; Etzioni, 1964).

Applying these concepts, we can see how decision-making processes within complex and expanding universities entailed significant challenges from rapidly changing environmental demands and ambiguous goals, as well as from the structural decentralization of academic responsibility to faculty (Ikenberry, 1971). That decentralization and the attendant deference to faculty expertise at the operating levels of departments was intended to ensure effectiveness and academic legitimacy. Differentiation and expansion enabled both faculty and university administrators to make fewer selective choices among valued activities, a luxury their contemporaries do not enjoy (Gumport and Pusser, 1995). The long period of expansion and differentiation may also have shaped a somewhat unrealistic perception of collegiality and shared governance, a proposition we address in the final section of this chapter.

By the 1970s, there was a growing sense of strain in universities: a recognition that expansion was not limitless, and that bureaucratic authority was not immune to breakdown. The perception in that era was that, given projected resource shifts, management's role was to shape structure (Balderston, 1974) and coordinate work flow and procedures in light of emerging concepts of efficiency and effectiveness, and to do so with an awareness of the limitations of planning models (Fincher, 1972).

Both conceptually and operationally, this planning approach gained currency through the decade of the 1970s and was proposed for both administrative and academic programs. Forecasts of enrollment declines and changing economic conditions prompted planners to engage in detailed academic priority setting. This required two stages: determining the overall inventory of academic programs, and prioritizing those programs (Shirley and Volkwein, 1978). The mission statement was given additional prominence in the planning process (Fuller, 1976), particularly in deliberations over quality and centrality, while program cost became an increasingly important factor. The result was a growing demand for planning that integrated decision making on academic priorities with decision making on resource allocation.

Into the 1980s, the activities of university management continued to focus on planning, and increasingly on strategic planning for linking goals and resources in an uncertain and complex environment. Economic perspectives and lessons from the for-profit sector were offered to university managers for their thinking about costs, revenue streams, market considerations, and the deployment of human resources to achieve goals (Hearn, 1988), although additional political and social considerations specific to the academic arena were offered for conceptualizing retrenchment in the 1980s (Mortimer and Tierney, 1979; Mingle and Associates, 1981; Keller, 1983; Hyatt, Shulman, and Santiago, 1984; Barak, 1984). Scanning the environment and evaluating revenue sources were two important foci of analysis (Cope, 1978; Hearn, 1988; Cope and Delaney, 1991). Resource allocation reform designed to preserve excellence under retrenchment was seen as a central component of university management (Hyatt, Shulman, and Santiago, 1984; Massy, 1994). Cost containment and the preservation of quality were key guides to the development of indicators and benchmarks of performance for institutions and their subunits. Such planning efforts were at times focused on particular fields of study, as in the case of reorganizing the biological sciences at UC Berkeley (Trow, 1983).

By the close of the 1980s, a number of economic problems for higher education had been identified as continuing challenges. Tuition escalation (Gladieux, Hauptman, and Knapp, 1994; Griswold and Marine, 1996), rising administrative costs (Leslie and Rhoades, 1995), and low productivity (Anderson and Meyerson, 1992) were often addressed, while innovative financial management strategies were sought to close the gap between the long-run growth rates of expense and revenue. The perspective of many planners was expressed in a decision rule for competitive institutional advancement: expand an activity as long as marginal value plus marginal revenue exceeds marginal cost (Hopkins and Massy, 1981). It was widely agreed that, as financial stress increased, more precise alignment of resource-dependent relationships would be a key strategy.

The nature of proposals for university realignment that emerged depended on whether the conceptualization and subsequent adaptation were guided by processes adopted from the for-profit sector (Guskin 1994a, 1994b; Mohrman, 1993; Dill and Sporn, 1995b), emerging networks similar to multinationals (Bartlett and Ghoshal, 1989; Ghoshal and Nohria, 1993), or principles inherent in the management of nonprofits (Oster, 1995; Albert and Whetten, 1985). The adoption of restructuring practices developed in for-profit, particularly corporate, settings, has become a central vehicle for the transition to contemporary university frameworks. However, this transition is not without its critics. As James (1990, p.77) pointed out, economic decision processes and priorities are based on assumptions that "clearly do not hold" for American colleges and universities. We revisit this point in more detail in the final section of this chapter.

Calls for Reform

By the early 1990s widespread fiscal challenges, particularly in state economies, prompted university planning literature to attend to shifting environmental demands. A recognition of a changing competitive context, environmental turbulence, and shifting demands led scholars and observers to suggest reforming delivery processes in order to better attune them to costs, quality, and markets (Guskin 1994a, 1994b; Pew Higher Education Roundtable, 1993a, 1994; Dill 1993–94; Dill and Sporn, 1995a). In this context, demands called for institutional redesign, with goals of lower costs and better student learning, more attention to teaching, and direct contributions to regional economic development (Guskin, 1994b; Massy and Zemsky, 1994; Southern Regional Education Board, 1994). Demands for teaching students more effectively at lower costs occurred across the higher education system and were assimilated under the banners of increased quality, productivity, and efficiency in higher education (Anderson and Meyerson, 1992; Massy, 1994).

The push for quality and efficiency arises from demands for response to resource constraints. In the early 1990s, public universities at every level faced declines in state appropriations, a fundamental source of revenue, to a degree unprecedented in the post–World War II era. Private and public universities alike were feeling a significant financial pinch, from a pattern of costs surpassing inflation and economic recession (Zemsky and Massy, 1990; Cole, 1993). At the time of this writing, a consensus is building among scholars and administrators of higher education that unlike the demands for retrenchment of the eighties, the political economic demands for change that are reflected in declining state appropriations are part of a structural shift in funding for higher education that goes beyond belt-tightening and is unlikely to be restored in the event of general economic recovery (Barrow, 1993; Cole, 1993; Kennedy, 1993; Pew Higher Education Roundtable, 1993b). As Zemsky and Massy have observed, "cost containment is much more than cost-cutting. Each of these institutions seeks a basic shifting of priorities along with substantial administrative redesign. They want to be not just leaner, but actually different institutions—more flexible, more able to focus their investments, simpler in their organization and management" (1990, p. 22).

University planners have had particular difficulty in coping with contemporary revenue shifts, as they have been accompanied by a multitude of contradictory, and often expensive, political economic demands generated by an array of competing interest groups (March and Olsen, 1995). These demands include insistence that access be preserved and enrollments increased, calls for cuts in outreach and moratoriums on new construction, demands for increased institutional revenue generation and limits on tuition and fee increases, promotion of privatization initiatives and calls for a return to essential land-grant missions, demands for new programmatic offerings, and, of course, demands to reduce higher education costs.

This attention to the magnitude and nature of costs in higher education has forced planners to focus on two fundamental questions: "Are we doing things right?" and "Are we doing the right things?" The former question has been given additional urgency by the emergence of, and increasing demand for, new technologies for evaluating and delivering educational products and services. A number of observers have begun to identify emerging possibilities for reorganizing administrative operations as well as for redesigning core academic processes, such as teaching and learning (Guskin, 1994a, 1994b; Pew, 1993c, 1994; Peterson, 1995) with enhanced, electronic, and interactive technologies. The goal is to apply new technological competencies to reduce the cost of production and consequently to educate more students without additional funding.

The question "Are we doing the right things?" has led planners to reconsider organizational identity (Albert and Whetten, 1985) and the future market for higher education in every sector. Some observers have noted that we are entering a new era of competitiveness (Cameron and Tschirhart, 1992; Stigler, 1993; Dill and Sporn, 1995a; Clark, 1995) accompanied by increasing student demand for marketable skills. This trend, as it attempts to match student "educational consumption" patterns with a rapidly changing national job market, has been characterized as a "new vocationalism" (Pew Higher Education Roundtable, 1993a, 1993b). In this arena, it is useful to note an important distinction between responding to direct student demand and planning to prepare students for a rapidly changing world (Jessop, 1993). We return to this point at the conclusion of this chapter.

A corollary aspect of the demand for new efficiencies and greater productivity is the growing interest among university planners in reorganization strategies adopted from corporations in highly competitive arenas. When applied to higher education, these strategies address a range of organizational processes that challenge how decisions are made, how information is shared, how students are taught, how students learn, how faculty work, how research is conducted and subsequently developed for marketing, and how auxiliary enterprises are managed (Peterson, 1995). The emergence of new technology is seen as a particularly important complement to these reorganization strategies. Taken together, heightened resource constraints, changing market demands, and emerging technological capabilities are part of a broader conjunction of forces calling for change in the business of higher education. A prime example of the external pressures for efficiency and responsiveness comes from Virginia. Early in 1994, as a portion of the General Assembly's appropriations act, each public senior institution of higher education and the Virginia community college system were required to submit long-range restructuring plans to sustain effectiveness while increasing enrollments but without increases in state appropriations. To ensure compliance, the state withheld a portion of each institution's education and general appropriation for the biennium until its restructuring plan could be approved by the State Council for Higher Education and the state secretary of education. To underscore the point, the secretary pledged to withhold funds from those schools failing to prove they were fundamentally changing the way they did business.

Approaches to Academic Restructuring

Restructuring has emerged as an imperative at the nexus of resource constraints, market demands, and technological possibilities. University planners are attempting to devise new management strategies and decision processes to facilitate access and quality improvements, reductions in bureaucracy, and the implementation of administrative and academic production efficiencies.

It is noteworthy in the contemporary context that academic reform and administrative reform, traditionally treated as quite separate arenas, are linked in the name of restructuring. Contemporary proposals also broaden the scope of responsibility for academic reform to include wider university participation and shift the locus of decision making on academic issues beyond faculty jurisdiction (Gumport, 1993; Guskin 1994a, 1994b). Although our focus is on academic restructuring, we give some consideration to incipient efforts in the administrative domain as well.

In analyzing emerging restructuring initiatives, we find it useful to identify three distinct strands of action: reengineering, privatization, and reconfiguring. Taken together, they constitute the essence of contemporary restructuring.

Reengineering

Proponents of change have advocated that the administrative domain should be restructured before the core academic processes of the university are (Pew Higher Education Roundtable, 1993a, 1993b, 1993c; Hyatt, 1993; Guskin 1994a, 1994b). There are a number of rationales for this, one being that the administrative actors who implement changes in either domain can address their "own side of the house" with less resistance (Guskin, 1994a, 1994b), and that for some time administrative expenditures have been growing more rapidly than those for instruction (Gumport and Pusser, 1995).

The initial approach to restructuring the administrative domain in response to economic retrenchment was reminiscent of the financial management approach of earlier decades, relying on discipline in budgeting, monitoring resource allocations for effectiveness, and cultivating new revenue streams. However, a new reengineering orientation has begun to emerge (Pew Higher Education Roundtable, 1994; Guskin 1994a, 1994b). When adapting corporate strategies that attempt to reengineer core work processes (Hammer and Champy, 1993), higher education organizations have been called upon to rethink the nature of the work to be done and to redesign processes as well as culture. The goal is to go beyond "cutting and combining" (Guskin, 1994a) and getting "meaner and leaner" for cost containment (Zemsky and Massy, 1990).

Key dimensions of this reengineering approach, particularly the effort to implement an organizational shift from a hierarchical bureaucracy to a network of interdependent work processes designed to address customer needs (Lembcke, 1994; Coate, 1993), have originated in premises from Total Quality Management (TQM) and similar reengineering processes (Seymour, 1992, 1994; Peterson, 1993). From this perspective, higher education managers can identify persistent quality problems and make structural modifications to improve the organizational performance of administrative operations. It remains to be seen whether these strategies address the changing nature of higher education administrative work itself, as new technologies increasingly challenge existing notions of expertise and authority (Barley, 1996).

In one case of administrative reengineering (at Antioch), the change process required that organizational units imagine themselves out of business, in order to envision the redesign of processes for delivery of administrative services. In effect, this gave the administration the opportunity of "closing down one central administration and starting a new one" (Guskin, 1994a, p. 28). In another case (University of Maryland at College Park), reengineering was utilized as part of developing a multifaceted enhancement plan, assessing existing organizational processes and procedures, as well as for inspecting specific linkages between revenue generation and resource utilization (Hyatt, 1993).

In a similar vein, late in 1993 the University of California convened a work group charged with exploring new approaches to human resource management that would address "unprecedented challenges by making unprecedented and fundamental changes in the structure and delivery of its administrative services" (Work Group on a New University Human Resources Management Framework, 1993, p. 1). Two key facets of the proposal were reorganization of campus information technology to provide enhanced communication and management information systems, and increasing reliance on outside organizations, wherever cost-effective, to perform campus administrative service. The work group's recommendations included a comprehensive redesign intended to shift the norms of the workplace, including recasting the role of administrative leadership: "[S]enior management commitment and support will be essential to help managers and staff overcome the profound resiliency of the University's bureaucratic culture" (Work Group on a New University Human Resources Management Framework, 1993, p. 2).

In each of these cases, cultural transformation is fundamental to the reengineering process. As one observer describes it, traditional bureaucratic relations of hierarchy and control are ostensibly being challenged by those of market and exchange, and of customers, products, and distribution (Tuckman, 1994). An important distinction arises with regard to the application of "market" approaches to higher education reform. Tuckman points out that the emergence of TQM and other quality-focused derivatives proposes a competitive market for resources within the institution, in addition to the traditionally acknowledged competition between institutions, and between higher education institutions and other providers of educational services. He suggests: "The introduction of TQM clearly allows further organizational change such as the breakdown in role demarcation, enhancing the development of a more flexible division of tasks. Its particular contribution to the current repertoire of organizational changes is not to construct market relations, but to create a way of seeing organizational relations as market relations" (1994, p. 731).

In the academic domain, a similar starting point for reengineering has been offered: a view of the academic enterprise as a network of interdependent work processes rather than a static, hierarchical structure of discrete units. There has also been some acknowledgment that administrative reengineering principles and redesign of processes cannot simply or appropriately translate onto academic operations, such as curriculum formation, teaching and learning, promotion and tenure, and admissions (Pew Higher Education Roundtable, 1993a; Fienberg, 1996).

It has been suggested that adapting quality reengineering principles to academic work requires a new approach to defining academic quality as well as a rethinking of the nature of academic work. Regarding the former, Guskin notes that "for decades universities and colleges have wanted to define academic quality in terms of resources—faculty scholarship and degrees, depth and breadth of curricular offerings, and the presence of topflight labs, libraries and facilities" (1994b, p. 24). He credits this definition of quality as a key catalyst in rising costs, proliferating disciplinary programs based on faculty interests, and increasing cost of student services. Guskin suggests a shift in the definition of academic quality from resources to results. This would ostensibly turn institutional focus from faculty productivity to student productivity; from faculty disciplinary interests to "what students need to learn"; and from faculty teaching styles to student learning styles, placing a priority on the student as customer. Guskin calls this overall process "outcomes" thinking and suggests it is the norm in health care, another arena where TQM has been used extensively. He sums up this way: "Returning to my basic point: the costs of education, the demand for enhanced learning outcomes, and rapid advances in technology will bring pressures for radical change in the administrative and educational practice of American higher education. Our need is twofold: to reduce student costs and increase student learning" (1994b, p. 25).

Reengineering academic work will involve rethinking the educational process itself, the way faculty work, and the standards of educational technology (Pew Higher Education Roundtable, 1993a, 1993c; Guskin, 1994a, 1994b; Breneman, 1995). Proponents of reengineering also presume that technology can help lower the cost of education and make the delivery processes of teaching and learning more efficient by using electronic and interactive technology for transmitting course material and communicating. Along the same lines, using technological advances to replace the notion of "credit for contact" with "credit for knowledge" will render the concept of "classroom time" a "quaint anachronism" (Pew Higher Education Roundtable, 1994, p. 3A).

Underlying this goal is the presumption that faculty need to be convinced to change how and what they teach. The issue from this perspective is not simply to get faculty to teach more students or to work harder; the idea is to get faculty to change how they work. As Massy (1992, p. 1) states it: "The problem is not whether professors are working hard, but rather how they are working and what they are working on." A key focus in this transition will be to encourage academic departments to reengineer delivery of courses and programs to maximize efficiency and effectiveness (Pew Higher Education Roundtable, 1994). Reengineering to reduce costs in the arena of student learning will presumably be applied in related academic arenas as well: in the research enterprise (Kennedy, 1993; Shapiro, 1990) and in maximizing the benefits of the service enterprise at a minimal cost (Southern Regional Education Board, 1994).

Privatization

A second and central rationale for contemporary restructuring initiatives is administrative redefinition of just how much of the "business" of higher education should be handled within existing structures and competencies. In a highly competitive environment, the thinking goes, certain traditional university operations can no longer effectively compete with for-profit entities offering the same services at lower cost. Although auxiliary enterprises that operate like for-profit entities have long been fixtures on many campuses, a growing trend toward private/public partnerships and direct private operation of university services has become increasingly apparent (Zusman, 1994). As one example of the expansion of auxiliary enterprises, in the University of California system over a recent twenty-five year period expenditures on auxiliary enterprises increased over 200 percent (Gumport and Pusser, 1995). In the University of Virginia system, once the initial round of legislatively mandated restructuring proposals are implemented on campuses, private companies will provide food service at twelve of the sixteen four-year campuses; eight campuses will have bookstores run by private firms; and on one comprehensive campus, George Mason University, over fifty campus services will be conducted by private contractors (Trombley, 1995).

Although implementation of privatization initiatives on campus to date has been primarily in the domain of administrative services, a number of proposals and shifting financial arrangements have also brought elements of privatization to the academic arena as well. In the case of UC, in 1994 differential student fees were implemented for selected professional schools, with a portion of the increases remaining in those schools. At the same time, introductory Spanish language classes were eliminated at the UC Berkeley campus and subsequently "outsourced" to the campus extension program. The UC Office of the President also intends to explore outsourcing a number of other introductory courses to outside providers (Gumport, 1994).

On a much larger scale, early in 1996 the same office requested regent approval to merge the University of California at San Francisco Medical Center and a number of UCSF hospitals and clinics with the Stanford University Hospital and various Stanford clinics, along with the clinical practices of the full-time medical faculty of both universities. The proposal called for the formation of a new nonprofit public benefit corporation to be known as "NEWCO." Under the proposed governance arrangement for NEWCO, UC would hold six seats on a seventeen-member board; consequently the governing board's actions would not be subject to the state's open meeting laws or public records act. Under the proposal, the University of California would also transfer more than one hundred million dollars of assets into NEWCO, an enterprise the regents' general counsel described as "not a public entity in the same sense as the UC" (University of California General Counsel of the Regents James E. Holst, speaking in public session, UC Regents meeting, July 18, 1996).

The higher education privatization trend is part of a broader shift in the provision of welfare functions in the United States, in which aid is increasingly delivered directly to consumers. A prominent example in higher education is the widespread adoption of high-tuition/high-aid financing models in public higher education institutions (Hauptman, 1990; Griswold and Marine, 1996). The past decade has seen a significant shift of the responsibility for funding student enrollments from the states to individual consumers in the form of tuition and fee increases, in some cases tied to increases in direct student loans (Gladieux, Hauptman, and Knapp, 1994). Nonprofit institutions are also increasingly shifting from direct provision of services to financing or arranging the provision of traditional services by third parties (Salamon, 1995). We address some of the implications of the privatization shift in greater detail later in this chapter.

Reconfiguring

The third strand of reorganization initiatives encompasses reconfiguration of university structures utilizing strategies adapted from corporate models. In essence, reconfiguring aims to reshape organizational structures in order to facilitate implementation of reengineering processes. As with reengineering, the ostensible goal of reconfiguring is to enhance organizational efficiency, flexibility, and response.

The network conceptualization is one of the more prominent examples of corporate restructuring strategies that may be applied to higher education. Extending the premise of adaptation to an increasingly competitive marketplace (Powell, 1990; Provan and Milward, 1995), in networked organizations there is a strong push away from vertical integration into more and smaller work units. The intention is organizational decentralization, downsizing of bureaucracies, growth of smaller units of enterprise, and development of extended networks of interaction. These modes of organization, which Powell calls "hybrid forms," flourish under rapidly changing environmental conditions, when large-scale organizations have reached their functional limits and there is a demand for rapid information transfer and decision making. A key challenge within this management orientation is to accommodate the differentiation needed for flexibility and horizontal work arrangements at the same time as achieving efficient integration of academic work (Dill and Sporn, 1995b).

A related aspect of network reconfiguration seen as particularly relevant to academic restructuring has been developed by Bartlett and Ghoshal (1989, 1990, 1994, 1995a, 1995b). According to these management theorists, success in a complex and competitive environment depends on a fit between environmental demands and strategy. Beyond this acknowledgment of resource dependence, organizational leaders must view their organizations as a portfolio of unified horizontal work processes, which are dynamic and in need of ongoing redesign. This view is intended to broaden the focus of managers: "As powerful as new structure can be, structure is only one instrument of organizational change, and a blunt one at that" (Bartlett and Ghoshal, 1995a, p. 88). Managers are to manage people and processes in order to build an organization based on a shared and internalized vision as well as efficiency in human resource management: "This means creating an organization with which members can identify, in which they share a sense of pride, and to which they are willing to commit. In short, senior managers must convert the contractual employees of an economic entity into committed members of a purposeful organization" (Bartlett and Ghoshal, 1994, p. 81).

Contemporary higher education research inspired by corporate strategies suggests that managers should view the university as a multiproduct organization and should adopt a more corporate form of organization and management. This may be thought of as a complement to the privatization initiatives that turn university auxiliary functions over to corporate providers. According to Dill and Sporn, the competitive environment makes a compelling case for this shift: "In particular, intra-national and international competition among universities and between universities and other organizations is increasing. This new environment will require that all universities that wish to compete in this emerging international market develop a more corporate form of organization and management, with the capacity to employ university resources, programs, and personnel, in a more flexible, adaptive, and efficient manner" (1995b, p. 212). From this perspective, universities need to create academic, research, and service profit centers that exploit core competencies (Prahalad and Hamel, 1990). This perspective also invites managers as well as all members of the organization to continuously reevaluate the organizational mission. Strategies are designed to focus on clarifying and internalizing organizational values. The focus on horizontal processes is intended to yield better access to information, more entrepreneurial activity, and ultimately a more competitive institution.

A recent University of California initiative offers a useful example of the network vision of reconfiguration as applied to higher education administration. As part of a comprehensive review of its human resources management, a university task force presented a set of recommendations that were intended to "embody the paradigm shift from the University's existing bureaucratic environment to a proposed network vision" (Work Group on a New University Human Resources Management Framework, 1993, p. 4). Recommendations included implementation of localized systems of administrative decision making, a move away from a focus on central administration to a focus on the department level of decision making, and redistribution of roles and responsibilities between the Office of the President and the individual campuses.

Another personnel challenge at the University of California, the large numbers of senior faculty taking advantage of early retirement incentives, is increasingly common across the nation and at multiple levels of the higher education system (Gilliam and Shoven, 1996). The extent of early retirements, and the necessity of replacing those faculty innovatively, hints at the potential scale of the application of network reconfiguration. Over the past three years, nearly two thousand UC ladder faculty have taken advantage of voluntary early retirement programs. A number of initiatives have been discussed as part of efforts to replace and realign those faculty positions. The systemwide Academic Planning Council has begun to pursue the emerging concept of "one system thinking" (University of California, Academic Planning Council meeting minutes, July–September 1994). The intent of the "one system" approach is to find ways to increase intercampus cooperation, examine redundancies in curricula, and reconfigure existing academic personnel commitments in order to sustain quality curricula while creating a more adaptable academic workforce and achieving broad cost savings.

Contemporary Restructuring: Challenges and Implications

The practices embodied in contemporary reengineering, privatization, and reconfiguring initiatives provide a guide to emerging academic restructuring proposals. They also point to a definition of restructuring as a managerial imperative, emerging from political economic demands for cost-cutting, efficiency, productivity, and competitiveness. Perhaps the most comprehensive set of restructuring proposals advanced to date emerged from the public higher education institutions of Virginia, referred to earlier in this chapter. Under legislative mandate, the state's public senior institutions and its community college system were required to prepare plans that would "effect long-term changes in the deployment of faculty, to ensure the effectiveness of academic offerings, to minimize administrative and instructional costs, to prepare for the demands of enrollment increase, and to address funding priorities as approved by the General Assembly" (Virginia General Assembly Appropriations Act, 1994).

The plan submitted by George Mason University is an excellent example of the array of forces and forms that engage contemporary planners. With regard to administrative functions, the report includes sections on "Privatizing for Better Service, Increased Effectiveness," "Innovative Outsourcing," and "Managing for Maximum Efficiency." In the academic domain the sections include "Public-Private Partnerships for Mutual Benefit," "Serving the Region: The Distributed University," "Technology's Role at the Distributed University," "Breaking the Faculty Mold," "From Input to Output Measures," and "The Virtual University" (George Mason University, 1994). George Mason's plan also hopes to significantly alter the university's academic culture. After reconfiguration, students will be able to take courses at twelve universities in the Washington Metropolitan area, receive instruction from faculty via electronic hookups, and access new curricula in instructional units located outside both departments and colleges.

Plans submitted by other Virginia universities include detailed sections on improving faculty productivity through incentives and technological innovation, curricular reform, economic development programs, and reconfiguration of academic disciplines, including the elimination of forty-seven degree programs (Trombley, 1995). The Virginia Community College System's (VCCS) plan began with a commitment to a complete review of curricula—over six thousand courses—in order to reduce redundancy and speed time to degree. VCSS also proposed a number of innovative applications of technology, including transformation of learning resource centers into instructional technology centers and development of comprehensive databases to track student progress over time and across cohorts.

The various Virginia plans demonstrate the extent of the contemporary shift in university management strategies. Moving beyond planning for resource constraints and rapidly changing environmental demands, a new set of university management initiatives is being developed that reposition and reconceptualize the higher education industry. These developments need to be considered in historical perspective and combined with lessons already learned from long-range strategic planning efforts (compare Schuster, Smith, Corak, and Yamada, 1994). Taking a long view, we are reminded that while much has changed in university life much has remained the same; the essential conservatism of academic structure and culture has protected universities from short-sighted adaptations (Kennedy, 1993; Kerr, 1995). Proponents of restructuring models adapted from contemporary corporate organizational reforms must also confront the enduring academic norms of individual entrepreneurialism and autonomy, a bundle of formidable obstacles that Bartlett and Ghoshal (1989) have called "administrative heritage." It is no surprise, then, that although a number of proposals have been launched, except where legislatively mandated relatively little academic restructuring has actually been implemented. Nonetheless, proposals for academic restructuring warrant thoughtful consideration, as changing environmental demands pose challenges for universities to depart from doing business as usual.

With that in mind, we now turn to some unresolved challenges for academic restructuring inherent in the structure and organization of today's postsecondary institutions. Identification of obstacles is valuable at this stage, because although academic restructuring is relatively untested, some problematic dimensions are apparent even in its nascent form. We address four areas of specific concern: restructuring based on initiatives developed in a for-profit context; challenges to academic autonomy; the changing nature of administrative work; and political economic resistance to restructuring, particularly to privatization initiatives.

First, a formidable challenge lies in the effort to base higher education restructuring initiatives on models developed in for-profit, primarily corporate, organizational realms. A fundamental difficulty arises from the absence of a clear and shared profit-maximizing goal within higher education organizations (James, 1990). Further, university missions have historically been ambiguous, core competencies difficult to define, outcomes assessment problematic, and outputs difficult to gauge. As Massy notes, "Achieving precise quality definitions and measures for higher education's outputs is difficult, if it is possible at all" (1990, p. 1). Measuring effectiveness in universities has been significantly more complicated than in for-profit organizations, where success is measured by an easily benchmarked "bottom line." A number of explanations have been offered for the difficulties in evaluating the efficiency of public-sector and nonprofit enterprises relative to private, particularly corporate, entities. These include the problem of defining efficient courses of action in public institutions beholden to a multitude of primary and contextual goals, the generally weaker incentives for executives in nonprofit institutions to find efficiencies, and the diffusion of authority that limits public-sector executives' ability to implement efficiencies (Wilson, 1989). It has also been argued that the professional motivations of nonprofit employees are ambiguous and that universities, along with other nonprofits, have more labor-intensive production processes than for-profits (Oster, 1995) as well as having highly complex professional work at the operating level (Mintzberg, 1994). University managers need to proceed with caution. As Columbia University Provost Jonathan Cole has noted (1993, p.6): "Of course research universities are not, cannot, and should not be organized in imitation of corporations. The process of decision-making is going to take longer than in the hierarchical culture of the corporate world. The goal is not to imitate the business community, but to take some lessons from it (especially in the administrative and business side of research universities)."

A related and equally significant concern for academic restructuring proposals is the challenge to academic autonomy. Universities must accommodate demands to maintain institutional competitiveness in a postindustrial environment while adapting to prepare students for competition in a changing global economy (Dill and Sporn, 1995a). The latter demand is for constructive and fundamental change, particularly in curricula and degree programs that will enable students to be proficient in new competencies for a global marketplace (Pew Higher Education Roundtable, 1994). Consequently, universities are called upon to simultaneously reduce the costs of their degrees and remain flexible in resource allocations to academic programs. As we have noted, these calls are increasingly taking the form of external mandates linked to university appropriations. Such shifts in the locus of control over the nature and pace of academic program change raise powerful questions for university autonomy.

While prior challenges to university autonomy have been characterized as an internal struggle between administration and faculty or as a struggle between campus and external political actors (Berdahl, 1990), it appears that the preservation of autonomy from increasing market demands has also become a central challenge (Slaughter, 1994; Altbach, 1994; Williams, 1995). University planners will be hard-pressed to respond to market demands for curricular change, while at the same time maintaining local control of academic programs.

The situation is further complicated by differing perspectives on academic purposes and processes among faculty as well as between faculty and administration (Peterson and White, 1992; Gumport, 1993). Academic restructuring proponents have stated that the fragmentation and entrepreneurialism of research faculty need to be mitigated in order for effective teamwork and horizontal integration to develop (Massy, 1994; Dill and Sporn, 1995b). In that light, the challenge shifts from rearranging organizational architecture to a more fundamental call for faculty resocialization and integration (Shapiro, 1990; Kennedy, 1993; Hastorf, 1996).

The mechanism for achieving this integration is not clear. Although attention in the recent restructuring literature is paid to faculty and faculty culture as impediments to academic restructuring (Massy and Zemsky, 1995; Massy, 1995), we suggest that such resistance as is found in the academic realm results from a complex of historical traditions and contemporary interactions (Clark, 1987; Altbach, 1994). A number of groups, including external resource providers, legislatures and coordinating councils, administrators and institutional governing boards, employee unions, and students, also possess distinctive cultures and interests in the shaping of a broad institutional academic culture, cultures and interests that need to be reconciled for innovative restructuring proposals to succeed. As Wilson explains, "in defining a core mission and sorting out tasks that either fit or do not fit with this mission, executives must be aware of their many rivals for the right to define it" (1989, p. 371).

Further, it is not clear that new forms of organization reduce the intrinsic competition in higher education between groups with varied interests and objectives. In the case of the University of California's proposal to create NEWCO, litigation was commenced by employee labor groups before the proposal had even been adopted. With such obstacles in mind, it appears that the involvement of a variety of interest groups, as part of a collective deliberation about academic purposes and values, is critical to implementation of academic restructuring initiatives.

Another challenge to contemporary academic restructuring comes from an enduring set of political economic demands that have not yet been sufficiently addressed by reengineering, privatization, or reconfiguration proposals. The recent restructuring literature addresses political economic challenges by suggesting that universities establish a position close to "the market" for higher education, as represented by demands from students, funders, and other political economic actors (Pew Higher Education Roundtable, 1993a, 1993b; Williams, 1995). Positioning for "the market" remains problematic on at least two dimensions: first, "market demand" in higher education is poorly defined, while the supply and relative quality of university "outputs" is particularly difficult to quantify (James, 1990). Second, public higher education has a unique history of public ownership shaping its dimensions. Private higher education is similarly bound by tradition and unique constituencies that render of limited utility any projections on the "commodification" of the "product." This is not to say that strategic positioning is not important for higher education institutions, or that market considerations will not influence the reshaping of academic priorities and programs. A key to successful planning is recognition that positioning in higher education is extremely difficult and is shaped by a multitude of demands that are, as noted, often contradictory.

Within the mix of political economic demands pressuring universities, the call for quality management strategies, the demand for excellence, and the directive to cut costs deserve special consideration. How to enhance academic quality while cutting costs is not yet clearly defined. The mandate to lower costs comes with widespread enthusiasm for new technologies intended to enhance delivery of educational products and services. However, whether technological advances for academic work will lower costs is not clear (Callan, 1995). Nor does implementation of quality management principles ensure lower costs (Seymour, 1994) or improvement in the quality of academic processes of universities (Fienberg, 1996). What is clear is that additional research and evaluation is needed on the efficacy of quality-improvement programs for higher education (Fienberg, 1996).

A similar case can be made for increased research into the changing nature of academic and administrative work (Barley, 1996). While much has recently been written about the potential influence of technology on the delivery of educational services (Massy and Zemsky, 1995; Green, 1995) and on reorganization of university structures and processes in light of changing contexts and technologies (Dill and Sporn, 1995a, 1995b), this emerging literature speaks more to the organization of academic and administrative work than to the nature of that work itself. As Barley (1996) notes, "Part of the problem is that our images of work and occupations are outdated. Remedying this situation will require developing new models of work and relations of production representative of the division of labor of a post-industrial economy." Building on Barley's analysis of the emergence of technicians and technical expertise in the labor force, we suggest that higher education restructuring for a postindustrial economy requires a recognition of the changing nature of academic and administrative work, as well as cultural and institutional changes.

The issue of increased privatization of university functions presents a number of concerns for postsecondary planners. Salamon (1995) points out that as the outsourcing of enterprises increases, managers are increasingly held accountable for the performance of programs removed from their control. Outsourcing and privatizing also raise significant issues with regard to public funding of higher education. Under the prevailing system, public universities receive state appropriations that are used in part to subsidize auxiliary enterprises and students as consumers of university services. As privatization increases, larger portions of the public appropriation are funneled to private entities, with the university serving as conduit. This may lead to increased demands for student vouchers as well as direct subsidy from funders to private-sector service providers, bypassing the university in the name of efficiency.

In the case of academic medical centers, many universities' efforts to compete in a capital-intensive and volatile arena dominated by large private providers has been accompanied by remarkably rapid shifts in bottom-line performance. The Regents of the University of California were described as "stunned" by a 1995 KPMG Peat Marwick analysis of the financial challenges faced by UC's five medical school hospitals (Russell, 1996). In a report to the regents in May 1996, the University of California Office of the President noted that "Numerous presentations to the Regents over the last several years have demonstrated that academic medical centers are imperiled by economic competition in their local markets and by significant reductions in support for medical education programs" (University of California, San Francisco, 1996). Although some privatization initiatives hold out the promise of increased efficiencies and cost savings, in a number of cases they may also render institutions increasingly vulnerable.

Taken together, these obstacles to academic restructuring illuminate an enduring challenge for higher education institutions: The implementation of contemporary organizational restructuring in all sectors depends on consensus. Literature from a variety of perspectives calls for the development of an internalized, shared vision and a clear understanding of organizational purpose (Bartlett and Ghoshal, 1990; Clark, 1993; Dill and Sporn, 1995b). Achieving a shared sense of purpose in a complex university, a mature organization with a variety of stakeholders, is extremely problematic. Strategic adaptation based on incomplete consensus or adversarial relations is far less likely to take hold or become institutionalized. In that light, generating broad participation in the creation of a consensus on whether and how to restructure may be the paramount challenge for contemporary university planners.

Further Reading

Those interested in further reading on the themes introduced in this chapter on academic restructuring may want to examine the volume edited by Dill and Sporn (1995a) on emerging demands for adaptation in higher education; the edited volume by Arrow, Cottle, Eaves, and Olkin (1996), as well as Cole (1993) and Kennedy (1993) in the special issue of *Daedalus,* for issues for research universities; Massy (1995), Massy and Zemsky (1995), Green (1995), and Guskin (1994a, 1994b) on possible implications of technology; and Barley's article (1996) on the changing organization of work.

References

Albert, S., and Whetten, D. "Organizational Identity." In L. L. Cummings and B. M. Staw (eds.), *Research in Organizational Behavior*, 1985, *7*, 263–295.

Altbach, P. "Problems and Possibilities: The American Academic Profession." In P. G. Altbach, R. O. Berdahl, and P. J. Gumport (eds.), *Higher Education in American Society*. (3rd ed.) Amherst, N.Y.: Prometheus, 1994.

Anderson, R., and Meyerson, J. (eds.). *Productivity and Higher Education*. Princeton, N.J.: Peterson's Guides, 1992.

Arrow, K., Cottle, R., Eaves, B., and Olkin, I. (eds.). *Education in a Research University*. Stanford, Calif.: Stanford University Press, 1996.

Balderston, F. *Managing Today's University*. San Francisco: Jossey-Bass, 1974.

Barak, R. J. *State Level Academic Program Review*. Denver: State Higher Education Executive Officers, 1984.

Barley, S. "Technicians in the Workplace: Ethnographic Evidence for Bringing Work into Organization Studies." *Administrative Science Quarterly*, 1996, *41*(3), 404–441.

Barrow, C. "Will the Fiscal Crisis Force Higher Ed to Restructure?" *Thought and Action*, 1993, *9*(1), 7–24.

Bartlett, C., and Ghoshal, S. *Managing Across Borders*. Boston: Harvard Business School Press, 1989.

Bartlett, C., and Ghoshal, S. "Matrix Management." *Harvard Business Review*, 1990, *68*(4), 138–145.

Bartlett, C., and Ghoshal, S. "Changing the Role of Top Management: Beyond Strategy to Purpose." *Harvard Business Review*, 1994, *72*(6), 79–88.

Bartlett, C., and Ghoshal, S. "Changing the Role of Top Management: Beyond Structure to Process." *Harvard Business Review*, 1995a, *73*(1), 86–96.

Bartlett, C., and Ghoshal, S. "Changing the Role of Top Management: Beyond Systems to People." *Harvard Business Review*, 1995b, *73*(3), 133–142.

Berdahl, R. O. "Public Universities and State Governments." *Educational Record*, 1990, *71*(1), 38–42.

Blau, P. "A Formal Theory of Differentiation in Organizations." *American Sociological Review*, 1970, *35*(2), 201–218.

Blau, P. *The Organization of Academic Work*. New York: Wiley, 1973.

Breneman, D. *A State of Emergency? Higher Education in California*. Report prepared for the California Higher Education Policy Center, San Jose, January 1995.

Callan, P. M. "An Interview: Robert Zemsky." *Cross Talk*, 1995, *3*(3), 2.

Cameron, K. S., and Tschirhart, M. "Postindustrial Environments and Organizational Effectiveness in Colleges and Universities." *Journal of Higher Education*, 1992, *63*(1), 87–108.

Cheit, E. *The New Depression in Higher Education*. New York: McGraw Hill, 1973.

Clark, B. R. *The Higher Education System*. Berkeley: University of California Press, 1983.

Clark, B. R. *The Academic Life*. Princeton, N.J.: Carnegie Foundation for the Advancement of Teaching, 1987.

Clark, B. R. "The Problem of Complexity in Modern Higher Education." In S. Rothblatt and B. Wittrock (eds.), *The European and American University Since 1800*. Cambridge, England: Cambridge University Press, 1993.

Clark, B. R. "Complexity and Differentiation: The Deepening Problem of University Integration." In D. Dill and B. Sporn (eds.), *Emerging Patterns of Social Demand and University Reform: Through a Glass Darkly.* New York: Pergamon Press, 1995.

Coate, L. "An Analysis of Oregon State University's Total Quality Management Pilot Program." In W. E. Vandament and D. P. Jones (eds.), *Financial Management: Progress and Challenges.* New Directions for Higher Education, no. 83. San Francisco: Jossey-Bass, 1993.

Cole, J. R. "Balancing Acts: Dilemmas of Choice Facing Research Universities." *Daedalus,* 1993, *122*(4), 1–36.

Cope, R. G. *Strategic Policy Planning.* Littleton, Colo.: Ireland Educational, 1978.

Cope, R. G., and Delaney, G. 1991. "Academic Program Review: A Market Strategy." *Journal of Marketing for Higher Education,* 1991, *3*(2), 63–86.

Dill, D. D. "Rethinking the Planning Process." *Planning for Higher Education,* 1993–94, *22*(2), 8–13.

Dill, D. D., and Sporn, B. "The Implications of a Postindustrial Environment for the University: An Introduction." In D. Dill and B. Sporn (eds.), *Emerging Patterns of Social Demand and University Reform: Through a Glass Darkly.* New York: Pergamon Press, 1995a.

Dill, D. D., and Sporn, B. "University 2001: What Will the University of the Twenty-First Century Look Like?" In D. Dill and B. Sporn (eds.), *Emerging Patterns of Social Demand and University Reform: Through a Glass Darkly.* New York: Pergamon Press, 1995b.

Durkheim, E. *The Division of Labor in Society.* New York: Free Press, 1933.

Etzioni, A. "Administrative and Professional Authority." In A. Etzioni (ed.), *Modern Organizations.* Englewood Cliffs, N.J.: Prentice-Hall, 1964.

Fienberg, S. "Applying Statistical Concepts and Approaches in Academic Administration." In K. Arrow, R. Cottle, B. Eaves, and I. Olkin (eds.), *Education in a Research University.* Stanford, Calif.: Stanford University Press, 1996.

Fincher, C. "Planning Models and Paradigms in Higher Education." *Journal of Higher Education,* 1972, 43(9), 754–767.

Fuller, B. "A Framework for Academic Planning." *Journal of Higher Education,* 1976, *47*(1), 65–77.

George Mason University. *The George Mason Plan: Recasting the University.* Sep. 1994.

Ghoshal, S., and Nohria, N. "Horses for Courses: Organizational Forms for Multinational Corporations." *Sloan Management Review,* 1993, *34*(2), 23–35.

Gilliam, K., and Shoven, J. "Faculty Retirement Policies: The Stanford Experience." In K. Arrow, R. Cottle, B. Eaves, and I. Olkin (eds.), *Education in a Research University.* Stanford, Calif.: Stanford University Press, 1996.

Gladieux, L., Hauptman, A., and Knapp, L. G. "The Federal Government and Higher Education." In P. Altbach, R. Berdahl, and P. Gumport (eds.), *Higher Education in American Society.* (3rd ed.) Amherst, N.Y.: Prometheus, 1994.

Green, K. C. "Academic Productivity and Technology." *Academe,* 1995, *81*(1), 19–25.

Griswold, C., and Marine, G. "Political Influences on State Policy: Higher-Tuition, Higher-Aid, and the Real World." *Review of Higher Education,* 1996, *19*(4), 361–389.

Gumport, P. J. "The Contested Terrain of Academic Program Reduction." *Journal of Higher Education,* 1993, *64*(3), 283–311.

Gumport, P. J. "Academic Restructuring in Historical Perspective: Shifting Priorities in the University of California." Paper presented at annual conference of Association for the Study of Higher Education, Tucson, Ariz., Nov. 9–13, 1994.

Gumport, P. J., and Pusser, B. "A Case of Bureaucratic Accretion: Context and Consequences." *Journal of Higher Education,* 1995, *66*(5), 493–520.

Guskin, A. "Reducing Student Costs and Enhancing Student Learning: The University

Challenge of the 1990s. Part I: Restructuring the Administration." *Change,* 1994a, *26*(4), 23–29.

Guskin, A. "Reducing Student Costs and Enhancing Student Learning: The University Challenge of the 1990s. Part II: Restructuring the Role of the Faculty." *Change,* 1994b, *26*(5), 16–25.

Hammer, M., and Champy, J. *Reengineering the Corporation: A Manifesto for Business Revolution.* New York: HarperCollins, 1993.

Hanson, K., and Meyerson, J. (eds.). *Higher Education in a Changing Economy.* Washington, D.C.: ACE/Macmillan, 1990.

Hastorf, A. "The University Fellows Program at Stanford: On Turning Scientists and Scholars into University Statesmen and Stateswomen." In K. Arrow, R. Cottle, B. Eaves, and I. Olkin (eds.), *Education in a Research University.* Stanford, Calif.: Stanford University Press, 1996.

Hauptman, A. M. *The College Tuition Spiral.* Washington, D.C.: ACE and College Board, 1990.

Hearn, J. C. "Strategy and Resources." In J. Smart (ed.), *Higher Education: Handbook of Theory and Research.* Vol. 4. New York: Agathon Press, 1988.

Hopkins, D.S.P., and Massy, W. *Planning Models for Colleges and Universities.* Stanford, Calif.: Stanford University Press, 1981.

Hyatt, J. A. "Strategic Restructuring: A Case Study." In W. E. Vandament and D. P. Jones (eds.), *Financial Management: Progress and Challenges.* New Directions for Higher Education, no. 83. San Francisco: Jossey-Bass, 1993.

Hyatt, J. A., Shulman, C., and Santiago, A. *Reallocation Strategies for Effective Resource Management.* National Association of College and University Business Officers (NACUBO), 1984.

Ikenberry, S. "The Organizational Dilemma." *Journal of Higher Education,* 1971, *43*(1), 23–34.

James, E. "Decision Processes and Priorities in Higher Education." In S. Hoenack and E. Collins (eds.), *The Economics of American Universities.* Albany: State University of New York Press, 1990.

Jessop, B. "Towards a Schumpeterian Workfare State?" *Studies in Political Economy,* 1993, *40*(Spring), 7–39.

Keller, G. *Academic Strategy: The Management Revolution in American Higher Education.* Baltimore: Johns Hopkins University Press, 1983.

Kennedy, D. "Making Choices in the Research University." *Daedalus,* 1993, *122*(4), 127–156.

Kerr, C. *The Uses of the University.* Cambridge, Mass.: Harvard University Press, 1963.

Kerr, C. "A Critical Age in the University World." *European Journal of Education,* 1987, *22*(2), 183–193.

Kerr, C. "Expanding Access and Changing Missions." *Educational Record,* 1994, *75*(4), 27–31.

Kerr, C. "Preface, 1994: A New Context for Higher Education." *The Uses of the University.* (4th ed.) Cambridge, Mass.: Harvard University Press, 1995.

Lembcke, B. "Organizational Performance Measures: The Vital Signs of TQM Investments." In D. Seymour (ed.), *Total Quality Management on Campus.* New Directions for Higher Education, no. 86. San Francisco: Jossey-Bass, 1994.

Leslie, L., and Rhoades, G. "Rising Administrative Costs: Seeking Explanations." *Journal of Higher Education,* 1995, *66*(2), 187–212.

March, J. G., and Olsen, J. P. *Democratic Governance.* New York: Free Press, 1995.

Massy, W. F. "A Paradigm for Research on Higher Education." In J. Smart, (ed.), *Higher Education: Handbook of Theory and Research.* Vol. 6. New York: Agathon Press, 1990.

Massy, W. F. "Restructuring Academe." Paper presented at Governor's Annual Awards Conference, Missouri Higher Education Commission, St. Louis, December 1992.

Massy, W. F. "On Values and Market Forces." *Pew Policy Perspectives,* 1993, *5*(1), (entire insert).

Massy, W. F. *Resource Allocation Reform in Higher Education.* Washington, D.C.: National Association of College and University Business Officers (NACUBO), 1994.

Massy, W. F. *Leveraged Learning: Technology's Role in Restructuring Higher Education.* Stanford, Calif.: Stanford Forum for Higher Education Futures, 1995.

Massy, W. F., and Zemsky, R. "Faculty Discretionary Time." *Journal of Higher Education,* 1994, *65*(1), 1–22.

Massy, W. F., and Zemsky, R. *Using Information Technology to Enhance Academic Productivity.* Paper based on Wingspread Conference, EDUCOM, The Ohio State University Press, Columbus, Ohio, June 1995.

Mingle, J. R., and Associates. *Challenges for Retrenchment.* San Francisco: Jossey-Bass, 1981.

Mintzberg, H. *The Rise and Fall of Strategic Planning.* New York: Free Press, 1994.

Mohrman, S. "Integrating Roles and Structure." In M. W. Galbraith, J. R., Lawler, E. E., III, and Associates, *Organizing for the Future: The New Logic for Managing Complex Organizations.* San Francisco: Jossey-Bass, 1993.

Mortimer, K. P., and Tierney, M. L. *The Three R's of the Eighties.* AAHE/ERIC Report no. 4. Washington, D.C.: AAHE, 1979.

Oster, S. *Strategic Management for Nonprofit Organizations.* New York: Oxford University Press, 1995.

Peterson, M. W. *Total Quality Management in Higher Education: An Annotated Bibliography.* Ann Arbor: Center for the Study of Higher Education, University of Michigan, 1993.

Peterson, M. W. "Images of University Structure, Governance, and Leadership: Adaptive Strategies for the New Environment." In D. Dill and B. Sporn (eds.), *Emerging Patterns of Social Demand and University Reform: Through a Glass Darkly.* New York: Pergamon Press, 1995.

Peterson, M. W., and White, T. "Faculty and Administrative Perceptions of Their Environments." *Research in Higher Education,* 1992, *33*(2), 177–204.

Pew Higher Education Roundtable. "A Call to Meeting." *Policy Perspectives,* 1993a, 4(4).

Pew Higher Education Roundtable. "A Transatlantic Dialogue." *Policy Perspectives,* 1993b, 5(1).

Pew Higher Education Roundtable. "An Uncertain Terrain." *Policy Perspectives,* 1993c, 5(2).

Pew Higher Education Roundtable. "To Dance with Change." *Policy Perspectives,* 1994, 5(3).

Pfeffer, J., and Salancik, G. R. *The External Control of Organizations.* New York: HarperCollins, 1978.

Powell, W. W. "Neither Market Nor Hierarchy: Network Forms of Organization." In L. L. Cummings and B. M. Staw (eds.), *Research in Organizational Behavior,* 1990, *12,* 295–336.

Powell, W. W., and Friedkin, R. "Organizational Change in Nonprofit Organizations." In W. W. Powell (ed.), *The Nonprofit Sector.* New Have, Conn.: Yale University Press, 1987.

Prahalad, C. K., and Hamel, G. "The Core Competence of the Corporation." *Harvard Business Review,* 1990, *68*(3), 79–91.

Provan, K., and Milward, H. B. "A Preliminary Theory of Interorganizational Network Effectiveness." *Administrative Science Quarterly,* 1995, *40*(1), 1–33.

Russell, S. "UCSF–Stanford Hospital Merger Forces Regent Decision: Vote Will Focus on Structure of Governing Board." *San Francisco Chronicle,* July 18, 1996, p. A17.

Salamon, L. *Partners in Public Service.* Baltimore: Johns Hopkins University Press, 1995.

Schuster, J. H., Smith, D. G., Corak, K. A., and Yamada, M. M. *Strategic Governance.* Phoenix: American Council on Education/Oryx Press, 1994.

Seymour, D. T. *On Q: Causing Quality in Higher Education.* New York: Macmillan, 1992.

Seymour, D. T. "The Return on Quality Investment." In D. Seymour (ed.), *Total Quality Management on Campus.* New Directions for Higher Education, no. 86, Jossey-Bass, 1994.

Shapiro, H. "Higher Education in a Changing Environment: Some Scholarly and Economic Imperatives." In K. Hanson and J. Meyerson (eds.), *Higher Education in a Changing Economy.* Washington, D.C.: ACE/Macmillan, 1990.

Shirley, R. C., and Volkwein, J. F. "Establishing Academic Program Priorities." *Journal of Higher Education,* 1978, *49*(5), 472–488.

Slaughter, S. "Academic Freedom at the End of the Century." In P. Altbach, R. Berdahl, and P. Gumport (eds.), *Higher Education in American Society.* (3rd ed.) Amherst, N.Y.: Prometheus, 1994.

Southern Regional Education Board (SREB). *Changing States: Higher Education and the Public Good.* Atlanta, Ga.: Commission for Educational Quality, 1994.

Stigler, S. "Competition and the Research Universities." *Daedalus,* 1993, *122*(4), 157–178.

Trombley, W. "Ambitious Reform Agenda: Restructuring in Virginia Higher Education." *Cross Talk,* 1995, *3*(3), 1–6.

Trow, M. A. "Reorganizing the Biological Sciences at Berkeley." *Change,* 1983, *15*(8), 44–53.

Tuckman, A. "The Yellow Brick Road: Total Quality Management and the Restructuring of Organizational Culture." *Organization Studies,* 1994, 15(5), 727–751.

Tyack, D. "'Restructuring' in Historical Perspective." *Teachers College Record,* 1990, *92*(2), 170–191.

University of California, San Francisco. *UCSF and Stanford Merger of Clinical Activities: Creation of "NEWCO Corporation."* Oakland: Office of the President, University of California, 1996.

Virginia General Assembly. Appropriations Act. March 1994.

Weber, M. *The Theory of Social and Economic Organization.* New York: Free Press, 1947.

Williams, G. "The 'Marketization' of Higher Education: Reforms and Potential Reforms in Higher Education Finance." In D. Dill and B. Sporn (eds.), *Emerging Patterns of Social Demand and University Reform: Through a Glass Darkly.* New York: Pergamon Press, 1995.

Wilson, J. *Bureaucracy.* New York: Basic Books, 1989.

Work Group on a New University Human Resources Management Framework. *Developing the UC Workforce for the 21st Century.* Improved Management Initiatives Task Force, 1993.

Zemsky, R., and Massy, W. "Cost Containment." *Change,* 1990, *22*(6), 16–22.

Zhou, X. "The Dynamics of Organizational Rules." *American Journal of Sociology,* 1993, *98*(5), 1134–1166.

Zusman, A. "Current and Emerging Issues Facing Higher Education in the United States." In P. Altbach, R. Berdahl, and P. Gumport (eds.), *Higher Education in American Society.* (3rd ed.) Amherst, N.Y.: Prometheus, 1994.

CHAPTER TWENTY-FOUR

TRANSFORMING FACULTY ROLES

Dorothy E. Finnegan

The financial straits in which higher education professionals find themselves today pose unprecedented challenges. Some institutions are rushing through white water around the looming boulders, while others are thrashing in the shoals. In either courseway, maneuvering to maintain financial stability is assuming more time, and few elements within the organization are exempt from potential jettison. In laying a course for the future, the common question is "What can we do without?" Equally important is "Who is to make the decisions?"

The myriad internal and external forces that influence the operations of our colleges and universities appear to take on a life of their own. We often anthropomorphize organizations, as if they were sentient and active agents—more importantly, as if these artificial systems bore responsibility for what occurs to their members. Thus, change can appear to occur without human intervention and in spite of human interference. However, humans as transcendental creatures have the "capacity to project [themselves] into the future by projecting a future and by pulling [themselves] toward it" (Etzioni, 1968, p. 32). Projecting a future requires analyzing contemporary currents and interpolations from those trends. Allan Cartter (1965), assuming that colleagues would take positive action if they were armed with data and analyses, claimed that the best projections should make poor predictions.

In this chapter, I project two futures for faculty. These projections are based on what I see as possibilities, given the contemporary state of the profession, first as it might evolve if modified by small course corrections and then as it might be if transformed by a sea change. I am concerned here with the contractual relationship between the faculty and their institutions—not a legal perspective, but rather the sociological compact that binds one to the other. The relationship of faculty to their institutions is not simple, however, since faculty have disciplinary allegiances that stretch beyond their institutions (Mintzberg, 1979). Their professional lives constitute a balance between autonomy, which ". . . sanctions the presence of specific knowledge and skills among members and their right for expert decisions," and accountability, which ". . . warns of obligations to others, within and outside the community" (Fasano, 1995, p. 1). In other words, within the context of their associations and institutions faculty have promoted their autonomy while creating and participating in constituent methods of accountability.

I use the concepts of autonomy and accountability as analytical elements that frame the current issues and actions affecting the sociological compact. The degree of autonomy for most faculty is decreasing, while the amount of accountability is increasing. Optimistic about the future of faculty based on current and projected technological advancements, I am simultaneously pessimistic about the professoriate's autonomy given the contemporary state of political and economic events and values. My contention is that current forces, *if not checked,* are leading to a deterioration of professional faculty autonomy that will be replaced by public accountability and to significant diminution of the importance of colleges and universities, and with that the emergence of transitory employment conditions for many faculty.

Scholars are faculty members only by virtue of being employed by an institution of higher learning (Light, 1974). The role of faculty can be transformed through a managed partnership of faculty and administrators working to strike an appropriate balance between autonomy and accountability. Opportunities abound for this partnership to effect positive change in the nature of the professorial role and, through those changes, the nature of the learning processes that take place within their institutions. Although some administrators have begun to redefine their compact with faculty, many maintain the traditional role by enforcing a composite of expectations, incentives, and rewards that in effect maintains the status quo.

I begin this chapter with two thumbnail sketches: the contemporary professorial role as it has evolved, and the current social arguments and action that seek to modify the role. After outlining emerging trends, I suggest areas ripe for transformation with (hopefully, as George Keller, 1996, has requested) creative alternatives rather than merely criticisms of contemporary practice.

La Fin de Siècle

The academic profession has evolved through a series of modifications since faculty began engaging students. Beginning in the Middle Ages, faculty have associated as professional colleagues within college and university structures (Haskins, 1967) rather than acting as independent contractors engaged by students. In the new American colonies, they associated under the leadership of a scholarly president. But within a century of that period, they began to realize autonomous professional status (Finklestein, 1984). By exploring and defining knowledge through rising disciplines, faculty continuously refined their relationships to each other and to their institutions (Metzger, 1987). At the end of the Progressive Era, higher education had diversified extensively. Presidents sought assistance from deans and others to define and manage the growing organizational complexity of their institutions. Since then, the professorial role has been influenced by administrative strategies and tactics aimed at ensuring the success of the institutions' mission.

Recent generations of faculty have clarified the professional role by advancing and sharing knowledge, developing utilitarian and aesthetic products for society, and self-regulating the quality of that knowledge and those products through the professional peer review and public market systems. Early stimulations for change in the faculty role were few in number and focused on the academy, thus allowing faculty to expand their autonomy.

At the end of the twentieth century, American faculty find themselves in a peculiar situation with regard to this balance of autonomy and accountability. As Radcliffe College President Linda Wilson (1995) has observed, the role of the faculty has become very complex: "They serve as educators, counselors, researchers, entrepreneurs, policy advisors, peer reviewers, public relations performers, financial managers, personnel managers, to name several of their roles *within the enterprise*" (Wilson, 1995, p. 115; emphasis in the original). In their professional role, faculty also are engaged in activities with colleagues within disciplinary or field associations. Autonomy is preserved through professional associations that safeguard the quality of the knowledge produced through public contributions. Faculty thus serve as scholars, peer reviewers, elected officials, mentors, editors, and consultants, to name several of their roles *within their invisible colleges.*

Without doubt, the degree to which—and the number of people to whom—faculty are accountable for their complex set of actions has escalated within the recent past. Thus, the demands on and alterations in the faculty role are accelerating. Multiple, complicated, and often contradictory contemporary forces, both within our institutions and external to them, are challenging the evolved definition and nature of the profession.

Institutional Exigencies

In three decades, the higher education system has moved from unprecedented growth to accelerated resource competition. Current institutional exigencies have been exacerbated by reductions in support on the national and state levels; with each response of academic personnel to these challenges, the faculty role has been affected.

With the 1960s' enrollment expansion, both the complement of faculty and the physical plant complexes enlarged and required substantial resources for maintenance. To support both, a new set of consumers had to be identified and wooed. Institutions established or expanded their master's and doctoral programs, drifting into new degree-granting categories (Aldersley, 1995; Finnegan, 1992; Birnbaum, 1988). The community college expansion of the 1970s magnified the competition for traditional-age students. Enrollments thinned across several sectors. Institutions coped by opening their doors to adult learners, who brought different learning needs and abilities to the classroom. As four-year-institution faculty slots diminished, the competition accelerated; this permitted administrators across the sectors to hire faculty with credentials that exceeded those of their seniors (Eimers, 1996; Finnegan, 1993; Queval, 1990; Krohn, 1992).

The newly constituted universities with their young research-oriented faculty lacked the prestige of the established institutions they sought to emulate in order to obtain resources for sustaining the graduate programs, faculty, and students. As the new faculty approached tenure and promotion, the academic ratchet (Massey, 1990) began; administrative and faculty expectations for publications jumped (Muffo and Robinson, 1981; Finnegan and Gamson, 1996). Even with recent appeals to institutions to emphasize teaching, the faculty's desire to expand available time for research continues to intensify (Finklestein, Seal, and Schuster, 1995).

Since the competition for diminishing resources has not abated, the products of faculty research, whether publications or practical goods, have gained in their utility to develop and maintain institutional prestige and resources. As such, the criteria for appointments, contract renewal, tenure, and promotion have spiraled upward as faculty compete for a limited number of employment slots. Across most sectors, faculty have had little choice but to pursue research agendas, often to the detriment of their institutional roles.

As the ratchet tightens, the number of publications and then the quality of journals and publishers gain prominence over measures of teaching. Then, external peer reviews of publication portfolios are added to the process. Thus, professorial autonomy substantially derives from a peer quality control system that governs publication and other scholarly activities; in other words, professional and institutional success for most faculty members is derived from a source external to the institution. Regardless of the fact that provosts and presidents recommend and governing boards ultimately award promotion and tenure, the autonomy of the faculty in controlling its membership and their activities has grown to considerable proportions. Administrators have relinquished their role in accountability by handing autonomy to operations within the invisible colleges of the disciplines.

With the new research-oriented faculty secured, research grants provided new sources of support across many institutions beginning in the 1980s (Feller and Geiger, 1993). Institutional coffers are supplemented by indirect cost-recovery funds and occasionally from royalties realized from patents and other products. Cost-recovery monies not only supply teaching surrogates but often replace research, travel, and equipment funds, thus making grant stalking even more essential and prevalent. Forty-one percent of the faculty employed across the sectors and surveyed in 1992 had conducted research with intramural or extramural funds within the preceding two years; not surprisingly, 60 percent of the public university faculty reported using research funds (Dey, 1995). By making the quest for grants a criterion for tenure and promotion, administrators further normalized not only scholarship but professional and external entrepreneurial behavior.

Finding new money is only one side of the budgetary coin. When looking for resources, the search involves only one set of tactics that have affected faculty. As nonacademic staff increased an "astounding" 60 percent from 1975 to 1985 (Wertz and Dreyfus, 1995), and as state and federal subsidies have diminished (Minter, 1991), administrators have had to reduce instructional budget expenditures. Composed heavily of personnel costs, budget reductions are realized by trimming the complement of full-time faculty.

Outsourcing auxiliary services, such as the campus bookstore and food service operations, has reduced expenditures for many colleges and universities since the 1980s, and increasingly so in the 1990s, by dispatching the accelerating cost of services to private contractors (Wertz and Dreyfus, 1995). Applying the same logic to the employment of faculty, use of long-term non–tenure-track instructors is pervasive (Gappa and Leslie, 1993; Chronister, Baldwin, and Bailey, 1992). Outsourcing faculty reduces the number of long-term contractual commitments to faculty and contains salary expenditures within the instructional budget. Recent faculty hires "are less likely to be in the tenure stream: fully 32.8 percent are not in tenure-eligible positions compared to 15.8 percent of their more senior colleagues" (Finkelstein, Seal, and Schuster, 1995, p. 12). Replacing tenurable faculty slots with temporary appointments—even though accrediting agencies have long advised administrators against this practice—complicates the role of the permanent faculty.

Faculty/student contact hours vary across types of institutions, but sector differentials in teaching loads do not explain the complexity of the workload. Except for specialized coursework, temporary faculty tend to be hired for introductory or survey courses, leaving upper-level courses to permanent faculty. Although we know that 69 percent of faculty have prepared a new course within the preceding two years of being surveyed (Dey 1995), we do not know why. How many different preparations? And at what level of complexity do faculty teach? A three-course/three-preparation load demands more scholarship and instructional preparation than a four-course/two-preparation load, albeit with less classroom time. Outsourcing lower-level courses may add to the claims on faculty time and energy in ways not perceived.

In addition, the quality of the academic programs is likely to be diminished. Regardless of how competent short-term contracted faculty are in the classroom, temporary personnel tend not to become involved with curricular planning and construction or serve in institutional governance roles (Chronister, Baldwin, and Bailey, 1992) since their priority logically rests with securing their own professional future. With fewer colleagues, the development and implementation of programs become burdens.

Faculty accountability for and encouragement to pursue institutional activities, namely, teaching and service, largely have been tied to institutional type (Clark, 1987). Student course evaluations provide the bulk of evidence of instructional competency, and contributions to institutional governance generally lack scrutiny. Indeed, the institutional press is for faculty to join the quest for organizational prestige and resources, while the faculty's own desire is to pursue scholarship for external recognition, salary supplements, and possibly mobility; between these two forces, faculty are pushed and pull themselves outside the walls of the campus. Surprisingly, most faculty continue to agree—at least they did in 1993—that they would choose to enter academe again (Finkelstein, Seal, and Schuster, 1995). As the external climate changes, substantial modifications to the role and careers of the faculty and the processes of accountability and autonomy could easily develop, changing faculty's career devotion.

The quest for prestige and resources has translated into new resources, in some cases stable or increased enrollments, in others grants and patents. Certainly, most nonacademics recognize the intrinsic and extrinsic value in applications of research, especially in medicine and engineering. However, since faculty autonomy and accountability practices largely do not make sense to external constituents, government officials and the public have entered into the arena of accountability. Accountability for these groups does not rest with the quality of professional abilities or with the contributions of the faculty, but rather with cost-benefit concerns. Explanations of the benefits of a college education and bases for the high cost of education have fallen short.

External Pressures

Public resources have been stretched to their limits; national, state, and local public officials are all seeking new sources of revenue as well as expenditure reductions. One potential source has been nonprofit organizations. When for-profit businesses challenged nonprofit income tax exemptions associated with unrelated business profits in the 1980s, the door opened to regulate and pressure institutions to pay their share of cost of the commonweal. More recently, universities and colleges have been targeted by local governments as a source of property tax revenue or community service user fees (Burns, 1996). On the other hand, public subsidies for higher education have proven to be one source for realized savings for state budgets (Hines, 1994), especially since public universities have found sovereign resources from their own fundraising efforts.

The erosion of public confidence in higher education has aggravated these new financial demands. Rising tuition rates, depreciating occupational prospects and financial profit for graduates, and escalating concerns about the skills of graduates have caused citizens to question the return on their civic investment. In many states, the legislative response has been to mandate what might be called valuation studies (that is, determination of the quantitative return for financial support) and to attempt their own modifications of the faculty role so as to force institutions to reduce their expenses.

The first public offensive tactic has been to question teaching loads. In response to the public outcry that assumes a direct relationship of time spent in the classroom to public benefit, at least twenty-three state legislatures have commissioned faculty workload studies within the past few years (*Chronicle of Higher Education Almanac Issue,* 1993; State Higher Education Executive Officers, 1994). The simplistic solution to the soaring cost of public higher education and to tuition increases appears to many to be increasing the hours faculty spend in the classroom. Absent an alternative, legislatively mandated teaching loads are not inconceivable (Layzell, Lovell, and Gill, 1996).

Tuition, although escalating, does not cover the cost of operations (Hansen and Stampen, 1993). Unfunded government regulations require personnel for compliance; delayed maintenance projects and infrastructure renovations can no longer be avoided (Association of Physical Plant Administrators of Universities and Colleges, 1989); and new technology is required to maintain instructional currency (Conditions of Education, 1995). Public institutions now supplement tuition revenue and state subsidies with private funds, while private institutions seek federal and state subventions to complement their fundraising. Both actions blur the formerly clean line between private and public institutions, but they also project an ability to balance the budget with decreased support.

The second line of public offense has been aimed at eliminating tenure, with legislative bills and proposals emerging in various states. The debate on the efficacy of tenure is muddied by disparate definitions and attributed consequences that divert consideration from the function and purpose of tenure. Concerned with faculty accountability in the classroom (State Notes, 1995), a South Carolina state representative introduced legislation to eliminate tenure in the public colleges. In Florida, the state Board of Regents, although desirous of eliminating tenure throughout the university system, agreed to experiment with a mixed tenure and multiyear contract system at a new campus opening in fall 1997 (Cage, 1995). A university administrator suggested that the new system might enable the state universities to fill short-term curricular needs (Cage, 1995), while a state regent submitted that removing tenure would avoid the costly litigation that can occur when a candidate's tenure application is rejected (Uhlfelder 1995).

As Layzell, Lovell, and Gill (1996) have noted, these issues point to a dissonance between the goals of the public and the faculty—and, I would add, the institutions. As faculty have become obsessed with satisfying the peer review system, it has snowballed into an essential component in a large proportion of promotion and tenure judgments. Without this external sanctioning of professional competence, ensuring continuous employment and rewards for faculty is most difficult. Professional autonomy and accountability practices for faculty thus have devolved in large measure to an extra-institutional process. It is no wonder that faculty have fled the classroom and service opportunities.

However, the public and its representatives have become concerned both with evidence (rather, the lack of it) that the cost of higher education produces the benefits it touts and with the high price tag that appears to support the scholarly agendas of individual faculty rather than the needs of society. The chasm is widening every year. Without serious intervention from the faculty themselves in concert with their administrators, "legislative solutions will be fashioned to 'fix' the situation" (Layzell, Lovell, and Gill, 1996, p. 93). This prediction may appear far-fetched, but in Virginia recently threats of abolishing tenure were used as a fiscal sledgehammer to secure implementation of accountability measures and to encourage institutional responsiveness. The state coordinating council was able to avoid legislative discussion of removing tenure by requiring post-tenure review processes that were coupled to an institution's funding of faculty salary increments.

The Challenges of the New Century

Given these issues, the consequences for the faculty are legion—that is, they will be if we do nothing about transforming our academic culture; our organizational structures; our employment requirements, norms, and rewards; and our daily activities. We can formulate our future, based at least on what we can extrapolate from current trends, or we can allow all vestiges of faculty autonomy and accountability to dissolve and be determined by external constituencies.

Wilson (1995) argues that personnel policies assume that faculty still derive support from a model of traditional gender roles. The traditional family that accommodates the faculty's contributions and achievements at great "sacrifice of personal life" no longer exists in the main; ". . . We need to recognize how very much the design features built into our institutions are linked to these out-of-date expectations and how much they therefore impede progress toward our goals of engaging talent effectively" (Wilson, 1995, p. 115). Indeed, the design features are linked also to bounded definitions of professional quality that are impeding external relations. But who is to define the meaning of faculty talent? In what ways should faculty talent be engaged? Finally, what does progress mean? If expectations and definitions are both stale, then transformation is essential. Transformation of the faculty role is going to happen whether it is generated from within or forced from without by economic exigencies.

Rost (1993) defines leadership as a collaboration in which leaders and followers develop mutual purposes projected for the common good; only through the establishment of these mutual purposes can real transformation occur. "Real transformation involves active people, engaging in influence relationships based on persuasion, intending real changes to happen, and insisting that those changes reflect their mutual purposes" (Rost, 1993, p. 123). Tinkering with incentives and rewards only modifies current practice, in an attempt to permit us to go on with business as usual. We are not living in a business-as-usual world. By analyzing the emerging social patterns, we can surmise elements of the transformation required in colleges and universities. Then, faculty and administrators can develop mutual purposes for the common good and not merely adjust the role of faculty.

The Information Age

Whether we look at its economy, politics, or education, the structure of our society has been defined within the Industrial Age, which is marked by bureaucracy, specialization, and boundaries. Most futurists agree that the Industrial Age is waning

(Sandel, 1996; Drucker, 1994; Rost, 1993). We have entered the early stages of the Information Age, or a knowledge society (Drucker, 1994), with extraordinary advances in technology that impact almost every facet of life. Arising economic patterns and political needs exhibit clues to potential elements of the new social order; they suggest possible transformations in higher education if it is to remain an active agent in society.

In a recent interview, Secretary of Labor Robert Reich called society's unfolding economy an "electronic capitalism in which investment decisions are made at the speed of an electronic impulse." Within this new economy, "the most rapidly growing job categories are knowledge-intensive" (Bennahum, 1996). "Knowledge workers" will constitute more than one third of the workforce in the United States by the turn of the century and "will give the emerging knowledge society its character, its leadership, its social profile" (Drucker, 1994, p. 64). Reich concludes that "technology and globalization have conspired to shift demand in favor of people with the skills, the right education, and the right connections, and against people without these attributes" (cited in Bennahum, 1996).

At the same time, the National Commission for Employment (Mishel and Bernstein, 1995) reports that the recent downsizing across most industries is forcing new patterns of employment. Downsizing has been used to encourage industry profit and to control federal spending. Employment growth has occurred in temporary positions, which, although accounting for only 2 percent of all jobs, are responsible for 20 percent of all new slots. Almost 19 percent of the workforce describe themselves as "self-employed" (Longworth and Stein, 1995). Successful companies, those marked by "sales growth and international market expansion," rely heavily on "contingent workers," that is, part-time and contracted employees (Kanter, 1995, p. 93). Job security and retiring from the sole career corporation have faded as employment norms. Langdon Winner, an RPI science and technology scholar, notes that "valued now are protean flexibility, restless entrepreneurialism and a willingness to dissolve social bonds in the pursuit of material gain" (1995, p. 5).

Within corporations, organizational culture is shifting from centralization and regulation to the opposite pole, moving away from the rational bureaucratic scheme that has dominated this century. Halal reports that "the most successful corporations today, MCI, Hewlett-Packard, ABB, have redistributed decision-making power to small 'internal enterprises' that are free to manage their own affairs. Where organizations were once 'vertically integrated' by hierarchical control, these internal enterprises are 'virtually integrated' over the growing grid of information networks as they buy and sell from one another and from outside firms" (1996).

Traditional boundaries are being crossed elsewhere. McClenon argues that "the nation-state is no longer universally the most appropriate form of sovereign government. A challenge for humanity in the twenty-first century will be the re-definition of appropriate governmental institutions and of the relationships be-tween nations and states" (1995, p. 1). Through the Industrial Revolution, American politics has operated according to economic theory rather than by a civic philosophy. Conservatives have promoted economic growth, while liberals have sought broad access to prosperity (Sandel, 1996). So the battle to differenti-ate individual civil liberties from group civil rights continues to plague us. "Find-ing and preserving the right balance between local, provincial, regional, and subcontinental government will remain an issue. The challenge for the United States, as a culturally diverse and heterogeneous nation, is to avoid internal frag-mentation and polarization, and to complete the incomplete task of racial justice while avoiding being divided by competing claims of group rights" (McClenon, 1995, pp. 2–3). Sandel (1996) posits that to achieve a democratic political authority, we face the challenges of devising a political institution capable of governing the global economy and cultivating the civic identity that is necessary to devise the moral authority required.

Between the new economic trends of fluidity and the floundering political modes of polarization, society needs to devise a workable *Weltanschauung*. Aca-demics can assume leadership as society works through influencing the value system, or they can maintain the status quo by keeping with a moribund system of faculty role requirements supported and encouraged by a restrictive reward sys-tem. If we do not transform our own goals, then politicians, corporate leaders, and proprietary administrators will fill the void (Burke, 1994). To some degree, these agents are already concentrating on the new society's needs.

Addressing entrepreneurial skills, the Open University, a proprietary institu-tion in Orlando, offers variable-length certificate programs that teach the skills re-quired in the cash-flow industry to buy, sell, and broker financial and debt instruments, that is, mortgages, promissory notes, contracts, lottery winnings, in-surance, and so on. According to its advertisements, students receive knowledge-intensive training and graduates are able to establish transportable careers that are not corporate-dependent.

From the corporate side, responsive learning and community building are surfacing as essential skills for the knowledge society. The software company Lightbridge defines itself as a "learning organization": "Managers set goals for education, and the company offers abundant courses in project management and software development techniques, as well as featuring a large library" (Kanter, 1995, p. 96).

Finally, concerned about cost and access—and wise to the potential of digi-tal technology—eleven western governors proposed in late 1995 to establish a vir-tual university to serve a multistate constituency. The university is projected to reduce future budgetary strains as the college population within these states increases over the next decade. Offering no instruction, the university will award credit by assessing students' mastery of postsecondary courses (Blumenstyk, 1995). By June 1996, the virtual university design, managed by the Western Governors' Association staff, already includes a draft of a virtual catalogue, competency assessment outlines in several broad content areas, and plans for legislative and accreditation policy agreements, among other artifacts of the new institution. A competency-based degree eliminates building new classrooms and faculty offices, long-term commitments to and relationships with additional "permanent" instructional staff, and operating capital for face-to-face instruction.

Carried to an extreme, these trends of campus downsizing, distance-learning cyberprograms, proprietary short courses, and industry in-service could translate into a drastic academic personnel innovation: privatizing or outsourcing faculty on a fairly large scale. If we do not reform ourselves, others will.

Transforming Faculty Talent

Three distinct areas within colleges and universities that affect faculty directly are ripe for transformation: organizational structures and their commitments, faculty personnel policies and practices, and faculty development. Examples of innovative practice and my own experience and thoughts pertaining to these three areas offer alternatives to current customs and trends.

Organizational Structures and Their Commitments. The structure of most colleges and universities reflects an "industrial paradigm" (Rost, 1993) that emphasizes productivity, whether measured by faculty publications or student/credit-hour loads. As hierarchical bureaucracies, colleges and universities often operate by top-down planning with personnel designated to departments and offices. Governing boards make policy, presidents propose policy, provosts and deans administer policy and manage annual operations through their staff, and faculty provide the primary services.

Faculty belong to disciplinary or field-specific departments or area divisions with personnel decisions and employment budget lines expensed to these units. Certainly, departments composed of active scholars engaged in similar subjects encourage more faculty productivity, but they also limit explorations of cross-disciplinary perspectives (Rost, 1993). Yet, within the past decades a considerable amount of knowledge has been advanced by scholars crossing discipline boundaries.

Models of interdisciplinary research centers do exist. Boston College maintains a Center for Corporate Community Relations, which provides training and research services to corporations in the community with the intent of fostering corporate community involvement. George Mason University houses the International Institute, with intramural centers that specialize in European Community studies and global market studies. GMU also sponsors the Center for Conflict Analysis and Resolution, which concentrates on conflict related to social fragmentation and multiculturalism (Potter and Chickering, 1991). The College of William and Mary, using a "cluster" concept, encourages faculty and students across several disciplines and fields to initiate research and application projects under a defined topic. The Environmental Policy Cluster, which commences in the fall of 1996, was planned by and supports faculty and students from biology, marine sciences, public policy, government, and law.

Reorganizing faculty into broad issue-related units to support collaboration in scholarship and curriculum would be a logical transformation, radical as that might be. At minimum, using the new corporate management model, faculty at least should be stimulated and rewarded to become "virtually integrated," to set up knowledge networks based upon broad issues with social impact. Knowledge networks using digital technology can invest scholars and students from across the country and the globe in discovering and applying knowledge. At Arizona State University, a faculty member facilitates a virtual seminar in global political economy "mediated through computer networks, electronic mail, and electronic archiving of materials" (Gonick, 1995). Participants include forty faculty members (scholars from Zimbabwe, Mexico City, Moscow) and, over the past two years, about 250 students from more than thirty countries. Students not only are connected to the world's foremost specialists but are required to collaborate in research projects with peers from other institutions.

When faculty are not segregated into disciplinary departments, the curriculum is more likely to assume an interdisciplinary character as well as to focus on student needs rather than the content of singular fields. Preparing graduates to confront combined, knowledge-intensive occupations is a task that we have only begun to address. Graduates need to be self-reliant and entrepreneurial, possessing a transportable skill set. They must learn to collaborate within issue-oriented teams, to take initiative, to find and analyze resources quickly, and to devise creative solutions (Kanter, 1995). Through interdisciplinarity, students can learn and practice stochastic thinking, generating and testing new models and approaches to new questions and problems. They also must learn to appreciate, value, and advocate the social bonds required for human life. Focusing on theories and concepts from only one paradigmatic perspective is no longer a viable path. Interdisciplinary units could engage faculty to cross boundaries that departments have maintained so rigidly. Further, faculty can model collaborative organizational behavior and foster these professional skills and personal traits, but only if the organizational affiliations, resources, and investments are in place (Ahrne, 1994).

Faculty Personnel Policies and Practices. If transformation is a goal, then the common purpose of our institutions must be determined by the administrators and faculty in concert. Realizing the common purpose cannot occur without the participation of the faculty. Revising the departmental structure does not in itself transform faculty activities unless new configurations are empowered, with at least some budgetary input and with units gaining direct involvement in personnel commitments.

To encourage collaboration within and across units, incentives and rewards must be provided that support team projects oriented toward the common purpose. Several innovative tactics can encourage and reward an individual's participation in preferred activities. Professional accounts, which are tax-free stipends, allow faculty who engage in the common purpose to purchase additional hardware and software, pay for professional expenses, or supplement travel allotments. Competitive, but institutionalized, course-releases permit faculty to plan, experiment with, or implement projects with unit members or with students. Entrepreneurial loans that require an operational plan and an amortized payback scheme support units that seek new revenue sources, whether in the form of enrollments, grants, or gifts.

Incentives and rewards are not the only elements that drive an individual's behavior. Every system also possesses disincentives: policies and procedures that threaten or punish inappropriate behavior indirectly. Disincentives that impede fostering common purposes must be identified and removed. Currently, in many research institutions, service to external constituents has gained prominence in the presidents' rhetoric, but it is often discounted in promotion and tenure decisions. Should a faculty member translate the experience into publication, the disincentive remains if empirical scholarship is prized over the dissemination of applied scholarship.

Transforming assessment and evaluation criteria to advocate the new common purpose is essential. About ten years ago, the cafeteria-style benefits-package concept addressed the variegated life choices of faculty. A cafeteria-style faculty role set would encourage new modes of faculty contributions. Although Ernest Boyer (1990) formulated a taxonomy of scholarship that broadens the definition of faculty activity, his taxonomy or any other set of redefinitions cannot work unless the prestige hierarchy inherent in faculty activities is recast. Indeed, major scholarly innovations are essential to the continued progress of intellectual thought and production of utilitarian goods. However, our current values-and-reward system, rooted in the late–nineteenth-century Americanized ideal of scholarship brought back from the German universities, prevents us from respecting other academic activities.

Patrick Terenzini's (1989) assessment cube for appraising student outcomes may be expanded to form a set of criteria to transform the assessment and evaluation system for faculty appointment and rewards. The criteria should include *purpose, object, level* (Terenzini, 1989), and *audience, quality, and effect.* Terenzini (1989) uses *purpose* to ask why. Does the assessment serve an accountability function, which is summative, or a developmental one, which is formative? *Object* refers to the type of product (Terenzini, 1989) and might employ Boyer's taxonomy of scholarship (1990): discovery, translation, application, and teaching. Being artificial, taxonomies place no intrinsic value on any one of the taxons. The forms of scholarship therefore may be accorded equal merit or differential merit depending upon the institutional and unit common purposes. *Level* refers to agency, that is, whether the activity emanates from solitary effort, individual effort that promotes the group, or collaborative group effort.

Once value is attached to the various forms of scholarship, the *audience* for whom the scholarship was created must be consulted. As long as the only audience from which we credit evaluations is the professional peer group, the system remains the same and only discrete research agendas are addressed. Given the four types of scholarship, audiences may include the traditional invisible colleges, students, other faculty and professionals, and citizen-clients. Finally, *effect* refers to the quality and efficacy of the scholarship. Most often scholarly products are counted and, depending upon the type of institution, perhaps ranked according to the exclusivity of the publishing agent. The actual quality of the product itself is often neglected, or at best evaluated as part of a package of products by outside reviewers. Likewise, the magnitude of influence and consequences that result from faculty products does not often enter the evaluation schemas we use. Rather, we rely on reputation—of the journal, the publisher, the peer reviewers, and even the number (but rarely the content) of citations for a substitute measure of effect.

Sternberg and Horvath (1995) define *experts* as persons who use knowledge in more effective ways, solve problems more efficiently, and apply more novel and appropriate solutions than novices do. While undergraduates certainly can be considered novices in a field, many professionals who work in such applied fields as local government, social services, and the schools fall at the midpoint on a continuum of expertise. Educated in their vocation, many lack new skills and access to new knowledge advanced since finishing their degrees. Faculty, on the other hand, spend their professional lives constructing "more nearly adequate problem models" (Sternberg and Horvath 1995, p. 13) within a field of knowledge and can provide and interpret new perspectives to applied professionals and illustrate new or alternative methods of solving problems.

An example illustrates the point. Often within rural or at least less urban areas, local officials serve in part-time elected positions. Although they understand the social politics of the area, they often do not have the expertise necessary to manage the municipality. Indeed, many of these officials have limited access to sources of instruction in basic procedures. Faculty educate nonspecialists by developing workbooks designed with local budget problems and conducting short-courses or on-site training in budgeting for elected local officials. This type of scholarship extends faculty expertise beyond the invisible colleges, and it challenges faculty to integrate knowledge by forging new perspectives.

As the range of acceptable products broadens, so must the measures and sources of evaluation. Publication of journal articles documenting a successful application is only one potential source to judge the quality and effect of a professional's activities. *Criteria-based* testimonies from recipients of consultations, reports detailing planning and implementation processes, and documentation of successful changes or outcomes are some of the ways that evaluations and assessments can include new and relevant audiences for translation and application scholarship. When a faculty member teaches her students the process of state legislative policy making and when, through a class project, a significant piece of legislation is passed, is this not scholarship? Are the audiences not identifiable? Are the quality and effect not apparent? When a faculty member writes a textbook that translates the field to undergraduates and is adopted by a multitude of faculty from across the country, is this not scholarship? Are the audiences not identifiable? Cannot the quality and effect be ascertained?

These scholarly activities require the same technical expertise and a similar amount of effort and time to create as a research project does. Yet heretofore, they have been considered less-than-appropriate activities and the audiences inappropriate evaluators of faculty expertise. The audiences that might be tapped for evaluations are available; the issue is credibility. So long as personnel committees and academic administrators hold sacred the scholarship hierarchy that posits empirical research as the pinnacle rather than as one point on a continuum of knowledge advancement, then alternative schemes and consequentially transformation will not be adopted.

Faculty Development. Internet conferences, learnware for adults, videoconferences, on-line books and journals, e-zines, Internet yellow pages, virtual libraries, asynchronous classes, computer-mediated communication, newsmedia, digital video—the technological innovations in merely the last three years are staggering. Keeping up with almost daily announcements of new applications of digital technology is virtually impossible. Incorporating the technology into our personal and professional lives presents new challenges for collaboration: refocusing instruction from teaching to learning, exploring and adopting new interactive distance and on-site digital technology systems, and integrating nonthreatening assessment processes to transform our institutions into continuous-improvement learning organizations.

Steven Gilbert of the American Association of Higher Education's Teaching, Learning, and Technology Roundtable has recently noted that "new applications of information technology can be used either to increase the isolation of individuals and further fragment our society or to support forms of collaborative work and sustain more effective communities" (Gilbert, 1996). The faculty role, though, continues to support individual action and products that have little direct impact on their institution's purpose and primary responsibility. Furthermore, it continues thus in a social environment in which future stable employment patterns are tenuous. Faculty would be more willing to collaborate with each other and their administrators if "the interaction is likely to continue for a long time, and the players care enough about their future together" (Axelrod, 1984, p. 182). I would add: if the players are convinced that their investment makes a difference.

In the common purposes we devise and the transformations that follow, faculty need the time to explore the resources and their potential, develop their individual and collective expertise, and reconceive many of their scholarly activities. Until participants agree and accept the need for transformation and not merely redefinition, dynamic change will not occur. A moratorium on annual normative business underscores the imperative nature of devising a common purpose and a new definition of the faculty role. Teams of faculty and administrators who normally do not work together but who are brought together to devise purposes and role definitions not only help to dissolve standing alliances but also forge new relationships and generate ideas that cross traditional boundaries. Simultaneous team sessions that explore common topics for which background literature is provided permit focused discussions, especially if teams are responsible to the larger unit for proposals on a regular basis. From the transformation of the organizational structure, a second phase, the translation of the educational activities, can proceed.

No longer is the concept of transforming our institutions from a teaching orientation to one of learning an eccentric idea. While disciplinary paradigms have provided the necessary epistemological structure to develop knowledge throughout the past century and a half and have provided the basic content for the curriculum, society now requires what Reich calls symbolic analysts, who "utilize the technology for problem-solving" (Bennahum, 1996). Knowledge workers must be able to acquire additional specialties rapidly (Drucker, 1994). With the amount of knowledge already universally accessible, and forecasted to be available through digital connections, learning how to consider knowledge—that is, how to apply, analyze, and evaluate—and learning how to utilize knowledge—that is, extrapolate, predict, synthesize, and create—become essential cognitive skills.

The focus on teaching, and especially on lecturing, is obsolete. One emerging approach is issue-oriented teams of students guided by faculty in problem-solving exercises. Applied fields have used case studies for some time, but a student-centered, issue-oriented approach is viable across a variety of knowledge areas and usually has many interesting outcomes. In his church history seminar, a faculty member at the International School of Theology in California combines class meetings with asynchronous on-line mentored discussions based on threaded open-ended questions. Linked on e-mail by a class listserver, students respond twice a week to the official discussion, but they also create informal content-based "whispers" among themselves as well as developing their own content-based discussion threads (Albrektson, 1995). Indeed, lecturing and passive leaning has been comfortable for both faculty and students, but students can learn to assume more responsibility and faculty can learn to facilitate rather than direct. What is needed are "curricula . . . driven by student needs and tested by feedback from students, employers, professional associations, and alumni" (Massy, 1996, p. 11) and by society's need to devise a workable economic and political framework.

Third, faculty and administrators must explore and adopt new interactive distance and on-site digital technology systems. Twenty-five years ago, when new external degree institutions were established, the higher education establishment was slow to accept their credibility. Today, numerous small colleges across the nation are affiliating with education consulting firms to develop a new market share by offering adult degree completion programs through short, tailored, cohort-based curricula. Other colleges and universities are investing in sophisticated uplink/downlink technology to attract new and, more specifically, additional students through distance-learning programs. Old Dominion University has partnered with the Virginia community colleges to offer upper-level baccalaureate coursework and degrees to distance students. In general, faculty are not prepared in their graduate work to teach, let alone to cope with, distance learning.

These new initiatives require the added skills of facilitating learning within a pattern of real-time, long-distance, and multisite classes. The initiatives require course objectives and teaching techniques that are learner-centered and oriented to skill mastery rather than faculty- and content-centered (Bork, 1995). The initiatives require new skills of interaction over computer time, rather than "face-time" in the office or classroom. Learning these skills, both instructional and technological, takes time, and it requires incentives, rewards, and contractual commitments.

As noted above, the appointment-and-rewards system for faculty must support any transformation that is to occur. Threats to autonomy in the form of abolishing tenure and the response of emphasizing post-tenure review demonstrate that we are not transforming from within, but rather reacting to accountability movements from without. Most faculty development programs described by scholars focus on helping new faculty to cope with the competing demands of teaching and research; as they try to cope, the probation clock ticks away. Recently, development programs for senior faculty have been discussed, but rejuvenation is situated within the clearly comfortable research mode as post-tenure review requires continued productivity. Are these appropriate forms of development that support our future?

Finally, a common purpose; a learning-centered environment; an inclusive and future-oriented appointment, incentive, and reward system; and an institutional commitment to transformation require integrating nonthreatening assessment processes to change institutions into continuous-improvement learning organizations. Unit and subunit goals, the individual faculty member's part in achieving those goals, and the institution's part in advocating the faculty member's scholarly goals must be defined; the progress of the three have to be assessed, feedback provided, and course corrections made. Clearly, individuals should be held responsible for their action and inaction, and eventually evaluation must occur; but an inappropriate reward system, including incentives and disincentives, should not stand in the way.

Evaluation for the untenured does not have to occur every year if bona fide assessments are accomplished. Post-tenure review does not have to be endured on a cyclical basis if bona fide assessments are accomplished. The unit's administrator can facilitate evaluation of unit goal accomplishments and the process of correcting the course and activities. As a part of that process, the administrator can assess the amount, quality, and effect that result from both the group's and the individual's efforts. When individuals choose not to participate, consequences must follow. Participants must be committed, but they must also feel a commitment from the institution.

Transformation is not easy. The development of the contemporary faculty role took decades. Unfortunately, I do not believe that we have decades to create a transformation. I do believe that change is in process. Whether the change occurs as a deliberate transformation on our part that reconceptualizes autonomy and assumes accountability—or as an unwelcome, reconfigured, and financially based set of employment procedures and requirements from external sources—is entirely up to us.

Further Reading

A variety of scholars are wrestling with issues related to the future of the faculty and higher education. Interested readers should consult R. Eugene Rice's work on the faculty role; his writings on transforming the faculty role span almost a decade and inspired Boyer's taxonomy (1990). Rice's latest paper, "Making a Place for the New American Scholar" (presented at the 1996 AAHE Conference on Faculty Roles and Rewards), continues his thought-provoking vision of the faculty perspective. Potter and Chickering's (1991) discussion of the role of government thoroughly outlines the boundaries that must be crossed if transformation is to occur. The anthology by Sims and Sims (1991) in which their chapter appears offers a number of insights by various scholars. The bimonthly newsletter *On the Horizon*, edited by James Morrison, is a tremendous source for challenging debate on future trends in and around higher education. Finally, I commend Joseph C. Rost's *Leadership for the Twenty-First Century* (1993) to all as a magnificent treatise on the concept of leadership (rather than leaders' behavior traits) that is eminently instructive about what can and should be accomplished for transformation.

References

Ahrne, G. *Social Organizations: Interaction Inside, Outside, and Between Organizations.* London: Sage, 1994.

Albrektson, J. R. "Mentored Online Seminar: A Model for Graduate-Level Distance Learning." *T.H.E. Journal,* Oct. 1995, 102–105.

Aldersley, S. F. "'Upward Drift' is Alive and Well: Research/Doctoral Model Still Attractive to Institutions." *Change,* 1995, *27*(4), 16–20.

Association of Physical Plant Administrators of Universities and Colleges. *Capital Renewal and Deferred Maintenance.* Critical Issues in Facilities Management, no. 4. Washington, D.C.: APPA, 1989.

Axelrod, R. *The Evolution of Cooperation.* New York: Basic Books, 1984.

Bennahum, D. S. "An Interview with U.S. Secretary of Labor Robert Reich." *MEME,* Jan. 24, 1996.

Birnbaum, R. "State Colleges: An Unsettled Quality." In G. T. Kurian (ed.), *Yearbook of American Universities and Colleges, Academic Year 1986–87.* New York: Garland, 1988.

Blumenstyk, G. "Campuses in Cyberspace." *Chronicle of Higher Education,* Dec. 15, 1995, pp. A19, A21.

Bork, A. "Distance Learning and Interaction: Toward a Virtual Learning Institution." *Journal of Science Education and Technology,* 1995, *4*(3), 227–244.

Boyer, E. L. *Scholarship Reconsidered: Priorities of the Professoriate.* Princeton, N.J.: Carnegie Foundation for the Advancement of Teaching, 1990.

Burke, J. C. "New Faculty Roles in New Learning Environments." Paper presented at the SUNY Conference on Instructional Technologies, Albany, June 1994.

Burns, C. F. "Rendering Unto Caesar: The Movement to Tax Colleges." *Planning for Higher Education,* 1996, *25*(1).

Cage, M. C. "New Florida University to Offer an Alternative to Tenure." *Chronicle of Higher Education,* June 2, 1995, p. A15.

Cartter, A. M. "New Look at the Supply of College Teachers." *Educational Record,* 1965, *46,* 267–277.

Chronicle of Higher Education Almanac Issue, 1993.

Chronister, J. L., Baldwin, R. G., and Bailey, T. B. "Full-time Non–Tenure-Track Faculty: Current Status, Condition, and Attitudes." *The Review of Higher Education,* 1992, *15*(4), 383–400.

Clark, B. R. *The Academic Life: Small Worlds, Different Worlds*. Princeton, N.J.: Carnegie Foundation for the Advancement of Teaching, 1987.

Conditions of Education, 1995. Vol. 2: Postsecondary Education. Washington, D.C.: National Center for Education Statistics, 1995.

Dey, E. L. "The Activities of Undergraduate Teaching Faculty." *Thought and Action: The NEA Higher Education Journal*, 1995, *11*(1), 43–62.

Drucker, P. F. "The Age of Social Transformation." *Atlantic Monthly*, 1994, *274*(3), 53–80.

Eimers, M. "Subtle Shifts in Tradition? What Faculty Find Rewarding at the Selective Liberal Arts College." Columbia: University of Missouri, unpublished manuscript, 1996.

Etzioni, A. *The Active Society: A Theory of Societal and Political Processes*. New York: The Free Press, 1968.

Fasano, C. "Balancing Autonomy and Accountability in the 21st Century: The Nature and Role of Systematic Monitoring in Education." *On the Horizon*. J. L. Morrison (ed.). Home page, Nov. 23, 1995.

Feller, I., and Geiger, R. L. "The Dispersion of Academic Research During the 1980s." Report to the Andrew W. Mellon Foundation. University Park, Pa.: Institute for Policy Research and Evaluation, Pennsylvania State University, 1993.

Finklestein, M. *The American Academic Profession: An Analysis of Social Science Research Since World War II*. Columbus: Ohio State University Press, 1984.

Finkelstein, M. J., Seal, R. K., and Schuster, J. H. *The American Faculty in Transition: A First Look at the New Academic Generation*. Preliminary report. Washington, D.C.: National Center for Education Statistics, U.S. Department of Education, 1995.

Finnegan, D. E. *Academic Career Lines: A Case Study of Faculty in Two Comprehensive Universities*. Doctoral dissertation, University Park, Pennsylvania State University, 1992.

Finnegan, D. E. "Segmentation in the Academic Labor Market: Hiring Cohorts in Comprehensive Universities." *Journal of Higher Education*, 1993, *64*(2), 621–656.

Finnegan, D. E., and Gamson, Z. "Disciplinary Adaptations to Research Culture in Comprehensive Institutions." *Review of Higher Education*, 1996, *19*(2), 141–178.

Gappa, J. M., and Leslie, D. W. *The Invisible Faculty: Improving the Status of Part-Timers in Higher Education*. San Francisco: Jossey-Bass, 1993.

Gilbert, S. W. "Making the Most of a Slow Revolution: Recommendations from the AAHE Teaching, Learning, and Technology Roundtable Program." Part 4. Posted on *Horizonlist*, Jan. 7, 1996.

Gonick, L. "The Virtual Seminar in Global Political Economy." *On The Horizon*. Home page, Nov. 18, 1995.

Halal, W. "Employee Welfare in a Turbulent Economy: A Likely Solution to the Brown-Shostak Dilemma." *On The Horizon*. Home page, Jan. 31, 1996.

Hansen, W. L., and Stampen, J. O. "The Financial Squeeze on Higher Education Institutions and Students: Balancing Quality and Access in the Financing of Higher Education." In D. W. Breneman, L. L. Leslie, and R. E. Anderson (eds.), *ASHE Reader on Finance in Higher Education*. New York: Ginn Press, 1993.

Haskins, C. H. *The Rise of Universities*. Ithaca: Cornell University Press, 1967.

Hines, E. *The Grapevine*. Sep.–Oct. 1994, no. 398. Normal, Ill.: Center for Higher Education.

Kanter, R. M. "Nice Work If You Can Get It." *The American Prospect*, 1995, *25*, 92–98.

Keller, G. "Let's Move Beyond Critical Thinking." *On the Horizon: The Environmental Scanning Publication for Educational Leaders*, 1996, *4*(1), 13–14.

Krohn, J. R. *Advancing Research Universities: A Study of Institutional Development, 1974–1986.* Unpublished doctoral dissertation, Pennsylvania State University, 1992.

Layzell, D. T., Lovell, C. D., and Gill, J. L. "Developing Faculty as an Asset in a Period of Change and Uncertainty." *Integrating Research on Faculty: Seeking New Ways to Communicate About the Academic Life of Faculty.* Conference report. Washington, D.C.: Office of Educational Research and Improvement, 1996, 93–110.

Light, D., Jr. "Introduction: The Structure of the Academic Professions." *Sociology of Education,* 1974, *47,* 2–28.

Longworth, R. C., and Stein, S. "Temp Work Replacing Lifetime Employment." *Washington Post,* Sep. 20, 1995, p. A4.

Massy, W. F. "A New Look at the Academic Department." *Policy Perspectives.* Philadelphia: Pew Higher Education Research Program, 1990.

Massy, W. F. "New Thinking on Academic Restructuring." *AGB Priorities,* 1996, *6,* 1–16.

McClenon, R. "Nation-States, 1000–2100." Essay posted on the Internet 2000 Talk List, 1995.

Metzger, W. P. "The Academic Profession in the United States." In *The Academic Profession: National, Disciplinary, and Institutional Settings.* Berkeley: University of California Press, 1987.

Minter, J. "Fiscal Facts, Trends, and Forecasts." *Educational Record,* 1991, *72*(2), 19–22.

Mintzberg, H. *The Structuring of Organizations.* Englewood Cliffs, N.J.: Prentice-Hall, 1979.

Mishel, L., and Bernstein, J. *The State of Working America.* Washington, D.C.: Bureau of Labor Statistics, National Commission for Employment, 1995.

Muffo, J. A., and Robinson, J. R. "Early Science Career Patterns of Recent Graduates from Leading Research Universities." *Review of Higher Education,* 1981, *5*(1), 1–13.

Potter, D., and Chickering, A. W. "The 21st Century University: The Role of Government." In R. R. Sims and S. Sims (eds.), *Managing Institutions of Higher Education into the 21st Century: Issues and Implications.* Westport, Conn.: Greenwood Press, 1991.

Queval, F. A. *The Evolution Toward Research Orientation and Capability in Comprehensive Universities: The California State System.* Unpublished doctoral dissertation, University of California, Los Angeles, 1990.

Rost, J. C. *Leadership for the Twenty-First Century.* New York: Praeger, 1993.

Sandel, M. J. "America's Search for a New Public Philosophy." *Atlantic Monthly,* 1996, *277*(3), 57–74.

Sims, R. R., and Sims, S. (eds.). *Managing Institutions of Higher Education into the 21st Century: Issues and Implications.* Westport, Conn.: Greenwood Press, 1991.

State Higher Education Executive Officers. *Update on Faculty Workload Activities.* Denver: State Higher Education Executive Officers, 1994.

State Notes. "South Carolina Lawmaker Would Abolish Tenure." *Chronicle of Higher Education,* Mar. 31, 1995, p. A24.

Sternberg, R. J., and Horvath, J. A. "A Prototype View of Expert Teaching." *Educational Researcher,* 1995, *24*(6), 9–17.

Terenzini, P. T. "Assessment with Open Eyes: Pitfalls in Studying Student Outcomes." *Journal of Higher Education,* 1989, *60*(6), 644–664.

Uhlfelder, S. J. "Reform Tenure Now: Addressing Florida's Failed System." *Outside the Lines.* Report on educational policy studies. Foundation for Florida's Future, Tallahassee, Fla., Aug. 1, 1995.

Wertz, R., and Dreyfus, J. V. "Privatization of Services on Campus: A Growing Trend in American Higher Education." *Privatization in Higher Education: Papers and Presentations.* Symposium and advanced workshop at the annual meeting of the National Association of College Auxiliary Services, Staunton, Va., Jan. 1995.

Wilson, L. S. "Beyond Conservation and Liberation: The Education of Our Aspirations." In *Looking to the Twenty-First Century: Higher Education in Transition.* The David D. Henry Lectures, 1986–93. Urbana-Champaign: University of Illinois Press, 1995.

Winner, L. "Who Will We Be in Cyberspace?" Paper presented at the Conference on Society and the Future of Computing, Durango, Colo., June 1995.

CHAPTER TWENTY-FIVE

SUSTAINING QUALITY ENHANCEMENT IN ACADEMIC AND MANAGERIAL LIFE

Theodore J. Marchese

Since the mid-1980s, the reigning management philosophy of corporate America has been quality management. The "quality first" movement began in the manufacturing sector; spread to services, health care, and government; and hit higher education around 1991. Total Quality Management (TQM)—or, as the movement is known in health care and education, Continuous Quality Improvement (CQI)—quickly became the academy's most talked-about management development in years. Attempts to implement it are visible on hundreds of campuses.

This chapter examines the history and core ideas behind quality management, and its successor movements of the present decade; looks at CQI implementation efforts in higher education; offers perspectives on its longer-term prospects in the academy; and concludes with tips on getting started.

The Triumph of Quality

The quality movement had its gurus—W. Edwards Deming, Joseph Juran, and Phillip Crosby—and later its business-school champions. But a fairer reading of its development is as a big tentful of ideas, old and new, that found coherence only when put together company by company in executive offices and on shop floors. In those companies, assortments of quality ideas have been picked up, discarded, modified, or recreated, always in a context of an enterprise's underlying work, sense of problem, and organizational culture.

Given this, there exists today no single, commonly accepted definition of quality management. What General Motors does in the name of quality is different from what Ford does; quality at Disney isn't the same as at Hertz or DuPont. Indeed, many companies today no longer speak of TQM or CQI, nor do they have a quality "program"; as Procter & Gamble CEO John Pepper told a college audience in 1996, "It's just the way we run the company." This "tentful of ideas" did, however, arise from a common impulse: survival. Xerox's David Kearns recalls walking down New York's West 47th Street in 1981 and seeing a Canon copier in a store window with higher quality and performance than a like Xerox product, yet with a street price lower than the *manufacturing* cost of his company's machine. At that moment, Kearns realized, the game was up: only a complete transformation of how his company worked would save it. For him, it was time to stop blaming the unions, government regulation, or the Japanese; it would be up to Xerox to remake itself.

What visionary executives like Kearns and Motorola's Robert Galvin took aim at was their own stagnant enterprises. In their eyes, the late–twentieth-century corporation had become bloated, self-absorbed, unresponsive, and repressive of talent; worse, it was fundamentally uncompetitive. The enemy was that great German invention of the late nineteenth century, the bureaucracy, with its functional units, layered responsibilities, work by the book, and command-and-control leadership. The urgent need was for organizational forms that were leaner, flatter, more focused, more quick-footed, and more humane.

To achieve this transformation, the movement's champions questioned everything and searched widely for ideas. By the mid-1980s a core set of "total quality" concepts had emerged, from systems thinking and statistical process control, industrial and humanistic psychology, management theory, and human and organizational development, plus lessons from earlier (mostly failed) improvement efforts such as quality circles. Quality's new champions looked widely for ideas because they wanted more than a change in management practice: they wanted an entirely new organization, one whose culture would be quality-driven, customer-oriented, marked by teamwork, and avid about improvement. The terms *corporate revolution* and *paradigm shift* were much in the air.

The movement took momentum through the eighties from the spectacular improvements its proponents claimed to achieve. At Ford, management layers were cut from twenty-seven to five; product reliability jumped 80 percent. At Motorola, productivity increases of 15 percent or more annually were realized for eight consecutive years; market share and profits soared. Xerox returned to health as it cut its manufacturing costs in half and machine defects by 90 percent.

Soon Federal Express, IBM, Westinghouse, Corning, American Express, and Hewlett-Packard were on board. The books, workshops, and consultants multiplied. In 1985, the U.S. Navy coined the phrase "total quality management." In 1987, Congress set up the Malcolm Baldrige National Quality Award; its seven criteria became a consensus statement of TQM values. In 1988, the Department of Defense mandated TQM for itself and all contractors; a Federal Quality Institute began pushing TQM across all departments and agencies. Surveys showed that buyers—nine of ten in 1990 versus three in ten in 1980—placed first value on quality (above price, styling, etc.); studies demonstrated that quality-oriented firms in fact did better in market share and profits. In banking and insurance, in electronics and hotels, from microchips to pet food, the word was out: consumers value *products* that work and last, and *service* that's prompt and dependable. TQM is the way to satisfy those consumer expectations.

The Core Ideas

However variously TQM was implemented, a core group of ideas fueled quality initiatives through the eighties.

Quality Comes First

The alpha and omega of TQM is its singular emphasis on quality as the defining aim of an organization. Quality in this view is not just an attribute of products or services; it is a mind-set, the soul of the company itself, an all-pervasive drive of such intensity that it defines a corporate culture. Just as geneticist Barbara McClintock's breakthroughs came when she was able to "think like corn," TQM enjoins managers to "imbibe" quality as the first aim of every aspect of their work.

International consultant Arman Feigenbaum observes that American corporate policy had been to "make it quick and cheaper, finance it cleverly, and sell it hard. The value of 'making it better' was left out. Firms now have to march to an entirely new drumbeat: quality" (Feigenbaum, 1991). Indeed, with Toyota the constant example, firms throughout the eighties were told that in the long run emphasis on gimmicks, frequent styling changes, and hard selling was counterproductive. Instead, quality practices would enable them to reduce "scrap, waste, and rework," and thereby their costs, while offering customers ever fitter and more reliable products or services, thus positioning themselves as the highest-value provider in the market. As they did so, customer appreciation and loyalty would grow, and with it market share and profitability. In this formula, then, quality becomes a firm's strategic advantage.

In the nineties, a quality focus has been no less important to firms, but the claims that it provides strategic advantage have been dampened. For one, as more and more firms pursue quality, the edge reaped by any one practitioner recedes. Instead of advantage, quality becomes a necessary, assumed practice—in competitive industries, no more than a ticket to play. For another, as IBM's stumbles have warned everyone, even a top-notch quality program is no substitute for good strategic thinking and market smartness.

Customer-Driven

In earlier days, quality was defined as what the craftsman or professional said it was. In industry, it was the absence of defects. The new dispensation is that quality is what the *customer* says it is, and the new corporate objective becomes providing goods or services that meet or exceed customer requirements, indeed that surprise or delight the customer.

In TQM companies, then, a keen sense of customer needs governs all activities. The cardinal rules are to identify explicitly who your customers are, know systematically their preferences and requirements, and commit to meeting them. Who are your customers? "Follow the product," urges Juran, know it in use; anyone who depends on the fitness of your work is a customer.

To the concept of *customer* there soon was added that of *supplier*, with both seen as crucial to, indeed part of, the organization. At Ford, the separate companies that supply parts to assembly lines are expected to meet Ford's quality requirements in full, every time, with a reciprocal expectation that Ford will help them do so. At the other end of the value-chain, dealers, purchasers, and even repair shops are thought of as customers to Ford (with requirements the company must meet), and as part of the company.

The identification of customer-supplier relationships extends to every individual, team, and work process inside a company. That is, each office or function depends on the fitness of prior work, just as other parties next along in the process rely on it being done well. In Ford offices and shop floors, people know the parties they depend upon and who depend on them; they state requirements to their suppliers and strive to meet or exceed those of their internal customers.

Writ large, the doctrine of customer focus is a call for everybody in the organization to get out of the cubbyholes they work in and talk with—*listen* to—the real parties they're serving. The aim is to break two bad habits of aging bureaucracies. One is that of the people in them (especially professionals) to assume they know best what the customer wants (or should want). In competitive markets, this is a fatal blindness or arrogance. The second is the tendency in older organizations for work arrangements to settle around the needs and preferences of employees, to the detriment of service and responsiveness. The customer orientation of quality management wants to crack open the mature enterprise's inward-looking, self-referential culture.

Continuous Improvement

Quality management rejects adages such as "If it ain't broke, don't fix it." It argues that customers, markets, technologies, and competitors change every day; what's good enough now will be suicidal tomorrow. Deming preached "constancy of purpose" on behalf of continuous adaptation and improvement; he and Juran describe quality as a "journey." Xerox President David Kearns proclaimed, "In the race for quality, there is no finish line." The boundaries of quality have to be pushed, year in and year out; whatever level you've achieved today has to be bettered tomorrow.

Simple as the concept seems, an embrace of constant improvement as imperative and ethic has profound consequences for an organization. It raises the need to rethink, all the time, all the processes that deliver value to customers. It implies management, production, personnel, information, supplier, and reward systems that are in gear and geared to the task. In a word, it is all (or most) of quality management.

Continuous improvement implies never-ending needs for organizational *learning*. A CQI-driven organization is always asking the question, "How can we get smarter and better at what we do?" The matter is so important that, as Deming and Peter Senge pointed out, all of CQI—its tools and processes—have as their heart and rationale the ability to contribute to organizational learning.

Making Processes Work Better

Every organization is a network of processes. In a college, these might range from single-purpose activities (generating a bill, advising a student) to cross-functional activities (enrollment management, general education). The aim is to identify those processes; enable the people who discharge them to understand their work in relation to customer needs ("Are we doing the right thing? How well?"); and, through problem-solving teams, set in motion process improvements.

In the old industrial paradigm, attention to quality began and ended on the shop floor; it was a matter to be controlled or "inspected in." In the new one, quality concerns reach in all directions. An absence of defects won't do; goods are followed out the door, where their quality is judged by how well they fit or exceed customer expectations in actual use. The new quality concerns reach backward from the shop floor, as companies develop stable relations with a smaller set of suppliers who agree to be partners in the quality-improvement process. Rather than a matter of inspection, then, quality becomes a larger organizational philosophy, incorporating sound, up-front design; attentive process management; and constant communication with customers and suppliers.

In the old bureaucratic world, work processes tended to cluster within neatly tiered departments, each with its own turf, aims, norms, and culture (manufacturing, finance, sales, purchasing, and so on). CQI wants to break down the walls between these "vertical silos." At Ford, for example, suppliers, designers, assemblers, dealers, purchasers, and repairpersons work together as a "horizontal team" to produce a car that is buildable, sellable, fixable, and a delight to the customer.

The Discipline of Information

Quality practitioners always want to see the data, and they want to see it in public, up on the wall in the shop or office. If you're serious about improving quality, they say, you have to be as specific as possible about what you mean by the word and systematically keep track of how you are doing in relation to it. CQI wants everybody's focus to be on central missions and the pursuit of quality; public, visible information systems let each person know what's important and how we're doing.

More largely, the central idea here is to get managers and work teams to move beyond decision making by personal impression, anecdote, or complaint; to develop habits of looking for and preferring systematic data aim to counter the bureaucrat's problem-chasing or beliefs in their own story-driven world. "Keep track, dig out the facts, look for the root cause," CQI enjoins. Process-improvement teams are taught to track meticulously every fault, complaint, breakdown, accident, shortage, or success that comes their way; every process, the University of Wisconsin's statistician George Box teaches, generates the data for its own improvement. A variety of relatively simple statistical tools—diagrams, charts, matrices, graphs, and checksheets—are deployed to these ends, not by experts in an administrative office but by workers themselves.

People

In Deming's view, 85 percent of all problems are traceable to the systems within which people work, and just 15 percent to individual failure. Stop attacking people, he admonished managers, look to your systems: "Drive out fear from the workplace!" (Deming, 1988). People *want* to do the right and better thing, they *want* pride in their work, CQI urges; the task of managers is to remove the system barriers that prevent people and teams from doing their best work.

From top management to the shop floor, within units and across functions, quality issues are attacked in teams. Teams are *not* the committees of old, but "self-directed work groups" with their own required competencies and protocols. CQI wants to marshall the collective efforts of everyone on quality's behalf; it believes that there will always be greater wisdom in a team than in the head of any one individual; and it believes that team ownership of a process and team learning are the keys to continuous improvement.

So that all employees can understand the corporate vision of quality, have the skills of teamwork and problem solving they need, and relate more effectively to customers, quality-driven firms invest heavily in human resource development. Across its various units, Motorola spends 2–6 percent of its salary budgets on training; IBM-Rochester invests 5 percent across the board; every Saturn employee spends at least one hundred hours a year in the classroom. Personnel systems in TQM companies rely less on incentives and rewards directed at the individual than on team-oriented recognition, honors, and celebration.

Finally, on behalf of these values, CQI partisans want fewer managers, at least of the old type—powerful figures in sole command of vertical authority structures, plus layers of middle managers devoted to oversight. They want leaders, of a new type: vision-givers, listeners, coaches, teamworkers themselves; committed to quality and customer needs; avid but patient for long-term ends; orchestrators and enablers of people-driven improvement. The leader's job is to nourish initiative and creativity throughout the organization, tend to the organization's systems and "white spaces" between work units, and nurture organizational learning.

Into the Nineties

CQI's basic "tentful" of ideas coalesced in the eighties. In the present decade, their fuller implications have been played out in a set of follow-on developments. Companies have instituted just-in-time delivery arrangements with suppliers to cut inventory costs; activity-based cost accounting now assigns costs to processes instead of budgets to functions; managers now undergo "360 degree" evaluation by their superiors, direct reports, suppliers, and customers; and so on.

At the same time, certain weaknesses or blind spots in the original CQI message have surfaced to prompt more fully blown, add-on movements, four of which are mentioned here.

Reengineering

The original expectation of TQM was that the patient, team-based work of process improvement would over time bring gains in quality and thereby market share, securing corporate profits and everyone's job. In the nineties, however, that formula often hasn't held. For one, companies may need breakthrough improvements *now*, not five years from now; for another, with most competitors practicing quality, price becomes more of a competitive requirement, which means cutting costs out of processes that include personnel costs. But as Hammer and Champy pointed out in their best-selling *Reengineering the Corporation* (1993), you can't expect the team "owners" of a process to come up with breakthrough solutions that imply laying off half their number; that's a job for parties outside the process.

In reengineering, then, SWAT teams of top managers and outside consultants descend on a process; take it apart; try to wring steps, time, and costs out of it; and put in place a new plan of work (often involving information technologies). What drives them is often a "stretch goal": to cut cycle time and costs by half, for example, with no loss in product or service quality.

Hundreds of companies have tried the Hammer and Champy formula, often with unhappy results. For a variety of reasons, a reported 70 percent of such interventions fail: the "outsiders" never understood the work well enough, technology wasn't the whole answer, the costs in employee morale outweighed the gains. To systems theorists, the organization that accomplishes a hundred small gains yearly always outperforms the competitor that relies on occasional home runs. In 1995, Champy renounced the earlier book's emphasis on "heavy blasting," arguing that authentic gains in performance could come only from the people within.

Benchmarking

If not through reengineering, how *does* an organization get breakthrough thinking? How can CQI work teams avoid an inward-looking, modest-goals mind-set? The reigning answer, now practiced by 80 percent of Fortune 500 firms, is benchmarking, the discipline of searching out and learning from "best practices" elsewhere.

Benchmarking appeared as a formal practice in the eighties (notably at Xerox) but took off only in the present decade, by which time a critical mass of industry leaders had quality programs, common processes were mapped and could thus be compared, and when needs for stretch gains were more apparent. In a typical benchmarking study, a firm identifies a process for improvement, assigns a team to the task (mostly, but not exclusively, people who work within it), carefully maps that process, gathers intelligence on parallel processes in other companies, identifies two or three best-in-class examples for further study, pays a formal visit to those companies, and then puts together all learnings for a redesign of the home process. The larger aim of benchmarking's formal studies is to get people out of their immediate foxholes to see for themselves creative, more effective ways of doing their work.

Through trial and error, a company like DuPont now finds that over 90 percent of its benchmarking studies lead to measurable gain; it has completed three hundred studies this decade, boosting quality and market share while cutting $1 billion in costs over that decade. The practice of benchmarking in industry (and in health care) is now driven by a widely accepted set of guidelines and a code of ethics and is aided by an industry-based International Benchmarking Clearinghouse in Houston.

Earlier this decade, benchmarking and reengineering were often posed as competing improvement strategies. In time, their proponents came to see that the two had similar goals of breakthrough improvement, customer focus, and out-of-the-box thinking; blended versions of the two came into vogue. Today, even CQI diehards recognize that "broken" processes often require outside intervention, while reengineering efforts are less prone to push aside the knowledge and involvement of process workers.

Learning Organizations

Working from the insight that CQI is about "getting smarter and better," an active group of academicians and consultants has been engaged in thinking more deeply about issues of organizational learning. Their touchstone is a book that appeared in 1990, *The Fifth Discipline: The Art and Practice of the Learning Organization,* by MIT's Peter Senge. In a host of books and articles since, people have probed the systems nature of the evolving organization; looked to learning theory for cues to its behavior; mined group dynamics and communications theory for corporate lessons; and speculated about the spirituality of work and servant leadership. While the practical application of these ideas has thus far been scant, they have nevertheless brought significant insight and conceptual depth to CQI practice.

In the corporate world, there is a parallel (if somewhat less ethereal) conversation going forward about "knowledge creation and use." That is, in large, diffuse enterprises, how can the business intelligence or lesson garnered by any one party—be it a person, team, or office—become that of the entire organization? How does local, personal learning become corporate? The issue is a difficult but crucial one for knowledge-based enterprise; these days, information technologies increasingly figure in the solution.

Planning

In olden bureaucracies, planning was a function done by professionals in an office; when strategic choices needed making, a powerful "big decisions" committee was rolled out. In quality organizations, where the top-down and the rational are suspect, alternative ways of planning have emerged, often with an eye to the frequent disconnect between what the plan says and what people in the organization actually do.

Quality practitioners in Japan evolved their own version of what Americans know as strategic planning, called *Hoshin* or "breakthrough" planning. It starts with a vision statement (typically for the next five years), from which come goals (with a customer orientation), work plans (for specific critical processes), and steps of deployment and execution, followed by monthly "audits" to monitor progress toward the vision. The central feature of *Hoshin* is the identification of no more than three or four fundamental quality improvements (the breakthroughs) for a given time span, followed by steps of deployment to ensure that *all* units in the organization work in their pursuit. *Hoshin* practitioners have developed their own set of planning tools (the matrix diagram, for example); they often put value statements in plans to emphasize that how things are done can be as important as their direction.

Hoshin planning can well be top-down, of course, except that its American practitioners often enact it with open-space and whole-system approaches to planning. In these, an entire office, plant, or workforce may set aside several days to jointly craft a vision statement, or to design a scenario for meeting breakthrough goals. The driving idea is that participants thus *own* that which they create, to the benefit of subsequent performance.

CQI practitioners argue that big decisions can indeed be made by powerful committees at the top—for example, the tough decisions about layoffs or ending a product line—but that the need just as often is for a decisive change in *culture*, which no committee can simply order up. To change a culture, they argue, you need the involvement and communication that the new, more participative forms of planning aim for.

Impacts on Higher Education

In the 1995 American Council on Education "Campus Trends" survey, 65 percent of all campuses report TQM/CQI activity (El-Khawas, 1995). The survey leaves to respondents the definition of *activity;* the one sure inference is that interest in quality management has been wide in higher education.

More concretely, and looking to actual implementation, the number of campuses on which quality management practices go forward is not the two thousand implied by the survey, but closer to several hundred. *Quality Progress* magazine runs an annual listing of campuses active in CQI; in September 1995 it found just under three hundred U.S. campuses to profile (Calek, 1995). That listing, put together by noneducators, has many glaring omissions (and some dubious inclusions); comparing several such lists, the magazine may undercount by half the number of active campuses. But if one asks, "On how many campuses is the pursuit of quality a fact of daily life?" the number may be closer to 100 (AAHE's Campus Coordinator's Network has 106 members). If one asks further, "On how many campuses has a 'culture of quality' taken root as a new, dominant norm?" the number falls below 10.

All these figures stand against the fact that there are thirty-six hundred U.S. campuses, most of whom are *not* actively engaged with CQI.

The *Quality Progress* survey does document a widely noticed phenomenon: that CQI practice is concentrated in public higher education (76 percent of cited institutions), mostly in large public universities and community colleges. Similarly, within the independent sector three-fourths of the listed campuses are universities, not liberal arts colleges. In all but a handful of cases, the implementation that prompted the listing is on the administrative side, not the academic. On the academic, examples from business and engineering schools predominate. One also notices that CQI activity is highest in states (the upper Midwest, parts of the South) where there is a strong community press for CQI that includes state government.

Why the Quality Effort Began

What reasons do campuses give for pursuing quality? Listserv discussions turn up a variety of impulses. In many cases, reformers seize on CQI as a way to fix dreadful service levels on campus; in others, the president, pressed by trustee or corporate believers in quality, starts a program to show responsiveness; on not a few campuses, the driver is a worry about competitiveness in admissions; and several start with the thought that CQI's participative ways will increase staff morale. In the case of business and engineering schools, employer pressure on behalf of quality has been strong. Few campuses, one notes, started with an idea of using CQI to cut costs or improve academic effectiveness.

What Are the Obstacles?

Given the interest and a flood of articles about CQI, what explanations are given for its often-meager implementation? David Entin's study (1993) of CQI efforts on ten Boston-area campuses and Daniel Seymour's look at twenty-one campuses with faltering CQI programs provide similar answers: it's too great a change, the time and effort are great, the reason and reward for this are unclear, the language is off-putting, the president doesn't buy in, nor does the faculty, and maybe it's just a fad. Interestingly, half a dozen of the original members of AAHE's Academic Quality Consortium (these were the twenty-two leading implementers in 1992) had by 1996 all but ended their quality efforts.

Administrative Applications

Corporate and health-care versions of CQI have often been undertaken with cultural transformation in mind. On campuses, the obstacles to that appear so great that more limited goals usually prevail, often having to do with a team-based effort to improve an administrative process within a given office. AAHE's CQI Project has tracked hundreds of such efforts, more than a few of which have recorded striking results:

- At the University of Pennsylvania, teams cut waiting times for late-night escort service by 50 percent and special calls by 70 percent, while doubling ridership.
- At El Camino College in California, 95 percent of the paperwork associated with payroll was eliminated, saving countless hours of faculty and secretarial time.
- At Kansas State, students now get their work-study checks in three days, not sixteen.
- At Samford in Alabama, transcript requests are fulfilled within a week, instead of three months.
- At the University of Wisconsin, graduate-school admissions decisions that used to take ninety-nine days are completed in sixty.
- At Belmont in Tennessee, a student's loan gets credited to her account within twenty-four to forty-eight hours, instead of four weeks.

Countless further examples can be adduced on behalf of a few summary points. One is that academic administration offers fertile ground for CQI efforts; they do work. Another is that elaborate preparation and training often are not necessary for projects like these; if anything, what teams need most is simple permission to form and act, after which their initiative and common sense takes hold. People *enjoy* doing this; morale and cross-unit communication go up.

Academic Applications

For a variety of reasons, quality management has made few inroads in mainstream academic life. There are, of course, the liabilities of CQI's industrial origins and vocabularies, plus the fact of its administrative flavor. More fundamentally, the academy's high emphasis on unit independence and individual autonomy runs counter to quality management's emphasis on teamwork and the needs of the whole. Whatever the claims for its ideas, CQI partisans find that academic culture remains remarkably resilient.

It is largely in professional schools—business, engineering, and health-related—that at least some faculty have examined the aptness of quality to their work. A good window into that conversation is offered by the thirty-one chapters in *Academic Initiatives in Total Quality for Higher Education,* edited by the University of Chicago's Harry Roberts (1995). Several chapters detail the work of innovators attempting to apply quality precepts in their teaching. By and large, these faculty have been led in two directions, to the formation of student teams (for study and projects) and to the use of frequent feedback (for teacher and student). Reading these chapters, one is glad for the prompting that quality seems to provide toward progressive practices, but one is left with the feeling that all this, in somewhat different vocabularies, is but the day's mainstream wisdom about teaching and learning.

The chapters on course and curricular design, by comparison, have fresh things to say. Individual courses have been designed from a customer-supplier perspective, so that they make sense for students in light of what's been studied before and will follow next. Whole sequences of courses have been rationalized to eliminate waste and duplication, saving student and faculty time. In business schools, entire MBA programs have been designed from scratch, replacing discrete courses and stand-alone teaching with seamless learning experiences. In engineering schools, students enroll in clusters of related courses, attack real-world problems in teams, and participate in their college's quality-improvement projects.

The Roberts book has no chapters on the assessment of student learning at the departmental and campus levels. For many arts and sciences faculties, however, the practice of assessment (which all institutional accreditors now require) has offered an introduction to quality ideas. (See Chapter Nineteen for a more extensive discussion on this topic.) Assessment's themes—sustained attention to learning goals and outcomes, to data and reflection on process improvement, to cross-functional programs such as general education—are directly analogous to those of the quality movement. In June 1995, 1,550 faculty and academic staff turned out for AAHE's National Conference on Assessment and Quality in Boston.

Finally, it is worth noting that quality ideas are in the air these days in higher education, at least among academic reformers. Whether or not people are "doing quality," concepts of continuous improvement; the delivery of value, teamwork, and collective responsibility; performance rewards for unit performance; and of vertical silos but horizontal processes have seeped into academic vocabularies and wider discourse—a not inconsiderable development.

But Will It Save Money?

The "rap" on CQI among more than a few campus leaders is that it's a fine way to improve services but a waste of time if you need to cut costs and recapture resources. The immediacy of the latter objective on hard-pressed campuses in the West and Northeast is one reason for CQI's weaker presence in those regions. Reports from the campus-based Pew Roundtables, devoted to restructuring, are often void of references to quality management; more than a few campuses have quietly brought in consulting firms to reengineer a necessary downsizing.

Recall that the original party line about CQI was that if one put quality and customers first, then market and financial gain would follow. It is a strategy for the long-term, not instant pudding, Deming taught. University of Kansas business professor Larry Sherr warns colleges that if "resources are being used unwisely, they cannot be found on the day you must retrench" (Sherr, personal communication). Fordham's Sylvia Westerman, examining campus experiences, observed that "TQM absolutely can achieve efficiencies, raise morale, show good stewardship of funds, and win public trust . . . but it's hard to make claims for cost-savings" (Westerman, personal communication).

Three observations are obtained. First, CQI can provide an important platform for determined cost cutting through reengineering; quality practitioners have already identified and mapped critical processes, for example. Indeed, that became the case in at least two Oregon institutions, Portland State and Oregon State, when voters there passed a drastic tax-reduction referendum. At Portland State, some $3 million in cumulative savings were wrung from administrative costs between 1992 and 1995.

Second, Japanese experience and U.S. research show that it is only when firms attack *cross-cutting* functions that they realize major gains in productivity and cost savings. So far, however, as noted earlier most campus CQI projects have addressed straightforward processes within single units. There are exceptions to note—the University of Maryland, for example—but also failures, such as at the University of Minnesota-Duluth, where a cross-functional project involving student recruitment and admissions brought disappointing results. No matter what the promise of gain in addressing universitywide problems—for example, in curbing course proliferation in general education or at the top of majors—it is difficult indeed to address such cross-functional situations in a collegiate ethos of semiautonomous units. Quality practitioners with the Hospital Corporation of America recommend several years of work and learning with single-function projects before pursuing more ambitious, cross-functional targets.

Third, benchmarking—another tool that requires a platform of CQI experience—has become a method of choice among corporate quality practitioners.

As noted before, DuPont has used benchmarking studies to wring $1 billion from its cost structures over a decade's time. But few campus CQI efforts have as yet the maturity to support benchmarking on behalf of cost reduction. Most of the twenty or so examples of collegiate benchmarking one could cite to date (in advisement practices, for example) have had gains in effectiveness, not efficiency, as their goal.

Reflection

In the short run, the outlook for a further spread of CQI in higher education and for its impacts is clouded. A fundamental obstacle is that most institutional leaders don't think their institutions have a quality problem—however they might be improved in other ways. Have cost structures risen? Do just half of all students graduate? Are there employer and public complaints? When, they ask, was it otherwise?

Nor do leaders, if they even think of the matter, believe they have a productivity problem. Former SUNY chancellor Bruce Johnstone has been beating the drums for campuses to attend to the productivity of learning; at AAHE's 1996 National Conference, he spoke to a largely empty hall.

In effect, academic leaders have yet to experience David Kearns' walk down West 47th Street, encountering the undeniable fact that mandates transformation. If campus leadership doesn't think it has a quality or productivity problem, why would it undertake the disciplines of CQI?

Meanwhile, other agendas compete for attention and precious time: diversity and affirmative action, tenured-in faculties, sagging indirect costs, soaring tuitions and unfunded student aid, binge drinking, distance learning, health and environmental concerns, accountability, school reform, and on and on . . . agendas that quality management, at first glance, doesn't seem to address. Public-campus leaders sense that quality improvements to undergraduate education count for little when it comes to state funding formulas; private-campus leaders know that undergraduate quality is a hard sell in admissions markets, with (at best) only longer-term payoffs.

In the short run, CQI's academic champions might well put away the three-letter banner and concentrate instead on bringing the core ideas of quality—such as teamwork, data, service, and process improvement—into the academy's wider, ongoing conversations about learning and teaching, curricula and departments, faculty roles and rewards, technology and restructuring.

Five years from now—in 2001—there's no telling where the academy will be. Distance learning may bring a flood of new competitors into our markets; acquisitions, mergers, and partnerships may be the order of the day; how education is funded and delivered may shift; breakthroughs in our understanding of human learning may occur. Conceivably, higher education's next five years could bring the order of changes that came to health care between 1990 and 1995. In 1990, quality management was an intriguing option taken up by a few medical centers; today it is an assumed practice across all types of the new provider organizations.

Getting Started

During 1994–95, three Continuous Quality Improvement Listserv (CQI-L) discussions took up questions of starting a CQI effort, generating advice for presidents and new CQI coordinators, and maintaining the momentum. Dozens of veteran practitioners and consultants contributed to these discussions, which, taken together, evoke five recommendations.

In-Depth Learning

There are more than a few examples of campuses that boldly announced a commitment to CQI and plunged ahead, only to stumble when they realized they hadn't fully grasped the reach and demands of quality management. At a private university in Minnesota, the stumbling so embarrassed an administration that a year-long moratorium had to be called on CQI efforts, during which campus leaders undertook a regimen of reading, seminars, visits, and retreats. Afterward, a better-grounded CQI effort was put in place.

Practitioners are unanimous on this point: understand what you are getting into. CQI is a total organizational philosophy, not a bite-sized bag of techniques. A president embracing CQI should know and believe it sufficiently to say, "This is the way I'll run my own office first." Indeed, he or she should know it well enough to teach it to others, and to articulate and defend it before the inevitable audience of skeptics.

Know the Aim

The ability to articulate and defend implies knowing *why* one is undertaking a CQI effort, a "question that gets begged four times out of five," according to one listserv skeptic. The aim may be fundamental and long-term—a significant boost in student attainment, for example, or a major change in university cost structures—or it may be more immediate and modest, such as improving campus communication, service, and morale. The CQI vision may encompass no more than a simple string of improvement projects, or it may look to deeper changes in campus culture.

It may apply to one part of the campus only—the administration, an engineering school, student affairs, the conference center—or the vision may contemplate CQI for the whole, all at once or bit by bit.

Whatever the case, knowing the *why* behind the undertaking helps choices get made, directs energies, and controls expectations. When the *why* gets begged, room is left for runaway hopes (or suspicions) that will do in the effort.

An interesting lesson from campus experience is that when the main impetus for CQI has been *external*—for example, government, employers, or the board want it—the internal implementation seems ever uphill. In many such cases, the president or sponsoring dean never quite has the time to learn CQI in depth, and internal parties (rightly) come to see the effort as someone else's agenda. Prospects for success are much better when the effort advances from a base of reason that is internal, mission-related, and connected to problems people want solved.

Start Smartly

The advice may seem obvious, but many campus CQI efforts came to be marked (and dogged) for years by their artless beginning: a puffed-up, jargon-filled introduction, coupled with inappropriate training, upon which followed the trivial, result-free project. The smarter start leads with thoughtful, up-front explanation (enabled by the steps above), just-in-time training tailored to task, and care in the selection of initial teams and projects.

The latter point bears emphasis: after the explanations, people will know CQI by its fruits. Savvy campuses pick initial projects that (1) have a high likelihood of success, (2) entail problems having high visibility, and (3) result in quantifiable, widely felt benefits, be they service or budgetary. Further, if the ultimate goal is to impact administrative and academic areas alike, some initial projects can have faculty benefit as an aim. Before long, and by using surveys and focus groups, the better-founded efforts begin letting customer feedback (perhaps not called that) drive the next rounds of project teams. The whole start, in short, positions CQI as commonsensical, effective, and very much worth the time and effort.

Think Longer Term

Over time, CQI aims to transform the way work gets done in the institution; it wants to change the system to unleash new levels of communication, creativity, and responsiveness. For CQI to take root and have such effects, campus systems—which are perfectly set up for the results we now see—have to be modified or replaced.

For example, existing governance mechanisms, such as the administrative council or faculty senate, don't have the reach or power needed to direct a CQI effort; a broad-based, influential quality council may need to be established. Similarly, CQI calls into question present ways of planning and budgeting, choosing and preparing leaders, collecting and sharing information, and of professional incentives and rewards. The need is to develop over time patterns of consistent integration and reinforcement across the institution.

Down the Road

Practitioners advise CQI newcomers to start slow, choose your targets, and build for the long run. Leave for later the more difficult steps one might better contemplate with experience: cross-functional projects, formal benchmarking, and business-process reengineering, even though these may be the steps needed for breakthrough gains. Leave for later, too, use of the Baldrige criteria as a template for planning and evaluation.

Further Reading

The best entry point to the written literature on quality management (through 1994) is the annotated bibliography by Peterson and Cameron (1995). The other recent and comprehensive listing of resources has been assembled by Brigham (1996). Brigham's CQI Project at AAHE has also published two dozen classic articles on the topic, in *CQI 101: A First Reader for Higher Education* (1994), and a compilation of institutional reports, *25 Snapshots of a Movement: Profiles of Campuses Implementing CQI* (1994). Another widely read "first book" is that of Seymour (1992).

References

Brigham, S. *Roadmap to Resources: Sources and Tools for CQI Implementation.* Washington, D.C.: American Association for Higher Education, 1996.

Calek, A. "'Quality Progress' Fifth Quality in Education Listing." *Quality Progress,* 1995, *28*(9), 27–73.

CQI 101: A First Reader for Higher Education. Washington, D.C.: American Association for Higher Education, 1994.

Deming, W. E. *Out of the Crisis.* Cambridge, England: Cambridge University Press, 1988.

El-Khawas, E. *Campus Trends: 1995.* Washington, D.C.: American Council on Education, 1995.

Entin, D. "Boston: Less Than Meets the Eye." *Change,* 1993, *25*(3), 28–31.

Feigenbaum, A. "Keynote Address." Presented at Second Annual Symposium on the Role of Academe in National Competitiveness and Total Quality Management, Los Angeles, Calif., 1991.

Hammer, M., and Champy, J. *Reengineering the Corporation.* New York: HarperCollins, 1993.

Peterson, M. W., and Cameron, K. *Total Quality Management in Higher Education: From Assessment to Improvement.* Ann Arbor, Mich.: Center for the Study of Higher and Postsecondary Education, 1995.

Roberts, H. V. (ed.). *Academic Initiatives in Total Quality for Higher Education.* Milwaukee: ASQC Quality Press, 1995.

Senge, P. *The Fifth Discipline: The Art and Practice of the Learning Organization.* New York: Doubleday, 1990.

Seymour, D. T. *On Q: Causing Quality in Higher Education.* New York: American Council on Education/Macmillan, 1992.

25 Snapshots of a Movement: Profiles of Campuses Implementing CQI. Washington, D.C.: American Association for Higher Education, 1994.

CHAPTER TWENTY-SIX

ASSISTING ECONOMIC AND BUSINESS DEVELOPMENT

Harvey A. Goldstein and Michael I. Luger

Research universities, like many other institutions in American society, have been undergoing significant change. Since at least the mid-1980s we have been witnessing a new confluence of forces that are shifting the traditional focus of U.S. universities from being centers of learning and purveyors of knowledge to being more complex organizations with multiple objectives and "products," so to speak.

One such emergent objective, particularly for publicly supported research universities, is to serve as an engine of local and regional economic growth and development. From a public economic development point of view, the argument that universities should serve this role is a compelling one. Whittled down to its bare essentials, it goes like this: (1) we are living in an increasingly knowledge-based and global economy; (2) to sustain themselves economically in this environment, regions have to be capable of generating and nurturing innovative individuals, businesses, and organizations on a continuing basis; (3) universities are *the* institutions with the resources to provide the stream of knowledge, know-how, and human capital to their respective regions as the fuel for innovation, entrepreneurship, and regional synergy.

From the universities' perspective, there is a separate set of internal pressures for having an explicit economic development role. These include falling enrollments due to demographic changes and increased competition from other institutions; reductions in revenue growth from government and private sources during economic downturns, and funding incompletely restored during subsequent recoveries; institutions' limited ability or unwillingness to downsize when faced with budget austerity; greater competition for the noneducational uses of government funds; rising equipment and facility costs due to more sophisticated technology; rapidly rising salaries in the sciences and engineering due to competition with private industry and the drop in the number of Ph.D.'s awarded in those fields; and higher expectations from the public for free services.

Public officials increasingly have relied on universities—especially publicly supported ones—as instruments of economic development policy, having at least *implicitly* accepted the argument above. During the past fifteen years they have launched a host of key technology-oriented programs and centers located on university campuses, or otherwise involving universities as partners. Some of these technology-oriented activities extend the traditional roles defined for universities, but some require universities to redefine their roles. University administrators, acutely aware of the external and internal pressures facing their universities, generally have been willing to accept an economic development role for their institution, although perhaps with more than a little privately held caution and reservation. Similarly, many members of university faculties, especially in the humanities, have softened their long-standing resistance to university-industry partnerships (see Klausner, 1988; and Luger and Goldstein, 1991).

In this chapter, we make the case that the modern research university, as a multiproduct organization, stimulates local and regional economic development in a number of different ways, which are identified. Second, relying in part upon the available empirical evidence, we suggest the contingent conditions upon which universities are likely to be *effective* instruments of economic development. Third, we discuss the normative issue of the desirability of universities' adopting an explicit economic development role, albeit from a limited, economic development perspective.

The University as a Multiproduct Organization

Several branches of the economics literature relate to the role of universities. Gary Becker (1975) and others writing in the human capital tradition consider universities (and other types of educational institutions) to be important to the degree that they make workers more productive and consequently enhance their value in the labor market. Griliches and Jaffe are among another set of economists who focus on the role of universities as loci of research and development (see, for example, Griliches, 1984, 1986; Jaffe, 1986, 1989; and Tratjenberg, Henderson, and Jaffe, 1992). A related literature discusses the importance of universities in knowledge creation, more generally (Romer, 1990; and Rosenberg and Nelson, 1994). Another branch of the literature places the university in the center of a web of input-output linkages and measures the impact of universities on their regions in terms of their spending multipliers. A large number of universities in the United States have conducted this analysis. Caffrey and Isaacs (1971) provide the standard methodology for studies of this type. Some researchers also discuss the attractiveness of universities to new and expanding businesses and, by aggregation, to research parks (Luger and Goldstein, 1991).

In fact, universities can be important in all these ways, and more. In this section, we present a conceptual model of the university as a multiproduct organization that may help us understand (1) why some universities are bigger engines of economic growth and development for their regions than others and (2) the trade-offs university administrators and economic development officials make regarding changes in the research university's mission or particular mix of outputs.

In many respects, universities behave like any other economic organization. First, they are affected by conditions in their regional environment. However, unlike private businesses, universities are not likely to move if local input prices rise, or the local demand for services wanes. Universities find other ways to respond to economic changes, including alterations in the mix and quality of their outputs. In addition, they often attempt to shape and restructure their regional environment, to improve the availability and quality of locally supplied inputs, including labor, infrastructure, amenities, and related knowledge-producing organizations.

Second, the mix and quality of universities' outputs have economic impacts that vary with distance. Some activities have a very local impact, while others can have a wider national, or international, impact, where the "spatial gradient" of the impacts can be relatively flat. But the spatial impact gradient is not shaped the same for all universities, for the same types of activities. Universities' size and certain internal characteristics, and the nature of the regional environment, affect the spatial pattern of economic impact for such functions as teaching or basic research.

In short, there is a two-way, dynamic relationship between what a university does and what happens in its regional environs. This relationship is important to understand, both for university decision makers who are concerned with the viability of their institutions and for local/regional officials who are interested in universities as potential stimulants of economic and business development.

We further conceptualize the modern research university as an organization that procures a set of inputs in order to produce a particular mix of outputs. The typical inputs include supplies, equipment, services, external funding, students, and labor of varying skill levels. But the set of inputs also includes the regional "milieu," which provides a set of amenities and other public goods more or less available to all individuals and organizations located within the region, as well as opportunities for *interaction* with other actors and institutions within the region.

Research universities have a much broader set of possible outputs today than they did twenty or more years ago. Today's set includes:

1. The creation of new "basic" knowledge through research
2. The creation of human capital through teaching (that is, knowledge transfer from faculty to students)
3. The transfer of existing know-how (technology) to businesses, governmental agencies, and other organizations
4. The application of knowledge to the creation and commercialization of new products or processes, or the improvement of existing ones (technological innovation)
5. Capital investment in the built form and in the equity of private businesses
6. Leadership in addressing critical social problems
7. Coproduction of a knowledge-based infrastructure
8. The creation of a favorable regional milieu

We briefly discuss these outputs and their expected, or hypothetical, economic and business impacts below.

Knowledge Creation

The creation of basic knowledge through research is the *raison d'être* of the research university. Tratjenberg, Henderson, and Jaffe (1992, p. 3) note that the scientific and technological literature defines basic research according to a focus on general scientific as opposed to particular technological questions. Those authors operationalize the concept by claiming that basic research is difficult for individual firms to appropriate. For that reason, the geographic impact of basic research is likely to be rather wide. Results obtained in a lab in California are likely to be useful over time in Tokyo and Massachusetts, as well as in California. There is some debate in the literature about the extent of the spatial spillover of the benefits of basic research. Tratjenberg, Henderson, and Jaffe conclude that "basic research results do not spill out as easily, as widely, or as quickly as the traditional view would suggest" (1992, p. 1). Relatively speaking, however, the geographic impact is wide (Cohen and Levinthal, 1989; Jaffe, 1989; and Jaffe, Tratjenberg, and Henderson, 1993).

Because basic research, by the Tratjenberg, Henderson, and Jaffe definition, is not directly appropriable, it is more likely to be funded by the government than by industry. Government funding can go directly to researchers for their time and equipment needs, and/or for the construction and operation of special government labs (for instance, North Carolina's Biotechnology and Microelectronics Centers). Both provide space and specialized equipment for use by university or industry scientists and engineers to conduct research. The work sponsored by those (and similar) facilities includes a mix of basic and appropriable research. We might conclude, then, that the basic research function of the university is not new, but some of the support structures for it are.

The fact that basic (and much applied) research is funded by the government leads to a different type of regional development effect, which is due to the distribution of that funding as opposed to the ultimate impact of the research. Though there has been considerable dispersion of federal research monies since 1980, those funds are still highly concentrated (Geiger and Feller, 1995). The ten greatest recipients of research dollars in FY 1990 still captured almost 18 percent of federal R&D funds in the United States (Geiger and Feller, 1995). This infusion of research dollars into selected local economies creates a wave of additional spending in the region that is an important source of regional growth.

Human Capital Creation

Knowledge transfer from faculty to students is regarded by many as one of the two primary functions of research universities. From a regional development perspective, there is no more important ingredient for sustained economic development than a creative, talented, and well-trained population. (The key role of universities in supplying such a labor force for a technologically rapidly changing economic environment was articulated as early as 1969 by a National Academy of Sciences report: "A key requirement in the attainment of social and economic objectives for a given region lies in the development of human capabilities and talents, and the attraction or retention of the most gifted and innovative segment of the population" 1969, p. v.) An economic impact to the region is realized when the increase in human capital leads to an increased stock of labor skills in the region and then to increases in businesses' productivity.

Certainly, the transfer of knowledge from faculty to students, in classrooms, tutorials, advising, and supervised instruction, is not new. However, some new tools are broadening the spatial incidence of a university's teaching function. Specifically, interactive teleconferencing is used increasingly to bring specialized instruction to far-flung locations. That trend is expected to intensify in coming years. The economic impact of knowledge transfer through teaching depends on the "flow" of students: where they come from prior to matriculation and where they locate after graduation. Universities that draw talented students from a wide geographical area, so-called national or world-class universities, and whose regional labor markets offer abundant job and career opportunities, would be expected to have the largest regional economic impacts, while on the other hand universities that mainly draw students locally but that tend to choose to leave the region for better career opportunities or perceived quality-of-life reasons may inadvertently contribute to a regional brain drain and have negative economic impacts.

Transfer of Existing Know-How

This output includes the outreach, extension, and public service functions originally associated with land-grant universities in the United States but now solidly established in most public and private research universities. It is analogous to the knowledge transfer function discussed above, except the "clients" for these services tend to be businesses, other private-sector and civic organizations, government agencies, and individual citizens, rather than enrolled students.

As a general category, the output is the application of existing knowledge to the improvement of a product or process, or problem solving. Organizationally, universities provide these services institutionally by such organizations as industrial (and agricultural) extension services, small-business assistance centers, business schools, economic and business research bureaus, medical clinics, or by individual faculty through consulting (paid or pro bono).

In many cases, this technology transfer role can be combined with the teaching (and research) function, with clients being local government in addition to private businesses. Administrators and faculty recognize that the local context can serve as a good laboratory for students, to test the applicability of theory to real-world problems in not only engineering and agriculture but also public health, the environment, social welfare, planning, and economic development.

Yet the know-how transfer function, unlike teaching and basic research, typically has an *explicit* economic development objective. Accordingly, the spatial gradient of the resulting economic impacts is fairly steep. More generally, the extent to which the benefits are localized depends on the nature of the services provided and the geographic location pattern of businesses that need or seek that assistance. Relatively recent delivery and marketing mechanisms such as new modes of communication and information transfer have tended to widen the spatial range of university clients.

Technological Innovation

This refers to the application of knowledge for the creation and commercialization of new products, or the improvement of existing ones. This output may receive the most publicity, and draw the most controversy, of all the universities' nontraditional activities. One reason for the controversy is that this type of research is usually appropriable, using Tratjenberg, Henderson, and Jaffe's (1992) terminology, and thus runs counter to the tradition of a university in which knowledge creation is regarded as an open process and the products of research are located in the public domain.

Often the output from the university is not a "final" product but instead arrives at the marketplace by way of corporate labs. In any event, application of knowledge to the creation and commercialization of new products normally requires ideas from university-based researchers to be patented and licensed to commercial producers. Intermediate steps include prototype development and testing.

The economic impacts of this output typically have a steeper spatial gradient than that for basic research, for several reasons. First, some university researchers spin off new firms themselves, either while on the university payroll or as an alternative to university employment. The choice between these two options is determined in part by university policy. Some universities make such commercial activity very difficult for faculty. Others, such as the University of Utah (see Luger and Goldstein, 1991), encourage academic entrepreneurship as an integral part of the official mission. In addition, firms in the university's region have a greater opportunity to learn about faculty research and enter into relationships than do businesses farther away. And during the prototype development and testing stages, the faculty inventor/researcher needs to be available. The extent of the regional effect depends in large part on the composition of the local economic base. If the invention/research result is useful to an industry that has a large local presence, the effect is large. However, there are many examples of the contrary case: when research conducted in one region is important for industry located far away. Goldstein and Luger (1993) conclude that the benefits from the research conducted at most of North Carolina State University's engineering labs redound to businesses outside the state of North Carolina.

Capital Investment

Universities (or the state, for public universities) spend considerable sums of money each year building, renovating, and maintaining facilities, such as classroom buildings, laboratories, administrative offices, and activity centers that are required to carry out their basic academic mission. They also frequently provide infrastructure, including internal roads, power stations, water delivery systems, athletic facilities, and student housing. Increasingly, universities have been developing facilities that support production of some of the "nontraditional" outputs, such as advanced technology labs, small business incubators, and research parks. A number of universities in the United States have begun to invest in start-up business ventures and commercial and residential real estate in their regions, sometimes using endowment monies, as a potential (if risky) source of revenue and as a way to influence the type and quality of development in the university's environs.

Whatever the motivation to undertake capital projects, through the spending multiplier process the direct plus indirect economic effects can be substantial. For example, Goldstein and Luger (1993) estimated that the construction of one proposed $55 million engineering research facility at North Carolina State University in Raleigh would generate a one-time increase in value of output by North Carolina businesses of $96 million. That translates into $30.5 million in new earnings paid to North Carolina households and approximately fifteen hundred new jobs, mostly in the construction sector. (In addition, the purchase of supplies, additional equipment, services, and labor to support the ongoing operations of the facility would lead to indirect increases in business activity in the state because of the spending multiplier. Goldstein and Luger estimated that on an annual basis there would be a net increase of $16.5 million to output by North Carolina businesses, $4.8 million in earnings paid to households, and 260 permanent jobs *above and beyond* the jobs and earnings paid for directly by North Carolina State University.) More generally, the magnitude of the economic impact of university investments depends upon the extent to which the investment realizes net, ongoing, economic activity vis-à-vis only construction activity, as well as the size of the investment itself. The spatial gradient of the impact falls off sharply since a large proportion of all investments tends to be located close to the university.

The construction and ownership of facilities and improvements by universities can have a negative effect on regions as well. Real property owned by public universities (that is, by the state) and facilities with academic uses, broadly defined, owned by many private universities in the United States are exempt from local property taxes. Most private universities in the United States are extended tax-exempt status as charitable organizations, as defined in §501.C.3 of the Internal Revenue Code. In-lieu-of-tax payments by the university to the local government sometimes are negotiated, but in many instances local governments with large universities forgo a considerable amount of tax revenue. The tax-exempt status of many of the new nontraditional facilities is the subject of some legal controversy.

Provision of Regional Leadership

Increasingly, top university officials and distinguished faculty are asked by public officials to serve on commissions, boards, and committees to provide leadership in addressing critical social, economic, and environmental problems. What universities can contribute in this role, in addition to their technical resources, is a certain type of moral authority and political clout to help forge consensus among conflicting interests toward a plan of action. Typical problem areas might be affordable housing, crime and safety, governmental efficiency, environmental hazards, and economic development itself.

In providing regional leadership, universities can influence economic development by contributing to the region's quality of life, specifically by making it more attractive as a place for the general population and business community to live, work, and invest. Of course, university interests are advanced by improvements in a region's quality of life: for example, faculty and student recruitment becomes easier and the number of nonuniversity R&D facilities in the region is likely to grow. Publicly supported universities located in regions that are cited as up-and-coming in location surveys are quick to take credit, whether or not they are actually responsible for the improved quality of life, as a way to curry favor in the state legislature. Livability comparisons are published periodically by *Money* magazine, *Places Rated Almanac,* and other books and journals.

Universities located in the larger and older cities in the United States historically have been the most active in community affairs and in consciously shaping community outcomes. However, in recent years, many universities in both North America and Europe located in economically lagging smaller cities and non-metropolitan areas, and in areas undergoing significant economic restructuring, have added this role to their mission statements.

Knowledge Infrastructure

In addition to the *direct* creation of knowledge, technology, and human capital, the research university is a key element of a region's knowledge infrastructure. Just as a high-quality, efficient physical infrastructure—transportation and communication facilities, and various public utility systems—is essential for a region to have the capacity for future growth and development, so is a knowledge infrastructure necessary for a region to grow creative and innovative organizations and individuals that can lead to sustainable economic development.

The knowledge infrastructure comprises individual repositories of scientific knowledge and technical know-how, linked together in largely informal networks of both electronic and face-to-face interaction. A well-developed knowledge infrastructure has a high density of differentiated knowledge generators, and a developed set of intermediary support services that provide possibilities for a high degree of interaction among them. Universities with policies that actively promote interaction of faculty and research units with other knowledge-producing organizations in the region tend to contribute more to the productivity of the knowledge infrastructure. Also, we would expect that universities located in large metropolitan regions with higher densities of knowledge-producing organizations are better able to generate regional synergy and entrepreneurial activity. Almost by definition, the economic impacts of the university's contribution to the knowledge infrastructure are highly geographically localized.

Regional Milieu

Finally, through the production of its previously mentioned outputs, the research university inadvertently creates a set of externalities that may be shared by a large number of other actors and, consequently, can lead to regional economic benefits (and costs). We include here the production of a distinctive type of *milieu*—in parts intellectual, cultural, social, and recreational—that certain individuals, businesses and organizations, particularly those involved with research and development functions, value highly. Universities affect the milieu of a region because the institutions themselves are often relatively large and employ a large concentration of highly educated and creative professionals who are willing to pay for high levels of public goods and amenities. That, in turn, attracts other highly educated professionals to the region who often have no direct ties with the university. The same dynamic, however, can lead to *negative* externalities as well. For example, a region that has experienced a high rate of growth based upon attracting new R&D activity can suffer from commercial gentrification whereby higher input costs such as labor place traditional businesses at risk. That eventually can lead to significant outmigration and sharply reduced economic growth as a result of the inability of many types of lower-paid, but necessary, nonprofessional workers to afford to live in the region. That has occurred, for example, in California's Silicon Valley (Luger and Goldstein, 1991).

This last type of output, as well as the coproduction of a region's knowledge infrastructure, is not well defined, and so the ensuing economic impacts are very difficult to measure. Because of that, and the fact that they are not intentional but instead are by-products of what the university does, their "value" is often ignored or dismissed. Yet the long-term trend of an increasingly knowledge-based economy strongly suggests that those university outputs may be among the most important in contributing to economic development.

By way of summary, the various output categories and their expected major economic impacts are depicted in Table 26.1. It should be pointed out that specific activities can overlap more than one of these outputs, and there are likely to be important complementarities between several of the categories. An obvious example is the production of new knowledge (research) and human capital creation in the training of many graduate students. Also, there is variation in the degree of opportunity costs for increasing production among types of outputs. For example, increasing technological innovation may require substantial additional

TABLE 26.1. UNIVERSITY OUTPUTS AND THEIR LIKELY GEOGRAPHIC IMPACTS.

Activity	Traditional or New Activity?	*Likely Geographic Impact*			
		Broadest	Broad	Narrow	Narrowest
Creation of new "basic" knowledge through research	Traditional	XX			YY
Application of knowledge to the creation and commercialization of new products	Traditional, new		XX		YY
Application of knowledge to the improvement of existing products and processes	Traditional, new			XX	
Creation of human capital through teaching	Traditional		XX		
Creation of physical capital and infrastructure	Traditional, new				XX
Leadership in addressing critical social problems	New				XX
Support services to other economic actors	New				XX
Creation of a favorable "milieu"	Traditional				XX

XX = spatial incidence due to activity's outcomes.

YY = spatial impact of spending on research, regardless of research results.

capital and staff resources with attendant opportunity costs, while the investment in buildings and infrastructure requires the use of the university's capital resources but few of its limited human resources. The university's provision of leadership and its contribution to the region's knowledge infrastructure have very low costs; furthermore, they can be highly complementary with its teaching, research, and public service activities.

The (Contingent) Local and Regional Economic Impacts of Universities

In the previous section, we conceptualized the university as a multiproduct organization. By using a combination of inputs, the university produces a set of outputs—some traditional, some fairly new—and by doing so, it influences its regional economic environment. Some traditional outputs, such as teaching and knowledge creation, do not have an intended economic development impact but can have important unintended impacts. Other outputs are produced *intentionally* to have a favorable economic impact on the region.

In this section, we collect some of the evidence about the local and regional economic impacts of universities by type of output identified above. Given the broad scope of relationships between a university and its region, and the evident difficulty of measuring them, it is not surprising that the amount and quality of evidence differ considerably. In many areas, the available evidence is anecdotal and plagued by obvious omissions and gaps.

The Regional Impact of University Expenditures

This type of impact results in generation of greater economic activity within the geographically defined region—usually measured in terms of increases in the value of output, household earnings, and employment—as a result of the university's purchase of inputs from businesses and households (labor) located within the region. The magnitude of the impact is most importantly a function of the size of the university (its aggregate annual purchases), the extent to which the university purchases its inputs from within the region and the density of interindustry linkages within the region, and, to a lesser extent, the mix of inputs purchased by the university.

Estimates of the output multipliers of research-oriented universities in the United States (using regional input-output models) range roughly from about 1.5 to 3.0. (Leslie and Brinkman, 1988, provide a table summarizing the magnitudes of multipliers estimated in a number of university economic impact studies.) That is, a university whose annual spending for inputs within the region is $10 million generates $15–30 million in total additional value of output throughout the region. The multiplier is toward the upper end for universities located within large and diverse metropolitan regions and toward the lower end for universities located in relatively isolated rural areas. Also, research universities tend to have larger *effective* impacts than other types of higher education institutions because they are able to leverage a significant amount of *external* sources of funding for research and training. Whether this type of impact is larger than for other regional organizations of comparable size depends on whether universities tend to purchase more of their inputs from within the region. That is likely to be the case compared to private multiple-location businesses, especially those with well-developed internal intermediate input networks (for example, vertically integrated companies). In the Goldstein and Luger (1992) study of the economic impacts of the University of North Carolina at Chapel Hill, the estimated output multiplier was 2.0. But in the ratio of total annual value of output directly and indirectly generated by the university to the amount of state government appropriations, the *effective* multiplier was closer to 4.0. The logic here was that the state appropriation was able to leverage outside revenue that would not have otherwise come into the state and generate economic activity.

Regional Impacts from the Creation of Human Capital Via Knowledge Transfer

The regional economic impacts accruing from the teaching and training function of particular universities are not usually estimated, in part because of the so-called attribution problem, and in part because of the large data requirements. There have been two traditions in the literature for estimating the aggregate economic value of higher education: the estimated contribution of education to national income, and the rates of return to investment in schooling. Summarizing the first group of studies, the contribution of education (as a whole) to increases in national income is roughly 10–20 percent. Approximately one-quarter of that can be attributed to higher education (Leslie and Brinkman, 1988).

The return on investment in higher education has been measured as the increase in wages and salaries by the students undertaking the investment. That measures the private returns to the individuals, but it may also be considered as a reasonable proxy for the increment to marginal productivity accruing to businesses employing such individuals. These studies, by Hansen (1963), Hanock (1967), Griliches and Mason (1972), Raymond and Sesnowitz (1975), and others, typically disaggregate individuals by level of schooling and demographic characteristics. In rate-of-return studies, producers' surplus is usually neglected in the measurement of productivity gains realized by the producing firms. Also, the use of wage and salary measures rather than total compensation, that is, including fringe benefits and working conditions, underestimates the rate of return on the order of 10–40 percent. Other non–market-induced benefits of investments in higher education, such as improved health, are usually ignored. For a complete typology of market and nonmarket impacts of investment in schooling, see Haveman and Wolfe (1984).

The definitions, methods, assumptions, and data vary considerably among the rate-of-return studies. Nonetheless, the general conclusion is that the private rate of return on investment in higher education in the United States is on the order of 10–20 percent (Leslie and Brinkman, 1988). The returns to graduate higher education are somewhat lower than for undergraduate education (5–15 percent).

A better measure of economic benefit would be the *social* rate of return, but that is more difficult to measure. It takes into account that some of the costs of higher education are publicly subsidized (making the social rate of return lower than the private rate), but also that there are external benefits of higher education that society as a whole receives (which would make the social rate higher than the private). Whether the social rate of return is higher or lower than the private rate is an empirical matter that depends on whether the external social benefits of higher education outweigh the public subsidization of the per-student costs of teaching/training. Of course, the actual rate of return in a particular case fluctuates around the average rate of return, depending upon academic field, gender, race, years completed, degree, and region. In any event, with data on the number of person-years of schooling and the average investment per student-year appropriately disaggregated, the marginal economic benefit to society at large of the teaching/training function of a given university for a unit period of time could be estimated.

Since we are specifically interested in the economic benefits accruing to the *region*, though, we can count only those trained who have become employed and remain in the same region. The proportion of students who take jobs within the same region and the amount of time they stay vary considerably from region to region. This depends upon the perception of the job opportunities for certain skill levels compared to other regions. The more specialized a job searcher's skills and educational training, the wider the geographic scope of his or her search, and the less likely she or he will stay within the region. Graduates of universities located within large metropolitan labor market areas are more likely to remain in the region than those from universities in small and isolated regions whose departure would contribute to a brain drain. This argument has an important policy implication: because of the difficulty disfavored regions have in keeping university graduates within their labor market, locating new universities or expanding existing ones in such regions may not generate the expected effects.

Amenity level may affect the decision to remain or move upon graduation. In the economic impact study of the University of North Carolina at Chapel Hill, Goldstein and Luger (1992) investigated the geographic flow of students between the time immediately preceding registration at the university and current location, for three separate cohorts (entering the university for the first time in 1973, 1978, and 1983). The results showed that over time the proportion of graduates that remained within the region increased as the regional labor market coincidentally expanded significantly, and the smaller the region of origin the more likely the former student is currently residing within the local labor market area. We are prone to ignoring the two-way, intimate relationship between a university and its regional environment. While this chapter focuses on the impacts of the university *upon* its regional environment, the regional environment is a critically important input, or determinant, of the set of outputs and impacts that a university can potentially generate.

The Regional Impacts from Technology Transfer

We use the term *technology transfer* to refer to the full array of stored know-how, expertise, hard and soft technologies, and problem-solving capacity that can be applied to and adopted by a range of private businesses, units of government, and nonprofit organizations in the region. (We recognize that in the course of applying existing knowledge and problem solving, new knowledge is sometimes gained. In practice, technology transfer and research can overlap, as can technology transfer and teaching/training. We believe the conceptual differences are still meaningful, though their separation in practice—and measurement—may in some cases be intractable.) Technology transfer encompasses many of the services often included in public service, as well as extension, technical and small business assistance, and individual faculty consulting. Technology transfer creates regional economic benefits when recipient organizations in the region become more productive or more innovative as a result of the know-how received.

Originally tied to the idea of land-grant universities, some types of technology transfer activity are now ingrained in just about every public university, and many private ones. Specific institutional programs vary. In a recent survey, over 50 percent of responding U.S. research and doctoral-granting universities indicated that they sponsored technical assistance centers, while about 13 percent had small-business assistance centers (Luger and Goldstein, 1991). Matkin (1990) has counted "several hundred" technical assistance programs (TAPs) sponsored by universities.

Estimates of the economic impacts of institutionally based technology transfer programs typically are based upon a count of program outputs (for example, number of clients assisted, or client-hours of assistance) and the recipient organization's self-assessment of the difference the assistance has made to the organization (such as changes in sales, employment, or productivity). Data generated from such self-assessments are subject to questions of both reliability and validity. As a result, there tends to be a lot of anecdotal information.

The magnitude of regional economic impacts depends largely on the amount of university inputs devoted to technology transfer. (In addition to dollars in resources to pay for staff time, the degree of commitment by the university's administration, the incentives provided to faculty and staff, and the effectiveness of the organization of service provision within the university—whether decentralized along essentially departmental lines or highly centralized through a public service or extension division with its own staff devoted to service provision—have often been cited as important internal factors.) The impact also is a function of the density and receptivity of the pool of organizations within the region, the degree to which the expertise and know-how within the university are appropriate for the needs of the region's businesses and organizations, and the compatibility of the styles of communication and other forms of interaction between the providers of services and the recipient organizations.

Most existing evaluations of technology transfer programs (including public service and extension activities) are anecdotal, reducing our ability to draw generalizable lessons. The studies at least suggest that universities' and clients' perspectives on technology transfer do not coincide. Universities generally prefer to integrate technology transfer operations with their teaching/training and research activities, as a way to demonstrate how responsive they are to external demands for public service and outreach and to economize on inputs. Many recipient organizations, on the other hand, prefer technology transfer to be detached from research and teaching/training activities (Matkin, 1990). Those clients' needs may not require Ph.D.-level expertise, while the responsiveness, timeliness, and pertinence of the services provided might be compromised by the university's attempt to meet a number of objectives. If that is true, universities could be judged to be less appropriate than others (on efficiency grounds) for providing technology transfer services.

University-Based Technological Innovation

Technology development here refers to a range of programs and institutional arrangements whose primary objective is to generate innovations that lead to new, commercially viable products or processes. (This would exclude those research projects, for instance, that yield commercial products that were not a primary objective of the research. While individual intentions are often difficult to measure at the institutional level, by contrast centers, institutes, programs, objectives, and mission statements may be more explicit.) The range of programs include patenting and licensing assistance offices, industrial liaison programs, centers for advanced technology (CATs), and joint university-industry research projects. From a regional economic development point of view, we would expect to see some combination of cost savings, increased sales, and increased employment within established businesses, and an increased incidence, and higher rate of survival, of technology-based start-up companies.

Among U.S. research-oriented universities, technology development has become almost as ubiquitous as teaching and research in the past fifteen years. Peters and Fusfeld (1983) found that about one-half of research universities surveyed had industrial liaison programs, although the vast majority had begun in the five-year period *since* 1978. In a 1990 survey of research and doctoral-granting universities, over 83 percent of the respondents indicated they had licensing/patenting assistance offices, while 82 percent had joint university-industry research projects under way (Luger and Goldstein, 1991).

As these activities have become more commonplace in the United States, less has been heard from critics of the university, who invoked ethical and moral principles to argue (mostly in the 1970s and early 1980s) that universities dedicated to the pursuit of knowledge and truth in an open community of inquiry should not be engaged in "research for profit" (Noble, 1977; Marsden, 1994).

The challenge has moved from the philosophical to the practical realm. Tight budgets put strains on the universities' ability to respond to demands for more technology development. In addition, faculty have little incentive to respond. Few are trained or acculturated to identify changes in the external environment that might affect what they do. The university reward structure is still based on scientific publications in refereed journals, not on inventions, patents, licenses, provision of technical assistance, and other types of technology transfer.

There is also the problem of measuring the effectiveness of university-based technology development programs. Generalizable studies that identify which particular models of university-based technology development are most effective under different conditions are almost nonexistent. In part, this is because the very processes of technological innovation remain black boxes, as Feller (1994) has noted. The existence of multiple models that vary widely—not only by technology field but also by institutional environment, regional and national setting, and particular human agents, and over time—would lead us to conclude, based on available evidence, that the critical success factors tend to be more idiosyncratic than systematic.

Despite this rather harsh assessment, there are at least some suggestive findings that have implications for what economic development role(s) universities should play. First, and not at all surprising, the regional impacts tend to be larger for universities located in larger metropolitan areas. This is simply due to a larger pool of organizations that potentially can realize economic benefit from technology developed within the university or jointly with nonuniversity personnel. On the other hand, there is more difficulty, particularly in macro-level studies, in disentangling the effects of the university's activities from other putative regional influences.

Second, large corporations (or their R&D branch plants) are more likely to benefit from the technology development activities in research-oriented universities than are existing small and medium-sized businesses. This is based on the observation that "academic research findings are seldom directly transferable into commercial innovations, requiring instead considerable technical and economic refining" (Feller, 1994, p. 23). Hence, those firms that are best able to keep informed of scientific and technological advances, and that possess the resources and internal R&D capabilities to take advantage of these advances, will be those most likely to benefit from direct affiliation and research collaboration with research universities. This assessment was made based on the experiences of what

Feller (1994, p. 23) calls the "university-industry model." It may be less true for the "product development model" and for models that we place in the category of technology transfer in this chapter.

Third, the economic benefits accruing to regions from the universities' technology development activities are small in comparison to the benefits those activities generate for society as a whole. They also are smaller than the share of regional benefits from technology transfer and teaching/training. This is a partial corollary from the two preceding paragraphs. Diffusion from universities and adoption by industry of technological innovations are only minimally inhibited by distance, while collaboration between university and industry scientists and engineers can be increasingly accommodated in university labs and centers without the need for separate location of corporate R&D facilities in the region. Also, just as large corporations enter into collaborative relationships with a portfolio of universities where researchers are doing cutting-edge work, no matter where located, research universities tend to be global rather than parochial in their search for the most fruitful collaborative arrangements. A survey of the research and technology development centers at the highly regarded College of Engineering at North Carolina State University in Raleigh, for example, indicated that the overwhelming majority of corporate and industrial affiliates of those centers were located out-of-state, despite the concentration of high technology businesses in the same Research Triangle region.

Direct Stimulation of New Business Start-Ups

Universities can stimulate business start-ups directly by providing equity funds for new technology-oriented businesses (thereby serving as a venture capitalist) and indirectly by generating entrepreneurs, faculty and graduates, who spin off new technology-oriented businesses. Universities also *indirectly* stimulate start-ups in several ways: through their research spending, generating small subcontractors for provision of intermediate inputs to research (Bania, Eberts, and Fogarty, 1987); through development of particular technological innovations that may spawn a number of new businesses, as discussed in the preceding section; and by contributing to a regional milieu favorable to entrepreneurial activity, discussed below.

Whether the stimulation is direct or indirect, the proportion of universities that make equity investments in new technology-based businesses actually is quite low, about 11 percent in 1990 (Luger and Goldstein, 1991), despite the wide attention given to a few groundbreaking cases in the late 1970s and early 1980s. Among the most widely known cases were Harvard University's investment in several biotechnology companies in which Harvard faculty capitalized on DNA research begun at the university. Other early leaders in the ownership of companies based upon research the university had sponsored were MIT (a number of ventures), Penn State (DMI), Boston University (Seragen), and the University of California at Berkeley (Engenics); it is to be noted that this list comprises a mixture of private and public universities.

There were a number of problems associated with these early cases around issues of financial and management conflicts, faculty opposition, and threats to the reputation and independence of the institution, in addition to financial risk (Matkin, 1990). This low incidence may be explained by the recognition that equity ownership could result in conflicts of interest for universities. At base, universities tend to be conservative in their investment policies. Public universities also may be subject to stringent oversight by the legislature or state treasurer. There is some indication that investment policies may be gradually loosening as universities gain greater fiscal autonomy and flexibility on the one hand, while forced to become more aggressive in seeking out new revenue sources on the other (see, for example, many recent issues of the *Chronicle for Higher Education*).

Business spin-offs directly from universities (without university ownership) are more common. Individual entrepreneurs are responsible for starting and successfully growing spin-offs. However, in many cases, universities initially "supply" the entrepreneurs and provide the infrastructure and support for many of the research projects that later spawn commercial opportunities for founding spin-off businesses.

The incidence of business spin-offs from universities has been investigated mostly as case studies of particular universities. Stanford University and MIT generated huge numbers of spin-off businesses in Silicon Valley in California and along the Route 128 corridor in Massachusetts, respectively, because they were able to take advantage of the explosion of national defense spending for applied research in the sciences and engineering from the late 1950s through the 1970s; those two cases have defined standards of success that almost all other universities and their regions cannot realistically emulate (Sirbu, Treitel, Yorsz, and Roberts, 1976; Dorfman, 1982; Saxenian, 1985; Krenz, 1988; Luger and Goldstein, 1991). Yet other research universities in the United States have stimulated more modest, but still significant, numbers of technology-based spin-offs, including the University of Utah, the three research universities of the Research Triangle region of North Carolina (Duke University, University of North Carolina at Chapel Hill, and North Carolina State University), and the University of Texas, Austin (Brown 1987; Luger and Goldstein 1991; Ko, 1993; see also Brett, Gibson, and Smilor, 1991).

By far, the most important predictor of university spin-offs is the history of previous spin-offs. Individuals who have successfully spun off businesses from their universities can serve as role models and sources of advice to potential faculty and graduate entrepreneurs and help lessen the perceived barriers. Other factors that help account for spin-offs are the policies of the university toward faculty entrepreneurship, the general incidence of technology-based start-ups within the region, and of course the base of support within the university for research in technology fields that are ripe for commercial innovations. With the possible exceptions of Stanford and MIT in the 1960s and early 1970s, universities have not generated as many direct regional economic benefits through their spin-offs as they have through their spending and teaching/training. However, we should not minimize the symbolic importance of a vibrant spin-off economy, especially the effect it can have on the attractiveness of a region as a high-tech location.

Contributions to a Region's Knowledge-Based Infrastructure and Milieu

Contributions to knowledge-based infrastructure and milieu are the most indirect and least well-defined ones that we consider, though they may very well end up being the most important. A region's knowledge-based infrastructure consists of the set of institutions and organizations, and their synergies, that support and increase the region's capacity for knowledge creation and dissemination, technological innovation, and entrepreneurship. Specific elements in addition to universities typically include public schools, community colleges, training institutions, sources of venture capital and other forms of business finance, and technical and managerial assistance, as well as information services providers, research institutes, and the network of small and medium-sized R&D firms already in the region.

Milieu is used here in a very inclusive way, to encompass aspects of culture, community tastes and demand for public goods, political attitudes, and "entrepreneurial spirit." The regional milieu of the type considered here can stimulate economic development by attracting to an area creative and talented people who seek proximity to others like themselves. A research university creates such a location dynamic almost by definition.

Knowledge infrastructure stimulates economic development by effectively lowering the costs faced by *individual* businesses for some of the critical inputs (for example, specialized labor skills, information, ideas, and intellectual stimulation) needed for successful innovations. It would be nearly impossible to attribute the regional development impacts to a single institution that forms part of the region's infrastructure, or even to separate the impact due to the infrastructure as a whole (because of such high degrees of overlap with other contributing factors). However, we observe a strong positive correlation between the degree of development of a region's knowledge-based infrastructure, including the prominence of one or more research universities, and its capacity for generating innovative businesses and sustained economic development. One can argue that the implied direction of causality may be the opposite: generation of a number of innovative businesses (brought about by other factors) makes it possible to build a more highly developed infrastructure, since one of the contributors to the infrastructure is a pool of successful entrepreneurs, talented scientists and engineers, R&D shops, and so on.

Measuring the effect of a regional milieu on economic development is an even more heroic task, partly because the concept itself is so slippery and partly because of the usual, but even more complicated, attribution problems. The best evidence is from studies of the location decisions of R&D and other high-technology firms, which show that the presence of research universities in the region was a very important factor even when the business did not expect to have any direct relationships with the university (Malecki, 1987; Luger and Goldstein, 1991; Ko, 1993). It is indeed unfortunate that perhaps the most cost-effective role (essentially zero cost), and potentially the one role that may become the most important in stimulating economic development in the coming decade, has been so difficult to measure.

Is the Economic and Business Development Role of Research Universities Desirable?

In this paper, we have argued that research universities adopted an explicit economic development role as a result of external pressures—related to the unfolding of a knowledge-based global economy and the demands this places on regions to remain competitive—as well as internal pressures such as shortfalls in more traditional revenue sources and rising costs. But fulfilling this new role is not cost-free. The necessary internal reallocation of resources and changes in organizational and management practices—to help make the university a more efficient producer of nontraditional outputs—are likely to create strains within the academy. And there are questions of whether universities have comparative advantages for stimulating economic development. If they do not have comparative advantages, or if the resulting strains and changes in organizational practices cannot be managed effectively, then other institutions may be more appropriate for these roles. If they do have comparative advantages, for what specific set of activities are universities best suited, and what kinds of organizational arrangements might be needed to enhance their effectiveness?

Capitalizing on Comparative Advantage

In addition to wanting to know which university activities are effective in stimulating economic development in a given situation, we also want to know whether those university activities are best conducted by universities as opposed to other types of institutions (private businesses, not-for-profits, etc.). This is tantamount to asking whether a legislature would maximize the return on a given appropriation in terms of economic development results by channeling the funds to a university as opposed to another type of institution.

To answer the question, we should ascertain the unique strengths of universities in general that give them comparative advantage. There are at least three. The first is the concentration of technical knowledge and expertise. That is not to say that professionals in industry are not equally intelligent and inventive. The difference is that the faculty at research universities are rewarded not only for creating new knowledge in specialized areas but also for keeping abreast of scientific and technical advances in broader areas of knowledge.

The second comparative strength of universities is their credibility, based on the perception that research is nonpartisan and scientifically rigorous. This perception is not always borne out, but to the extent that scholarly research must pass through peer review before it is published, it is generally more credible than industry or special-interest-group research (Long, 1992).

A third comparative advantage for universities is their pool of talented but inexpensive labor: the students. While some might consider this exploitative, student involvement in explicit economic development activities represents synergistic benefits to the university, faculty, *and* students, if it passes the test of providing valuable learning experiences or research training.

These advantages are not granted or made available to universities automatically. Universities need to develop and cultivate them. Technical knowledge and expertise in broader areas of knowledge requires interaction and cooperation between faculty members who are experts in their respective fields. Credibility of a university disappears easily when its research does not meet a certain level of quality. Since a few bad examples can cause major damage, universities are well advised to develop mechanisms that guarantee the minimum quality of their output. Students as qualified but inexpensive labor are only a comparative advantage for a university when the faculty can add a learning and training component to the work and provide necessary supervision and mentoring.

Provided universities develop and cultivate their comparative advantages, what do these suggest about the use of public funds for various activities? First, knowledge transfer—from faculty to students in the classroom, and faculty (and research staff) to other economic actors via the provision of technical and managerial assistance, expert testimony, and consulting—draws directly on the first unique strength of universities. Private consultants certainly do the second type of knowledge transfer as well, and in many cases with good results. However, the second unique strength of the university discussed above would suggest that university-based knowledge transfer generally would be more credible (in terms of quality and neutrality).

Concentration of technical expertise also supports the basic research function. This is research that has many potential applications. Industry is at least as well suited to conduct applied research that results in improvements to its products or specific new products that the business can commercialize. In fact, the best research marriage between universities and industry is the combination of basic research strength with industry knowledge of applications. This point is made as well by Rosenberg and Nelson (1994), who warn universities away from research with specific industry applications. An exception could be made for R&D in industries or countries dominated by small and medium-sized firms that do not have their own R&D capacity. Then, universities can fill important gaps and prime the pump of private R&D. Rosenberg and Nelson provide numerous examples of how state universities developed productive research programs affiliated with small local industries.

The availability of willing students who do not yet command a market wage provides unique opportunities for universities to engage in labor-intensive public service activities, in particular those that would serve as a training ground for professional (or preprofessional) students.

The Appropriate Mix of Activities

The preceding discussion suggests that there is a legitimate basis for university involvement in all of the activities that we have identified, both traditional and new. That does not mean, however, that all are appropriate for every university. Like private business, a university may find it preferable to specialize and pursue only a certain set of activities. As we have shown earlier, not all activities are equally likely to lead to regional economic development.

In summary, university spending on supplies, facilities, and employee wages and salaries, and related student and visitor spending, have significant regional development consequences via multipliers. Knowledge transfer also has considerable regional development effects, especially in regions with a large enough job base to retain graduates. Students trained in the local university are more productive. So are businesses and governments in the region that have received technical and managerial assistance from the university. The third set of activities with highly localized effects are those relating to public service and leadership; that is most pertinent for universities in larger and more urban settings.

Creation of new technologies and improvements in existing technologies also have an impact gradient, but it is flatter than for the activities mentioned above. Spin-offs are likely to be located in the same region, but creation of specialized knowledge can be appropriated by businesses anywhere in the world.

The mechanisms for all these transfers require cooperation from local and regional businesses, government institutions, and policy makers, as well as time to develop. For example, businesses have to adjust to the demands of the university, its faculty, and its students in order to make the multiplier effect work. Similarly, when there is no tradition of technical and managerial assistance to government at the university, government officials have to spend some time with university representatives explaining their needs and constraints. The initial stages are characterized by uncertainty and misunderstanding, until the partners develop a basis of trust and a common language.

Taking on new responsibilities is not without risk for universities. As we have seen, the set of requests and expectations universities face has broadened considerably in recent years. Because of limited resources, no university can fulfill all these requests simultaneously. Therefore, universities have to decide about their product mix; they have to analyze such questions as, Which requests are essential for the long-run development of the institution? Are there market niches the university can occupy? What are the short- versus long-run implications of a certain strategy?

When the university chooses a certain product mix and targets a specific market—such as serving the local or regional economy—the adjustments and resource allocations it has to make have implications for its structure and development potential. In order to serve the targeted market most efficiently, the university develops structures that are suitable for this specific need but may be ill suited for other functions. Structures and instruments that prove to be adequate under today's conditions may be hampering the university's future ability to adjust to changes in its dynamic environment.

Such rigidities may result not only from a university's operation in the past. They may also be the result of externally imposed regulations, particularly in the case of publicly supported universities. Such regulations might make a university appear to be lacking entrepreneurial spirit.

Conclusion

As a result of fundamental changes in society and the economy, universities today face a broader and more complex set of demands than a few decades ago. In addition to the traditional teaching and research functions, universities today are expected to provide leadership and infrastructure, stimulate the economy through technology transfer and expenditures, and create a milieu that is favorable to economic and societal development. Our analysis suggests that there is a legitimate basis for universities to get involved in all of these activities, although it may not make sense for each institution to take on the whole set of responsibilities. Whether a certain university should become actively involved in a specific function depends not only upon the university and its structure but also upon the region and its economy.

Taking on new functions may entail new and challenging management tasks for university administration. At best, it needs to target the appropriate new areas for the university and balance new and old requests. It is likely, however, that taking the necessary steps will encounter opposition and cause stress within and outside the organization. Managing these periods of crisis by communicating the aims and long-term perspective of restructuring and by carefully balancing its costs and benefits is a major task for university leaders. In order to drive the development process rather than be driven by it, university administration needs a long-term perspective in addition to considerable managerial competence. To be able to take the steps required for the new set of demands, universities will need sufficient flexibility in and control over their internal structure and operation (Neave, 1995; Williams, 1995).

Further Reading

The theoretical foundations of the work reported here come from various literatures, including human capital (Becker, 1975), invention and productivity (notably Griliches, 1984; and Jaffe, 1989), and endogenous growth (Romer, 1990). Luger and Goldstein (1991), Malecki (1987), and Saxenian (1985) place knowledge creation within a regional, or geographic, context. Feller (1990) and Feller (1994) are two particularly valuable explications of the role universities play as instruments of technology and economic development policy. Finally, readers may find several case studies of interest, including Goldstein and Luger's analysis of the regional economic development impact of the University of North Carolina at Chapel Hill (1992), and of North Carolina State University's College of Engineering (1993).

References

Bania, N. R., Eberts, R., and Fogarty, M. "The Role of Technical Capital in Regional Growth." Paper presented at the Western Economic Association Meetings, Santa Barbara, Calif., July 1987.

Becker, G. *Human Capital: A Theoretical and Empirical Analysis.* New York: National Bureau of Economic Research, 1975.

Brett, A. M., Gibson, D., and Smilor, R. W. *University Spin-Off Companies.* Lanham, Md.: Rowman & Littlefield, 1991.

Brown, W. S. "Locally-Grown High Technology Business Development: The Utah Experience." In W. S. Brown and R. Rothwell (eds.), *Entrepreneurship and Technology: World Experiences and Policies.* White Plains, N.Y.: Longman, 1987.

Caffrey, J., and Isaacs, H. H. *Estimating the Impact of a College or University on the Local Economy.* Washington, D.C.: American Council on Education, 1971.

Cohen, W. M., and Levinthal, D. "Innovation and Learning: The Two Faces of R&D." *Economic Journal,* 1989, *99,* 569–596.

Dorfman, N. S. "Massachusetts' High Technology Boom in Perspective: An Investigation of Its Dimensions, Causes, and of the Role of New Firms." Unpublished manuscript. Cambridge, Mass.: Center for Policy Alternatives, Massachusetts Institute of Technology, 1982.

Feller, I. "Universities as Engines of R&D-Based Economic Growth: They Think They Can." *Research Policy,* 1990, *19*(4), 335–348.

Feller, I. "The University as an Instrument of State and Regional Economic Development: The Rhetoric and Reality of the U.S. Experience." Paper prepared for the Conference on University Goals, Institutional Mechanisms, and the Industrial Transferability of Research, Stanford University, Mar. 18–20, 1994.

Geiger, R. L., and Feller, I. "The Dispersion of Academic Research in the 1980s." *Journal of Higher Education,* 1995, *66*(3), 336–360.

Goldstein, H. A., and Luger, M. I. *Impact Carolina: The University of North Carolina at Chapel Hill and the State's Economy.* Report prepared for the UNC-CH Bicentennial Observance. Chapel Hill, N.C.: University of North Carolina at Chapel Hill, 1992.

Goldstein, H. A., and Luger, M. I. *The Economic Impact of North Carolina State University's College of Engineering on the State.* Unpublished report prepared for the College of Engineering, North Carolina State University. Raleigh, N.C.: North Carolina State University, 1993.

Griliches, Z. *R&D, Patents, and Productivity.* Chicago: University of Chicago Press, 1984.

Griliches, Z. "Productivity, R&D, and Basic Research at the Firm Level in the 1970s." *American Economic Review,* 1986, *76*(1), 141–154.

Griliches, Z., and Mason, W. "Education, Income, and Ability." *Journal of Political Economy,* 1972, *80*(3), 74–103.

Hanock, G. "An Economic Analysis of Earnings and Schooling." *Journal of Human Resources,* 1967, *2*(3), 310–346.

Hansen, W. L. "Total and Private Rates of Return to Investment in Schooling." *Journal of Political Economy,* 1963, *71*(2), 128–140.

Haveman, R. H., and Wolfe, B. L. "Schooling and Economic Well-Being: The Role of Nonmarket Effects." *Journal of Human Resources,* 1984, *19*(3), 377–407.

Jaffe, A. "Technological Opportunity and Spillovers from R&D: Evidence from Firms' Patents, Profits, and Market Value." *American Economic Review,* 1986, *76*(5), 984–1001.

Jaffe, A. "Real Effects of Academic Research." *American Economic Review,* 1989, *79*(5), 957–970.

Jaffe, A., Tratjenberg, M., and Henderson, R. "Geographic Localization of Knowledge Spillovers, as Evidenced by Patent Citations." *Quarterly Journal of Economics,* 1993, *108*(3) 577–598.

Klausner, S. Z. "Dilemmas of Usefulness: Universities and Contract Research." Paper presented to the American Bar Foundation, Apr. 18, 1988.

Ko, S. "The Incidence of High Technology Start-Ups and Spin-Offs in a Technology-

Oriented Branch Plants Complex." Unpublished doctoral dissertation, University of North Carolina at Chapel Hill, 1993.

Krenz, C. "Silicon Valley Spin-Offs from Stanford University Faculty." Unpublished manuscript. Stanford, Calif.: Stanford University Business School, 1988.

Leslie, L., and Brinkman, P. T. *The Economic Value of Higher Education.* New York: ACE/Macmillan, 1988.

Long, E. L., Jr. *Higher Education as a Moral Enterprise.* Washington, D.C.: Georgetown University Press, 1992.

Luger, M. I., and Goldstein, H. A. *Technology in the Garden: Research Parks and Regional Economic Development.* Chapel Hill, N.C.: University of North Carolina Press, 1991.

Malecki, E. J. "The R&D Location Decision of the Firm and 'Creative' Regions." *Technovation,* 1987, *6,* 205–222.

Marsden, G. M. *The Soul of the American University: From Protestant Establishment to Established Nonbelief.* New York: Oxford University Press, 1994.

Matkin, G. W. *Technology Transfer and the University.* New York: American Council on Education/Macmillan, 1990.

National Academy of Sciences. *The Impact of Science and Technology on Regional Economic Development.* Washington D.C.: National Academy of Sciences, 1969.

Neave, G. "The Stirring of the Prince and the Silence of the Lambs: The Changing Assumptions Beneath Higher Education Policy, Reform, and Society." In D. D. Dill and B. Sporn (eds.), *Emerging Patterns of Social Demand and University Reform: Through A Glass Darkly.* New York: Pergamon Press, 1995.

Noble, D. *America by Design.* New York: Knopf, 1977.

Peters, L. S., and Fusfeld, H. I. *University-Industry Research Relationships.* Washington D.C.: National Science Foundation, 1983.

Raymond, R., and Sesnowitz, M. "The Returns to Investments in Higher Education: Some New Evidence." *The Journal of Human Resources,* 1975, *10*(2), 139–154.

Romer, P. "Endogenous Technological Change." *Journal of Political Economy,* 1990, *98,* S71–S102.

Rosenberg, N., and Nelson, R. "American Universities and Technical Advance in Industry." *Research Policy,* 1994, *23,* 323–348.

Saxenian, A. "Silicon Valley and Route 128: Regional Prototype or Historic Exceptions?" In M. Castells (ed.), *High Technology, Space, and Society.* Thousand Oaks, Calif.: Sage, 1985.

Sirbu, M. A., Treitel, R., Yorsz, W., and Roberts, E. B. *The Formation of a Technology-Oriented Complex: Lessons from North America and European Experiences.* Unpublished manuscript, Massachusetts Institute of Technology, Center for Policy Alternatives, Cambridge, Mass., 1976.

Tratjenberg, M., Henderson, R., and Jaffe, A. "Ivory Tower versus Corporate Lab: An Empirical Study of Basic Research and Appropriability." (Working Paper No. 4146.) Cambridge, Mass.: National Bureau of Economic Research, August 1992.

Williams, G. "Reforms and Potential Reforms in Higher Education Finance in Europe." In D. D. Dill and B. Sporn (eds.), *Emerging Patterns of Social Demand and University Reform: Through A Glass Darkly.* New York: Pergamon Press, 1995.

CHAPTER TWENTY-SEVEN

UNDERSTANDING THE GLOBALIZATION OF SCHOLARSHIP

David William Cohen

Since the late 1980s, "internationalization" has become one of the most constantly articulated goals of North American higher education. The theme has been much voiced by university leaders and has been the subject of a number of national conferences. The meanings attached to the concept have been open to wide interpretation among diverse communities of administrators and faculty both within and outside the university. While the calls for internationalization have constituted significant motors of change in the organization of academic training and research, they have also created tensions over the planning of change and the disposition of resources.

It is certain that ideas and objectives concerning internationalization motivated in the late 1980s and early 1990s will carry influence in higher education for years to come; it is also certain that internationalization—as a concept, a goal, a mandate—will both attract new interpretations and produce changes in universities and colleges that can hardly be anticipated today. As with other mandates, a broad commitment that hardly seems contestable opens upon an unknown future. The challenges are substantial for leaders and planners within higher education in North America. This chapter addresses some of the present challenges and opportunities for higher education in respect to this moment, one in which substantial changes in the political and economic order of the wider world (the world outside North America), whose outcomes are hardly predictable, are accompanied by calls for significant transformation in the organization of research, training, and administration in higher education.

The "Capital Infrastructure" of International Academic Research and Training

From the end of the Second World War through the 1980s, the North American university underwent development as the principal site for research, analysis, and training on the wider world, with a vast growth of expertise in the university lodged in both older and newer disciplines and in international and area centers. Research universities as well as liberal arts colleges have made vast investments in the development of these resources, guided and supported in significant ways by major foundations and the federal government.

These investments in the cultivation of area and international expertise were often justified, if not also motivated, by reference to the support of American interest amidst Cold War conflict, though at least one observer has suggested, from a survey of publications by area specialists between 1976 and 1981, that fewer than 6 percent of these publications "had any possible relevance to military or strategic planning" (Lambert, 1990, p. 732). While university-based expertise would at times oppose American policy in the Cold War theaters, the Cold War imperative was nevertheless constantly used as a major rationalization for the expansion of—and, in hard times, defense of—federal support for international and area studies (Scott, J. C., 1994). While university-based expertise would at times be substantially ignored in the formulation of U.S. foreign policy—and might, even where implemented, not achieve the objectives sought—Congress, federal agencies, and foundations continued to support area and international research and training in the universities via invocation of national interest.

The end of the Cold War removed a well-rehearsed argument on behalf of continued federal subsidy of research and training in area and international studies. While national-interest arguments could still be generated and command attention, and while new challenges, anxieties, and enemies could be identified or imagined, the end of the Cold War had a profound effect on how North American research universities addressed the wider world.

This period of transition and transformation in the academy continues today, and it would be no simple matter to write a history of the experience only a half decade or so after the fall of the Berlin Wall and the disappearance of the Soviet Union from the world system. But three observations can be made about the changes in the university's address to the wider world, changes that have accompanied or are consequences of the end of the Cold War.

1.   A dynamic change has occurred in the relative authority of different branches of expertise away from international relations and balance-of-power attentions toward an array of other disciplinary and subdisciplinary attentions. While one may observe a reconfiguration of the academic disciplines, the nature of the end of the Soviet Union and the disappearance of socialist states and socialist ideology have sustained the former Soviet sphere as the most important field of address of university-based international expertise.

2.   Fuller recognition has come within the American academy of the significance and power of expertise based in institutions in other countries, with a much-enhanced American interest in drawing upon and collaborating with this expertise. World region studies, or area studies programs and centers, in the United States have substantially transformed themselves from an "orientalist" guise—that the Western academy commanded expert authority and that the rest of the world would be the proper subject of that expertise—toward a position of being the means of access, within the American academy, to expertise based in universities and related institutions in other countries around the globe (Anderson, 1994).

3.   There has been a sometimes reluctant acknowledgment of the power of expertise lying outside the university, whether in North America or abroad.

While the North American university has been able to accommodate—or at least begin to adjust to—the first two elements of transition and transformation, the third element noted above is itself a major challenge to the capacity of university-based expertise to act in and upon the world, not to mention rising to the challenge of producing a fresh generation of expertise capable of comprehending and serving a much-transformed world. Along with briefly extending the first two observations, this chapter gives specific focus to the third observation, because it appears to lay before American higher education a most significant challenge.

The Fate of Academic Expertise

From the mid-1980s, new formations of expertise have developed outside the academy, developing within nongovernmental and nonuniversity organizations. Recent world changes, including the end of the Cold War, have produced a remarkable growth of international expertise in such fields as conflict resolution, debt, environmentalism, health, human rights, military conversion, the oppression of women and ethnic minorities, refugees, and the protection of indigenous peoples. Consulting firms, philanthropic organizations, and advocacy groups have become major information-gathering (as well as information-interpreting) agencies, have gained a purchase on formal policy making, are reshaping the ways in which Americans address the wider world, and are constituting a new economy of expertise.

International expertise is arguably constituting itself as an international civil society with common approaches to local, regional, and global issues; shared languages of discussion; and comparable institutions shaping research and activism; as well as shared values and goals, particularly in respect to enhancement of the guilds of international expertise across the globe and to motivation and enforcement of "international standards." Through the 1980s and 1990s, funding agencies have given important sustenance to these developments, a consequence of a prevailing distrust of state-directed projects and programs.

Now operating outside any possibility of being constrained or foiled by accusations of serving the interests of international communism, and moving rather easily across national borders, international expertise today is challenging and even altering, perhaps forever, long-standing concepts of sovereignty and noninterference. The increasing salience of arguments about "basic needs" and "global standards" overpowers older notions of the nation-state being the nexus of definition of values and rights through national constitutions and the entity's responsibility for the welfare of its population. These developments continue to be elaborated by new attentions, including international standards on pollution, occupational safety, child labor, and scientific experimentation. In all this, the university, its leaders, and its faculty—along with foundations and other funding agencies—face a significant challenge, and also considerable opportunity, in the recognition that neither the academy nor the United States today commands a predominant position in respect to producing knowledge of the world.

One may also observe how guilds of international expertise pronounce themselves "the development community" (Cooper, 1994; Ferguson, 1990) or "the human rights community" or "the disarmament community," replacing the older topographies defined by ideological difference and national interest. For example, in documentation and analysis of famine relief requirements in Somalia between 1982 and 1992, this international expertise may define itself at one moment as independent of the interests of particular states (replicating in a sense the political self-presentation of the old and now virtually forgotten "nonaligned bloc"). At another, such expertise may be reckoned the very medium of state or metropolitan or western or American influence upon the world. While claiming "global addresses," these "epistemic communities" (Zald, 1995) of experts are, on closer examination, clearly seated amidst tensions among local, national, global, and professional values (Cooper, 1994; Lee, 1995; Malkki, 1995).

To comprehend the workings of these communities requires unique research and representational capacities, well outside the frameworks that were long standard in academic scholarship; powerful expositions of the complexities of the work of these organizations and communities may find their way into publications outside the academic sphere. A good example is Joe Kane's 1993 piece in *The New Yorker*, "Letters from the Amazon," which looks at struggles over the exploitation of heavy crude oil and indigenous peoples in the Ecuadorian Amazon. The experts who seek to define and control the issues in the Amazon, who seek to move simultaneously in both local and international spheres, and who claim to know and speak for indigenous peoples do not fare well in Kane's treatment. Notwithstanding Kane's productive skepticism, these days "on the ground" authority (proclaiming itself to be "in the villages" or "just back") anoints individuals as experts on countries that, we see on reflection, are thickly structured in international and regional economic and social contexts that are hardly "the ground" at all.

It is, of course, commonplace to bewail the failures and inexactitudes of experts. Why couldn't experts predict the end of the Cold War, or the disintegration of the Soviet Union, and why couldn't they comprehend the logic of Saddam Hussein's campaigns? Or anticipate the popular enthusiasm for Mohammed Farah Aidid's resistance to United States and United Nations intervention in Somalia? Or recognize the impossibility of finding anyone who could command and sustain legitimacy as a spokesperson for indigenous peoples of the Amazon? Or predict the Rwanda genocide? Or even predict descendant outcomes in neighboring Zaire, Burundi, and Tanzania? Or provide cautionary advice on the tumultuous consequences of the breakup of the Yugoslavian federation?

The question goes beyond competency, beyond recognizing that the "experts"—such as those trained within the American university—may not have been sufficiently trained or skilled to predict or imagine the direction or the pace of recent change. The question goes to the fate of expertise, and to the fate of particular kinds of expertise, with the appearance of a global intellectual apparatus and the internationalization of expertise through the general globalization of professions. The interests of the new self-professed global experts may not be unambiguous, but clearly they are constructed differently from the interests of those experts—for example, the Kremlinologists—who were expected to predict the disappearance of socialist states across the globe.

Such guilds are having a profound effect on how countries, or nations, are known and addressed within the global arena. Such organizations as the Nature Conservancy and the World Wildlife Fund have emerged as major nongovernmental players on the global environmental stage, even operating as major contractors for the U.S. Agency for International Development.

"Global" Values and American Professions

In the North American academy, the transition toward a grammar of global values is perhaps exemplified most clearly in the recent and growing appearances of specialties in "human rights law" or "international human rights" or "women's rights" within the registers of faculty interests and expertise in the catalogues of American law schools, in the internationalization of law conferences, in the enlarged presence of human rights within the programs of professional meetings of lawyers and legal scholars, and in the increasing importance of international conferences examining national and global standards in respect to the rights of persons. Outside the academy, one may observe mailboxes overflowing with appeals for the support of organizations documenting and challenging human rights abuses; one cannot absent oneself from the international economy of advocacy. In Washington and other world capitals, one may note the active and visible presence of nongovernmental organizations stressing advocacy on a global scale.

In respect to the pivotal field of human rights, reporting on human rights concerns since the Carter Administration has emerged as a primary medium of communication about the conditions of life and the practices of government of more than a hundred nations across the globe, paralleling the post–World War II growth of national economic indicators as measures of conditions in the non-Western countries. This expansion of human rights reporting has accompanied, but also been a part of, the centering of human rights concerns within the practice of international diplomacy. In a front-page story on the debate in 1994 over the U.S. government's reading of China's human rights record, *The New York Times* quoted Winston Lord, assistant secretary of state for East Asian and Pacific affairs: "When I was working for Henry Kissinger in the 1970s, I tended to meet with think-tankers and academics, purely on political security issues. Today, I find myself going from a meeting with Amnesty International or Asia Watch in the morning to one with the Chamber of Commerce in the afternoon" ("China's Human Rights Record," 1994). Indeed, many scholars are noting a saturation of the political field (national and international) across the globe by what Mary Ann Glendon has called "rights talk," displacing other forms of interest articulation and other languages of political and social action. And there is no doubt that attention to women's status and women's rights has become a most dynamic impulse within international policy planning in the fields of development, health, and population planning, as well as human rights.

This centering of expertise, and of the professions of experts, is not simply an academicist assertion. One sees across the world diverse and significant challenges to claims of expert authority. One can recognize that from, say, 1945 to 1960, local nationalisms developed against old imperial structures in settings in which expertise found responsive claimants on any side of any contest. But since the mid-1980s, one notes that the local nationalisms seen exploding throughout the world develop against bureaucrats, intelligentsias, and *nomenklaturas,* and against their claims as experts to represent history, define policy, and determine the new forms of community.

The opening of virtual global "conversations" concerning local, regional, and international issues has been accompanied, quite obviously, by extraordinary ruptures in the expectations of so many experts seeking to realize what they have fashioned as global norms. What may seem natural, normative, and obviously correct to one party may appear threatening, intrusive, oppressive, or revolutionary to another; this may be noted quite clearly in the field of population and fertility control. Across Africa, the history is still to be written of the emergence and adoption of "national population policies" over the past decade and a half. The pressures of international organizations, including the United Nations Fund for Population, the World Health Organization, and the Economic Commission for Africa, have been important in producing "national policies" that include population targets, contraceptive utilization goals, and related programs; but historical examination reveals important resistances across Africa to command policies mandated from abroad. Questions may be asked about whether these policies are, indeed, "national"; whether the negative effects on the governance capacity of African states through their taking on key policies and programs effectively mandated from outside outweigh any asserted benefits to African societies and to development; whether, in fact, resistance to state authority has moved into less visible but perhaps more significant and influential channels.

At the same time that the realization of "global" values seems to evade efforts of American experts to produce and induce change outside the folds of American civil society and professional life, the American professions and American professional education face the challenge of assessing how open its protocols of training are to the differences and subjectivities of practice, context, and principle in other cultures and societies. For universities and professional schools, some of the conversations within which change is asserted as necessary are motivated by claims for relevance by international students and claims for sensitivity on the part of domestic students who identify with the values of a multicultural and multiethnic society. In some cases, arguments for opening the curriculum are restrained by the observedly conservative nature of faculties; in other cases, restraints are produced by professional and accrediting bodies charged with regulating professional life under the umbrella of American civil law and civil procedure. Leaders and planners within the setting of American higher education face incredible challenges in attempting to deal with these diverse "motions in the system."

What is the stake of academic scholarship and higher education in the emergence and growth of self-defining and self-confident international and transnational communities of expertise operating in fields around the globe? What is our role in conceptualizing domains of interest; aggregating power, resources, and visibility; defining standards of practice for governments and international agencies; organizing collection of new kinds of data in a wide range of social, cultural, economic, and environmental fields (and giving powerful valences to their readings of data); practicing investigations and enforcement; and establishing the legitimacy and value of certain kinds of expertise before international, national, and local bodies?

Where in this setting is the late twentieth century Western university, replete with expertise of virtually every kind, yet organized around academic disciplines and professions, organized by long established guild practices relating to teaching, research, publication in established journals and constrained by obeisance to objectivity and reproducible findings?

Can American-seated frameworks of scholarship, including not only colleges and universities but also funding agencies and scholarly societies, respond to the challenges to academy-based expertise around the world, globally, and within the United States (American Council of Learned Societies, 1995)?

Is the North American university able to challenge its students to recognize the complexities that attach to guilds of practice and disciplines as they travel internationally?

An Agenda for Internationalization

These questions draw attention to the changing sites and dimensions of diverse communities of expertise. The questions are substantially speculative, and they may require "longer conversations." But to constitute a programmatic opening, I assert that the American research university and its students, faculty, and administration can play a major role in comprehending a world both made and unmade by the work of such communities of international experts who—simultaneously constructing their own bases of authority—aspire to establish global norms and standards, and push the edges of globalization.

A first opening is a growing awareness within American higher education (and the American research establishment) that, as with most of the world's resources and population, most of the world's expertise (if it can be thought of as an aggregate) is located outside North America. Yet more than any other institution, the American research university commands a capacity to recognize and draw into its programs of training and research sections of significant expertise located outside the United States. Within the United States, area studies centers and programs, many of them designated as National Resource Centers by the Department of Education, occupy commanding heights in their capacity to identify, translate, and draw upon this expertise within their agendas for training, research, documentation, and public programs. As well, through such familiar activities as study-abroad programs and visiting-professor programs like the Fulbright, American universities and colleges move expertise internationally, bringing into the American academy scholarship not otherwise available. At the same time, they are positioning American scholars in settings abroad where not only are the opportunities for learning and collaboration greatly magnified but there are also unique opportunities to observe the relative status and force of expertise within and outside the academy in settings outside the United States. Contracts, treaties, and agreements between American universities and counterparts abroad expand the potential surface area of exchanges, increasing the possibilities for access to expertise, resources, and research opportunities outside the United States. Rebecca Scott has suggested, as a means of "guarding against the arrogance of heavily metropolitan expertise, . . . the early, thorough, and reciprocal incorporation of multiple voices from precisely those regions where the uniform application of general theories is likely to appear threatening and intrusive. . . . [W]e should try to conceive of expertise as transnational right from the start, rather than only in application" (1994, p. 8).

Secondly, American higher education is, at this moment, extraordinarily well positioned to provide linguistic and cultural training to enhance the capacities of expert authority and to make possible, through translation and novel learning experiments, communication of heretofore recondite and largely inaccessible bodies of learning into the classrooms and laboratories of American colleges and universities. Paradoxically, as area studies and non-Western language and literature programs defend their usefulness—absent the ready argument of national strategic interest—students and faculty in professional schools increasingly recognize the values of specialized language training and culturally based learning opportunities (classroom, internships, overseas residencies) within professional education. The American research university, and the liberal arts college, most certainly have to devise new and enhanced modes of providing training in a growing range of languages, not only because of the opening of so many arenas to on-the-ground expertise but also because the processes inhering within what is meant by globalization also involve the reawakening of interests of second-generation immigrants and transposed national and ethnic communities in the study of the cultures, histories, and languages of their lands of origin. Enhancing the values of linguistic facility within international expertise inevitably strengthens the role of those American institutions capable of providing such facility.

Equally, those being trained within the professions and undertaking research, consultancy, and service internationally increasingly recognize the local, concrete contingencies of practice, work, management, service, exchange, entrepreneurship, and investment, and come to understand the importance of working in languages beyond English, even where English appears to be adequate for certain kinds of communication.

Attention to language and culture within professional schools sits amidst a recognition of various possible synergies within the American research university between, on the one hand, the traditional seats of international and area expertise in academic departments and, on the other, the arenas of agenda-defined interest and expertise in professional schools, many of which are themselves marked by increasing attention to internationalization: of expertise, of the professions and standards of professional practice, of the opportunities developing in fields of professional activity for professional school graduates, and of core issues in the fields of interest. Through internships and travel fellowships, and through new courses and seminars, the university can—and in some respects does—offer opportunities to students and faculty in international and area studies to identify arenas of practical activity, investigation, and advocacy that lie outside the long-standing frameworks of their academic and professional training, arenas that create opportunities for the flow back and forth of critical insight and reflection on the role of academic and professional expertise in their address to the wider world.

With the recognition of broader, more diverse, and more international domains of expertise, there is both opportunity and responsibility to assess the historical formation of scientific authority, ethics, methods, and epistemology of university-based research in North America. As the university seeks to play an enhanced role in the constitution of international expertise beyond the academy itself, it should seek to enrich its courses and seminars in methodology with questions that engage the state and fate of disciplinary methodology in a world where the operative contexts and effects of expertise are changing remarkably. It would be a stunning transformation of the "laboratories" in which expertise is nurtured. The American research university should press its students—prospective leaders in their fields—to become sensitive to issues both broad and narrow relating to methods in their disciplines and professions. It should also press them to engender a sense of responsibility for generating high-level conversation concerning the values and utilities of specific disciplinary and interdisciplinary methodologies, not only those traditionally taught but also those realized within fields of practice around the globe. One should not only seek accomplishment and expertise within a discipline but also recognize how methodologies, epistemologies, and research designs develop through the specific histories of disciplines and subdisciplines in local, "school," and national contexts. What is the meaning of *discipline*? What are the characteristics and challenges of interdisciplinary, multidisciplinary, and trans-disciplinary research?

The American research university may further challenge its students and faculty to recognize the complexities that attach to guilds of practice and disciplines as they travel internationally. In what ways do standards of practice in the disciplines develop from specifically local, national, and historical contexts? How do such values operate as a culture, as a sociology, and an economy of practice in a different setting? What is the architecture of the disciplines, in an international framework? How do values, epistemologies, practices, and paradigms move transnationally and globally? How is the course of professionalization of academic disciplines altered by the enlarged global context of production, reproduction, and work of professionals? A colleague, Michael Kennedy, has remarked that "When we think about comparative studies and theory, we should not only think about sites (abroad) as possible data points available for the reformulation of a theory, but also think of them as potential sites of the reconstruction and reimagination of what theory is, what it is we should be asking, and what are the questions that need to be addressed" (personal correspondence, 1996).

Moreover, the American research university, with its massive libraries and immense and accessible data resources, may productively encourage its scholars to examine their own responsibilities and capacities in the development of new bodies of data, and the refinement of those existing and ongoing, and to grasp the nature of data among other categories of global commodities in a changing global order. How do data "exist"? What are the properties and, in a sense, sociologies of data? Whose "property" are data, and how are property rights in data established? How do data change in the process, or as a consequence, of their collection? How do data become standardized, and also authorized, in the production of data sets and data packages, including censuses, databases, and economic and demographic tables? How should the researcher, and the research university, address state-constituted data, and historic and ongoing collection programs, at the juncture of science and the state? What are the responsibilities of scholars or researchers for the production and reproduction of data? Are there "new bodies of data" in the world, and what are the implications of such data for method and for disciplines? And what are the values and possibilities of fresh programs of data collection?

The American research university, its faculty, and its students have recognized with increasing acuity that opportunities to reach out from the United States to the wider world, to draw on expertise abroad, to develop new fields of research, and to utilize unique laboratories and sites abroad are predicated on reciprocities, collaborations, and affiliations, between the American institution and counterparts abroad, that are occasionally and presently threatened by various proposals to restrict immigration to the United States. Faculty exchange programs, training of students from abroad, student exchanges, specific research collaborations, and coauthoring have been important means of sustaining and extending this international reach, though in truth these are more modest efforts than those of the early twentieth century, in which American institutions undertook formal establishment and operation of colleges and research institutes abroad. While such investments are unlikely today, the American research university—or some of its parts—may see more appropriate and powerful opportunities in linkages to nonacademic institutions abroad: specialized laboratories, think tanks, design centers, international corporations, museums, libraries, and archives; and if American research universities are to be successful in their post–Cold War reach into the international sphere, they certainly have to contribute anew to the development of corresponding facilities abroad. It is not enough for an American university or college to have enhanced Internet and distance-learning capacity if prospective collaborating institutions abroad are without comparable and compatible capacity. Such innovation and flexibility in collaborative endeavors might enable, or be accompanied by, modes of research, instruction, learning, practice, publication, and dissemination that would, in the contemporary American university, seem unsettling if not strange and unfamiliar.

Finally, within American higher education is located the possibility, and the as-yet unrealized potential, of critical examination and comprehension of the practice, constitution, force, and effect of expertise as it operates upon the world (Lee, 1995). The internationalization of professions and expertise is not simply or satisfactorily the extension of American expertise into and onto the wider world. The American research university can do more to bring its students and faculty toward a more confident and a more productively skeptical engagement with such processes of globalization of expertise even as many in *our community* themselves may operate with significant and positive impact in the forefront of such international expertise. A first step is to recognize that international expertise—as a culture, as a sociology, and as an economy—is itself a subject receiving important study.

Reshaping Institutional Order

This is a large agenda for the post–Cold War North American university as it seeks to address changes in the organization and production of expertise globally. Within this agenda, there are several key issues facing leaders of North American research universities, deans of constituent schools and colleges, and leaders of undergraduate institutions.

1.   Those bearing responsibility for planning and overseeing institutional change in the light of internationalization mandates must take account of extant "capital" investment in faculty, libraries, laboratories, and programs. How can prior investments and extant intellectual capital be directed toward refreshed goals through incentives for faculty, opportunities for retraining, and new administrative arrangements?

2.   Those charged with planning internationalization must recognize the opportunities for building bridges to new bodies of expertise not simply through faculty hires or rearranging intra-institutional resources but rather through constituting strong working relations with institutions abroad. Such relations might involve now-conventional arrangements such as undergraduate study-abroad exchanges and faculty exchanges; they might yet come to involve joint interinstitutional degree programs. What are the possibilities of moving students through the programs of several institutions toward a specific degree not feasible at the American institution alone?

3.   Those stylizing new protocols of training within the rubric of internationalization might assess how far international service and internships can be integrated as required elements within professional and academic training, not as an added value element but as fundamental to the formation of a scholar or professional. How long will American higher education continue to support—through arranging options and requirements—the division of academic and professional trajectories between domestic and international spheres?

4.   It is much observed that the call for internationalization comes at a time of observed decline in expectations that students need to master languages other than English (and Spanish). Will leaders of American higher education join with leaders in other sectors of education to encourage—give positive symbolic support for—study and mastery of languages other than English and Spanish?

5.   American-based professional societies and professional credentialing and accreditation bodies have vast influence over the shape and content of American higher education. As "guild organizations," they are predictably resistant to opening their training protocols to different and alternative modes, including protocols for professional training and service in other countries, or protocols more appropriate to those engaged in international and transnational professional life. The answer is not necessarily to export American standards for training to other societies, as such expertise, such practice, may not be appropriate in other settings beyond North America. Moreover, one observes in some professions a tightening of American professional training protocols amidst the effects of globaliza-

tion, including the migration of specialists toward economies offering greater opportunities. How will the leaders of American higher education—presidents of universities and colleges, deans, trustees, and visitor committees—address demands and needs for more flexible training protocols? What scope for innovation is possible, and how may such scope be stretched?

6. Leaders and planners in American higher education enter the discussion of internationalization with the recognition that extant structures and resources dedicated to research and training were developed incrementally—investments made toward momentary needs and opportunities—without significant regard for coordination. There are economies and values attached to extant arrangements, and some high-level university administrators may see the competition among discrete entities as not only positive in terms of generating quality but also cheaper in that contest and debate long defer decisions to reorganize and to invest fresh resources. However, internationalization as a mandate provides a substantial moment for building resources together to realize efficiencies, through integration and coordination, and moreover to give opportunity for a centeredness to planning and critique within international academic programs. Integrative models of organization—by their nature more visibly resourced—are arguably more likely to engage activist faculty and students resources and more likely to effect change in institutional routines. More important, integrated models may be better at maintaining viability and strength against the threats and fears of loss of federal dollars.

7. Lastly, leaders and planners in American higher education must recognize that the coincidences between American corporate moves toward internationalization and those of the American university are not always compatible. Corporations have specific interests in elaborating internationalization as a means of enlarging markets and creating efficiencies in contracting, production, and distribution. Internationalization in the university domain must involve not just these elements, which may or may not be seen to have practical value for American higher education, but also elaboration of expertise to master the complexities of contingencies of value and effect in the workings of corporate capital globally and to assist students—the next generations—to understand both the material and ethical domains of global economic and cultural change. How will universities manage the simultaneous calls for corporate partnerships and for comprehension of the workings of corporate capital within and upon the world?

Further Reading

For a discussion of some of the debate over allocation of resources among competing approaches to international studies, see Jacob Heilbrunn, "The News from

Everywhere," *Lingua Franca,* May–June 1996, pp. 49–56. For a discussion of changing approaches to the "global" within scholarship beyond the United States, see Lee (1995). *Public Culture* and, in recent years, *Foreign Affairs* have published a number of articles and reviews that touch on or frame debates over internationalization and globalization in the academy and in public policy fields. *The Internationalization of Scholarship and Scholarly Societies* (American Council of Learned Societies, 1995) is a valuable statement of issues facing American educators.

References

American Council of Learned Societies. *The Internationalization of Scholarship and Scholarly Societies.* ACLS Occasional Paper, no. 28. New York: ACLS, 1995.

Anderson, B. "The Changing Ecology of Southeast Asian Studies in the United States, 1950–1990." In C. Hirschman, C. F. Keyes, and K. Hutterer (eds.), *Southeast Asian Studies in the Balance: Reflections from America.* Ann Arbor, Mich.: Association for Asian Studies, 1994.

"China's Human Rights Record." *The New York Times,* February 6, 1994.

Cooper, F. "Development Knowledge and the Social Sciences." *ii: The Journal of the International Institute of the University of Michigan,* 1994, *1*(2), 22, 24.

Ferguson, J. *The Anti-Politics Machine.* Cambridge, England: Cambridge University Press, 1990.

Kane, J. "Letter from the Amazon: With Spears from All Sides." *New Yorker,* Sep. 27, 1993, pp. 54–79.

Lambert, R. "Blurring the Disciplinary Boundaries: Area Studies in the United States." *American Behavioral Scientist,* 1990, *33*(6), 712–732.

Lee, B. "Critical Internationalism." *Public Culture,* 1995, *7*(3), 559–592.

Malkki, L. H. *Purity and Exile: Violence, Memory, and National Cosmology Among Hutu Refugees in Tanzania.* Chicago: University of Chicago Press, 1995.

Scott, J. C. "Foreword." In C. Hirschman, C. F. Keyes, and K. Hutterer (eds.), *Southeast Asian Studies in the Balance: Reflections from America.* Ann Arbor, Mich.: Association for Asian Studies, 1994.

Scott, R. "Response: Transnational Expertise." *The Journal of the International Institute of the University of Michigan,* 1994, *1*(1), 7–8.

Zald, M. "Progress and Cumulation in the Human Sciences After the Fall." *Sociological Forum,* 1995, *10*(3), 455–479.

NAME INDEX

A

Academic Senate for California Community Colleges, 424
Ackoff, R. L., 377
Adelman, C., 274
Adlrich, H. E., 394, 400
Ahrne, G., 491
Albert, S., 458, 460
Albrektson, J. R., 496
Aldersley, S. F., 482
Allen, W. A., 414, 418, 420, 429
Allport, G. W., 416
Alpert, D., 131, 156
Altbach, P. G., 27, 28, 85, 86, 470, 471
Althoff, E. J., 302
American Association for the Advancement of Science, 37, 38, 44
American Council of Learned Societies, 555
Anderson, C. J., 130, 157
Anderson, R., 458, 459
Anderson, R. E., 94, 104
Anderson, V. J., 369
Angelo, T. A., 369

Apple, E., 439
Apps, J. W., 436
Arce, C. H., 405, 406, 415
Argyris, C., 345, 346
Armajani, B., 58, 62, 115, 122, 123
Arns, R. G., 350
Arredondo, S., 47, 48, 49, 50, 64, 174, 175, 190
Arrow, K., 473
Ashworth, K. H., 292, 294
Association of Governing Boards, 58, 63
Astin, A. W., 366, 367, 412, 413, 422
Austin, N., 345
Axelrod, R., 495

B

Baggett, J. M., 367, 372
Bailey, T. B., 483, 484
Balderston, F., 457
Baldridge, J. V., 89, 90, 103, 104, 130, 135, 156, 342, 389
Baldwin, R. G., 483, 484
Bania, N. R., 538

Banta, T. W., 367, 379
Barak, R. J., 349, 350, 352, 374, 457
Bardach, E., 399
Barley, S., 454, 462, 472, 473
Barnes, C. A., 193
Barrow, C., 459
Bartlett, C., 91, 97, 104, 466, 469, 473
Barzelay, M., 122, 123
Bateman, M., 58, 63
Baugher, K., 373
Bazluke, F., 411
Becher, T., *xv*, 88, 95, 104
Becker, G., 522, 545
Benjamin, R., 185, 187, 188
Bennahum, D. S., 488, 495
Bensimon, E. M., 154, 156, 192, 194, 195, 196, 197, 198, 200, 201, 202, 239
Benson, J. K., 394, 400
Berdahl, R. O., 27, 28, 47, 48, 50, 63, 85, 86, 470
Berg, D. J., 291, 295, 305
Berger, 348
Bergquist, W. H., 236, 237, 244, 245

SUBJECT INDEX

A

Access: as basic goal of federal aid, 43; and electronic delivery systems, 59–60; and financial aid, 35; societal commitment to, 59

Accountability: and assessment, 55, 175–176, 361, 362–364, 375, 376; and performance reporting, 55, 175–176, 375–376; in program review, 374; and regional accrediting agencies, 74–76, 82–83; and resource allocation, 16, 185–187, 361, 458–459, 460

Accreditation: agencies, 70–72, 82; and assessment, 373; diversity and quality criteria in, 424–425; quasi-governmental role of, 71, 82; prescriptive approach to, 54; regional, 74–76, 82–83; specialized, 76–77, 83–84

Administration/administrators. *See* Chief academic officer; Leadership

Admissions standards, 59

Advanced learning, defined, 108

Affirmative action, 10, 411–412

American College Testing, Work Keys program, 112

American Council on Education (ACE), 130

Area studies programs. *See* International academic programs

Assessment, 360–378; accountability dimension in, 55, 175–176, 361, 362–364, 375, 376; in alternative delivery formats, 371; campus-centered, 363; conventional grading approaches, 369; credentialing role of, 373; curricular and classroom, 368; embedded, 368, 372–373; and external communication and reporting, 375–376; of faculty, 492–494; instructional, 364–366, 372; mandate, shift in, 360–361; movement, 55–56; naturalistic techniques in, 367–369; organization and administration problems in, 376–378; as outcomes movement, 360–361, 366–367; per-

formance-based, 363–364; portfolio, 367, 368–369; program performance, 374–375; in program planning, 375; and quality management, 365, 372; in redesign and restructuring, 153, 365–366; student and academic, 131; systems, 492–494; technical evolution in, 366–370

Assets data, 279–281

B

Baldrige Award, 15, 16, 504

Benchmarking, 509–510, 515–516; data networks, 176–177

Budgeting: allocation priorities, 185–187; environment context in, 289–290; and fundraising, 311, 314; and institutional cuts, 167, 185–187; performance budgeting, 292, 293–294, 300; and program review, 354; responsibility center budgeting, 292, 295–296, 300; strategy, 167–168, 289; for technology, 328; tools and techniques, 302;